Children's
Literature
Review

Guide to Gale Literary Criticism Series

For criticism on	Consult these Gale series
Authors now living or who died after December 31, 1959	*CONTEMPORARY LITERARY CRITICISM (CLC)*
Authors who died between 1900 and 1959	*TWENTIETH-CENTURY LITERARY CRITICISM (TCLC)*
Authors who died between 1800 and 1899	*NINETEENTH-CENTURY LITERATURE CRITICISM (NCLC)*
Authors who died between 1400 and 1799	*LITERATURE CRITICISM FROM 1400 TO 1800 (LC)* *SHAKESPEAREAN CRITICISM (SC)*
Authors who died before 1400	*CLASSICAL AND MEDIEVAL LITERATURE CRITICISM (CMLC)*
Authors of books for children and young adults	*CHILDREN'S LITERATURE REVIEW (CLR)*
Dramatists	*DRAMA CRITICISM (DC)*
Poets	*POETRY CRITICISM (PC)*
Short story writers	*SHORT STORY CRITICISM (SSC)*
Black writers of the past two hundred years	*BLACK LITERATURE CRITICISM (BLC)*
Hispanic writers of the late nineteenth and twentieth centuries	*HISPANIC LITERATURE CRITICISM (HLC)*
Native North American writers and orators of the eighteenth, nineteenth, and twentieth centuries	*NATIVE NORTH AMERICAN LITERATURE (NNAL)*
Major authors from the Renaissance to the present	*WORLD LITERATURE CRITICISM, 1500 TO THE PRESENT (WLC)*

ISSN 0362-4145

volume 49

Children's Literature Review

Excerpts from Reviews,
Criticism, and Commentary
on Books for Children
and Young People

Alan Hedblad
Thomas McMahon
Deborah J. Morad
Editors

GALE

DETROIT • LONDON

STAFF

Alan Hedblad, Thomas McMahon, Deborah J. Morad, *Editors*

Cindy Buck, Sheryl Ciccarelli, Melissa Hill, Motoko Fujishiro Huthwaite, Paul Loeber, Carolyn C. March, Adele Sarkissian, Gerard J. Senick, Diane Telgen, Martha Urbiel, Kathleen L. Witman, *Contributing Editors*

Karen Uchic, *Techincal Training Specialist*

Joyce Nakamura, *Managing Editor*

Susan M. Trosky, *Permissions Manager*
Maria L. Franklin, *Permissions Specialist*
Sarah Chesney, Edna Hedblad, Michele M. Lonoconus, *Permissions Associates*

Victoria B. Cariappa, *Research Manager*
Norma Sawaya, *Project Coordinator*
Barbara J. McNeil, Gary J. Oudersluys, *Research Specialists*
Jeffrey D. Daniels, Tracie A. Richardson, Cheryl D. Warnock,
Robert Whaley, *Research Associates*
Phylllis P. Blackman, *Research Assistant*

Mary Beth Trimper, *Production Director*
Carolyn A. Fischer *Production Assistant*

Gary Leach, *Graphic Artist*
Randy Bassett, *Image Database Supervisor*
Robert Duncan, Michael Logusz, *Imaging Specialists*
Pamela A. Reed, *Imaging Coordinator*

Address until September 15, 1988:
835 Penobscot Building
Detroit, MI 48226-4094

Address after September 15, 1998:
27500 Drake Road
Farmington Hills, MI 48331-3535

Library of Congress Catalog Card Number 76-643301
ISBN 0-7876-2026-2
ISSN 0362-4145
Printed in the United States of America

10   9   8   7   6   5   4   3   2   1

Contents

Preface   vii
Acknowledgements   xi

Preface

Literature for children and young adults has evolved into both a respected branch of creative writing and a successful industry. Currently, books for young readers are considered among the most popular segments of publishing. Criticism of juvenile literature is instrumental in recording the literary or artistic development of the creators of children's books as well as the trends and controversies that result from changing values or attitudes about young people and their literature. Designed to provide a permanent, accessible record of this ongoing scholarship, *Children's Literature Review (CLR)* presents parents, teachers, and librarians—those responsible for bringing children and books together—with the opportunity to make informed choices when selecting reading materials for the young. In addition, *CLR* provides researchers of children's literature with easy access to a wide variety of critical information from English-language sources in the field. Users will find balanced overviews of the careers of the authors and illustrators of the books that children and young adults are reading; these entries, which contain excerpts from published criticism in books and periodicals, assist users by sparking ideas for papers and assignments and suggesting supplementary and classroom reading. Ann L. Kalkhoff, president and editor of *Children's Book Review Service Inc.,* writes that "*CLR* has filled a gap in the field of children's books, and it is one series that will never lose its validity or importance."

Scope of the Series

Each volume of *CLR* profiles the careers of a selection of authors and illustrators of books for children and young adults from preschool through high school. Author lists in each volume reflect:

- an international scope.

- representation of authors of all eras.

- the variety of genres covered by children's and/or YA literature: picture books, fiction, nonfiction, poetry, folklore, and drama.

Although the focus of the series is on authors new to *CLR*, entries will be updated as the need arises.

Organization of This Book

An entry consists of the following elements: author heading, author portrait, author introduction, excerpts of criticism (each preceded by a bibliographical citation), and illustrations, when available.

- The **Author Heading** consists of the author's name followed by birth and death dates. The portion of the name outside the parentheses denotes the form under which the author is most frequently published. If the majority of the author's works for children were written under a pseudonym, the pseudonym will be listed in the author heading and the real name given on the first line of the author introduction. Also located at the beginning of the introduction are any other pseudonyms used by the author in writing for children and any name variations, including transliterated forms for authors whose languages use nonroman alphabets. Uncertainty as to a birth or death date is indicated by question marks.

- An **Author Portrait** is included when available.

- The **Author Introduction** contains information designed to introduce an author to *CLR* users by presenting an overview of the author's themes and styles, biographical facts that relate to the author's literary career or critical responses to the author's works, and information about major awards and prizes the author has received. The introduction begins by identifying the nationality of the author and by listing the genres in which s/he has written for children and young adults. Introductions also list a group of representative titles for which the author or illustrator being profiled is best known; this section, which begins with the words "major works include," follows the genre line of the introduction. For seminal figures, a listing of major works about the author follows when appropriate, highlighting important biographies about the author or illustrator that are not excerpted in the entry. The centered heading "Introduction" announces the body of the text.

- **Criticism** is located in three sections: **Author's Commentary** (when available), **General Commentary** (when available), and **Title Commentary** (commentary on specific titles).

  - The **Author's Commentary** presents background material written by the author or by an interviewer. This commentary may cover a specific work or several works. Author's commentary on more than one work appears after the author introduction, while commentary on an individual book follows the title entry heading.

  - The **General Commentary** consists of critical excerpts that consider more than one work by the author or illustrator being profiled. General commentary is preceded by the critic's name in boldface type or, in the case of unsigned criticism, by the title of the journal. *CLR* also features entries that emphasize general criticism on the oeuvre of an author or illustrator. When appropriate, a selection of reviews is included to supplement the general commentary.

  - The **Title Commentary** begins with the title entry headings, which precede the criticism on a title and cite publication information on the work being reviewed. Title headings list the title of the work as it appeared in its first English-language edition. The first English-language publication date of each work (unless otherwise noted) is listed in parentheses following the title. Differing U.S. and British titles follow the publication date within the parentheses. When a work is written by an individual other than the one being profiled, as is the case when illustrators are featured, the parenthetical material following the title cites the author of the work before listing its publication date.

    Entries in each title commentary section consist of critical excerpts on the author's individual works, arranged chronologically by publication date. The entries generally contain two to seven reviews per title, depending on the stature of the book and the amount of criticism it has generated. The editors select titles that reflect the entire scope of the author's literary contribution, covering each genre and subject. An effort is made to reprint criticism that represents the full range of each title's reception, from the year of its initial publication to current assessments. Thus, the reader is provided with a record of the author's critical history. Publication information (such as publisher names and book prices) and parenthetical numerical references (such as footnotes or page and line references to specific editions of works) have been deleted at the discretion of the editors to provide smoother reading of the text.

- Centered headings introduce each section, in which criticism is arranged chronologically; beginning with Volume 35, each excerpt is preceded by a boldface source heading for easier access by readers. Within the text, titles by authors being profiled are also highlighted in boldface type.

- Selected excerpts are preceded by **Explanatory Annotations,** which provide information on the critic or work of criticism to enhance the reader's understanding of the excerpt.

- A complete **Bibliographical Citation** designed to facilitate the location of the original book or article precedes each piece of criticism.

- Numerous **Illustrations** are featured in *CLR*. For entries on illustrators, an effort has been made to include illustrations that reflect the characteristics discussed in the criticism. Entries on authors who do not illustrate their own works may also include photographs and other illustrative material pertinent to their careers.

Special Features: Entries on Illustrators

Entries on authors who are also illustrators will occasionally feature commentary on selected works illustrated but not written by the author being profiled. These works are strongly associated with the illustrator and have received critical acclaim for their art. By including critical comment on works of this type, the editors wish to provide a more complete representation of the artist's career. Criticism on these works has been chosen to stress artistic, rather than literary, contributions. Title entry headings for works illustrated by the author being profiled are arranged chronologically within the entry by date of publication and include notes identifying the author of the illustrated work. In order to provide easier access for users, all titles illustrated by the subject of the entry are boldfaced.

CLR also includes entries on prominent illustrators who have contributed to the field of children's literature. These entries are designed to represent the development of the illustrator as an artist rather than as a literary stylist. The illustrator's section is organized like that of an author, with two exceptions: the introduction presents an overview of the illustrator's styles and techniques rather than outlining his or her literary background, and the commentary written by the illustrator on his or her works is called "illustrator's commentary" rather than "author's commentary." All titles of books containing illustrations by the artist being profiled are highlighted in boldface type.

Other Features: Acknowledgments, Indexes

- The **Acknowledgments** section, which immediately follows the preface, lists the sources from which material has been reprinted in the volume. It does not, however, list every book or periodical consulted for the volume.

- The **Cumulative Index to Authors** lists all of the authors who have appeared in *CLR* with cross-references to the biographical, autobiographical, and literary criticism series published by Gale Research. A full listing of the series titles appears before the first page of the indexes of this volume.

- The **Cumulative Index to Nationalities** lists authors alphabetically under their respective nationalities. Author names are followed by the volume number(s) in which they appear.

- The **Cumulative Index to Titles** lists titles covered in *CLR* followed by the volume and page number where criticism begins.

A Note to the Reader

CLR is one of several critical references sources in the Literature Criticism Series published by Gale Research. When writing papers, students who quote directly from any volume in the Literature Criticism Series may use the following general forms to footnote reprinted criticism. The first example pertains to material drawn from periodicals, the second to material reprinted from books.

[1]T. S. Eliot, "John Donne," *The Nation and the Athenaeum,* 33 (9 June 1923), 321-32; excerpted and reprinted in *Literature Criticism from 1400 to 1800,* Vol. 10, ed. James E. Person, Jr. (Detroit: Gale Research, 1989), pp. 28-9.

[1]Henry Brooke, *Leslie Brooke and Johnny Crow* (Frederick Warne, 1982); excerpted and reprinted in *Children's Literature Review,* Vol. 20, ed. Gerard J. Senick (Detroit: Gale Research, 1990), p. 47.

Suggestions Are Welcome

In response to various suggestions, several features have been added to *CLR* since the beginning of the series, including author entries on retellers of traditional literature as well as those who have been the first to record oral tales and other folklore; entries on prominent illustrators featuring commentary on their styles and techniques; entries on authors whose works are considered controversial; occasional entries devoted to criticism on a single work or a series of works; sections in author introductions that list major works by and about the author or illustrator being profiled; explanatory notes that provide information on the critic or work of criticism to enhance the usefulness of the excerpt; more extensive illustrative material, such as holographs of manuscript pages and photographs of people and places pertinent to the careers of the authors and artists; a cumulative nationality index for easy access to authors by nationality; and occasional guest essays written specifically for *CLR* by prominent critics on subjects of their choice.

Readers who wish to suggest authors to appear in future volumes, or who have other suggestions, are cordially in-vited to contact the editor. By mail: Editor, *Children's Literature Review,* Gale Research, 835 Penobscot Bldg., 645 Griswold St., Detroit, MI 48226-4094; by telephone: (800) 347-GALE; by fax: (313) 961-6599. Address after September 15, 1998: 27500 Drake Road, Farmington Hills, MI 48331-3535.

Acknowledgments

The editors wish to thank the copyright holders of the excerpted criticism included in this volume and the permissions managers of many book and magazine publishing companies for assisting us in securing reproduction rights. We are also grateful to the staffs of the Detroit Public Library, the Library of Congress, the University of Detroit Mercy Library, Wayne State University Purdy/Kresge Library Complex, and the University of Michigan Libraries for making their resources available to us. Following is a list of the copyright holders who have granted us permission to reproduce material in this volume of *CLR*. Every effort has been made to trace copyright, but if omissions have been made, please let us know.

COPYRIGHTED EXCERPTS IN *CLR*, VOLUME 49, WERE REPRODUCED FROM THE FOLLOWING PERIODICALS:

Appraisal: Children's Science Books, v. 1, Winter, 1967; v. 2, Fall, 1969; v. 7, Fall, 1974; v. 9, Spring, 1976; v. 12, Spring, 1979. Copyright © 1967, 1969, 1974, 1976, 1979 by the Children's Science Book Review Committee. All reproduced by permission.—*Australian Book Review,* May, 1993; April, 1994; December, 1994; January, 1995; November, 1995; September, 1996. All reproduced by permission.—*Booklist,* v. 61, June 15, 1965; v. 62, May 1, 1966; v. 63, May 15, 1967; v. 64, May 1, 1968; v. 65, November 1, 1968; v. 65, July 15, 1969; v. 66, May 1, 1970; v. 68, October 1, 1971; v. 72, May 1, 1972; v. 70, December 15, 1973; v. 70, January 15, 1974; v. 72, January 15, 1976; v. 73, April 1, 1977; v. 74, February 15, 1978; v. 75, September 1, 1978; v. 75, June 1, 1979; v. 76, July 1, 1980; v. 78, July, 1982; v. 79, February 15, 1983; v. 80, November 15, 1983; v. 80, January 1, 1984; v. 81, March 15, 1985; v. 82, October 15, 1985; v. 82, March 1, 1986; v. 82, May 15, 1986; v. 85, September 1, 1988; v. 85, May 1, 1989; v. 86, September 15, 1989; v. 86, December 15, 1989; v. 86, March 1, 1990; v. 86, July, 1990; v. 87, October 15, 1990; v. 87, November 1, 1990; v. 87, February 1, 1991; v. 87, January 1, 1991; v. 88, October 1, 1991; v. 88, January 15, 1992; v. 88, February 1, 1992; v. 88, March 1, 1992; v. 88, March 15, 1992; v. 88, April 1, 1992; v. 88, April 15, 1992; v. 88, July, 1992; v. 89, December 1, 1992; v. 90, November 15, 1993; v. 90, October 15, 1993; v. 90, September 15, 1993; v. 90, February 15, 1994; v. 90, March 15, 1994; v. 90, May 1, 1994; v. 91, April 15, 1995; v. 92, March 15, 1996; v. 93, December 15, 1996; v. 93, February 15, 1997. All reproduced by permission.—*Books for Keeps,* n. 51, July, 1988; n. 56, May, 1989; n. 65, November, 1990; n. 71, November, 1991; n. 74, May, 1992; n. 80, May, 1993. © School Bookshop Association 1988, 1989, 1990, 1991, 1992, 1993. All reproduced by permission.—*British Book News Children's Books,* June, 1987. © The British Council, 1987. Reproduced by permission.—*The Bulletin of the Center for Children's Books,* v. 17, June, 1964; v. 18, May, 1965; v. 18, July, 1965; v. 19, November, 1965; v. 19, July/August, 1966; v. 20, November, 1966; v. 20, December, 1966; v. 20, June, 1967; v. 21, March, 1968; v. 21, April, 1968; v. 22, January, 1969; v. 24, October, 1970; v. 24, December, 1970; v. 25, November, 1971; v. 27, March, 1974; v. 27, May, 1974; v. 29, July-August, 1976; v. 30, May, 1977; v. 32, July-August, 1979; v. 33, May, 1980; v. 33, July-August, 1980; v. 37, November, 1983; v. 37, April, 1984; v. 42, October, 1988; v. 43, October, 1989; v. 44, October, 1990; v. 45, September, 1991; v. 46, November, 1992. Copyright © 1962, 1963, 1964, 1965, 1966, 1967, 1968, 1969, 1970, 1971, 1974, 1976, 1977, 1979, 1980, 1983, 1984, 1988, 1989, 1990, 1991 by The University of Chicago./v. 47, December, 1993; v. 47, March, 1994; v. 47, June, 1994; v. 47, July/August, 1994; v. 48, July/August, 1995; v. 49, May, 1996; v. 49, June, 1996; v. 51, October, 1997. Copyright © 1993, 1994, 1995, 1996, 1997 by The Board of Trustees of the University of Illinois./v. 2, September, 1957; v. 15, May, 1962; v. 16, January, 1963; v. 16, April, 1963; v. 16, June, 1963. Copyright © 1957, renewed 1985; Copyright © 1962, renewed 1990; Copyright © 1963, renewed 1991 by The University of Chicago. All reproduced by permission.—*Catholic Library World,* v. 37, December, 1965; v. 49, November, 1977. Both reproduced by permission.—*Children's Book Review,* v. III, October, 1973. © 1973 by The Five Owls Press Ltd. All rights reserved. Reproduced by permission.—*Children's Literature: Annual of The Modern Language Association Group on Children's Literature and The Children's Literature Association,* v. 12, 1984; v. 6, 1997. Both reproduced by permission.—*Children's Literature Association Quarterly,* v. 5, Summer, 1980; v. 8, Spring, 1983; v. 11, Summer, 1986. All reproduced by permission.—*Christian Century,* v. LXXVI, December 2, 1959. Copyright © 1959, renewed 1987 Christian Century Foundation. Reproduced by permission.—*Christian Science Monitor,* v. 56, May 7, 1964; v. 57, May 6, 1965; v. 58, April 3, 1966; v. 61, May 1, 1969; v. 62, October 17, 1970. © 1964, 1965, 1966, 1969, 1970 The Christian Science Publishing Society./September 30, 1947; v. 45, November 12, 1953; v. 50, May 8, 1958; v. 52, May 12, 1960; November 16, 1961; v. 54, May 10, 1962; v. 55, May 9, 1963. © 1947, renewed 1975; © 1953, renewed 1981; © 1958, renewed 1986; © 1960, renewed 1988; © 1961, renewed 1989; © 1962, renewed 1990; © 1963, renewed 1991 The Christian Science Publishing Society. All rights reserved. All reproduced by permission from *The Christian Science Monitor.*—*Commentary,* v. 8, July, 1949 for "Uncle Remus and the Malevolent Rabbit" by Bernard Wolfe. Copyright © 1949, renewed 1977 by the American Jewish Committee. All rights reserved. Reproduced by permission of the publisher.—*Fine Print,* v. VIII, July, 1982 for a review of "Alice in Wonderland" by Edward Guiliano. Reproduced by permission of the publisher.—*The Five Owls,* v. 8, March-April, 1994. Reproduced by permission.—*Growing Point,* v. 22, September, 1983 for a review of "Adrift" by Margery Fisher; v. 24, September, 1985 for a review of "Little Brother" by Margery Fisher; v. 25, July,

COPYRIGHTED EXCERPTS IN *CLR,* VOLUME 49, WERE REPRODUCED FROM THE FOLLOWING BOOKS:

Arbuthnot, May Hill. From *Children and Books.* Third Edition. Scott, Foresman and Company, 1964. Copyright © 1964 by Scott, Foresman and Company. Reprinted by permission of Addison Wesley Educational Publishers Inc.— Bader, Barbara. From *American Picturebooks from Noah's Ark to the Beast Within.* Macmillan Publishing Company, Inc., 1976. Copyright © 1976 Barbara Bader. All rights reserved. Reproduced with the permission of the author.— Blount, Margaret. From *Animal Land: The Creatures of Children's Fiction.* William Morrow & Company, Inc., 1975. Copyright © 1974 by Margaret Ingle-Finch. All rights reserved. Reproduced by permission of the author.— Bone, Robert. From *Down Home: A History of Afro-American Short Fiction from Its Beginnings to the End of the*

Children's
Literature
Review

Allan (Stuart) Baillie

1943-

Scottish-born Australian author of fiction, picture books, short stories, and retellings.

Major works include *Little Brother* (1985), *Riverman* (1986), *Drac and the Gremlin* (1989), *The China Coin* (1991), *Songman* (1994).

INTRODUCTION

One of the most acclaimed Australian authors of literature for children and young adults to have emerged in the 1980s, Baillie is considered a talented writer whose books are both exciting adventure stories and insightful depictions of the feelings of the young. Recognized as one of the few Australian authors to base some of his books outside of Australia, he sets his works, which include realistic fiction, fantasy, and picture books, in both historical and contemporary periods as well as in both real and imagined places. Baillie is celebrated for the authenticity and immediacy of his stories, which often revolve around political events at which the author was present, such as the war in Vietnam or the student protest at China's Tiananmen Square; in addition, he is acknowledged for providing young readers with thorough descriptions of history, culture, and locale. Characteristically, Baillie's young male and female protagonists learn about themselves by surviving physical and emotional crises, often the result of harrowing quests or encounters with natural disaster. In addition to physical survival and the search for identity, Baillie addresses such themes as war, tyranny, the meaning of courage, and the importance of knowing one's family history; he underscores his works with a strong sense of justice and respect for humanity and its values. Critics usually view Baillie as the creator of complex and demanding books that, despite the seriousness of their themes, reflect the author's wit and humor as well as his distinctive personal stamp. Several of these works, which Baillie writes in a direct, authoritative style, are considered both ambitious and significant. Writing in *Books for Keeps*, Valerie Bierman calls Baillie "a first-class writer with the power to stretch children's imaginations and make them think." *Junior Bookshelf* reviewer Marcus Crouch asserts, "Allan Baillie is a mature writer who knows exactly what he is doing and how to do it. . . . With him the Australian scene, which has produced so many fine stories recently, is in good hands."

Biographical Information

Born in Prestwick, Scotland, Baillie lived in England until the age of seven, when he and his family moved to Australia. Growing up in both bush towns and coastal cities, he had an idyllic childhood; he has written of this time,

"Learned to swim in a cove with a cave of many sinister bones, built go-karts for the dusty road that plummeted past my place, and very often sat in the sprawling apricot tree, read books, and gorged myself." At about the age of nine, Baillie wrote a poem that was printed in a children's supplement of the Melbourne *Sun*. "To make up for this terrible lapse," he later wrote, Baillie started a gang of schoolmates; in retaliation, his headmaster asked Baillie to write and produce a play about the Nativity. "It was terrible, hideous," Baillie remembers, "But it left me with a very strange itch." Moving to Melbourne, Baillie was asked by a teacher to write a puppet play, which he based on *Treasure Island*; at thirteen, he wrote and illustrated his first book, a science fiction novel. Continuing to write science fiction, Baillie was asked by a teacher to produce a radio play, for which he adapted a chapter from one of his stories. When he was fourteen, he won a short story contest and was paid for his effort. During Baillie's last year in high school, a letter that he wrote to the editor of the Melbourne *Sun* was published as an article. On the strength of this article, Baillie was hired after graduation as a cadet journalist at the *Sun* and also sold his first short story to a newspaper. At twenty-one, while fencing with a friend, Baillie was pierced between his left eye and the bridge of his nose; the accident left him partially paralyzed and with a speech impediment. "But something had happened to me since the accident," Baillie wrote. "The most obvious part of that was an obsession with pushing out my personal envelope, the hell with anything else. I learned to drive my way, to swim, to write. . . . I started to figure that everything that happened to me after the accident was a bonus, a gift. And you don't throw away gifts like that. . . ." After working as a feature writer for the *Sun* for another year, Baillie left to, as he says, "wander the world."

Before returning to Australia, Baillie traveled to Asia, India, Europe, and Central America. He worked for newspapers in Sydney and Auckland, New Zealand, where he wrote an unpublished adventure novel about his experiences in Guatemala and British Honduras. While he was traveling in Thailand, Baillie became interested in Cambodian culture and went to Cambodia and Laos as a freelance journalist; two months after he left Cambodia, the Vietnam war began. In 1975, Baillie published his first adult novel, *Mask Maker,* the story of a teacher who becomes involved in the Laos mountain war and the opium trade. In 1979, Baillie returned to Cambodia to cover the war between Vietnam and the Khmer Rouge; he remembers, "I stumbled from bleak story to story in the camps: fathers bundled into a midnight bus, families cut down to a single survivor, little girls pointing out other children for execution. . . ." Returning to Australia, Baillie tried unsuccessfully to write a novel about his experience; when his wife, Agnes, came to him with a newspaper clipping about four Lebanese boys and a dog who were rescued from a crate in the Mediterranean, Baillie used the story as the basis for his first book for children, *Adrift* (1983).

Since the publication of that first juvenile novel, Baillie has used his experiences to create many of his works. For example, *Little Brother* was inspired by the author's memory of Vuthy, a boy he met in one of the Thai camps who had escaped execution by the Khmer Rouge; Baillie decided to tell the story of Cambodia from the viewpoint of the boy, who dodged bullets and fought starvation to travel into Thailand by foot, rickshaw, truck, and buffalo cart. "After *Little Brother,*" Baillie wrote, "I . . . began a system for writing books that has stayed with me to this day. Get an idea, go to where the idea sparked, research, come home and write the thing." Baillie continued his travels and, after serving as a writer and editor for various periodicals and for the Australian Broadcasting Corporation, became a full-time writer in the late 1980s. In 1987, he toured China as a delegate of the Children's Book Council of Australia, and was inspired to write *The China Coin,* the story of a teenager—half Australian and half Chinese like his own daughter—who comes to China looking for her roots. In 1989, Baillie experienced the student uprising against the Chinese government at Beijing's Tiananmen Square, an event that is a major part of *The China Coin.* "I thought," Baillie wrote, "that a book like *Little Brother* could happen to a writer only once in a lifetime. I was wrong." His experience in China also inspired the picture books *The Boss* (1992) and *Rebel!* (1994) and

affected his science fiction novel *Magician* (1993). For *Songman,* a historical novel for young adults about the Aboriginal people in Australia before the arrival of Captain Cook, Baillie traveled to the Yolgnu settlement in Arnhem Land and was taught the aboriginal way of life for six weeks; this work, he has written, "seems to be a culmination of my moving about and the books I have done." In addition to his books for children and young people, Baillie has contributed short stories to anthologies and magazines in Australia, China, Great Britain, and the United States.

"The centrepiece of all my books," Baillie told Karen Jameyson of *Horn Book,* "is simply to get read, to construct a book like a trap in an attempt to grab the reader, shake him, and—just maybe—never let him go."

Major Works

In his first book, *Adrift,* Baillie reworks the true story that originally inspired him by focusing on schoolboy Flynn and his five-year-old sister, Sally, who are swept out to sea with their cat on an empty crate off the shores of Sydney, Australia. During their two-day ordeal, the children, who have no tools, food, or protection, face hunger and thirst as well as a storm and a shark before being rescued; through his experience, Flynn draws on unexplored inner resources and also comes to a better understanding of his father. A critic in *Publishers Weekly* notes that *Adrift* "offers a harrowing look at survival without losing sight of the protagonists' character. . . . Fans of *The Cay* and *The Red Badge of Courage* should be equally taken with this well-crafted yarn." Hazel Rochman of *Booklist* claims, "Like Paulsen's *Hatchet* and all the best survival stories, this is also about the inner journey to take responsibility and find your way home." *Books for Keeps* reviewer Valerie Bierman notes, "It says much for the author's skill as a storyteller that the tension between two children and a cat sitting on a drifting crate remains for the entire book." In *Little Brother,* which is set at the beginning of the Vietnam invasion, Baillie changes his protagonist's name to Vithy but otherwise keeps many details of the real boy's story intact. Separated from his older brother Marig in their escape from the Khmer Rouge, eleven-year-old Vithy reaches a refugee camp in Thailand and works in the hospital there; he is reunited with Marig, whom he has given up for dead, after he agrees to go to Australia at the request of a doctor who has befriended him. Although some critics see the circumstances in which the brothers reunite as somewhat far-fetched, most consider *Little Brother* to be an exceptional story. Writing in *Voice of Youth Advocates (VOYA),* Barbara Flottmeier says, "Novels that foster an understanding of another culture and history are rare, and those that are interesting and written for young adults are rarer still. Such a novel is *Little Brother. . . .*" *School Library Journal* contributor John Philbrook concurs: "This excellent tale of courage and survival lends real life flesh to textbook facts. . . . It should be mandatory reading for anyone working with Southeast Asian youth." Writing in *Books for Keeps,* Valerie Bierman claims that *Little Brother* is "a gem which deserves to become a classic, if only to demonstrate to children the futility and cruelty of war." *Riverman* outlines how ten-year-old Brian Walker, a Sydney boy who first appeared as a minor character in *Adrift,* journeys to Tasmania to stay with his great-uncle Tim, who has agreed to help him with his school project on family history. Uncle Tim shows Brian "Walker's Tree," a huge, thousand-year old pine that he discovered as a youth in 1912, and tells him about his own boyhood: when Tim's father is killed in a mine explosion, the boy goes with his forester uncle into unexplored territory in search of sellable timber; through his experiences, which include facing tigers and the dangers of the river as well as the pain of losing his father, Tim grows to the status of "Riverman." Writing in *Growing Point,* Margery Fisher says, "A pioneering past is brought to life in an old man's words. . . ."

Baillie's next book, *Eagle Island* (1987), is his first for young adults: it outlines how Lew, a hearing-impaired teenager, and his nemesis, the delinquent Cal, come to face each other on an eagle-inhabited island in the Great Barrier Reef; Lew accidentally comes across a stash of drugs with which Cal is connected. "A first-rate novel," writes *British Book News Children's Supplement* contributor Margaret R. Marshall, who adds that the story is "not about a deaf teenager but about teenagers, one of whom who happens to be deaf." With *Drac and the Gremlin,* Baillie makes his first contribution to the picture book genre. This book, for which the idea came to Baillie in a dream, joins a fantastic adventure with Jane Tanner's naturalistic illustrations. The pictures depict a young girl and her little brother as they play in a suburban yard, but the text describes their activities differently: the girl calls herself Drac, the Warrior Queen of Tirnol Two, and her brother is the Gremlin; together they save the White Wizard's planet from the Terrible-Tongued Dragon. "[T]his clever juxtaposition of science fiction and artistic realism makes for an interesting mix," writes Ilene Cooper of *Booklist,* who calls the book "a testament to the rich fantasy world of children." Baillie's interest in science fiction emerges fully in *Megan's Star* (1988), a young adult novel set in the twenty-first century about a teenage girl with paranormal powers who is unhappy at home and is called a witch at school. Wandering around in suburban Sydney, Megan rescues Kel, a boy with psychic gifts who has escaped from the scientific institution where he is being exploited. Megan and Kel go to the moon and beyond; Kel stays on one of the planets they have discovered, but Megan decides to return home. Writing in *Growing Point,* Margery Fisher says, "The idea of a girl trying to break out of a lonely, constricting life is deepened by superb descriptions of movement in space . . . ; there is a positive imaginative thrust in the story which should strongly affect the reader and make any question of literal belief irrelevant." *Books for Keeps* reviewer George Hunt adds, "I found this moving and exciting story put me back in touch with those aspects of SF which originally attracted me to the genre. . . ." Baillie's second science fiction novel for young adults, *Magician* (1993), is set thousands of years into the future when the last remaining humans are living in a desert in Australasia;

the story describes how young Kim leads his people from the desert to a more suitable planet with the help of an alien being. Writing in the *School Librarian,* Jessica Yates says, "this parable is thought-provoking and yet punchily told."

Two of Baillie's most highly regarded works are *The China Coin* and *Songman.* In *The China Coin,* eleven-year-old Leah goes with her mother from Australia to China in order to trace her roots and search for the holder of the other half of a broken coin being held by her mother. Leah journeys from village to village, meeting relatives and learning about the culture of her ancestors. The Australians also develop a close relationship with one of their relatives, Ke, a student activist who has the missing half of the coin. Leah and her mother follow Ke to Beijing and then to Tiananmen Square; during the protest, Leah is left with the two halves of the coin as a symbol of the division among her people. Writing in *Magpies,* Kevin Steinberger notes that this "superbly constructed novel . . . will not be quickly forgotten," while Adrian Jackson of *Books for Keeps* calls *The China Coin* "a wonderful book where the events in Peking are re-seen in a living context, to shock and horrify as well as deepen our understanding of particular history and the bonds which unite us all." Set in Australia in 1720, *Songman* describes how Yukuwa, a sensitive Aboriginal boy who is not particularly adept at hunting or fishing, learns to accept himself and to find a place in his community. Yukuwa travels to Macassar with his adopted father Dawu, his close friend Jago, and the traders who come every year to his home among the Yolngu people of Arnhem Land. While in the Macassars, Yukuwa learns how to make dugout canoes and Dawu finds a wife and decides to stay. On the voyage home, Jago is killed when the boat in which he and Yukuwa are traveling is attacked by pirates. Yukuwa, who is greatly affected by his experiences, accepts the fact that he will never be a good hunter or warrior and decides to be a songman so that he can sing "of laughter, anger, terror, and, sometimes, of the soft pain Jago has left." Writing in *Reading Time,* Sophie Masson says, "*Songman* is a mould-breaker of a book; an unusual and engrossing look at a relatively unexplored period of history. . . ." *Australian Book Review* critic Pam McIntyre claims, "[Yukuwa is] one of the most realised characters of recent YA fiction," and notes, "This is a book with much to offer . . . that should find readily the readership it deserves." Writing in *Junior Bookshelf,* Marcus Crouch claims that with *Songman* Allan Baillie "pays his most moving tribute to Australia," while *Magpies* reviewer Agnes Nieuwenhuizen calls the novel Baillie's "best book yet."

Awards

In 1983, Baillie won the first Kathleen Fidler Award in the category of middle grade fiction for *Adrift;* this award, presented by the National Book League in the United Kingdom, is given to unpublished manuscripts for young readers by Commonwealth authors. In 1988, *Riverman* won the International Board on Books for Young People (IBBY)

Award in the Australian writing category. In 1989, *Drac and the Gremlin* was named Picture Book of the Year by the Children's Book Council of Australia; *Little Brother* was named a Book of the Year Highly Commended by the same group in 1986. *The China Coin* won the Australian Multicultural Children's Literature Award in 1992. Baillie has also received awards for his short stories as well as several fellowships and grants.

GENERAL COMMENTARY

Valerie Bierman

SOURCE: "May We Recommend Allan Baillie," in *Books for Keeps,* No. 51, July, 1988, p. 17.

It's not often that a relative newcomer writes a string of unputdownables. . . .

Anyone reading Allan Baillie's books will quickly realise that he has his own distinctive style; a flair for creating suspense, an uncanny knack of understanding an emotional crisis in children, and all revolving around a search, either for adventure or, more often, for identity.

Born in Scotland in 1943 but emigrating to Australia seven years later, much of his own character, either unwittingly or by design, frequently surfaces in his books. His obvious sympathy and understanding of disability stems from an accident at the age of 21 which left him semi-paralysed and with a speech impediment.

His writing career began when he worked as a journalist and published some short stories. After reading about the newly founded Kathleen Fidler Award, he decided to submit a manuscript of a children's novel; *Adrift* went on to win the Award. As with all Baillie's books it was based on fact. His wife Agnes had given him a newspaper cutting about four Lebanese boys and their dog being washed out to sea on an old raft. This spark of an idea grew into a full-length novel having as its core characters Flynn, his young sister Sally and, a nice touch, their cat Nebuchadnezzar. As in all good adventure tales it begins with a holiday. But here similarity ends.

> Flynn turned and saw something angular and black moving on Sally's shoulder. There was blood in the water. He kicked until he could breathe and tried to lift the cat off Sally but the cat was sinking its claws into her head. Sally had closed her eyes and was whimpering from the pain. She screamed when Flynn tried to pry a claw from her head. The cat made a sound he had never heard before, like a snake about to strike, and then bit his hand. Sally screamed until water flooded into her mouth.

The three manage to scramble aboard their crate and as the shoreline recedes further into the distance, Flynn reflects that they are in trouble—big trouble. It says much for the author's skill as a storyteller that the tension between two children and a cat sitting on a drifting crate remains for the entire book.

The next book resulted from his years covering the Vietnam war, a deeply disturbing experience for Allan Baillie. He had toyed with the idea of writing an adult novel for years, then realised that perhaps the horrors of war could best be conveyed through the eyes of a child—to give a child's innocent view which often has a clarity and understanding lacking in adults. *Little Brother* is based on a chance meeting with a 16-year-old boy he found bandaging the wounds of a Khmer Rouge soldier. The boy had lost everything—family, friends, home—and lived a fearful existence in the jungle. The boy's experiences were used as a background to the character Vithy, separated from his elder brother while fleeing from the Vietcong. *Little Brother* means a great deal to Baillie. It is his favourite book—a gem which deserves to become a classic, if only to demonstrate to children the futility and cruelty of war.

Then two books followed in rapid succession. *Riverman* takes the reader back to 1912, to Tasmania where Tim's dad has been laid off from the smelter and has gone to Queenstown to find work. On his return they've planned a trip up the river to find the Thunderer, a huge waterfall that no-one has ever seen. Then there is a fire in a mine— and Tim's Dad is down there. . . .

His childhood comes to an abrupt end and Tim is determined to prove that although he is derisorily known as The Shrimp, he can take his place with the men. He journeys up river with his uncle, copes with the scorn of the others, and draws on an inner strength to overcome the deep pain of his father's death.

Eagle Island, a racy thriller and Allan Baillie's most *Australian* novel, is set on an island in the Great Barrier Reef. Lew, the hero, is deaf. Col, his most hated enemy, picks on him at school because of his odd way of speaking. Lew's one pleasure in life is his catamaran, which his parents had been against at first. "'How can he sail something like that?' she said, or he thought she said . . . "He'll drown." How can he *not* sail it? Here's something he can do as well as other kids.' Lew was going to forget about Col for two weeks as he set sail for the distant Whitsundays; he could almost forget about being deaf. The trip is vividly described and the word pictures of the wealth of wildlife make fascinating reading. (I defy anyone to read of Lew cooking a coral trout without their mouth watering!) This idyllic life is rudely interrupted by the appearance of Col, and their encounter turns into a deadly game of hide and seek. *Eagle Island* should be lapped up by older readers.

1988 sees the latest Baillie offering, *Megan's Star,* no doubt his most challenging and complex work so far. For the first time the central character is female—Megan, who reluctantly has to look after her small brother Walter, otherwise known as Goblin. Their mother works all day and their father has walked out on them. . . .

Set in the 21st century *Megan's Star* is an interesting mix of science fiction and traditional adventure story. It reveals yet another layer of Allan Baillie's talent.

There's more to come. . . . Here is a first-class writer with the power to stretch children's imaginations and make them think. His books deserve to be far more widely read—this is a writer well worth discovering.

Karen Jameyson

SOURCE: "News from Down Under," in *The Horn Book Magazine,* Vol. LXVII, No. 4, July-August, 1991, pp. 493-95.

"The centrepin of all my books is simply to get read, to construct a book like a trap in an attempt to grab the reader, shake him, and—just maybe—never let him go." Allan Baillie accomplishes what he sets out to do. Across Australia—and, increasingly, in other countries as well—his books are opened, and traps snap shut. For such a friendly, good-hearted human being, this talented writer has certainly done more than his share of ensnaring unsuspecting readers.

I've been a victim myself. Not long after arriving in Australia, I began reading *Little Brother* on a train ride home one evening. The author's books had been recommended to me, but I was mostly just curious to see how an Australian writer coped with a Cambodian setting. No sooner had I made it through the first page than—SNAP!—Baillie had himself another literary prisoner. A kind lady elbowed me at the last train stop. "Must be a beaut book," she remarked, as I collided numbly with seats, doors, and passengers on my way out. And so it is. The novel tells the story of the young boy Vithy on his desperate and treacherous run in war-torn Kampuchea. Separated from his only living relative, an older brother named Mang, Vithy has determined that he will get to the border, hundreds of kilometers away, where he believes Mang may be waiting. Dodging the Khmer Rouge, terrorized by the unfamiliar forest environment, and basically struggling for survival, Vithy perseveres in his arduous journey.

Taut, clear writing, fast pacing, and an intensely vivid backdrop distinguish *Little Brother.* Although the ending has been criticized as being less realistic than the rest of the narrative, young readers seem to respond favorably, and the title's overall effect is undeniable: we are with Vithy every step and stumble of the way.

This sort of vivid physical setting typifies Baillie's writing. It's one of the strengths that has helped earn his six novels widespread critical acclaim and a place in the hearts of young readers. His characters' actions and metamorphoses usually intertwine quite snugly with their immediate environment—whether it's Cambodia, the Tasmanian wilderness, the Whitsunday Islands, a suburban Sydney neighborhood, or contemporary China.

In the picture book *Drac and the Gremlin,* written by Baillie and illustrated by Jane Tanner, physical surroundings become almost a member of the cast of players. With an ingenious interplay of fantasy and reality the book tells two stories. While the illustrations show two children romping with their pets in the yard, the text relates the fantastical saga of Drac, the Warrior Queen of Tirnol Two, and the Gremlin of the Groaning Grotto, who is "quick, quiet as a spider, and very, very dangerous." In these circumstances the garden setting takes on a whole new life.

The environmental force of water comes streaming through Baillie's work again and again. In *Hero* the action revolves around the Sydney flood of 1986, as the waters of the Hawkesbury River rise and threaten to overwhelm an outer suburb. The penetrating wetness practically oozes through the pages. Against that backdrop Baillie has braided together three strands of story—of character, actually.

Aside from attending the same school, Darcy, Pam, and Barney could scarcely be more different from one another. Each youngster grapples with personal and quite distinct inner turmoils revolving around home and family. None of them has any particular interest in the other two. But as the flood peaks, the three find themselves thrown together like pebbles and must somehow manage to reach inside themselves to confront a life-threatening situation.

Divided into chapters and written in the third person, the novel moves from one child's perspective to the next. So just as we become completely immersed in Darcy's struggles and actions, for instance, we switch to Barney's story. While Baillie demands a lot of his readers with such a technique, the structure is a remarkably effective one for conveying character. We come to understand each of these young people well. We feel sharply their individual problems. As a result, the climactic scene simply swells with poignancy.

Just as ambitious in another way, the author's latest novel, *The China Coin,* will be published by Viking in Australia in late 1991. As part of a 1988 Children's Book Council delegation traveling to China, Baillie became inspired with several ideas for books set in that country. He subsequently returned to China with his family in tow—his Chinese wife and their daughter and son—to research the titles. They trekked together through areas described in the novel, ending in Beijing in the spring of 1989. Although the rest of the family left at that point, Baillie stayed on and was in the country during the events of Tiananmen Square.

The result is a fascinating, moving, at times heart-wrenching story, set in China in May and June of 1989. Following her father's death, Leah, an Australian-born Chinese girl, has journeyed to China with her mother, seeking the missing half of an old coin which they hope will elucidate some family history. The search is challenging. In fact, the entire experience turns out to be an amazing emotional hodgepodge in a country creaking and swaying under the weight of student demonstrations. Baillie's skill at communicating a setting and the characters involved with that setting once again lifts his narrative to soaring heights. Streaked with political unrest, populated with a riveting cast of characters, dusted with a touch of romance, and pulled along always by the mystery of the broken coin, the novel will undoubtedly trap a few more readers and—"just maybe"—never let them go.

TITLE COMMENTARY

ADRIFT (1983)

Margery Fisher

SOURCE: A review of *Adrift,* in *Growing Point,* Vol. 22, No. 3, September, 1983, pp. 4132-33.

[A dangerous journey in australian waters not far from Sydney] is described in *Adrift,* the first book chosen for the Kathleen Fidler Award for fiction for the 8-12 age-group. . . . Allan Baillie has been alert to suggest the ebb and flow of courage, the moments of resentment and despair, which direct the actions of schoolboy Flynn when because of a careless accident he and his little sister Sally float out to sea on an empty crate with the family cat. Thirst, a prowling shark, storm, the restless animal, all exact from Flynn the utmost ingenuity and endurance he can muster, his feeling of responsibility for the small girl changes its scope during the hours of danger; there is time also in the two-day ordeal for him to remember moments in the past. These moments bring him to a better understanding of his father, who has made a necessary (but to Flynn an unjustified) move from the country to difficult town life. Flynn sees only what a boy of his age could be expected to see of adult constraints and problems; the author weaves his reflections and memories skilfully into the hour-by-hour events of the down-coast voyage to its fortunate conclusion. The book is tightly constructed on a plan that makes for variety and forward movement and holds the readers attention with aptly chosen details of wind and weather.

D. A. Young

SOURCE: A review of *Adrift,* in *The Junior Bookshelf,* Vol. 47, No. 6, December, 1983, p. 253.

Flynn, who must be about twelve, is carried out to sea, with his five-year old-sister Sally, and a mangy cat on an old crate. They are subject to all the hazards of the sea. They have no provisions, no tools and no protection from the hot sun, the rain or the storm. They survive and in so doing demonstrate courage and a will to live. It is quite a harrowing story in itself and complicated by a series of flashbacks which concern Flynn's difficulty with his family relationships. He doesn't get on with his Dad and as he

battles with the elements to keep himself and his sister alive he remembers and reflects upon significant events in the past. I cannot help feeling that this is a sophisticated technique for eight to twelve-year-olds. Flynn's thinking is articulated in a very mature way which might puzzle even a bright young reader.

Its merits as a novel make it a well-deserved prize winner but one wonders if they make it an attractive read for the age range concerned.

Hazel Rochman

SOURCE: A review of *Adrift,* in *Booklist,* Vol. 88, No. 14, March 15, 1992, p. 1356.

In an exciting survival adventure set in Australia, Flynn, his little sister, Sally, and her cat jump into an old crate they find floating by the rocks. At first it's a game, like pirates after treasure, but before they know it, they're swept out to sea. Adrift. And no one knows they're there. For two days, they cope with thirst, hunger, heat, exposure, shark, storm, and terrible loneliness. As Flynn struggles in the great circle of sea, he talks to his dad in his head, angry at the way things have changed between them since drought and bushfire drove them from the sheep farm to the city. Always, Dad's hunched back seems turned to Flynn. At the same time, Dad is his role model, and Flynn finds courage and resourcefulness he didn't know he had, as well as a new tenderness for his sister. Some of the realistic details don't bear too close scrutiny (does no one even glimpse them as they drift out?), but you know they're going to make it. Like Paulsen's *Hatchet* and all the best survival stories, this is also about the inner journey to take responsibility and find your way home.

Phyllis G. Sidorsky

SOURCE: A review of *Adrift,* in *School Library Journal,* Vol. 38, No. 5, May, 1992, p. 111.

Walking along a beach, Flynn and his younger sister, Sally, discover a large crate and get it to float in a cove. Flynn imagines himself to be a pirate, but must resign himself to taking his whiny sister and her pesky cat aboard. When the box begins drifting out to sea, Sally refuses to abandon her cat, leaving them no other choice than to stay on the box and gravitate toward the horizon. The children suffer from overexposure to the sun, thirst, nighttime cold as well as boredom and fear. While trying to cope with these overwhelming problems, Flynn recalls happier times through stream-of-consciousness images and flashbacks and, while despairing of rescue, reevaluates his feelings for his father. In due course, after even more harrowing episodes, the children reach land and a rescue boat comes into view. While there seems to be a surfeit of perilous episodes, Baillie makes it all sound plausible. This is a survival tale set in Australia, but it is also the account of a boy realistically developing insight into his family and himself. While readers may empathize with his predicament, the story may be too introspective for a broad readership.

Publishers Weekly

SOURCE: A review of *Adrift,* in *Publishers Weekly,* Vol. 239 No. 21, May 4, 1992, p. 57.

Ever since the farm failed, Flynn has had to take care of his baby sister. Now, on vacation, that means walking along the seashore for hours until Sally finds her share of shells. Then Flynn finds a big crate—a perfect pirate ship—and he and Sally climb aboard. The tide carries them away from land, and the boy soon realizes that they are in serious trouble. Several boats pass them and, as in Steven Callahan's novel (also titled *Adrift*), Baillie's narrative shows how the successful survivor learns to make his own luck. Flynn rigs a sail from his shirt, and the children eventually make their way home. Based on a true incident, the novel offers a harrowing look at survival without losing sight of the protagonist's character. Flynn wrestles with his feelings for his sister and with the changes in his parents that give him an adult's responsibility before he's ready. Fans of *The Cay* and *The Red Badge of Courage* should be equally taken with this well-crafted yarn.

📖 LITTLE BROTHER (1985)

Margery Fisher

SOURCE: A review of *Little Brother,* in *Growing Point,* Vol. 24, No. 3, September, 1985, p. 4492.

Separated from his older brother in their escape from forced labour under the Khmer Rouge, Vithy, the *Little Brother* of the title, has no map to guide him out of Kampuchea; he must follow Mang's plan to get over the border into peaceful Thailand somehow but his eleven years have always been organised by others and the dangerous enforced independence is not easy. Finding food, putting together a rackety bicycle from a graveyard of discarded machines, hiding from distant figures who have to be assumed to be hostile, Vithy eventually reaches a refugee camp and there waits anxiously for news of the brother whom he fears has been shot, working meanwhile in the hospital, where he discovers that 'the enemy' is not unlike himself. By the time he is reunited with Mang the six or seven years between them seem to have telescoped, for Vithy has grown up. Without any exaggerated sentiment Allan Baillie has described the long journey to freedom entirely from the boy's point of view; jungle, road, ruined temple, refugee camp, all appear vividly before our eyes but in an entirely practical way as Vithy makes his dangerous way across country to the border. Compact, well planned and full of lively detail of place and people, this book offers stimulating reading to children around nine or ten for whom stories are all too often filleted and bland.

R. Baines

SOURCE: A review of *Little Brother,* in *The Junior Bookshelf,* Vol. 49, No. 5, October, 1985, p. 224.

Pursuit is close behind the two fleeing boys when Vithy sprains his foot. After concealing his younger brother Mang leads the soldiers away through the forest, but a single shot rings out . . . Vithy is left with nothing but the determination to find Mang, and his brother's instruction to "follow the lines of war" to the border.

Allan Baillie's well told and exciting story is set against the background of the Vietnamese war. He writes authoritatively with the style and pace of a former newspaper reporter of the tragic and terrifying circumstances which existed in that place at that time, highlighting the dangers which beset Vithy by contrasting them with the boy's memories of his former happy family life.

Vithy eventually reaches a refugee hospital on the border of Thailand where an Australian woman doctor befriends him. She contrives a happy ending, leaving the reader wishing that it might be so.

Carolyn Phelan

SOURCE: A review of *Little Brother,* in *Booklist,* Vol. 88, No. 10, January 15, 1992, p. 939.

Fleeing from the Khmer Rouge soldiers, Vithy becomes separated from his older brother, Mang, as they try to escape from Cambodia into Thailand. Vithy, numbed by the deaths of his other family members, must now endure separation from Mang and confront the possibility of Mang's death. As Vithy makes his dangerous journey, he comes to rely on his own wits and instincts. Historical novel, adventure, and character study, this book takes readers to another place and time, giving a sense of the culture and traditions of the Cambodian people and an even stronger sense of individual and family loss brought about by war. . . . First published in Australia, Baillie's novel offers children a vivid glimpse of a sympathetic character whose life is changed irrevocably by forces beyond his understanding.

John Philbrook

SOURCE: A review of *Little Brother,* in *School Library Journal,* Vol. 38, No. 3, March, 1992, p. 237.

Brothers Mang and Vithy, having escaped the Khmer Rouge, are being pursued through the Cambodian jungle. When the younger boy sprains his ankle, Mang leads their recent captors away from him. A single shot rings out and he does not return. Vithy, about 11, now sets out to accomplish the brothers' original plan of escaping to the Thai border, hoping to be reunited with Mang. The story is set at the beginning of the Vietnamese invasion, so there is danger of being caught in the crossfire, but also room for kindness from strangers as the Vietnamese have liberated much of the countryside from the vise of the Khmer Rouge. There are also well-integrated vignettes of earlier, happier times as Vithy recalls his life with his parents and little sister, all since murdered. The highly believable plot leads the boy to his goal and a refugee hospital, where an Australian doctor befriends him and engineers his re-settlement with her in Sydney. The novel is well written and realistically developed, Vithy being so nicely drawn in varying emotions that one suspects that he is based on a real person. No heavy-handed theme dominates the text, yet it conveys a chilling glimpse of what many Cambodian children have had to endure. . . . This excellent tale of courage and survival lends real life flesh to textbook facts and will be welcomed in most collections. It should be mandatory reading for anyone working with Southeast Asian youth.

Barbara Flottmeier

SOURCE: A review of *Little Brother,* in *Voice of Youth Advocates,* Vol. 15, No. 3, August, 1992, p. 166.

Novels that foster an understanding of another culture and history are rare, and those that are interesting and written for young adults are rarer still. Such a novel is **Little Brother,** a heartbreaking novel of one young boy, Vithy, and his escape from the Khmer Rouge in Cambodia to Thailand during the Vietnam War.

Vithy and his older brother Mang escape from enforced labor in the high rice paddies in Cambodia, intending to find freedom from their captors. When Mang uses himself as a decoy to lead the soldiers from his injured brother, Vithy is left alone in the terror-ridden forests and hills to fend for himself and search for the Thai border with the freedom it represents. This is the story of struggle and survival much like *Hatchet* by Gary Paulsen but it also is the revelation of a foreign culture: its joys and fears, beauty and devastation; its family relationships and the indomitable will of a people to survive.

This story would be a good companion to *Children of the River* by Linda Crew, particularly good for Social Studies units but just as good for an exciting read. The cover art appears a bit juvenile and the story will have to be sold at first.

📖 *RIVERMAN* (1986)

Margery Fisher

SOURCE: A review of *Riverman,* in *Growing Point,* Vol. 25, No. 2, July, 1986, pp. 46, 50-51.

A Sydney boy arrives in Tasmania to stay with his great-uncle who is to help him with a school project on his family's history. Expecting to be given letters to read or

photographs to look at, Brian is surprised to be taken on a long journey into the mountains and shown a group of trees which is in fact one single, massive Huon pine more than a thousand years old. The family history Uncle Tim relates goes back to his own boyhood of pioneer days, when his father was killed in a mine explosion and the lad went with his roaming forester uncle Larry and his gang far into the unexplored country in search of saleable timber. Hardships and accident moved him painfully out of boyhood and gave him the status of **Riverman** as he faced the challenge of turbulent river passages and a wilderness of tangled bush and steep ranges. If we seem to enter fully into the boy's experience, as I think we do, it is mainly because of the vitality, the pictorial quality of a narrative which is more than half description. A pioneering past is brought to life in an old man's words as he offers a city boy a vigorous example of his family's endeavours.

Elizabeth Barry

SOURCE: "Pining Among the Piners," in *The Times Literary Supplement,* No. 4375, February 6, 1987, p. 145.

As part of his research for a school project on family history, ten-year-old Brian Walker travels from his home in Sydney to Tasmania and meets Great Uncle Tim, a tiny wizened old man, certainly "a bundle of puzzles", possibly "as mad as a parrot". Tim knows about things like cannibals and tigers and he takes Brian on a journey to show him "Walker's Tree" and to recount its place in family's legend.

This brief, present-day prologue sets up a historical perspective which is immediately dispensed with as the reader is plunged into an account of events in Zeehan, Silver City in 1912. Tim takes over the centre of the stage and we are told of the death of his father in a mining accident and of a wild, illicit ride on a record-breaking steam-train "Mount Lyell Number Three". Such are Tim's despair and despondency, however, that his Uncle Larry decides to take him on a trip up-river with his fellow piners (loggers). The trip is ostensibly to find a waterfall, but we understand that it will help Tim forget his loss and make a man of him.

The main part of the book describes the journey, the smashing, grinding battle with the river and all its hardships, from the dank piners' huts, in which it is up to Tim to light the fire, to Tasmanian tigers. There is enough excitement and real danger in the journey to help Tim grow up but there are additional emotional hazards in his mourning his father and in his relationships with Larry (who is hard on the boy in order to hide his own feelings and for his good). At the journey's end there is the discovery and naming of Walker's Tree, a gigantic Huon pine, and a bizarre but moving journey back to civilization when Larry (who has been blinded), carries Tim (who has been lamed) on his back to act as his eyes.

Allan Baillie's way with this somewhat rich material is to

get in close and move it along fast. The details of Tim's steam-propelled ride at the start of the book are clear and, presumably, historically accurate, but the sweep of the train through the dramatic landscape is never slowed; the descriptions of the sights and smells of the river are not clogged with too much information about button grass or bowyangs, not even about Walker's Tree itself, which was pushing out shoots "when people in Europe still had stone-tipped spears". When it comes to fighting the elements, sheer excitement carries the day. There is more than just skill with high adventure, though; Baillie, who won the Kathleen Fidler Award in 1983, also writes sensitively about Tim's feelings and does not overdo the masculine world of the rivermen. In contrast to the pace and sweep of the adventure story, the return to "real" life in the book's epilogue is a comparatively tame tying-up of loose ends: "They don't call it Deception Gorge any more, just the Great Ravine with rapids like the Churn, Coruscades, Thunderush, the Cauldron."

David Bennett

SOURCE: A review of *Riverman*, in *Books for Keeps*, No. 56, May, 1989, p. 76.

You don't get many novels set in turn-of-the-century Tasmania! For Tim Walker it looks as though his diminutive size will make it extra tough for him to find a niche in the gritty, aggressive, pioneering world of his father and Uncle Larry. But when that world destroys the father, the uncle takes Tim on a voyage up the Franklin River to fell Huon Pines, and Tim discovers more than danger— wider horizons, he also learns a lot about himself and how to live with grief. It's a very boyish book but I doubt it'll make too many strong waves.

EAGLE ISLAND (1987)

Margaret R. Marshall

SOURCE: A review of *Eagle Island*, in *British Book News Children's Books*, June, 1987, p. 28.

Allan Baillie has a powerful style, seen in his award winning books *Adrift* and *Little Brother* and evident in this story of two teenage boys, Col a delinquent in conflict with Lew, who is deaf. Set in Australia's Great Barrier Reef, the sympathetic yet positive treatment of Lew's deafness and the references to his gang, the Flying Finger Mob (sign-language communication), are skilfully woven into the plot so that the story is not about a deaf teenager but about teenagers, one of whom happens to be deaf. Pace, tension and action come as Col searches for a metal box dropped in to the Reef from a plane. Lew is revelling in the solitude of his eagle-inhabited island, where his deafness is no handicap, until Col invades his privacy, their respective boats are destroyed and the ugly contents of the box are revealed. There is some excellent characterization, some memorable description and a contempo-

rary sting in the tail, making a first-rate novel with appeal for boys aged twelve to sixteen.

A. R. Williams

SOURCE: A review of *Eagle Island*, in *The Junior Bookshelf*, Vol. 51, No. 3, June, 1987, p. 129.

Allan Baillie tells a straightforward story of a deaf boy's adventure which is threatened by the greed of small-time criminals involved in drug running as a result of his accidentally coming upon a cache of drugs near his 'personal' island retreat. This is his Border Island, around 20S 149E, among the Whitsunday Islands off the north east coast of Queensland between the Australian mainland and the Great Barrier reef. Only some two miles long and one and a half miles wide, it is a limited area for the classic climax of hide-and-seek which Mr. Baillie organises for his closing sequence. For sailors there is much of interest in Lew's coping with navigation and survival at sea. In the accompanying map one 'l' is twice squeezed out of 'Molle'; otherwise the cartography is informative and relevant.

MEGAN'S STAR (1988)

Margery Fisher

SOURCE: A review of *Megan's Star*, in *Growing Point*, Vol. 27, No. 4, January, 1989, pp. 5088-89.

In *Megan's Star* the improbable is used as a way of presenting the character of a girl who feels she is a misfit, both at school where she is teased as a witch and at home where her father has left with a younger woman and her librarian mother is perpetually tired and despondent. Megan's reputation at school comes partly from her loner habits and partly from her unwise exploration of a power of foreknowledge. At first this power had alarmed her; then, wandering in the suburb of Sydney where she lives, she pulls out of a fallen house a boy with kinetic and ESP gifts who has escaped from a scientific institute where he is being extensively examined and exploited. Hiding in an old warehouse, Kel encourages Megan to join him in achieving Distant Vision by which they voyage together to the Moon and beyond; here Kel elects to stay on a planet where they have found alien intelligences but Megan prefers to return to her unsatisfactory but familiar world. The idea of a girl trying to break out of a lonely, constricting life is deepened by superb descriptions of movements in space, a worthy image for her emotional vacillation; there is a positive imaginative thrust in the story which should strongly affect the reader and make any question of literal belief irrelevant.

George Hunt

SOURCE: A review of *Megan's Star*, in *Books for Keeps*, No. 65, November, 1990, p. 11.

Megan, a troubled adolescent living in a vividly depicted coastal metropolis, rescues Kel while he's on the run from vivisectors intent on probing the source of his psychokinetic ability. He reveals Megan's own powers to her, and together they embark on a celestial odyssey.

I found this moving and exciting story put me back in touch with those aspects of SF which originally attracted me to the genre: the description of links between Earth and Universe, and the sheer fascination of seeing different worlds through the eyes of an imaginative writer.

📖 *DRAC AND THE GREMLIN* (1989)

[The following essays are by Baillie and illustrator Jane Tanner and describe their collaboration on Drac and the Gremlin.]

Allan Baillie

SOURCE: "Jane Tanner and I," in *Reading Time,* Vol. 34, No. 1, 1990, pp. 4-6.

For me *Drac and the Gremlin* has become a touchstone. It spans my career in writing children's books, from *Adrift* into the Future, and it has given me some of my best moments—the sort of moments that make children's writing a deep pleasure.

The beginning of *Drac* was in 1983, when Bob Sessions bought my first kids book, *Adrift,* for Nelson and assigned Jane Tanner to do a cover for the book—in two days! (That cover is still being printed by Nelson for their Young Australia edition.)

I loved the cover then, and met Jane when we were in Canberra for the CBCA 1985 Book of the Year. We were both on short lists, her for her work in Margaret Wild's *A sea in my bedroom,* me for *Adrift.*

Neither of us won anything so we retreated to the pub and sulked. Until Jane said: "Baillie, why don't you write a picture book?"

Jane flew back to Melbourne and I sagged into the guest bed of CBC Canberra president Lynn Fletcher, thinking I didn't know anything about writing picture books, couldn't do it, why didn't Tanner bag her head?

At about 1 am I woke and sat up in bed. I think I hissed: "I've got it!" The entire thing—the idea, the plot, the characters—had been dumped on me while I snored. Later Fletcher was muttering something about royalties for the guest bed.

It took me a while, but I was able to work out where the idea came from. I had often gazed wistfully out my home-office window and watched my kids, Lynne and Peter, play in the back yard. Play? More like murder each other.

And I could remember how I had shot a hundred bandits with a bent stick in an afternoon.

Well, I went home and wrote the story with brackets showing Jane what the reader saw. Like: The Terrible Tongued Dragon is upon them! (A floppy-eared dog with long tongue bounces about.)

Jane had trouble working it out until her daughter led her through it, but she said yes. Whereupon she came up to the Baillie house in Sydney, with some idea of having a little holiday.

Hah! She was locked in a cell with some paper and pencils, fed on bread and water until she produced a storyboard. (Perhaps I exaggerate, but what do you expect from a kids' writer?) She would think up an idea, and I'd make a change at my end of the house, and the house would sound like an elephant charge as we swapped thoughts. Then Jane took her storyboard outside to pose Lynne and Peter with the dog and cat, before her camera. After that we did have a very short holiday.

The rest of the production story is really hers. She sold the book to a dubious Sessions with a few roughs and my fourth draft. Sessions had left Nelson and established himself as an independent publisher. Jane replaced the photos of my kids and animals with local kids and animals, which she could use any time.

Time passed. We signed contracts, Sessions kicked me toward my tenth draft, *Riverman* and *Eagle Island* followed *Little Brother.* There was evil muttering in the jungle about stewing slow artists.

But suddenly Sessions is on the phone, joyful, excited, flapping round the office. He has one of Jane's completed colour illustrations and—we have a book!

Steady, steady . . .

He'll send a colour photo, a little washed out, to show me what we're getting.

The picture is of Drac talking to the transmogrified White Wizard, the little girl with the butterfly on her shoulder.

Have we ever got a book!

But that was almost all I saw of the colour pages before publication. Jane is superstitious and will not allow any author to see any colour work in process for his/her book. The pencil roughs are fine, but colour is taboo. So when I visit her, the studio is locked, blinds are down and the lock is blocked.

But she did invite me to appear on a TV show with her and she had to take some of the Drac art with her. She was thinking of asking me to wear a blindfold . . .

Sessions—now boiling tea at Penguin—pushed me up to my thirteenth draft and Jane came up to Sydney again, this time to display some work in a Penrith gallery. I would pick her up and we would have a little holiday before she goes back to Sydney. Despite the rain.

Except the Nepean River broke its banks, trapping me and hundreds of motorists on flooded roads and Jane standing in ankle-deep water outside the locked gallery, waiting for me to appear. What do you do in situations like that? Well, I sat in my dry car, looked at the rain and thought up a book. Called *Hero,* which I wasn't.

Megan's Star was released—a more serious version of Drac?—and Drac was finally published.

And things began to happen. A class was challenged to try their hands at producing Drac-type yarns and came up with one tentacle, one red eye monster (vacuum cleaner) and a galaxy gun (rotary hoist). A library had a Drac fancy dress party, we received masterpieces of the Terrible Tongued Dragon, and Jane's work was touring Australia with Dromkeen.

I disappeared into China to research a book, became involved in the Beijing massacre and came back quivering and angry. The CBCA awards affair at Hobart helped pour me back together again.

Now Jane and I are working together—of a sort. She is doing the paperback cover of *Megan's Star* and the new paperback cover of *Eagle Island.* She has done the hardback cover of *Hero*—hers by right—and if I can ever get the China novel right she has promised to do the cover of *The broken coin.*

Jane Tanner has showed me that I can write a picture book. Now my highest ambition is to think up a script that she cannot resist.

Just to watch it come alive. Once more.

Jane Tanner

SOURCE: "Allan Baillie and I," in *Reading Time,* Vol. 34, No. 1, 1990, pp. 5-6.

Drac and the Gremlin taught me many things. Technically it helped me with depth of field and setting a figure into an environment. It also freed me up a little in the use of paint and understanding something of light and movement.

It taught me about the tactile and powerful recollections of childhood locked away in the back of our brains. In helping me to identify with the characters it enabled me to bring them to life.

Most of all it taught me another stage of working in a democratic and respectful way with an author: to see us as equal storytellers.

My initial challenge to Allan was offered about more than

just wanting a good story . . . I wanted to look at the "shape" of a book. How is it read? What *is* integration of text and picture? I had read *Adrift* and really admired Allan's truthful, observed writing. It would be quite a change for him to leave out his wonderful descriptive passages and let the pictures do some of it for him. I felt I could trust Allan's sense of adventure to produce something different. He didn't disappoint me . . . I was delighted with the story of Drac and the irony/conceptualizing it contained.

Brackets from authors to explain text and "what pictures to put where" are absolutely taboo with me. If the story is clear and well written they're not needed. Instructions deny the illustrator's skill at interpreting and bringing their own contribution to the book. Why then would I pay attention to Allan's? Because *this time* the text needed explanation just as in the finished book the pictures do the explaining. I needed Allan's view of the twist as a *starting point* but I did not stick exactly to his instructions . . . they were a diving board for me to leap off.

Drac and the Gremlin evolved as pictures and text changed to accommodate each other. Although Allan's basic story never altered, the form and shape of the book was moulded in a very plastic way. Allan even changed the length of some text after the art work was completed which affected the design of those pages. It took initiative to accommodate these changes and that was its own reward.

It is true that I am quite secretive with my work in progress. I'm not so much superstitious as protective of the creative process.

My pictures evolve from roughs which are merely records of ideas. In the idea stage they can be discussed and changed. The "finished" art work requires a complex and private sculpturing of the image out of its background and each picture is connected to the next like a piece of music. Until I've resolved all the elements to my own satisfaction I cannot permit others to involve themselves in the process any more than a writer would ask for opinions at each paragraph. I will, however, invite constructive criticism if I feel blocked and in need of a fresh viewpoint.

A successful book is usually the product of a number of peoples involvement. Bob Sessions leaves the stamp of his critical mind on the books he publishes. He is unstinting in his enthusiasm and standards of excellence. I also had John Nicholson's advice with type and finished layout. Add to this one of the most patient and generous of children's writers and you've got the climate in which I was fortunate to be working.

Ilene Cooper

SOURCE: A review of *Drac and the Gremlin,* in *Booklist,* Vol. 85, No. 17, May 1, 1989, p. 1544.

In this imaginative book, the text tells one story while the pictures reveal something else. Listeners will hear about Drac, the Warrior Queen of Tirnol Two, who is in dreadful danger from the Gremlin of the Groaning Grotto. The duo's adventures continue through a jungle and across a sea; at least, that's what the words say. But in the pictures Drac and the Gremlin are depicted as two suburban children whose jungle is the backyard. There's a lot going on here: a wizard (Mom) who transforms herself into a butterfly; a fight with the Terrible Tongued Dragon (the family dog); and finally the reward of the Twin Crimson Cones of Tirnol Two (ice cream). The action is all handsomely illustrated by Tanner's full-color artwork. The oversize pictures, which have the look of photographs, grab attention with some arresting close-ups. The story could not stand on its own, but this clever juxtaposition of science fiction and artistic realism makes for an interesting mix. From Australia, this is a testament to the rich fantasy world of children.

Marcia Hupp

SOURCE: A review of *Drac and the Gremlin,* in *School Library Journal,* Vol. 35, No. 12, August, 1989, p. 114.

A young girl and a younger boy play at fantasy amidst the "jungles" (garden), "bubbling seas" (lawn sprinkler), and "black volcano" (smoking barbecue) of their Australian backyard. Enemies at first, the girl ("Drac, the Warrior Queen") and the boy ("the Gremlin of the Groaning Grotto") unite to rescue the "White Wizard," repelling both "General Min" (their cat) and the "Terrible Tongued Dragon" (their dog). At this point, their mother interrupts their play to award them the "Twin Crimson Cones of Tirnol Two" (ice cream cones) for their valor—and this, more than anything, illustrates all that is wrong with this book. It is all too clearly an adult rendering of a child's fantasy. The lavish illustrations leave nothing to the imagination, exposing the fantasy at every turn, while the text seems almost voyeuristic in its intrusion into the private world of the child's imagination. Ironically, this betrays the free spirit that it tries, but fails, to celebrate.

Marcus Crouch

SOURCE: A review of *Drac and the Gremlin,* in *The Junior Bookshelf,* Vol. 53, No. 6, December, 1989, p. 262.

Drac the Warrior Queen and the Gremlin fight out their fantasy wars in the back garden. They are in fact a little girl and her younger brother. Jane Tanner's highly competent pictures bring them to life; they have all the appearance of portraits of real children. This does not make them more endearing. The determined 'cuteness' of these precocious infants soon becomes wearisome, and the story seems to go on for a long time. The drawing of the Australian settings is beautiful, and one wishes that Ms Tanner had harnessed her talents to a more profitable theme.

Liz Waterland

SOURCE: A review of *Drac and the Gremlin,* in *Books for Keeps,* No. 71, November, 1991, p. 7.

Truly sensational illustrations linked to a very clever story explain why this large-format picture book won the title 'Picture Book of the Year '89' in Australia.

The story is just the sort young children tell themselves while playing . . . all about wizards, white witches and terrible-tongued dragons. It delves into the world of the imagination and creates a wonderful impression of magic and adventure.

Alongside the story run the pictures showing what's really happening . . . the dragon is the family hound and Queen Drac, the warrior queen of Tirnol Two, is a little girl playing, with her brother, the Gremlin for the purposes of this adventure, in their garden. Very satisying and full of invitations to talk and imagine. Highly recommended.

HERO (1990)

Marcus Crouch

SOURCE: A review of *Hero,* in *The Junior Bookshelf,* Vol. 54, No. 3, June, 1990, p. 139.

Hero is the story of an actual event, the Sydney floods of 1986, as witnessed and shared by three children of very different characters and backgrounds. Pam has a wealthy, domineering and aggressive father. Barney is the serious and responsible younger son of a farmer. Darcey has a drunken brute of a father and a hopeless mother. He himself is at war with the world. They all go to the same school but have nothing else in common. Then the flood brings them together and tests each one to the limit. Each reacts in an unpredictable way. Afterwards they are changed, but not too much. There are no miracles.

Allan Baillie is a mature writer who knows exactly what he is doing and how to do it. He has his narrative firmly under control. He describes the violent scene with great strength but—despite the title—without heroics. In a crisis like this there is no room for heroism, only for reactions to stress. His three principals, each subject to close scrutiny, are shown through their actions. He avoids analysis. The effect is the more convincing. A great deal is packed within these few pages, and one wishes there had been more room to develop some promising lines. I would like to have got to know Marge better. Marge is the poor girl who lives in a 'dump' but who rises briskly and without fuss to a crisis. Sadly Marge slips out of the story early on. Barney's family too calls for closer acquaintance than we are allowed. These are not criticisms, just an indication that Mr. Baillie is full of ideas fighting to get out; he cannot be contained within these covers. With him the Australian scene, which has produced so many fine stories recently, is in good hands.

Margery Fisher

SOURCE: A review of *Hero,* in *Growing Point,* Vol. 29, No. 2, July, 1990, p. 5369.

A natural disaster is used to offer more than one definition of the term in **Hero.** In 1986 a serious river flood hits the Sydney suburb of Richmond. When the pupils are sent home at mid-day from school, three of them get into difficulties. Pam Browning misses the bus home because she goes back to collect her local history project; Darcy Harris, a disruptive boy with a surly father, steals a trial bike to have fun in the flood water; Barney Stevens, a farmer's son, tries in vain to save a frightened calf in a water hole. After several narrow escapes the three young people find themselves together near the river just as Pam's father, realising he has left it too late to cross the submerged bridge to look for his daughter, makes a fatal attempt to drive over a ford. When the car is held in deep water the two boys have to act. What can they do? And which of them is the more heroic, practical Barney or police-ridden, furious Darcy? The interaction of moods as the two boys and the girl face unexpected peril is matched almost symbolically by the wild confusion of wind and water, while switches in time provide for the reader more information about their personalities and home background. This latest of Allan Baillie's adventures setting problems for the inexperienced young to solve is perhaps his most powerful tale so far.

David Bennett

SOURCE: A review of *Hero,* in *Books for Keeps,* No. 74, May, 1992, p. 19.

Three very different children, caught up in different circumstances and places in the same flood, are dramatically brought together, learning through the experience a great deal about themselves, their families and each other. This is a fast-paced, suspense story, written so that you keep turning the pages and become involved with the individual characters and their plight. There are shades of Ivan Southall's work, which would be worth resurrecting for comparison and contrast.

📖 *THE CHINA COIN* **(1991)**

Kevin Steinberger

SOURCE: A review of *The China Coin,* in *Magpies,* Vol. 6, No. 5, November, 1991, p. 32.

One of the indelible images of the 20th century will surely be that brave, anonymous student confronting the column of tanks rumbling towards Tiananmen Square in June, 1989. Similarly, this superbly constructed novel which culminates in a desperate flight from the terror of that insurrection will not be quickly forgotten.

It is a story of a quest, the archetypal journey punctuated by trials and ordeals, the protagonists driven resolutely against huge odds by belief in their goal. For Australians, Joan and her eleven year-old daughter, Leah, it is a long journey across China seeking Joan's ancestral village and family and the origin of an ancient coin bequeathed to her by her father. As they journey into the centre of China they observe a gathering uprising by students against the Communist regime—a parallel quest for democracy. The journeys become inextricably linked after the Australians locate their Chinese family and Leah develops a close rapport with one of them, Ke, a student activist. They follow him to Beijing and Tiananmen Square.

Through clipped prose and abbreviated dialogue Baillie skilfully simulates the urgency and rapidity of events leading up to the rebellion's violent finale. The relief that the Australians feel as they are trucked off to an evacuation aircraft is fairly palpable. There, all the strands of this compelling, multi-layered novel are drawn together as Leah contemplates the coin and all that it symbolises of their China journeys.

The China Coin is written with an authentic voice; there is much of the author and his family in it. Typically, Baillie has extensively explored and researched the history and locale of his novel. While the background to the revolution is deep and complex, he manages to weave essential details into the story without congestion. Highly recommended.

Marcus Crouch

SOURCE: A review of *The China Coin,* in *The Junior Bookshelf,* Vol. 55, No. 6, December, 1991, p. 257.

One of the most remarkable of last year's novels, William Bell's *Forbidden City* dealt urgently, and very close to the events, with the massacre of Tiananmen Square. Now, less urgently but with equal passion and even more commitment, comes another book on the theme.

Bell's hero was a Canadian boy caught up in the crisis by chance and seeing it, inevitably, as a sympathetic outsider. The players in Allan Baillie's drama see the action through Chinese eyes. The two reactions could not be more different. Leah is Chinese in part and at first reluctantly. She sees herself as Australian. The Chinese part of her inheritance comes in the shape of half a coin, with a letter from her dying grandfather urging her Chinese mother to seek out its other half and with it her lost family. Father has died, and with his death mother has become joan, a changed woman. Chinese perhaps but with 'a Swiss watch, a New Zealand blouse, an Australian skirt. English walking shoes, with an American magazine on her lap.' As they move deeper into China Joan becomes more at home. Leah fights against the influences that press upon her. In each city they meet evidence of unrest, to Joan's distress—she is haunted by childhood memories of rioting. From clue to clue they follow the trail of the coin and find their destination in an ancient village remote beyond the railway. A forgotten family welcomes them warmly, and Leah finds herself involved in their affairs and with Ke, a young student committed to the cause of reform. Ke goes to Beijing to support the weakening protest, and Joan and Leah, sight-seeing on their way back to Australia, are not quite witnesses to the death-throes of the revolution. Leah is left with the two halves of the coin, a symbol of a divided people.

This is strong stuff and at times bitter stuff, but *The China Coin* is rich too in humour, in sharp observation, and with an abundance of loving warmth. This is a novel, not a politico-social document, and everything is seen in human terms. There are vivid portraits, from sketches like the half-demented Communist woman encountered on the train and Heng, the village's Party boss whom Leah, by one glorious, probably costly action, manages to frustrate, to studies of complex relationships of which that between Leah and her troubled mother is the most difficult. After all, the central character of this rewarding novel is not Leah but China herself, infinitely vast, deeply suffering, shaped by centuries of patient endurance.

Laurie Copping

SOURCE: A review of *The China Coin,* in *Reading Time,* Vol. 36, No. 1, 1992, p. 28.

When Leah sets out with her Chinese mother, Joan, to trace family and the mystery of the broken coin, she is embarking on an enthralling journey culminating in the horror of Tiananmen Square. After her English father dies she takes up the quest with her mother. As they journey from village to village, meeting relatives and absorbing the atmosphere of ancient cultures they are drawn inexorably towards Beijing. Baillie succeeds splendidly in creating an array of interesting characters who treat Leah and her mother as honoured guests.

Two themes are interwoven with great skill. We have the story of the broken coin as the search continues for the other half, while, at the same time, we feel the tension of student marches leading to the massacre. At this point it is important to realise that Baillie, who was in China at the time, does not engage in over dramatic language, but rather creates the scene in sorrowful tones.

This is a gripping novel well up to the high standards of this much respected author. Like all good books about a journey, there is a useful map and a diagram of Tiananmen Square. Jane Tanner's cover illustration is quite striking as we see Leah and Ke, in contemplative mood before a background of the Square. *The China Coin* is an important addition to Baillie's growing list of significant works.

Frances Wood

SOURCE: A review of *The China Coin,* in *The School Librarian,* Vol. 40, No. 1, February, 1992, p. 30.

Leah Waters, a half-Chinese, half-Australian teenager, visits China with her mother, and they try to find Joan's family. They bring with them half a Chinese coin, left to Joan by her father who departed from China in 1936, taking his family to Penang. In their search for the other half of the coin, they travel to Canton, Shanghai, up the Yangtse to Sichuan province, and return to Australia via Peking. As they arrive in Canton, the student movement of 1988 reaches its height and they leave Peking in the aftermath of the bloody suppression of the movement in Tian an men Square.

There are many strands to the book. The reactions of Leah and her mother to China are very different. To Leah, her mother becomes almost unrecognisable as she reveals a street-wise attitude to grasping money-changers, jealous relatives and prevaricating officials. The student movement and its danger remind Joan of the anti-Chinese riots she witnessed as a child in Penang, while for Leah, innocent and idealistic, the students are heroes. The book is full of complex details about China and particularly provocative in its revelation of the problematic relationships between overseas Chinese and their 'back-home' cousins. For questioning teenagers this could well provoke much further reading, about recent political events in China and the centuries-old question of the Chinese diaspora and its significance. To which end, I'd recommend, among others, Zhang Xinxin and Sang Ye's *Chinese Lives: An Oral History of Contemporary China* and Lynn Pan's *Sons of the Yellow Emperor: the Story of the Overseas Chinese.*

Adrian Jackson

SOURCE: A review of *The China Coin,* in *Books for Keeps,* No. 80, May, 1993, p. 17.

The events of Tiananmen Square in 1989 are brought to life in a startlingly fresh and dramatic way which combines the excitement of plot and character with a sense of the deeper layers of story and history that lie embedded in China's current events.

Leah, half-Chinese, visits China with her mother to try to reunite their half of an ancient coin with its partner left behind in their 'home' village. This physical joining is a very clever metaphor for a range of broken relationships and the continual effort to mend personal, cultural and political divisions. It's a wonderful book where the events in Peking are re-seen in a living context, to shock and horrify as well as deepen our understanding of particular history and the bonds which unite us all.

📖 *THE BOSS* (1992)

Melanie Guile

SOURCE: A review of *The Boss,* in *Magpies,* Vol. 7, No. 5, November, 1992, p. 27.

The early morning peace of a rural Asian family is shattered as "a bump and a shout shook the house". The Boss, an overconfident, meddlesome preschooler, is out of bed and on duty. His job is to "rule the world" and he sets about it, tolerated if not indulged by the long-suffering villagers. However, he meets his match in the farm animals who share his own sense of purposeful independence but move to a different rhythm. When, exhausted by his own bossy vigilance, he falls asleep, "the geese march[ed] over his hand" and all nature—human and animal—re-establishes its own directions.

Baillie's is a fine, assured text, ironic, understated and funny: "'Ah. The Emperor of China', sighed his mother". The tone is comic but it's underscored by unsettling insights into the nature of aggression itself. The Boss's outsized military hat is a disturbing symbol of unwieldy power: domination for its own sake. Peace is active, Baillie suggests, and re-asserts itself in spite of interference, but not without cost. The Boss is not an especially sympathetic character until his mother reclaims him, sleepy and vulnerable—but what about tomorrow? And the future . . . ? [Fiona O'Beirne's illustrations] are not a match for the text with rather wooden characterisations and lack of detail in the landscape settings (so important to the plot.) They echo but don't extend the text. Harassed parents will appreciate this book, and preschool to lower primary readers will gain from it.

📖 *MAGICIAN* (1993)

Stephen Matthews

SOURCE: "From the Word Go," in *Australian Book Review,* No. 190, May, 1993, pp. 59-60

Allan Baillie . . . is already well-established and *Magician* will enhance his reputation, despite the disconcertingly pervasive use of portentous capital letters for Significant Objects in the Story—the Guardians, the Darkness, the Cube, the Tower, the Gate, the Beast and many more. Set in a superstitious, myth-bound future many centuries hence, *Magician* is the story of Kim, who lives in an isolated coastal village and becomes one of the Guardians, whose task it is to help Maldaur avert a return of the darkness, which brought to an end the age of the Golden People. When an odd-looking alien arrives and is set upon by Kim's fellow Guardians, Kim comes to question Maldaur's encouragement of blind xenophobia in the guise of defence against the Darkness. Resounding with myth and allegory, and peopled by sharply realised characters, *Magician*'s vivid picture of a difficult, though not desperate, future, is marred a little by its over-intricate plot.

Jessica Yates

SOURCE: A review of *Magician,* in *The School Librarian,* Vol. 41, No. 4, November, 1993, p. 164.

Allan Baillie is Australian by adoption, having moved from Scotland as a child. He has written in several genres, mainly adventure stories. In *Megan's Star,* his first SF novel, he treated a theme which has become an Antipodean trademark: the alien or superpowered child. His new book, *Magician,* is also SF. The blurb gives away the setting: thousands of years in the future. The remnants of humankind are living on the edge of a desert in Australasia, operating by a mixture of high-tech and caveman culture. People are named by the community's teacher-librarian after characters from books, apart from, I think, their dogmatic leader Maldaur. As the book opens, a group of youngsters is going through a rite of passage to make them Guardians. Maldaur has often lectured them about the possible return of the Darkness, which destroyed civilisation hundreds of years ago. Thus, when a spaceship lands, the Guardians beat up the alien who emerges. The alien is secretly rescued by Kim, the hero, who learns his secrets, and that a wondrous city still operated by robots exists beneath the desert. It turns out that the legend of the Darkness has been distorted, and that the alien is good, and has come to save the rest of humanity from certain death. The story becomes a contest of wills between Maldaur, who calls the alien a 'magician', and Kim, who believes the alien's scientific explanation of what is happening to planet Earth. Thus in fact Maldaur has been the 'magician', deceiving his people with the monopoly of advanced Earth inventions: a 'magic' staff and flying 'pod'. This parable is thought provoking and yet punchily told, with an excellent cover illustration. I hope that Allan Baillie will go on writing children's SF, having made such a good start in the genre.

A. R. Williams

SOURCE: A review of *Magician,* in *The Junior Bookshelf,* Vol. 57, No. 6, December, 1993, p. 238.

Allan Baillie has peered into the future thousands of years hence to find the home of a small group of surviving humans. They inhabit a small valley blocked at one end by an ever-increasing desert and at the other by a sea populated by lethal black fish. Living conditions are harsh. What keeps them going are the legends they have of their past and the dangers that face them in the future. They are ruled by Maldaur who reminds them constantly of the need to be watchful and prepared to face up to the coming of the Darkness.

The story line involves the arrival of a visiting alien who puts to flight the myths by which Maldaur holds the community in thrall. Kim, one of Maldaur's young Guardians, is the one who challenges his master's authority and with the aid of the alien leads the exodus from the inhospitable valley to a more welcoming planet.

In this short book there are two themes competing for the available space: the creation of an entirely new but completely credible environment and the fleshing out of a group of its inhabitants and their interaction which will capture the reader's interest. Moreover there is hidden in this dense matter reflections on such things as totalitarianism and power by thought control. 'Sometimes people make up myths so they don't have to face the truth.'

All of which makes this a difficult book to read. It has to be taken slowly, thoughtfully and reflectively if anything like its true worth is to be enjoyed.

THE BAD GUYS (1993)

Virginia Lowe

SOURCE: A review of *The Bad Guys,* in *Magpies,* Vol. 8, No. 3, July, 1993, p. 32.

Hulk, Nose, Sweet Eddie and Wheels, the narrator, are part of the Crew. While camping, they encounter two other gangs of kids, the Tribe and the Nerds, and, being "the bad guys," make as many difficulties for everyone as possible. They terrify with ghost disguises, they set up then cheat in a home-made boat race. And their badness always backfires right up until the end, when Wild Alice and her Tribe are going to have to eat the Nerds' disgusting smelling cooking.

These are believable gangs of kids, with the girls neatly ahead on intelligence and brawn. David Cox's drawings, reminiscent of Quentin Blake's, add to the fun. Everyone, including the pup Spectre, are drawn as mean, if a little insecure. As with the text, however, we know we are seeing it all through Big Wheels' eyes. Maybe all is not as it seems.

Baillie writes sympathetically and excitingly for this age group, and the book itself is pleasantly and invitingly produced. A sure-fire winner as book-bait but with interesting angles about relationships and about unreliable narrators as well to make for quite fascinating discussion.

REBEL (1994)

Publishers Weekly

SOURCE: A review of *Rebel,* in *Publishers Weekly,* Vol. 241, No. 4, January 24, 1994, p. 54.

Subdued illustrations [by Di Wu] dampen the inherent drama of this story, based on a real-life incident that occurred in Rangoon. Things look pretty grim for a small Burmese village when a general and his troops march in, flattening the school playground with their tanks and announcing the conditions of the new regime. The general's pomposity is punctured, however, by a small act of rebellion: a child flings a thong from the schoolhouse and bonks him on the head. Enraged, the dictator orders everyone out of the building, thinking to easily nab the one-shoed culprit. The children and their teachers outwit him by appearing barefoot en masse, and the laughter of villagers and soldiers alike causes the general such humiliation that he and his forces retreat. It's a bracing tale of

courage in the face of tyranny, and Baillie makes the most of it. Wu is a competent illustrator; his faces in particular are enormously expressive and full of humanity, but a drab palette of khaki, olive and off-white creates a visual blandness.

Kirkus Reviews

SOURCE: A review of *Rebel,* in *Kirkus Reviews,* Vol. LXII, No. 3, February 1, 1994, p. 137.

With "long columns of crunching, hard-faced soldiers," the General and his artillery march over Burma's dusty plains to order a playground destroyed while children watch. Then, as he boasts of his plans ("You will give me half of everything you make . . . the children will learn only of my heroic battles . . . "), a child's thong flies from a window and knocks off his hat. Furious, he demands a lineup to identify the thongless culprit, but even his own troops dissolve in laughter when the whole school steps forth—barefoot. Based on a true incident that occurred in Rangoon, the simply told story epitomizes the senseless injustice of despotism and how courage and humor may counter its excesses. The Chinese-born artist caricatures the general in a cartoon style rendered in soft pencil and watercolors; informal in tone, Wu's illustrations are effective in relaying the strong message, while the subtle diversity of expression on the faces conveys a range of intense feelings. A valuable offering, suggesting a variety of creative uses.

Lynne T. Burke

SOURCE: A review of *Rebel,* in *The Five Owls,* Vol. 8, No. 4, March-April, 1994, p. 85.

The General and his tiny army clank noisily across the Burmese countryside into the schoolyard. At his command, tanks destroy the school's fence and playground as children watch from inside the classrooms. In the village, rude soldiers kick down doors and wave their guns in the air to round up the rest of the townspeople. The General tells them that they are his people now and must do his bidding. "You will give me half of everything you make, and at school the children will learn only of my heroic battles and my glorious victories."

At that moment, a tattered sandal is flung from the school. It skims over the heads of the villagers and soldiers and hits the General on the head, knocking his hat into the dust. The General is furious at such disrespect and orders all the children outside so that the rebel—the one-shoed one—can be identified and punished. But as soon as the children are assembled, both townspeople and soldiers cannot suppress their laughter: all the children have come out of the school barefoot. In disgust, the General breaks his baton and leaves. Tyranny has been defeated by laughter, the ultimate weapon in a culture where saving face is a valuable asset and losing control is a humiliating liability.

This story is based on an actual incident that occurred in Rangoon recently. Members of the Burmese community spoke about it at a meeting of Amnesty International at which Allan Baillie was present. . . .

This is not merely a story about the history of modern Burma or a lesson about the power of laughter and the potential of youth. At its heart is a plea to every person who sees evil in the world to have the courage to be a witness, to stand up for truth and justice.

Meredith Sorenson

SOURCE: "Bully Books," in *Australian Book Review,* No. 159, April, 1994, pp. 66-8.

Allan Baillie's **Rebel** illustrated by Di Wu is a book about a bully. . . . [The] bully is the leader of an invading army. . . . Baillie tells us in an afterword that 'the heart of this story is true. It happened in 1990 at a school in Rangoon.' Apart from the political nature of its text, however, this is much more your standard picture book. Unlike 'real' life, there is nothing bleak, ultimately terrifying or unresolved here—good does win out over evil. There is, as has been the 'norm' in picture books since once upon a time, hope.

Rebel has the form of a parable. The General marches in and bullies and terrorises a village, but right in the middle of his 'mean' speech he is hit on the head by a small battered thong. The General rants and raves and demands that all the children be brought from the school so the one who is wearing only one thong can be found. The message, of course, is one of solidarity as all the children are revealed to have taken off their shoes. And when the hard faces of The General's soldiers begin to twitch with laughter and the towns-people begin to giggle, the General flees.

There is a story about Hitler that his closest aides wouldn't let him see *The Great Dictator* because they felt the sharpness of Chaplin's satire may have pierced the bubble of the man's own inflated image of himself. And **Rebel** clearly shows what a powerful weapon laughter can be.

The image of solidarity of the oppressed, the small battered thong winning against all the guns and weapons of war, gets a good airing here too. Baillie is much aided in this task by the illustrations of Di Wu. Reminiscent of Kathe Kollwitz's drawings about the suffering of the downtrodden individual within an oppressive regime, they do achieve a haunting beauty at times—although the interplay between the words and images is rather stilted and literal.

For all the potential violence of the story, this is a quiet book. Baillie's text is restrained and in the best tradition of the parable, lets the story do all the work. The result is a very effective piece of communication in which the message reigns supreme. After reading **Rebel** you'd have to be a bully or a fascist to think pushing nice people around is tough.

📖 *SONGMAN* (1994)

Sophie Masson

SOURCE: "An Interview with Allan Baillie About *Songman,*" in *Reading Time,* Vol. 39, No. 1, February, 1995, p. 5.

[The following is an interview by Sophie Masson.]

Allan Baillie's latest novel, **Songman** is a mould-breaker of a book; an unusual and engrossing look at a relatively unexplored period of history: pre-1770 Australia, and beyond that, Macassar (now on the Indonesian island of Sulawesi). I spoke with the author recently about the idea which led to the book, and the many months (in fact, eighteen months) of work the author had to undertake.

"**Songman** went through about seven or eight drafts," Allan Baillie said. "It was not an easy book to write! The characters had to ring true, the dialogue had to sound right, I had to incorporate heaps of research without allowing it to sound like a turgid lecture . . . My editors and I went back and forth, back and forth, over it till we were satisfied . . ."

The novel, which tells of a Yolngu (Arnhem Land) boy, Yukuwu's voyage to Macassar in 1720 and what he sees there, is also the account of his growing to maturity and the realisation of just what his life's meaning is. He goes as a newly-made young man; he returns as a Songman, weaver of the magic of songs, of the word, keeper of the soul of a people. It had its beginning in a visit the author made to the National Maritime Museum in Sydney, where he discovered that coastal Top End Aborigines had been in contact with Macassans for hundreds of years before Captain Cook's visit to the East Coast of Australia.

"To me, the Aborigines were a land bound people, I hadn't realised they had this contact," Allan said. "I thought, hey, there's certainly a story in this! And then, fortuitously, I was invited by the School Libraries Association of Northern Territory to come on a visit there, and I started asking questions. I discovered that everyone in the Northern Territory knew of it, and I was introduced to a lady called Annie Mathews from Nhulunbuy who said, oh you should come up my way, there's lots of people who could talk about it there! To cut a long story short, I did go up there, to Yirrkala and other places, where I was given a lot of fantastic help, asked lots of questions. . . . I was asked a lot of questions, too! I was even given a skin name. . . ." He paused, and laughed, ruefully. "They called me Birrkngu Ganambarr, which means, old, old grandfather like a praying mantis! Well, I guess I was older than most of the group there!"

After that, Allan returned to Sydney, where he wrote the first thirty pages, returning to the Territory to vet the work with the group, who approved it: something which

Allan Baillie felt was most important. "They don't want people barging in there, taking stories, not consulting, and so forth. Anyway, after that, I went off to Sulawesi for two and a half weeks and researched that end of things, then back to Yirrkala and more work! The writing was hard, there was no doubt about it. In the beginning, I had more people in it than a Russian novel, I just couldn't control the cast, and all the research that kept trying to force its way in."

And how difficult was it, I asked, to get into the skin of his diverse characters?

"It goes back to writing books about Cambodia, China and so on—no matter how foreign these people seem, no matter how long ago they lived, basically, we are the same. We may be separated by race, culture, time, place: but we are all human. It might seem naive to say that, but it's not, really: it's like an actor getting into a part. Like an actor, I have to think, OK, so and so would do this, would feel like this, would eat this, and so on. And when I'm writing, I'm actually that character, I'm inhabiting it."

He said, too, that because Yolngu culture is still so strong, and because things are still done in much the same way in Sulawesi, it was not as difficult as it might appear to get into the flavour and feeling of the past. "The living culture of Yolngu is still very, very strong and vivid, so it was also a question of observing as well as asking . . . and in Sulawesi, I got to see how the boats were made, how they were sailed, in much the same way as they would have been back then. . . ."

One of the things that particularly struck Allan in his research was how much respect there was between the Macassans and the Aborigines. "They learnt from each other: they approached each other from a position of equals, different but equal. The Aborigines learnt a great deal about Macassan culture without having their culture fouled up; they could give and take without pressure. In fact, when the whites moved to the area, the Aborigines more or less knew what they were after; they could put it in context and contact, on this coast at least, was less traumatic than in other places."

And why had nobody approached this before, I asked?

"Well, I think many of us just didn't know anything about it! We were brought up on the glories of Britain or whatever, not on contact with our northern neighbours. Until I stumbled over it, I knew nothing about it—but I must say people in Northern Australia knew all about it, it just doesn't get disseminated much down here. And I wanted to show, too, what a rich culture there was here before Captain Cook,—and not just an inward-gazing one, but a confident, proud one that traded and exchanged. I wanted to write a story of an Aboriginal boy who is not affected by having trouble with the whites. I didn't want to go over that ground. That is what they had in 1720, something complete and rich and not necessarily parochial at all."

Agnes Nieuwenhuizen

SOURCE: "Know the Author: Allan Baillie," in *Magpies*, Vol. 10, No. 1, March, 1995, pp. 16-18.

[The following is an interview by Agnes Nieuwenhuizen.]

"I had written as a Cambodian (**Little Brother**) and as a Chinese (**The China Coin**) and I didn't get shot, so I felt I could attempt to write from an Aboriginal point of view. I believed I should have a go at writing about our people. I was spurred on by hearing politicans and judges saying that there was no civilisation in Australia before Captain Cook. Not quite fair is it?"

The preceeding passages introduce **Songman** and sets the scene for an extensively researched historical novel. **Songman** is a deeply felt, beautifully written testament to the civilisation, culture and lifestyle that flourished in just one part of Australia before the white man came.

Having a "go" and a sense of fairness and justice are hallmarks of Allan Baillie's life and work. Coming "home" in this novel is perhaps also an indication of Baillie's confidence and mastery as a writer. For **Songman** is ambitious in its scope, courageous in its stance and masterly in its execution. Bailie was last interviewed for *Magpies* in 1987. Then he said: "You can tell a story in your own backyard, but if you put the same story somewhere else, it gains atmosphere." Curiously, Baillie has been one of the few Australian writers for young people to set his stories off shore. Here, however, he demonstrates that our own backyard can yield many many fascinating stories and plenty of "atmosphere", although these elements are enhanced and enriched by the Macassan scenes and connections.

The novel starts with a long, leisurely section evoking and detailing the life of the Yolngu people who still live in and around Arnhem Land. "I wanted to show that this is how it was; this was the civilisation people claimed didn't exist. In his 1975 book, *Triumph of the Nomads*, Geoffrey Blainey pointed out that the Aboriginal people had a better standard of life, before the coming of the white man, than many other nations and people at the time. This observation stayed with me."

"I was also interested in showing that there had been contact between Aborigines and others. I had found out that there is a tree which grows in Madagascar that also appears in the north west part of Australia. There were pirates operating out of Madagascar and I played around with the idea of writing about a pirate boy who came here. Then I came across a small section in the National Maritime Museum in Sydney showing how the Madagascans had been trading with the Aborigines at least 500 years ago. I was rivetted by this because I had assumed that the Aborigines had been totally land bound. So I thought 'if I don't know about this, there must be many others who don't and might like to find out'."

"At about this time I was invited by SLANT (School Library Association of the Northern Territory) to come and talk about *The China Coin.* While I was in Darwin, I asked if anyone could help me make contact with the Aborigines of the area. I was introduced to Annie Matthews who invited me to the Aboriginal settlement at Yirrkala. In fact when she went off on holidays she left me with her house and I was able to stay there for a whole month—all I had to do was a bit of watering."

The last time I had interviewed Allan Baillie was in 1989. I listened to him describing his travels through war-torn Cambodia out of which came *Little Brother.* He told me about a boat run up the Gordon River and about wandering through the Tasmanian wilderness during his honeymoon, many, many years before the appearance of *Riverman* (1986). During that trip he was told about a tree that was over three thousand years old. He said: "Sometimes things develop very slowly . . . that tree . . . was actually the very first idea I had for a children's book—long before *Adrift* (1988) . . . I've got this passion for trees. I wrote the book when the Franklin River was in trouble . . . it's definitely a conservation and history book. It's looking at the cradle. I'm saying: 'This is what we have'." (*No Kidding,* 1991)

The "history" in *Riverman* was about mining as well as old trees. *The China Coin* (1991) is, according to Baillie, also 'very much a historical novel, though I didn't know it was going to be that until I started'. Originally planned as a book exploring links between two countries and cultures when an Australian-Chinese girl (like Baillie's daughter) is moved back to her ancestral village, the book changed dramatically when Baillie found himself witnessing the Tianamen Square massacre. "That changed my novel. The book now finishes two days after the massacre."

So "looking at the cradle", saying: "this is what we have, who we are and who we were", are central themes and concerns for Baillie. Add to this an abiding love of the sea and boats and a predilection for giving his characters plenty to battle with. "The event, perhaps a disaster, will bring out special qualities in a character . . . all my books have that same element. Give 'em hell."

All these elements are indeed present in *Songman.* Having established where the idea came from I wanted to know more about the research. Baillie makes it all sound so easy. He jokes about expeditions to research a book being a good excuse for him to indulge his love of adventure and the outdoors. Everyone seems willing to help him. As well as Annie Matthews, he made contact with Steve Fox, who manages the local arts centre. Fox introduced him to Nguliny Burarrwanga (also known as Barbara). Baillie says: "She became my tutor. Without her, the book would not have existed." At this stage we have a look through a thick album of photos detailing Baillie's stay in Arnhem Land and his three weeks around Ujung Pandang (formerly Macassar in Sulawesi).

Baillie says: "After a short period, I was made part of the family." How did he establish the credibility? How did the Yolngu people respond to him wanting to write about them? "They had never heard of me. But I showed them some of my books. They were especially keen on *Drac and the Gremlin.* I was worried about them telling me to get out, that I was not one of them. But the idea was so strong with me that I had to have a go. What they said was: 'That's a great idea', and they helped me enormously."

Some of the photographs show a corroboree. Baillie explains: "While I was there, a very important person died. Of course I was not allowed to find out this person's name. There was an eight day corroboree. People came in from everywhere. Because I was one of the family, I was supposed to take photos. Some did not come out because sand got into the camera. Look this is Baillie with ochre [a photo of Allan with painted face]".

"My month with the Yolngu was an absolute delight. We went on a sort of walkabout, though we used cars. We went fishing and hunting for crabs. We went to a place called Crocodile Beach and lived in grass shelters."

Then about the book: "I had decided the Yolngu had to read the book and if they didn't like it, that's it. After the first thirty pages they said: 'That's pretty good'. I made some terrible cultural blunders. The people of Arnhem Land must have the most complicated relationships. They must have known several thousands of years ago that sooner or later the academics would appear and all this would drive them mad!"

After the third draft, Baillie got in touch with a lecturer, Michael Cooke, who had edited a book about the contact between the Yolngu and the Macassans. Cooke sent the manuscript out to teachers he was teaching. "This was exactly what I wanted", said Baillie.

Songman went through eight drafts and took Baillie two years of reading, research and writing. The carefully documented acknowledgements show the care and respect shown by both the author and his publisher. It is a stylish book, with a cover by Mark Sofilas, who was the contributing artist to another recently published book about a darker incident in Australian history, *The Burnt Stick,* written by Anthony Hill. The publishers, justifiably, have high hopes for *Songman.* . . .

Songman starts with a shark attack, introducing and linking the two main characters. Dawu, the testy elder and Yukuwa who is his spiritual son. Yukuwa saves Dawu, but Dawu has lost a foot in the encounter. He had also been having marital problems. Baillie explains: "Partly I wanted to show that essential relationships are and remain the same between people. It's why I write books like this. But also, Dawu had to be fragile in the way he lives so he could be shaken away from his life. Without a foot, and with his marriage in tatters, he has to make a change to move. He looks at the much more sophisticated boats of the Macassans and says to himself: 'I can do this.

I can become a boat builder.' To do this he has to go to Macassar." And Baillie, too, is forced to spend a lot of time watching the Macassan boat builders and messing around with his beloved sea and boats.

In Ujung Padang he again finds the right person. "He took me to his family and showed me how they were living. Things had not changed much in 200 years. I spent a lot of time on the beaches. It was a hard life. I watched them still making boats the way they used to. They don't use plans. They still use adzes. They 'find' boats in the shape of a tree."

Baillie brought to the interview a replica of the boats the Macassans used on their trips to Arnhem Land to fish for trepang. The Yolngu welcomed the annual visit and helped in the fishing. They hated the taste and texture of trepang. Baillie has fun with all this.

There is a full sized replica of such a boat in the Darwin Museum. Another of Baillie's sources, Peter Spillett, had one built. It was sailed to Darwin by a crew including Macassans and Aborigines. "There was a big ceremony at Nhulunbuy when it arrived. The world wide media coverage resulted in such boats now being built for rich yachties. And I am still waiting for a ride!"

Some of the more dramatic and densely written passages are at sea and demonstrate the skill of the Macassan sailors, others show the Yolngu boy confronted with a busy, strange, frightening meeting of cultures. Yukuwa becomes good friends with Jago, the Macassan boy, during the voyage to Jago's home and during the time they spend in Jago's village on the island of Celebes. When they travel to Macassar we see a colonial power at work through the eyes of the innocent, curious Yukuwa, and at another level, through the eyes of the more knowing and experienced Jago. Why are people behind bars? Why are the boys told to avoid the Dutch? They witness a hanging.

"I was writing about three civilisations. I wanted to balance them against each other. I wanted to say things about the Aboriginal standard of life. I wanted it all to flow and make a good story. I created the character of Hals, the Dutch pastor because I wanted a good Dutchman to offset the empire. I looked at paintings, read about life in Holland at the time and before. I thought, this is a man who has the job of being a religious under the thumb of the colonials. He provided a point of contrast, a human face for Yukuwa."

During the eight re-writings, several characters disappeared, though there is still a big cast. "My publishers commented that the book read a bit like a Russian novel. So I discarded characters and somewhere in all this Yukuwa stopped being an 'Aboriginal person' and became a real person. I know him. It took four drafts before I knew Dawu. The greatest thing about writing is when a character *turns* and you know exactly what he would and wouldn't do or say."

Towards the end of the book, Yukuwa and Dawu both make important and independent decisions about their futures. Baillie did not believe that the boat building experience and time in Macassar was strong enough to provide a resolution for Yukuwa's future. He said: "They had to share a deeper, more profound experience". There is a short but deeply moving funeral and this finally enables Yukuwa to return home and recognise and accept his role as songman.

Despite the seriousness, even solemnity, of much of *Songman,* there is a great deal of wit and humour. Like Baillie, his protagonists always have a healthy sense of self-mockery and fun. Much of the cross cultural contact is conveyed and sharpened by the wry tone and humour. About the following passage, Baillie said: "I wanted to have a go at the savage bit." Early in their friendship, before Yukuwa's trip to Macassar, the boys have this conversation which seems to encapsulate the art of Allan Baillie in his best book yet:

"Are you a savage?"

"What's a savage?"

"My mother says you are all savages," said Jago.

"She has been here?"

"She has never left Macassar, but she knows everything."

"What's a savage?"

"Oh, they're black like you . . . "

Yukuwa looked at Jago. This poor boy is only deep brown, like ironwood. Macassar must be a long way west, where the sun goes at the end of the day and it is too tired to burn people a proper black.

"And they don't wear anything."

"Why?"

"Why what?"

"Why do you wear things?"

"Because we are not savages."

Pam MacIntyre

SOURCE: "Black Lines," in *Australian Book Review,* No. 167, December, 1994 and January, 1995, pp. 56-7.

Songman describes [a] time, 1720, before Cook and when the Macassan sailors and traders were visitors to the Yolngu people of Arnhem land. Rich in place, history, adventure, character, culture, this is a fascinating, gripping story of little known aspects of the past. Yukuwa, an ordinary boy, not a good hunter nor fisherman but a brave boy who feels and thinks and notices, is firmly at its centre. Yukuwa and his father—not his true father but Dawu, the one who has taught him and been there for all the important moments of his life—travel to the Celebes to learn how to make dugout canoes, on the return journey of the Macassan traders who come to Marege seasonally for the trepang (sea slugs). The mode of telling this story is realistic—although it is full of the spirits and demons of the Yolngu People. . . .

[The] world is viewed from the point of view of a young person seeing things for the first time. Boy and Sarah Jane see trains, cars, aeroplanes but Yukuwa, in Macassar sees imprisoned men, a hanging and a repressive balanda (Dutch) justice system. So straightforward and simple is Baillie's retelling that the reader too, sees afresh, as if for the first time, from Yukuwa's cultural position and therefore with his shock.

Baillie too is concerned with reconciliation, particularly cultural. Yukuwa encounters the Bugis, the Macassans, the Toala, the Barra and even the Balandas in the form of the tragic Pieter Hals. . . . Yukuwa does mature and this underpins the story of his friendship with Jago, and the father-son relationship with Dawu. Personal relationships are where tolerance and understanding are learnt, as is the pain of letting go. Yukuwa must learn that each person finds their own place. He experiences pain, terror, confusion, but remains himself, one of the most realised characters of recent YA fiction, to become the Songman. This is a book with much to offer. It combines exciting adventures, humour, intriguing historical, cultural and geographic detail in a moving gentle story that should find readily the readership it deserves.

Moira Robinson

SOURCE: A review of *Songman,* in *Magpies,* Vol. 10, No. 1, March, 1995, p. 30.

An unusual story set in 1720 which describes how Yukuwa and his adopted father Dawu, whose tribe lives on the coast of Arnhem Land, travel to Macassar with the traders who come every year for the trepang. In Macassar Dawa finds a wife and decides to stay; Yukuwa sails back to Australia for the next trepang season, but on the way the boat is attacked by pirates and his closest friend, Jago, is mortally wounded. Back with his tribe, Yukuwa accepts that he'll never be a good hunter or warrior but that he can try to be a songman and sing 'of laughter, anger, terror and, sometimes, of the soft pain Jago has left'.

This is a curate's egg of a book. In some ways its the best thing that Allan Baillie has written. He's managed to write an unusual historical novel about Aborigines without resorting to capital letters or stilted language. At the same time he has preserved the impression of Yukuwa's difference and sensitively portrayed his attempts to make sense of an alien culture. The character of Yukuwa with his self doubts, his inferiority complex and vulnerability is extremely well drawn and there's some wonderful writing, but—the fatal but—the book is slow slow slow and the

adventure promised on the front jacket doesn't materialise until twelve pages before the end. For readers who know nothing about Indonesia's colonial history, the book would be very confusing—it's pretty confusing anyway—and I don't know how many readers would persevere to the end.

Marcus Crouch

SOURCE: A review of *Songman,* in *The Junior Bookshelf,* Vol. 59, No. 4, August, 1995, pp. 141-42.

Scottish-born Allan Baillie here pays his most moving tribute to Australia which has been his home for most of his life. This is not a familiar Australia; not a hint of *Neighbours* or even of Pamela Wrightson. Captain Cook will not arrive for more than half a century. Even the Dutch have not sighted these coasts. Baillie's hero is a young aborigine, adventurous and timid, and his eyes look beyond his own country to the islands from which brown traders come. When they return in their precarious canoes Yukuwa goes with them, and so does his nominal father (in the tribe, as in some animal communities, the chief sires the children and farms them out to titular parents). The boy has already paid his debt to Dawu by rescuing him, at the cost of a foot, from a shark, and it is appropriate that Dawu should share the perils of the voyage. Less appropriate perhaps but at least happily Dawu finds happiness in Macassar with a recently, and dramatically, widowed young woman, and he chooses to stay far from home. Yukuwa returns after a dangerous voyage, and at home discovers that he has a new role in the community. He may still not be able to throw a spear, but he can sing a song which records his experiences. He is now the songman.

The author makes his most impressive points very quietly, without heroics. These remote beings, with their difficult names and with motives, traditions and actions, who in less able hands would remain anonymous and inexplicable, claim complete surrender by the reader. No difficulties are glossed over, no conflicts ignored, but these are real people and events and we share their grim experiences most gladly, recognising that each tribe and race has acquired its own wisdom. It is a long book but never a tedious one. The action moves steadily, sometimes swiftly, and the story unfolds with total conviction.

Cecilia J. Hynes-Higman

SOURCE: A review of *Songman,* in *The School Librarian,* Vol. 43, No. 3, August, 1995, p. 116.

Once I had persevered with this novel, I began to enjoy it, but the first few chapters are slow, confusing and lacking in narrative interest. The storyline is never strong even when launched but the characters develop, as does the sense of location and culture. The novel is set in northern Australia before the time of Captain Cook, and charts the growing awareness of a teenage boy who, on the brink of adulthood, meets people from very different cultures from that of his own tribe. First he makes friends with a boy from a tribe which lives on a distant island beyond any experience of his own; then he accompanies him home, where he meets Dutch settlers—his first sight of white men and all the strange trappings of civilisation that they brought with them. When he returns home, his new experiences have not only changed him from boy to man but have also laid the foundations for a vocation as one of the tribe's songmen, telling tales of adventure.

This would prove quite a challenge for all but the enthusiastic fluent reader. It does not rate among Allan Baillie's best works.

DREAM CATCHER AND OTHER STORIES (1995)

Peter Nicholls

SOURCE: "Horrors Upfront, Horrors Half Glimpsed," in *Australian Book Review,* No. 176, November, 1995, pp. 60-1.

[Horror, the uncanny, and the macabre] is familiar ground for Alan Baillie, whose *Dream Catcher* contains thirteen recent (1988-1995) stories, three of them horror of the non-supernatural variety, and one fantasy. The remainder consist of one joke, and eight tales of ordinary human relationships, five of them distinctly gloomy.

Baillie's horror is not really different in kind to his more mundane stories; both kinds often turn on one or more older kids making some kind of terrible mistake. A somewhat austere writer, whose short sentences have cruel clarity, Baillie is severe on mistakes. Sometimes the kid in question survives sadder but wiser; four or five times we are left icily to contemplate ruined young lives. This is not a very *entertaining* collection; even the joke story ('Silent Night') has Santa's sleigh shot down, mistaken for a UFO. In person Baillie may be charming and amusing, but he's somewhat minatory on the page.

With single-minded professionalism, every story makes just one point, normally a moral point, astringently. There are no side tracks, decorations, *rococo* twists and turns. We know from his novels that Baillie can be a lot more relaxed than this, but even here there are things to enjoy, mostly the precision with which he occasionally captures an epiphany of adolescent feeling.

The more horrific stories: in 'The Gun' a boy takes a gun he finds in the attic to school; he is miserable, it is loaded, disaster ensues; in the title story 'Dream Catcher' a boy is put into a hypnotic trance by his friend's eccentric auntie and appears to go back in time to the age of the Brownshirts in 1920s Germany, but the truth is horridly contemporary; in the savagest of all, 'Bones', over-imaginative children accidentally kill their old, ill, next-door neighbour, thinking him wrongly to be some kind of bogeyman.

There is a subtler shudder to be found in two of the best stories in the book. 'Cheat!' has a girl learning that plagiarism is not always intentional, and is just saved from behaving badly through vanity and grievance. 'The Champion' in pungent, physical prose tells of a school-boy cross-country runner who finds in himself a capacity for brutality, and dismays both himself and a young admirer by what he has done. But the best story in the book (and this one is not just linear) is 'Castle Hawksmere' about the fantasy lives of lads still just on the childhood side of puberty, and how their leader, a girl who was just one of the boys, is suddenly a young woman and metaphorically a thousand miles away from their lives.

SECRETS OF WALDEN RISING (1996)

John Marsden

SOURCE: "Secret Township," in *Australian Book Review,* No. 184, September, 1996, pp. 58-9.

If you're a word in Allan Baillie's new book you'll have to work pretty damn hard. Baillie doesn't like passengers: 'Dad did not even look up. He shook his head. "It's dead, just a hunk of iron."' Sometimes the words have to work too hard. They get strained to their limits: 'Wilson creaked his long frame forward into the sun, twisting a grey-streaked sideburn.'

But maybe that's appropriate. In this story of rural Australia everyone and everything are strained to their limits. This is writing stripped of its decorative frills. It's as bare as the brown paddocks that Baillie describes. A stringent vocabulary for a drought-diseased landscape. Gradually it has its effect, until you're no longer in your dingy little office, watching that stingy ray of sunlight . . .

Instead you're in the harsh and horrible town of Jacks Marsh. It's the end of the road. Clancy never made it this far out. If you know Australia you'll recognise Jacks Marsh, with its boring school, the butcher that sells only lamb and beef, a tin-shed garage, and the ghastly Terminus Hotel. The people who live here have only one thing in common: they're failures. Sometimes that can be a bond; sometimes it's not enough.

So we have Harry, old and lonely and confused. We have murderous Lean Wilson, landlord of the Terminus, which he describes as the 'goddamn end of everything'. Tony Lee, of Chinese descent, shut out from part of his heritage by the Anglo boys. Bago, son of a failing farmer. Most importantly there's Brendan. He's not as interesting as Bago, but he's the central figure of *Secrets of Walden Rising.* Brendan and his father have fled tough memories in Britain, and arrive in Australia dreaming of making their fortunes. It doesn't happen. Brendan clings to the belief that everything will be prosperous when the rain comes, but the reader can't be entirely convinced.

Brendan's bullied at school. The main sequence describing this, when Elliott knees him and Bago delivers a king-hit, is a terrific piece of writing, capturing the seemingly senseless, almost dispassionate brutality of playground bullies. Late in the book Baillie lets Bago off the hook a little, when we realise Bago's bullying is partly a reaction to his unhappiness at having to shoot the drought-stricken sheep. Bago's poddy-lamb, Groucho, is about the only thing to which he can show any affection, but Bago has to shoot him too. Truly, in Jacks Marsh, you kill that which you love. Baillie doesn't explain the bullying away too glibly; it's more that he's searching for a meaning for behaviour that often defies understanding.

Gradually, out of this grim environment, Walden emerges. It's not Thoreau's pond. It's a decayed town that's been drowned for fifty years, but is slowly revealed in the dam as the drought leaches away the water. Dreams of secret worlds figure prominently in the adolescent psyche, and Baillie gives us a satisfying and believable one, a world that the boys are eventually able to explore.

When they do, they find what appears to be treasure, but it has no value. Bago isn't bothered: he believes the real treasure is the rain that has at last started to fall. The rain might be redemptive, although in the world of Jacks Marsh it's hard to believe anything could be. Certainly people long for rain, and it's the lack of water which leads to the emergence of the sinister ghost town. One starts to think that the rain's the only hope. Everything made by humans is worthless. Buildings are abandoned and down they fall. The metal rooster on the weathervane is evil and has to be 'shot'. The bulldozer, unused for two years, is made to work again, but is immediately employed for the shot sheep. Thunderbolt's money—the treasure—provokes murder, but is rubbish, literally.

For most of the book mateship barely exists. There are traces of it but it doesn't do much good to anyone. Women are irrelevant. Sure there're a few women mentioned in passing, and Brendan's memories of the mother who abandoned him shadow his thoughts and are part of his guilty memories. But all the characters of consequence are male.

Many writers have seen the bush as redemptive in itself. Nature as the great healing force. But in Baillie's bush 'everything has prickles, thorns, barbs and stings'. There's nothing inside or outside Jacks Marsh to make anyone feel good about anything.

So, we're talking bleak here. Yet this is an intelligent and interesting novel. One longs for relief from the grimness but Baillie is an uncompromising writer. The only real relief, the only real redemption, apart from the unconvincing rain, is a tentative friendship that evolves. It seems that mateship has something to offer after all. One can only hope that it will serve and sustain the boys better than it has their elders. When your parents and other adults fail you, Baillie seems to be saying, kids have only got each other.

DRAGONQUEST (1996)

Allan Baillie

SOURCE: "DragonQuest," in *Reading Time,* Vol. 41, No. 2, May, 1997, p. 5.

I have had so much fun with [illustrator] Wayne Harris over *DragonQuest* that I have been forgetting where it started. It was a tiger. There were several tigers, but it came down to one.

In my youth I had been fascinated by *The Man-Eaters of Kumaon* by James Corbett. Corbett had the job of hunting rogue tigers in the jungles of India when they developed the habit of hunting people instead of hunting animals.

One of Corbett's scenes has stayed with me: A young woman is edging slowly along a very narrow track cut into a high cliff toward her village. People from the village have been killed by a man-eater, she is alone and she is nervous. She looks along the track ahead and sees the tiger treading toward her . . .

I felt a whisper of that woman's fear when I saw a magnificent Bengal Tiger, big as a small horse, prowling round its little island in the Western Plains Zoo at Dubbo.

Corbett thought the Indian villages backing on the jungle would lose something precious if there were no tigers left to chill the nights. And China paints tiger pictures and dreams of what might have been.

It is precious to know there are still jungles out there, with elephants, gorillas, orangutans living their way. But maybe it is even more precious to have something that still touches in us the terror of our distant ancestors. To know in the world we have dominated that there are animals that could still consider us as prey.

Possibly the woman on the cliff—she was badly scarred, but survived by falling backward as the tiger leapt, catching its massive body with her legs and swinging it off the cliff—might agree with Corbett a long time afterward.

The boy in *DragonQuest* says it for me: I don't want to kill the last dragons, it is everything to know that they are there.

Wayne Harris

SOURCE: "DragonQuest," in *Reading Time,* Vol. 41, No. 2, May, 1997, p. 5.

I had been wanting to illustrate a mythic story and Allan certainly managed to write a marvellous one with *DragonQuest.*

It's important to find the tone that the illustrations will eventually have and with this book I spent a long time looking at artists of the early Renaissance such as Piero della Francesca and Ucello, and at Breugel and Bosch. I wanted to avoid pastiche but felt that something in the spirit of these artists would provide the key to a sense of enchantment.

The book is constructed so that each double page spread represents a specific point on the journey and I tried to make each of those moments distinct in tone and atmosphere. I gave the pictures a sinuous sense of design and brushstroke, so that you have the feeling that the environment itself is alive and bewitched.

I also realised that the book is about the way that the male quest changes from generation to generation and I really approved of the young boy's refusal to conquer and slay and his preparedness to accept that knowledge itself is empowering.

DragonQuest's landscape is very much the internal landscape of myself as a young boy and it was a book that I found myself reluctant to leave. It was quite a journey to illustrate; it demanded that I submerbge myself totally in its mythic environs and ultimately on its completion it was like waking from a heady and potent dream.

Additional coverage of Baillie's life and career is contained in the following sources published by Gale Research: *Contemporary Authors New Revision Series*, Vol. 42; *Something About the Author*, Vol. 87; and *Something About the Author Autobiography Series*, Vol. 21.

Aileen (Lucia) Fisher

1906-

American author of fiction, nonfiction, poetry, and plays.

Major works include *Going Barefoot* (1960), *Listen, Rabbit* (1964), *Valley of the Smallest: The Life Story of a Shrew* (1966), *We Alcotts: The Life of Louisa May Alcott as Seen Through the Eyes of 'Marmee'* (1968), *Out in the Dark and Daylight* (1980).

INTRODUCTION

Since her prolific writing career began in 1932, Aileen Fisher has published children's literature in several genres, including poetry, nature fiction, biographies, and plays. Best known for her verse for preschoolers and primary graders, Fisher defines a poem as a "rhythmical piece of writing that leaves the reader feeling that life is a little richer than before, a little more full of wonder, beauty, or delight." In such poetry books as *Up the Windy Hill* (1953), *Where Does Everyone Go?* (1961), *In the Middle of the Night* (1965), and *My Cat Has Eyes of Sapphire Blue* (1973), she, as a contributor in *The New York Times* wrote, "lights the commonplace moment with wonder": the natural world of plants and animals—her most frequent and beloved subject matter—is at once described with impeccable accuracy and rendered magical through poetic language. Fisher's rhymed verses are usually very short or in longer, narrative form and often open with a query or musing, which leads to observations on nature. She is praised for her "simple, quiet style" and for her ability to "see the outdoors," M. F. Birkett commented, "both as a naturalist and a poet." She is further applauded for her ability to understand children's hopes, fears, and curiosities; thus, despite their often humorous undertones, her poems never degenerate into comic jingles intended simply to amuse their readers. Fisher has set several books in the Colorado mountain region where she has lived for many years, including *Trapped by the Mountain Storm* (1950), and *Valley of the Smallest: The Life Story of a Shrew* (1966), which, among other awards, was named an American Library Association Notable Book. With longtime friend Olive Rabe, she has written biographies of Louisa May Alcott and Emily Dickinson. Yet Fisher remains characteristically modest about her accomplishments and is inspired by the pleasure she derives from recollecting her own youth during the writing process. "I enjoy writing for children. I especially enjoy writing verse," she acknowledged, "It gives me such a good chance for remembering how things looked and felt and *were* when I was a child."

Biographical Information

Born in 1906, Fisher was raised on a forty-acre farm in

Iron River, Michigan, near the Wisconsin border. During her childhood she spent a great deal of time outdoors—swimming and fishing in the river, gardening, and tending to her family's farm animals. She attended the University of Chicago for two years before later transferring to the University of Missouri where she earned a Bachelor of Arts degree in journalism. After graduation, Fisher returned to Chicago to work at the Women's National Journalistic Register and the Labor Bureau. She began publishing poems in children's magazines during this period, but it was not until 1932, when she moved to a 200-acre ranch in Colorado with Olive Rabe, that she decided to make writing her career. The following year she published her first volume of children's verse, *The Coffee-Pot Face,* which treats subjects found in many of her subsequent books: nature, such as ladybugs and icicles; familiar, everyday objects, such as armchairs; and common childhood conditions or experiences, such as stomachaches. Since the publication of *The Coffee-Pot Face,* which was chosen as a Junior Literary Guild Selection, Fisher has produced over 100 works. Among the biographies that she and Rabe co-wrote, and one about Joan of Arc that she published on her own, her favorite was on Emily Dickinson, whom Fisher admires for her insights into nature and meditations on life, death, eternity, and immortality. Writing full time has made it possible for Fisher to pursue a lifestyle similar to that of her childhood: she avoids cities, traffic, pollution, travel, and crowds, and embraces country life and all the pleasures it provides her—being near animals, mountain climbing, hiking, working with wood, gardening, and reading. A disciplined author, Fisher writes for four hours a day on average, in long-hand, drawing on both recollections of her youth and extensive biological research.

Major Works

In *Going Barefoot,* a little boy impatiently longs for the June days when it will be warm enough for him to go barefoot outside. As the late winter and early spring months pass, he envies the animals who scamper across the ground without catching cold, comparing the claws, paws, and feelers of the animals to human footwear. Fisher's lilting verse captures this blissful childhood experience, which culminates in great happiness for the boy when he is finally allowed outside without his shoes and socks on. In a similar vein, Fisher addresses another common childhood experience in *Listen, Rabbit,* a narrative poem recounting the story of how a young boy once wanted a pet, but became resigned to befriending—and not taking home—a wild rabbit. As the boy follows the rabbit through the changing seasons, he eventually finds a nest of young bunnies and comes to the bittersweet acceptance that most animals should stay in their natural surroundings. The rabbit, whether jumping openly or eluding the boy, provides an appealing focus for young readers.

Fisher's award-winning book *Valley of the Smallest: The Life Story of a Shrew* demonstrates her unique blend of keen observation and poetic sensibility. In minute detail, she describes the ecology of a Colorado Rockies valley near her home, focusing on how the tiny shrew helps stem the infestation of the Pandora moth, which threatens a stand of lodgepole pines. *Valley of the Smallest* not only conveys a sense of quiet beauty as the animals discover snow and other wonders of mountain life, but achieves a measure of suspense in its depiction of survival in the wild. In *We Alcotts,* Fisher and Olive Rabe use a creative approach to biography. Narrated as if by Louisa May Alcott's mother, who was portrayed in *Little Women* as Marmee, the biography draws from journals, letters, and other writings of the Alcotts to explore the nature of the Alcotts' marriage, the family's moral convictions and beliefs, and the literary aspirations of Louisa. Like the fictional March family, the Alcotts emerge as a loving, self-sacrificing clan as Fisher and Rabe treat the reader to an inside look at nineteenth-century family life.

Consisting of 140 short poems, *Out of the Dark and Daylight* is a collaboration between Fisher and illustrator Gail Owens about the four seasons and the holidays that fall during each. As in most of her poetry, Fisher uses figurative language to describe the natural world of plants and animals—toadstools become elves' hats, a cocoon is a sleeping bag for a butterfly, and the grass a jacket for

the earth. Her poems are, according to M. F. Birkett of *School Library Journal,* "brief, fresh, deft, and often illuminating, and they are pleasant to read alone or aloud."

Awards

Several of Fisher's works were designated Notable Book of the Year by the American Library Association, including *Going Barefoot* in 1960, *Where Does Everyone Go?* in 1961, *My Cousin Abe* in 1962, *Listen, Rabbit* in 1964, *In the Middle of the Night* in 1965, and *Valley of the Smallest: The Life Story of a Shrew* in 1966. Fisher received the Western Writers of America Award for juvenile fiction in 1967 and the Hans Christian Andersen Honor Book in 1968 for *Valley of the Smallest: The Life Story of a Shrew.* She was also bestowed with the National Council of Teachers of English Award for Excellence in Poetry for Children in 1978.

AUTHOR'S COMMENTARY

[*In the following essay, Fisher and Olive Rabe discuss the writing of their fictionalized biography* We Alcotts: The Life of Louisa May Alcott as Seen Through the Eyes of 'Marmee.']

Aileen Fisher and Olive Rabe

SOURCE: "Writing About the Alcotts," in *The Horn Book Magazine,* Vol. XLIV, No. 5, October, 1968, pp. 541-44.

Several years ago, before we even thought of writing about the Alcotts, we reread *Little Women*—not from any nostalgic feeling carried over from girlhood, but for a very practical reason. What was there about this book that had made it live for a hundred years?

On the very first page of Louisa M. Alcott's most famous book, we found several answers to our question. *Little Women* immediately catches the reader's attention by exceptionally good dialogue, which makes the characters live as real people. Right in the beginning the author establishes differences between the four leading actors in their warm family setting, differences that make the story move. Jo, Meg, Beth, and Amy are as natural and spontaneous today as they were when the great-grandmothers of present-day readers followed their dreams and adventures.

It did not take us long to realize that the continuing popularity of *Little Women* rested on a firm foundation. But how, we wondered, had the author acquired the skill to build such a foundation? What preparation did she have for turning out a best seller? Our wonderment increased when we discovered that the handwritten manuscript of 402 pages, begun with reluctance in May, 1868, was finished by the 15th of July of the same year. And in addition Louisa had squeezed in the writing of three short stories.

How did she do it? Before long we found ourselves thinking it would be fun to discover some of the answers by writing a book about Louisa and her family. And so we were off again on the long road of research that precedes the writing of a biography.

We found a wealth of material available. But the research would have been an almost impossible task had not Ednah D. Cheney, long a friend of the Alcotts, carefully collected Louisa's letters and journals, and published them the year after her death; and had not the late Professor Odell Shepard labored over Bronson Alcott's fifty handwritten volumes of journals and condensed them into a few printed books. A great deal of other work had likewise been done for us by the biographers of famous men and women who played a part in the lives of the Alcotts.

We both read the books that would give us the basic background of the family and the period. Then we divided some of the reading that radiated from the center. One of us concentrated on the Hawthornes, Margaret Fuller, Lydia Maria Child, and the Peabody sisters; the other on Emerson's life and journals, Transcendentalism, and communal-living projects like Brook Farm and Bronson Alcott's own Fruitlands. We both worked on Thoreau because we were both eager to reread *Walden* and some of his journals.

As we read, we took time to write little "episodes" that we thought might work into the story—sometimes only a few sentences or paragraphs, sometimes several pages. And this brings up a question we are often asked—how can two people write a book together?

Actually we did not write *We Alcotts* together in the sense of sitting opposite each other, figuring out sentence after sentence. Together we decided on the ground to be covered and worked out a rough framework for the chapters. Then we each worked on the same chapter separately, incorporating our episodes. Next one of us undertook to meld the two versions together, after which the other edited, cut, and revised. During this process whole episodes had to be removed, to keep the story from becoming too diffuse. In the end we both agreed on the final version.

Our rough framework leaned heavily on a chronology which we added to continuously throughout our reading. Every year had a page or more of its own, which covered the events and activities, large and small, not only of the Alcotts but of their close friends and contemporaries. Every time we saw a date, down it would go on the proper yellow sheet of the chronology. Not knowing for several months just where we would start or end our story, we had to take in a wide sweep of years, beginning with the birth of Bronson Alcott in 1799 and ending with his death and Louisa's in 1888.

Soon after we started reading and taking notes, we had to decide upon our point of view to make the writing of the episodes possible. We narrowed it down to two possibilities. We could use the point of view of the omniscient observer, as had Louisa's other biographers, where everything appears through the eyes of a third person. This method has the advantage of covering happenings offstage and on, but it lacks intimacy. Our other possibility was to do as we had done in *We Dickinsons*—have a member of the family tell the story. This method is more restrictive, since everything has to be within the experience of the narrator. Yet, in many ways we felt it would make for a warmer story. And it seemed to us that the most natural point of view would be that of Marmee, the hard-working, loving, courageous mother who kept the family going.

During the long months of gathering material, before we even started to organize the book, we found Bronson Alcott's character and ideals capturing our interest. So strongly did we feel this influence that we were impelled to write to our editor, saying we feared Bronson would run away with the story. What should we do about it? She wrote back reassuringly, telling us not to worry but to let the book develop as it would.

In the end we found that all we had to do was make a slight change of emphasis in our subtitle. Originally it had read: "The story of Louisa M. Alcott and her family. . . ." We changed this to "The story of Louisa M. Alcott's family . . . ," which emphasized the entire family cast instead of making too great a star of Louisa.

And now we come to the unanswered question of how Louisa was able to write her best seller in so short a time with so sure a hand.

When she sat down in her attic hideout at Orchard House to work on the "girls' story," which an editor had asked for, she was thirty-five years old. She had already been writing for many years. As early as her tenth birthday her mother had given her a pencil-case with a note saying, "I have observed that you are fond of writing, and wish to encourage the habit." At an early age Louisa had begun to keep a journal of her thoughts and activities, thus carrying on a tradition of the Alcott family. When she was eight, she surprised her mother with her first poem.

Her first story was published when she was twenty years old. From then on more and more of her writings found their way into print, and this success gave her needed encouragement. She loved to write and had a natural facility of expression. Each new story she tackled with fervor, applying herself to it with such concentration that sometimes she forgot to stop to eat. In this way she formed the work habits that enabled her to put in fourteen hours a day writing *Little Women.*

Louisa's talent for making things happen on stage, instead of telling the reader about them in cold exposition, dated back to her childhood experience of writing plays with Anna and producing them. As she grew up, Louisa's interest in writing plays and acting in them continued. At one time in her early twenties she was so stage-struck she would actually have deserted her writing to become a professional actress, had not her mother objected. Louisa's dialogue throughout *Little Women* shows this flair for the dramatic.

She was never held back by having to search for the right way to say something, because her father's tutoring had given her a thorough grounding in grammar and sentence structure, and ease of expression. Listening for years to her father's famous table talk and to her mother's well-told stories of life in the May family, Louisa learned naturally how to highlight her own writing. Then, too, she had her material at her fingers' ends—actual family experiences—and so had no need to do research.

Another facet of her apprenticeship, which enabled her to keep the reader in suspense, was her writing of "lurid" tales, unsigned or under pseudonyms. These tales she dashed off at great speed, without taking time to edit or revise. She found a ready market for them and felt that they gave her needed relaxation.

But even with all these advantages, turning out a book like *Little Women* in so short a time was an amazing accomplishment. Our writing of the biography of this prolific producer proved to be a much more time-consuming, though always enjoyable, task.

GENERAL COMMENTARY

Kathleen D. Kevorkian

SOURCE: "Aileen Fisher, Poet: An Overview," in *Children's Literature Association Quarterly,* Vol. 5, No. 2, Summer, 1980, pp. 25-27.

Aileen Fisher has created in her body of work a testimony to the wonder of nature and its creatures, in poetry and verse which is eminently accessible to children. Her works are evocative of awe, wonder and delight in the natural world. The format of her work falls into two catgories:

1) Poetry collections

2) "Nature-verse picture books." Of her collections, I deal with these three: *Skip Around the Year* (1967); *That's Why* (1946); and *Feathered Ones and Furry* (1971).

In *Feathered Ones and Furry,* the poem **"The Furry Ones"** best sums up the scope of vision that appears throughout all her books:

> I like
> the furry ones—
> the waggy ones
> the purry ones
> the hoppy ones that hurry . . .

> The snuggly ones
> the hug-ly ones
> the never, never
> ugly ones . . .
> all soft
> and warm
> and furry.

In any body of poetry there will be some poems that are thin, and certainly Miss Fisher has such. But when she is at her best and strikes a chord, it can be just right. In **"After School,"** the speaker lists all the needs her new puppy has and muses, "And every day I wonder/ what I used to do *before.*"

Or, in **"Chipmunk,"** her turn of phrase rivals David McCord's "Sadiebug:"

> You ought
> to be called
> a quickmunk
> instead of a
> chippity chipmunk.

A fine, clever turn also occurs in the brief **"Merry Christmas":**

> Before he tunneled
> to reach his house
> he wrote "Merry Christmas"
> in white, in mouse.

This, coupled with **"Footprints,"** in which she writes of wintertime animal tracks, are examples of her recurrent delight in and attention to tracks as a key to communication with wildlife.

> Their snowy footprints
> write it out . . .
> and I know how to read!

Time and again in her verse and picture books, tracks appear. This theme might especially speak to the youngster who has recently learned to read, or who longs to do so, to whom both animal tracks and the printed word represent a mystery to be unraveled.

It is a comfortable perch from which Miss Fisher's speaker views the world, a comfortable human nest with nurturing loved ones nearby. In **"Sleepyheads,"** she writes of pity for the creatures:

> They're all asleep
> on Christmas Day
> poor things . . .
> I wouldn't want to be them.

While throughout Fisher's books there is frequent comparison with the creatures, the speaker is content with her humanness.

That's Why, collected in 1946, contains some poems that

make a repeat performance in *Feathered Ones and Furry,* and in some cases they would better have been retired for good. Here, again, there are animal tracks marching through, such as in **"Rabbit Tracks."** There is about this collection a shadow of A. A. Milne, most evident in the poems that deal with a child's exasperation with adults and their ways. **"Mother's Party,"** for instance,

> "What's your age?"
> and
> "What's your name?"
> EVERY lady was the same . . .

sounds very like Milne's "Politeness."

This collection is noteworthy for the number of poems dealing with themes of a child's perspective of childhood. A youngster certainly would identify with the speaker in **"Plans":**

> When I make Plans
> that are grand and vast,
> even more grand than
> the time-before-last,
> HOW can my Mother
> say "NO!" so fast?

In later works Fisher's scrutiny shifts to creatures and wildlife instead.

Skip Around the Year (1967) is a utilitarian collection, noteworthy for its ecumenical and humanitarian posture, celebrating Christian, Jewish, and national and international holidays. The final **"Remember the Sabbath"** is perhaps the best in the book:

> Friday for the Muslims,
> Saturday for Jews,
> Sunday for the Christians—
> What different days we choose!
> But is it so important
> When Sabbaths end or start,
> So long as we remember
> to set one day apart?

It is, however, in her "nature-verse picture books" that Miss Fisher is most successful. In that format, when the poems are paired with an illustrator whose style is congruent with the evocative nature of her words, a reader can be slowly drawn through an experience with nature. The themes of these picture books are the same: a youngster discovers that he or she is akin to a creature or to the world of nature. In some, like *My Mother and I* (1967) and *In the Middle of the Night* (1965), there is an added element of closeness to a parent while also being close to nature, creating a unity and a spirit of one among all.

The universal theme of awe and delight in creatures occurs over and over, again and again, yet in the picture book format it never stales. It is a theme which seems best suited to the leisurely route of this format. The comparison between the speaker and the creatures occurs re-peatedly as well, continually pointing up similarities and differences.

In *Going Barefoot* (1960), there is an extended comparison between various forms of animal feet and assorted kinds of human footwear, leading quite naturally to the subject of tracks again. Also present in this book is a child's questioning of what we adults take for granted: the predictable cycle of the seasons. Many children, especially young ones, aren't yet convinced of the certainty of it all, and "When can I go barefoot?" is a question youngsters care about.

Among the especially appealing lines that occur in her picture books are these from *Going Barefoot:*

> But not in boots that cowboys use,
> only, of course,
> in their "birthday shoes."

Where Does Everyone Go? (1961) also deals with an annual cyclical occurrence: the approach of winter. *Like Nothing at All* (1962) is a child's eye-view of animal camouflage, while *Listen, Rabbit* (1964) deals with the bitter-sweet of unfulfilled possessiveness when a child encounters a creature that must stay in its natural world. *We Went Looking* (1968) might be called a lesson in animal camouflage and serendipity.

It is the picture book which, in a library setting, is most accessible to children's browsing, while poetry books usually must be sought after. It is also these picture books which reach the child at an especially formative time, and perhaps they might instill a reverence, a wonder, and a delight in the world and its creatures. Who knows—perhaps these books may initiate a lifelong realization of and an empathy for living things, and an ecological awareness of the planet as a whole.

At this time, when a high percentage of children live in fractured families and in urban environments, Miss Fisher grants them the perspective of a secure child-viewer safe in his or her observation of wildlife.

No hawks here, no vicious beasts, no violence—is it an unreal world that she depicts? A realist might balk, but children do learn the cruelties of life first-hand soon enough. It is this that she offers as her gift: a love for the creatures and a harmony with the world as a whole. Aileen Fisher, winner of the 1978 National Council of Teachers of English award for excellence in poetry for children, has done for her readers an immense service.

X. J. Kennedy and Dorothy M. Kennedy

SOURCE: "Tradition and Revolt: Recent Poetry for Children," in *The Lion and the Unicorn: A Critical Journal of Children's Literature,* Vol. 4, No. 2, Winter, 1980-81, pp. 75-82.

Writers for children are, to be sure, under no obligation

to favor subjects from technology or modern urban life. To a young child, everything is new—including things that have enlisted readers of children's poetry for generations. We are still seeing—as in Aileen Fisher's recent large gathering, *Out in the Dark and Daylight*—collections of pleasant, innocuous nature poems, hardly different in form or content from children's verse that was current fifty years ago. At her best, Fisher can be skilled, touching, and accurate in depicting animals, gardens, and the shifting seasons; although most American children at the moment must find her world somewhat strange in its perfect exclusion of cars, airplanes, city streets, television, and fast-food dispensaries. Still, she has a knack for making the ordinary into the memorable: A jack-o'-lantern has "a tooth up north and two down south." Fisher's only concession to the contemporary is to begin her lines with lower-case letters; but she is one of the few poets writing serious lyrics (not merely comic jingles) that can be relished by some youngsters of five, six, or seven.

Janice M. Bogstad

SOURCE: "Is There Poetry in Children's Poetry?," in *The Lion and the Unicorn: A Critical Journal of Children's Literature,* Vol. 4, No. 2, Winter, 1980-81, pp. 83-92.

[Aileen Fisher's] *Anybody Home?* illustrated by Susan Bonners is actually just one poem with irregular rhythm and end rhymes, while *Out in the Dark and Daylight* illustrated by Gail Owens is a collection of over 125 short poems which concern the everyday life of children who have access to a natural environment.

As is often the case with books for very young readers (4-7 and 5-10, respectively) both of these carry on a narrative in part through pictures that accompany the poetry. *Anybody Home?* is more illustration than text, and Bonners' illustrations are delightfully descriptive. The subject of the poem is the homes of creatures such as squirrels, badgers, raccoons, and other mammals. Illustrations, corresponding to the lines of poetry, show a young girl visiting these homes.

> I'd like to see,
> near the top of a tree
> a house made of leaves
> with rounded eaves,
> where a squirrel might be
> asleep in his clothes,
> with his tail for a blanket
> across his nose.

In this particular example, each set of four lines is the occasion for a full-page drawing, the first of a girl climbing the tree to see her squirrel's house, the second of the squirrel wrapped up in his tail. Words and pictures together are what make this book interesting. The closest that this text comes to real poetry is in its use of end rhyme, which is never sustained for longer than a couplet or the alternating second lines of two couplets. Even the

rhythm of these short lines is choppy. However, the combination of text and drawings was delightful in many ways. It could be almost a fantasy text for children who had never been to a meadow or stream. The educational value of such a book is also obvious, as it describes the actual habitations of these several animals, all mammals. Since the picture-narrative involves a child, it appeals to her or his private world. However, it is not a very exciting example of poetry. The children I surveyed seemed to understand it readily but were not very enthusiastic about it.

Four large two-page interiors as well as illustrations for some of the poetic selections draw together the texts of *Out in the Dark and Daylight* into a narrative covering the four seasons. Thus, through title and interiors, the author has provided indications of the passage of time, from dawn to dusk and through Summer, Autumn, Winter, and Spring. Since the poetry in this collection is all by Aileen Fisher, her attempts at ordering the pieces into a framework to assist her readers in contextualizing them may have been more easily achieved than with a more heterogeneous collection.

Ms. Fisher writes nature poetry and attempts to create through it a private relationship between her children, who never appear as characters except as part of the illustrations, and the world of nature. Again, they do not speak very well to children who have no tactile experience of nature, despite the fact that the poetic imagery evoking natural scenes, sounds and smells, is quite often marred by metaphor which uses human scenes as the vehicle—a **"Mouse Dinner"** with the mouse using a napkin leaf; **"Daisy World"** is one of daisy cities, towns, and suburbs. There are many more examples of this reductive metaphor, and they are characteristic of children's poetry in the other collections. It is often nice, peaceful, and idyllic. It is seldom evocative of the new, the unusual, or the exciting, nor does it dare to depict the troublesome or fearful imaginations of childhood. **"Good Night"** characterizes three family members in the most stereotypic of terms: Father with paper and moustache, Mother with knitting and a barely present Grandma.

Despite the fact that Fisher's poetry didactically clings to a false sense of "normalcy," it doesn't teach anything in the sense of expanding one's perceptions or one's perspective. While I found many of the pieces to be pleasant and some merely bothersome, others were particularly offensive; an example noted by other critics is titled **"Looking Around"** and bears quotation:

> Bees
> own the clover,
> birds
> own the sky,
> rabbits,
> the meadow
> with low grass and high.

Perhaps this was intended to instill in the child some sense that animals have rights as well as people. The travesty of investing animals with property rights, however, is obvious to most of us.

Ethel L. Heins

SOURCE: A review of *We Alcotts* and *We Dickinsons,* in *The Horn Book Magazine,* Vol. LXI, No. 3, May/June, 1985, p. 338.

Two fine examples of fictionized biography successfully employ a difficult literary device. From contemporaneous source material the authors re-create the lives of two famous, close-knit, nineteenth-century, New England families—in each book letting one member narrate the reminiscences. The Alcotts emerge as a loving, self-sacrificing household whose story illuminates a reading of *Little Women;* while Emily Dickinson's enigmatic personality, her mystical preoccupations, and her rare poetic talent are revealed in an intense, intimate memoir.

TITLE COMMENTARY

THAT'S WHY (1946)

Virginia Kirkus' Service

SOURCE: A review of *That's Why,* in *Virginia Kirkus' Service,* Vol. XIV, No. 9, May 1, 1946, p. 222.

There are too few competent books of verse about everyday things for small children, and this one fills a real need. Gay verses about the things they find important— the soda cracker crunch of snow, the fun of being rain-soaked, the shortness of the misnamed all-day-suckers, and so on. The author of **Coffee Pot Face,** etc., has a real talent for simple, charming verse, bright, amusing rhymes, lilting rhythms, and direct sharp silhouette illustrations.

Lois Palmer

SOURCE: A review of *That's Why,* in *The New York Times Book Review,* May 26, 1946, p. 31.

In this collection of verses children will be surprised that a grown-up has caught so accurately their impressions of the world they are exploring. There are so many wonderful things to see and hear, rabbit tracks, June bugs, snails, moonlight, sunset, the wind in the field and in the trees. Miss Fisher has written gay rhymes about all these and about many other thoughts which children have. Parents and children will enjoy together such ones as this on **"Eyes":**

> *Two eyes of Mother's*
> *are all I can see.*

> *But she's got OTHERS*
> *she uses on me.*

OVER THE HILLS TO NUGGET (1949)

Florence M. Hensey

SOURCE: A review of *Over the Hills to Nugget,* in *Library Journal,* Vol. 74, December 1, 1949, pp. 1827-28.

Appealing story to give to fourth-fifth-graders and slow sixth-graders who like family and pioneer books. Papa has a ranch in Colorado, and Ernie and the whole family work against odds, including a fire, to make a go of it. Filled with family spirit and daily doings which delight many children. Format with its creamy pages and good-sized type is pleasing. Many illustrations in black-and-white by Sandra James.

Sarah Chokla Gross

SOURCE: "Colorado Pioneers," in *The New York Times Book Review,* December 11, 1949, p. 20.

Mother's caster set and her Star of Bethlehem pieced-quilt were the only two fine possessions she had to remind her, and father, and the three Brett children of another kind of life than that in the Colorado Territory. The farm above Nugget was better than dismal Skillet Gulch, but it meant plenty of hard work and little cash. Thus, when Charley Whiskers told Mrs. Brett of a bargain in cows, in father's absence, she and young Ernie decided that to raise money to buy the cow they'd best sell the quilt and caster.

Of pioneering in mining country, of sacrifice (with a happy outcome), and of the excitement a family found as they worked together, Aileen Fisher has made a story that fairly races along. Sandra James' drawings authentically call up the West of the Eighteen Seventies.

TRAPPED BY THE MOUNTAIN STORM (1950)

Virginia Kirkus' Service

SOURCE: A review of *Trapped by the Moutain Storm,* in *Virginia Kirkus' Service,* Vol. XVIII, No. 17, September 1, 1950, p. 516.

This little book answers the question children often ask when a storm is in the offing—"what will the animals do." When a storm came to the Rockies in February the Old Ewe was one of the first to smell the warning. Then gradually all the animals and birds began to seek shelter—the mountain lion, the water oussel, the rabbit, the martin, the deer. But there are enemies to contend with, and the author has caught the excitement of the double danger, as strange bedfellows are met in the shelters, and the more hardy animals take advantage of the confusion to hunt. A fresh and entertaining tale of the ways of wild animals. Illustrations in black and white by J. Fred Collins.

📖 *UP THE WINDY HILL: A BOOK OF MERRY VERSE WITH SILHOUETTES* (1953)

Ellen Lewis Buell

SOURCE: "Poems of Childhood," in *The New York Times Book Review,* August 9, 1953, p. 14.

Like Mrs. Fisher's **That's Why** and **Inside a Little House,** this is a collection of cheerful verses and jingles, whimsical rather than lyric in tone. For the most part they are concerned with such everyday subjects as **"A Picnic," "The Rag Bag," "Scissors"** and **"Leftovers."** Mrs. Fisher is no rival of Stevenson (Robert Louis), but her verses are full of little jokes—of the kind children themselves like to make. She has also a shrewd knowledge of childhood failings as,

> *I won't play house*
> *with Mary Lou:*
> *she always wants*
> *to be Mama too.*

Rae Emerson Donlon

SOURCE: "Cooking, Crafts, Riddles, Reading," in *Christian Science Monitor,* November 12, 1953, p. 11.

At this point, an adventure in reading poetry would not be amiss—and in a just-right kind of book, because of the lovely silhouettes with which the poet herself, Aileen Fisher, has illustrated almost every poem:

> When you stop to think of it,
>   isn't it funny—
> the wiggle-y nose that there is
>   on a bunny,
> the smartness of bees to know
>   all about honey,
> the difference in days that are
>   rainy or sunny,
> the way that our legs can be
>   walky or runny,
> the things you can buy, if you
>   just have the money—
> When you stop to think of it,
>   isn't it funny?

This is a delightful sample of the verse in this collection for children from six to nine. Each poem has an idea that will be a help in memorizing and repeating dramatically. Decidedly this is a book for the quiet family hours and will be treasured for long years by its possessor.

📖 *OFF TO THE GOLD FIELDS* (1955)

Virginia Kirkus' Service

SOURCE: A review of *Off to the Gold Fields,* in *Virginia Kirkus' Service,* Vol. XXIII, No. 13, July 1, 1955, p. 418.

A home-styled story of the Colorado gold rush in 1859 takes eleven- year-old Joel away from his Iowa farm family for some adventures with his wanderer uncle, Jake. Starting out for Pike's Peak in the spring, Joel is kept on tenterhooks by the mysterious provisions Uncle Jake has loaded into his wagon. Then as they journey West, the new friends made add experiences as valuable as the gold they find. The mysterious load turns out to be well-stored provisions that come in handy in time of need. Warm and light.

Nina Brown Baker

SOURCE: "Covered Wagon Trek," in *The New York Times Book Review,* November 13, 1955, p. 38.

In this amusing, fast-paced story of a boy's trek to the Colorado gold fields, Joel and his Uncle Luke join their covered wagon to a long procession headed for "Pike's Peak or Bust!" On the trail they meet disappointed prospectors creeping home, with "Busted!" for their new and bitter slogan. But uncle and nephew from Iowa press on, meeting dangers and difficulties.

Skillfully entwined with the exciting story line is a thread of mystery which tantalizes from the first page until nearly the last. What was in the great sealed barrel that Uncle Luke guarded so carefully from mishap? Joel could not guess, for all his trying. Neither could the Indians who almost succeeded in stealing it. Neither, to be frank, could this reviewer.

Jennie D. Lindquist

SOURCE: A review of *Off to the Gold Fields,* in *The Horn Book Magazine,* Vol. XXXII, No. 1, February, 1956, p. 30.

There is a freshness about this lively pioneer story that sets it far above the average. The principal characters are Uncle Luke who decides to leave his farm and go by covered wagon to Pike's Peak for gold; Joel, his eager young nephew, who is allowed to go with him; and tomboy Debbie from another wagon in the train. An unusual touch is Uncle Luke's mysterious big barrel firmly secured in the middle of his wagon and guarded most carefully. No one can persuade Uncle Luke to tell what is in the barrel and Joel, Debbie and the reader are kept guessing until the end. Miss Fisher's writing deserves better bookmaking. Children will be troubled by such things as the double spread placed so that one half of Joel's head comes on one page more than an inch from the other half on the page opposite. But they will love the story.

📖 *ALL ON A MOUNTAIN DAY* (1956)

F. L. S.

SOURCE: A review of *All on a Mountain Day*, in *Saturday Review*, Vol. XXXIX, No. 46, November 17, 1956, p. 58.

The action in this book takes place during one day in the high Rocky Mountains. Each chapter tells of the ingenious ways a mountain creature—snowshoe rabbit, porcupine, grouse, coyote, bob cat, pack rat, water ouzel, marmot, and deer—finds food for her young and protects them. There is a real feeling for these animals and the part each plays—the hunted and the hunters—in the overall pattern of nature.

Booklist

SOURCE: A review of *All on a Mountain Day*, in *Booklist*, Vol. 53, No. 7, December 1, 1956, p. 180.

In a book reminiscent of the author's ***Trapped by the Mountain Storm,*** an episodic story chronicles the happenings of one day in the lives of nine Rocky Mountain animals. The problems of protecting and caring for the young, the constant struggle for survival against natural enemies and the elements, and the interrelationship of the animals of the wildlife community are perceptively and vividly portrayed. A little sentimental but true to nature and interesting.

C. E. Van Norman

SOURCE: "Up in the Rockies," in *The New York Times Book Review*, December 16, 1956, p. 16.

It happened "all on a mountain day, to the wild folk of the Rockies: to the Snowshoe Rabbit, the little Grouse, the Porcupine, the young Marmot, the Coyote who liked to play his tricks, the Pack Rat, the Water Ouzel, the impatient Fawn, and the Bobcat." The paths of the nine crossed and each, in turn, became the hunter or the hunted. But when a storm broke over the mountain, all found a common need—to seek protection from Mother Nature's violence.

The adventures of the nine animals are skillfully interwoven with facts about their homes and habits. The personality of each emerges clearly, without having been humanized by description or conversation. The last pages contain a "Who's Who" of the characters, and many attractive black-and-white sketches [by Gardell D. Christensen] add to the value of this nature book.

📖 *A LANTERN IN THE WINDOW* (1957)

Jennie D. Lindquist

SOURCE: A review of *A Lantern in the Window*, in *The Horn Book Magazine*, Vol. 33, No. 3, June, 1957, p. 224.

How twelve-year-old Peter in 1851 went rather reluctantly to work for his Uncle Eb and Aunt Ellie on their farm by the Ohio River. What he really wanted to do was get a job on a river boat; nothing exciting ever happened on farms, he thought. However, he soon realized that strange things were going on at Uncle Eb's and gradually by putting two and two together discovered that the farm was part of the Underground Railroad. He became as eager as his Aunt and Uncle to help the slaves and by his willingness and ingenuity proved his worth. Miss Fisher writes in a lively manner and by the introduction of eleven-year-old Betsy, a high-spirited neighbor girl, makes this a story that will appeal to girls as well as to boys.

Booklist

SOURCE: A review of *A Lantern in the Window*, in *Booklist*, Vol. 53, No. 22, July 15, 1957, p. 587.

Twelve-year-old Peter, who lived for the day when he could work on a river boat, came to help on his Quaker uncle's farm on the Ohio River believing that nothing exciting ever happened on a farm. When he discovered that Uncle Eb's farm was a station of the Underground Railroad and had a part in helping the fugitives, Peter not only found out how wrong he had been about the lack of excitement but also came to appreciate the Quaker way of life and to realize the importance and satisfaction in helping others. Not essential but a well-told, enjoyable story.

Bulletin of the Center for Children's Books

SOURCE: A review of *A Lantern in the Window*, in *Bulletin of the Center for Children's Books*, Vol. 2, No. 1, September, 1957, p. 7.

When young Peter first went to stay with Uncle Eb and Aunt Ellie on their Ohio River farm, he was more excited at the prospect of seeing the river boats than of being of help to his uncle. His one ambition was to get a job on a boat and someday to work up to the position of river pilot. Then he became aware of the unusual happenings around his uncle's farm, learned that the farm was a station on the Underground Railroad, and came in time to realize that helping his uncle carry on his anti-slavery activities was more important than being a river pilot. Although the story follows a fairly well-worn pattern, it is acceptable where there is need for more materials on this period.

☐ *RUNNY DAYS, SUNNY DAYS: MERRY VERSES* (1958)

Virginia Kirkus' Service

SOURCE: A review of *Runny Days, Sunny Days,* in *Virginia Kirkus' Service,* Vol. XXV, No. 14, July 15, 1957, pp. 478-79.

Small verses with a child's eye view of the world ponder jack-o'-lanterns, ant hills, kites and puddles with simple words, and just a few stanzas. The meter is lilting and even and humor makes it suitable for reading aloud to toddlers or for children through third grade to read to themselves. The author's silhouettes of cut paper illustrate the short poems.

Lois R. Markey

SOURCE: A review of *Runny Days, Sunny Days,* in *Library Journal,* Vol. 83, No. 6, March 15, 1958, p. 106.

A pleasing and useful collection of verse similar in content and style to the author's *Up The Windy Hill.* The wonder and delight of small children in nature and in everyday events is amiably presented in short verses with large print, good spacing, and attractive silhouettes. Can be read by third-graders independently but will also be enjoyed when read aloud to very young children.

Silence Buck Bellows

SOURCE: "Time to Rhyme," in *Christian Science Monitor,* Vol. 50, No. 138, May 8, 1958, p. 16.

These poems are as full of surprises as a child's thoughts. In fact, that is the way they are presented. In each one a child speaks, in the language of a child. It is this quality, rather than poetic value, which makes the verses charming. For instance:

> Cats who walk
> by daylight
> squint through just a slit,
> but evening cats
> have lantern eyes
> with both the lanterns lit.

This is one of the best in the book, from a poetry-content point of view.

Anzia Yezierska

SOURCE: " . . . and Some Poetry as Well," in *The New York Times Book Review,* June 1, 1958, p. 18.

Less introspective than Miss Miller, Aileen Fisher moves swiftly from mood to mood, as a child responds to the changing influences of the external world. In *Runny Days, Sunny Days* she lights the commonplace moment with wonder. **"Remembering"** is one of her most vivid poems. "Do you suppose that butterflies/ fluttering around/ remember they were caterpillars/ once, upon the ground?/ And if they DO remember, do/ they make a singy sound/ because they're through with walking/ with their noses to the ground?"

☐ *SKIP* (1958)

Virginia Kirkus' Service

SOURCE: A review of *Skip,* in *Virginia Kirkus' Service,* Vol. XXVI, No. 14, July 15, 1958, p. 502.

When Skip, a Border collie, goes blind, Krissy's happy life on a Colorado farm becomes overcast with worry. Her father, with a farmer's practical outlook, has no use for helpless animals, considering them an extravagance, and Krissy is sick with the thought that he will send Skip away. Turning all her love and ingenuity toward training Skip to be useful despite his infirmity, she succeeds, and in the end, her pet acquits himself to the satisfaction of the entire happy family. A nice little girl, a nice dog, and a nice farm, momentarily threatened by misfortune, all add up here to an expected but ingratiating story.

Virginia Haviland

SOURCE: A review of *Skip,* in *The Horn Book Magazine,* Vol. 34, No. 6, December, 1958, pp. 468-69.

Any girl or boy who loves a pet will be moved by this story of the Colorado farm child, Krissy, and the border collie, Skip, who "was *hers* more than anyone else's." Krissy's fear of losing Skip begins, early in the story, when she discovers that he is blind, and increases in agonizing intensity until Skip himself proves his worth to the farm. The clear individuality of each member of the family, busy with separate and cooperative projects, and the conviction of Krissy's special love of animals and the out-of-doors raise this story above the average in family and pet stories.

Booklist

SOURCE: A review of *Skip,* in *Booklist,* Vol. 55, No. 9, January 1, 1959, p. 243.

The shattering discovery that Skip, the family's border collie, is blind not only saddens Krissy but makes her fearful of losing him because her father holds that every animal on the farm must pay its way. Krissy's efforts to keep the dog she loves and the way in which Skip proves his worth on the farm are told in an appealing story which, while not exceptional, is convincing in its characterizations and its picture of a modern farm family.

Ellen Lewis Buell

SOURCE: "Krissy and Friend," in *The New York Times Book Review,* February 1, 1959, p. 32.

What good is a blind cow dog on a small ranch where every animal has to pay its way? That was what Krissy would have to prove to her practical, hard-pressed father when he discovered, as he inevitably would, that Skip, the beloved collie, had gone blind. Krissy, trying to delay that time of decision, secretly training Skip to live and work in darkness and then trying desperately to convince her father of the dog's usefulness, is a sturdy, touching figure—especially to anyone who has ever championed a pet of doubtful value. And because the others of Krissy's family are portrayed in firm, realistic strokes, this is also a good story of people working through hard times together.

📖 *FISHERMAN OF GALILEE* **(1959)**

Virginia Kirkus' Service

SOURCE: A review of *Fisherman of Galilee,* in *Virginia Kirkus' Service,* Vol. XXVII, No. 13, July 1, 1959, p. 451.

The story of Simon Peter from his meeting with Christ on the Sea of Galilee to his final reunion with the crucified Lord, this story embraces most of the familiar episodes as related in the Gospels. It is with an almost miraculous consistency that Aileen Fisher robs her story of its grandeur and intensity, employing a style and scope more congenial to a mechanical teen-age romance than to anything remotely resembling the biblical original. This attempt to bring the life of Peter into modern context fails on the most basic point for in impoverishing the style and texture of the original, the immensity of the story is lost, where more faithful adaptation despite "archaisms," have made their impact for the past two-thousand years.

Christian Century

SOURCE: "The Religious Year," in *Christian Century,* Vol. LXXVI, No. 48, December 2, 1959, p. 1407.

We hope Miss Fisher will pardon us for including her book among children's books: hers is an adult book that deserves reading to or with older children. The big fisherman narrates the events which he witnessed. Like many expansions of biblical narratives, this volume is rather overloaded with exclamation points. Stark and dramatic illustrations by John De Pol frame the story well.

Ellen Lewis Buell

SOURCE: "The Great Teacher," in *The New York Times Book Review,* December 20, 1959, p. 16.

In a novel, *Fisherman of Galilee,* Aileen Fisher gives us a dual portrait of Jesus and St. Peter, and she, too, fills in the background with illuminating details. Quietly, simply, Simon Peter tells of Christ's life, from His baptism to His last appearance to His disciples. This is not only an account of Christ's work, teaching and miracles as seen by a loving follower, but also a study of the latter's growing faith and understand[ing]— and also uncertain of his own strengh to live up to Jesus' faith in him. It is these very human doubts which give to this thoughtful study a poignant sense of immediacy.

Ruth Hill Viguers

SOURCE: A review of *Fisherman of Galilee,* in *The Horn Book Magazine,* Vol. 36, No. 2, April, 1960, p. 145.

The ministry of Jesus is seen here through the eyes of Simon Peter from his first acquaintance with the Nazarene who said, "Follow me and I will make you fishers of men," to the resurrection and the words, "I will be with you always." This is a reverent, intensely interesting account, filling in the Bible record with details which make vivid the background and the personality of Simon Peter and others of the disciples. A book for any age and for all the year, but especially appropriate at the Easter season.

📖 *GOING BAREFOOT* **(1960)**

Virginia Kirkus' Service

SOURCE: A review of *Going Barefoot,* in *Virginia Kirkus' Service,* Vol. XXVIII, No. 5, March 1, 1960, p. 183.

A little boy waits for barefoot days, for those soft June days when shoes are no longer necessary for children to wear. By March he begins to envy the animals who run over the cold ground without a thought of sniffles. He ponders on their ways, on the fact of shoes, on the difference between claws, paws, and feelers. And then, before he knows it, his mother turns the calendar page and he, too, can venture out in barefoot freedom. This rhymed text imparts a substantial amount of naturalist information in a pleasant and animated fashion. The colorful illustrations of Adrienne Adams partake of the author's happy facility to couch fact in playful terms.

Pamela Marsh

SOURCE: "A Time to Dance, A Time to Read," in *Christian Science Monitor,* Vol. 52, No. 142, May 12, 1960, p. 1B.

For some, spring is to put on silly new hats, for others (those under four feet) it is to kick off silly old shoes. Aileen Fisher's verses and Adrienne Adams' delicately misty water colors in *Going Barefoot* show that this author-artist team knows all about the feeling of "a barefooted morning or afternoon when the side walk's warm and the grass and clover are green velvet carpets that feet run over . . . [and the] tickle of grasses, prickle of hay, trickle of water along the way." There is plenty of by-the-way information for the 4-8's about rabbits and deer and raccoon and other barefoot animals and the prints they leave. And plenty of freshness and rhythm and joy, too.

Booklist

SOURCE: A review of *Going Barefoot,* in *Booklist,* Vol. 56, No. 18, May 15, 1960, p. 575.

A little boy waiting impatiently for the wonderful month of June when he can go barefoot thinks about the insects, birds, and animals whose "toes are free to squiggle and squish, wherever they be, whenever they wish," without having to wait for the month of the Barefoot Moon. A picture book whose spontaneous rhyming text and pleasing drawings in color and in black and white create a happy mood of anticipation and discovery.

M. W. Brown

SOURCE: A review of *Going Barefoot,* in *The Horn Book Magazine,* Vol. 36, No. 3, June, 1960, p. 209.

Anyone old enough to remember, or young enough to anticipate, the ecstasy of the first day warm enough for going barefoot outdoors will find that blissful experience captured in the beautiful swinging rhythms of these poems, so perfectly in harmony with Adrienne Adams' lovely, soft-colored pictures. As a child waits through winter and spring for the magic time to come, he watches and envies the rabbits, raccoons, birds, and other animals who are so gloriously free of shoes.

SUMMER OF LITTLE RAIN (1961)

Virginia Kirkus' Service

SOURCE: A review of *Summer of Little Rain,* in *Virginia Kirkus' Service,* Vol. XXIX, No. 7, April 1, 1961, p. 331.

Attempting to penetrate the mind and instincts of beaver and squirrel, this narrative depicts realistically and from the animal's viewpoint, detailed seasonal and environmental effects on both these creatures, transferring our attention consistently from one to the other. In the last months of winter, the frozen pond with its overlay of water created a threat to the beaver lodge beneath the surface. Summer drought on the other hand, exposed the lodge entirely and eventually made it necessary for the beaver and her kits to move to another pond and begin the arduous building of a new dam. The squirrel's most pressing problem was gathering adequate food while his mate judiciously taught her young the elements of squir-

relhood. And at all times, simultaneously hovering over the animals of the forest are the dangers of fire, flood, drought and the jaws of a portentous enemy. Certainly a great deal of valuable insight into the ways of the wild is here deftly imparted, but the overall effect is loose and rambling.

Will Barker

SOURCE: "Survival in the Mountains," in *The New York Times Book Review,* May 7, 1961, p. 26.

Aileen Fisher's newest book, like her **All on a Mountain Day,** is the story of a plant and animal community on the eastern side of the Rocky Mountains and especially of two animals within this community—a female beaver and a male pine squirrel.

The story begins in mid-April, when ice still coats the pond of the beaver and when the winter food supply of the squirrel is nearly exhausted. Indeed the whole wildlife of this community, is threatened by the after-effects of a forest fire—unknowingly started two years earlier by a group of upstream campers. How the beaver, the squirrel, and the other wildlife survive in spite of conditions resulting from the forest fire and a season of little rain is the core of the narrative.

The author well portrays the life in this natural community. She has done well, too, in showing how the act of an individual, or a group, can affect an entire area. But I wish she had not personified her animals—the female beaver is given to such reflections as "For her youngsters' sakes she regretted the hot dry summer. Young ones should be full of joy and play." This tendency and the use of clichés prevent **Summer of Little Rain** from being among the best of its kind. There are attractive illustrations in black and white [by Gloria Stevens], and a short selected bibliography.

Virginia Haviland

SOURCE: A review of *Summer of Little Rain,* in *The Horn Book Magazine,* Vol. 37, No. 3, June, 1961, p. 279.

Miss Fisher keeps company with Chipperfield and the Georges in vivid, moving description of animal life—here a March-to-autumn view of Beaver and Squirrel, their families and enemies on the east side of the Rockies, where she herself lives. Her book speaks as a graphic plea for conservation in a picture of the disaster wrought by forest fire and loss of trees. Woodland beauty; authentic horrors of natural excesses in ice storm, drought, and flood; the playfulness of the animals and their meeting with enemies all have sensitive treatment by this poet-author, to make superb reading-aloud for summer campers and individual reading for nature-lovers in the middle group of children. There are many line drawings [by Gloria Stevens], full of action.

Booklist

SOURCE: A review of *Summer of Little Rain,* in *Booklist,* Vol. 58, No. 1, September 1, 1961, p. 31.

Beautifully written, sensitive story of a beaver family and a squirrel family whose lives are threatened by the summer drought that follows a devastating forest fire in the watershed above their home territory. The effects of the fire on all aspects of plant and animal life are vividly portrayed. Without resorting to personification, the author gives the animals individuality, and the reader is held by the suspense of their struggles to survive. The story is appealing and gives a good lesson in conservation. . . .

WHERE DOES EVERYONE GO? (1961)

Ellen Lewis Buell

SOURCE: "In Season," in *The New York Times Book Review,* October 15, 1961, p. 42.

For reasons best explained by naturalists, autumn in America is gayer, brighter, more joyous than anywhere else. After the long summer there is a quickening in the air and for children it is a time for doing and a time of discovery. Aileen Fisher and Adrienne Adams have captured that feeling in *Where Does Everyone Go?,* a companion volume to *Going Barefoot.* Here a little boy wonders what happens to the birds, the insects, the animals who have so suddenly vanished and even though the answers include migration, hibernation and death, there is no sense of loss but rather a feeling of the rightness of the cycle. Because the verses move so lightly, so quickly and because Adrienne Adams' pictures are so evocative there is that feeling of wonder and excitement which belongs to the season, especially as the narrative moves into the eager anticipation of the first snowstorm.

Booklist

SOURCE: A review of *Where Does Everyone Go?,* in *Booklist,* Vol. 58, No. 5, November 1, 1961, p. 166.

A little boy wonders—and learns by exploring and questioning—about where the butterflies, frogs, and furry animals go in the fall "when the days get short and the sun gets small and leaves go skidding on every breeze . . . and at night the edges of puddles freeze." This enticing picture-book story by the author and the illustrator [Adrienne Adams] of *Going Barefoot* is recounted in buoyant, rhyming text and in evocative drawings in lovely fall colors and in black and white.

Rod Nordell

SOURCE: "Gentle Pencils," in *Christian Science Monitor,* November 16, 1961, p. 2B.

Gently penciled, gently colored autumn leaves [by Adrienne Adams] scud across the end papers of this small-boy's-eye view of changing seasons. Where do ladybugs go in the fall? Where do frogs go in the winter? The answers come easily in Miss Fisher's rhyming text, which adds a breath of humor now and then to the snugness of hibernators and the bustle of people planning not to sleep through the snow. In the tawny shades of apple-picking time, or the skisuit-vividness of later days, Miss Adams's pictures are a delight, but even the black-and-white pages have a soft gradation, from the black nose of a deer to the white chest of a squirrel, that gives them a special atmosphere.

M. W. Brown

SOURCE: A review of *Where Does Everyone Go?,* in *The Horn Book Magazine,* Vol. 38, No. 1, February, 1962, p. 43.

The author and artist who celebrated Spring and Summer in *Going Barefoot* have made an even more beautiful book about Fall. (There are surely too many books about seasons around, but this is one not to be missed.) Aileen Fisher's verse is fine— "What happens to everyone/in the Fall/when the days get short/and the sun gets small/and leaves go skidding/on every breeze/and apples are picked/ from the apple trees/and at night the edges/ of puddles freeze?" The illustrations [by Adrienne Adams] in lovely pastels, soft grays, and occasional flashes of brilliant autumn colors show falling leaves, migrating birds, hibernating animals, and human beings in a variety of autumnal activities. A beautiful book.

LIKE NOTHING AT ALL (1962)

Virginia Kirkus' Service

SOURCE: A review of *Like Nothing At All,* in *Virginia Kirkus' Service,* Vol. XXX, No. 8, April 15, 1962, p. 385.

A walk in the woods during each of four seasons results in surprises not bargained for. Nature's protective colors keep a rabbit, a fawn, a grouse and a weasel well hidden until their quick movements separate them from their surroundings and reveal their identity to the child. Dressed in brown hat and green smock the child too attempts to blend into the woods like "nothing at all." Miss Fisher's fresh original verse and Leonard Weisgard's penetrating illustrations in one color create a most satisfying blend.

Zena Sutherland

SOURCE: A review of *Like Nothing At All,* in *Bulletin of the Center for Children's Books,* Vol. 15, No. 9, May, 1962, p. 141.

A read-aloud book with a verse text that describes some

of the animals whose protective coloration makes them hard to see; the soft and attractive illustrations are printed on palest green. The text carries through the seasons of the year, as a small girl conveys her enjoyment of the outdoor world. Rhyme and rhythm are good; text and illustrations [by Leonard Weisgard] are well-matched.

Silence Buck Bellows

SOURCE: "'A Featherweed to Twirl'," in *Christian Science Monitor*, May 10, 1962, p. 2B.

Everybody knows that wild animals have ways of looking like nothing at all when they wish not to be seen; but the 4-8's reading this book will know it with a difference. Following the poem's eager child through the woods in each of the four seasons, we discover shy woodland animals almost invisible in their protective surroundings, all presented with an enchantment that is compounded of a child's wonder and a poet's skill.

Saturday Review

SOURCE: A review of *Like Nothing At All*, in *Saturday Review*, Vol. XLV, No. 19, May 12, 1962, pp. 36-37.

What a nice, woodsy, spring-like book—using light brown and green so successfully that it really does seem to go through the four seasons it depicts. Aileen Fisher's poetic text and Leonard Weisgard's atmospheric illustrations seem made for each other, and the way in which the light green wash is carried on the text page is also pleasing.

The child who is in theory the narrator begins with an account of a spring walk: "wild-flowers/springing up eagerly/and robins/singing inside of me!"—then takes other seasonal walks, discovering that animals have what is more formally known as protective coloration, but aptly described as "looking like Nothing at All." Finally the child tries a little of this herself.

Booklist

SOURCE: A review of *Like Nothing At All*, in *Booklist*, Vol. 58, No. 22, July, 1962, p. 796.

Walking in the woods in the spring, summer, fall, and winter and being startled each time by the movement of an animal whose protective coloring prevents it from being seen while it is motionless, a little girl becomes aware of how conspicuous her brightly colored clothes are. Taking her mother's old green, paint-splotched smock and her father's old brown hat and donning them in the woods the following spring, the child, too, blends in with the surroundings and is successful in hiding playfully from her family. A delightful picture book with a buoyant, rhyming text and pleasing illustrations [by Leonard Weisgard] in green and brown tones.

Ruth Hill Viguers

SOURCE: A review of *Like Nothing At All*, in *The Horn Book Magazine*, Vol. 38, No. 4, August, 1962, p. 365.

In each season a little girl goes into the woods and sees something that looks mostly like "nothing at all": in the spring, a cottontail rabbit invisible in the grass; in the summer, a spotted fawn among the ferns, dappled by the sun; in the fall, a grouse; and in the winter, a white weasel. Then she surprises her family by making herself look "like nothing at all." The poetry of the text and the illustrations [by Leonard Weisgard] in very dark brown and white on soft green background make this a beautiful book.

I WONDER HOW, I WONDER WHY (1962)

Virginia Kirkus' Service

SOURCE: A review of *I Wonder How, I Wonder Why*, in *Virginia Kirkus' Service*, Vol. XXX, No. 17, September 1, 1962, p. 825.

A random sampling of assorted objects of wonder—this attempts self-consciously to reflect the fascination children find in the world around them. The spinning earth, apple trees, a windy day, the growth of seeds, the moon and the stars—all of these are open to those who would explore and embellish with imagery. Yet one has the feeling that the adult imposes her own reactions in each case. The childlike quality necessary to form a basis for identification is missing here. Even Carol Barker's illustrations are too bright and too busy and the whole is too precocious.

William Turner Levy

SOURCE: A review of *I Wonder How, I Wonder Why*, in *The New York Times Book Review*, November 11, 1962, p. 3, 61.

The verses here are miraculously short and rhythmically delightful. Because they so effectively encourage curiosity, they start their readers thinking. The world around us—its living creatures, anthills, roads and sky—seems more intimately ours to understand as a result of Aileen Fisher's art. It is calmly realistic with a charming query into the impossible possibility of people living on a moon which, after all, shrinks in certain phases. The book is illustrated with a bright and cheery touch that appears much easier to accomplish than it is.

Times Literary Supplement

SOURCE: A review of *I Wonder How, I Wonder Why*, in *Times Literary Supplement*, Vol. 62, No. 3222, November 28, 1963, p. 972.

I Wonder How, I Wonder Why is . . . a pretty book, with little verses about the things that puzzle small children—how does the hen get the yolk inside the white, how does a mole know when it's time to get up, how do seeds know what kind of flower to grow into? An adult reader has an uneasy feeling that it is really a book about children being cute, and a second uneasy feeling that perhaps child listeners would demand the real answers to these questions and be disillusioned by adult ignorance, but no one, old or young, could fail to be charmed by the illustrations [by Carol Barker].

MY COUSIN ABE (1962)

Zena Sutherland

SOURCE: A review of *My Cousin Abe,* in *Bulletin of the Center for Children's Books,* Vol. 16, No. 5, January, 1963, p. 78.

Abraham Lincoln's cousin, Dennis Hanks, tells about Abe and his family in an unusual biography, an excellent one. Dennis knew and loved Abe from birth; they were neighbors in Kentucky, lived in the same household in Indiana, moved on together to Illinois—Dennis being wed by then to Abe's step-sister. The writing is faithful to the vernacular and the viewpoint is consistently that of Dennis himself: a convincing technique that makes the book seem truly a family story, with a cousinly affection and pride giving a warm and intimate picture of Abraham Lincoln.

I LIKE WEATHER (1963)

Virginia Kirkus' Service

SOURCE: A review of *I Like Weather,* in *Virginia Kirkus' Service,* Vol. XXXI, No. 6, February 15, 1963, p. 181.

Once again, this "poetess" attempts to illuminate a child's world, peering eagerly, skipping gleefully, wandering wistfully—all in verse—verse in which the rhymes are pushed, forced, and the meter is bumpy and ragged. A boy and his very plain dog seek out all the joys of the four seasons of the year. The artist [Janina Domanska] has squeezed these pleasures and activities into illustrations which demand more space, and the use of many colors does not add any vitality.

Zena Sutherland

SOURCE: A review of *I Like Weather,* in *Bulletin of the Center for Children's Books,* Vol. 16, No. 8, April, 1963, p. 126.

A read-aloud picture book about the seasons of the year, with illustrations [by Janina Domanska] (both black and white and full color) that are gentle and evocative. Following the cycle of the year, the rhyming text tells, through the voice of a small boy, of the special delights of each of the seasons. Some of the lines and concepts seem patterned, but much of the text has freshness and vitality.

Melvin Maddocks

SOURCE: "Something to Give," in *Christian Science Monitor,* May 9, 1963, p. 2B.

Sometimes it's only by running and running and jumping, sometimes it's only by dancing and shouting that a 4-8-year-old can express the exuberance of a new season just arriving. Only once in a while someone like Aileen Fisher finds just the right words for them. "I like it /when it's sprinkly, /when sunny drops are twinkly /on leaves that still are crinkly." She tells about otters and ducks, summer "shimmery and sunny, /yellower than honey" and swimming children, windy days and rainy days, snowy ones and quiet nighttime too. Janina Domanska's pastel drawings are an important part of the book. Despite the gentleness of their color and their soft outlines, her children and animals are lively enough to leave the page.

Virginia Haviland

SOURCE: A review of *I Like Weather,* in *The Horn Book Magazine,* Vol. XXIX, No. 3, June, 1963, pp. 274-75.

A poetic picture book—it might be called a series of poems—in which a boy, accompanied by his faithful spaniel, talks of how and why he enjoys all the seasons and days with their "different kinds of smells and sounds and looks and feels and ways." The realistic pictures [by Janina Domanska] project moods in soft colors, sometimes in penciled grays and blacks. The text frequently contains the fresh imagery of good poetry and has many onomatopoetic words; when the boy wonders to himself or talks to the animals or the reader, the lines revert to plain narrative. Teachers will enjoy sharing this, as a whole or in such excerpts as the poetic description of the first snow.

CRICKET IN A THICKET (1963)

Virginia Kirkus' Service

SOURCE: A review of *Cricket in a Thicket,* in *Virginia Kirkus' Service,* Vol. XXXI, No. 16, August 15, 1963, p. 797.

Thirty-nine poems with nature as the theme. This is a rhymed view of the out-of-doors—from beetles through trees—that presents the world of nature on its best or most endearing behavior. The poems do not employ a difficult vocabulary nor do they demand or provide much in the way of new insights. [Feodor] Rojankovsky's black and white drawings decorate each page.

Saturday Review

SOURCE: A review of *Cricket in a Thicket,* in *Saturday Review,* Vol. XLVI, No. 38, September 21, 1963, p. 42.

> Out of the trees
> with rustly sleeves
> fall wonderful colorful autumn leaves . . .
>
> Everything falls from There to Here . . .
> No wonder we call it
> the fall of the year.

Now that crickets are "singing" at the tops of their "voices" and the leaves will soon be turning, this should be a useful and pleasant little book to have around the house. Children like Aileen Fisher's verses, and they will enjoy the [Feodor] Rojankovsky illustrations, which are realistic and charming. Some science-wise children may spurn the more imaginative touches; but, on the whole, children are imaginative, too.

Paul Engle

SOURCE: "There's Every Sort of Poem for Every Kind of Child," in *The New York Times Book Review,* November 10, 1963, p. 2.

Aileen Fisher's book, **Cricket in a Thicket,** wavers from fresh to trite, but Feodor Rojankovsky cannot illustrate a children's book without illuminating it. He is quite as astonished as I am at the lines: "Centipedes/have more than 30 feet to wash/when they get dirty." And he agrees with Miss Fisher's shrewd comment on caterpillars: "They just eat what by and by/will make them be a butterfly." Alas, fancy falters, and a poem on **"Moles"** lists the obvious things: sun climbs, grass bends, winds race, stars twinkle. It is simply unfair to a child to assure him that blue birds "twitter gentle little rhymes." The best of Miss Fisher is the charm, however slight, of her mouse poem: "She's not afraid/of the dark at all/though the night's so big/and herself so small." The poor poems are for age eight (at the risk of distorting its taste) and the good are for age twelve.

Ruth Hill Viguers

SOURCE: A review of *Cricket in a Thicket,* in *The Horn Book Magazine,* Vol. XXXIX, No. 6, December, 1963, p. 59.

Beautiful drawings in black and white on every page [by Feodor Rojankovsky] illustrate an enchanting collection of nature poems. Kindergarten and even very young children will especially appreciate the imagery, humor, and the careful, varied meter and rhyme. "A mouse goes out/ in the dark of night/ without a lantern/or other light./ She's not afraid/ of the dark at all,/ though the night's so big/ and herself so small."

LISTEN, RABBIT (1964)

Virginia Kirkus' Service

SOURCE: A review of *Listen, Rabbit,* in *Virginia Kirkus' Service,* Vol. XXXII, No. 6, March 15, 1964, pp. 289-90.

A very patient, observant and gentle boy watches through the seasons for a wild rabbit first sighted in the fall. His attempts to get close to it through autumn and winter teach him about the behavior of rabbits and the nature of wild things. In the spring, his patience is rewarded with a glimpse and a touch of the rabbit's fur-lined nest with five bunnies curled inside. Told in rhyme in the words of the boy, this is a quiet poem with a full story in it. Mr. [Symeon] Shimin's beautifully drawn illustrations, many in full watercolor, catch exactly the mood established by Miss Fisher.

Silence Buck Bellows

SOURCE: "The Poetry Shelf: New Voices and Old," in *Christian Science Monitor,* May 7, 1964, p. 6B.

In this charming and tender narrative poem a little boy tells the story of how he wanted a pet. When he saw a wild rabbit, he hoped it might be his pet; but if the rabbit didn't want to leave the field, just to be friends would be enough. It is difficult, though, to get to be friends with a rabbit. There are too many things to frighten it away. However, patience and love are rewarded. The boy doesn't exactly get a rabbit for a pet, but he gets something even better. This book has all the suspense of good narration and all the beauty and appeal of good poetry.

Zena Sutherland

SOURCE: A review of *Listen, Rabbit,* in *Bulletin of the Center for Children's Books,* Vol. 17, No. 10, June, 1964, p. 154.

A lovely, lovely picture book. The rhymed text is gentle, the illustrations [by Symeon Shimin] are beautifully soft, and the two are completely in harmony. A small boy sees a rabbit and he loves it; there are pets in his home, but nothing that belongs just to him. All through the wintertime the boy wonders how the rabbit is—now and then he sees the rabbit, but it always flashes away. One day the boy finds a nest of young, and he closes in joy, "I hadn't a pony or pup to pet,/But I/had a nest/like a fur-lined cup/ And *five baby rabbits* to watch grow up!"

Virginia Haviland

SOURCE: A review of *Listen, Rabbit,* in *The Horn Book Magazine,* Vol. XL, No. 3, June, 1964, p. 275.

A companion to the poet's **Going Barefoot** and other

picture-poetry books, this long poem expresses a boy's enchanted anticipation of making friends with a wild rabbit he has spied in the field. Summer turns to fall, fall to winter, and then there is spring when "I hadn't a rabbit/ exactly, yet,/ But I/ had a nest/ like a fur-lined cup/ And *five baby rabbits*/ to watch grow up!" Sunset, rainy, snowy, moonlit, and pale-green spring scenes have a maximum of atmosphere and lovely color with the jumping or hiding rabbit always an appealing focus. Children may notice changing details of costume for the boy and his sister, from page to page for the same adventure; but the total effect of great beauty will transcend this flaw.

George A. Woods

SOURCE: A review of *Listen, Rabbit,* in *The New York Times Book Review,* July 26, 1964, p. 26.

Listen rabbit, this boy intends no harm. Friendship is his goal. He has sought you the whole year through: spying you first on the edge of the summer sky; worrying how you manage in rain and hail; dreaming of your dance on the moonlit lawn; seeing you hunched up against autumn's air; following your tracks in the telltale snow (wondering, he'd "like to know/can you hear the quiet/of windless snow/falling like star dust/ashy white, falling like feathers, fluffy, light?"), finally discovering a special secret of yours amid the bursting buds of spring.

Aileen Fisher's narrative poem describes these timorous encounters between boy and rabbit, always conveying the patient expectation that maybe tomorrow they will be friends. Running through the poem is a fidelity to the timid, elusive side of nature, and a responsiveness to the beauty of the ever-changing seasons. [Symeon] Shimin's literal illustrations, line and delicate wash tints, are pleasing.

IN THE MIDDLE OF THE NIGHT (1965)

Virginia Kirkus' Service

SOURCE: A review of *In the Middle of the Night,* in *Virginia Kirkus' Service,* Vol. XXXIII, No. 6, March 15, 1965, p. 309.

Fear of the dark is a widely shared pre-schooler reaction and the reassuring books come few and far between. This is a long poem about a little girl whose birthday wish to see the night is granted. Her report serves to remove the imagined horrors from night in the woods as it follows the girl and her father on their walk. Her flashlight reveals a world of small nocturnal creatures busy with their normal round. That the unending balance of nature is in full force is mentioned so casually and blithely—"Watch out, little mouse, in your velvet blouse/You'll stay under cover/if you are wise,/for the owl wants a dinner that's just your size."—removes the menace traditionally associated with the situation by disengaging the first person

of the poem from any concern while she finally arrives at a sense of oneness with the whole night scene. The bibliotherapeutic possibilities perhaps outweigh anything that might be said about the poem as poetry and, the fact that the night has been dressed by Adrienne Adams in the same rich black and jewel colors she used for *Cabbage Moon* makes it well worth looking at.

Zena Sutherland

SOURCE: A review of *In the Middle of the Night,* in *Bulletin of the Center for Children's Books,* Vol. 18, No. 9, May, 1965, p. 128.

A poem about the night, with illustrations [by Adrienne Adams] that are attractive in black-and-white and beautiful on those pages that are in color. A little girl who wonders what the out-of-doors is like at night is given a nocturnal walk as a birthday present. It is just what she wants; she is not disappointed, but is enthralled by the quiet beauty and by the glimpses into the secret world of night animals. A peaceful and a satisfying book, evoking the hushed excitement of a child's first experience of a country night, written with a restrained imagery in a style appropriate for the small girl who is speaking.

Barbara S. McCauley

SOURCE: "Through a Child's Eyes," in *Christian Science Monitor,* May 6, 1965, p. B2.

What is more natural, this delightful poem asks, than for a little girl to wonder about "the middle of the night," when children are supposed to be asleep? Adults scoff, but she wants just one birthday gift—a night in the woods. Her father walks with her and shares the moonlit fantasy through a child's eyes. [Adrienne] Adams' illustrations beautifully capture the feeling of wonder:

> It was even better
> than I had dreamed;
> and my Father seemed
> not tall, and me small,
> but as if we'd become
> sort-of-the-same size,
> looking with surprise
> through the same kind of eyes.

Barbara Novak O'Doherty

SOURCE: A review of *In the Middle of the Night,* in *The New York Times Book Review,* May 9, 1965, p. 4.

Aileen Fisher's *In the Middle of the Night* illustrated by Adrienne Adams . . . deals with a child's curiosity, this time about the night, and the discoveries in nature the little girl makes with her father on the night of her birthday are sensitively described by the author in verse: "What would be in sight/ in the only-a-little-light/ of the middle of the night?" Here Adrienne Adams does have a larger format, but the drawings are too arbitrary to be successful.

Ethel L. Heins

SOURCE: A review of *In the Middle of the Night,* in *The Horn Book Magazine,* Vol. XLI, June, 1965, p. 268.

Even without words, the beautiful pictures, some in black and soft gray, others in full, luminescent color, would convey both a mood and a story. But a freely poetic text sharpens the images and deepens the sensations. A little girl longs to explore the nocturnal mysteries of the out-of-doors in the country; but the grownups say, "You're not a cat, you know,/ with lantern eyes glowing/ to show where you're going/ so you won't stub your toe./ Besides, what would you see/ when things that are creepy/ and peepy/ and leapy/ are most of them sleepy . . . / as *you* should be?" And then, for her birthday present, the child chooses, above all, to have a walk in the dark with her father. A lovely book, full of appreciation for the wonders of sky, woods, and field in the nighttime world.

Booklist

SOURCE: A review of *In the Middle of the Night,* in *Booklist,* Vol. 61, No. 20, June 15, 1965, p. 996.

All a little girl wants for her birthday is permission to stay up, and outdoors, all night to see the small creatures that inhabit the nighttime. An understanding father stays with her as, flashlight in hand, she explores the wonders of meadow and wood, of grass and sky, from sunset to dawn. The poetic style lends itself well to reading aloud and both the text and the illustrations will give the young listener a reassurance that the night is a place of beauty and wonder, with no room for fears.

ARBOR DAY (1965)

Zena Sutherland

SOURCE: A review of *Arbor Day,* in *Bulletin of the Center for Children's Books,* Vol. 18, July, 1965, p. 160.

One of a series of books about national or religious holidays, this title has a rather slight text. The first part of the book describes the destructive carelessness of the early settlers and the erosive forces of nature; the second part discusses the work of Sterling Morton in Nebraska and the adoption of Arbor Day by other states, the holiday now being nationally observed. There is so small an amount of material available on Arbor Day that the book will be useful, but the end of the text gives very little information—possibly because the observance is simply the formal planting of trees. The writing style is rather choppy.

 ### *WE DICKINSONS: THE LIFE OF EMILY DICKINSON AS SEEN THROUGH THE EYES OF HER BROTHER AUSTIN* (written with Olive Rabe, 1965)

Virginia Kirkus' Service

SOURCE: A review of *We Dickinsons,* in *Virginia Kirkus' Service,* Vol. XXXIII, No. 16, August 15, 1965, p. 825.

A more accurate title would have been *We Dickinsons; The Life of Emily Dickinson as Seen Through the Eyes of her Brother Austin as Imagined by Aileen Fisher and Olive Rabe.* Poor Emily Dickinson; not only has the self-imposed solitude of her life been a favorite of prying eyes and imaginations, but here she has been turned into a fictional character in a weak attempt to improve on reality. Hopefully the readers will understand that this first person account isn't the real Austin Dickinson speaking (it's never really explained). Hopefully also they will look elsewhere (perhaps Polly Longsworth's *Emily Dickinson: Her Letter to the World*) for a more accurate assessment of her life. In this book she comes through mainly as a sweet suburban girl of a genial family background, who adored plants, animals, and cooking. Rather a disappointment to the teenager who has always considered Emily Dickinson a romantically enigmatic figure.

Johanna Hurwitz

SOURCE: A review of *We Dickinsons,* in *School Library Journal,* Vol. 12, No. 1, September, 1965, p. 166.

Two books about Emily Dickinson have appeared this year. The first was *Emily Dickinson: Her Letter to the World,* by Polly Longsworth which is a straight factual account of the poetess' life. *We Dickinsons* will be much more difficult for catalogers to place. It is the life of Emily as Miss Fisher and Mrs. Rabe imagine her brother Austin saw her. As in Aileen Fisher's *My Cousin Abe,* the authors have striven to write an intimate portrait of their subject based on sound research but using poetic license and imagination, and have done a good job. Emily is more vivid here than in the Longsworth biography, and this book may well serve as an introduction both to the woman and to her poetry. Many poems are quoted in the text.

Zena Sutherland

SOURCE: A review of *We Dickinsons,* in *Bulletin of the Center for Children's Books,* Vol. 19, No. 3, November, 1965, p. 43.

A biography in which the authors have used an unusual technique, and used it most successfully: the book is written as though the author were Emily's brother Austin. Thus the intimate observations seem reminiscence rather than fictionalization; both Austin's personality and the attitudes that reflect the times and his environment are consistently maintained. The biographee is viewed with sympathy rather than with adulation.

Sr. M. Lucille

SOURCE: A review of *We Dickinsons: The Life of Emily Dickinson As Seen Through the Eyes of Her Brother Austin,* in *Catholic Library World,* Vol. 37, No. 4, December, 1965, p. 272.

This is a delightful biography of Emily Dickinson. Relying chiefly on letters written by her to members of her family and friends, and on her poems, the biographers have revealed the poet's sensitive, affectionate nature, and her keen intellect. Always shy, Emily, who could be quite animated in a gathering, tended to avoid people more and more as she grew older in order to be alone with her thoughts. Perhaps the best quality of the authors' effort is that their story shows that Miss Dickinson did not withdraw from people, but withdrew rather because she needed the solitude and time to express her thoughts in concise and beautiful poetry. For young people just discovering Emily Dickinson, this is an enlightening and "alive" portrait of a great poet.

Ethel L. Heins

SOURCE: A review of *We Dickinsons,* in *The Horn Book Magazine,* Vol. XLI, No. 6, December, 1965, p. 642.

A publishing coincidence has brought forth in the same year two important, though wholly different, treatments of an endlessly interesting subject. Polly Longsworth's *Emily Dickinson* was essentially an objective biography—exquisite, discriminating, and restrained. *We Dickinsons* is a piece of biographical fiction which, despite a few weaknesses of style, convincingly employs a difficult narrative device. From material found in Emily's voluminous letters, the authors have created a verbal portrait in the form of a first-person reminiscence by the poet's fiercely devoted brother. Both books in their own way emphasize Emily's rare independence of spirit, her joy in family and friends, her withdrawal from the world, her quick, impish wit, her astonishing dexterity with words, her cryptic, penetrating verse, her exultation with life, and her mystical preoccupation with God and eternity. But this new book becomes a personal memoir—emotional, intimate, informal—revealing the poet as a beloved, though enigmatic, member of a close-knit family.

Shulamith Oppenheim

SOURCE: A review of *We Dickinsons,* in *The New York Times Book Review,* January 16, 1966, p. 36.

"The Poets light but lamps—Themselves—go out—." Written in 1864 this is one of the loveliest among the thousand odd poems discovered after Emily Dickinson's death. In her own case she was mistaken. Emily Dickinson, the woman and poet, has never "gone out." Her poetry, intensely autobiographical, impeccably executed, is continually being reinterpreted in the light of her enigmatic life. Biographers are especially fortunate. There are always enough shadows surrounding her life behind the hemlock hedge to warrant a new approach, a fresh interpretation. But in the book *We Dickinsons* shadow and substance are confounded. Established facts are reworked or simply ignored to suit the authors' design. Perhaps the trouble stems from the narrative technique—Emily seen by her brother Austin, two years older than she. For whatever reason, the life he depicts does not reveal his sister's unique qualities of mind and spirit. Her love affair with life, that "gratuitous glee," her struggle with questions of faith and death and immortality do not emerge. Very few of her poems have been included, and that, too, is unfortunate. Emily Dickinson is still "her own best biographer."

IN THE WOODS, IN THE MEADOW, IN THE SKY (1965)

Virginia Kirkus' Service

SOURCE: A review of *In the Woods, In the Meadow, In the Sky,* in *Virginia Kirkus' Service,* Vol. XXXIII, No. 18, September 1, 1965, p. 900.

It's another collection of short poems about nature, on the order of *Cricket in a Thicket.* The rhythms are sprightly and catchy, very readable and very recitable. Practically all of these selections assume the rather precious intonation and viewpoint of the child—a continually delighted child who finds the outdoors the perfect playground for his simple games. The images are many, simple, visual, but commonplace. The black and white drawings [by Margot Tomes] are a carefree accompaniment.

Priscilla L. Moulton

SOURCE: A review of *In the Woods, In the Meadow, In the Sky,* in *The Horn Book Magazine,* Vol. XLI, No. 6, December, 1965, pp. 640-41.

In character and subject, the poems are similar to those of *Cricket in a Thicket,* an earlier collection of proven popularity with primary-grade children. The words and the construction are simple, the meter and the rhyme pronounced, the imagery childlike. Illustrations have a sun-and-shadow, wind-caressed quality that evokes a carefree, lyric mood. The restlessness, the curiosity, the joy of childhood are here—also the perception and the humor. "Trees are full of holes—/between the leaves, I mean./ But if you stand away enough/ the holes fill up with green." Children will be happy to read and quick to recall the poems and pictures in a distinguished volume.

Zena Sutherland

SOURCE: A review of *In the Woods, In the Meadow, In the Sky,* in *Bulletin of the Center for Children's Books,* Vol. 19, No. 11, July/August, 1966, pp. 177-78.

A collection of poems, some of which have been previously published in periodicals, with illustrations that are attractive. The poems are divided into those about (or set in) the woods, the meadow, and the sky; there is little variation in approach or subject: and not much variation in the quality of the selections. Some few seem stilted, but many are quite charming; the greatest number are pleasant, lacking either great vigor or imagery but having no real weakness.

📖 *BEST LITTLE HOUSE* (1966)

Virginia Kirkus' Service

SOURCE: A review of *Best Little House,* in *Virginia Kirkus' Service,* Vol. XXXIV, No. 5, March 1, 1966, p. 239.

This is a long rhyme about a little boy disquieted at the disorganization of his home as his parents prepare to move to a new house. After a restless night spent dreaming of houses underscored by the enlivened musicians from his music box, his mother suggests, "Take your flute and we'll go on a tour with a toot-toot-toot." They toot around some woodland paths with mother pointing out and describing the housing of ants, wasps, mice, raccoons, etc. until they're led to a yard where the boy's father is waiting with a dog house and, " . . . there inside on a bed of hay a not-very-big-little puppy lay, waiting for someone to come and play and rollick and frolic from bush to tree . . . waiting for someone who looks like ME." It's an arch and aimless ending to a wandering mood nature piece. The swiftly sketched illustrations are best on the examples of animal architecture, worst on faces and figures and alternate between color pages and black and white.

Booklist

SOURCE: A review of *Best Little House,* in *Booklist,* Vol. 62, No. 17, May 1, 1966, p. 875.

In sprightly rhymed verses the author tells the story of a small boy whose unhappiness at moving from his familiar home in town is changed to joy when his mother shows him the many unusual houses of insects and other small creatures who live near his new home in the country. Despite the rather insipid portrayal of human faces, the drawings in soft glowing colors and in black and white are pleasing and informative. An inviting introduction to the wonders of nature as well as a childlike interpretation of adjustment to change.

Carolyn H. Lavender

SOURCE: "On the Trail of Animals," in *The New York Times Book Review,* May 8, 1966, p. 43.

Aileen Fisher's *Best Little House* is a change from the animal stories, for it describes in verse the dismay a boy experiences when he moves to the exurbs:

> *"Way out there*
> *at the edge of town*
> *there wouldn't be houses*
> *up and down.*
> *Who would I know?*
> *How would I play?*
> *Why did anyone move away"?*

The boy's discovery of nature's little houses (a wasp's nest, a mouse's hole) and his amazement in finding the wonder of the country is delightful. Arnold Spilka's illustrations are sensitive, as befits the story.

Ethel L. Heins

SOURCE: A review of *Best Little House,* in *The Horn Book Magazine,* Vol. XLII, No. 3, June, 1966, p. 299.

In another of her poetic picture-storybooks, the author again reveals her identification with the world of nature and her sensitivity to the thoughts and feelings of children. A small boy is moving to a new house and is fearful of the loneliness to come: "Way out there/ at the edge of town/ there wouldn't be houses/ up and down./ Who would I know?/How would I play?/Why did *anyone* move away?" But as she walks with him on the very first morning, the boy's mother shows him all sorts of snug little houses occupied by fascinating new neighbors: the paper house of the hornets, the sand house of the ants, the mud huts of the wasps, the tree holes of the birds, and the spun-silk cocoon of the butterfly; then back at home, the boy finds the happiest surprise-house of all. Responsive illustrations [by Arnold Spilka]—some drawn in black and white, others painted in warm, naturalistic color—accompany the verses.

Zena Sutherland

SOURCE: A review of *Best Little House,* in *Bulletin of the Center for Children's Books,* Vol. 20, No. 3, November, 1966, p. 41.

A read-aloud picture book with verse text, the simply drawn, large scale illustrations using, on alternate double-page spreads, black and white and full color in soft tones. The story is told by a small boy who is sad at leaving his familiar house to go live in the country. His mother takes him on a nature walk and the boy is fascinated by the many marvelous structures his mother finds: the potter wasp's jar, the papery sack of the hornet, the curled green leaf of the leaf-roller moth. The best little house of all is the small house that the boy finds at the end of his walk, a dog house with a new puppy that has been given by parents who understand that the child will feel lonely in a new place. Although the story seems a bit extended in dealing with the problem of adaptability, with the charming pages on natural science, and with the interim section, in which the boy plays his music-box and dreams, it never becomes weighty—the writing is lightly affectionate in tone, neither sentimental about the adjustment nor heavily instructive during the sequence of the country walk.

📖 *VALLEY OF THE SMALLEST: THE LIFE STORY OF A SHREW* (1966)

Virginia Kirkus' Service

SOURCE: A review of *Valley of the Smallest,* in *Virginia Kirkus' Service,* Vol. XXXIV, No. 19, October 1, 1966, p. 1050.

"One of the most common, yet least familiar, of all our American mammals" is here treated in a manner which fully compensates for past neglect. Aileen Fisher's text takes one shrew through the year, searching for food day and night, fighting the Deer Mouse and the Weasel, giving birth and tending her young, weakening and falling prey to an owl. Each of the other animals is followed down his own paths, and even a Man appears, to demonstrate the interdependence of living things. Only occasionally does the author compromise her objectivity, but even on these occasions she is not sentimental. (After a Garter Snake invades the Shrew's nest—"Her babies, naked, blind, deaf, and entirely helpless, were gone."—but she does not mourn.) Adding to the effectiveness throughout are crisply delineated, carefully textured drawings by Jean Zallinger in black-and-white. . . . If you want shrews handled with loving care, this is for you.

Marian Sorenson

SOURCE: "Of Birds, Beasts, Beetles, and Butterflies," in *Christian Science Monitor,* April 3, 1966, p. B11.

One of the most interesting books this fall is devoted to the shrew, that tiny animal with the rapid metabolism which makes it eat more than twice its own weight in food each day. *Valley of the Smallest,* by Aileen Fisher, tells of the strain this remarkable little animal must live under. Also included are the deer mouse, the ground squirrel, the weasel, and the horned owl who inhabit the shrew's world. A rare glimpse for 10s and up of one of the world's smallest animals.

Henry B. Kane

SOURCE: "Ways of the Wild," in *The New York Times Book Review,* November 6, 1966, p. 58.

Valley of the Smallest, by Aileen Fisher, is the life story of a shrew. The setting is a mountain valley in the Rockies, but it could be anywhere as the story recites the pattern of this masked shrew's life. The shrew has a constant struggle to find food—and not to serve as food for other creatures. These tiny animals, bundles of nervous energy, are constantly on the go, winter and summer. The story is authoritative, well written, and beautifully illustrated by Jean Zallinger.

Zena Sutherland

SOURCE: A review of *Valley of the Smallest,* in *Bulletin of the Center for Children's Books,* Vol. 20, No. 4, December, 1966, p. 57.

An exceptionally good book on the life cycle of an animal, written in a smooth narrative style, yet never popularized or sentimental. The tiny shrew is an animal, not a winning personality; in describing her life, fraught with danger, the author gives a fine picture of the whole ecology. The illustrations, handsome and realistic in black and white, have both softness and strength. A list of suggested readings and an index are appended.

Science Books & Films

SOURCE: A review of *Valley of the Smallest,* in *Science Books & Films,* Vol. 2, No. 3, December, 1966, pp. 214-15.

With a beautiful narrative style characteristic of good nature writing, and based on a serious study of background literature (listed in her bibliography), the author has created a lively "novel" about "one particular shrew" in a Colorado mountain valley. From this narrative the young reader may pleasantly become aware of basic facts of the life-history and ecology of a fascinating and little-known mammal.

Virginia Haviland

SOURCE: A review of *Valley of the Smallest,* in *The Horn Book Magazine,* Vol. XLII, No. 6, December, 1966, p. 728.

In this companion to ***All on a Mountain Day*** the naturalist pictures the ecology of a valley of the Colorado Rockies. The interest centers on the smallest animal there, the shrew, and on the problem of the infestation of the Pandora Moth, which threatens a stand of lodgepole pines with death. A sharp observer, with a poet's imagination, the author records what she has seen near her mountain home. Her account is both more vivid and more suspenseful than most nature books depicting survival in the wild. The Shrew, a frenetically active creature, is always "whiskering" or "whizzing" around near the beaver flat where she has her tunnel home, for she must eat often and has to make frantic dashes to safety from Weasel, Owl, and other predators. A government entomologist detects not only the existence of the Pandora Moth but also the part that the hungry Shrew and her fellows have played in saving the lodgepole trees. There is a beauty in the description of the animals' discovery of snow and in the treatment of many other aspects of mountain life, making this book well worth sharing aloud. Exquisitely textured soft-pencil drawings [by Jean Zallinger] give added dimensions to the personalities of the animals and the emotional atmosphere of the action.

Appraisal: Children's Science Books

SOURCE: A review of *Valley of the Smallest*, in *Appraisal: Children's Science Books*, Vol. 1, No. 1, Winter, 1967, p. 5.

In this distinguished presentation, the current knowledge about the life of shrews is woven into a narrative that highlights the life story of a single shrew—a long-tailed shrew who lives out her brief life in a Rocky Mountain setting in Colorado. Although the narrative is a sympathetic one in its portrayal of the drives that keep this small mammal constantly alert, it is objective and unsentimental. Beautiful prose, spare and effective, and remarkably lovely drawings make this an outstanding introduction to the life story of these miniature animals. Heightened perception and observation should result from careful reading of this text.

📖 MY MOTHER AND I (1967)

Kirkus Service

SOURCE: A review of *My Mother and I*, in *Kirkus Service*, Vol. XXXV, No. 31, April 1, 1967, p. 406.

A little girl feeling lost because her mother has gone to take care of her gran thinks about things without mothers—Bug, Frog, Butterfly—and consoles herself with her father's reassurance that "*you* have a mother/ the whole year through/ . . . except just now/ for a week or two." Discovering the reproductive habits of insects and amphibians seems to us a dubious consolation for the loss, even temporarily, of a mother. Despite the pleasant watercolor illustrations, you have to accept the premise and welcome the attendant nature lore to enjoy this slight rhymed introspection.

Publishers Weekly

SOURCE: A review of *My Mother and I*, in *Publishers Weekly*, Vol. 191, No. 14, April 3, 1967, p. 56.

Don't let the title of this one mislead you. It is no attempt to cut in on the profits from that florist's creation, Mother's Day. It is the gentle story of a walk through spring with a small girl who discovers beetles and bugs, logs and frogs. And her mother. Now I'll go commercial—

with Aileen Fisher's light-hearted verses, and Kazue Mizumura's misty spring pictures, *My Mother and I* is a book *I* would love to get for Mother's Day.

Eve Merriam

SOURCE: "Well, They Rhyme," in *The New York Times Book Review*, May 7, 1967, p. 45.

In *My Mother and I,* by Aileen Fisher the watercolors by Kazue Mizumura are limpidly lovely, but the verse story made me a bit queasy. A little girl, whose mother has had to go away to visit *her* mother, who is sick, scampers about asking a bug, a frog, and a butterfly where their mothers are. At the same time she reminds the creatures that she really and scientifically knows they don't have mothers that stay with them. You'll be relieved to know that "Gran" recovers, "Mum" returns, and the little girl is happy she's not an oyster, shrimp, newt, or lizard because they don't have mothers to go on play outings with them.

Saturday Review

SOURCE: A review of *My Mother and I*, in *Saturday Review*, Vol. L, No. 19, May 13, 1967, pp. 50-51.

If you are a small girl who loves a country walk with her mother, and the year is at spring, and the walk has been planned, it is shattering to come home to an empty house and have a neighbor tell you that mother has gone away on an emergency visit. Sad to think of all the creatures that don't know their mothers: tadpoles and butterflies, bugs and frogs. "'Without a mother . . . who cures your itches?' I asked. 'And warns you away from the ditches? And answers your whys and whats and whiches?' He hadn't a single word to say. He just looked hurried, and scurried away." The book communicates both a love of nature and warm feeling for close family ties. The illustrations are quite attractive, particularly in the soft colors and subtle suggestion of line.

Booklist

SOURCE: A review of *My Mother and I*, in *Booklist*, Vol. 63, No. 18, May 15, 1967, p. 991.

A little girl comes home from school bursting with anticipation of a promised walk to the top of the hill with her mother only to find that Mother has been called away for a week or two. During Mother's absence the disappointed child observes and thinks about the many small creatures with no mothers at all and as a result is all the more joyful over her mother's return. In this sensitive story the author once again reveals her understanding of young children and her feeling for nature. Lovely watercolors reinforce the mood conveyed by the lilting rhymed text.

Zena Sutherland

SOURCE: A review of *My Mother and I,* in *Bulletin of the Center for Children's Books,* Vol. 20, No. 10, June, 1967, p. 152.

A charming book, both in the beauty of its illustrations and in the gentle quality of the rhyming text. Elated by the spring, a small girl looks forward to a day outdoors with her mother; when mother is called away because of her own mother's illness, the lonely child thinks about the creatures she sees and the fact that many of them never know their mothers. Of a frog: "I knew he hadn't a mother at all, not since the day he was just a small spot in an egg, in a black-and-white ball in jelly-like slime. (My mum read me that in a book one time.)" The nature lore is accurate and simply presented; the text is warm without being sentimental.

Virginia Haviland

SOURCE: A review of *My Mother and I,* in *The Horn Book Magazine,* Vol. XLIII, No. 4, August, 1967, p. 459.

The poet-naturalist again offers a provocative occasion for an illustrator to complement her lyrical description of the beauty and joy in a child's wonder-filled discoveries in the outdoor world. In the quiet story a little girl comes home after school to find that her mother is not waiting to take a promised walk because *her* mother is ill and needs her. Comforted by a neighbor, the child goes out alone, sees a bug, a frog, and a butterfly, and realizes that *they* have never known a mother. The bright paintings, alternating with those in soft gray wash, have the freshness of colors not yet dry.

📖 *SKIP AROUND THE YEAR* (1967)

Kirkus Service

SOURCE: A review of *Skip Around the Year,* in *Kirkus Service,* Vol. XXXV, No. 20, October 15, 1967, p. 1277.

A little collection of sing-song celebrations that slights no one: Lee balances Lincoln, and Jewish holidays are generously represented. The purpose is worthy but the rhymes are weak, as per *Abraham Lincoln:* "His lot was hard/and his future bleak—/Abraham Lincoln/of Pigeon Creek./ He studied law/ though a backwoods boy—/Abraham Lincoln/ of Washington./ Rarely a man/ more loved than he—/Abraham Lincoln/ of history." This is one of the most banal of the bunch; others are trite and stilted.

Barbara Gibson

SOURCE: A review of *Skip Around the Year,* in *School Library Journal,* Vol. 14, No. 1, November, 1967, p. 58.

Teachers always need holiday material so it is very handy to have a collection of poems covering several holidays in one volume, including Jewish, Christian, and national holidays. Miss Fisher has arranged the poems chronologically, following the year from New Year's Eve to Hanukkah and Christmas. Unlike some holiday collections which are weighted with cliches, this collection brings added meaning to holidays through an emphasis on giving: spreading seeds for birds on Valentine's Day, leaving May baskets, and collecting coins for UNICEF on Halloween are a few of the ideas transmitted through these thoughtful poems. The illustrations [by Gioia Fiammenghi] reflect the imagery in the poems through familiar symbols interpreted to fit the deeper meaning in the poetry.

Zena Sutherland

SOURCE: A review of *Skip Around the Year,* in *Bulletin of the Center for Children's Books,* Vol. 21, No. 7, March, 1968, p. 108.

A collection of holiday poems that move through the calendar year; the verses are brief, varied in form and mood; the illustrations are lively and sometimes humorous. The author has included, in addition to the usual legal holidays, commemorative occasions like Arbor Day, and Christian and Jewish holidays, such topics as Voting Day, The Red Man Speaks, and the birthday of Robert E. Lee. Not unusual, but useful.

📖 *UP, UP THE MOUNTAIN* (1968)

Kirkus Service

SOURCE: A review of *Up, Up the Mountain,* in *Kirkus Service,* Vol. XXXVI, No. 13, March 1, 1968, p. 254.

In another of Miss Fisher's instructive, evocative versifications—better to look at than to listen to, better to listen to than to think upon—a family that missed spring in the south goes trekking up a mountain to find it. "Every one thousand feet/ we climb/ up a mountain/ most any time,/ up through the woods/ and past the trees,/ weather gets colder/ by three degrees—/ about the same/ as driving as far/ as six hundred miles/ to the north by car." The illustrations [by Gilbert Riswold] shimmer and glow but the text is a long-playing laggard.

Booklist

SOURCE: A review of *Up, Up the Mountain,* in *Booklist,* Vol. 64, No. 17, May 1, 1968, p. 1042.

A picture-book story in verse, similar to the author's *In the Middle of the Night,* evokes the freshness of mountains in summer. A family on a camping trip climbs into cooler weather, finally reaching a spot so high they must seek shelter from a sudden snowfall. The mood of appreciation of nature's beauties is heightened by the wholesome prettiness of the pictures [by Gilbert Riswold].

Steve Rybicki

SOURCE: A review of *Up, Up the Mountain,* in *Library Journal,* Vol. 93, No. 9, June 15, 1968, p. 2538.

"Spruces were spires/of a woodsy church,/and some of the stars came down to perch,/and a sickle of moon/ cut through the dark,/and a meteor fell/like a blown-out spark. . . . " The majesty of a forest is described in narrative verse in this story of a family which walks from summer to winter as they scale a mountain. The iambs dance along supporting the joy of discovery which the story imparts, and the attractive drawings are good portrayals of many aspects of the great outdoors. Both love and knowledge of nature are evident in this slim, picture-book plug for nature appreciation.

📖 *EASTER* (1968; reissued as *The Story of Easter,* 1996)

Kirkus Service

SOURCE: A review of *Easter,* in *Kirkus Service,* Vol. XXXVI, No. 14, March 15, 1968, p. 339.

A non-denominational Easter is virtually a non sequitur and this treatment probably won't please anyone entirely; neither is it likely to offend very many. The first half is devoted to customs as derived from old spring festivals— decorating, rolling and hunting eggs; awaiting the Easter bunny—and from the practices of the Early Christians— donning new clothes. The second half telescopes the life of Jesus, and especially the events of Holy Week, as prelude to the Resurrection which "is the great message of Easter." Condensation leaves some questions unanswered (including ultimate responsibility) and the use of "Biblical" quotes is inconsistent ("this fellow . . . stirreth up"); the illustrations [by Ati Forberg] are primarily decorative. The result is supplementary reading rather than inspiration, safe enough that you won't be sorry.

Zena Sutherland

SOURCE: A review of *Easter,* in *Bulletin of the Center for Children's Books,* Vol. 21, No. 8, April, 1968, p. 125.

A simply written, straightforward account of the events of Holy Week and of the ways in which they are observed is preceded by a more general discussion of Easter customs in the Christian faith. Some of these, seeming secular, have religious origins; some have been incorporated from pre-Christian celebrations of the springtime. The

illustrations [by Ati Forberg], effective in design, enhance the text and are appropriate to its dignified tone.

Kirkus Reviews

SOURCE: A review of *The Story of Easter,* in *Kirkus Reviews,* Vol. LXIV, No. 23, December 1, 1996, p. 1736.

First published in 1968 and newly illustrated by [Stefano] Vitale, this is a history of the Christian celebration of Easter that, after briefly recounting the story of the Resurrection, links the holiday to other spring festivals, covers the ancient custom of giving the gift of an egg (a symbol of the new life of spring), and includes contemporary customs, such as the fashionable stroll down New York City's Fifth Avenue after church on that day. Also included are instructions for egg decoration and a recipe for hot cross buns. Even the recipe demonstrates the clear, informative prose of Fisher, whose expert organization leads from topic to topic. Vitale's illustrations are a marvel; each full-page picture is filled with details that reflect the times, the flora, and the culture of the era shown, colored with a range of appropriate earth tones. Every element of design makes this an inviting addition to the holiday shelf, even for those already owning the original book with Ati Forberg's illustrations.

Ilene Cooper

SOURCE: A review of *The Story of Easter,* in *Booklist,* Vol. 93, No. 8, December 15, 1996, p. 729.

Beginning with the biblical story of Jesus' life and resurrection, Fisher explains the Easter season to the primary-grade set. She then moves on to the spring festivals that people celebrated before Christianity spread and shows how symbols of these festivals, such as eggs and rabbits, were incorporated into Easter. Fisher's telling, first published in 1968, is low-key and accessible, though at times more explanation could be made (she tells readers Good Friday is God's Friday, but she doesn't explain the derivation of Maundy Thursday). What sets this apart from other Easter books is [Stefano] Vitale's new artwork, which is as fresh and alive as spring itself. Both the biblical scenes and those showing traditional Easter celebrations are handsomely rendered and full of interesting detail. Information on making Easter eggs and a recipe for hot cross buns complete the attractive package.

Publishers Weekly

SOURCE: A review of *The Story of Easter,* in *Publishers Weekly,* Vol. 244, No. 4, January 27, 1997, p. 97.

Fisher condenses and makes plain the Bible accounts of the Passion and Resurrection of Christ and introduces young readers to the Easter season traditions from around the world in her newly reissued picture book. While Christians rejoice in the new life of Jesus on this important holiday, the whole world celebrates the rebirth of spring, whether it be by elaborately decorating Easter eggs or by strolling in an Easter parade. Fisher is careful to include Easter lore and symbols from many nations, and she also skillfully draws several parallels between this holiday and Passover. [Stefano] Vitale's richly textured paintings on wood range from glorious icon-like portraits of Jesus to scenes of frolicking children hunting for Easter eggs. The informative text, including directions for baking hot cross buns and egg-decorating ideas, offers many points for family discussion.

Celia A. Huffman

SOURCE: A review of *The Story of Easter,* in *School Library Journal,* Vol. 43, No. 3, March, 1997, p. 174.

A welcome reissue of Fisher's **Easter,** newly illustrated. While much of the content remains the same, the text in many instances has been rearranged and adapted. Sentences have been edited for a smoother flow. Terminology has been altered occasionally to reflect both gender and multicultural sensitivities. Scriptural excerpts are not as prolific and are often paraphrased. The White House egg roll is the only noticeable deletion. Selected activities have been included, e.g., a recipe for hot-cross buns and directions for decorating eggs, but no cautions are extended concerning working with an adult. [Stefano] Vitale's oils on wood panels are a wonderfully effective addition. Their clear, crisp, stylized and almost iconographic appearance provides a highly effective match to Fisher's text. Along with the full-page illustrations, the artist enhances the presentation with border panel motifs that mirror a folk-art style similar to that of the traditional Pysanki eggs. Fisher's attention to Biblical accuracy, in combination with the discussions of customs and origins, results in a fine addition to the holiday shelves. It complements Gail Gibsons's more basic *Easter.*

WE WENT LOOKING (1968)

Kirkus Service

SOURCE: A review of *We Went Looking,* in *Kirkus Service,* Vol. XXXVI, No. 21, July 1, 1968, p. 686.

The pretense of looking for a badger, in singsong rhyme, is nevertheless an irresistible album of plants and animals. Miss Angel fixes on natural scenes—a sparrow feeding her young's pink-red mouths, a lizard swallowing a mosquito, tree roots and stalks of foxglove—and realizes an elegant simplicity through a use of color and stance reminiscent of Beatrix Potter. An underwhelming text records the search, unsuccessful ("but we only saw a Woodchuck . . . Grackle . . . Toad . . . Bumblebee . . . ") "Till the day we looked for SHREWS!" The lines won't attract listeners but the volume is as gracefully designed and lettered as a fourteenth-century Book of Hours.

Warren Chappell

SOURCE: A review of *We Went Looking,* in *The New York Times Book Review,* September 15, 1968, p. 30.

The theme here is serendipity. An unsuccessful search for a badger is rewarded by glimpses of dozens of other creatures, all decoratively composed and ably rendered by an English calligrapher-illuminator, Marie Angel. Aileen Fisher provides a simply-rhymed text, of less than three hundred words, which is an itinerary of the search. The text has been transcribed in a capably written calligraphic roman.

Booklist

SOURCE: A review of *We Went Looking,* in *Booklist,* Vol. 65, No. 5, November 1, 1968, p. 308.

"We" went looking for a badger—north, south, east, and west—but, though we saw a woodchuck, a lizard, a mockingbird, some minnows, and other small creatures and "half wore out our shoes, . . . we didn't see a Badger . . . Till the day we looked for Shrews!" Delicately drawn colored pictures [by Marie Angel] and melodious verse are felicitously combined to provide an enticing close-up view of nature.

Zena Sutherland

SOURCE: A review of *We Went Looking,* in *Bulletin of the Center for Children's Books,* Vol. 22, No. 5, January, 1969, p. 77.

A longish, lilting nature poem in which a slow perambulation through the wilds affords glimpses of no sought-for badger but of many other animals. The poetry's quiet mood is matched by the delicate details and subdued tones of the small, precise pictures [by Marie Angel]. Each illustration has a brief line of text above and another below, the whole effectively framed by wide, restful space. The lack of plot or action may limit the book's appeal to those children who enjoy the elegant, pressed-flower charm of the pictures or the rhythm of the verse.

WE ALCOTTS: THE LIFE OF LOUISA MAY ALCOTT AS SEEN THROUGH THE EYES OF 'MARMEE' (written with Olive Rabe, 1968)

Kirkus Service

SOURCE: A review of *We Alcotts,* in *Kirkus Service,* Vol. XXXVI, No. 22, August 15, 1968, p. 910.

The story of Louisa M. Alcott's family as seen through the eyes of 'Marmee,' mother of *Little Women:* simulated autobiography that is true to events, to the thoughts of its "author," to her manner of expression—without mimicry. In short, a considerable *tour de force,* much more successful then *We Dickinsons.* The Alcotts were a singular family and Abba May Alcott, fending off destitution and criticisms of her philosopher-hewer husband, was its linchpin; she was not simply "Marmee" (a tag happily held in check here), she best-friended Lydia Maria Child, knew what Emerson and Thoreau were about, sympathized with Abolitionists and Transcendentalists. Utopians, however, she mistrusted for their deemphasis on the family, and "her" account of the Fruitlands consociation is both ludicrous and tragic. All these experiences formed Louisa May Alcott and her books (Fruitlands became "Transcendental Wild Oats"); Louisa herself, her sisters, a legendary aunt, a European lover, brief acquaintances, peopled them. Happily again, "Marmee" does not anticipate the parallels or insist upon them. Better informed and more informative than Meigs' *Invincible Louisa,* less stodgy and reverent than Sandford Salyer's *Marmee* (a *young adult* biography), this is also a delight: Abba Alcott putting up a family post box, Bronson Alcott dispensing wisdom and apples, Louisa vowing, at fourteen, to pay *all our debts*—seen with knowing affection, told without sentimentality.

Publishers Weekly

SOURCE: A review of *We Alcotts,* in *Publishers Weekly,* Vol. 194, No. 11, September 16, 1968, p. 71.

It seems only fitting that on the 100th anniversary of the publishing of her *Little Women,* there should be a new biography of Louisa M. Alcott. It's more than fitting, it is an astute as well as a refreshing idea to tell not only her story but the story of her family, for of course, *Little Women was* her family. To tell it through the eyes of Marmee, the mother of the Alcott girls and so, the mother of the March girls, was inspired. Well, why not? Look who wrote it!

Elizabeth Janeway

SOURCE: A review of *We Alcotts,* in *The New York Times Book Review,* September 29, 1968, p. 46.

Another telling of Louisa Alcott's story, *We Alcotts,* is offered by Aileen Fisher and Olive Rabe, who have attempted to freshen it by regarding it through the eyes of Mrs. Alcott, the "Marmee" of *Little Women.* Though the authors have worked from "the journals, letters and other writings of the Alcotts as well as those of friends and relatives; also [from] critical studies of the Alcott family," I can't feel that their version adds much to Miss Meigs's account, and the flatness of tone in which Mrs. Alcott is presumed to speak is daunting.

Paul Heins

SOURCE: A review of *We Alcotts,* in *The Horn Book Magazine,* Vol. XLIV, No. 5, October, 1968, p. 540.

The authors of *We Dickinsons* have again in a fictionalized biography re-created the atmosphere of the daily life of a nineteenth-century family. From a background of meager meals and idealism, woodchopping and neighborly contacts with Emerson, Thoreau, and Hawthorne, the Alcott family emerges as an interdependent group of laboring and loving people. In a deceptively simple style, the wife of Bronson Alcott and the mother of Louisa May recounts the joys and vicissitudes of her married life, and the moral and literary development of her most famous daughter. "Much of the dialogue incorporates sentences, words, and phrases from the writings of the Alcotts, Ralph Waldo Emerson, Henry Thoreau, and others."

Readers of *Little Women* and of Cornelia Meigs's *Invincible Louisa* will realize that there were three invincible Alcotts— "Marmee" and Bronson as well as Louisa. If Bronson Alcott, the educational theorist and experimenter, retained his serene but impractical idealism until the end, Mrs. Alcott in turn heroically supported him, though she had to struggle with the problems of everyday life. "No matter how conscientiously I economized or how hard my husband worked, we rarely were able to meet our monthly expenses. . . ." Her patience was often tried: "I was surprised to hear how often my husband said . . . , 'I sat and watched the fountain in the Common for several hours today.'" And she was well aware of the complexity of her situation: "Though I sometimes lost my temper and patience with him, I still thought him the greatest, most idealistic man I knew."

Despite the plain living and high thinking of the Alcotts, one senses drama in the life of the family: the decision of Abba May, at the age of twenty-seven, to marry Bronson Alcott, a man inferior to her in social station; the decision of Bronson, after his disastrous experiment in communal living at Fruitlands, to withstand the temptation of joining the Shakers and leaving his family. The story ends when "Marmee" receives her copy of *Little Women* and Louisa announces that she can now repay the Alcott debts. As in *Little Women,* "Marmee" has the last word. Quoting from Bronson "that human life is a very simple matter . . . 'Breath, bread, health, a hearthstone . . . a wife and children . . . and a task life-long given from within,'" she adds, "And these are the gifts we Alcotts have had all along. . . . "

The story-biography captures the aura of the mutual lives of the Alcotts, permits them to speak for themselves, and reveals the humor as well as the rigors of their situation. It also discloses anew the tantalizing closeness between the Alcotts and the Marches, and thus sharpens one's realization of Louisa May's inventiveness.

Booklist

SOURCE: A review of *We Alcotts,* in *Booklist,* Vol. 65, No. 5, November 1, 1968, p. 308.

A vitalized, unsentimental account of life in the Bronson Alcott household based on authentic firsthand sources and narrated by Bronson's wife, Abba May Alcott. Because of the nature and scope of both Abba May's and Bronson's interests and activities, the book offers illuminating sidelights on many of the controversial issues of the times in addition to giving a lively picture of the poverty-stricken but emotionally fulfilling and mentally stimulating home life which exerted a profound influence on Louisa May Alcott.

Saturday Review

SOURCE: A review of *We Alcotts,* in *Saturday Review,* Vol. LI, No. 45, November 9, 1968, pp. 69-70.

"He was moderate, I impetuous. He was modest and humble, I forward and arbitrary. He was poor, but we were both industrious." Thus wrote Abba May, a Boston gentlewoman who was captivated by Bronson Alcott's charm and who, through the long years of their financial woes and intellectual plenty, continued to think her husband a genius, even when his impractical ideas reduced the family to a cottage where there was little beyond love. The book is imbued with the appropriately decorous attitudes of the nineteenth century, liberally sprinkled with anecdotes about Louisa, and given vigorous added interest because of the Alcott's passionate concern about abolition of slavery, permissive educational methods, and the intellectual and literary movements of the times. Could any Alcott lover resist?

📖 SING, LITTLE MOUSE (1969)

Pamela Marsh

SOURCE: "Looking-glass Land," in *Christian Science Monitor,* May 1, 1969, p. B4.

For *Sing, Little Mouse* Aileen Fisher has written a verse as tuneful as any mouse could hope to be, about a boy's search for a mouse with a voice like a trilling bird. As for Symeon Shimin's illustrations, he has managed to show a couple of boys at their listening quietest, gentle but not sentimental. Where color has been used, it is reproduced with all the look of fresh paint.

Kirkus Reviews

SOURCE: A review of *Sing, Little Mouse,* in *Kirkus Reviews,* Vol. XXXVII, No. 42, May 15, 1969, p. 556.

Sing, Little Mouse is in the same key as *Listen, Rabbit,* and youngsters who hearken to the one will likely respond to the other. A towhead who's heard of a mouse that can sing importunes his family until father brings home a big book about mice and the two discover that the "white-footed, light-footed" Deer Mouse is a sometime singer. Following the clue of a Deer Mouse's tracks in the snow, the boy finds its hole, then, when spring comes,

camps overnight with his brother nearby. A rainstorm sends them scurrying home but ("Can you guess what I saw/ in my very own house?") the mouse has come too, in a sleeping bag, and favors the boy with trills and twitters before he's returned to his home. The most tangible, most forceful illustration shows the Deer Mouse magnified up front; most of the others, in color and black-and-white, are in a vein of misty lyricism that's Symeon Shimin's signature. Aileen Fisher's long narrative poem is similarly vaporous, even vapid. But the pair have their staunch adherents.

Booklist

SOURCE: A review of *Sing, Little Mouse,* in *Booklist,* Vol. 65, No. 22, July 15, 1969, p. 1274.

The author and the illustrator of **Listen, Rabbit** here combine talents in a poetic picture-book story of a small boy's desire to hear a mouse sing. After learning from a book his father brings home that "A White-Footed Mouse/is sometimes heard/to sing a song/like a trilling bird," the boy accidentally captures one and later rewards his tiny songster for its clear, sweet trilling and twittering by setting it free. Aileen Fisher's light, gay rhymes and [Symeon] Shimin's expressive drawings in black and white and in pastel colors portray mood and action with warmth and charm.

📖 CLEAN AS A WHISTLE (1969)

Kirkus Reviews

SOURCE: A review of *Clean As a Whistle,* in *Kirkus Reviews,* Vol. XXXVII, No. 26, September 1, 1969, p. 924.

"Isn't it fun/ to be young and dirty/ instead of grown-up/ and clean/ and thirty!" What starts out as a blithe celebration of living like animals— "who just live free/ in the wilds for years/ without a washing/ behind the ears"— turns into a long-winded-lady-like lesson on the hygienic habits of each species. Delivered by a fairy-godmother type who dwells in a quaint cottage in the woods. And who twists their words so that every time they ask how to find the *path* home, she launches into another kind of *bath.* Of course they finally get the idea ("A bath!"), whereupon she gets the idea ("A path!"), whereupon they go down the path, presumably to have a bath. They've already taken a drubbing.

Ethel L. Heins

SOURCE: A review of *Clean As a Whistle,* in *The Horn Book Magazine,* Vol. XLVI, No. 1, February, 1970, pp. 31-32.

Three children go to play in the woods and have a wonderfully muddy, messy time. And they start for home, determined to remain as free, unwashed, and uncombed as the forest animals. But they lose their way and meet a deaf old woman who misunderstands them the more they try to explain their predicament. " . . . we were lost/ and must have a *path*/ at any cost./ 'In a rush to get home,'/ I said quite clear./ 'You must have a *bath?*'/ She cupped her ear./ 'And a *brush and a comb,*/ did you say, my dear?'" And amiably garbling their words, she describes the grooming habits of each of the woodland creatures. "'My animal friends,'/ the old woman said/ with a jog of her feet/ and a bob of her head,/ 'are clean as a whistle/ and very well-bred.'" Sepia drawings, [by Ben Shecter] showing three old-fashioned, carefree, grimy children, match the wood-brown print of the rhymed text.

IN ONE DOOR AND OUT THE OTHER: A BOOK OF POEMS (1969)

Kirkus Reviews

SOURCE: A review of *In One Door and Out the Other,* in *Kirkus Reviews,* Vol. XXXVII, No. 28, October 15, 1969, p. 1116.

Although many of these rhymes are too cute and coy, a few do have a hold on simple childhood experiences. The subjects are familiar enough—the weather, pets, what happens when company comes—and often they end on an up note, as in this boost for campfire picnics: "Cheese and jelly-bread are good,/ but toasted buns are better . . . / and for a week/ I still can smell/ the campfire on my sweater." But most of the verses are just passing, and the slightly shaggy illustrations don't make the grade either.

Ramona Weeks

SOURCE: "Focus on Seasons Sounds and Rites of Passage," in *The New York Times Book Review,* November 9, 1969, p. 46.

In One Door and Out the Other, by Aileen Fisher, opens with verses about breakfast and spring crocuses and ends with poems about Christmas and bedtime. In between are poems about neighbors, birthdays, picnics, goldfish and school. Several of the characters are memorable. I became fond of Mrs. King, who came to visit "one day in spring,/and let me flash/with her diamond ring." The cumulative effect of the book, with illustrations by Lillian Hoban, is slight but pleasant.

Carolyn Giambra

SOURCE: A review of *In One Door and Out the Other,* in *School Library Journal,* Vol. 95, January 15, 1970, p. 232.

With the energy of young children, these 63 whimsical little poems run "In one door and out the other!" through

the daily experiences in a family household. Many poems center on seasonal themes, from the first signs of spring to the favorite Christmas tree. Others reveal the sentiments of a child as he views his parents, friends, toys and animals and comments on whispers, squirting water fountains, company, etc. The poems are aptly illustrated [by Lillian Hoban] with a profusion of small black-and-white drawings, which young readers will identify with and delight in.

JEANNE D'ARC (1970)

Kirkus Reviews

SOURCE: A review of *Jeanne d'Arc,* in *Kirkus Reviews,* Vol. XXXVIII, No. 3, February 1, 1970, p. 106.

Filling a need at the very least, this is a simple, faithful rendition punctuated by full-page color illustrations—pastels in effect if not in fact—the whole becoming the only suitable projection of Jeanne's being available for the younger child. The drama is largely interior—in the Holbein-fine heads particularly—and this might be considered the girl's Jeanne in contrast to the martial vigor of Boutet de Monvel. But what is straightforward tinged with spirituality rather than spirited is nevertheless not maudlin or melodramatic, a sizable commendation in itself.

Booklist

SOURCE: A review of *Jeanne d'Arc,* in *Booklist,* Vol. 66, No. 17, May 1, 1970, p. 1098.

Briefly but dramatically Fisher narrates Joan of Arc's experiences from her first visions to her death at the stake seven years later. Conversations, thoughts, and emotions attributed to the Maid and other characters make the presentation more intimate than accurate perhaps, but do serve to give the reader a personalized view of the facts. The full-page illustrations [by Ati Forberg] in color and in black and white are vivid and romanticized. Large print for easy reading.

Barbara Wersba

SOURCE: A review of *Jeanne d'Arc,* in *The New York Times Book Review,* May 24, 1970, p. 30.

Saints and heroes are extraordinarily difficult to write about—perhaps because they are at once too strange and too familiar. Joan of Arc is no exception.

To adults, the drama will seem rather stale as the Maid of Orleans hears her voices, has the Dauphin crowned King, and is finally condemned by her Church. To children ignorant of the story, there will also be something missing—for Joan's life and death are implausible without passion. She was not, after all, merely a religious teen-ager who was able to ride a horse. Nor was she a medieval Bernadette Devlin. If anything, she was an extreme product of the Middle Ages—and her fanaticism and piety can be understood only in that context.

Ati Forberg's full-color illustrations are quite sensitive, the drawings of faces in particular, but the book remains less the journey of a saint than a biography of a very nice girl.

Diane Farrell

SOURCE: A review of *Jeanne d'Arc,* in *The Horn Book Magazine,* Vol. XLVI, No. 3, June, 1970, p. 304.

"Although she was not beautiful, her face was filled with the light of her spirit, and her eyes glowed with the purpose of her mission." A young, gentle, eager Joan proceeds through these pages with dignity, humility, and a quiet inner strength to fulfill her inescapable destiny. The short, straightforward account of the life of Joan of Arc adheres closely to historically verifiable facts. The full-page illustrations and the double spreads [by Ati Forberg] are dramatic pencil drawings, colored with luminous pastels. Easily the most appealing and the most beautifully illustrated biography of the saint for young readers that is currently available.

Saturday Review

SOURCE: A review of *Jeanne d'Arc,* in *Saturday Review,* Vol. LIII, No. 26, June 27, 1970, p. 39.

Even a peasant girl of eleven understood that France must be united or it would perish, and little Jeanne wished she could be a soldier and fight for her country. When she first heard the voices, Jeanne told nobody, but she obeyed their directions. The familiar story is beautifully retold for young readers, with just enough historical background and a reverent simplicity that is echoed in the illustrations [by Ati Forberg]. Softly drawn, with a bold economy of line, the pictures of the Maid and the portraits of simple peasant faces and brooding courtiers are stunning.

Zena Sutherland

SOURCE: A review of *Jeanne d'Arc,* in *Bulletin of the Center for Children's Books,* Vol. 24, No. 2, October, 1970, p. 24.

At last, a fine book about the Maid of Orleans for younger readers, handsomely illustrated [by Ati Forberg] with pictures (some black and white, some in color) that have a grave beauty. The writing is simple and dignified, and the story is well-suited to the middle grades reader also because of the clean, large print, the amount of historical information, and the fact that the retelling begins in Jeanne's eleventh year.

BUT OSTRICHES . . . (1970)

Kirkus Reviews

SOURCE: A review of *But Ostriches . . . ,* in *Kirkus Reviews,* Vol. XXXVIII, No. 14, July 15, 1970, p. 741.

Most birds fly But OSTRICHES . . . And "Most birds surely/ walk quite poorly. But OSTRICHES,/ mind you,/ are truly fleet/ by using only/ their horny feet/ with pads underneath/ to stand the heat/ of the African sand/ of ostrich-land." "(And they *don't,* by the way,/ with danger at hand/ go bury their heads/ in the sunny sand.)" Variously enjoining, informing, reminding, comparing, and always resuming the refrain, the internal rhyme and differentiating line-drawings introduce some of the idiosyncrasies of the ostrich: height, weight, foot-shape, pet-ability— "You'd better beware:/ That gleam in the ostrich's eye,/ that glare/ suggests you conduct yourself/ with care"; polygamous nesting "The sum of the eggs,/ in case you've wondered,/ may be numbered/ at half a hundred,/ with all the parents cooperating/ by taking turns/ with the incubating." No substitute but quite likely a stimulus to the older, ordered Zim . . . and a rollicking read-aloud, join-and-repeat-aloud parrotable poem on its own.

Publishers Weekly

SOURCE: A review of *But Ostriches . . . ,* in *Publishers Weekly,* Vol. 198, No. 4, July 27, 1970, p. 74.

The blurb on the jacket of this book about ostriches says it all: "Poet and naturalist Aileen Fisher muses in verse about ostriches and their peculiarities." For I can't think of anyone around whose musings I'd rather read than Aileen Fisher's, nor any pictures I'd rather look at than Peter Parnall's, which do indeed "capture the strange dignity . . . as well as (the) comic and endearing bumptiousness" of ostriches, those true eccentrics in the world of nature.

Zena Sutherland

SOURCE: A review of *But Ostriches . . . ,* in *Saturday Review,* Vol. LIII, No. 38, September 19, 1970, p. 35.

"Over the streams/ and over the shallows/ Over the marigolds and mallows/ Over the meadows/ and the narrows/ Orioles fly/ and hawks, and sparrows./ But OSTRICHES . . ." Thus, combining silky poetry and observations on bird life, permeated with humor and illustrated [by Peter Parnall] with delicate felicity, the redoubtable Aileen Fisher draws a profile of the ostrich. He does not bury his head in the sand; he has a communal incubating system; he sings not, neither does he fly. All in all, delectable.

Virginia Haviland

SOURCE: A review of *But Ostriches . . .*, in *The Horn Book Magazine,* Vol. XLVI, No. 5, October, 1970, p. 470.

The long-legged ostrich with his outsized, kicking, two-toed feet has occasioned humorous rhymes typical of the author's earlier musings on nature. She compares this idiosyncratic creature to other birds, and [Peter Parnall's] clean-lined pen sketches give them all alert personalities. In the various comparisons of eggs, sounds, nests, and toes, as well as of size, many smaller birds appear: the hummingbird, the wren, barnyard fowls, the whooping crane, and the trumpeter swan. The verses should be read to the child viewing the pictures, for their liveliness greatly enhances the meanings of the words they so perfectly support. "But OSTRICHES . . . / no one/ has ever said/ there's much of a tune/ in that periscope head./ Canaries/ are vastly preferred/ instead."

Christian Science Monitor

SOURCE: "Pumpernick, Pimpernell, Pudding and Friends," in *Christian Science Monitor,* October 17, 1970, p. 15.

Ostriches don't really stick their heads in the sand; and singing is not one of their talents. But they do run very quickly on their two-toed feet, using only one toe at a time. (Most birds have four toes on each foot, "three in front and one in back." So we learn from *But Ostriches . . . .*)

In happy verse and whimsical illustrations, poet-naturalist Aileen Fisher and artist Peter Parnall tell us what ostriches are really like. Facts about other birds also dance off the pages in snappy rhythm.

Here education is not a chore but a joy, an eagerness to read further to discover how these tall, stately, non-flying birds differ from our neighborhood robins and sparrows. The reader is as pleased and surprised by his new discoveries as he is by the clever way in which they are presented.

Zena Sutherland

SOURCE: A review of *But Ostriches . . .*, in *Bulletin of the Center for Children's Books,* Vol. 24, No. 4, December, 1970, p. 58.

Good for nature study, delightfully illustrated, and a pleasure to read aloud, this book of flowing poetry contrasts with humorous wit the ostrich and other birds. Pattern: "Most birds surely/ Walk quite poorly/ Most birds merely / hop around/ They're securest/ swiftest, surest/ on their wings/ *above* the ground," and at the turn of a page, "But OSTRICHES . . ." So, in most palatable fashion, the habits of the ostrich are explored and explained. The spare

precision of the [Peter] Parnall pictures resembles the anatomical exactness of Ravielli's work.

FEATHERED ONES AND FURRY (1971)

Kirkus Reviews

SOURCE: A review of *Feathered Ones and Furry,* in *Kirkus Reviews,* Vol. XXXIX, No. 14, July 15, 1971, p. 742.

"I like the furry ones—/ the waggy ones/ the purry ones/ the happy ones/ that hurry." But then, "I like them feathery too—/ I certainly, certainly do." Thus begin the two blandly impartial title poems that set the tone for this collection of coy and innocuous little animal rhymes. The verses are technically conventional, with rhythm and rhyme schemes ranging from mildly pleasant to flatly predictable; the worn-out subjects include a cat given a male name who "pretty soon" had kittens (this one ends with an exclamation mark) and a speculation on how the birds know when it's time to migrate. The black lino-cuts [by Eric Carle] are attractive, but their tone too solid for the feathery-furry text. With so many superior collections of animal rhymes in print, this one is easily dismissible.

Ethel L. Heins

SOURCE: A review of *Feathered Ones and Furry,* in *The Horn Book Magazine,* Vol. XLVII, No. 5, October, 1971, pp. 473-74.

A collection of poems about the animal world in all seasons: cats and kittens, dogs and puppies, ponies, chipmunks, weasels, squirrels, and mice, as well as many kinds of birds from sandpipers to pelicans. Some of the verses are new; some are reprinted from periodicals and from the author's early books. The author sees nature not in its fury and violence but in its gentleness and benign relationship to man. "My puppy can't speak English,/she doesn't know a letter,/ but her wiggles and her wriggles/ when she sees me get my sweater/ and her raggle-taggle waggles/ when I pack a lunch and pet her/ are just as good as talking is . . . /and maybe even better." One cannot say that this is great poetry, but in idea and expression, the verses are childlike and appreciative. Seldom is a book of poems so handsomely designed, so beautifully illustrated. The linoleum cuts—black figures on alternating pages of white and beige—[by Eric Carle] are elegant but not austere, humorous and affectionate but not sentimental.

Booklist

SOURCE: A review of *Feathered Ones and Furry,* in *Booklist,* Vol. 68, No. 3, October 1, 1971, p. 150.

Illustrated with eye-catching linoleum cuts [by Eric Carle], this is a collection of 55 poems about birds and animals by a well-known writer of poetry for children. The poems, nearly half of which originally appeared in magazines and in other books by the author, are uneven in quality, but many of the short rhythmical verses will strike a responsive note with children who have a pet, want one, or simply enjoy animals.

Zena Sutherland

SOURCE: A review of *Feathered Ones and Furry*, in *Bulletin of the Center for Children's Books*, Vol. 25, No. 3, November, 1971, p. 42.

Simply written poems about animals, in a book illustrated with handsome linoleum cuts [by Eric Carle] in black on white or beige pages. The tidiness of meter and rhyme are exemplified by **"A Robin."** "I wonder how a robin hears?/ I never yet have seen his ears/ But I have seen him cock his head/ And pull a worm right out of bed." The appeal of the subjects and the level of writing make this a good book for reading aloud to younger children as well as for independent reading.

📖 *MY CAT HAS EYES OF SAPPHIRE BLUE* (1973)

Booklist

SOURCE: A review of *My Cat Has Eyes of Sapphire Blue*, in *Booklist*, Vol. 70, No. 10, January 15, 1974, p. 541.

Simple rhymes that describe without straining for effect the multifaceted nature of cats and their activities. Every page is generously decorated with Marie Angel's feline portraits in the trompe l'oeil vein—each hair finely drawn over muscles rippling in a myriad of typical poses. A friendly little book for budding cat afficionados to pore over.

Ethel L. Heins

SOURCE: A review of *My Cat Has Eyes of Sapphire Blue*, in *The Horn Book Magazine*, Vol. L, No. 1, February, 1974, p. 59.

A pair of cat-lovers—a poet-naturalist and a nature painter [Marie Angel]—have combined their talents to create a tour de force that cannot fail to surprise and delight other feline fanciers. The still-hesitant young reader will be rewarded by the simplicity of "Fur of cats,/ it seems to me,/ is wired with/ electricity." Yet, any reader or listener will find in the poems accurate echoes of distinctive cat behavior. "How calmly she sits/ and stares at the scenery,/ How lithely she flits/ through thickets and greenery,/ How deftly she hits/ at a ball that is dear to her,/ How fiercely she spits/ when a dog comes too near to her." The exquisitely meticulous cat portraits—which so easily could have strayed into sentimentality—are totally representational, yet strikingly expressive. Whether they are elegant

Siamese or handsome varieties of the honest *felis catus,* the cats, with every hair under control, are captured in fluid motion, acrobatic posturing, statuesque alertness, or sleepy repose.

📖 *DO BEARS HAVE MOTHERS, TOO?* (1973)

Zena Sutherland

SOURCE: A review of *Do Bears Have Mothers, Too?*, in *Bulletin of the Center for Children's Books*, Vol. 27, No. 9, May, 1974, p. 142.

A collection of poems addressed to animal young by their mothers is illustrated by pictures [by Eric Carle] that take full advantage of the oversize pages. The pictures—large in scale, bright, handsome, executed in a combination of collage and other media—are excellent for group use as well as for individual lap-lookers. The poems are breezy and fresh, with moments of humor and a permeating mood of mother love. Sample: "Cygnets, you must practice early/ not to be unkempt or surly/Swans have quite a reputation/ we are known in every nation/For our grace and comely beauty/To uphold this is your duty." A beguiling book.

📖 *ONCE WE WENT ON A PICNIC* (1975)

Kirkus Reviews

SOURCE: A review of *Once We Went on a Picnic,* in *Kirkus Reviews,* Vol. XLIII, No. 21, November 1, 1975, p. 1224.

It's the kind of a morning that just goes by, as four children set out for a picnic in the park but nibble away their lunch and their time on sidewalks, stoops and a vacant lot where they observe ants, a grasshopper, a water strider in a puddle, and other examples of the less pestilent forms of urban wildlife. Fisher's rhymed text sacrifices the jubilant bounce of **Going Barefoot** for a more natural walking pace, but, in the process, all the bug watching, cookie munching and sandwich trading becomes so ordinary that you question the likelihood of the children's happy realization: "We had gone on a picnic/ All along the way." Still, Tony Chen's clear, wide awake shoots and blossoms (his flowers as usual take center stage and the birds and animals outshine the people) project a fair day for mite-sized serendipity.

Barbara Eileman

SOURCE: A review of *Once We Went on a Picnic,* in *Booklist,* Vol. 72, No. 10, January 15, 1976, p. 684.

Four children start off on a picnic but are sidetracked by a series of explorations. They stop to watch a hungry spider, a city of ants, a cricket, a June bug, a bumblebee, a cobweb, and a puddle left by the rain. And as they watch they nibble and nibble on their goodies—until they realize their picnic has been happening all along the way. Fisher rhymes the tale in an easy flowing style, while [Tony] Chen pictures the "spangling morning" with fresh-looking, idyllically precise drawings of colorful plants and animals. Readers are invited along on the excursion, and a map of the flora and fauna, with identifying page numbers, is included for them. A nature lesson in a most inviting form.

Diane Holzheimer

SOURCE: A review of *Once We Went on a Picnic,* in *School Library Journal,* Vol. 22, No. 6, February, 1976, p. 38.

A rhymed account of the adventures of four children on their way to a park for a picnic. The verse is forgettable and precious in places, but the slight story is an appropriate vehicle for the spectacular full-color wash illustrations [by Tony Chen] of the numerous plants and animals encountered along the way. These beautiful and delicately rendered pictures of chipmunks and hummingbirds, milkweed and geraniums invite scrutiny. A map at the end of the book identifies and lists by page number the over 70 creatures and plants that appear, just in case some were missed or not identified correctly.

Carol L. Reiner

SOURCE: A review of *Once We Went on a Picnic,* in *Science Books & Films,* Vol. XII, No. 1, May, 1976, p. 39.

Large, colorful and detailed illustrations [by Tony Chen] should make this book quite appealing to young children. The theme is observation of plants and animals by a group of children picnicking, and a pictorial summary of plants and animals is provided in the back of the book. The word content is quite advanced for young children, and many expressions used may not be easily understood. The length and wording of some passages are quite complex, thus the book does not always make for smooth, easy reading. The shorter passages of four lines or less which rhyme are quite charming, however, and will catch the attention and interest of young children. The subject matter in this book should provoke much curiosity, since young children adore looking for animals and small insects. Because of the numerous animals and plants presented, this book would be useful in the classroom in conjunction with a unit on nature or classification, and it lends itself to being read repeatedly by second or third grade children.

I STOOD UPON A MOUNTAIN (1979)

Kirkus Reviews

SOURCE: A review of *I Stood Upon a Mountain,* in *Kirkus Reviews,* Vol. XLVIII, No. 5, March 1, 1980, p. 282.

Oh dear. Aileen Fisher has written a text about a little girl standing on a mountain wondering "How did it all happen?" and getting various answers from various folks ("from an egg," says an old mountaineer; "from a Word," says a black woman; "from fire," says an Indian; "from an explosion," says a boy); and Blair Lent has illustrated this wishy-washy paean to the wonderful American world with wishy-washy pictures which include double-page watercolors of the surf breaking on the shore, the desert at sundown, and a New England village in the snow. "Wonderful world!" is in fact the little girl's greeting to each of her informants-to-be—and one wonders who save a hippie grandmother would find any of this engaging.

Mary M. Burns

SOURCE: A review of *I Stood Upon a Mountain,* in *The Horn Book Magazine,* Vol. LVI, No. 2, April, 1980, pp. 163-64.

Imbued with childlike curiosity, the rhythmic text explores the ancient cosmological problem of the earth's origin. The questioner, a young child awed by the vistas she beholds, is shown in four diverse settings representing the seasons of the year. In each location she wonders, "How did it all happen?" and each time she encounters different people with explanations ranging from the metaphysical to the scientific. The little girl is not disturbed by the divergence of opinion but with the confident serenity of childhood accepts the possibility that there may be many answers. She finds at last her own explanation: She is "filled with a wonder/ that needs no answer,/ no answer at all." The luminous watercolor illustrations, a departure in style for the artist [Blair-Lent], underscore the controlled emotion of the text, at the same time conveying the splendor of a mountain landscape in spring, a pulsing ocean in summer, a rich-hued desert in autumn, and a snow-clad village in winter. In contrast to the magnificence of the double-page spreads which depict the seasonal vistas, other pages delineate the child and her companions in subtle character studies. A celebration of nature, childhood, and beauty—less intimate, perhaps, than Robert McCloskey's *Time of Wonder* but warmer in feeling than Uri Shulevitz's *Dawn.*

Kathy Piehl

SOURCE: A review of *I Stood Upon a Mountain,* in *School Library Journal,* Vol. 26, No. 8, April, 1980, p. 92.

During each of the seasons, a little girl looks at the world and wonders how it came into being. Every time, she encounters someone who offers another explanation of the earth's origin. Did the world start as an egg or a fire? Did it begin at the impulse of the Word of God or because an explosion wracked the universe? What existed before the fire, the egg, the Word, the mass of matter? The girl concludes that the wonder she experiences in viewing the world is more important than a precise answer about earth's beginning. In gentle language, Fisher promotes a spirit of tolerance and appreciation of natural beauty rather than any particular view of creation. [Blair] Lent's watercolors, especially the delicately shaded two-page landscape vistas that depict each season, will foster in readers the same sense of wonder the girl experiences.

Zena Sutherland

SOURCE: A review of *I Stood Upon a Mountain,* in *Bulletin of the Center for Children's Books,* Vol. 33, No. 9, May, 1980, p. 171.

In flowing, vibrant watercolor [Blair] Lent pictures the ocean, the desert at sunset, the verdant hills, and other natural scenes of beauty, as a small child wonders how it all began. The free pattern of poetic thought is deftly adapted to a simple sequence and repetition; each time the child greets someone with "Wonderful world," she gets a different explanation of how the world began. There are many answers, she concludes, but "I am still / filled with a wonder / that needs no answer / no answer at all." A book for a quiet moment, a book to stimulate conjecture, a book to encourage awareness of the environment.

📖 *OUT IN THE DARK AND DAYLIGHT* (1980)

X. J. Kennedy

SOURCE: "Children's Verse," in *The New York Times Book Review,* April 27, 1980, p. 47.

Children more civilized than mine may enjoy parts of Aileen Fisher's *Out in the Dark and DayLight,* with drawings by Gail Owens. Miss Fisher is a true poet, no mere light versifier. Brief, gentle nature poems follow the round of the seasons. The best abound with insight: a bird's wings "hinge wide," birch trees pack "buds all waxed and new," shoes are houses you shut your feet in. "Snowy Benches," a four-line poem, is beautifully concise:

> Do parks get lonely
> in winter, perhaps,
> when benches have only
> snow on their laps?

Unluckily, Miss Fisher's diction can get cutesy. Birds have "little hoppy, scratchy feet," a rabbit's neck is "hunchy furry." Rhymes seem forced, as in the title poem, which couples "Out in the dark and day light" with "Out in the park and play light." For 20 fine poems, you'll have to read 147 pages, some repetitious. If I had to take another one about crickets in thickets or the habits of rabbits, I'd scream.

Zena Sutherland

SOURCE: A review of *Out in the Dark and Daylight,* in *Bulletin of the Center for Children's Books,* Vol. 33, No. 11, July, 1980, p. 211.

Soft, grainy pencil drawings [by Gail Owens], realistically detailed and deft in their evocation of light and shadow, illustrate a collection of poems, many of which were originally published in magazines. Although the poems are not grouped, the arrangement of selections follows the cycle of the year; some are as specific as **"Summer Stars,"** or **"Early Snow,"** while others (**"Mother Cat,"** or **"All That Sky"**) are more general. Most of the poems are about some aspect of nature; less frequent are those that speak of a child's emotion or attitude, as do **"Going Calling"** and **"Birthday Present."** The poems are brief, fresh, deft, and often illuminating, and they are pleasant to read alone or aloud; the book could be used for reading aloud to pre-readers as well as by the independent reader.

Betsy Hearne

SOURCE: A review of *Out in the Dark and Daylight,* in *Booklist,* Vol. 76, No. 21, July 1, 1980, p. 1606.

A more poetically zealous and larger collection than *Morning Noon and Night-time, Too, . . .* this combines some lyrical passages with many of Fisher's characteristically personalized commonplaces, as in **"Wind Circles"**: "Without a pen, / without a hand, / without a pair of glasses, // The broken stalks / so bent and tanned / among the scattered grasses // Draw curves and circles / in the sand / with every wind that passes. // And I / can't draw them half as grand / in school, in drawing classes." Almost all the selections are strictly rhymed, metered, and related directly or tonally to child readers in simplest terms. The occasional reliance on "filler phrases" ("and That's what I hope, / hope, hope I'll get.") is irritating, but this is balanced by more original images ("Do parks get lonely / in winter, perhaps, // when benches have only / snow on their laps?"). [Gail] Owens' carefully shaded black-and-white drawings elaborate many of the poems and mark seasonal transitions in the content.

Kirkus Reviews

SOURCE: A review of *Out in the Dark and Daylight,* in *Kirkus Reviews,* Vol. XLVIII, No. 15, August 1, 1980, p. 981.

"The west wind plays a merry tune/ upon the pines all afternoon—/ the music swells and ebbs./ I wonder if a little breeze,/ too small to play upon the trees,/ can play on spider webs?" Fisher's modest nature poems ask many such small, fanciful questions— "Is a star/ too far/ for a rabbit to see?" "What do beetles think about/ in places where they crawl?"—and confide small musings with about the strength of breezes that might register on spider webs. "I should think [the Chickadee] would like a pair of earmuffs" is one last line, and "toadstools" are seen as hats which the elves have put out to dry. There are a few child-catching images (dandelions are "buttons on the lawn"). But overall—as in a Halloween poem that goes "We . . . jump like goblins/ and thump like elves/ and almost manage to scare ourselves," and one on a day's berry-picking that ends "I dreamed I *still/* kept picking, picking"—both the thoughts and their expression are customary and commonplace.

Mary F. Birkett

SOURCE: A review of *Out in the Dark and Daylight,* in *School Library Journal,* Vol. 27, No. 1, September, 1980, p. 58.

In her 140 poems presented here, Fisher celebrates nature as it changes throughout the seasons. Divided into four sections introduced by soft black-and-white drawings depicting each season, the poems describe with detail, accuracy, and imagination life in the small worlds of insects, plants, and animals. Toadstools become elves' hats, a cocoon a sleeping bag for a butterfly, and grass a jacket for the lawn with dandelions for buttons. Holidays are a part of each season, and poems about Halloween, Thanksgiving, Christmas, and Easter are included. Fisher sees the outdoors both as a naturalist and a poet, couching precise biological observations in figurative language.

ANYBODY HOME? (1980)

Barbara Hawkins

SOURCE: A review of *Anybody Home?,* in *School Library Journal,* Vol. 27, No. 3, November, 1980, p. 60.

Fisher successfully addresses the curiosity young children feel about the natural world around them. They are curious about who lives " . . . in a secret burrow/ beside a brook/ in a log or furrow,/ or under rocks. . . ." And they will smile as the final lines of the poem are read. The soft black-and-white half-tone illustrations [by Susan Bonners] are the perfect complement for this verse. Some show a little girl having the experiences wished for in the poem; others are beautifully framed sketches of the animals and their homes. A good book for reading aloud, whether in the library or during private time between parent and child.

Kirkus Reviews

SOURCE: A review of *Anybody Home?,* in *Kirkus Reviews,* Vol. XLVIII, No. 22, November 15, 1980, p. 1460.

"I'd like to look/ in a meadowy nook/ at the small grass house/ of a mother mouse/ in a velvety blouse." In *Going Barefoot* rhythms but without that ebullience, a little girl imagines peeking inside not only the mouse house but also a coon hole in a tree, a beaver mound, a squirrel nest, or a fox or bear lair. "But if I should see/ a home near a tree,/ and someone in black/ with stripes down his back/ and his tail in the air,/ I wouldn't just stare/ I'd run!" That will do for a closing, but only at a routine level. [Susan] Bonners' soft black illustrations bring out the hushed and delicate nature of this kind of poking about, but the compositions tend toward the conventionally cute and the stillness has an artificial quality.

Virginia Haviland

SOURCE: A review of *Anybody Home?,* in *The Horn Book Magazine,* Vol. LVI, No. 6, December, 1980, p. 632.

The pictured rhymes express a repetition of wishes—the cravings of a child to meet the wildlife whose domiciles she has found. She knows that the meadow grasses hide a mother mouse with "six pink babies" and that a hole in a tree shelters "a curled-up coon/ who sleeps by the sun/ and prowls by the moon." The lines vary in freshness and precision of words—from a forced and ordinary "as I rove and roam" to "with a claw for a comb/ and his tail for a chair" and "with his tail for a blanket/ across his nose." Knowing that the skunk has a unique weapon, the little girl says: "I wouldn't just stare/ and think it was fun . . . / I'd run." The deep gray drawings [by Susan Bonners] have the proper perspective to illuminate meadow and woodland scenes, furry animals with beady eyes, and an attractive little girl full of curiosity and investigative energy.

RABBITS, RABBITS (1983)

Zena Sutherland

SOURCE: A review of *Rabbits, Rabbits,* in *Bulletin of the Center for Children's Books,* Vol. 37, No. 3, November, 1983, p. 48.

Small, neat, and appealingly verdant, the light, bright paintings [by Gail Niemann] are nicely appropriate for an assortment of equally bright, brisk poems. All of the selections are brief and lilting, and they range from agreeable to memorable, with Fisher's usual unobtrusive control of rhythm, rhyme, and meter. Sample, **"Spring Fever"**: "When green tints the meadows/and gold shines the tree/and Winter is over/and rivers run free/do you feel all leapy/and hoppy . . . like *me/*Rabbit?"

Ilene Cooper

SOURCE: A review of *Rabbits, Rabbits,* in *Booklist,* Vol. 80, No. 6, November 15, 1983, p. 496.

Twenty-one soft and sweet poems capture different aspects of a rabbit's life, physical characteristics, habits, environment, and even some speculation on the nature of its thoughts. The poetry also takes the rabbits through the year, and readers will become sensitive to the nuances of season when they read (or listen to) lines such as these about the rabbits' Christmas: "They have little spruces to celebrate under, / where snow has made pompons / with silvery handles, / and frost has made tinsel / and icicle candles." Paired with the poems are delicate watercolors [by Gail Niemann] with rabbits escaping their borders and making this book experience as pleasing visually as it is aurally.

Ethel L. Heins

SOURCE: A review *Rabbits, Rabbits,* in *The Horn Book Magazine,* Vol. LIX, No. 6, December, 1983, pp. 720-21.

From toy bunnies to real-life rabbits, the long-eared animals maintain their favored position as a subject of literature for young children. The award-winning poet has assembled twenty-one of her own poems in a slender, inviting volume, which opens with **"Early Spring":** "Rabbit,/ with those ears you grow/ you should be/ the first to know/ signs of Spring/ before they *show.*" Proceeding through the year in all kinds of weather, one then encounters rhymed, rhythmic celebrations of plain brown rabbits, cottontails, a jack rabbit, and the snowshoe hare. "Do Rabbits have Christmas,/ I wonder, I wonder?/ They have little spruces to celebrate under,/ where snow has made pompons/ with silvery handles,/ and frost has made tinsel/ and icicle candles." The illustrations are particularly successful; from fresh spring greens to the sharp white of snow against a dark blue sky, the seasonal colors—except for one or two garish lapses—and the winsome creatures add undeniable appeal.

Joan W. Blos

SOURCE: A review of *Rabbits, Rabbits,* in *School Library Journal,* Vol. 30, No. 6, February, 1984, pp. 57-58.

These 21 poems are predominately for lovers of rabbits, Aileen Fisher fans and those looking for Easter poems. Others are regretfully advised that in some of these poems the imagery defers to the rhyme, so that "daffy-down-dillows" rhymes with the "cottony pillows" made by their soft little tails. [Gail] Niemann debuts as an illustrator here, working well with watercolor as she makes lovely meadows and woods and rabbits in lively postures.

📖   *WHEN IT COMES TO BUGS* (1986)

Karey Wehner

SOURCE: A review of *When It Comes to Bugs,* in *School Library Journal,* Vol. 32, No. 9, May, 1986, pp. 72-73.

The bright, multicolored, nonspecific illustrations of spiders, insects and their environs make up the biggest and best part of this slight poetry collection. Eighteen short poems offer general observations on and feelings about

dragonflies, beetles, caterpillars, crickets, etc. Half of the poems, have appeared in earlier collections by Fisher; **"Little Talk"** and **"Mrs. Brownish Beetle"** have been included in several anthologies as well. The poems are well written and the rhyming, for the most part, is smooth, simple and easy on the ear; however, many are so short they seem overwhelmed by the full-page (sometimes page and a half) full-color illustrations [by Chris and Bruce Degen] that accompany them. Most of the poems share the same tone of gentle appreciation of nature. **"Little Talk"** and **"Crickets"** have the sharpest imagery. There's not much of a mix of poetic rhythms and imagery, which becomes a bit tiresome in such a short collection. Itse's *Hey Bug! and Other Poems about Little Things* and Griffen's *A Dog's Book of Bugs* are more imaginative, fuller treatments of similar material.

Carolyn Phelan

SOURCE: A review of *When It Comes to Bugs,* in *Booklist,* Vol. 82, No. 18, May 15, 1986, p. 1394.

Bugs might seem an unlikely source of inspiration, but Fisher has come up with 18 short, satisfying, child-oriented poems on the subject. With the ability to create rhymes and the skill to keep them flowing naturally, without the inevitable clunk of many versifiers, Fisher writes short poems about nature with the voice of childhood. Here is **"When It Comes to Bugs"** in its entirety: "I like crawlers, / I like creepers, / hoppers, jumpers, / flyers, leapers, / walkers, stalkers, / chirpers, peepers . . . / I wonder why / my mother thinks / that finders can't be keepers?" The accompanying illustration shows a boy sitting on the back steps, his net fallen to the ground, a jar in his hands containing a butterfly. We do not see his mother, but above his head her hand stretches, index finger eloquently pointing toward the yard. The pictures, each illustrating a short poem on a single- or double-page spread, are as simple, lively, and direct as the text. Chris Degen fashioned the vibrant line drawings on scratch-board, while Bruce Degen did the curiously electric color overlays—a successful joint venture. Here's a good source of poems to read aloud, at home, or in the classroom when bugs are in season.

📖   *THE HOUSE OF A MOUSE* (1988)

Carolyn Phelan

SOURCE: A review of *The House of a Mouse,* in *Booklist,* Vol. 85, No. 5, November 1, 1988, p. 482.

These 19 poems reflect Fisher's thoughts and imaginative suppositions about the ways of mice. The selections have a childlike quality, a combination of close observation and simple, though sometimes ingenuous, expression. A good example is the title poem: "The tiny world of Meadow Mice / can't be very safe or nice / When nibbly sheep and crunchy cows / make earthquake trembles as they browse, / and horses plunk a giant hoof beside (or on) a Mouse's roof. / I'm glad my house is stronger far / than Mouse's houses ever are." Deeply shaded pencil drawings illustrate the book with delicacy and precision [by Joan Sandin]. Brightened with blue-and-yellow washes, the artwork heightens the book's appeal by playing on children's affinity for these small animals while staying within the bounds of naturalism. A good choice for a primary-grade classroom with mice in residence.

Kathleen Whalin

SOURCE: A review of *The House of a Mouse,* in *School Library Journal,* Vol. 35, No. 5, January, 1989, p. 70.

The tone of this collection of 19 of Fisher's poems about mice, aided by [Joan] Sandin's color pencil drawings of big-eyed mice, is slightly too precious. Lines like "You'd think a bear had broken in/ instead of just a Mousikin" (from **"House Guest"**) or "curling together/ (as Mouselings do)/ rosy and dozy/ and squeaky new" (from **"Surprise"**) create only the common image of cute mice and undermine the effect of some of her fine poems such as **"Snow Stitches"** ("That's the one/ whose footprints show/ like stitches in the new white snow"). *Mice Are Rather Nice,* selected by Vardine Moore, contains four wonderful Fisher mouse poems, including **"Snow Stitches,"** and offers a much richer and more imaginative look into the world of mice. Poems about mice/ can be rather nice/ but *The House of a Mouse* falls short.

📖 *ALWAYS WONDERING: SOME FAVORITE POEMS OF AILEEN FISHER* (1991)

Leone McDermott

SOURCE: A review of *Always Wondering: Some Favorite Poems of Aileen Fisher,* in *Booklist,* Vol. 88, No. 3, October 1, 1991, p. 319.

This amiable collection ponders the pleasures and puzzles of a child's daily life. There are poems on family, pets, losing a tooth, and the first day of school, among other subjects. Many poems express wonder at the natural world and delight in the seasons: "I like fall: / it always smells smoky, / chimneys wake early, / the sun is poky." The verses are fresh and simple, half-musing and half-humorous in tone, with satisfying rhythm and rhyme. New readers will find the poetry easy to read and memorize, while young children will enjoy hearing it read aloud. Teachers and librarians may also find useful the section of 16 poems on major holidays.

Barbara Chatton

SOURCE: A review of *Always Wondering,* in *School Library Journal,* Vol. 37, No. 12, December, 1991, pp. 109-10.

This collection of 80 of Fisher's poems captures the fascination and excitement of growth, the seasons, and the ways of small living things as experienced by young children. *Always Wondering* is an apt title as many of the poems are speculative: How is growing done? How does the chick know how to get out of the egg? The verse is simple, the thoughts brief. Each poem holds the kernel of an idea about nature. The selections are perfect for posting in classrooms and libraries; for sharing aloud while watching mice, rabbits, and insects; and for reading to open up doors into the world. Many of the entries appeared in Fisher's *Feathered Ones and Furry, I Wonder How, I Wonder Why,* and *In the Woods, In the Meadow, In the Sky,* but this book will introduce a new generation of children to her poetry. Sandin's lovely pencil sketches open each of the volume's four sections. Like Shirley Hughes's *Out and About,* this collection has a child's eye as its focus. A fine addition to the poetry shelves.

Joel Chandler Harris

1848-1908

American author of short stories, novels, folklore retellings, and journalism.

Major works include *Uncle Remus, His Songs and His Sayings: Folklore of the Old Plantation* (1880), *Nights with Uncle Remus: Myths and Legends of the Old Plantation* (1883), *Daddy Jake the Runaway, and Short Stories Told after Dark by Uncle Remus* (1889), *Uncle Remus and His Friends: Old Plantation Stories, Songs and Ballads* (1892), *The Tar-Baby, and Other Rhymes of Uncle Remus* (1904), *Told by Uncle Remus: New Stories of the Old Plantation* (1905).

Major works about the author include *The Life and Letters of Joel Chandler Harris* (by Julia Collier Harris, 1918), *Joel Chandler Harris, Folklorist* (by Stella Brewer Brookes, 1950), *Joel Chandler Harris: A Biography* (by Paul M. Cousins, 1968), *Joel Chandler Harris* (by R. Bruce Bickley, Jr., 1978), *Critical Essays on Joel Chandler Harris* (by R. Bruce Bickley, Jr., 1981).

The following entry presents criticism on the various "Uncle Remus" collections.

INTRODUCTION

Although during his time he was well-known as a journalist and humorist, Harris is remembered today for his enduring yet controversial character, Uncle Remus, and the African American folktales he related. Harris's intent in recording these tales was, as he noted in the introduction to his first collection *Uncle Remus, His Songs and His Sayings: Folklore of the Old Plantation,* to "preserve the legends" as he had heard them on the plantation, in the dialect prevalent at the time. Designed to be read aloud, these tales of Brer Rabbit, Brer Fox, and other anthropomorphized animals were wildly popular with white audiences during the late nineteenth century, and engendered a number of imitators as well as serious scholarly interest in the folklore of African Americans. Framed by the narration of Uncle Remus, a kindly ex-plantation slave who instructs a group of young white boys, the tales tell the adventures of a series of "creeturs" who must use guile and brains to outwit stronger and more powerful animals. As the author himself recognized, the situations in which the vulnerable yet clever Brer Rabbit found himself were particularly meaningful for the similarly powerless slaves who told the tales; these situations also made the stories appealing to children.

The role of the narrator has been the subject of much controversy, for as a former slave who looks back with nostalgia on pre-Civil War times, Uncle Remus has been identified by many with the "happy darky" stereotype that whites perpetuated to downplay the evils of slavery. Some critics, however, have observed that Uncle Remus is a complete character—although one troubling to modern sensibilities—who makes observations on the stories and the world around him. The transformation of Uncle Remus the persona into Uncle Remus the stereotype by early audiences and critics (one suggested Remus demonstrated "the whole range of the Negro character") has made critical assessment of Harris's work problematic. Nevertheless, many commentators have had praise for both the author's rendering of plantation dialect and of his faithful interpretation of the folktales. Others have observed that by popularizing these tales, Harris helped to create a new type of children's story: the animal fantasy. While the debate over Uncle Remus continues, few challenge the value of the tales themselves—the legacy of a people and a culture which survived slavery and oppression—and Harris's role in preserving them for modern audiences. As African-American author and critic Julius Lester remarked in the introduction to his retelling of the tales, "Whatever one may think about how Harris chose to present the tales, the fact remains that they are a cornerstone of Afro-American culture and continue to be vital."

Biographical Information

Harris's sympathy for those overlooked or mistreated by society can be traced to his origins as a poor, illegitimate child growing up in Georgia. Born in 1848 outside of Atlanta to Mary Harris, an unmarried woman, Harris was further distinguished by his startling red hair and freckled complexion, which led to extreme shyness and a stutter. He attended public schools until the age of thirteen, when he was hired as a printer's apprentice for the *Countryman,* a weekly newspaper produced on a local plantation. It was there, Harris later recounted, that he "became familiar with the curious myths and animal stories that form the basis of the volumes accredited to 'Uncle Remus.'" Harris borrowed from the plantation's library and started to write for the *Countryman,* contributing pieces until 1866, when the paper folded after General Sherman's forces overran the plantation. For the next ten years young Harris worked for various newspapers in the South, ending with the *Savannah Morning News.* In Savannah he met and married Esther LaRose, who bore him nine children, three of whom died in childhood.

In 1876, Harris began working as an editorial paragrapher for the Atlanta *Constitution* and eventually rose to the position of associate editor. While there he became known for his humorous anecdotes, but he also wrote editorials, many of which focused on the need for compassion and reconciliation in the South of the Reconstruction era. Although he was an apologist for slavery, believing it had helped "civilize" Africans, Harris also had ideas that were considered rather liberal for his time. He advocated public education for African Americans, opposed the deportation of blacks to Africa, considered minstrel shows debasing and offensive, and invariably opposed stereotypes of African Americans as idle or unthrifty, insisting that people should be judged as individuals.

The genesis for the Uncle Remus stories occurred in 1878, when the journalist was asked to assume responsibility for a column of anecdotes and sketches "authored" by a black character. Various sketches and stories featuring a character name Uncle Remus were published in the paper in the years 1878 and 1879, and their popularity led to the appearance of the book *Uncle Remus, His Songs and His Sayings: Folklore of the Old Plantation* in 1880. Harris left the staff of the *Constitution* in 1900, but was coaxed out of retirement in 1907 to edit and write for *Uncle Remus's Magazine,* which his son Julian helped to found. Harris's health began to fail the following year, and he died of acute nephritis and chronic cirrhosis of the liver on July 3, 1908. Reserved to the end (he never read his stories to an audience, even his children), he requested that no monuments be erected in his honor. Instead, his works, originals as well as numerous adaptations, have endured for more than a century.

Major Works

Harris's first book was the one that made his reputation; the thirty-four stories in *Uncle Remus, His Songs and His Sayings* introduced his audience to Uncle Remus and his stories of the foibles and virtues found in a community of animals. The collection features the most famous of Uncle Remus's stories, "The Rabbit and the Tar-Baby," in which the feisty Brer Rabbit finally meets his match in a silent, passive statue made of tar created by his nemesis Brer Fox, and later escapes the fox's trap by using reverse psychology and asking not to be thrown into a briar patch. The book was an immediate success, going through four editions within just a few months and selling thousands of copies yearly for over two decades. *Nights with Uncle Remus: Myths and Legends of the Old Plantation* features seventy-one additional animal tales, but introduces two new narrators, Daddy Jack and Aunt Tempy, who compete with Remus in their storytelling.

Harris's next two collections avoided animal fables of the Remus type; *Mingo and Other Sketches in Black and White* (1884) and *Free Joe and Other Georgian Sketches* (1887) were local-color stories focusing on poor whites and blacks of the South, and were more prone to stereotype. Considered his best longer work, the autobiographical novel *On the Plantation: A Story of a Georgia Boy's Adventures During the War* was published in 1892 and marked the beginning of a period when Harris wrote very few Uncle Remus stories. Instead, the author produced children's stories, novels, more local-color pieces, and essays. None of these works approached the success of his Uncle Remus stories, however, and by 1904 he returned to his most popular subject, penning the new collections *The Tar-Baby, and Other Rhymes of Uncle Remus* and *Told by Uncle Remus: New Stories of the Old Plantation.*

The community of animals featured in the Uncle Remus folktales closely resembles a human one, with characters who talk, wear clothing, work, maintain households, and argue over money, women, food, and status. While the Uncle Remus framework presents the stories as being told to a child—and the tales have long been considered children's literature—many of the tales feature violent resolutions to the conflicts, with characters being boiled alive, served in soup, or stung to death by bees. The typical story involves a relatively powerless animal, such as the rabbit, terrapin (turtle), or bullfrog, pitted against a more powerful opponent, such as the fox, bear, or wolf. The weaker animal, however, usually has the benefit of more wit, guile, or wisdom than the stronger one, and eventually triumphs over his enemy. As Uncle Remus and the other narrators relate these stories, they intersperse their own commentary, opinion, and instruction to their young listeners, providing additional insight into the era and society that formed the tales.

Critical Reception

Initial critical opinions of Harris's work reflected its popularity, with reviewers praising its reproduction of dialect and folklore and the character of Uncle Remus. Mark Twain named the author America's "only master" of "Negro dialect," while *The New York Times* called *Uncle*

Remus, His Songs and His Sayings "the first real book of American folklore." Even at this early date, however, critics expressed reservations about Harris's apologetic tone toward slavery and use of the word "nigger," observing that this worked against the tolerance and understanding that the sharing of African-American folklore otherwise promoted. Nevertheless, most early observers tended to agree with William Malone Baskerville, who wrote in 1897 that the Uncle Remus stories were "the most valuable and, in [this] writer's opinion, the most permanent contribution to American literature in the last quarter of this century."

Early twentieth-century critics who were beginning to assess the place of Harris's work in American literature tended to focus more on Uncle Remus than the folktales themselves, judging the character a unique literary creation who was as realistic a reflection of the "negro character" as had ever been created. A 1933 essay by African-American writer Sterling A. Brown began a period of re-evaluation, as many critics began to question how valuable the folktales could be when encased in a framework that perpetuated old, stereotypical ideas of race. Even into the 1940s, however, some commentators ignored addressing this issue even as they recommended *Uncle Remus, His Songs and His Sayings* as an American classic. A controversial 1949 essay by Bernard Wolfe brought racial issues to the fore, however, exploring how Uncle Remus and Brer Rabbit contain conflicting perceptions of African-American response to white oppression: the "prototype of the Negro grinnergiver" on the one hand and the "symbol . . . of the Negro slave's festering hatred of the white man" on the other. Subsequent critical assessments have debated whether Uncle Remus is stereotype or character, whether the dialect is a colorful vernacular or an unintelligible hindrance, whether the folktales as Harris wrote them are valuable for a modern audience or not, and whether the tales would have survived into the present without the author's intervention.

While today Harris's work still evokes strong reactions—both favorable and unfavorable—critics in the later part of the twentieth century are more inclined to recognize that the Uncle Remus stories reflect the mind of a complex man whose conflicting racial sympathies were a product of his times. As Nina Mikkelsen wrote in 1983: "If, in 1880, white Southerners had the best opportunity to record the black man's experience, then it is fortunate that the white Southerner who did it was Harris, a man with a listening ear, a strong literary talent, and a humorous spirit. When Remus and the animals talked to Harris they didn't tell him everything. But they told him enough to create a Southern and an American literature of lasting value."

Awards

For his contributions to American literature, Harris was elected to the American Academy of Arts and Letters in 1905. *Uncle Remus, His Songs and His Sayings* was awarded a Lewis Carroll Shelf Award in 1963.

AUTHOR'S COMMENTARY

Joel Chandler Harris (essay date 1880)

SOURCE: Introduction to *The Complete Tales of Uncle Remus,* Houghton Mifflin Company, 1955, pp. xxi-xxvii.

I am advised by my publishers that this book is to be included in their catalogue of humorous publications, and this friendly warning gives me an opportunity to say that however humorous it may be in effect, its intention is perfectly serious; and, even if it were otherwise, it seems to me that a volume written wholly in dialect must have its solemn, not to say melancholy features. With respect to the Folk-Lore series, my purpose has been to preserve the legends in their original simplicity, and to wed them permanently to the quaint dialect—if, indeed, it can be called a dialect—through the medium of which they have become a part of the domestic history of every Southern family; and I have endeavored to give to the whole a genuine flavor of the old plantation.

Each legend has its variants, but in every instance I have retained that particular version which seemed to me to be the most characteristic, and have given it without embellishment and without exaggeration. The dialect, it will be observed, is wholly different from that of the Hon. Pompey Smash and his literary descendants, and different also from the intolerable misrepresentations of the minstrel stage, but it is at least phonetically genuine. Nevertheless, if the language of Uncle Remus fails to give vivid hints of the really poetic imagination of the Negro; if it fails to embody the quaint and homely humor which was his most prominent characteristic; if it does not suggest a certain picturesque sensitiveness—a curious exaltation of mind and temperament not to be defined by words—then I have reproduced the form of the dialect merely, and not the essence, and my attempt may be accounted a failure. At any rate, I trust I have been successful in presenting what may be, at least to a large portion of American readers, a new and by no means unattractive phase of Negro character—a phase which may be considered a curiously sympathetic supplement to Mrs. Stowe's wonderful defense of slavery [*Uncle Tom's Cabin*] as it existed in the South. Mrs. Stowe, let me hasten to say, attacked the possibilities of slavery with all the eloquence of genius; but the same genius painted the portrait of the Southern slave-owner, and defended him.

A number of the plantation legends originally appeared in the columns of a daily newspaper—*The Atlanta Constitution*—and in that shape they attracted the attention of various gentlemen who were kind enough to suggest that they would prove to be valuable contributions to myth-literature. It is but fair to say that ethnological considerations formed no part of the undertaking which has resulted in the publication of this volume. Professor J. W. Powell, of the Smithsonian Institution, who is engaged in an investigation of the mythology of the North American Indians, informs me that some of Uncle Remus's stories appear in a number of different languages, and in various modified forms, among the Indians; and he is of the opinion that they are borrowed by the Negroes from the red men. But this, to say the least, is extremely doubtful, since another investigator (Mr. Herbert H. Smith, author of *Brazil and the Amazons*), has met with some of these stories among tribes of South American Indians, and one in particular he has traced to India, and as far east as Siam. Mr. Smith has been kind enough to send me the proof sheets of his chapter on "The Myths and Folk-Lore of the Amazonian Indians," in which he reproduces some of the stories which he gathered while exploring the Amazons.

In the first of his series, a tortoise falls from a tree upon the head of a jaguar and kills him; in one of Uncle Remus's stories, the terrapin falls from a shelf in Miss Meadows's house and stuns the fox, so that the latter fails to catch the rabbit. In the next, a jaguar catches a tortoise by the hind leg as he is disappearing in his hole; but the tortoise convinces him he is holding a root, and so escapes; Uncle Remus tells how the fox endeavored to drown the terrapin, but turned him loose because the terrapin declared his tail to be only a stump root. Mr. Smith also gives the story of how the tortoise outran the deer, which is identical as to incident with Uncle Remus's story of how Brer Tarrypin outran Brer Rabbit. Then there is the story of how the tortoise pretended that he was stronger than the tapir. He tells the latter he can drag him into the sea, but the tapir retorts that he will pull the tortoise into the forest and kill him besides. The tortoise thereupon gets a vine stem, ties one end around the body of the tapir, and goes to the sea, where he ties the other end to the tail of a whale. He then goes into the wood, midway between them both, and gives the vine a shake as a signal for the pulling to begin. The struggle between the whale and tapir goes on until each thinks the tortoise is the strongest of animals. Compare this with the story of the terrapin's contest with the bear, in which Miss Meadows's bed cord is used instead of a vine stem. One of the most characteristic of Uncle Remus's stories is that in which the rabbit proves to Miss Meadows and the girls that the fox is his riding horse. This is almost identical with a story quoted by Mr. Smith, where the jaguar is about to marry the deer's daughter. The cotia—a species of rodent—is also in love with her, and he tells the deer that he can make a riding horse of the jaguar. "Well," says the deer, "if you can make the jaguar carry you, you shall have my daughter." Thereupon the story proceeds pretty much as Uncle Remus tells it of the fox and the rabbit. The cotia finally jumps from the jaguar and takes refuge in a hole, where an owl is set to watch him, but he flings sand in the owl's eyes and escapes. In another story given by Mr. Smith, the cotia is very thirsty, and, seeing a man coming with a jar on his head, lies down in the road in front of him, and repeats this until the man puts down his jar to go back after all the dead cotias he has seen. This is almost identical with Uncle Remus's story of how the rabbit robbed the fox of his game. In a story from Upper Egypt, a fox lies down in the road in front of a man who is carrying fowls to market, and finally succeeds in securing them.

This similarity extends to almost every story quoted by Mr. Smith, and some are so nearly identical as to point unmistakably to a common origin. . . .

Professor Hartt, in his *Amazonian Tortoise Myths,* quotes a story from the *Riverside Magazine* of November, 1868, which will be recognized as a variant of one given by Uncle Remus. I venture to append it here, with some necessary verbal and phonetic alterations, in order to give the reader an idea of the difference between the dialect of the cotton plantations as used by Uncle Remus, and the lingo in vogue on the rice plantations and Sea Islands of the South Atlantic States:

> One time B'er Deer an' B'er Cooter [Terrapin] was courtin', and de lady did bin lub B'er Deer mo' so dan B'er Cooter. She did bin lub B'er Cooter, but she lub B'er Deer de morest. So de noung lady say to B'er Deer and B'er Cooter bofe dat dey mus' hab a ten-mile race, an' de one dat beats, she will go marry him.
>
> So B'er Cooter say to B'er Deer: "You has got mo' longer legs dan I has, but I will run you. You run ten mile on land, and I will run ten mile on de water!"
>
> So B'er Cooter went an' git nine er his fam'ly, an' put one at ebery mile-pos', and he hisse'f, what was to run wid B'er Deer, he was right in front of de young lady's do', in de broom-grass.
>
> Dat mornin' at nine o'clock, B'er Deer he did met B'er Cooter at de fus mile-pos', wey dey was to start fum. So he call: "Well, B'er Cooter, is you ready? Go long!" As he git on to de nex' mile-pos', he say: "B'er Cooter!" B'er Cooter say: "Hullo!" B'er Deer say: "You dere?" B'er Cooter say: "Yes, B'er Deer, I dere too."
>
> Nex' mile-pos' he jump, B'er Deer say: "Hullo, B'er Cooter!" B'er Cooter say: "Hullo, B'er Deer! you dere too?" B'er Deer say: "Ki! it look like you gwine fer tie me; it look like we gwine fer de gal tie!"
>
> W'en he git to de nine-mile pos' he tought he git dere fus, 'cause he mek two jump; so he holler: "B'er Cooter!" B'er Cooter answer: "You dere too?" B'er Deer say: "It look like you gwine tie me." B'er Cooter say: "Go long, B'er Deer. I git dere in due season time," which he does, and wins de race.

The story of the Rabbit and the Fox, as told by the Southern Negroes, is artistically dramatic in this: it progresses in an orderly way from a beginning to a well-defined conclusion, and is full of striking episodes that suggest the culmination. It seems to me to be to a certain extent allegorical, albeit such an interpretation may be unreasonable. At least it is a fable thoroughly characteristic of the Negro; and it needs no scientific investigation to show why he selects as his hero the weakest and most harmless of all animals, and brings him out victorious in contests with the bear, the wolf, and the fox. It is not virtue that triumphs, but helplessness; it is not malice, but mischievousness. It would be presumptuous in me to offer an opinion as to the origin of these curious myth-stories; but, if ethnologists should discover that they did not originate with the African, the proof to that effect should be accompanied with a good deal of persuasive eloquence.

Curiously enough, I have found few Negroes who will acknowledge to a stranger that they know anything of these legends; and yet to relate one of the stories is the surest road to their confidence and esteem. In this way, and in this way only, I have been enabled to collect and verify the folklore included in this volume. There is an anecdote about the Irishman and the rabbit which a number of Negroes have told to me with great unction, and which is both funny and characteristic, though I will not undertake to say that it has its origin with the blacks. One day an Irishman who had heard people talking about "mares' nests" was going along the big road—it is always the big road in contradistinction to neighborhood paths and bypaths, called in the vernacular "nigh-cuts"—when he came to a pumpkin-patch. The Irishman had never seen any of this fruit before, and he at once concluded that he had discovered a veritable mare's nest. Making the most of his opportunity, he gathered one of the pumpkins in his arms and went on his way. A pumpkin is an exceedingly awkward thing to carry, and the Irishman had not gone far before he made a misstep, and stumbled. The pumpkin fell to the ground, rolled down the hill into a "brush-heap," and, striking against a stump, was broken. The story continues in the dialect: "W'en de punkin roll in de bresh-heap, out jump a rabbit; en soon's de I'shmuns see dat, he take atter de rabbit en holler: 'Kworp, colty! kworp, colty!' but de rabbit, he des flew." The point of this is obvious. . . .

The difference between the dialect of the legends and that of the character-sketches, slight as it is, marks the modifications which the speech of the Negro has undergone even where education has played no part in reforming it. Indeed, save in the remote country districts, the dialect of the legends has nearly disappeared. I am perfectly well aware that the character-sketches are without permanent interest, but they are embodied here for the purpose of presenting a phase of Negro character wholly distinct from that which I have endeavored to preserve in the legends. Only in this shape, and with all the local allusions, would it be possible to adequately represent the shrewd observations, the curious retorts, the homely thrusts, the quaint comments, and the humorous philosophy of the race of which Uncle Remus is the type.

If the reader not familiar with plantation life will imagine that the myth-stories of Uncle Remus are told night after night to a little boy by an old Negro who appears to be venerable enough to have lived during the period which he describes—who has nothing but pleasant memories of the discipline of slavery—and who has all the prejudices of caste and pride of family that were the natural results of the system; if the reader can imagine all this, he will find little difficulty in appreciating and sympathizing with the air of affectionate superiority which Uncle Remus assumes as he proceeds to unfold the mysteries of plantation lore to a little child who is the product of that practical reconstruction which has been going on to some extent since the war in spite of the politicians. Uncle Remus describes that reconstruction in his "A Story of the War," and I may as well add here for the benefit of the curious that that story is almost literally true.

GENERAL COMMENTARY

The New York Times (essay date 1880)

SOURCE: "'Negro Folklore,'" in *Critical Essays on Joel Chandler Harris,* G. K. Hall & Co., 1981, pp. 3-6.

We are just discovering what admirable literary material there is at home, what a great mine there is to explore, and how quaint and peculiar is the material which can be dug up. Mr. Harris's book [*Uncle Remus, His Songs and His Sayings*] may be looked on in a double light—either as a pleasant volume recounting the stories told by a typical old colored man to a child, or as a valuable contribution to our somewhat meagre folk-lore. Descanting but slightly on such *mise en scene* as the author has very wisely chosen, still admiring the happy little bits of by-play, with which the numerous stories are introduced for the delectation of "Miss Sally's" 7-year old child, we would rather confine ourselves to the strange myths which are still kept alive by the negroes in Southern plantations, and the dialects, which curious subjects Mr. Harris has cleverly arranged and presented to us with a great deal of skill and judgment.

To Northern readers the story of Brer (Brother-Brudder) Rabbit may be novel. To those familiar with plantation life, who have listened to these quaint old stories, who have still tender reminiscences of some good old Mauma who told these wondrous adventures to them when they were children, Brer Rabbit, the Tar Baby, and Brer Fox come back again with all the past pleasures of younger days. . . .

Of late there have been many variations of one particular story, **"The Rabbit and the Tar Baby,"** presented to an admiring public, but Mr. Harris, through Uncle Remus, presents the pure unalloyed version. There is a delightful nonsensicality about some of these stories, as **"How Mr. Rabbit Saved His Meat,"** which cannot but please even the most prosaic reader. . . .

Mr. Harris's book is altogether excellent of its kind, and in preserving certain quaint legends, and giving us exactly the sounds of the negro dialect, he has established on a firm basis the first real book of American folk lore.

The Spectator

SOURCE: A review of *Uncle Remus and His Legends of the Old Plantation,* in *The Spectator,* Vol. 53, No. 2753, April 2, 1881, pp. 445-46.

This charming little book [*Uncle Remus and His Legends of the Old Plantation*] appears to be written by a partisan of "the peculiar institution," and so very thorough a partisan, that he speaks of Mrs. Stowe's "wonderful defence of slavery as it existed in the South." "Mrs. Stowe," he goes on, "let me hasten to say, attacked the possibilities of slavery with all the eloquence of genius; but the same genius painted the portrait of the Southern slaveowner, and defended him." In the same sense, and no other, Mr. Harris obviously regards this book as a defence of the slave-system. Because it depicts the slave of the old plantations as often warmly attached to the family in which he was domesticated, as full of sympathetic qualities, full of humour and fancy, and full, too, of a certain kind of social independence, Mr. Harris appears to suppose that it is an apology for the system. In reality, this book illustrates the habits of cunning, deceit, and dishonesty, and the delight in them, in which even these highly favourable specimens of the slave were steeped, quite as much as it illustrates their attachment to the house to which they belonged, and their fascinating qualities of head and heart.

However, the interest of the book is not in its illustrations of slavery, but in its picture of the kind of imaginations in which the negro slave most delighted. In his preface, Mr. Harris says:—

> The story of the Rabbit and the Fox, as told by the Southern negroes, is artistically dramatic in this; it progresses in an orderly way from a beginning to a well-defined conclusion, and is full of striking episodes that suggest the culmination. It seems to me to be to a certain extent allegorical, albeit, such an interpretation may be unreasonable. At least it is a fable thoroughly characteristic of the Negro; and it needs no scientific investigation to show why he selects as his hero the weakest and most harmless of all animals, and brings him out victorious in contests with the bear, the wolf, and the fox. It is not virtue that triumphs, but helplessness; it is not malice, but mischievousness.

And, perhaps, that admission is quite sufficient—if anything were needful for that purpose—to cancel the effect of all the author's admiring insinuations as to the value of the institution which has produced these charming legends. Mr. Harris should have said, "It is not virtue that triumphs, but cunning," for mere "helplessness" can never triumph; and the object of all these legends is to show that races of inferior physical strength are *not* helpless, but more able to help themselves by cunning than their adversaries by tooth and claw. However, whatever be the drift of the author, the idea of preserving and publishing these legends in the form in which the old-plantation negroes actually tell them, is altogether one of the happiest literary conceptions of the day. And very admirably is the work done.

What strikes us most, perhaps, is the curious simplicity of the trickery which is supposed to win the victory over superior force. The rabbit, who is always, or almost always, the negro's hero amongst animals,—sometimes the terrapin, a kind of fresh-water tortoise, we believe, takes

his place,—gets out of his scrapes by the sort of inventiveness which, if it were conceivable at all, would be not so much an evidence of his superior cunning, as of the infinite and immeasurable gullibility of the fox, or wolf, or bear with whom he has to contend. And evidently the imagination of the negro delighted itself more in grotesquely exaggerating in every way this gullibility of the stronger races, than even in dwelling upon the cunning of the weaker races. These legends embody better the contempt of the weak for the humorously-exaggerated stupidity of the strong, than their delight in the astuteness of the weak. One of the earlier stories, however, tells how the rabbit is, at first, taken in by the fox, who makes a sort of lay figure of a baby all smeared over with tar, which is called a "tar-baby." The curiosity of the rabbit entangles him with this sticky lay-figure, so as to put him in the fox's power, though he afterwards outwits the fox. . . .

Nothing could show better how the negro imagination ran riot in imputing stupidity to those who were known to be stronger than themselves, than the charming legend where the Rabbit actually boasts that his family has always made a riding-horse of the Fox, with the express intention *not* of putting him on his guard, but of making him into a ridinghorse, and succeeds none the less. The touches of humour in the story are exquisite. The refusal to account for Miss Meadows in any way beyond stating that she was "in the tale"; the demeanour of Brother Rabbit when Miss Meadows and her daughters are laughing at him, sitting there "sorter lam like," and then crossing his legs and winking his eye "slow"; making his false boast, and paying his "'specks," and "tipping his beaver," and walking off as stuck-up as a "fire-stick"; and the description of the fox looking as "peart as a circus pony" in the saddle and bridle and blinkers in which he tamely came on purpose to prove that he had never been the Rabbit's riding-horse; the account of the putting-on of the spurs; the fault the fastidious horseman finds with his horse for losing his pace; and the old negro's final objection to giving out more cloth at one time than is needful for one pair of trousers,—are all telling features in a most humorous tale. But, for ourselves, we think we even prefer the story of the contest of the Fox with the Terrapin, in which, again, a degree of stupidity is attributed to the fox far more charmingly grotesque than the cunning attributed to the tortoise. . . .

Brother Terrapin, allowing to himself that when the fox comes up "he'd sorter keep one eye open," his pococurante way of saying he'd been "lounjun 'roun'," and "suffer'n," and his gentle patronage of the fox for not knowing what trouble is; his ill-advised indignation at the idea that his tail had been burnt off, and the unfortunate demonstration of the existence of that member into which it surprises him; and finally, the extraordinarily simple trap into which the fox falls by being led to suppose that he had got hold of a stump-root, and not of the terrapin's tail, are all of them charming touches of humour, and of humour obviously enjoying the consciousness of its own extravagance. So, too, when the rabbit gets the wolf into the chest, and before beginning operations against him, deliberately goes to the looking-glass to wink at himself; and again, when the political indignation of the crayfishes breaks out because the elephant "puts his foot down" on one of them, and they "sorter swawmed tergedder, en draw'd up a kind o' peramble wid some wharfoes in it, en read her out in de 'sembly"; and once more, when we listen to the delightful bravado with which the old negro parades the fine, bushy tail of the rabbit of old times, in the hope of exciting his little auditor's wonder, we appreciate the popular humour of these legends as we have hardly ever appreciated any humour so gay and childlike. . . .

What could be more admirable than the dignity with which Uncle Remus confronts what the boy has inferred from what he said, with what he actually said, and accuses him of false witness, and reduces him to abject submission, before he will consent to go on a single syllable with his story? In such touches lies the charm of this fascinating little volume of legends, which deserves to be placed on a level with *Reineke Fuchs* for its quaint humour, without reference to the ethnological interest possessed by these stories, as indicating, perhaps, a common origin for very widely-severed races.

The Nation

SOURCE: A review of *Nights with Uncle Remus: Myths and Legends of the Old Plantation,* in *The Nation,* Vol. 37, No. 959, November 15, 1883, p. 422.

Mr. Harris's reputation was made at a single stroke by his **Uncle Remus, His Songs and His Sayings,** which appeared just three years ago in book form. It was then seen that, in spite of his disclaimer that he was simply a chronicler of negro folk-lore, he was an exquisite humorist, whose mastery of the negro dialect and skill as a story-teller placed him in the front rank of American writers. He now comes forward with a second volume, no longer a medley, but wholly given up to the "creetur" tales which made the first so enjoyable and so valuable, and thus proves the sincerity of his protest that he was a man with a mission. The mine of which he first fairly revealed the richness has, meantime, been still further opened up by his own explorations and the help of friends, until in addition to the thirty-four of the former series we have seventy-one new tales placed before us. It cannot be supposed that the vein is worked out, even if it should seem that the best ore lay on the surface. Opinions will differ as to whether there is anything in the present collection to be preferred, say, to the **"Tar Baby,"** the explanation of Brer Possum's love of peace, or the trial of strength in which Brer Tarrypin surpasses Brer B'ar. But in all other respects, unquestionably, this work more than holds its own, and indeed, regard being had to the literary skill displayed in setting so large a number of stories, must be thought an extraordinary *tour de force.*

The ease and confidence with which Mr. Harris haudles his materials are shown in various ways. There is a certain development in the two leading characters. "The lit-tle boy" is felt to be getting older and more mature; Uncle Remus grows more mellow, and his finer traits are brought out by contrast with an aged "Affiky" man, Daddy Jack, from the rice plantations, and with two of the women house servants. These three new-comers all relieve Uncle Remus in telling stories, and Mr. Harris's crowning art lies in maintaining the peculiar speech and psychic quality of each. In other words, he drives a dialectic four-in-hand with unrivalled dexterity. Nothing could be better here than the way in which Daddy Jack takes a tale away from Uncle Remus and proceeds to tell it himself, but the former will not father it, and quietly resumes: "Now, den, we'er got ter go 'way back behrme dish yer yallergater doin's w'at Brer Jack bin mixin'us up wid. Ef I makes no mistakes wid my 'membrence, de place wharbouts I lef' off wuz whar Brer Rabbit had so many 'p'intments fer ter keep out der way er de t'er creeturs dat he 'gun ter feel monst'ous humblyfied." Another striking example is a succession of three variants of one theme, told by Uncle Remus, Daddy Jack, and Aunt Tempy respectively. Space fails us, however, to quote freely from these laughable pages.

The Dial

SOURCE: A review of *Nights with Uncle Remus,* in *The Dial,* Vol. IV, No. 44, December, 1883, p. 195.

Everybody will welcome another collection of stories by Uncle Remus (**Nights with Uncle Remus,**); for whether we regard them as contributions to the science of folk-lore, illustrations of dialect, or simply as good stories, few recent publications have met with equal favor. It is a good thick volume too, containing seventy-one stories, a few of which have already seen the light in the pages of magazines, and on the average the stories will, we think, be found fully as good as those in the first collection. We learn from the preface, that "the thirty-five legends in the first volume were merely selections from the large body of plantation folklore familiar to the author from his child-hood, and these selections were made less with an eye to their ethnological importance than with a view to presenting certain quaint and curious race characteristics, of which the world at large had either vague or greatly exaggerated notions." The present volume undertakes to be as complete as it could be made, although no doubt other legends exist which somebody will by and by pick up. The skill with which the tales are introduced, the descriptions of the old man's demeanor, and his by-talk with the little boy, all show a high degree of dramatic power on the part of the author.

Mark Twain (essay date 1883)

SOURCE: "America's Immortally Shy Master of Negro Dialect," in *Critical Essays on Joel Chandler Harris,* G. K. Hall & Co., 1981, pp. 53-54.

[The following excerpt is from "Uncle Remus and Mr. Cable," a chapter from Twain's Life on the Mis-

sissippi which was published in 1883. In 1882, Harris visited Twain and author George Washington Cable in New Orleans in order to discuss Twain's proposal for a joint lecture tour; Harris, who was extremely shy and even refused to read the Uncle Remus stories to his own children, eventually declined the offer.]

Mr. Joel Chandler Harris ("Uncle Remus") was to arrive from Atlanta at seven o'clock Sunday morning; so we got up and received him. We were able to detect him among the crowd of arrivals at the hotel-counter by his correspondence with a description of him which had been furnished us from a trustworthy source. He was said to be undersized, red-haired, and somewhat freckled. He was the only man in the party whose outside tallied with this bill of particulars. He was said to be very shy. He is a shy man. Of this there is no doubt. It may not show on the surface, but the shyness is there. After days of intimacy one wonders to see that it is still in about as strong force as ever. There is a fine and beautiful nature hidden behind it, as all know who have read the Uncle Remus book; and a fine genius, too, as all know by the same sign. I seem to be talking quite freely about this neighbor; but in talking to the public I am but talking to his personal friends, and these things are permissible among friends.

He deeply disappointed a number of children who had flocked eagerly to Mr. Cable's house to get a glimpse of the illustrious sage and oracle of the nation's nurseries. They said:

"Why, he's white!"

They were grieved about it. So, to console them, the book was brought, that they might hear Uncle Remus's Tar-Baby story from the lips of Uncle Remus himself—or what, in their outraged eyes, was left of him. But it turned out that he had never read aloud to people, and was too shy to venture the attempt now. Mr. Cable and I read from books of ours, to show him what an easy trick it was; but his immortal shyness was proof against even this sagacious strategy, so we had to read about Brer Rabbit ourselves.

Mr. Harris ought to be able to read the negro dialect better than anybody else, for in the matter of writing it he is the only master the country has produced.

The Critic (essay date 1889)

SOURCE: "Daddy Jake the Runaway," in *Critical Essays on Joel Chandler Harris,* G. K. Hall & Co., 1981, pp. 17-18.

Putnam County, Georgia, bids fair to become the classic soil of the South as Athens is dubbed by Milton the "eye of Greece"; for in this famous country the immortal "Uncle Remus" is at home. . . .

This new collection of Mr. Harris's Negro stories [*Daddy Jake the Runaway and Short Stories Told After Dark*] rotates about the year 1863, and has the War of the Con-

From The Favorite Uncle Remus, *written by Joel Chandler Harris. Illustrated by A. B. Frost.*

federacy for its dramatic background. The core of the tales, however, is the inexhaustible curiosity of the "little boy"—here "bisected," as it were, into a boy and a girl. These charming infants—Lucien and Lillian—ply the "old man" of the former collection—now rechristened "Daddy Jake"—with the usual childish multitude of questions; they are as eager for a "story" as ever; and Brer Coon and Brer Rabbit are nearly as fertile in these as the living ones are in skipping and scampering offspring. It is Aesop come to life again after his reincarnation in an Ethiopian mould. Aesop, too, was a slave, like Uncle Remus and Daddy Jake and Epictetus and many and many another of the great philosophers and saints; and the fables of Greece and Rome and India are hardly more striking than the Negro "marooners" in their simple *naïveté* and imaginative humor. It will probably never be practicable to separate the myths of Putnam County from the myths of the broader "Africa" from which they spring; yet one must always be thankful that an artist has arisen fearless enough to seize and publish them with all their accompaniment of quaint dialect and Southern plantation life. They have value for the philologist as well as for the lover of comparative mythology.

"Uncle Remus" is here, too, in *propriâ personâ;* for after the introductory story is concluded, we have a new cycle of Remus legends and animal fables. . . .

One at least of these new stories has a remarkable variant or parallelism in a Kafir legend of South Africa, and all thirteen show the undiminished vivacity of Uncle Remus's recollection. The book is delightfully printed, and forms a most auspicious prelude to the burst of "juvenile" books soon to come.

The Nation

SOURCE: A review of *Uncle Remus and His Friends,* in *The Nation,* Vol. 55, No. 1433, December 15, 1892, pp. 455-56.

In a very graceful and modest preface to **Uncle Remus and His Friends,** Mr. Joel Chandler Harris closes his memorable series; and certainly when we are shown the old man at the telephone and the phonograph and in an electric car, Uncle Remus begins to have a *fin de siècle* air preliminary to his translation. Yet we marvel afresh at the delineator's art, his extraordinary versatility in narration, and his ever-extending vocabulary and phraseology. In other words, of exhaustion, either on the part of Mr. Harris or of his material, there is no sign in this final volume, which includes some secular negro songs and some episodes illustrative not of the old plantation, but of present Southern problems and perplexities, such as the exquisite **"Some Advice to a Colored Brother," "Views on the African Exodus," "Called to Account by the Preacher,"** and the **"William Henry"** adventures. It is curious to notice the consciousness, on Mr. Harris's part, of a certain danger to childish morals from much familiarity with his animal fables. He touches on this in his prelude to **"Brer Billy Goat's Dinner,"** and later on he tells a tale (**"The Man and his Boots"**) expressly by way of deprecating any confusion "'twix' creetur doin's en folks' doin's." "How de name er goodness," he asks "the little boy," "kin folks go on en steal en tell fibs, like de creeturs done, en not git hurted? Dey des can't do it." It will perhaps be surprising if parents do not at least have to trace prankishness and mischievousness to the same exemplars. Another reflection which occurs to us is, that Mr. Harris has added Uncle Remus to the gallery of popular negro types to which belong Topsy and Uncle Tom. Millions are reading of them all—have been reading of the earlier two for forty years. How much has been done by this means towards breaking down the unchristian prejudice against color? How much will that prejudice be strengthened by introducing to the nursery, through Mr. Harris's classic pages, the word "nigger" used opprobriously (as it is in fact) by colored people one towards another?

John Habberton (essay date 1893)

SOURCE: "'Uncle Remus and His Friends': Uncle Remus Is 'Just the Same as Ever'," in *Critical Essays on Joel Chandler Harris,* G. K. Hall & Co., 1981, pp. 23-24.

It is high time for a new book from Unc' Remus [***Uncle Remus and His Friends: Old Plantation Stories, Songs, and Ballads with Sketches of Negro Character***], for the older ones have been thumbed to pieces in thousands of families. The old man is just the same as ever, and his home audience consists principally of the little boy, but the stories and songs are new, and quite as funny as the old ones. Thousands of bedtime hours will be made merry for the little ones by this new collection of tales, and hundreds of thousands of boys and girls at the North will wish, in spite of their comfortable homes and good parents, they could have been born down South and slipped down to the old darkey's cabin with that other "little boy" who seems as important to Remus as Boswell was to Johnson. As to Mr. Harris, scores of writers envy him the honor which will be done him in the future—long distant may it be—when some tourist will scrawl on his tombstone "Author of Uncle Remus."

Thomas Nelson Page (essay date 1895)

SOURCE: "'Immortal Uncle Remus'," in *Critical Essays on Joel Chandler Harris,* G. K. Hall & Co., 1981, pp. 55-57.

[The following excerpt is from a review of the 1895 edition of Uncle Remus, His Songs and His Sayings, *also known as the "Frost" edition because of its illustrations by artist A. B. Frost. The critic was a popular American novelist and short story writer as well as a former ambassador to Italy. As a writer, Page is recognized for his portraits of Virginia plantation life; his novel* Red Rock *(1898) and short stories are often compared to Harris's local color tales.]*

Fifteen years ago, out of a region known rather for its acting men and talking men than for its writing men (though several volumes of sketches wonderfully racy of the soil had come from it, even in the old times), there appeared a book so humorous and unlike all that had gone before it that, though at first sight it seemed to be in an almost unknown tongue, the public at once seized on it, first with curiosity and then with delight. It purported to be a record of the stories, songs and sayings told or sung by an old negro—a former slave—to the little grandson of his old master and mistress, and on the outside the stories were a series of fables of animals and birds, relating in the main to the strife between Brer Fox and Brer Rabbit, and these stories were recognized by those who had been brought up in the South as at core the same which they had heard in their childhood from the old "uncles" and "aunties" of the plantation. But there was more. Instead of the old darkies, there was the best storyteller of the time to make his characters as real as the wolf in Little Red Riding Hood, or the Beast who kept Beauty captive. Some found in the book animal-myths valuable as links in the chain with which they hope[d] to penetrate the mysterious and always vanishing recesses of the ethnological labyrinth. Others welcomed it as a contribution to the history of the negro race, in which they were philanthropically interested. But the great majority found in it more. Under the apparently unknown tongue when they had mastered it sufficiently to appreciate its soft elisions and musical inflections, were found to lie humor, wit, philosophy, "unadulterated human nature" and a charming picture of the relation between the old family servant and the family of his master.

It possessed, besides, that fidelity to life, that simplicity of recital and that subtle, indefinable essence which is the unmistakable birthmark of genius. It brought back to them their youth, and changed them to children again, yet with a quickened apprehension which only age and experience can give. With Miss Sally's little boy they sat and heard not mere stories of animal life, but discerned under them wit, wisdom and the philosophy of life. The narrator became no longer only Miss Sally's Little Boy's Uncle Remus, but their Uncle Remus, as well, and Brer Fox and Brer Rabbit took their places among the small but distinguished company who, touched by the light of genius, have become immortal in the realm of literature.

Mr. Harris has achieved the distinction of creating three characters who have already taken their place in this high company. Brer Fox and Brer Rabbit are familiar characters in our speech and have oftener than once been cited as illustrations in the House of Commons and in our own highest deliberative assembly. As might have been foreseen, this success has raised a host of imitators and followers, who have as a rule caught only the outside and followed after a long interval. The result has been a deluge of what are called "dialect-stories," until the public, surfeited by them, has begun almost to shudder at the very name. These writers have supposed that they were writing dialect when they were only writing distorted words and illiterate grammar, not knowing that the master here has used the vehicle only to carry the thought, and that the secret of his craft lies not in the manner so much as in the matter. Herbert Spencer says that, "Astonished at the performances of the English plough, the Hindoos paint it, set it up, and worship it, thus turning a tool into an idol: linguists do the same with language." Uncle Remus, with all his lingo, might be as dull as any of the other stories which, based on the mere counterfeit of mutilated words, have followed in his shining track, but for the stuff which is in it. It is not the abbreviated words nor the elision; but the habit of thought as of speech, the quaint turn of phrase overflowing with humorous suggestion, where sometimes a word carries a whole train of thought, which make up the dialect of Uncle Remus, nor yet is it only these; but it is far more the knowledge of animals, particularly of the animal, Man—"the unadulterated human nature"—which constitutes the stuff in all his stories, and makes them what they are when taken together, perhaps almost the best contribution to our literature which has been given since the war. No wonder it opened the way for others.

No man who has ever written has known one-tenth part about the negro that Mr. Harris knows, and for those who hereafter shall wish to find not merely the words, but the real language of the negro of that section, and the habits of mind of all American negroes of the old time, his works will prove the best thesaurus. The old-time negro is passing away, and his speech with him, as a certain type of old-time gentleman is passing. The new issue, that suc-

ceeds him, may be more gifted in grammatical speech, more able to fulfil the intricate demands of a truly independent Pullman-Portership; more able to hoe the new row of free and insolent citizenship, or to represent the government at home or abroad; and perhaps he will find in time his proper historiographer. But to some who knew the other, the true gentility of the Uncle Remuses, in however homely a garb, calls forth from the past memories which we would never wish to forget; and to us Mr. Harris has done an inestimable service.

The new edition now brought forth by Messrs. Appleton is worthy of the matter. It is in beautiful new type, in a warm, dignified and fitting binding, and is copiously illustrated by Mr. A. B. Frost, with illustrations so apt and admirable—that is, so truly illustrative of the spirit of the work—that Mr. Harris graciously says in his preface that Mr. Frost has made the book his. Whether he has done this or not, he has undoubtedly added to it the additional lustre of his genius, which has this exceptional merit that it is as distinctly American and original as Mr. Harris's own. One could not say more.

William Malone Baskerville

SOURCE: "Joel Chandler Harris," in *Southern Writers: Biographical and Critical Studies, Volume I,* Publishing House M. E. Church, South, 1897, pp. 41-88.

[*The following excerpt is from an essay that is usually considered the first substantial biographical and critical study of Harris. A professor at Vanderbilt University, Baskerville called Harris's plantation folklore stories "the most valuable and the most permanent contribution to American letters in the last quarter of this century."*]

Middle Georgia is the birthplace and home of the raciest and most original kind of Southern humor. In this quarter native material was earliest recognized and first made use of. A school of writers arose who looked out of their eyes and listened with their ears, who took frank interest in things for their own sake, and had enduring astonishment at the most common. They seized the warm and palpitating facts of everyday existence, and gave them to the world with all the accompaniments of quaint dialect, original humor, and Southern plantation life. . . .

In their earlier writings it is a homely wit, in which broad humor and loud laughter predominate; but tears are lurking in the corners of the eyes, and genuine sentiment nestles in the heart. In more recent times the horizon has widened, and there has been a gain in both breadth of view and depth of insight. Genius and art have combined to make this classic soil. . . .

[To] Putnam County was awarded the honor of giving birth to "Uncle Remus," a vertiable Ethiopian Æsop, philosopher, and gentleman, and to the "Little Boy," whose inexhaustible curiosity and eagerness to hear a "story" have called forth the most valuable and, in the writer's opinion, the most permanent contribution to American literature in the last quarter of this century. . . .

A number of things enhanced the value of [*Uncle Remus, His Songs and His Sayings*]—the wealth of folklore, the accurate and entertaining dialect, the delightful stories, the exquisite picture of "the dear remembered days." But the true secret of the power and value of "Uncle Remus" and his "Sayings" does not lie solely in the artistic and masterly setting and narration. The enduring quality lies there, for he has made a past civilization "remarkably striking to the mind's eye," and shown that rare ability "to seize the heart of the suggestion, and make a country famous with a legend." But underneath the art is the clear view of life, as well as humor, wit, philosophy, and "unadulterated human nature." We can get little idea of the revelation which Mr. Harris has made of negro life and character without comparing his conception and delineation with the ideal negro of "My Old Kentucky Home," *Uncle Tom's Cabin,* and *Mars Chan* and *Meh Lady,* and the impossible negro of the minstrel show. . . .

[No] one has equaled the creator of "Uncle Remus," one of the very few creations of American writers worthy of a place in the gallery of the immortals; and he should be hung in the corner with such gentleman as Col. Newcome and Sir Roger de Coverley, and not very far from Rip Van Winkle, my Uncle Toby, and Jack Falstaff.

Before the war Uncle Remus had always exercised authority over his fellow-servants. He had been the captain of the corn pile, the stoutest at the log rolling, the swiftest with the hoe, the neatest with the plow, the leader of the plantation hands. Now he is an old man whose tall figure and venerable appearance are picturesque in the extreme, but he moves and speaks with the vigor of perennial youth. He is the embodiment of the quaint and homely humor, the picturesque sensitiveness—a curious exaltation of mind and temperament not to be defined by words—and the really poetic imagination of the negro race; and over all is diffused the genuine flavor of the old plantation. With the art to conceal art, the author retires behind the scenes and lets this patriarch reveal negro life and character to the world. Now it is under the guise of Brer Rabbit, after his perilous adventure with the tar baby and narrow escape from Brer Fox as he is seen "settin' cross-legged on a chinkapin log koamin' de pitch outen his har wid a chip," and "flingin' back some er his sass, 'Bred and bawn in a brier patch, Brer Fox; bred and bawn in a brier patch!'" Another phase is seen in **"Why Brer Possum Loves Peace,"** a story of indolent good nature, questionable valor, and nonsensical wisdom: "I don' min' fightin' no mo' dan you doz, sez'ee, but I declar' to grashus ef I kin stan' ticklin.' An' down ter dis day," continued Uncle Remus, "down ter dis day, Brer Possum's boun' ter s'render w'en you tech him in de short ribs, en he'll laff ef he knows he's gwine ter be smashed for it." This whimsical defense of inborn cowardice has a touch of nature in it which makes it marvelously akin to Sir John's counterfeiting on Shrewsbury plain. But the prevailing interest is centered in Brer Rabbit's skill in outwitting Brer Fox and the other animals, which is managed with

such cleverness and good nature that we cannot but sympathize with the hero, in spite of his utter lack of conscience or conviction. But the chief merit of these stories, as Mr. [Thomas Nelson] Page has remarked, springs directly from the fact that Uncle Remus knows them, is relating them, and is vivifying them with his own quaintness and humor, and is impressing us in every phase with his own delightful and lovable personality. Mr. Harris's skill in narrative is well-nigh perfect, and the conversation, in which his books abound, is carried on with absolute naturalness and fidelity to life. The habit of thought as well as of speech is strikingly reproduced. Not a word strikes a false note, a scene or incident is out of keeping with the spirit of the life presented. No one has more perfectly preserved some of the most important traits of Southern character, nor more enchantingly presented some of the most beautiful phases of Southern civilization.

Other phases of negro character, very different from those presented in the "Legends," appeared in the "Sayings" and in various "Sketches," which reproduce "the shrewd observations, the curious retorts, the homely thrusts, the quaint comments, and the humorous philosophy of the race of which Uncle Remus is a type." But in *Nights with Uncle Remus, Daddy Jake the Runaway,* and *Uncle Remus and His Friends* we returned again to the old plantation home; "daddy," "mammy," and the "field hands" lived once more with their happy, smiling faces; songs floated out upon the summer air, laden with the perfume of rose and honeysuckle and peach blossom, and mingled with the rollicking medley of the mocking bird; and we felt that somehow over the whole life the spell of genius had been thrown, rendering it immortal. But it is with and through the negro that Mr. Harris has wrought this wonder, for as Mr. Page says: "No man who has ever written has known one-tenth part about the negro that Mr. Harris knows, and for those who hereafter shall wish to find not merely the words, but the real language of the negro of that section, and habits of mind of all American negroes of the old time, his works will prove the best thesaurus." . . .

[If Mr. Harris] should never give us a masterpiece of fiction like his beloved *Vicar of Wakefield, Ivanhoe, Vanity Fair,* or *The Scarlet Letter,* we shall still be forever grateful for the fresh and beautiful stories, the delightful humor, the genial, manly philosophy, and the wise and witty sayings in which his writings abound. His characters have become world possessions; his words are in all our mouths. By virtue of these gifts he will be enrolled in that small but distinguished company of humorists, the immortals of the heart and home, whose genius, wisdom, and charity keep fresh and sweet the springs of life, and Uncle Remus will live always.

The New York Times Saturday Review of Books (essay date 1904)

SOURCE: "'The Tar-Baby and Other Rhymes of Uncle Remus': Harris's Saga-Man Is a Poet of 'Style and Distinction'," in *Critical Essays on Joel Chandler Harris,* G. K. Hall & Co., 1981, pp. 42-43.

Some one has called the rhymes of Uncle Remus indispensable, and the adjective is hardly too strong for the fact. Certainly we do well to cherish to the uttermost a strain that is never to be replaced or imitated. Beside these songs of the ancient negro our own popular songs are thin and acrid. Uncle Remus is a poet with style and distinction and humor and pathos and joy of heart. He opens to us a simple world full of both wisdom and folly, in which tropical temperaments take their ease and find ready expression for a luxuriant imagination. Mr. Harris in all his collections has maintained the characteristic indigenous quality of the negro chants and ditties, and the present collection [*The Tar-Baby and Other Rhymes of Uncle Remus*] is particularly rich in archaeological value. . . .

In the camp meeting songs we have the fervor and intensity lacking in the songs of the plantation, and in the dancing songs we have the pure essence of irresponsibility, the ecstasy of pagan joy, the racial harmony, with exuberant forms of sentiment. Uncle Remus is more than a delightful story-teller—he is a saga-man of a race that has been almost entirely obliterated and that no possible combination of circumstances can restore.

The Nation

SOURCE: A review of *Uncle Remus,* in *The Nation,* Vol. 87, No. 2245, July 9, 1908, pp. 26-27.

Brer Fox, perhaps, might be able to explain why the great classics of the world's light literature should have been produced by men of serious interests, on the whole. . . .

It was not a professional student of folklore, but a Southern journalist, that first gave to the world the adventure of Brer Rabbit with the Tar Baby.

The field which Joel Chandler Harris opened has since been industriously ploughed by the folklorist and the short-story writer, to the greater glory of both. We have had reams of negro fable and tradition that come probably nearer to the scientific standard of anthropologic truth than the earliest narrative of Uncle Remus, and we have had fictive tales of negro belief that are, at first hand, cleverer in plot and dialogue, and more startling in orthography, than the colloquies of Brer Fox and Brer Rabbit. But whether Uncle Remus's combination of just that measure of truth with just that measure of art which makes permanent literature, has been equalled by others, is quite a different question. As a matter of fact, Mr. Harris, in his own later histories of Uncle Remus, showed a falling away from the perfect balance he struck in the first stories. He was deflected, sadly enough, too much towards the truth; began to gather negro lore with professional ardor, and let the formal side suffer. The decline, of course, was from the high standard which he himself had set. Compared with most of the grist that has come from the negro dialect fiction mill, what Uncle Remus had to say always carried with it something of the earth's freshness which it

is not given to the clever magazine writer to put into his pages.

How near to a real folklore, in the sense of a native store of crude belief, Uncle Remus has brought us, will remain for years, we suppose, a mooted question with those interested in negro anthropology. The negro in the South is in more ways than one a source of vexation to the student of ethnic evolution. It will not do to bind the mind of the negro too closely to his African ancestry. What the plantation hand believes now that is to us primitive, what he often says, what he often sings—is it an inheritance brought over from the Dark Continent, or is it the perversion of what he learned in this country from the white man long ago, and what the white man has forgotten? When Anton Dvoràk declared that a national American school of music would be developed on the basis of our negro melodies, evidence was brought forward to show, we believe, that his supposed native negro music has its origin in old Methodist revival hymns set to European tunes. Into voodoo, so far as our knowledge of that dark realm goes, not all that enters is African; Indian and European superstitions are mixed in the hodgepodge. The attempt has been made to trace the history of meaningless words in negro song and dialect back to an African vernacular; but with no apparent success. How much of Uncle Remus that is not Joel Chandler Harris comes from the banks of the Congo, and how much was born on the banks of the Rappahannock and the Chattahoochee, has not yet been shown.

The elements are common, of course, to all peoples. Brer Rabbit and Brer Fox and Jedge B'ar do the same things, more or less, as Coyote, Fox, and Bear among the Plains Indians. But as our children know them they are thrice removed from the tales the original mind of Africa must have evolved regarding them, or their entrancing beasts' counterparts. Extra-African legend has imposed itself on the atavistic belief to make up the creed of the American negro, and the white man who tells the story for his whiter brethren introduces his own modifications. Perhaps we shall not get to the real kernel of the African's soul until one of his own race, following in the steps of a Paul Laurence Dunbar, shall act as interpreter. Until that problematic day, Uncle Remus may rest safely on his laurels. That they will ever be in serious danger, we greatly doubt.

Julia Collier Harris

SOURCE: "'Uncle Remus: His Songs and His Sayings'," in *The Life and Letters of Joel Chandler Harris,* Houghton Mifflin Company, 1918, pp. 142-60.

[The critic, the wife of Harris's eldest son Julian La Rose Harris, published a biography of her father-in-law—from which the following excerpt is taken—ten years after his death. In his Joel Chandler Harris *(1968), R. Bruce Bickley, Jr. calls* The Life and Letters of Joel Chandler Harris *"valuable for its liberal inclusion of previously unpublished letters and reminiscences of Harris's family and friends."]*

Father was in the habit of saying that his career as a writer was wholly "accidental." His insistence on this point was, of course, largely due to his humble estimate of his talents. But the lover of "Uncle Remus" who has fallen under the spell of the old man's humor, tenderness, and dramatic force, is inclined to disagree with the author's own theory of his success, and to believe that aside from all accidents, happy or otherwise, he was bound to fulfill his destiny as a creator of characters that "wind themselves around our hearts and owe little to circumstance." . . .

It was some time in 1878 that there occurred in the course of father's work an incident which became the means of releasing [the] rich store of myths and legends which had slumbered for years in an obscure compartment of his memory. Sam W. Small had been conducting in the *Constitution* a column of anecdotes and sketches in which a negro character, "Uncle Si," figured. When the *Constitution* changed hands, Mr. Small withdrew from the paper, and Captain Howell applied to his new editorial assistant, asking him to carry on the series if possible. This, father was not inclined to do, but he agreed to furnish something in another line. "Uncle Remus's" songs, sayings, and fables was the result. . . .

Other "songs" were contributed throughout 1877, and . . . character sketches of the old man followed in 1878-79, together with the animal stories, including the one about the Tar-Baby. Of all the "Uncle Remus" legends written during twenty-five years and gathered into five separate volumes, the **"Tar-Baby"** story is perhaps the best loved. Father received letters about this story from every quarter of the civilized world. Missionaries have translated it into the Bengali and African dialects; learned professors in France, England, Austria, and Germany have written, suggesting clues as to its source; it has been used to illustrate points in Parliamentary debates, and has been quoted from pulpits and in the halls of Congress.

The great popular success of the legends was a matter of strange surprise to their author. It was "just an accident," he said; and added, "all I did was to write out and put into print the stories I had heard all my life"!

When asked by an interviewer [James B. Murrow] if any particular negro suggested "the quaint and philosophic character which he had built up into one of the monuments of modern literature," he replied:—

"He was not an invention of my own, but a human syndicate, I might say, of three or four old darkies whom I had known. I just walloped them together into one person and called him 'Uncle Remus.' You must remember that sometimes the negro is a genuine and an original philosopher."

On being asked how the legends happened to be put into book form, their author continued:—

"The representative of a New York publisher came to see me, and suggested an 'Uncle Remus' book. I was astonished, but he seemed to be in earnest, and so we picked out of the files of the *Constitution* enough matter for a little volume, and it was printed. To my surprise, it was successful." . . .

Father took great interest in the illustrations for the book. . . .

Not until Mr. A. B. Frost brought the skill of his pencil and the inimitable inventiveness and vigor of his imagination to bear upon Brer Rabbit and Brer Fox did their "compiler" feel a thrill of satisfaction—I might say of enthusiasm. He expressed this later on when he wrote to Frost, "You have breathed the breath of life into these amiable brethren of wood and field. . . . The book was mine, but you have made it yours, both sap and pith."

It seems a commonplace now to speak of the "success" of "Uncle Remus," since for two generations the old man and his "amiable brethren of wood and field" have been the dearest friends of thousands of children all over the world—for the book has been translated into many languages. But it may not be known that the collected stories were a conspicuous success from the day they appeared on the market. . . .

The book was favorably noticed in every paper of any importance in the country, and scientific publications devoted columns to its value as a contribution to folk-lore.

The stress laid upon this aspect of the stories always amused father. He once had occasion to write a review of some folk-tales of the South-west, and in this connection he said:—

"First let us have the folk-tales told as they were intended to be told, for the sake of amusement—as a part of the art of literary entertainment. Then, if the folk-lorists find in them anything of value to their pretensions let it be picked out and preserved with as little cackling as possible."

Certainly Uncle Remus was capable of following his own advice, for the quality most conspicuously absent from the tales is pedantry.

"It is but fair to say that ethnological considerations formed no part of the undertaking which has resulted in the publication of this volume," wrote the author in the introduction to the ***Songs and Sayings.*** Nevertheless, he had most carefully investigated the genuineness of all the tales, and in every case had sifted out the variants and had taken pains to retain the version which seemed to him most characteristic, after which he proceeded to give it "without embellishment and without exaggeration."

Whether or not father had anything more than a passing interest in folk-lore *before* the stories were published, he certainly made some study of the subject later on. He was a subscriber to the *Folk-Lore Journal,* published in London, and his library was well stocked with the folk-lore of different nations; but never for one instant did the humorist and imaginative writer separate himself from his "bump of locality" and get lost in the complicated mazes of ethnic or philologic investigation,—for which let the sophisticated and overwise children of the present generation be duly grateful! . . .

Before leaving the subject of the first volume of "Uncle Remus" stories, I cannot refrain from quoting a paragraph of the introduction, in which father touches on the prowess of their hero, Brer Rabbit, proceeding to link up his salient characteristics with the psychology of the negro. It is in reference to the almost invariable conquest of the fox by the rabbit that the author says:—

"It needs no scientific investigation to show why he (the negro) selects as his hero the weakest and most harmless of all animals, and brings him out victorious in contests with the bear, the wolf, and the fox. It is not *virtue* that triumphs, but *helplessness;* it is not *malice,* but *mischievousness.*"

Indeed, the parallel between the case of the "weakest" of all animals who must, perforce, triumph through his shrewdness, and the humble condition of the slave raconteur is not without its pathos and poetry.

Finally, the reader not familiar with plantation life is counseled to "imagine that the myth-stories of Uncle Remus are told night after night to a little boy by an old negro who appears to be venerable enough to have lived during the period which he describes—who has nothing but pleasant memories of the discipline of slavery—and who has all the prejudices of caste and pride of family that were the natural results of the system." I have been asked many times if my husband, the eldest son of the family, was "the little boy" of the stories. He was not; and strangely enough, father never told these stories to his own or any other children. His rôle was to record, not to recount. In a letter to Joe Syd Turner, one of his old playmates, and the son of Joseph Addison Turner, of Turnwold, written in 1883, shortly before the publication of the second volume of "myths and tales of the old plantation," father said:—

"Did it never occur to you that *you* might be the *little boy* in *Uncle Remus?* I suppose you have forgotten the comical tricks you played on old George Terrell, and the way you wheedled him out of a part of his gingercakes and cider. Lord! those were the wonderfullest days we shall ever see."

The aftermath of the appearance of *Uncle Remus: His Songs and His Sayings,* demonstrated to father, with peculiar force, one thing: that he was to be educated in the subject of folk-lore whether he willed it or not! I am certain that when "Uncle Remus" received his first greeting from the English-speaking public, his creator was ignorant of the fact that variants of the legend were to be found among so many of the primitive peoples.

Concerning the number of communications from various parts of the globe which came on the heels of the first volume of tales, father once said:—

"To be frank, I did not know much about folk-lore, and I didn't think that anybody else did. Imagine my surprise when I began to receive letters from learned philologists and folk-lore students from England to India, asking all sorts of questions and calling upon me to explain how certain stories told in the rice-fields of India and on the cotton-fields of Georgia were identical, or similar, or at least akin. Then they wanted to know why this folk-lore had been handed down for centuries and perhaps for thousands of years. They wanted to know, too, why the negro makes Brer Rabbit so cunning and masterful. These letters came from royal institutes and literary societies, from scholars and from travelers. What answer could I make to them? None—none whatever. All that I know—all that we Southerners know—about it, is that every old plantation mammy in the South is full of these stories. One thing is certain-the negroes did not get them from the whites: probably they are of remote African origin."

In a letter, dated December 14, 1880, from James Wood Davidson, for whose volume, *Living Writers of the South,* father had prepared an index when general factotum of the *Monroe Advertiser,* the writer said of **Uncle Remus:**—

"It is the only *true* negro dialect I ever saw printed. It marks an era in its line—the first successful attempt to write what the negro has actually said, and in his own peculiar way. After so many dead failures by a hundred authors to write thus, and after the pitiful *niaiseries* of the so-called negro minstrels, **Uncle Remus** is a revelation."

Father, however, did not claim to be the pioneer in this field; he justly and generously maintained that the first accurate and artistic depicter of the negro was the young Texan, Irwin Russell, who died in the early days of his promise, and whose book of verses, *Christmas Night in the Quarters,* portrays the negro with sympathy and fidelity. . . .

But Irwin Russell made no attempt, in his short career, to perfect himself in the dialect of the negro. It was in the truth and flavor of negro characterization that he excelled. Either because of the fineness of his ear or the accuracy of his memory or the wonderful assimilative power of his mind, or the combination of all three, father obtained an early and a complete mastery of the dialects of the American negro. In an interview in 1881, Walter H. Page, now American Ambassador to the Court of St. James, says: "I have Mr. Harris's own word for it that he can *think* in the negro dialect. He could translate even Emerson, perhaps Bronson Alcott, in it, as well as he can tell the adventures of Brer Rabbit."

And Thomas Nelson Page, now American Ambassador to Italy, who has himself so beautifully depicted certain phases of life in the South during and following the Civil War, accurately appraised father's knowledge of the "old-time" negro and his vernacular when he wrote: "No man who has ever written has known one-tenth part about the negro that Mr. Harris knows, and for those who hereafter shall wish to find not merely words, but the real language of the negro of that section, and the habits of all American negroes of the old time, his works will prove the best thesaurus."

Such appreciations as this and others from his colleagues were, of course, gratifying to father, who, nevertheless, in his almost incredible humility, was skeptical of all praise. But the tributes that pleased him most were those that came from children, or from men and women who found their childhood memories revived by these legends of the old plantation. . . .

Sometime during the course of this year a letter had come from Mark Twain, expressing his admiration for *Uncle Remus,* and proposing that father should visit him in Hartford at some early date, adding that he would like to discuss some outlines of negro fables which he had, one in particular being a "ghost story." Father replied to him. . . .

In his reply, Mr. Clemens commented on his friend's modest estimate of his abilities:—

"You can argue *yourself* into the delusion that the principle of life is in the stories themselves and not in their setting, but you will save labor by stopping with that solitary convert, for he is the only intelligent one you will bag. In reality the stories are only alligator pears—one eats them merely for the sake of the dressing. 'Uncle Remus' is most deftly drawn and is a lovable and delightful creation; he and the little boy and their relations with each other are bright, fine literature, and worthy to live. . . . But I seem to be proving to the man that made the multiplication table that twice one is two."

Mr. Clemens offered some advice regarding the publishing of a second volume of tales and sent the outline of the "ghost story" (called in his version "The Golden Arm"), which had been told him in childhood by his "Uncle Dan'l," a slave of sixty years, before the flickering blaze of a kitchen fire. Father was familiar with a variant of this story and afterward developed it in the dramatic **"Ghost Story"** told by 'Tildy, and incorporated in *Nights with Uncle Remus.* Mr. Clemens was anxious for father to appear with him in readings, and followed up this letter with a request that father meet him in New Orleans, where he was to stop for a few days in the course of a trip down the Mississippi River with Mr. Osgood, the publisher, to discuss this and other matters. . . .

It was inevitable that the impediment in his speech and his "immortal shyness" should combine to make it impossible for "Uncle Remus" to recount the exploits of "Brer Rabbit" from the platform.

H. E. Harman

SOURCE: "Joel Chandler Harris: The Prose Poet of the South," in *South Atlantic Quarterly,* Summer, 1918, pp. 243-48.

As a story teller [Mr. Harris] had few equals, but his material was crude and the dialect difficult and practical-

ly unknown, outside of the South. But when he wove into these stories of negro lore and the crude life of the swamp and the field a thread of poetic inspiration, his pages took on a new lustre. There came up before the reader ideals of beauty which did not seem to belong to the lowly surroundings where the simple plot was laid. The dim fireside of the negro cabin became something different from the original; upon the dusky face of the old slave a new light shone, and down through the sedge-covered field and up the rough hillside of pines and dogwood, there spread a halo of romance, which the reader had never seen or dreamed of before.

John Herbert Nelson

SOURCE: "Uncle Remus Arrives," in *The Negro Character in American Literature,* McGrath Publishing Company, 1926, pp. 107-19.

[The following excerpt is from a controversial study of African Americans in American literature written by a professor at the University of Kansas; the critic, who originally began his work as his doctoral dissertation at Cornell, writes in his preface that he "was attracted to certain American fictional types, particularly to the negro—perhaps the best portrayed of them all."]

If justice be done him, Joel Chandler Harris will be known to the future as the supreme interpreter of the American negro in his most attractive period of development. In the transitional period just after the Civil War, when the old negro of slavery times had not been quite supplanted by the free-born generation which we know today; in a day when the old negro was suspicious of the new, and the new was scornful of the old; in an age when the old loyalty and the new independence were still existing side by side; when the group of rural phenomena which had once formed the whole of the negro's surroundings, and had supplied all the material for the play of his fancy, was rapidly being enlarged to include all the man-made contrivances of the city—it was in this time that Harris lived and wrote. The negro of his writings, who belonged to the eighties and nineties of last century, has passed from the stage, and into his place has stepped the free American black—a quite different person. . . .

Most of the great creators of characters in our language— Shakespeare, Chaucer, Thackeray—have interpreted their own race, have worked with characters whose ways of thinking have been largely the same as the author's. But Harris has gone outside himself, and has entered into the thoughts and feelings of a human type different from his own in spirit, in psychology and emotional temper, in disposition, in talents and preferences; and has laid bare the very soul that he found there. . . .

Far from being an uninspired and perfunctory journalist, as some would have us believe, Harris was at heart a poet. Here and there in his pages one runs across passages of surprising beauty which flash out all the more forcibly because they are embedded in prose marked by simplicity and directness. His style suited perfectly his material, and so well did he blend excellent material with simple dignity, directness of expression, and sincerity of feeling that his best books have become classics. Despite his modest contentions, then, he was much more than a mere recorder of folk-stories.

The stories are themselves by no means to be despised. They comprise most of the oral tradition and literature of the quarters, and are written in such realistic form that they might well have been taken down verbatim—as indeed some of them were. Yet, valuable though they are, their setting and the characters who tell them are worth far more. . . .

[We] tolerate the stories to get what comes with them—the scene in the humble cabin, the incidental remarks of the speaker, the characterization of the story-teller himself. All Harris required was the bare outline of the folk-tale; he gave it its dressing, putting it in words he knew the speaker would use—words which he had heard used over and over again.

In depicting the negro Harris was, in his best work, a consistent realist. . . .

Remus's every word and action suggest the actual; we are cast under no illusion in reading of them, but feel that they belong to life. . . .

Uncle Remus's stories told to Miss Sally's "little boy" are ever mixed with remarks about the world around him. . . .

In all these remarks his dialect is the best to be found anywhere; it is convincing to the very smallest phrase. It was largely, or mainly, because of his mastery of the vernacular that Harris achieved his triumph. . . .

In reporting realistic negro dialogue Harris has never been surpassed. He reproduced a thousand homely phrases to be found nowhere else in print. Other writers have given individual words, phrases, and speeches as genuine as his; but in successfully continuing the dialect through page after page, even through volume after volume, without becoming artificial or involved and without lapsing into mere provincial English, he stands alone. So uniformly excellent is his work that any page of it will show the greatness of his mastery.

Harris treated the negro not as a type, but created distinct personalities. . . .

[It] is well nigh impossible that there will ever arise another Uncle Remus. He is as distinct a personality as the Wife of Bath or Bottom the Weaver or Colonel Newcome, and yet he is more than an individual. Despite an obvious individuality, he typifies the whole negro race as it was in that momentary and evanescent phase following emancipation. . . .

Never was a story-teller—not even the immortal Scheher-

azade herself—so abundantly supplied with material. Never was material fresher, more free from conventionality, more pleasingly naive and original. Into the primitive land of negro folk-lore—a well-ordered little world, peopled with comfortably dressed, fun-loving, talkative beasts, strangely human in their foibles—Uncle Remus enters with the confidence of guide and interpreter, and fully informs the little boy of the various misadventures of lumbersome Brer Bear, of would-be shrewd and daring Brer Fox, of vicious Brer Wolf, and others, all of whom fall victim to the inordinately lucky and unscrupulous hero, Brer Rabbit—the most picaresque of all picaresque figures. Uncle Remus knows the personal history of all the animals—of the whole forest tribe, from mammoth Brer Elephant to inconspicuous Brer Mud "Turkle."

We are not long in discovering, what Harris and many others pointed out, that the animals are the negroes themselves, and that Brer Rabbit represents the ideal hero of their primitive dream world—an individual able, through craft and downright trickery, to get the better of a master class seemingly unbeatable. The ideals of the animals are the negro's; their prying dispositions, their neighborli-

From The Favorite Uncle Remus, *written by Joel Chandler Harris. Illustrated by A. B. Frost.*

ness, their company manners, their petty thefts, their amusements are all the negro's; Brer Rabbit likes the same kind of food, the same brand of fun, as his interpreter does: he has the same outlook on life. Even the hopeless incongruity of this animal world—the rabbit and the fox owning cows, and hurting their "hands," and feeling an elementary kind of responsibility for their families—is part and parcel of the negro spirit. It is a product of his primitive outlook on life, of a poetical feeling that takes no account of the hard logic of consistency.

All this Uncle Remus shows about his race without detracting from his own distinct individuality. He is always consistent, always the same genial exponent of the psychology of the negro. Although he looks with longing eyes to the past, he is not exactly sentimental about the matter; he brings the past so vividly into the present that he actually lives it over again; and moreover he never forgets the immediate moment—with its duties, its dinners, its "sunshine niggers," its talk, and its leisure. He is at once a child of the present and a torch-bearer from the past, and yet, though eminently typical of his race, he is as much an individual as Sam Weller.

More enjoyable than the stories he tells are their setting and Remus's incidental comments. Practically any of the stories will show much about the old man himself. Note, for instance, how the setting of **"Brother Mud Turtle's Trickery"** is employed advantageously in character portrayal:

> "I don't like deze yer tales 'bout folks, no how you kin fix um," said Uncle Remus, after an unusually long pause, during which he rubbed his left hand with the right, in order to run the rheumatism out. "No, suh, I don't like um, kaze folks can't play no tricks, ner get even wid der neighbors, widout hurtin' somebody's feelin's, er breakin' some law er nudder, er gwine 'ginst what de preacher say.

> "Look at dat an what I des been tellin' you 'bout. He let de udder man fool 'im en ketch 'im, en mo' dan dat, he let um tote 'im off to de calaboose. He oughter been tuck dar; I ain't 'sputin' dat, yit ef dat had been some er de creeters, dey'd er sholy got loose fum dar."

This passage is filled with suggestions about the speaker; it emphasizes his love of "getting even" with his neighbors by a kind of trickery which, while effective, will hurt nobody's feelings, his inconsistency, his lack of sympathy for some of the white man's established conventions, his fear of the law, and his respect for religious tenets. Moreover, it shows his particular idiom and a distinctive habit of speech, of repeating himself when he is pleased with a statement or when he is firmly convinced of his opinion— "I don't like um," repeated. . . .

Here the whole range of the negro character is revealed so thoroughly that even during the narrative proper one is conscious of the pervading personality of the speaker.

Possibly, however, he appears to still greater advantage in

certain sketches, not folk-tales at all, which Harris included, along with the folk-stories, in **Uncle Remus: His Songs and His Sayings** and **Uncle Remus and His Friends.** Strange to say, these sketches have been neglected by critics, yet they are not only as delightful as anything Harris ever wrote, but have no interest but Uncle Remus—not even the slight distraction of a folktale. . . .

[All the skits are] excellent; and in each one of them appears the same quaint old man. Never for a moment does he deviate from the personality which Harris first conceived about 1880.

Uncle Remus is truly one of the great products of American literature—a lasting embodiment of what the American negro was during the period of development when he was most original and attractive, and a character which will insure Harris lasting fame. He is, to be sure, no great tragic figure, no suffering hero, torn by conflicting desires, dominated by an overwhelming passion, ruined by unworthy ambitions or mad desires, subjected to the trial of death or dire disgrace; his soul receives no such test as that afforded by a Goethe or a Shakespeare—lacking which it cannot of course measure up to the great spirit of Faust or Hamlet. But surely Harris's accomplishment is, for all that, not small. To set the negro forth in his happy, his whimsical, his pathetic mood, convincingly, true to nature, alive and breathing—to have done this is much—is, perhaps, all of which any white author, great or small, would be capable.

Sterling A. Brown

SOURCE: "Negro Character as Seen by White Authors," in *The Journal of Negro Education,* Vol. II, No. 2, April, 1933, pp. 179-203.

[The following excerpt is from a seminal essay by African American author and critic Sterling A. Brown. In his Joel Chandler Harris, *R. Bruce Bickley, Jr. writes, "Overtly sociological approaches to Harris began in the 1930s with the work of the black author Sterling Brown. Brown thought Uncle Remus one of the classic characters in American literature, but he still saw him as a stereotypical portrait of the prewar contented slave, an image that influenced later literary portraits of the black man. Decades later, Brown's views were still being echoed by black critics."]*

The Negro has met with as great injustice in American literature as he has in American life. The majority of books about Negroes merely stereotype Negro character. It is the purpose of this paper to point out the prevalence and history of these stereotypes. Those considered important enough for separate classification, although overlappings *do* occur, are seven in number: (1) The Contented Slave, (2) The Wretched Freeman, (3) The Comic Negro, (4) The Brute Negro, (5) The Tragic Mulatto, (6) The Local Color Negro, and (7) The Exotic Primitive. . . .

It can be said . . . that all of these stereotypes are marked either by exaggeration or omissions; that they all agree in stressing the Negro's divergence from an Anglo-Saxon norm to the flattery of the latter; they could all be used, as they probably are, as justification of racial proscription; they all illustrate dangerous specious generalizing from a few particulars recorded by a single observer from a restricted point of view—which is itself generally dictated by the desire to perpetuate a stereotype. All of these stereotypes are abundantly to be found in American literature, and are generally accepted as contributions to true racial understanding. Thus one critic [John Herbert Nelson], setting out imposingly to discuss "the Negro character" in American literature, can still say, unabashedly, that *"The whole range of the Negro character is revealed thoroughly,"* in one twenty-six-line sketch by Joel Chandler Harris of Br'er Fox and Br'er Mud Turtle.

Joel Chandler Harris is better known for his valuable contribution to literature and folk-lore in recording the Uncle Remus stories than for his aid in perpetuation of the "plantation Negro" stereotype. Nevertheless, a merely cursory study of Uncle Remus' character would reveal his close relationship to the "Caesars," "Hectors," "Pompeys," *et al.* of the pro-slavery novel, and to [Thomas Nelson] Page's "Uncle Jack" and "Uncle Billy." In Uncle Remus's philosophizing about the old days of slavery there is still the wistful nostalgia. Harris comments, "In Middle Georgia the relations between master and slave were as perfect as they could be under the circumstances." This might mean a great deal, or nothing, but it is obvious from other words of Harris that, fundamentally, slavery was to him a kindly institution, and the Negro was contented. Slavery was:

> . . . in some of its aspects far more beautiful and inspiring than *any* of the relations between employers and the employed in this day.

Anne Thaxter Eaton

SOURCE: "Unicorns and Common Creatures," in *Reading with Children,* The Viking Press, 1940, pp. 97-118.

A friendly introduction to **Uncle Remus Stories** by Joel Chandler Harris should come very early in a child's life. Here is a book of sheer delight and a humor that is deep and genuine. No child who has had a good Negro nurse will ever forget her, for of all the adults with whom he has associated in childhood she it was who was most nearly able to enjoy what he enjoyed in the same way. This ability to see from the child's standpoint, this spontaneity and joy in story-telling that belongs to the American Negro, Joel Chandler Harris understood and embodied in his Uncle Remus books.

To a child avid for reading the dialect will be no obstacle. Northern nine-year-olds, in fact, whose only contact with the South had come through Joel Chandler Harris's books, have been known not only to read the Uncle Remus stories to themselves but to essay reading them aloud to other children. Should children be deterred, however, by

words with which they are unfamiliar, it is the plain duty of parents, teachers, and librarians to introduce them to this great piece of American literature. There is no better book for the family where reading aloud is the custom, even though there is no expert in Negro dialect present to do the reading.

Thomas H. English

SOURCE: "In Memory of Uncle Remus," in *The Southern Literary Messenger,* Vol. II, No. 2, February, 1940, pp. 77-83.

[An American critic and educator who was the curator of the Joel Chandler Harris Memorial Collection at Emory University, English edited Seven Tales of Uncle Remus *(1948), a book that R. Bruce Bickley, Jr. calls "the last [edition] of original Harris stories"; the volume includes two tales that the editor discovered in manuscript at the Harris Collection. English also edited Harris's novel* Qua: A Romance of the Revolution *(1946) and the letters collection* Mark Twain to Uncle Remus, 1881-1885 *(1953). In addition, he is the author of* A. B. Frost and His Predecessors Illustrating Uncle Remus *(1978) as well as the co-author with Bickley of* Joel Chandler Harris: A Reference Guide *(1978).]*

Shortly after joining [the Atlanta *Constitution,* Joel Chandler Harris began] the series of Negro dialect sketches for which he created the character of Uncle Remus, who was to reach his full stature as the teller of the folk tales of the old plantation with the publication of the original Tar-Baby story in July, 1879.

Uncle Remus caught on immediately. To many of the older generation he brought nostalgic memories of childhood friends in the quarters, house servants or field hands, who had told them long ago the tales of Brer Rabbit and Brer Fox in the very manner which Joel Chandler Harris had made his own. To the youngest generation he brought a story-telling art inexpressibly droll and irresistibly taking, which, while it avoided the Sunday-school morality of so much juvenile literature, yet was interpenetrated with an earthy wisdom that gave direction and force to fancy and humor. . . .

If *Uncle Remus* is not an American classic, then our literature has not yet produced one. . . .

There is no lack of recognition of the part played by Mr. Harris as the channel by which was transmitted the repertory of folk tales that, with the spirituals, most fully represent the untutored genius of the Negro slave. The folk tales, with their store of racial wisdom and tang of racial genius, might have passed into oblivion had it not been that at a fortunate moment the body of traditional matter was recorded by one of another race whose ripe talents included in the highest degree both critical insight and sympathy. It is a fact too seldom insisted on that Uncle Remus is at least as great a creation as Brer Rabbit.

Uncle Remus is great because he is a persuasive human figure in a recognizable background. The tales that he tells are great because in them we hear the tones of a human voice vibrant with the overtones and undertones of a rich personality.

Bernard Wolfe

SOURCE: "Uncle Remus and the Malevolent Rabbit," in *Commentary,* Vol. 8, No. 1, July, 1949, pp. 31-41.

[The following excerpt is from what is often considered the most provocative essay to have been written on Uncle Remus. Wolfe maintains that although Harris admired and identified with African Americans, at his core he refused to accept the racial themes of his tales and was unable to transcend his prejudice. In addition, the critic notes, Uncle Remus's smiling face concealed real malevolence toward the white race, exemplified in the behavior of Brer Rabbit.]

Uncle Remus—a kind of blackface Will Rogers, complete with standard minstrel dialect and plantation shuffle—has had remarkable staying power in our popular culture, much more than Daddy Long Legs, say, or even Uncle Tom. . . .

For almost seventy years, Uncle Remus has been the prototype of the Negro grinner-giver. Nothing ever clouds the "beaming countenance" of the "venerable old darky"; nothing ever interrupts the flow of his "hearty," "mellow," "cheerful and goodhumored" voice as, decade after decade, he presents his Brer Rabbit stories to the nation.

But Remus too is a white man's brainchild. . . .

When Remus grins, Harris is pulling the strings; when he "gives" his folk stories, he is the ventriloquist's dummy on Harris's knee.

The setting for these stories never varies: the little white boy, son of "Miss Sally" and "Mars John," the plantation owners, comes "hopping and skipping" into the old Negro's cabin down in back of the "big house" and the story telling session gets under way. Remus's face "breaks up into little eddies of smiles"; he takes his admirer on his knee, "strokes the child's hair thoughtfully and caressingly," calls him "honey." The little boy "nestles closer" to his "sable patron" and listens with "open-eyed wonder."

No "sanctions of fear and force" here, Harris insists—the relationship between narrator and auditor is one of unmitigated tenderness. Remus "gives," with a "kindly beam" and a "most infectious chuckle"; the little boy receives with mingled "awe," "admiration," and "delight." But, if one looks more closely, within the magnanimous caress is an incredibly malevolent blow.

Of the several Remus collections published by Harris, the first and most famous is **Uncle Remus: His Songs and His Sayings.** Brer Rabbit appears twenty-six times in this book, encounters the Fox twenty times, soundly trounces him nineteen times. The Fox, on the other hand, achieves only two very minor triumphs—one over the Rabbit, another over the Sparrow. On only two other occasions is the Rabbit victimized even slightly, both times by animals as puny as himself (the Tarrypin, the Buzzard); but when he is pitted against adversaries as strong as the Fox (the Wolf, the Bear, once the whole Animal Kingdom) he emerges the unruffled winner. The Rabbit finally kills off all three of his powerful enemies. The Fox is made a thorough fool of by all the weakest animals—the Buzzard, the Tarrypin, the Bull-Frog.

All told, there are twenty-eight victories of the Weak over the Strong; ultimately all the Strong die violent deaths at the hands of the Weak; and there are, at most, two very insignificant victories of the Strong over the Weak. . . . Admittedly, folk symbols are seldom systematic, clean-cut, or specific; they are cultural shadows thrown by the unconscious, and the unconscious is not governed by the sharp-edged neatness of the filing cabinet. But still, on the basis of the tally-sheet alone, is it too far-fetched to take Brer Rabbit as a symbol—about as sharp as Southern sanctions would allow—of the Negro slave's festering hatred of the white man?

It depends, of course, on whether these are animals who maul and murder each other, or human beings disguised as animals. Here Harris and Remus seem to differ. "In dem days," Remus often starts, "de creeturs wuz santer'n 'roun' same like fokes." But for Harris—so he insists—this anthropomorphism is only incidental. What the stories depict, he tells us, is only the "roaring comedy of animal life."

Is it? These are very un-Aesopian creatures who speak a vaudeville dialect, hold candy-pulls, run for the legislature, fight and scheme over gold mines, compete for women in elaborate rituals of courtship and self-aggrandizement, sing plantation ditties about "Jim Crow," read the newspapers after supper, and kill and maim each other—not in gusts of endocrine Pavlov passion but cold-bloodedly, for prestige, plotting their crafty moves in advance and often using accomplices. . . . Harris sees no malice in all this, even when heads roll. Brer Rabbit, he explains, is moved not by "malice, but mischievousness." But Brer Rabbit "mischievously" scalds the Wolf to death, makes the innocent Possum die in a fire to cover his own crimes, tortures and probably murders the Bear by setting a swarm of bees on him—and, after causing the fatal beating of the Fox, carries his victim's head to Mrs. Fox and her children, hoping to trick them into eating it in their soup. . . .

One dramatic tension in these stories seems to be a gastronomic one: *Will the communal meal ever take place in the "Animal" Kingdom?* . . .

Remus is not an anthropomorphist by accident. His theme is a *human* one—neighborliness—and the communal meal is a symbol for it. His moral? There are no good neighbors in the world, neither equality nor fraternity. But the moral has an underside: the Rabbit can never be trapped.

Another tension runs through the stories: *Who gets the women?* In sex, Brer Rabbit is at his most aggressive—and his most invincible. Throughout he is engaged in murderous competition with the Fox and the other animals for the favors of "Miss Meadows en de gals."

In their sexual competition the Rabbit never fails to humiliate the Fox viciously. "I'll show Miss Meadows en de gals dat I'm de boss er Brer Fox," he decides. And he does: through the most elaborate trickery he persuades the Fox to put on a saddle, then rides him past Miss Meadows' house, digging his spurs in vigorously. . . . And in sex, it would seem, there are no false distinctions between creatures—all differences in status are irrelevant. At Miss Meadows' the feuds of the work-a-day world must be suspended, "kaze Miss Meadows, she done put her foot down, she did, en say dat w'en dey come ter her place dey hatter hang up a flag er truce at de front gate en 'bide by it."

The truce is all to the Rabbit's advantage, because if the competitors start from scratch in the sexual battle the best man must win—and the best man is invariably Brer Rabbit. The women themselves want the best man to win. Miss Meadows decides to get some peace by holding a contest and letting the winner have his pick of the girls. The Rabbit mulls the problem over. He sings ironically,

> Make a bow ter de Buzzard en den ter de
>   Crow
> Takes a limber-toe gemmun fer ter jump
>   Jim Crow.

Then, through a tricky scheme, he proceeds to outshine all the stronger contestants.

Food-sharing, sex-sharing—the Remus stories read like a catalogue of Southern racial taboos, all standing on their heads. The South, wearing the blinders of stereotype, has always tried to see the Negro as a "roaringly comic" domestic animal. Understandably; for animals of the tame or domestic variety are not menacing—they are capable only of mischief, never of malice. But the Negro slave, through his anthropomorphic Rabbit stories, seems to be hinting that even the frailest and most humble of "animals" can let fly with the most bloodthirsty aggressions. And these aggressions take place in the two most sacrosanct areas of Southern racial etiquette: the gastronomic and the erotic.

The South, with its "sanctions of fear and force," forbids Negroes to eat at the same table with whites. But Brer Rabbit, through an act of murder, *forces* Brer Fox and all his associates to share their food with him. The South enjoins the Negro, under penalty of death, from coming near the white man's women—although the white man has free access to the Negro's women. But Brer Rabbit flauntingly demonstrates his sexual superiority over all the other animals and, as the undisputed victor in the sexual competition, gets his choice of *all* the women.

And yet, despite these food and sex taboos, for two solid centuries—for the Rabbit stories existed long before Harris put them on paper—Southerners chuckled at the way the Rabbit terrorized all the other animals into the communal meal, roared at the Rabbit's guile in winning the girls away from the Fox *by jumping Jim Crow.* And they were endlessly intrigued by the O. Henry spasm of the miraculous in the very last story, right after the Fox's death: "Some say dat . . . Brer Rabbit married ole Miss Fox. . . ."

An interesting denouement, considering the sexual fears which saturate the South's racial attitudes. Still more interesting that Southern whites should even have countenanced it, let alone revelled in it. . . .

Significantly, the goal of eating and sex, as depicted in Uncle Remus, is not instinct-gratification. The overriding drive is for *prestige*—the South is a prestige-haunted land. And it is in that potent intangible that the Rabbit is always paid off most handsomely for his exploits. Throughout, as he terrorizes the Strong, the "sassy" Rabbit remains bland, unperturbed, sure of his invincibility. When he humiliates the Fox by turning him into a saddle-horse, he mounts him "same's ef he wuz king er de patter-rollers." ("Patter-rollers," Harris cheerfully points out, were the white patrols that terrorized Negro slaves so they wouldn't wander off the plantations.)

Brer Rabbit, in short, has all the jaunty topdog airs and attitudes which a slave can only dream of having. And, like the slave, he has a supremely cynical view of the social world, since he sees it from below. The South is the most etiquette-ridden region of the country; and the Rabbit sees all forms of etiquette as hypocritical and absurd. Creatures meet, address each other with unctuous politeness, inquire after each other's families, pass the time of day with oily clichés—and all the while they are plotting to humiliate, rob, and assassinate each other. The Rabbit sees through it all; if he is serene it is only because he can plot more rapidly and with more deadly efficiency than any of the others.

The world, in Brer Rabbit's wary eyes, is a jungle. Life is a battle-unto-the-death for food, sex, power, prestige, a battle without rules. There is only one reality in this life: who is on top? But Brer Rabbit wastes no time lamenting the mad unneighborly scramble for the top position. Because it is by no means ordained that the Weak can never take over. In his topsy-turvy world, to all practical purposes, the Weak *have* taken over. In one episode, the Rabbit falls down a well in a bucket. He can get back up only by enticing the Fox to climb into the other bucket. The Fox is duped: he drops down and the Rabbit rises, singing as he passes his enemy:

> Good-by, Brer Fox, take keer yo' cloze
> Fer dis is de way de worril goes
> Some goes up en some goes down
> You'll git ter de bottom all safe en soun'.

This is the theme song of the stories. The question remains, who sings it? The Rabbit is a creation of Uncle

Remus's people; is it, then, Uncle Remus singing? But Uncle Remus is a creation of Joel Chandler Harris. . . .

There is a significant difference in ages—some hundreds of years—between Uncle Remus and Brer Rabbit. The Rabbit had been the hero of animal stories popular among Negroes from the early days of slavery; these were genuine folk tales told by Negroes to Negroes and handed down in oral form. Uncle Remus was added only when Harris, in packaging the stories—using the Negro grin for gift-wrapping—invented the Negro narrator to sustain the dialect.

Harris, then, fitted the hate-imbued folk materials into a framework, a white man's framework, of "love." He took over the animal characters and situations of the original stories and gave them a human setting: the loving and lovable Negro narrator, the adoring white auditor. Within this framework of love, the blow was heavily padded with caresses and the genuine folk was almost emasculated into the cute folksy.

Almost, but not quite. Harris all his life was torn between his furtive penchant for fiction and his profession of journalism. It was the would-be novelist in him who created Remus, the "giver" of interracial caresses; but the trained journalist in him, having too good an eye and ear, reported the energetic folk blow in the caress. Thus the curious tension in his versions between "human" form and "animal" content.

Before Harris, few Southerners had ever faced squarely the aggressive symbolism of Brer Rabbit, or the paradox of their delight in it. Of course: it was part of the Southerner's undissected myth—often shared by the Negroes—that his cherished childhood sessions in the slave quarters were bathed in two-way benevolence. But Harris, by writing the white South and its Negro tale-spinners into the stories, also wrote in its unfaced paradoxes. Thus his versions helped to rip open the racial myth—and with it, the interracial grin. . . .

[The South] could not shake off the feeling that Brer Rabbit's overtones were more than just funny. And Harris, too, wavered. To a British folklorist editor he wrote, suddenly reversing himself, that the stories were "more important than humorous." And in the introduction to his book he explains that "however humorous it may be in effect, its intention is perfectly serious. . . . It seems to me that a volume written wholly in dialect must have its solemn, not to say melancholy features."

What was it that Harris sporadically found "important," "solemn," even "melancholy" here? It turns out to be the *Americanism* of Brer Rabbit: "it needs no scientific investigation," Harris continues in his introduction, "to show why he [the Negro] selects as his hero the weakest and most harmless of all animals. . . . It is not virtue that triumphs, but helplessness. . . . Indeed, the parallel between the case of the 'weakest' of all animals, who must, perforce, triumph through his shrewdness, and the humble condition of the slave raconteur, is not without its pathos."

A suggestive idea. But such a "parallel" could not have been worked out in the African jungle, before slavery; it implies that Brer Rabbit, after all, was born much closer to the Mississippi than to the Congo. . . . This crucial sentence does not occur in later editions. Instead we read: "It would be presumptious [*sic*] in me to offer an opinion as to the origins of these curious myth-stories; but, *if ethnologists should discover that they did not originate with the African, the proof to that effect should be accompanied with a good deal of persuasive eloquence.*"

In this pressing sentence we can see Harris's whole fragmented psyche mirrored. Like all the South, he was caught in a subjective tug-of-war: his intelligence groped for the venomous American slave crouching behind the Rabbit, but his beleaguered racial emotions, in self-defense, had to insist on the "Africanism" of Brer Rabbit and of the Negro. Then Miss Sally and Mars John could relish his "quaint antics" without recognizing themselves as his targets.

Against the African origin of Brer Rabbit one may argue that he is an eloquent white folk-symbol too, closely related to the lamb as the epitome of Christian meekness (the Easter bunny). May not the Negro, in his conversion to Christianity, have learned the standard Christian animal symbols from the whites? Could not his constant tale-spinning about the Rabbit's malevolent triumphs somehow, in some devious way, suggest the ascent of Christ, the meekness that shall inherit the earth; suggest, even, that the meek may stop being meek and set about inheriting the earth without waiting on the Biblical timetable? . . .

The Harris research technique, we learn, was first-hand and direct. Seeing a group of Negroes, he approaches and asks if they know any Brer Rabbit stories. The Negroes seem not to understand. Offhandedly, and in rich dialect, Harris tells one himself—as often as not, the famous "Tar-Baby" story. The Negroes are transfixed; then, suddenly, they break out in peals of laughter, kick their heels together, slap their thighs. Before long they are swapping Rabbit yarns with the white man as though he were their lifelong "hail-feller." "Curiously enough," Harris notes, "I have found few Negroes who will acknowledge to a stranger that they know anything of these legends; and yet to relate one of the stories is the surest road to their confidence and esteem."

Why the sudden hilarity? What magic folk-key causes these wary, taciturn Negroes to open up? Harris claims to have won their "esteem"; but perhaps he only guaranteed them immunity. He thinks he disarmed the Negroes—he may only have demonstrated that he, the white bossman, was disarmed.

And how much did the Negroes tell him when they "opened up"? Just how far did they really open up? Harris observes that "there are different versions of all the stories—the shrewd narrators of the mythology of the old plantation adapting themselves with ready tact to the years, tastes, and expectations of their juvenile audiences." But there seem to be gaps in Harris's own versions. At tantalizingly crucial points Uncle Remus will break off abruptly—"Some tells one tale en some tells nudder"—leaving the story dangling like a radio cliff-hanger. Did these gaps appear when the stories were told to Harris? When the slave is obliged to play the clown-entertainer and "give" his folk tales to his masters, young or old, his keen sense of the fitting might well delete the impermissible and blur the dubious—and more out of self-preservation than tact.

Of course, the original oral stories would not express the slave's aggressions straightforwardly either. A Negro slave who yielded his mind fully to his race hatreds in an absolutely white-dominated situation must go mad; and the function of such folk symbols as Brer Rabbit is precisely to prevent inner explosions by siphoning off these hatreds before they can completely possess consciousness. Folk tales, like so much of folk culture, are part of an elaborate psychic drainage system—they make it possible for Uncle Tom to retain his facade of grinning Tomism and even, to some degree, to believe in it himself. But the slave's venom, while subterranean, must nonetheless have been *thrillingly* close to the surface and its symbolic disguises flimsier, its attacks less roundabout. Accordingly his protective instincts, sensing the danger in too shallow symbolism, would have necessarily wielded a meticulous, if unconscious, blue pencil in the stories told to white audiences.

Harris tried hard to convince himself that Uncle Remus was a full-fledged, dyed-in-the-denim Uncle Tom—he describes the "venerable sable patron" as an ex-slave "who has nothing but pleasant memories of the discipline of slavery." But Harris could not completely exorcise the menace in the Meek. How often Remus steps out of his clown-role to deliver unmistakeable judgments on class, caste, and race! In those judgments the aggressions of this "white man's nigger" are astonishingly naked. . . .

[In] **"The Wonderful Tar-Baby Story"**—advertised on the dust-jacket as the most famous of all the Remus stories—Remus reverts to the question of pigmentation. ("There are few negroes that will fail to respond" to this one, Harris advises one of his folklore "legmen.") The Fox fashions a "baby" out of tar and places it on the side of the road; the Rabbit comes along and addresses the figure. Not getting any answer, he threatens: "Ef you don't take off dat hat en tell me howdy, I'm gwineter bus' you wide open." (Here the Rabbit's bluster reads like a parody of the white man's demand for the proper bowing-and-scraping etiquette from the Negro; it is a reflection of the satiric mimicry of the whites which the slaves often indulged in among themselves.) He hits the Tar-Baby—his fist sticks in the gooey tar. He hits it with the other hand, then kicks it—all four extremities are stuck.

This is "giving" in a new sense; tar, blackness, by its very yielding, traps. Interesting symbol, in a land where the mere possession of a black skin requires you, under penalty of death, to yield, to *give,* everywhere. The mark of supreme impotence suddenly acquires the power to render impotent, merely by its flaccidity, its inertness; it is almost a Gandhi-like symbol. There is a puzzle here: it is the Rabbit who is trapped. But in a later story, **"How Mr. Rabbit Was Too Sharp for Mr. Fox,"** it turns out that the Rabbit, through another cagey maneuver, gets the Fox to set him free from the tar-trap and thus avoids being eaten by his enemy. The Negro, in other words, is wily enough to escape from the engulfing pit of blackness, although his opponents, who set the trap, do their level best to keep him imprisoned in it. But it is not at all sure that anyone else who fell victim to this treacherous black yieldingness—the Fox, say—would be able to wriggle out so easily.

The story about **"A Plantation Witch"** frightens his young admirer so much that Remus has to take him by the hand and lead him home to the "big house." And for a long time the boy lies awake "expecting an unseemly visitation from some mysterious source." Many of the other stories, too, must have given him uneasy nights. For within the "gift" that Uncle Remus gives to Miss Sally's little boy is a nightmare, a nightmare in which whites are Negroes, the Weak torture and drown the Strong, mere blackness becomes black magic—and Negroes cavort with cosmic forces and the supernatural, zipping their skins off at will to prowl around the countryside terrorizing the whites, often in the guise of rabbits. . . .

[How] was it that Harris could apply his saccharine manner to such matter, dress this malevolent material, these nightmares, in such sweetness and light? For one thing, of course, he was only recording the tottering racial myth of the post-bellum South, doing a paste-job on its fissioning falseface. As it happened, he was peculiarly suited for the job; for he was crammed full of pathological racial obsessions, over and above those that wrack the South and, to a lesser degree, all of white America. . . .

[Harris] was *awed* by Uncle Remus. It was the awe of the sophisticate before the spontaneous, the straitjacketed before the nimble. But was the Negro what Harris thought him to be? It is certainly open to question, for another irony of the South is that the white man, under his pretense of racial omniscience, actually knows the Negro not at all—he knows only the falseface which he has forced on the Negro. It is the white man who manufactures the Negro grin. The stereotype reflects the looker, his thwartings and yearnings, not the person looked at; it is born out of intense subjective need.

Harris's racial awe was only an offshoot of the problem that tormented him all his life: the problem of identifying himself. He was caught in the American who-am-I dilemma, one horn of which is white, the other often black. And there is abundant proof that, at least in one compartment of his being, Harris defined himself by identifying with the Negro. . . .

Harris seems to have been a man in permanent rebellion against his own skin. No wonder: for he was driven to "give," and it was impossible for him to give without first zipping out of his own decorous skin and slipping into

Uncle Remus's. To him the artist and the Negro were synonymous.

And Harris virulently *hated* the Negro, too. . . .

What stillborn novelist can be undilutedly tender towards the objectivization of his squelched alter-ego, whose oral stories he feels impelled to "draw on" all his life?

Most likely, at least in Harris, the love went deeper than the hate—the hate was, in some measure, a *defense* against the love. *"Some goes up en some goes down."* Who sings this theme song? A trio: the Rabbit, Remus, *and* Harris. Literally, it is only a rabbit and a fox who change places. Racially, the song symbolizes the ascent of the Negro "Weak" and the descent of the white "Strong."

But to Harris, on the deepest personal level, it must have meant: the collapse of the "perfectly decorous" (inhibition, etiquette, embarrassment, the love that is never wild, the uncreative journalist-compiler, the blush and the stammer) and the triumph of the "wildly extravagant" (spontaneity, "naturalness," the unleashed subjective, creativity, "Miss Meadows en de gals," exhibitionism, the folk-novelist). The song must have been *deliciously* funny to him. . . .

The Remus stories are a monument to the South's ambivalence. Harris, the archetypical Southerner, sought the Negro's love, and pretended he had received it (Remus's grin). But he sought the Negro's hate too (Brer Rabbit), and revelled in it in an unconscious orgy of masochism—punishing himself, possibly, for not being the Negro, the stereotypical Negro, the unstinting giver.

Harris's inner split—and the South's, and white America's—is mirrored in the fantastic disparity between Remus's beaming face and Brer Rabbit's acts. And such aggressive acts increasingly emanate from the grin, along with the hamburgers, the shoeshines, the "happifyin'" pancakes. . . .

Increasingly Negroes themselves reject the mediating smile of Remus, the indirection of the Rabbit. The present-day animated cartoon hero, Bugs Bunny, is, like Brer Rabbit, the meek suddenly grown cunning—but without Brer Rabbit's facade of politeness. "To pull a Bugs Bunny," meaning to spectacularly outwit someone, is an expression not infrequently heard in Harlem.

There is today on every level a mass repudiation of "Uncle Tomism." Significantly the Negro comedian is disappearing. For bad or good, the *Dark Laughter* that Sherwood Anderson heard all around white New Orleans is going or gone.

The grin is faltering, especially since the war. That may be one of the reasons why, once more, the beaming Negro butler and Pullman porter are making their amiable way across our billboards, food labels, and magazine ads—and Uncle Remus, "fetchin' a grin from year to year," is in the bigtime again.

Stella Brewer Brookes

SOURCE: "General Description of the Uncle Remus Books," in *Joel Chandler Harris: Folklorist,* The University of Georgia Press, 1950, pp. 43-62.

[*"It does seem especially curious that of all the articles written about Harris,"* noted Brookes in the preface of the volume from which the following excerpt is taken, *"strangely enough there is left untouched an analysis of the folklore in his Uncle Remus books. The purpose of the present volume is to supply this lack."* In the first part of her book, Brookes analyzes *"the background—environmental and literary—to which the writing and publication of the Uncle Remus books are ascribable."* In the second part of the book, Brookes analyzes the folklore in the ten volumes of Uncle Remus stories; this part, the author claims, *"may claim to be an innovation."* In her acknowledgments, Brookes thanks Julian La Rose and Julia Collier Harris, the son and daughter-in-law of Joel Chandler Harris, for their critical reading of her manuscript.]

The Uncle Remus stories came to the world as a novelty—a genre not readily classifiable—a curious salmagundi of folklore, of picturesque locale, of humor (frequently bordering on pathos), of vital characterization, of spicy wit and quaint dialect. To the North, they were a revelation of the unknown; to the South, they were an eye-opener to the charm of the familiar.

To most Americans, the chief ingredient was humor. It was a new kind of humor in the history of American literature. Coming from a race good natured in the face of affliction, there was in it a propinquity of smiling and weeping, a wit which grew out of the fact that the ability to make an owner smile often saved a harsh lash. The odd quips and quiddities, the satirical and philosophical turns of thought, were heightened by the use of dialect—the best representation which has yet been given. Though humorous, Harris's portrayal seems genuinely sympathetic. . . .

It remains to be said here that the success of the first Uncle Remus book was instantaneous, but that when one seeks to find the secret of that success, it seems to be in no one merit. Perhaps there was nothing unique about what Harris did; maybe it was the combination of many things, or the innovation of a few things which caught the public eye and held it. In the series of Uncle Remus books three elements deserve consideration: the pattern, the characters, and the chronological order of volumes. . . .

Uncle Remus calls for special emphasis. Harris retires behind the scene and allows the wise, genial old man not only to tell the stories but also to express psychological and philosophical reactions to the world in which he lives. Upon the inquiry of an interviewer as to who suggested the character, Harris replied that he was not an invention of his own but a human syndicate of three or four old negroes whom he had just "walloped together".

Despite this remark by Harris, and the statements of most critics that Uncle Remus represents a whole race, what Harris gave to literature was not a Character but a Portrait. Uncle Remus was an individual—a distinctive personality. As Irvin S. Cobb has the hero of *J. Poindexter Colored say* of himself, "I ain't no problem, I'se a pusson; I craves to be so regarded." Well might Uncle Remus say, "I ain't no race, I'se an individual; I craves to be so regarded." Harris's aim was not to give a picture of an entire race; what he did was to choose from that race a dramatic human figure that appealed to him as picturesque and moving. It is true that he used the plantation as the background against which the old man's figure was silhouetted, for Uncle Remus could not have existed independently of his setting. Yet, he was a genius in the art of story-telling—few there were in fiction or in real life who could reach his stature. Story-telling is an art and Uncle Remus was an artist.

Perhaps [Fred Lewis] Pattee's statement concerning Uncle Remus best explains his status: "Harris embodied the results of his studies not in a type, but in a single negro personality to which he gave the breath of life. Harris's negro is the type plus the personal equation of an individual—Uncle Remus is one of the few original characters that America has added to the world gallery." . . .

Uncle Remus was not the first plantation story-teller in fiction; but none had so completely revealed himself as did he. Herein lay the essence of Harris's art: one is convinced, after reading the ten books, of the careful and complete delineation of the man. Harris reveals Uncle Remus's method: "He liked to be asked for a story so that he might have an opportunity of indulging in a friendly dispute, a wrangle of words, and then suddenly end it all by telling the tale that happened to be on his mind at the moment. In short, he delighted to whet the expectations of the youngster, and arouse his enthusiasm."

Harris uses the dramatic monologue as a principal means of character revelation, though brief descriptions of the old man interpolated throughout the stories add to the graphic presentation. The dramatic monologue was certainly no new form in literature, but Harris put it to new uses, aided by his unrivalled power of language and his accurate knowledge of folk speech. What makes Uncle Remus so true to life is that Harris captured not only what the man said, but his manner of saying it, his every gesture. To transfer these to the printed page was indeed a difficult art, but these are the touches that elevate Harris's character to originality, and establish for him the reputation as master in the art of creation of atmosphere and specifically the creation of a character who breathes. The old man is fond of pictorial instruction, much of which is found in conversation carried on with fidelity and naturalness. The venerable fabulist was apparently Harris's embodiment of the aim stated in the Introduction to his first book, ". . . to present the picturesque sensitiveness—a curious exaltation of mind and temperament, not to be defined by words."

Various are the roles which Uncle Remus plays. Some-times he scourges mischief: "I boun' I ain't gwine ter fix you up no mo' contraptions, ef dat's de way you does—massycreein' de cats, en de Dominicker chickens, en de Lord knows what! Ef you er huntin' war, des go up yonder whar dat ar Dominicker hen got de young chickens; go up dar en 'sturb her, en ef she don't make you squall de first letter er my name ain't Remus". . . .

Sometimes he is the philosopher. . . .

He is always engaged in some form of activity—oiling the harness, half-soling shoes, making a horse collar, grinding his axe; in the midst of these occupations he spins the tale, with which are mixed many other ingredients. He indulges in aphorisms, shrewd observations, curious retorts, homely thrusts—all of which become a commentary on life. Sometimes the criticism takes a pungent turn; often one notices a felicity of phrase abounding in similes and metaphors; frequently there is a poetic release where his words move with rhythm and flow with eloquence. There are passages which reveal an imagination which may come from the Celtic strain in Harris. Note how he describes old times, " . . . way back yander when de clouds wuz thicker dan what dey is now, an' when de sun ain't had ter go to bed at night ter keep fum being tired de next day." He delighted in mouth-filling, many-syllabled words, some of which seem nonsensical, but appealed to him because of their sonority. Uncle Remus also talks of gossip, "De word went 'roun' an' when it come back ter whar it started, it ain't look like itse'f;" he knows something of the gossip-monger, "She had a tongue wid salt en pepper on it."

So distinct a personality as Uncle Remus may never again be chronicled. His naive drollery, his whimsical incongruities, his aphorisms, quaintly expressed—all peculiar to himself—make up his character. He caught them from no one and to no one has he imparted them. . . .

The ten Uncle Remus books, though varying in a few aspects, have the same substance—there is the same pattern of the old man as principal raconteur and the little boy as listener; there is the same consistency of the human characters; there is the same atmosphere of reality environing these characters; and there is the same philosophy of the genial Uncle Remus whose treasury of anecdote is rich and distinctive. Harris had the genius to preserve the legends most of which he had imbibed during his youth, but he had also the gift of vivid characterization. Uncle Remus is one of the great products of American literature. The first books had immediate and widespread success and projected their author before readers of every part of America and some foreign countries. From a purely artistic standpoint Harris's books must always be included among the masterpieces of American literature.

Margaret Taylor Burroughs

SOURCE: "Uncle Remus for Today's Children," in *Elementary English*, December, 1953, pp. 485-91.

[For many years, Uncle Remus has been] the symbol of American Negro folklore, unchallenged and uncontested.

It is not the intention of this critical article to deprecate the position that Joel Chandler Harris, creator of Uncle Remus, earned for himself in American or regional literature by his writings. Certainly he made a great contribution merely by bringing to the attention of the world the existence of Negro folklore and stories, regardless of the manner in which he adapted them for purposes of his own chronicling.

It is my intention to open up discussion and thinking on Uncle Remus among persons who feel that the folk stories of the Negro should be available and intelligible to all and that the work of Joel Chandler Harris should be critically reviewed in searching out the reasons why these classics are seldom read today.

Negro Americans, through their animal stories, folk legends, myths, and proverbs bequeathed to them from their African forbears, have contributed a vast treasury of folklore to American life and literature; yet their contributions are, for the most part, totally unknown and unrecognized today.

The folklore phase of the Negro's cultural heritage has been bottled up for years. Since an appreciation and knowledge of our country's folklore is important for young Americans, giving them a sense of continuity and an awareness of their family's roots in the past, it is necessary that the stopper be removed from the bottle. While this is important for all young Americans, it is especially necessary for young Negro Americans who too often grow to adulthood believing that "they just growed, like Topsy."

Whenever Negro folklore is mentioned, the works of Joel Chandler Harris are brought to mind. They have been regarded both in his time and in the present as the last word on the subject. They have been revered as models of "true Negro dialect," and students interested in the characterization of the antebellum Negro have sought them out. Too, in Joel Chandler Harris' wake sprang forth a whole school of writers with stories told by faithful uncles, aunts, and aunties. It seems that their common purpose was more to cast a golden glow over the South before emancipation than to set forth authentic folklore.

Arthur Huff Fausett, educator, author, and folklorist, states in *The New Negro* that the Remus stories were based on original folk tales told by African slaves and their descendants. While Joel Chandler Harris admits this freely, the lay public seem to be under the impression that they are the exclusive creative product of one man. These stories are a part of the cultural heritage of the American Negro. And only a small part at that. . . .

Joel Chandler Harris stated that the purpose of his volumes was to create or revive in the readers an interest in and an enjoyment of the simple folktales and the charm of plantation life in the South. He accomplished his purpose; his works are no doubt of great interest to students of dialect and the antebellum South. However, this very dialect in which the stories are encased has deprived generations of Americans of the enjoyment of reading and hearing them read. So that while his intentions were of the best, it is apparent that his version of this material has done harm as well as good.

Joel Chandler Harris aimed to wed the legends to the quaint dialect through which they had become a part of the home life of every Southern family. He felt that his attempt would be a failure if the language did not give "vivid hints of the poetic imagination of the Negro, embody his quaint and homely humor and suggest his picturesque sensitiveness, and that without the dialect the tales would lack vitality."

Students of language may find this "true Negro dialect" a goldmine for research, but it is the dialect which renders the stories unintelligible. Also this mutilation of English spelling and pronunciation has often been mistaken as the present mode of speech ascribed to the Negro.

Many critics and scholars have lauded Joel Chandler Harris' handling of dialect. Stella Brewer Brookes in a comprehensive study of his life and works states, "No one in his day, nor has there been one since who has found the writing of the type of dialect with which he enriched the literature, 'easy'." Similarly no one today, with few exceptions and particularly in the case of young people, finds the reading of this type of dialect 'easy.'

But is it true that the dialect is so integrally a part of the legends and sayings? In its original form this material was not written or told in dialect. . . .

Do [the Aesop] fables, which are a part of the language and literature of peoples all over the world, lose their irony and bite by being written in clear, standard English? . . .

In my opinion, Negro myths and animal stories lose nothing by being written in English. In retelling or rewriting the stories, it is not the dialect itself that should be broken away from, but rather the stereotyped limitations too long imposed on "Negro dialect." Further, this type of dialect is a medium that is not capable of giving expression to the varied conditions of Negro life in America and much less is it capable of giving the fullest interpretation of the character and psychology of the Negro. . . .

Joel Chandler Harris' stories make their most powerful appeal and impression through the character of Uncle Remus. He is drawn as "an old negro. . . who has nothing but pleasant memories of the discipline of slavery and who has all the prejudices of caste and pride of family that were the natural results of the system . . . . He considered himself a partner in the various interests of the plantation." It is just this type of character projection that contorts these tales from their true plane. In all true folk tales, the story-teller is inconsequential, taking no prominent place and giving the stories an impersonal character. Uncle Remus plays such an important part, that he, and not the stories, is alone remembered.

Joel Chandler Harris takes it upon himself to interpret the character of the Negro instead of merely retelling the tales. The result is a composite picture of the antebellum Negro that fits neatly into the stereotyped conception of the Negro so dear to some Americans. These writings have been quoted as apologia for the system of slavery. Here are some instances from **Uncle Remus, His Songs and Sayings** which cause teachers, librarians, and parents who are interested in better human relations to place this volume high on the shelf:

> The book is peppered with such offensive terms as "nigger," "darkey," and "coon". . . .

Or commenting on the subject of Freedom, Remus says:

> "Dey er movin'. Dey er gitten' so dey bleeve dey ain't no better den wite fokes. W'en freedom come out de niggers sorta got dere humps up, an' dey staid dat way twel bimeby dey begun to git hongry, and den dey begun fer ter drap inter line right smartually an now dey er ez palaverous ez dey wuz befo' de war."

On the subject of education for the Negro, this apologist for white supremacy philosophizes:

> "W'at a nigger gwineter l'arn outen books? I kin take a bar'l stave and fling mo' sense inter a nigger in one minnit dan all de school houses betwixt dis an de state er Midgigin . . . Wid one bar'l stave I kin fa'rly lif de vail of ignunce. Education . . . hits de ruinashun er de country . . . . Put a spellin' book in a nigger's hans en right den an dar' you loozes a plowhan'."

Finally the Remus stories have been praised because "they brought out the quaint humor" of the Negro. It is just this intrusion of a dominant note of humor which falls in line with an unfortunate but general procedure in our country of regarding anything which bears the Negro tradition as inherently comical and only worth being laughed at. The simple, dullwitted character who mutilates English over the radio; or shuffles hat in hand across the movie or TV screen; or who grins forth with popping eyes and thick lips from the comics and cartoons; and whose antics are so thoroughly enjoyed by millions of Americans, men, women, and children, all good people, bears a strange resemblance to our "hero" Uncle Remus.

The quaint and sentimental humor so popularly prized in the Remus stories is, more often than not, merely an overtone. In the true Negro folktales, it is not necessary to draw upon sentiment to recognize their masterful quality. Moralism, sober and grim, irony, shrewd, and frequently subtle is the fundamental mood and tone. A sterling example of this is a West African folk story ["Talk"] from Harold Courlander and George Herzog's collection, *The Cowtail Switch.* . . .

Until the qualities observed in such stories as "Talk" are brought back to the Negro folk stories, more and more generations of children will be denied the cultural wealth of true Negro folklore.

May Hill Arbuthnot

SOURCE: "Old Magic: American Negro Tales," in *Children and Books,* third edition, Scott, Foresman and Company, 1964, p. 266.

Joel Chandler Harris became interested in collecting the tales he heard the plantation Negroes telling. Born in Georgia and raised on such stories as a child, he knew the Negro's dialect, humor, and picturesque turns of speech. Moreover, he had a deep love for the stories and for the fine people who told them. In the character of Uncle Remus, a plantation Negro, Harris embodied the gentleness, the philosophy, the shrewd appraisal of character, and the rich imagination of all Negro storytellers to whom he had listened. Into the mouth of Uncle Remus, he put the stories he gathered first-hand. It was a labor of love performed with sensitive perception and fidelity.

The stories are mostly talking-beast tales, and the hero is Brer Rabbit, the weakest and most harmless of animals, but far from helpless. Through his quick wit, his pranks, and his mischief, he triumphs over the bear, the wolf, the fox, and the lesser animals. Like the French "Reynard the Fox," he is a trickster, but unlike Reynard, he is never mean or cruel, only a practical joker now and then, a clever fellow who can outwit the big brutes and turn a misfortune into a triumph. No matter what happens to him or what he does, he remains completely lovable.

These stories are, of course, reminiscent of the talking-beast tales of other countries. Some of them may have had their roots in India, but it is generally agreed that most of them originated in Africa or were created in this country. Variants of "The Tar Baby" are found in many lands, but there is a special flavor to the Uncle Remus stories. They show a homely philosophy of life, flashes of poetic imagination, a shrewd appraisal of human nature, a childlike love of mischief, a pattern and style unsurpassed by any other beast tales.

These stories do have their limitations, and the dialect is chief of them. Children in the South may be fortunate enough to hear these tales read by adults who can do justice to the flavorsome dialect. A. A. Milne's British father read these tales aloud to his children, dialect and all, and they loved them. However, it is the dialect that makes the stories almost unintelligible to most children and adults. When the stories are turned into standard English, they retain their witty folk flavor, just as tales translated from the Norwegian or East Indian or American Indian do. Perhaps translation is the answer here, too.

Other objections to these stories are raised by modern American Negroes. . . .

These objections point up the fact that the great body of

seven hundred *Uncle Remus Tales* will survive chiefly as source material for gifted storytellers. Where else in any collection of folk tales can you find such droll revelations of human nature—antic, sagacious, witty? And where else can you find a colorful dialect so lovingly and perfectly recorded by a scholar with an ear for the euphony of speech?

Louis D. Rubin, Jr.

SOURCE: "Uncle Remus and the Ubiquitous Rabbit," in *The Southern Review,* Louisiana State University, Vol. X, No. 4, October, 1974, pp. 787-804.

The enormous disparity between the reception of Mrs. Stowe's novel [*Uncle Tom's Cabin*] by the American reading public, and that public's response, less than thirty years afterward, to the Uncle Remus tales, did not lie . . . in the depictions of the black protagonists. Rather, it was the relationship of the black men to the resident whites that made the difference. Mrs. Stowe showed Uncle Tom as mocked, beaten, starved, his humanity denied, his virtue unrewarded. Harris showed Uncle Remus as honored, pampered, respected, his simplicity and gentleness cherished by his grateful and indulgent white patrons. Thus if the northern reading public could feel that it was not Mrs. Stowe's version of black-white relationships, but Joel Chandler Harris', that typified life in the South, then the proper response was not to send armies southward to trample out the vintage where the grapes of wrath were stored, but to let the underlying amicability and mutual trust of black-white relationships down there exist free of the meddling of northern politicians and the blunders of misguided reformers. And this, all in all, was what the stories of Joel Chandler Harris and his imitators helped to accomplish. . . .

Clearly, it is not the folk tale subject matter as such that provides the chief appeal of the Uncle Remus stories, though when he began publishing them Harris discovered to his surprise that he was indeed contributing to the literature of folklore and that the same stories of rabbit, fox, wolf, terrapin, raccoon, and opossum that plantation Negroes in Georgia had told to him were known to ethnologists the world over, with their counterparts existing among the Indians of North and South America, the bushmen of Australia, and the Moro tribesmen of the Philippines. The appeal lies in the way that they are told, and in the dynamics of the relationship between Uncle Remus, the successive little white boys who listen, and the animal protagonists of the tales themselves, notably Brer Rabbit. The animal legends were necessary to Harris for the basis of his stories; when he exhausted his stock of recollections he advertised for more, and his readers supplied him with new materials. But Mark Twain was quite right when he told Harris that "in reality the stories are only alligator pears—one merely eats them for the sake of the salad dressing." The importance of the stories is that, because of their content and the associations they had for Harris, they enabled him to tap wellsprings of creativity hitherto unknown and fully available to him in no other form. When he tried to do it through other guises, it was never the same. In the Uncle Remus stories Harris was indeed able to *see* the world as a black man did, and also to sense *why* the black man looked at it in that fashion.

The important thing to remember about the Uncle Remus stories is that not merely the old Negro telling the stories, but the animal protagonists themselves, are southern rural blacks. What they do is inseparable from the idiom used to describe their actions. It is Brer Rabbit, and occasionally Brer Terrapin, whose antics provide the plot of the stories. The various tricks that Brer Rabbit plays on the fox, the wolf, the bear, the cow, and sometimes even Mr. Man himself, all exhibit his cunning and his resourcefulness, and it is this that Uncle Remus most admires as he relates them. Sometimes Brer Rabbit acts in order to procure food, sometimes to protect himself from being eaten, sometimes to avoid work while enjoying its benefits. At times his chief motivation is that of gaining revenge for attempted attacks on himself or his family. His dignity is also very important to him; he is quick to avenge any insult or slight. Sometimes, too, he will go to work on his fellow creatures merely in order to keep them mindful of his identity. Occasionally he is prompted by sheer mischievousness; in company with Brer Terrapin he will suddenly decide to have some fun with the others.

Harris knew very well that the rabbit was a Negro. In the preface to the second published volume, *Nights with Uncle Remus,* he declared of the black man's preference for the rabbit as hero of his folklore that "it needs no scientific investigation to show why he selects as his hero the weakest and most harmless of all animals, and brings him out victorious in contests with the bear, the wolf, and the fox. It is not *virtue* that triumphs, but *helplessness;* it is not *malice,* but *mischievousness.*" Several critics have pointed out, however, that strictly speaking, this last is not true of the Uncle Remus stories, for usually Brer Rabbit is more than merely mischievous; he can be quite malicious at times, and he is very much set on maintaining his prestige and reputation. Often his triumphs are based on the instinct for sheer survival rather than on any taste for prank playing. But it is something of a mistake to allegorize these stories, as some have done, merely as showing the Negro rabbit using his helplessness and his apparently insignificant status as weapons against the white power structure in the guise of the fox, bear, and wolf. The matter is a trifle more complex than that. What the rabbit exemplifies is the capacity to survive and flourish in a world in which society can be and often is predatory. The rabbit confronts life; the realism with which his situation is depicted, as Louise Dauner shows, "precludes any sentimentality . . . both life and death must be fatalistically accepted" ["Myth and Humor in the Uncle Remus Tales," *American Literature,* XX (1948)]. The power is in the hands of the strong; the weak cannot trust to any supposed belief in benevolence or fair play, for the real rules are those of power. That this had profound implications for the situation of the black man in rural southern society is obvious; yet what makes the stories work so well is not any direct political and social allegory, but the realism with which Harris can view the life he is depicting.

It is not that Harris was, consciously or unconsciously, trying to allegorize the plight of the black man; these are not parables of protest, and their success comes because they are not thus shaped. If they are moral, they are so as all good art is moral: through depicting the actualities of the human situation and by implication contrasting them with what we hold to be ideal. Through his instinctive identification with the black man. Harris was able to depict society as it confronted the underdog (or underrabbit, perhaps). Writing about animals, he could describe humans, and with a realism that was not subject to verification by the rules of poetic justice. A slave—or a sharecropper—must accept things as he finds them, not as he might like for them to be. "De creeturs dunno nothin' 'tall 'bout dat dat's good en dat dat ain't good," Uncle Remus tells the little white boy. "Dey dunno right fum wrong. Dey see what dey want, en dey git it if dey kin, by hook er by crook. Dey don't ax who it b'longs ter, ner wharbouts it come fum. Dey dunno de diffunce 'twix' what's dern en what ain't dern." In telling about the animals, Harris did not have to shape the morality and motivations of his characters in accordance with what the ideality of his time and place decreed ought to be; he could view their actions and responses in terms of what truly *was*. Uncle Remus could accept harsh actualities in a way that a white narrator might not have been able to do, because the experience that was Remus'—the experience of the plantation slave, as Harris had been privileged to perceive it—was all too elemental, and devoid of merely sentimental gestures. "In dem days," Remus tells the little boy on another occasion, "de creeturs bleedzd ter look out fer deyse'f, mo' speshually dem w'at ain't got hawn en huff. Brer Rabbit ain't got no hawn en huff, en he bleedzd ter be his own lawyer." Harris knew this, but it was only when writing of Negro life in the guise of the animals that he could, as a writer, tell what he knew.

Writing about black experience in the form of animal stories, therefore, served to liberate Joel Chandler Harris' imagination. It provided him with a technique whereby a writer who had been a shy, stammering, red-headed, illegitimate youth and faced social realities in a way that was direct and unprotected, could draw upon what he knew and create stories that imaged reality as few other writers of his time and place were able to do. He could make use of his humor, his awareness of the savageness and the remorseless nature of human circumstance, his sense of fatality, without the inhibitions of the genteel literary tradition, social respectability, or southern racial imperatives.

The Uncle Remus animal stories are not tragic; they are comic. But the comedy is decidedly not that of foolish, childlike darkies, the standard fare of local color. It is not comedy sweetened by sentiment. When, for example, in the story entitled **"Why Mr. Possum Has No Hair on His Tail,"** the rabbit and possum decide to raid the bear's persimmon orchard, and the rabbit decides to have some fun and informs the bear that Brer Possum is up in his persimmon trees, it is not Brer Rabbit who gets punished, either for his collaboration in theft or his betrayal of his accomplice. The possum is the one who suffers; he is shaken down from the tree, flees, and just as he escapes through the fence the bear grabs his tail in his jaws and rakes it forever clean of fur. The rabbit enjoys the spectacle thoroughly. The aggression, the pleasure taken in the possum's discomfiture, the cleverness of the rabbit, are amusing, but only because the characters are animals; one cannot imagine Harris or any other such writer suggesting a similar outcome to a story involving people. Yet the characters *are* people—black people. Thus was Harris enabled, however obliquely, to deal with reality, whether white or black.

As for the narrator, Uncle Remus enjoys the whole account. *He,* of course, wouldn't do such things; for he is the kindly, noble local color retainer. But he tells the little white boy about a world in which such things do happen, and then, when the little white boy occasionally becomes disturbed by the indifference of the creatures to conventional ethics, reminds him that rabbits, foxes, bears, possums, terrapins, and the like cannot be judged by human standards. As Louise Dauner says, "In Uncle Remus we have the symbol of the wisdom of Things-As-They-Are, a realistic acceptance and humorous transmission of the strenuous conditions and paradoxes of life. In Brer Rabbit we have the inescapable irony of the Irrational, coupled with man's own terribly humorous struggle for survival." Truly, the implications of the Uncle Remus stories are ferocious—as ferocious as those of the Mother Goose poems.

Only in the animal stories can Harris deal in such an unsentimental version of reality. Those Uncle Remus stories which are not centered on animal fables achieve no such directness, nor did they enjoy any such popularity as the animal tales. In those Atlanta sketches, Uncle Remus is all but undistinguishable from a hundred other literary plantation uncles. . . .

It must be said that except perhaps for one or two stories such as **"Free Joe and the Rest of the World,"** the only work of Harris' that has importantly survived its day are the animal stories. To some extent this may be ascribed to the format of the Uncle Remus stories; Harris was able to handle such episodes of 1500 to 2500 words with a formal expertness that he was not able to bring to longer, more complicated stories, and when he sought to work at the novel length he was out of his depth. In this respect his journalistic limitations stayed with him always; once he exceeded the length of the newspaper format he got into trouble. Yet this by itself will not suffice as an explanation. . . .

The real difficulty would seem to be that except when he was writing about life as experienced by southern Negroes in the guise of rabbits, terrapins, and other animal creatures, he became too much the sentimentalist, and all too unwilling or unable to look at life without making everything come out right. There *had* to be happy endings; village life had to be shown as sweet, tolerant, without prejudice; slaves had to be treated with kindness; seducers had to have hearts of gold; blacks during the Reconstruction and afterward had to be loyal to the white folks. Only in the tales told by Uncle Remus do people steal, lie, and triumph even so; only in them do people live by their wits and enjoy it; only in them are deception and trickiness portrayed as virtues, and economic necessities as more binding than moral imperatives. Harris never read any of the animal tales to his own children. "I was just thinking," the little boy remarks to Uncle Remus after an episode in which Brer Rabbit cleverly steals Brer Fox's provender, "that when Brother Rabbit got the chickens from Brother Fox, he was really stealing them." To which Remus replies, "Dey ain't no two ways 'bout dat. But what wuz Brer Fox doin' when *he* got um? Pullets an' puddle ducks don't grow on trees, an' it's been a mighty long time since dey been running' wil'. No, honey! Dey's a heap er idees dat you got ter shake off if you gwine ter put de creeters 'longside de folks; you'll hatter shake um, an' shuck um. . . . Folks got der laws, an' de creeturs got der'n, an' it bleeze ter be dat away." Life in the world of Uncle Remus is no picnic; as he remarks upon another occasion "ef deze yer tales wuz des fun, fun, fun, en giggle, giggle, giggle, I let you know I'd a-done drapt um long ago. Yasser, w'em it come down ter gigglin' you kin des count ole Remus out."

Was Harris fully aware of what he was doing in those stories? Such remarks as that just quoted seem to leap out of the page with startling clarity. What are they doing there at all? We know, as noted before, that Harris was quite aware that he was writing about black people. It seems inevitable that, having heard the stories under the circumstances that he did, he would have known that they were not, in their symbolic action, without relevance to the daily lives of the blacks. Yet before we go too far in crediting Harris with any secret racial subversiveness— and for a modern reader the temptation is all too real— we must remember that very little in his non-animal stories involving black people in the South will validate any such theorizing, while there is a considerable evidence to show that Harris was of his time and place, and that however benevolent his attitude, he did not transcend his circumstance. Furthermore, whatever it may have been that Harris intended, and whether consciously or unconsciously, his audience surely did not read the stories as subversive. In their time the stories seemed only to confirm the stereotype of the contented darkie. They told readers that the black man was happy and contented. They seemed to glorify life on the old plantation.

He was a curious man—not at all the simple sage of Snap-Bean Farm that he is made out to be, but a very private and complex person. It is as if there were two Joel Chandler Harrises—the journalist, citizen of Georgia, and man of letters who wrote pleasant, optimistic, moral tales in which right triumphed and the plain folk were good and kind; and the fiercely creative artist, his uncompromising realism masked to the world and to the other Harris as well by the animal tales format, one who saw life devoid of sentiment and unclouded by wishful thinking.

Margaret Blount

SOURCE: "Folklore and Fable," in *Animal Land: The Creatures of Children's Fiction*, William Morrow & Company, Inc., 1975, pp. 23-41.

Perhaps the best folklore animal, and certainly the most famous, is Brer Rabbit. Though later in time than the *Reynard* cycle or Aesop, in treatment and essence he is earlier and more primitive and has the genuine amoral wily innocence that fairytale animals lack. Hans Andersen sometimes leaves one full of an odd, cold sadness, however delicate the allegory and beautiful the image; compared with this, Grimm's folklore tales are like tomato sauce out of a bottle, and Brer Rabbit comes out of the same jar, full of humour and rather undeserved retribution, of which Uncle Remus offers no explanation except that it *was* so, in the old days when the animals could talk. These African stories modified and translated into an American setting, have one or two Aesop themes such as 'The Tortoise and the Hare', 'The Wolf and the Lamb', 'The Dog and the Meat', transformed and improved on, brought to life—the folklore version being a jollier one than the fable. . . .

On the whole the Uncle Remus stories are kindly in that the weak animals always win. The whole saga concerns a weak animal winning, and celebrates the victory of a creature that has no natural weapons, only speed, concealment and cunning, and the reversal of nature and the likely gives great delight. Everyone wants the weak and innocent to win and the tyrant to be defeated, and enjoyment is increased by Brer Rabbit's sly confidence, his deceits and trickeries that are full of outrageous resource and happy zest. Until the very end, most of the animals survive to hunt again and they all seem to belong to some wonderful American past when the Beasts 'had sense, same like folks', and the humans were not too obtrusive—indeed, did not even have proper names, but were addressed ambiguously as Miss Meadows or Mr Man. Their function was to provide farms and roads and a vaguely law-abiding background against which the animals eat-or-be-eaten existence could function more effectively.

Part of the charm of the *Brer Rabbit* stories is the vernacular way in which the animals talk. Their natural, funny, adult conversations are turned to childlike motives of hide and seek, being one up and outwitting your neighbour by being sharper than he is; a game spiced with danger because they are animals after all, the Fox is *really* out to eat the Rabbit, the evasions concern life or death; but the talk is all casual understatement as neat and careful as a game of tennis played by opponents who are so used to each other's styles that they have a sort of wary relaxation, an alert yet unstrained pleasure in countering and turning the other's attack. . . .

One had the feeling that if one had been lucky enough to live in America in this golden age, these witty talking animals would have been in one's backyard or farm or briar patch. . . .

Brer Rabbit was as near a man as a rabbit could ever be; he 'sorter pull his mustarsh and say . . .' The game of chase was exciting and constant; like Tom and Jerry, the prey was always elusive and cunning, the hunter indefatigably animal and incredibly naive, with no one really getting hurt until the strange, rather brutal deaths which come with the stories 'the sad end of—' and the saga is over.

The Tar Baby story is the classic of the collection, with its refrain 'Tar Baby ain't sayin' nothing' and Brer Fox, he lay low'; and the wonderful riposte of 'born an' bred in a briar patch', when the Fox, thinking he has given the Rabbit a fate worse than death, is persuaded to throw his prey among the brambles. The Fox is always the real victim, the Rabbit only the apparent one; the battle is conducted with conversation, those careful, stylised, once-removed remarks in which neither animal says what it means; an elaborate, cumulative game of double dealing in which the Rabbit always *knows.*

The other lucky animal that outwits the rest and is never hurt is the terrapin, even more passive and defensive than the rabbit and at times one up on both Rabbit and Fox. . . .

The way the animals end—as if Tom and Jerry had suddenly become serious and the consequences of each violent act became real instead of imaginary—is death, always in a cruel form. The Bear is stung to death by Bees, the Wolf scalded in a chest, the Fox's head served up in a stew to his unsuspecting wife and children; and the game is finally over. The wise-cracking gaiety is marred, but perhaps one can here, as in Grimm, accept the 'fates' of the bad characters because they have a certain amount of non-animal guilt and wickedness; but the end still seems out of place. It is happier to think of Brer Rabbit at last marrying one of the Gals.

Robert Bone

SOURCE: "The Oral Tradition," in *Down Home: A History of Afro-American Short Fiction from Its Beginning to the End of the Harlem Renaissance,* G. P. Putnam's Sons, 1975, pp. 19-41.

Joel Chandler Harris is in bad odor among the younger generation of literary men. The blacks, who tend to equate Uncle Remus with Uncle Tom—sometimes, one suspects, without having read either Harris or Stowe—reject the Uncle Remus books out of hand. And sympathetic whites, who hope thereby to ingratiate themselves with the black militants, are fond of giving Harris a gratuitous kick in the shins. Both responses are regrettable, for they blind their victims to the archetypal figure of Brer Rabbit, who is not only a major triumph of the Afro-American imagination, but also the most subversive folk hero this side of Stagolee.

Harris did not invent the animal fables that constitute the imaginative center of the Uncle Remus books. But he did transpose them to the written page, thus saving them from possible oblivion. It was through Harris that a major figure in the pantheon of American folk heroes saw the light of day. Brer Rabbit, who has kindled the imagination of black writers for almost a century, came loping into view in 1880. But Clio, the muse of history, is no respecter of race. It was a white man of the deep South who forged the missing link between the Afro-American folktale and the Afro-American short story.

The rehabilitation of Joel Chandler Harris was no part of my original intent. As a journalist, after all, he was an active propagandist in the cause of white supremacy, and as a literary man, a leading proponent of the plantation myth. Still less did I intend—nor do I now propose—to serve as an apologist for Uncle Remus, who is principally a figment of the white imagination. But the Brer Rabbit tales themselves are something else again. A product of the Afro-American oral tradition, these magnificent folktales must not be allowed to languish simply on the grounds that a white Georgian was the first to write them down.

So perhaps some modest effort at rehabilitation will be tolerated by the young. Out of simple justice, then, let it be entered on the record that, whatever else he was, Joel Chandler Harris was a complicated man, full of neurotic conflicts and self-deceiving ways; a Southern maverick, capable of stubborn orthodoxies and equally tenacious heresies where black people were concerned; an admirer of black folklore, and an ethnologist of strict integrity, to whom black Americans owe a considerable debt for the preservation of their folk heritage; and a catalytic agent of prime importance in the history of the Afro-American short story.

Our final judgment of this man and his work cannot be a simple one. If the Uncle Remus books perpetuate the proslavery myths of the plantation tradition, they also contain one of the sharpest indictments of the institution in American literature. . . .

[What] precisely is the relationship of the Brer Rabbit tales to the animal legends of West Africa? Do the folktales of the American Negro represent a survival of African culture in the New World? Joel Chandler Harris was inclined to think so. Basing his opinion on the latest findings of contemporary scholarship, he wrote of the animal tales, "One thing is certain—the Negroes did not get them from the whites: probably they are of remote African origin."

At the same time, Harris recognized that some Afro-American folktales were more African than others. He knew, for example, that the stories told on the cotton plantations of central Georgia were strikingly different from those recounted in the rice-growing districts of the Georgia coast. To accommodate these differences in his fiction he invented Daddy Jack, a narrator who came straight from Africa and told his tales in Gullah dialect. By creating a coastal counterpart of Uncle Remus, Harris anticipated, if only at the level of artistic intuition, some of the conundrums that have yet to be resolved by modern scholars. . . .

What seems beyond dispute is that a very ancient African tradition survived the middle passage, and served as a basis for renewed creative efforts in the Western Hemisphere. At the same time, we must insist that the Brer

Rabbit tales were conceived not by Africans, but Afro-Americans. For these tales reflect the social conditions and historical experience of black slaves on the continent of North America. They represent the first attempt of black Americans to define themselves through the art of story-telling; a heroic effort on the part of chattel slaves to transmute the raw materials of their experience into the forms of fiction. . . .

How faithful was Harris to his folk sources? In the process of writing down the animal fables, and providing them with a narrative frame, to what extent did he impose his own values and point of view as a white Southerner? At this point, a crucial distinction must be drawn between the kernel and its husk. It is undeniable that the external wrappings of the Brer Rabbit tales function to perpetuate the plantation myth. But the tales themselves were never tampered with. As a conscientious if amateur ethnologist, Harris respected their integrity. . . .

Of crucial importance to the present study is the point in time when [the] oral tradition surfaced, transcended its folk origins, and became incorporated into the literary culture of nineteenth-century America. That moment occurred in 1880, with the publication of the first book of Uncle Remus tales. . . .

Uncle Remus: His Songs and His Sayings was an instantaneous popular success. Within a matter of months the book passed through four editions. It was soon followed by a second volume, *Nights with Uncle Remus.* Six such books eventually appeared, whose impact on American culture has yet to be properly assessed. Harris had established a new literary mode whose first fruits included Charles Chesnutt's *The Conjure Woman* (1899) and Don Marquis' *The Lives and Times of Archie and Mehitabel* (1916). Later works in the same line of descent would include William Faulkner's *The Sound and the Fury* (1929), Ralph Ellison's *Invisible Man* (1952), and John Updike's *Rabbit Redux* (1971).

Uncle Remus: His Songs and His Sayings was the book that launched the plantation revival of the 1880's. It was, in point of fact, the first major literary statement of the New South. As such, it bore the historic burden of revealing to the nation the current state of the Southern soul. Was the defeated South in a repentant frame of mind, or unregenerate in its defense of slavery? The answer, when it came, seemed unequivocal. The new generation of Southern writers, by their revival of the plantation myth, seemed determined to idealize the old regime, mitigate its harshness, cloak it in a haze of nostalgia, and thereby justify the restoration of white supremacy.

Joel Chandler Harris, who was, after all, a political commentator for a major Southern newspaper, was entirely orthodox in this respect. There is nothing in his characterization of Uncle Remus that violates the spirit of the plantation myth. On the contrary, it is the author's avowed purpose to create a sympathetic, nostalgic, and untroubled portrait of plantation life before the war. The point of view, he tells us frankly, will be that of an old Negro

"who has nothing but pleasant memories of the discipline of slavery—and who has all the prejudices of caste and pride of family that were the natural results of the system. . . . "

Harris' unconscious motivations were something else again. Guilt is an elusive state of mind, whether in a man or nation. Seldom appearing to the conscious mind in its own guise, it assumes a thousand Protean shapes and forms. Dramas of the soul involving guilt are more likely to be enacted in the dark than before the bright glare of television cameras. Hence Harris' fascination with the subliminal world of the black folktale. Folktales are allied to dream states, and possess something of the magical fluidity of dreams. Precisely because they deal with buried feelings, they confront us with blurred outlines, veiled analogies, hints and correspondences. They thus permit us to know and not to know at the same time.

At some deeper level of artistic intuition, Harris must have known that Uncle Remus was not the whole story, and perhaps not even the true story, of slavery times. Through the character of Uncle Remus he gave form to the white man's fantasy of being loved by his slaves. But there was another perspective from which to view chattel slavery, as Harris was well aware from his lonely adolescent years at Turnwold. That was the black slave's point of view, as embodied in his folklore. Try as he would, Harris could not bring himself to suppress it. This ghost is present in the Uncle Remus books, just as inescapably as it is buried in the nation's consciousness.

Whatever the intentions—conscious or unconscious—of Joel Chandler Harris, the Uncle Remus tales confront us with two distinct, and ultimately irreconcilable, versions of reality. One is white, the other black, and they are embedded in a two-tier or split-level structure consisting of (1) a narrative frame, and (2) an animal tale. Dramatically, the tales shift from the human to the animal plane; from Uncle Remus and the little boy to Brer Rabbit and the other woodland creatures. Linguistically, they shift from standard English to Negro dialect, so that the very texture of the prose announces unmistakably the transition from a white to a Negro world.

The two fictive worlds of the Uncle Remus tales are in fact the divided worlds of the American South. They are the segregated and yet curiously interlocking worlds of the two races, of the Big House and the slave quarters, of Euro-American and Afro-American culture. Their uneasy coexistence in the Uncle Remus books is a tribute to the capacity of the human mind for self-deception. For if the one world is nostalgic and sentimental, the other is utterly subversive; if the one is steeped in fantasy and wish-fulfillment, the other is immersed in the harsh realities of American slavery. On the literary plane, these tensions are reflected in the conventions of pastoral and antipastoral.

Consider the tableau that sets the tone of the Uncle Remus books. The figures of Uncle Remus and Miss Sally's little boy cling to one another in pastoral innocence and peace. The boy rests with his head against the old man's arm or sits on his knee, as Uncle Remus strokes and caresses the child's hair. It is a picture of utter confidence and trust, mutual tenderness and love. In a word, the scene is idyllic. What it proclaims to the reader is this: "There is nothing to be afraid of, or even upset by, in these animal fables; they are merely quaint legends or harmless children's stories."

Now consider the central images of the folktales themselves. Far from creating an atmosphere of tranquility and love, they convey a world of unrelieved hostility and danger, violence and cruelty, terror and revenge. In one tale, Brer Rabbit lures Brer Wolf into a large wooden chest, bores holes in the top, and scalds him to death with boiling water. In another, he persuades the animals whom he has robbed to submit to an ordeal by fire, and as a consequence, the innocent Brer Possum is killed. In a third, having caused Brer Fox to be beaten to death, Brer Rabbit attempts to serve up his enemy's head in a stew to his wife and children.

The tales are full of beatings, tortures, savage assaults, and deadly ambushes. They reproduce, in their jagged images of violence, the emotional universe of the Negro slave. How else should the black imagination respond to the brutalities of the American slave system? What other images would be commensurate with its inhumanity? If the flagrant sadism of the Brer Rabbit tales offends, it is well to remind ourselves that violence and cruelty were the mainstays of the institution. If the white imagination is content to linger over the smiling aspects of the slave estate, it would be strange indeed if the black storyteller should follow suit.

The Brer Rabbit tales preserve not so much the dramatic features as the moral atmosphere of slavery. What they are about, in the last analysis, is the black slave's resistance to white power. Hence the effort to "contain" this subversive theme in a pastoral frame. But in the tales themselves, an unrelenting state of war obtains between Brer Rabbit and his powerful antagonists. It is a war to the knife, without truce or quarter or forgiveness. The moral vision projected in these tales is that of men who have been brutalized, degraded, rendered powerless—and yet who manage to survive by dint of their superior endurance and mother wit, their cunning artifice and sheer effrontery.

The world of Brer Rabbit is a pathological world, both emotionally and morally. There is nothing normal about being a slave, and nothing normal about the black man's response to an intolerable situation. Absolute power produces absolute desperation; all moral scruples are discarded in a fierce effort to survive. This is the explanation for the code of conduct that is celebrated in these tales. Deceit and trickery, theft and betrayal, murder and mayhem are endorsed as appropriate responses to the slave condition. Such are the ruthless expedients of Brer Rabbit, who can survive in Hell by outsmarting the Devil. Having been raised in a brier patch, he is one tough bunny.

Uncle Remus and Brer Rabbit stand in the relationship of

mask to countermask. Uncle Remus, the creation of Joel Chandler Harris, is one of many masks employed by the Plantation School to justify the restoration of white supremacy. But Brer Rabbit, the creation of anonymous black slaves, may be thought of as a countermask which contravenes the pastoral charade and exposes the harsh reality. . . .

The most profound of the Brer Rabbit tales is the famous story of the Wonderful Tar-Baby. Brer Fox, hoping to trap Brer Rabbit, makes a figurine of sticky tar and places it in his victim's path. Brer Rabbit, attempting to exchange polite salutations with the stranger, is infuriated by his silence: "Ef you don't take off dat hat en tell me howdy, I'm gwineter bus' you wide open." But the Tar-Baby maintains his silence, so Brer Rabbit lams him with one fist. "Ef you don't lemme loose, I'll knock you agin," says Brer Rabbit, and the other fist is stuck fast. Whereupon he kicks and butts, only to find himself completely mired in the tar.

Hubris is the subject of this story. For once Brer Rabbit oversteps himself, taking on the white man's ways of arrogance and willfulness, and bullying the tarry representative of blackness. To bully is to be cruel and overbearing to others weaker than oneself, and for this psychological indulgence Brer Rabbit pays with one of his few abject defeats. On a deeper plane, the tale is concerned with the relationship of will and circumstance. To *force* circumstance, to browbeat or intimidate it, to want one's way no matter what, is a fatal attitude. For circumstance is sticky stuff that seems pliable enough, but leaves us, if we fight it, with a nasty problem of extrication.

The sequel to this tale, **"How Mr. Rabbit Was Too Smart for Mr. Fox,"** delineates the proper relationship of will to circumstance. Brer Rabbit has been trapped, but he retrieves his error by *collaborating* with the force of circumstance, now embodied in the figure of Brer Fox. He manipulates his adversary by appealing to what Poe has called the imp of the perverse. As Brer Fox casts about for a means of killing his captive, Brer Rabbit counters each proposal by saying in effect: burn me, hang me, drown me, skin me, but whatever you do, don't fling me in that brier-patch. Which of course is the inevitable outcome, and Brer Rabbit skips off shouting triumphantly, "Bred en bawn in a brier-patch, Brer Fox—bred en bawn in a brier-patch!"

The brier-patch is an eloquent image of the uses of adversity. Lacking the defensive equipment of the porcupine, the rabbit borrows his defense from his environment; a hostile universe is thus converted to a sanctuary and a home. Such is the nature of antagonistic cooperation, as defined by Albert Murray in *The Hero and the Blues*. The nimble footwork, quick wit, and boundless invention of Brer Rabbit are called forth precisely by adversity. He is thus the forerunner of the blues hero who is equal to all emergencies and can extricate himself from any difficulty. This quality of improvisation in the face of danger, or as Hemingway would put it, grace under pressure, is in Murray's view the basis of the blues tradition.

From The Favorite Uncle Remus, *written by Joel Chandler Harris. Illustrated by A. B. Frost.*

The Tar-Baby stories bring our discussion of the Brer Rabbit tales to a fitting close. For these are the supreme fictions of the folk imagination, as memorable for their esthetic form as for the wisdom they impart. When we consider that the artists who created these and similar animal fables were illiterate slaves, we can only stand in awe of their achievement. By this act of creativity they vindicated their humanity and established their claim upon the highest faculty of man: the moral imagination. In so doing they transformed their lives and overcame the limits of their low estate. They accomplished, in short, the crucial metamorphosis of a fate endured into a fate transcended.

Margery Fisher

SOURCE: "Brer Rabbit," in *Who's Who in Children's Books: A Treasury of the Familiar Characters of Childhood,* Holt, Rinehart and Winston, 1975, pp. 53-54.

[Uncle Remus's] acceptance of his situation reflects a way of life which is naturally unacceptable to the present day, nor is the dialect of the stories immediately accessible, though with patience and a little thought it can be understood easily enough. The particular value of using Uncle Remus as story-teller is that tales whose motifs and plots are familiar all over the world are given a special authenticity by him. Because the old man treats the world of Brer Rabbit as if it were real (and gives it a history of its own through his references to an earlier Golden Age when there was no dissension among the animals), it becomes

totally real to the listener. No questions of scale or probability arise. It seems equally possible for Brer Rabbit to rob a vegetable garden or to think out the stratagem of the Tar Baby like a mischievous boy or to outdo Brer Fox in polite social amiabilities with Miss Meadows and the girls like a leisurely Southern gentleman. When these fables and folk tales are retold nowadays we receive them as beast fables full of amusing but representative characters; told by Uncle Remus, the characters are seen as individuals.

Nina Mikkelsen

SOURCE: "When the Animals Talked—A Hundred Years of Uncle Remus," in *Children's Literature Association Quarterly,* Vol. 8, No. 1, Spring, 1983, pp. 3-5, 31.

[There are 185 Uncle Remus] tales in all, of literary and historical importance for the moral and social viewpoints they directly and indirectly express, for the framing device of the old man's comments and the young boy's questions, for the humor and picturesque language, and above all, for the continuously intriguing question of whether or not Harris was able to deal with the literary matter of another race.

Thematically, the Uncle Remus tales set forth a rural, Southern, mythology, a code of behavior for the underdog, in which cunning and subterfuge replace open resistance, neither debate nor compromise being a possibility within the master-slave relationship. The underdog trickster who survives and triumphs in these stories is most often the rabbit, as is often the case in both Indian and African tales. . . .

Neither superhuman nor possessing magic powers, Brer Rabbit is quite frequently all too human, guilty at times of foolish and prideful actions, at other times of illegal or amoral ones. Yet always he survives, for small and defenseless as he is, his more powerful opponent invariably exercises less intelligence.

In Harris's first book, *Uncle Remus: His Songs and His Sayings,* at least eleven survival tactics are implemented by seven trickster figures: the rabbit in eighteen stories, the terrapin in three, the turkey buzzard, the frog, and the fox each in two, and the possum and crayfish each in one. In some stories, the trickster uses a combination of tactics; in others he employs several varieties of one particular tactic. . . .

Deception is the major underpinning of many stories. . . .

Nights With Uncle Remus, Harris's second book, depicts additional survival strategies. . . .

While the stories themselves spoke of civil strife among the animals, of public and private humiliations, of thievery, trickery, and life and death stakes, the framework surrounding them showed human kindness, patience, decency, and respect between the man and the boy. The framing device also helped to clarify many aspects of the tales, and because so many stories opened with the child's commentary on the previous story, it also served as a unifying device for interrelating the tales. On an artistic level, the framework enabled Harris to create the illusion of the spoken voice, as when, in **"Mr. Fox and the Deceitful Frogs,"** he describes Remus speaking terrapin talk—a "peculiar gurgling, jerky, liquid sound," says Harris, "made by pouring water from a large tub." The framework also enabled Harris to enhance the mood of a story. In **"Where the Harrycane Comes From,"** Remus first instructs the boy about rain clouds, as the sky turns "dark and threatening," later they move inside the cabin to watch the approaching storm and listen to the story.

In both the stories and the framework, Harris hoped to reflect what he felt was the black man's most prominent characteristic, his "quaint and homely humor," as well as what he felt would reveal the "poetic imagination of the Negro." Humor in the tales arises from comic expressions that juxtapose humor and animal behavior, as when Sis B'ar says, "If I wuz ter lef my ole man money-pus layin' 'round dat a-way, he'd des natally rip up de planks in de flo, en t'ar all de bark off'n de trees", and from proverbs such as "Don't kick 'fo you ere spurred." There are word fusings such as "reckermember," witty and descriptive comparisons like "De little Rabbits dey went inter der hole in de cellar, dey did, like blowin' out a candle," and rhythmical phrasings. . . .

Harris's diligence as an amateur folklorist is noteworthy. Not only was he quite anxious to preserve the stories in the exact form in which he heard them, the dialect, as he said, of the cotton plantation (as well as, in the second volume, of the Sea Islands' Gullah), he was also careful to verify every story he heard, retaining the particular version that seemed to be the most "characteristic," and to present it "without embellishment and without exaggeration." But unanswered questions still remain. As a white man, could Harris really judge what was truly characteristic of the black man? Furthermore, at a time when the stories themselves had as their major thrust the survival tactic of subterfuge, could they have been fully understood by Harris or any white man?

Throughout the years of slavery, the animal fables had been transmitted orally by storytellers to members of the black culture both to entertain and to inculcate social values; the most effective devices of humor and language pattern had been preserved and refined in many cases through numerous tellings, and characters and events had evolved as symbols for power struggles among individuals and institutions. The black child and adult were thus taught such survival tactics as passive resistance, no-work "work" ethics, and the value of entertaining a white audience, all through the safety of allegory. (According to Harris few black people ever acknowledged to strangers that they even knew anything of the legends, surely few divulged the allegorical meanings of the tales to Harris or any white person). Concerning **"Brer Rabbit's Laughing Place,"** for example, it is unclear whether Harris

understood, as did the black man, that "laughing place" meant a particular place, the Underground Railroad. In the framework of the tale, he seems to be interpreting the term in a very different way, as the imaginative capability, something he thought the child and the whole postwar era lacked, as when Remus says, "Dem wuz laughin' times, an'it look like dey wain't never comin' back."

The new little boy of this book, the child of the earlier child who has, by 1905, grown up, is "intensely practical." His imagination, Harris says, is "unaccompanied by any of the ancient illusions that make the memory of childhood so delightful. He had a contempt for those who believed in Santa Claus". (Harris takes up the same subject two years later in an essay for the *Uncle Remus Magazine,* entitled **"Santa Claus and the Fairies,"** in which he countered the theories, prevalent in his day, that children had need of the practical, with what he felt children needed: the possibility of faith in ideal truths.) This second child is only "infrequently disturbed by laughter" and then only in the company of Uncle Remus. What he needs, Remus tells him, is a laughing place "whar you kin go an' tickle yo'se'f an' laugh whedder you wanter laugh er no." The child replies that he knows he has such a place, and it is here with Uncle Remus. "Why you are my laughing place," he cries.

Harris had found his own "laughing place" as a youth listening to the stories of the animal antics on Turnwold Plantation, and he had managed to convey this laughter, this "poetic imagination" and "quaint and homely humor" to his countrymen. But did he realize that the black man saw "laughing place" as a metaphor for something entirely different, for freedom? Certainly Remus's statement—that he had no occasion to go to the rabbit's laughing place, yet if he could walk fifteen or sixteen miles a day like he used to, he could go right now and put his hand on the spot—is suggestive of the physical journey of the Underground Railroad. And when Harris describes Miss Squinch Owl as "a little fowl not much bigger dan a joybird laughin' herse'f blin' when dey wa'n't a thing in de roun' worl' fer ter laugh at," who tells the other animals, "You all dunner what laughin' is . . . You can't laugh when you try ter laugh", the evidence seems to become even more obvious. "Who mought de lady be?" Brer Bull asks. "Dey all say dey dunno," says Remus, "an' dey got a mighty good reason fer der sesso, kaze Miss Squinch Owl, she flies at night wid de bats an' de Betsy Bugs." How much of the owl character the reader is to associate with such heroines of slavery as Harriet Tubman and Sojourner Truth, who also flew at night with the bats and the bugs, is left unsettled, for Remus soon moves into the story itself, with the fox asking to see Brer Rabbit's laughing place and the rabbit taking him to a pine thicket and telling him that running "full tilt" through the vines and bushes will tickle him so much that he won't be able to stand up for laughing. When the fox runs to the East and runs to the West and jams "his head in a hornet's nes'," Brer Rabbit can only reiterate that it is his laughing place and no place for the fox, which suggests that the white man will only be tricked (and tormented) if he tries to discover the place.

The white man obviously would not be tormented for discovering the black man's sense of humor (a literal interpretation of the story) or his imagination (Harris's interpretation in the framework of the story). But the stakes would have been much higher if the white man had discovered the black man's escape route to freedom. If the story makes sense only within the context of racial implications, it is difficult to imagine that by 1905 Harris did not notice these subtleties, and perhaps he did. But that did not mean Remus thought the boy should be burdened with them, especially this particular boy, who was just learning to laugh himself.

In his own day, Harris's stories reached a predominantly white audience (and a fairly wide one, the first book selling 4,000 copies annually for two decades), and although the published stories had both the humorous and educative value that they had always had for the black audience, there was this difference—that white adults appreciated the *universal* experience displayed (no doubt also finding a certain amount of comic relief in associating the "quaint" dialect and "homely humor" of Remus and the animals with a race of people they often regarded as either humorous childlike figures or quaint curiosities).

White children, who often found themselves in the position of the underdog in domestic power struggles, could easily identify, with the tactics of the rabbit trickster.

While succeeding generations and changing values have produced a culture very different from Harris's own, the stories have not lost their appeal. Records and cassettes of several Remus tales, told in a rural black vernacular by notable storyteller Jackie Torrence, are now available from Weston Woods, Weston, Connecticut, and several editions of the first, second and third volumes remain in print. In addition, at least seven illustrated collections are available for children today. Jane Shaw's *Uncle Remus Stories* illustrates modern practices of revision concerning the books. Although original speech patterns have been maintained, phonetic spellings have been standardized, vocabulary occasionally updated and long passages of the earlier framework abbreviated; and the sketches and sayings, so often picturing Remus as obsequious and ignorant (capable of such remarks as "No use talkin' boss—Put a spelling book in a nigger's han's, en right den en ear' you loozes a plow-hand"), have been eliminated entirely.

Also, black authors have begun to publish their own collections of animal tales (many corresponding to those Remus told). Books like William J. Faulkner's *The Days When the Animals Talked* and Julius Lester's *The Knee-High Man* provide both black and white children with additional historical background for the tales, as well as the more realistic picture of the slave telling his stories to a black adult or child rather than a white one. As Simon Brown (the former slave who told Faulkner the tales) says, "Willie, unless a slave knew how to outthink his master or overseer, he might not get enough to eat in the wintertime . . . Now I was too smart to ever go hungry. . . . I was too much like Brer Rabbit. I used my head the same

way he did." The animal tales of Faulkner and Lester also substitute standardized speech patterns and spellings for Harris's earlier attempts to replicate syntax and the exact sound of speech in print.

But even after revision has prepared the tales for a modern audience, it is invariably Harris's version that we remember, for the comic situation and the dialogue, for the original expressions, and above all, for the common thread that binds the tales: in trickery there is strength—and equality. . . .

Admittedly, the tales reflect Harris's nostalgic dream for an idealized plantation life, which he felt the black person remembered with only pleasant memories (highly questionable indeed), as well as an era when the black man's humor and language could be described as "quaint" and he could be categorized as a "type"—weak, harmless, helpless, and mischievous—faint praise for people strong enough to survive the rigorous labor of the cotton and rice fields and imaginative enough to entertain the white man and his children, while never yielding up all their secrets. Yet Remus and his stories have a great deal to tell us about a time when the only hope of survival for an entire race was through the tactics tricksters of every culture have employed.

Although Harris could not escape absorbing many of the now dated attitudes and locutions of his own age and culture, he was to become himself the magician for which he was searching in 1879, catching and storing up from the black antebellum experience that unique and original material "as new as the world, as old as life." If, in 1880, white Southerners had the best opportunity to record the black man's experience, then it is fortunate that the white Southerner who did it was Harris, a man with a listening ear, a strong literary talent, and a humorous spirit. When Remus and the animals talked to Harris they didn't tell him everything. But they told him enough to create a Southern and an American literature of lasting value.

John Goldthwaite

SOURCE: "The Black Rabbit: Part One," in *Signal,* No. 47, May, 1985, pp. 86-111.

[*English critic Goldthwaite is the author of perhaps the most controversial essay about Harris to have appeared since Bernard Wolfe's "Uncle Remus and the Malevolent Rabbit" (1949). In the following excerpt, Goldthwaite states that the publication of* Uncle Remus, His Songs and His Sayings *in 1880 was "irrefutably the central event in the making of the modern children's story." The essay was originally published in two parts, in the May and September 1985 issues of Signal.*]

As busy as children's story has been with the comings and goings of the mouse, the bear, and the cat, . . . and as ancient as two of these are in the literature, modern make-believe does not begin with them. The homely explanation for what children read and watch today and where it comes from is rabbits. Arrange the major works of make-believe from the past century in chronological order and there emerges a clear line of descent going back as far as Potter's Peter, the first animal-child hero in a story, and then back a little farther still, to the 1880s, when the coming generation of fantasists was still impressionable and its members all within imagining range of the same ideas and images. What we find in that decade is what we should expect to find, given the otherwise inexplicable proliferation of animals in story over the next decade and a half. *The Jungle Books* and *Just-So Stories,* the *Hollow Tree Stories* of Albert Bigelow Paine, the tales of Beatrix Potter, *The Wind in the Willows,* and *Old Mother West Wind* and *Uncle Wiggily*—the appearance of all these books within fifteen years of each other indicates that in the 1880s story must have taken a significant turn in their direction; and in fact what we do find happening in that period is the beast fable suddenly shedding its ancient moralizing intent and taking on the affective weight of modern prose fantasy. In 1880 one creature in particular is put forward in print who, becoming a favourite with the reading public, will open up new possibilities for storytelling—possibilities that will be apparent to everyone at much the same time. . . .

It is from this hare, the first animal personage in children's story, that modern make-believe springs; it is the force of his personality on the public imagination that caused a shift in the direction of story—his and the personality of the old man telling us about him; and it is with him, Brer Rabbit, and with his teller, Uncle Remus, that any look into the origins of our modern nursery lore rightly ought to begin. . . .

Joel Chandler Harris's protest that 'There is nothing here but an old Negro man, a little boy, and a dull reporter,' delivered in alarm at the number of children, folklorists, and other correspondents descending on him through the mails, is characteristic of the repertoire of disavowals the shy author suddenly had to adopt to get himself through the day. The 'nothing' was of course something brand-new in story. Chaucer's pilgrims, Scheherazade, and the titular Mother Goose notwithstanding, never before had the image of the storyteller or the occasion of the telling been made so real to life or so appealing as with this old Negro and this compliant white child. And it was not just the conception of the book that was new, or even of the first importance, though it seemed so at the time to Mark Twain and others; it was the tales themselves: here, within an old man's memory of plantation life and transcending it onto an international stage, was a world still very much alive and kicking, a realm of make-believe unlike anything that had appeared in American letters or indeed anywhere, delivered with the air of a thing freshly discovered. Around and about its neighbourhoods roamed characters unknown to fantasy, speaking in accents of English few had ever heard outside the South and which none had ever seen in print (the dialect of regional writers and minstrels was exposed as wholly bogus; the rhetoric of contemporary fiction, as florid and tiresome).

As they told of their hero Brer Rabbit, these tales were, and sounded in every syllable, as big as life and twice as natural. So real were they and so real seemed their putative black narrator that southern children introduced to the real author by Twain, who had taken Harris in tow, disbelieved that this portly white man could possibly be their Uncle Remus. In New Orleans a crowd was overheard whispering, 'Look, he's white.' But that was the luck of these tales: whereas all but a few like 'The Tar Baby' would surely have been lost as the Civil War disrupted the flow of story from one generation to the next and Negroes born into the troubles of Reconstruction became less and less interested in what the old-timers had to tell, the tales instead passed safely through an honest scribe and into literature. Harris's genius had been to recognize virtue in men and story and to succumb to it. What he rescued of the oral tradition he reproduced faithfully: not one of the tales is whitewashed with whimsy or bathos or cheap effects (a fate that would catch up with them, however, in Walt Disney's *Song of the South*). Harris retold them according to the best tellings he had heard, from men he had troubled himself to know since boyhood. . . .

[After the publication of *The Complete Uncle Remus* in 1955,] the book that had become all the rage on publication and which for seventy-five years had been an honoured classic of American letters simply runs out of credibility and evaporates into the haze of history. Talking in dialect and the image of a slave as a man contented with his lot (more or less) did an injury, blacks knew, to their children, and whites, with the rise of the civil rights movement of the 1960s, quickly abandoned the work as an embarrassment. An Uncle Remus may have been the right, the necessary, choice of character for the telling of these tales, but he was, everyone agreed, the wrong one for the preserving of them. By 1976 a Bicentennial-inspired survey of children's-book professionals could yield, consequently, a list of the ten best American children's books of the previous two hundred years on which no place could be found for the one book that for its art and historical importance ought to have headed the list. In 1980 the centennial of *Songs and Sayings* passed with hardly a whisper of recognition. No mention at all is made of the work in most modern histories of American children's books.

There is an undue irony in the absence of *Uncle Remus* from a tally of home-grown greats. Harris himself had declared, in an 1879 call for a native Southern fiction that would transcend the merely provincial, that there could come out of the South no contribution to our understanding of what was American that did not incorporate the black character and no advance out of the old rhetoric into a clear, colloquial prose that did not acknowledge the black contribution to spoken English. 'I want you to illustrate the matter in your own way, which is preeminently the American way,' Harris wrote A. B. Frost in 1892 as they prepared *Uncle Remus and His Friends* for publication. 'We shall then have real American stuff [sic] illustrated in real American style.'

Real American tales as real Americans told them, pictured by an American with an instinct for the real earth on which make-believe must stand. It is one of the few happy pairings in children's literature, this collaboration in black and white—equal to Tenniel's *Alice* and to Shepard's *Wind in the Willows,* a book that descends from it. Today, despite several efforts to recast the tales into Standard English, *Uncle Remus* is an unbook. No one can rightly object to this eclipse on extraliterary grounds. We can regret that the best of all American books ever handed down to children is a book we cannot in good conscience read them. We can regret, too, that a body of folklore equal to Grimm's or the *1001 Nights* is a heritage black students are unlikely to know in its pure form, as their great-grandparents spoke it. We can regret that to enjoy these tales at all we must take ourselves to some Preservation Hall of the imagination, but we cannot deny that justice was due.

What does need correcting, however, is the regrettable fact that the only American children's book to exert a profound influence on storytellers at home and elsewhere has become a book without critical standing. In its own day so famous as to make the usual kinds of acknowledgement by the next generation of storytellers superfluous, it is, in the absence of overwhelming testimony, seen now as a work of no apparent importance whatsoever. Its influence on the major English fantasists from Kipling to Milne and on such popular Americans as Thornton Burgess and Howard Garis, from whom so much of our nursery reading derives, has gone unremarked, as far as I can discover, by any writer on children's literature. Yet before the publication of *Uncle Remus* in 1880 there was nothing like, and for fifty years after there was little else of note in make-believe but the *Uncle Remus* order of serial adventures in the countryside. However else we regard the book, it is irrefutably the central event in the making of modern children's story. . . .

Thirty years ago it could be assumed the reader would have some familiarity with *Uncle Remus,* but this is no longer the case. And anyway, a literature in which even a sneeze is heroic ('Bimeby he sneeze—*huckychow!*') is a literature that wants quoting. As we listen we should remember that although Harris's dialect is a phonetic approximation it is nevertheless the genuine article and not the mugging of an Al Jolson in white gloves and black face. Harris, from having spent as much time on Negro back porches as anywhere else in his boyhood, could by his own account think in dialect—his fellow Southerners, remember, had at first assumed that he *was* black. We have, as well, Mark Twain's word (in *Life on the Mississippi*) that 'in the matter of writing it he is the only master the country has produced'.

Keeping this in mind as the historical basis for the telling, we should perhaps however abandon the term dialect and in its place substitute the word style or voice. Dialect is a linguistic not a literary tag; it suggests the language in question is a degraded English rather than a form of expression with its own legitimacy. Think of *Uncle Remus* as story, as make-believe, and the dialect becomes the right and happy sound of the world being created in the

tales. Harris himself denied there was anything degraded about it: 'The difference between real dialect and lingo is that the first is preservative, while the latter is destructive, of language. Judged by this standard the negro dialect is as perfect as any the world ever saw.' And of its stylistic advantages: 'It has a fluency all its own; it gives a new coloring to statement, and allows of a swift shading in narrative that can be reached in literary English only in the most painful and roundabout way.' The stories he attempted to write for children in Standard English in the 1890s, in fact, are so painful and roundabout in contrast to the *Uncle Remus* tales it seems natural to conclude that through the black style of speaking Harris found a release into storytelling that was not otherwise available to him.

The dialect affords us a release into the tales as well: this perfectly rendered it deflects us straightaway into something we see is make-believe and catches us believing before we can think not to. It would not help us to believe to say of a character in any other way that when he laughed 'he laff en laff twel he hatter hug a tree fer ter keep fum drappin' on de groun'.' But *Uncle Remus* is tall-tale stuff calling for tall words, and these are the right words to inhibit our scepticism. A fear of language, a self-consciousness in its use, so common to Harris's mannered times, is quite foreign to these tales. In the line 'Ole Miss Goose she wuz down at de spring, washin', en b'ilin', en battlin' cloze' there is not the faintest echo of an author caught in the act of thinking twice before speaking. The event and its expression are perfectly married. Miss Goose exists, the clothes exist, the eternal battle between them exists, and we ourselves are as natural to the scene as if we had happened upon it while out for a stroll. That 'fluency all its own' allowed Harris—like Lewis Carroll a stutterer—to forget that he himself existed and to become one with the tale he was telling. Consequently there is the purest delight in listening to *Uncle Remus* and to the variety of things its language can do. Harris's easy virtuosity with the dialect catches each tale in mid-leap, like Brer Rabbit himself. Rendered into Standard English the stories can (as many editions attest) only sit there in the rhetorical mud like Brer Fox with 'a spell er de dry grins'. . . .

I cannot think of another American children's book that does not sound lifeless and slack by comparison. . . .

What we hear in *Uncle Remus* is the real world talking itself alive through the voices of the people living in one corner of it. They are talking animals, true, but they are living just next door. Their tales are fantasy, but what we hear in them is the noise of our neighbours. . . .

[Everywhere] in *Uncle Remus*—both in the frame stories concerning Uncle Remus and the little boy and within the tales themselves—we are moving in small, sometimes accidental steps away from the pure economy of the fable and toward the more sustained fantasy of the next generation of storytellers.

Uncle Remus points us toward a number of modern genres, and not all of them literary. It points us toward the wisecracking M.G.M. cartoons of the 1940s and toward the more benign satire of newspaper strips like *Pogo.* It points us toward our modern love of parody in general, and even in a way toward rock 'n' roll. And, apposite to this study, *Uncle Remus* is taking us forward into modern children's story. Not all the tales in *Uncle Remus* take a fearsome turn; in fact most do not. There are stories that, beyond exhibiting a human immediacy never before granted animals in story, have a great friendliness and gentle humour about them; and it is from these that the beast fable becomes redirected toward a new audience in the children's room. . . .

It is with two *Uncle Remus* fables of 1880 and 1892 that we see attention beginning its shift to young children in children's story. The tales are **'A Story About the Little Rabbits'** *(Songs and Sayings)* and **'Why Brother Wolf Didn't Eat the Little Rabbits'** *(Friends: 'The Fresher the Better').* . . .

What we have . . . in **'The Fresher the Better'** and **'A Story About the Little Rabbits'** is something quite new in make-believe, the first truly affecting portrait of young children in their literature. They run at their own pace, *blickety-blickety,* behind the *bookity-bookity* gait of the grownups; they are granted the right to cry when things aren't going well, and the moment help is in sight, toting that jug of molasses, all peril is forgotten and it's '"Lemme tas'e, daddy! Lemme tas'e, daddy!"' Those urchin bodies gathered in the road in their jeans and homespun in Frost's picture of them are, though rabbits, real children, never before seen in make-believe at this tender age outside *Mother Goose* and a few toy books. They are a portrait of the very young that will enable the next generation of storytellers to reimagine children's literature along entirely new lines.

John Goldthwaite

SOURCE: "The Black Rabbit: Part Two," in *Signal,* No. 48, September, 1985, pp. 148-67.

One feature of animal fantasy distinguishing it from folklore is the presence in the former of a memorable place for the story to happen, while in folklore the place is perfunctory. You cannot map the settlement in which these tales occur, the way you can map Grahame's riverbank, or Milne's hundred-acre wood, or Jansson's Moomin Valley. There is no detail in the text by which to orient the brers' quarters one to the other or to chart the progress of their comeuppances; nor would there be, considering that such tales must serve as well in Virginia and Texas as in Georgia. Harris located Brer Rabbit and his neighbours in the truck patches and woodlots behind a plantation in middle Georgia, but nothing in the tales themselves so restricts them. They were local to every corner of the South; the absence of any interior geography follows from their nature as folklore. At least we can say this—theoretically it is true; but in actuality there is something mappable in the stories after all—a named place in the settlement that, providing a geographical centre, localizes events to itself.

An actual map of 'de neighborhoods' is impossible; but focusing on this one identifiable dot we can almost make out, along the periphery of our vision, the details of some storybook American township emerging—a Yoknapatawpha County of the animal world. . . .

It is interesting . . . that Harris could find 'few Negroes who will acknowledge to a stranger that they know anything of these legends'. It is interesting but not surprising. Prisoners don't ordinarily share their jokes with their jailers, and certainly not if the jokes are at the jailers' expense. These were tales told on the sly, a private literature for slaves and a few white children. They gave a free place to live together, at least in story, to a people who must otherwise live kenneled like dogs in other people's backyards. They are a literature of captivity, of irreverent reports passed from one prisoner to the next. Like other captives in history the blacks created their lamentations and their satires. The lamentations we hear in spirituals and blues; the satire, in the trickster tales.

The tales are satirical of course in the sport they make of the strong in behalf of the weak but clever, or of the foolish, who lose their heads for wanting to be in the fashion. But the real satire in these tales lies in the language itself. It is the master's English, but inflected in such a way as to make it, like Brer Rabbit, as big as life and twice as natural. Black English is the sound of constricted souls insisting on life, their life, through every syllable. It becomes a way of knowing yourself by the way you speak another man's lingo, when his lingo has been forced on you. What is being satirized by the language of these tales, ultimately, is the stultification of a life lived in Standard English. . . .

I do not want to overstate the case for *Uncle Remus*—my sole subject here being children's story—but I do think its impact on English speaking culture between 1880 and the 1950s, both in and out of literature, is greater than would ordinarily be conceded to any book both accessible to children and hugely popular. Greater and also difficult to assess: the books appealed to so many readers from so many levels of society and for so many reasons, and spilled over into the culture so generally, that tracing their aftereffects would be as delicate a business as digging branch lightning out of a sand dune. It is easy enough to demonstrate their influence on popular forms of entertainment, quite another thing to unearth any solid influence on serious literature. Yet given its presence in literate households *Uncle Remus* must have helped set the imaginative terms of their knowing for several generations of readers (to borrow a phrase from Roger Sale), and so I think it must be reckoned a contributing, if unlikely, cause of modernism—helping to change, for example, the way that we speak in prose and the way that fiction came to be organized in the first decade of the century.

But clearly this shift of emphasis in how we read the world and retell it in turn is most easily seen where the main energy of *Uncle Remus* was discharged, in children's story. Tales of makebelieve before 1880 were variations played out all on a human theme; their heroes were young adults or children sent into the world to be put at physical and spiritual risk, and rewarded, usually, with the honorific 'grown-up'. With *Uncle Remus* a new cast was brought on stage and all that changed. Our perception of story changed, and our perception of how time passes and our appreciation of how much of our life is a life in the world and how much a passage through it. Before *Uncle Remus* story was a curtain rising on our expectations and setting again when the tale was done with us. We fell with Alice down the rabbit hole and woke with her at dream's end, to say goodbye. However resonant her adventures in Wonderland, they were a singular experience in our minds. They were singular because we each perceive ourself to be a singularity in the world, one sensibility heeding its own progress towards the grave, and reflexively we look to art for news of our fellow travellers. But with *Uncle Remus,* or any open-ended saga, we can break free of this habit of imagining, to perceive ourselves members in good standing of the community that will survive us. If our own lives, our singular stories, are inexorably falling off into the future, here in the serial duration and death are an illusion: we are invited to live awhile where time is arrested and the world peopled, unchanged, forever.

How this shift in our response to story came about becomes clearer, perhaps, when we go beyond what story meant to the slave and look at what it could *not* mean to him. And what it could not mean to him was freedom—the freedom to go where he would like to go in his imagination and to be what he would like to be. Before the modernism of Kafka and Beckett this freedom, or the promise of it, was the given of almost all Western literature, however pessimistic this or that work may otherwise have been about man's free will and his pursuit of happiness.

The slave stories of *Uncle Remus* are precursors of modernism in this one sense, then: they were not, they could not be, anything like the European model of popular story, which from the fairy tale to the novels of Scott and Dickens had taken the form of the romance. This type of story, which begins in Western civilization with *The Odyssey* and continues on the cheap today, a slave simply hasn't the wherewithal to tell. There are no heroic exploits in his storypack to pull out for the amusement of his own or his master's children. The man can have no dreams of glory to relate when he knows that 'sold South' will be the extent of his travels. There will be no embryo Robin Hoods gestating in his lore, no Sinbads cruising his seas, no Jacks setting out to slay giants and win a kingdom. A slave cannot send a corn-rowed Alice to argue some sense from the nonsense of the master's world or imagine a soul unfolding as that world works on the instincts of a Pinocchio. A black Pinocchio does not grow up to be a real boy; he grow up to be the master's 'boy'. The only kingdoms he can hope to gain are Canada or Kingdom Come; the only giants he can hope to slay are hunger, fear, and pain. Little in his inherited stock of images from Africa and nothing in his life as a captive would lead the slave to dream such dreams or tell such tales. A Robert Louis Stevenson is free to contemplate his possibilities, walk out of his life, and reappear aboard some westward-sailing ship, the man of his choice. But a slave can do no such thing, and his kind of story will be different. The hero he imagines for himself must stay put, like himself, and survive in place. Never mind the keys of any kingdom but the last; the rewards he will conjure up will be a decent supper and the victory of getting through the day.

In celebrating those who must beat the odds wherever fate has made them resident, however, the slave storyteller has one great advantage over the roving ego of the romantic looking to wrest a story from his contest with the world: the slave is immune to the pathos that underwrites all such dreams of glory. Romanticism is a solitary sport and the slave's life is of necessity communal. The romantic hero is born an orphan and dies alone, having lived to rewrite the world in his image. The slave's hero is born to the community, its legitimate son, and, being one with the community, is immortal. Black storytellers fell into this immortality of communal laughter over solitary tears by simply, but with genius, making the best imaginative use of the terms of their bondage. Stepping back, so to speak, into the woods and swamps surrounding the plantation, they could imagine themselves in another, a more natural, 'neighbourhood' and let their minds wander—'studyin' en laffin'' and getting even—down the same paths and through the same silences as the fox and the rabbit.

When you have gained at least the stealthy freedom a fox or a rabbit enjoys you can find in the dangers of slave life an object for play, and before long you will be building an imaginable life in the midst of an unimaginable one. Become a rabbit running free through the neighbourhoods, and what began as a compensation for your hardships can take on a life of its own. And the more you talk about your dream self and share him with the neighbours, the field hands, the children, the more you will warm to the game and gain speed, until you have outrun the master's English into an exuberance of your own, a verbal release from having had to talk like a nigger all day. As he gains in velocity your hare takes on the weight of reality, and you, too, when the master says you are dirt, will emerge from this course of story as big as life and twice as natural; your secret self having attained by imaginative acceleration the weight of a man who lived before the slave time and will live long after it.

This disclosure of *Uncle Remus,* that a people so confined could tell stories so exuberant, proved a happy discovery for certain readers at the turn of the century who were themselves looking for a release into some new order of available reality. What these readers shared, Kipling excepted, was what the slaves had shared, and what freed blacks continued to share: an immunity to the glory of empire-building and an unfamiliarity with that ghostly emotion that underwrites all tales of romance, the pathos of the dying fall. Colonialism, after all, becomes, however you play it, a glorious bore, and worse, a burden of guilt, having led only to more slaves. The idea of empire was going bankrupt even in Kipling's day. And the dying fall, whether one is dying for love or for country, what is it but another way of saying, they'll be sorry when I'm dead? Unless of course you happen to survive your adventures in the world, in which case you must either come home to puzzle out the remainder of your life or else end up some adulterous sot in the outback, awaiting your Somerset Maugham. So it is no wonder that a book like *Uncle Remus* would have had great appeal for certain readers at the close of the century, as the terms of romance literature became less and less plausible.

Inevitably, many of these readers would be women. . . .

[A] reader like Beatrix Potter might have responded to the exuberant disclosure of the work, seeing a parallel between the plight of black American slaves and her own constrained existence as the daughter of a starchy upper-middle-class family for whom schooling and a profession were nothing she need worry her little head over. . . .

Uncle Remus revealed that stories fit for readers to read could be made of such modest stuff as she had at hand.

This message was welcome news as well to a number of men of the period who found themselves geographically and emotionally distanced from a popular culture that, when not fatuously reinventing fairies, was metaphorically forever heading West. For Kenneth Grahame, Thornton Burgess, Howard Garis, and, later, A. A. Milne, the reality of make-believe lay—as it does with young children—less in the haunted past or some unconquered elsewhere than in the present and the local. These writers, when they dreamed, saw the world from the point-of-view of a six-year-old—often times with sophisticated embellishments, but nonetheless looking up at the world from below and out at the world from a recalled centre of childlike perception. For them the contemporary taste for the sentimental lullabies of Eugene Field, as he looked back on childhood and lied for our tears, or the quasi-religious bathos of Oscar Wilde's fairy tales, were poor substitutes for the active pleasures of making believe; the calling-all-boys dreams of glory of a Howard Pyle or an N. C. Wyeth, with their nostalgic King Arthur and costume-party buccaneers, were romance too much degraded into the merely picturesque to suggest any possibilities for living that could be conveyed to children. The sum effect of such literature is to leave us feeling it is more pleasant to retreat into day-dreams than to reimagine the world from the realities at hand.

Make-believe, to feel right and promising, would now instead have to be found closer to home. The publication of *Uncle Remus* gave this need a place and a way to happen. By anthropomorphizing the fauna of the rural neighbourhoods *Uncle Remus* gave storytellers fresh material with which to reconstruct the world in terms that could be at once familiar and magical with suggestion. A new set of images, see what you can build. This is what we find in the best work of the next fifty years or so: worlds are being made on the *Uncle Remus* model that comprehend the myriad details, speaking voices, variables

of time and space, and allusions necessary to evoke a world. The fields and briar patches of the rural South, the ponds and creeks, cart roads, kitchens, and front porches brought to life in *Uncle Remus*—together with the sense conveyed there of a world properly evolved to its fulness—these particulars and this sense we find Potter, Grahame, and Milne transposing and adapting to the English countryside; Kipling (the only traveller in this generation of stay-at-homes) to the more exotic jungles of India; Thornton Burgess to the fields of Massachusetts; and in time Jean de Brunhoff to an Africa that lay just around the corner from Paris, Walt Kelly to Georgia's Okefenokee Swamp, and Tove Jansson to the coast of Finland. . . .

[These authors] were guided by *Uncle Remus* both as a great wonder tale and, more practically, as a virtual blueprint for how such a literature should be organized and spoken. For some, like Grahame, it would be a matter of only a moment's recognition; for others, like Potter, a matter of back-and-forth reference and experimentation over many years. However brief or prolonged the influence, the results would be strikingly similar from storyteller to storyteller as a host of previously unspoken desires, images, and affinities comes to life in story at the turn of the century, and without, for some time thereafter, many lies being spun about the world under the guise of writing for children. For a while after *Uncle Remus* the world as retold in story could be comical, savage, sentimental, rude, serene, and all the same world in the telling. If the fairy tale and romance could only repeat the motion of our individual lives—which, as children quickly come to know, leads to the grave—the serial adventure could harbour these stories within a larger landscape that replicated the lived life of the world. With Mole and Rat, Peter Rabbit, Pooh, Old Mother West Wind's children, Mowgli's brothers, Uncle Wiggily, and the rest another kind of truth about the world can now intercede to stall time and mortality indefinitely in our behalf. Nor is that sense of well-being we experience while reading their stories a spurious feeling: the world has been fully accounted for in each of them. . . .

Several writers have elected as the most magical words in children's literature the phrase 'over the hills and far away' from *Mother Goose*. For me they are Stevenson's evocation of that big thing in the sky once worshipped by the old Egyptian boys whose lost toys he dreamed of discovering on his travels: 'Great is the sun, and wide he goes/ Through empty heaven without repose'. . . . It is something like this vision, investing the world with simplicity and greatness, that must have presided over the work of Kipling, Potter, Grahame, Burgess, and later, Milne and de Brunhoff. Their tropism for such a light made them fill worlds. And while they would restrict themselves to one or another neighbourhood—as they were restricted, most of them, by their own lives—it was wholly realized worlds they wanted to make, not just the cosier corners usual to children's books. Only whole worlds like Brer Rabbit's and whole books like *Uncle Remus* gave them satisfaction equal to their need to acknowledge the loneliness and ferocity of life and yet have the world be this great and this benign. For them, the storytellers who had to stay put, *Uncle Remus* was the sun that went wide and without repose.

Opal Moore and Donnarae MacCann

SOURCE: "Cultural Pluralism: The Uncle Remus Travesty," in *Children's Literature Association Quarterly,* Vol. 11, No. 2, Summer, 1986, pp. 96-99.

It is a perpetual tug-of-war to decide who will "own" and interpret the art and artifacts of the Black American—determine the use to which historical and cultural materials will be put. This subtle war of wills ensues as a natural result of scholarly Black resistance to further intellectual colonization. The resisters confront the reluctance of white America to relinquish its illegitimate and unnatural proprietorship of valuable and persuasive materials. The nature of this ongoing struggle is encapsulated in the steadily increasing efforts to restore Joel Chandler Harris's Uncle Remus to the 'canon' of children's literature.

This misdirected energy in behalf of the Harris version of classic Black folktales has kept pace with the efforts of Black scholars and writers to offer more creditable versions and presentations of the same (as well as other) Black folk material. For instance, Uncle Remus reappears in Macmillan's textbook for children's literature courses, *Classics of Children's Literature* edited by John W. Griffith and Charles H. Frey. In an article in the *Children's Literature Association Quarterly,* Nina Mikkelsen argues for Harris's version of the Black folktale because "it is invariably Harris's version that we remember." And in a two-part article appearing in *Signal,* John Goldthwaite goes even further, crediting Harris with inspiring the major advances in imaginative children's literature over the seventy year period from 1880 to 1950.

It is not for absence of reputable alternative materials that Harris's Remus is being revived. There are texts that offer the Black folktale in a balanced presentation, emphasizing the weight and substance of the story (as contrasted with Harris's depiction of Remus as the prototype of the national 'darky' character). The reasons for the Remus revival probably have less to do with the merits of alternative materials than with Mikkelsen's observation: that Harris's Remus-creation is the image already seared in the mature American psyche. The larger-than-life, shuffling, sho-nuffing, grinning image is the sugartit appeasement from which America has refused to be weaned. The contradictions and interpretive difficulties presented by the Remus figure as mouthpiece for the Black folktale are anxiously overlooked, or dismissed with a sympathetic nod. . . .

[The] variety of objections leveled against Harris's vision of the folktales turns on the conviction that Remus is *not,* and never was, the right presenter of the tales (that is, if importance is to be given to preserving their context, complexity, and texture). Such objections are decidely textual—raising substantive questions of authenticity and

intent—and cannot be brushed aside as nervous-Nelly liberalism, or the over-sensitive nail-biting of a finicky modern Black aesthetic.

Challenges to the authenticity of Harris's work take issue with the "packaging" of the tales more often than with the tales themselves, allowing for the numerous variations and omissions that are possible in an orally preserved story. The charges leveled against Harris are that *he,* rather than the tales, is "inauthentic"; that Remus is a mouthpiece crafted out of stereotype to camouflage, efface, misdirect, or mute the pungency and irreverence of the tales; and that the appropriation of the tales is a bald misuse of the material. Attempts to determine whether it is use or misuse must begin with Harris himself—a man seemingly as contradictory and problematic as his stumbling creation.

In explaining their use of the Harris texts, Griffith and Frey maintain that Harris "grew up on intimate terms with black storytellers." It is an assertion that suggests something more than the four years, from age thirteen, that Harris worked as printer's assistant for *The Countryman,* a newspaper owned by a Georgia planter. R. Bruce Bickley, Jr., a biographer of Harris, says [in his *Joel Chandler Harris,* 1978] that Harris gained access to the tales during hundreds of hours spent in the "quarters" when he had time on his hands between printings. No doubt Harris did have some contact with Black workers and overheard some number of exchanges, but the texture of Harris's adolescent (and later) encounters with Black storytellers is mostly speculation. It cannot be assumed, for example, that four years of employment with a southern planter afforded him an "intimate" relationship with the plantation's slaves. Nor can it be assumed that his collecting of Black folktales reflects on his politics or indicates some unusual affinity for, or understanding of, the Blacks themselves.

In his *Signal* article John Goldthwaite repeats the assumption of Griffith and Frey—that Harris' interest in the tales stemmed from an early contact with the stories. He writes: "Harris retold [the tales] according to the best tellings he had heard, from men he had troubled himself to know since boyhood." These kinds of statements, which claim an unusual intimacy and camaraderie between Harris and his Black sources, are perhaps designed to establish Harris's authority over the material (by suggesting his love of it) as much as to assert the authenticity of his material. However, any clear evidence of his interest in Black folklore stems from the period when a number of columnists were inventing fictional Black informants.

Emphasis on Harris's "intimacy" and "long time familiarity since boyhood" seem designed to soften the obvious fact that the social commentary and worldview of the Black folktale is in direct opposition to that of a press corpsman of the post-Reconstruction "New South." Harris would rapidly achieve notoriety writing for the reactionary *Atlanta Constitution*—the newspaper that spearheaded the 'New South's program to nullify the brief promise of Reconstruction and reconstitute the Black population as a cheap, exploitable labor force.

Prior to Harris's use of a Black stand-in, the *Constitution* had employed another columnist, Sam W. Small, who also created a fictional Black narrator. His "Old Si" mouthed the views of the 'New South' in the exaggerated "Negro dialect" made popular through minstrelsy. Southern writers used this as a method of condemning the reforms that would have fully enfranchised the Black population. . . .

When Small quit, Harris was offered the opportunity to try his hand at a similar type of column. Harris adopted the familiar format and device—white political commentary delivered through a 'new' Negro mouthpiece. . . .

It would appear that "Old Si" and propagandist convention were the more immediate inspiration for Harris' later works, rather than the trailing idyllic reminiscences of a youth spent in intimate exchanges with a multitude of Black Remus prototypes.

R. Bruce Bickley's claim that "Harris became one of the most sensitive interpreters of the Southern Negro" is too generous. Such an assertion would not seem possible given the vigor with which Harris applied his trade, ridiculing the strivings of Blacks for a symbol of freedom: "The colored people of Macon celebrated the birthday of Lincoln again on Wednesday. This is the third time since last October." Or, as [Bernard] Wolfe has pointed out [in his essay "Uncle Remus and the Malevolent Rabbit"], making light of the harsh reality of lynch "law" that necessitated specific civil rights legislation. . . .

Undoubtedly Bickley is attempting to draw a distinction between one Joel Chandler Harris and another. It is doubtful, however, that any such clear distinction can be made. Harris' manipulative political mouthpiece and its direct evolution into the story-telling Remus is too proximitous. It would be naive to expect that the latter could depart radically from his politically inspired progenitor.

At best, Uncle Remus is an ambivalent creation—suggesting a corresponding ambivalence in Harris. At times he is drawn sympathetically, as when he "dis'member'd" his own name or got "some er de facks mix up 'mong deyse'f," reminding the reader of his advanced age, his vulnerability, and possibly, an encroaching senility. At other times, he is the head-scratching "stage darky" as when he remarks to the child, in *Told by Uncle Remus,* "De fus' thing when I get ter de house I'm gwinter be weighed fer ter see how ol' I is. Now, whar wuz I at?" And, as Louis J. Budd asks in his essay on Harris, "Did any black actually say 'surgeon er de armies' for 'sergeant at arms'?"

It is a difficult task to find the fine line between the exaggerated clowning of the minstrel entertainer and the exaggerated dialect usage employed by Harris. Griffith and Frey state that "Harris took great pains to represent phonetically the dialect of the Southern blacks . . . ." But is it a representation or a misrepresentation of Black speech when Uncle Remus calls Atlanta "'Lantmatantarum?" And what is the real purpose of the extensive "eye" dialect—

misspellings that nevertheless represent correct pronunciation such as prommus, minnit, frum, wimmen, rashuns, masheen, cubberd? What does it do but create as wide a gulf as possible between the speech (which represents the intelligence) of the Black character and that of the white. The speech of the little boy and the anonymous narrator in the Remus stories is the flattest standard English. Not even a trace of the quite distinctive Southern "tongue" betrays itself in the speech of either.

Goldthwaite claims that "the real satire in these tales lies in the language itself. It is the master's English, but inflected in such a way as to make it, like Brer Rabbit, as big as life and twice as natural." Is "familious wild wunner nudder" an inflection?

Harris himself disavowed any link between his use of dialect and "stage Negro" dialect, stating that the latter was an "intolerable misrepresentation." But while he rejects some features of minstrelsy, he embraces others. For example, the unabashed vulgarity that characterized minstrel shows by the second half of the nineteenth century is not to be found in these works. However, his aim in emphasizing and enlarging the language was, he says, "to wed the (legends) permanently to the quaint dialect . . . and to give the whole a genuine flavor of the old plantation." This "quaint dialect" was the style employed by Irwin Russell, a Mississippian whose poems were published in the 1870s. Harris wrote an introduction to the collected verses, *Christmas Night in the Quarters and Other Poems* (1888), praising the poems and Russell for capturing in his dialect "the old-fashioned unadulterated negro, who is still dear to the Southern heart." This "unadulterated negro" resembles the 'newly industrious' Black character that Harris and the *Constitution* praised in propagandistic sketches. . . .

While Harris was, as he said, inspired by this dialect, he in turn inspired others. . . .

There is some indication that such dialect "affectations" thwarted the preservation of Afro-American folktales. Alice Bacon, the leader of the folklore society at Hampton Institute, described in 1898 how difficult it was to procure new examples of folk traditions in the schools. It was "almost impossible for (teachers) to gather from their pupils any folk-lore at all, so certain are they, if they have any, that it is something only to be laughed at . . . ." Contrary to the claim that without Harris the tales would have been lost, it can be argued that his minstrel-evoking dialect made them objects of mockery and hence more difficult to collect after 1880.

But, even though dialect versions were embarrassing to Black children, the tales themselves had durability. Goldthwaite asserts that, had Harris not intervened, "all but a few like **'The Tar Baby'** would surely have been lost as the Civil War disrupted the flow of story from one generation to the next . . . ." This is an extremely dubious speculation. For more than a century the "flow of story" had not been interrupted; the original conditions that generated and fostered storytelling were still in evidence in post-Civil War America: isolating racial oppression, multi-generational family structures, the historical verbal emphasis. These conditions did not alter significantly even with the mass migration to the North. The stories were the tools that 'travelled light,' entertaining, socializing, teaching, protecting, comforting. In 1880, violence against Blacks was on the increase. The cunning schemes and victories of Brer Rabbit were as pertinent as ever. In fact, storytelling did not seriously falter until modern gadgetry—radio, movies, T.V.—began to usurp the functions of the story ritual.

If the tales are viewed as a kind of psychological weapon against tyranny, there is an ultimate irony in Harris's propagandistic editorials (through Remus) about the work ethic, and, on the other hand, Remus's narration of stories celebrating Brer Rabbit, a work-saboteur *par excellence.* Yet there seems to be little doubt that Harris perceived the tales as allegories when he writes: "The parallel between the case of the 'weakest' of all animals, who must perforce, triumph through his shrewdness, and the humble condition of the slave raconteur, is not without its pathos." However, Harris deleted this sentence from his introduction to later editions of *Uncle Remus: His Songs and His Sayings,* again suggesting his ambivalence, or discomfort with certain aspects of the tales. Or perhaps it was the active conflict of warring selves: the professional journalist and aspiring novelist wishing to preserve the tales intact vs. the Old/New South journalist needing to subvert their message with the myth of the contented slave. The critic, Bernard Wolfe, has suggested just such an inner conflict as an explanation for the wide disparities and contradictions in Harris's work. Whatever the answer, Wolfe sums it up in a few words: "Harris's inner split— and the South's, and white America's—is mirrored in the fantastic disparity between Remus's beaming face and Brer Rabbit's acts."

Those who are now arguing to re-establish Harris within the children's literature canon are amazingly uncommitted to the stories themselves. Clearly, it was content as well as lively presentation styles that enabled the tales to endure, unwritten, until the last century. But, with Remus, comes a return to obsolete attitudes and historical perspectives. . . .

How can this distortion be perceived as "real to life?" And what of Black children? What is their importance in this wave of white nostalgia? If the tales are perceived [in the words of Mark Twain] as "alligator pears," bland except for the "dressing" and presented in this manner, then there is nothing positive or useful for Black children to receive.

Harris may be perceived by his proponents as "the most sensitive interpreter of the Southern Negro" in his time. Fortunately, the tales no longer require the interpretation of the "outsider" narrator. *Black Folktales,* retold by Julius Lester, presents fifteen stories in a lively, assertive voice. A more recent publication is Virginia Hamilton's *The People Could Fly,* which presents the stories clearly enough for children to read on their own, and includes

brief explanatory materials which discuss the dialect and the origins of the works.

Unlike Harris's retellings, these are not likely to make Black children believe that their culture is "something only to be laughed at" as the children of Harris's era feared.

Charles Frey and John Griffith

SOURCE: "Joel Chandler Harris: The Uncle Remus Stories," in *The Literary Heritage of Childhood: An Appraisal of Children's Classics in the Western Tradition,* Greenwood Press, 1987, pp. 139-45.

The place of the Uncle Remus stories by Joel Chandler Harris among the classics of children's literature is problematic in the extreme. On the one hand, there is no denying that they have had great impact on child audiences over the past century. Clearly Harris meant them for children (in the framework he contrived for them, Uncle Remus tells his stories to a little boy), and they have been both immensely popular and praised by critics ever since the first publication of the book *Uncle Remus: His Songs and His Sayings* in 1880. . . .

On the other hand, Harris's rendering of the Uncle Remus stories is so thoroughly entangled with the moral and emotional implications of slavery and racism that it may be impossible for the general reader in the late twentieth century to read and enjoy them simply and directly. Not only is the Southern black dialect in which they are written sometimes difficult for a modern reader to understand, it is unhappily reminiscent of minstrel-show humor; furthermore, Harris unmistakably intends a kind of defense of Old Southern racial hierarchy in his portrayal of Uncle

From The Favorite Uncle Remus, *written by Joel Chandler Harris. Illustrated by A. B. Frost.*

Remus as a simple, genial old black who happily serves as a plantation laborer and entertainer to the son of the white folks he works for.

It is in this last connection that the Uncle Remus books can be offensive. Harris thinks of Uncle Remus and the little boy as two child-like personalities in charming communion with each other and through a rich stock of folktales. Within limits, Uncle Remus sets the rules in the friendship: He sometimes scolds the little boy for misbehaving, takes umbrage when the boy asks impertinent or skeptical questions about the stories, and manipulates the boy to pilfer pies and cakes and other treats from the big house. But essentially Uncle Remus and his little companion meet on equal terms, two simple, idle people who both like stories. The stories themselves may show that Uncle Remus, the teller, has wit and perspicacity far beyond those of a seven-year-old; but his dealings with the little boy otherwise do not.

The reason for this, of course, is that Harris invented the exchanges between Uncle Remus and the boy; he did not invent the tales. And it is the tales—authentic folklore, reaching back to Africa and other Old Worlds and shaped by American slave culture—that make the Uncle Remus books worthy of consideration.

The world of Uncle Remus's tales is populated primarily by animals, though they are animals in only a few incidental respects: Brer Rabbit was born and bred in a briar patch, Brer Tarrypin lives in a shell, the characters are capable of eating one another, and a few stories claim to explain about tails—why rabbits have short ones, why possums have hairless ones, and why the ends of foxes' are white. Mainly, though, these animals are people (more or less of Uncle Remus's own social class) going by animal names: They talk, wear clothes, live in houses, cook and clean, and fight over money, food, women, and status in purely human ways.

Compared with the folktale societies of the Brothers Grimm or Joseph Jacobs, the characters in Uncle Remus's world show a remarkable degree of social involvement. Their principal form of livelihood is farming (they are apparently sharecroppers or squatters who spend a certain amount of their time clearing new ground), with a little hunting and fishing on the side; but visiting is what they do most, often dropping in on "Miss Meadows en de gals," an undefined circle of females who sponsor candy-pullings and other soirees, courting, and gossip. "Society" is all around these characters. Even Brer Fox and Brer Rabbit feel some obligation to invite each other to dinner and to accept such invitations.

Enemies or not, the critturs practice good manners. . . .

Quite a lot of Uncle Remus's narrative is devoted to . . . courtly greetings. . . .

Each one of these friendly greetings is prelude to a violent physical attack by the speaker against the one he is greeting. For, despite all this socializing, the world of

Uncle Remus's tales is no happy, loving community, no A. A. Milne Hundred Acre Wood; lions do not lie down with lambs here. On the contrary: The elaborate sociability and good manners of the Brers and Sisses ornament a world of great competitive ferocity, treachery, and brutality. . . . The courtesy of Uncle Remus's characters is like the courtesy the wolf shows Little Red Riding-Hood just before he devours her. It is a system of pretense, a habitual means of keeping people off-guard. . . .

Society is important in these stories, because society confers status, and the desire for status, to the Uncle Remus characters, is on a par with the desire for survival, money, and food. Most of the stories in *Uncle Remus: His Songs and His Sayings* center on pranks of one sort or another. The prankster may get his pay-off in taking somebody else's string of fish, or somebody else's crop, or somebody else's life; but whatever the trophy, an important part of his victory is in having looked smarter or quicker or more deceitful than his rival in the eyes of the community. To be the butt of a prank is to feel outcast; to lose a contest of wits is to feel "mighty lonesome," unable to hold one's head up in company.

Much of the imaginative force of each of these stories (and they probably should be judged and appreciated one by one, each as a separate idea, rather than as "chapters" in a "novel") depends on the artfulness or ingenuity or inherent suitability of the pranks they contain.

By all odds the most famous of the Uncle Remus stories is **"The Wonderful Tar-Baby Story,"** a yarn with a concept as compact, economical, and inevitable as "The Three Billy Goats Gruff" or "Little Red Riding Hood." The basic idea is that anyone as clever, sassy, and impressed with himself as Brer Rabbit is, is most vulnerable not to an antagonist who matches him maneuver for maneuver, but to one who just sits there—who isn't even alive. Being the embodiment of impudence and brash vitality, Brer Rabbit demands that the world react to him, either to challenge him or pay him respect. The Tar-Baby, of course, will do neither. Brer Rabbit is a counter-puncher who depends on his opponent's misguided momentum for his victories. He is therefore frustrated by an opponent who won't talk and won't hit back and won't let go.

The story's humor depends on our seeing it from Brer Fox's point of view. We are supposed to laugh with Brer Fox as he lays low in the bushes and watches Brer Rabbit's progression from sprightly sociability ("Mawnin'! . . . Nice wedder dis mawnin'") to irritation ("Youer stuck up, dat's w'at you is") to anger ("Ef you don't take off dat hat en tell me howdy, I'm gwineter bus' you wide open") to panic ("Tu'n me loose, fo' I kick de natal stuffin' outen you"). The pleasure we take in this is the primitive, amoral pleasure of an appropriate trick well-played (comparable to the scene in which Puss in Boots gets the ogre to turn into a mouse by appealing to his pride, or to Hans Christian Andersen's rogues getting the vain emperor to walk through the streets naked). For the duration of this one story, there is no use thinking of Brer Rabbit as "the good guy." Here he is just the cocky guy, and the plot simply spells out one of the comic implications of his cockiness.

"How Mr. Rabbit Was Too Sharp for Mr. Fox" is a symmetrical counterpart to **"The Wonderful Tar-Baby Story."** At the end of that first tale, Uncle Remus said a number of things could possibly have happened after Brer Fox caught Brer Rabbit. Even so, there is a neat balance or sense of completion in this account of how Brer Rabbit saves himself and recovers his dignity.

If **"The Tar-Baby"** showed the folly of cockiness, **"How Mr. Rabbit Was Too Sharp for Mr. Fox"** shows the folly of blind vindictiveness. Brer Fox is too incensed at Brer Rabbit, too resentful of his boasting and his uppityness, to think straight. . . .

If Brer Fox had any proper selfish use for Brer Rabbit—if he wanted to eat him, say, or make him his slave to do his work for him—this would be an entirely different story. But all Brer Fox wants is to "hurt Brer Rabbit bad ez he kin," and that, in effect, leaves the choice of punishments up to Brer Rabbit himself, since only he can really know what he would hate worst. Once this logic is established in the story, Brer Rabbit is master of the situation. All he has to do is name his preferred treatment, and the furious Brer Fox is obliged to give it to him.

The tale leaves one with the odd double impression that Brer Fox knows Brer Rabbit both too well and not well enough. He's fully aware of the legend of Brer Rabbit—the legend Uncle Remus refers to in introducing the story, of Brer Rabbit's dominance as "a monstus soon creetur" who was "at de head er de gang w'en any racket wuz on han'." But Brer Fox doesn't know, or doesn't remember, that Brer Rabbit comes from the briar patch—a fairly obvious fact about him. This may not be strictly realistic, but in a sense it is appropriate. Brer Fox hates Brer Rabbit impersonally, as it were, for his position in the neighborhood. He is hypnotized by Brer Rabbit's reputation and so plays right into Brer Rabbit's hands, never realizing what he would know if he were thinking personally about Brer Rabbit, i.e., that he was bred and born in the briar patch. . . .

The heart of Uncle Remus lore is the trickster tales, the ingenious, surprising, acrobatic judo maneuvers of adversary against adversary, and humor is the appropriate tone for telling them. Stories of all kinds are about struggle, to be sure; but struggle in a Brer Rabbit tale takes place in a psychic arena different from that, say, between Snow White and her stepmother (where youthful beauty and bitter self-love contend against each other), or that between Mowgli and Shere Khan (where honorable pride contends against mean-spirited envy). Brer Fox and Brer Wolf may die, but there is nothing tragic or pathetic about them; Brer Rabbit may win the hand of "one er de gals," but there is nothing romantic about him; and he may show a subtle grasp of psychological motivation equal to Solomon's in the story of the two mothers, but there is nothing wise or profound about him. He is, as Uncle Remus says, "the soones' man ez ever wuz," and the mood in which to talk of him is anarchistic joy.

Margery Fisher

SOURCE: "Joel Chandler Harris: 'Nights with Uncle Remus'," in *Classics for Children & Young People,* The Thimble Press, 1986, p. 19.

How close can an English child come to Uncle Remus and Brer Rabbit? I have no idea what my father decided about pronunciation when he read the stories to me, but as I don't remember having any difficulty in understanding what was going on or in adopting the animals as nursery individuals, I imagine that the verbal rhythms sounded right. My response to the stories now is complicated because I met the characters a second time as interpreted by Kipling's Stalky and his friends; stories already brightly coloured became, as it were, fluorescent. For the past three or four decades these transplanted and transmuted African folktales have, understandably, been set aside; the situation seems to be changing in the 1980s. Even if we cannot accept the subservience of Uncle Remus, mediator of the tales, it is surely legitimate to look behind the historical circumstances of slavery to the broad, free-coasting humour, the gentle wisdom and affection in the old man's actual dialogue with his small listener and in his joyous reconstruction of the sardonic-comic idiom of 'Miss Meadows and the gals'.

As for the tales themselves, they speak of the ageless need of the disadvantaged and the oppressed for a form of satirical, pathetic or burlesque fable that would provide them with a cryptic way of defining their troubles and so supply a kind of surreptitious redress for them. The Brer Rabbit stories contain many worldwide folklore motifs, especially in the trickster tales, but the special nature of their oral tradition has added poignancy to their universal theme of the weak outfacing the strong. They are robust, vivacious neighbourhood tales, but they are broad enough as well for comment on the global human condition. They are funny, cruel, perceptive, absurd. They have nothing and everything to do with animals, a fact that is bound to endear them to the young and to prick adults with stirring, often uncomfortable thoughts. . . .

[Children] should listen to rich, rolling sentences which satisfy their taste for slapstick comedy and provide an outlet for their frustrations as junior, subordinate members of the human race.

Julius Lester

SOURCE: A foreword to *The Tales of Uncle Remus: The Adventures of Brer Rabbit,* Dial Books, 1987, pp. xiii-xx.

[An acclaimed author of fiction and nonfiction, reteller, and editor as well as an educator and authority on African American history and culture, Lester has published two well-received volumes of African American folktales, Black Folktales *(1969) and* The Knee-High Man and Other Tales *(1972), as well as essays on black traditional music and tales. The au-*

thor has retold Harris's Uncle Remus tales in The Tales of Uncle Remus: The Adventures of Brer Rabbit *(1987),* More Tales of Uncle Remus: Further Adventures of Brer Rabbit, His Friends, Enemies, and Others *(1988), and* Further Tales of Uncle Remus: The Misadventures of Brer Rabbit, Brer Fox, Brer Wolf, the Doodang and All the Other Creatures *(1990). The following excerpt is from Lester's introduction to his first Uncle Remus collection.]*

The Uncle Remus stories of Joel Chandler Harris represent the largest single collection of Afro-American folktales ever collected and published. Their place and importance in Afro-American culture is singular and undisputed. . . .

Although Harris never studied folklore, and was embarrassed when others acclaimed him a folklorist, his integrity regarding the tales was exemplary and remarkable.

All of the tales were collected from blacks. Often Harris collected two or three versions of the same tale, and then chose the best version to publish. If he doubted a story's Afro-American roots, he did not use it.

Harris's other concern was language. Possessing a remarkable ear, he recognized that the tales could not be divorced from the language of the people who told them. Thus, he made a conscious and diligent effort to put this language on paper. In the absence of actual recordings, the Uncle Remus tales as put down by Harris are the most conscientious attempt to reproduce how the slaves talked, at least in one area of the South.

It is questionable whether the tales would have been so popular if Harris had not created a character named Uncle Remus as storyteller. By Harris's own admission, Uncle Remus was a composite of three former slaves he knew who had told him some of the tales.

As a character, Uncle Remus represents the "faithful darky" who, in Harris's words, "has nothing but pleasant memories of the discipline of slavery." He identifies wholly with his white master and mistress, espouses their value system, and is derisive of other blacks. There are no inaccuracies in Harris's characterization of Uncle Remus. Even the most cursory reading of the slave narratives collected by the Federal Writer's Project of the 1930s reveals that there were many slaves who fit the Uncle Remus mold.

Uncle Remus became a stereotype, and therefore negative, not because of inaccuracies in Harris's characterization, but because he was used as a symbol of slavery and a retrospective justification for it. This reflects the times in which the Uncle Remus tales appeared.

In 1876, the year the first Uncle Remus tale was published in the *Atlanta Constitution,* Rutherford B. Hayes "stole" the Presidency by promising the South that he would end Reconstruction and withdraw Federal troops in return for the South's votes in the electoral college. Be-

ginning the following year, the nation's attitude was to let the South deal with its problems—meaning the freed slaves—as it saw fit, in an attempt to heal the wounds inflicted by the Civil War.

In such a political and moral climate Uncle Remus became a symbol of that reconciliation. He was the freed slave who not only had no bitterness toward his former enslavement, but looked back nostalgically to a time he considered better. The white majority could take comfort in Uncle Remus because he affirmed white superiority and confirmed an image of black inferiority many whites needed. Harris's Uncle Remus permitted whites to look to the future free of guilt about the past.

Uncle Remus is the most remembered character from a literature that justified slavery by portraying blacks who found slavery a haven, and freedom a threat and imposition.

It would be unfair and inaccurate to ascribe unseemly motives to Joel Chandler Harris in his creation of Uncle Remus. A writer should be judged on his total oeuvre. In this context, Harris's work is varied in its depiction of blacks and their attitudes toward slavery.

If there is one aspect of the Uncle Remus stories with which one could seriously disagree, it is the social setting in which the tales are told. Uncle Remus, and sometimes other blacks, tell the stories to an audience of one—a little white boy, the son of the plantation owner. While such a setting added to the appeal and accessibility of the tales for whites, it leaves the reader with no sense of the important role the tales played in black life.

The telling of black folktales, and indeed tales of all cultures, was a social event bringing together adults and children. That folktales are now considered primarily stories for children is an indication of our society's spiritual impoverishment. Traditionally, tales were told by adults to adults. If the children were quiet, they might be allowed to listen. Clearly, black folktales were not created and told for the entertainment of little white children, as the Uncle Remus tales would lead one to believe.

Reading the original Uncle Remus tales today is not an easy task. The contemporary reader is offended by the dialect, if that reader is able to decipher it. (It is almost like reading a foreign language.) The reader is also uncomfortable with the figure of Uncle Remus, his attitudes, his use of the word "nigger," and his sycophancy. Because Uncle Remus is a character with whom blacks and whites are uneasy today, the tales themselves have become tainted in many minds. This is unfortunate. Whatever one may think about how Harris chose to present the tales, the fact remains that they are a cornerstone of Afro-American culture and continue to be vital.

The purpose in my retelling of the Uncle Remus tales is simple: to make the tales accessible again, to be told in the living rooms of condominiums as well as on front porches in the South.

Additional coverage of Harris's life and career is contained in the following sources published by Gale Research: *Contemporary Authors,* Vol. 137; *Dictionary of Literary Biography,* Vol. 91; and *Major Authors and Illustrators for Children and Young Adults.*

Edith (Thacher) Hurd
1910-1997

Clement (G.) Hurd
1908-1988

Edith Thacher Hurd (Also wrote as Juniper Sage, a joint pseudonym with Margaret Wise Brown): American author of picture books.

Clement Hurd: American author and illustrator of picture books.

Major works include *The Runaway Bunny* (written by Margaret Wise Brown and illustrated by Clement Hurd, 1942), *Goodnight Moon* (written by Margaret Wise Brown and illustrated by Clement Hurd, 1942), *The Day the Sun Danced* (1965), *Monkey in the Jungle* (written by Edna Mitchell Preston and illustrated by Clement Hurd, 1968), *Catfish* (1970), *The Mother Beaver* (1971), *Under the Lemon Tree* (1980).

INTRODUCTION

Widely celebrated for their child-centered approach to picture books, the Hurds are credited with helping to shape the direction of contemporary children's story telling and illustration. In a collaboration in which Edith authored the stories and Clement crafted the pictures, the two created books reflecting the everyday experiences that preschoolers and primary graders have with the people, events, and objects around them. Although the Hurds often collaborated with other artists and authors, as a husband-wife team they created science story books, which contain a wealth of interesting facts and pictures presented in an easy-to-read fashion. Covering a broad range of topics—from nature and wildlife to trucks and tugboats—these information stories are an alternative to conventional stories of fantastic or whimsical adventures and characters.

The Hurds are praised for combining rhythmic narratives and colorful textured prints to create pace, mood, and setting, thus giving children a multi-sensory experience. Edith establishes the pace of the story through tone and tempo, which is complemented by Clement's use of darks and lights, bright or gentle colors, and subtle shading to indicate gradual changes in the setting or atmosphere. Clement is further hailed for his ability to replicate patterns and textures of the environment using wood blocks, grains and other natural materials. As *Booklist* once noted, Edith's "quiet" narration of the baby's birth in *The Mother Whale*, for example, reflects the "tranquility and vastness" of the sea and its inhabitants, while Clement's blue and green prints match the mood of the text. In a similar vein, Joseph Stanton applauded Clement's cozy

and inviting illustrations for *Goodnight Moon* as "key to the success" of Margaret Wise Brown's story.

Throughout their careers, the Hurds have received widespread recognition for capturing the freshness and wonder of their young audience. Although Clement once remarked that he never felt really sure that he was creating pictures that spoke directly to children, *Publishers Weekly* recognized the "vitality and timelessness" of his illustrations, despite significant changes in the world and attitudes toward children's responses. Enthusiastic about children's responses to their books, the Hurds collaborated on many animal stories, such as *Catfish* and *No Funny Business* (1962), that appeal to children's love of action through exaggerated and zany misadventures. Using humorous situations and plenty of pictures, the Hurds created stories featuring animal characters with unique and lively personalities that small children cannot resist. On a different note, they produced works geared toward science and discovery that represent the detail of nature's cycle accurately, yet poetically.

Biographical Information

Born in New York City, Clement Hurd began painting and drawing at the age of thirteen at St. Paul's boarding school, where he was influenced by his teacher, a watercolorist. Spending most of his childhood in New York and Locust, New Jersey, he attended Yale University and studied at the Yale School of Architecture for one year before training in Paris under the direction of painter Fernand Leger. In 1933, with the Great Depression at its worst, Clement returned to New York where he supported himself as a freelance artist by painting murals in homes and doing other small design jobs. Impressed by one of his bathroom murals, Margaret Wise Brown sought him out to illustrate one of her children's books. Brown, who later collaborated with Clement on eight picture books, including *Runaway Bunny* and *Goodnight Moon,* was an editor of Young Scott Books, an unconventional publishing house known for producing books "bold in their child-oriented point of view," as Edith Hurd explained, "and unusual in choice of illustrators and authors."

Clement joined the Bank Street College Writer's Laboratory, a training center for those interested in writing nursery literature. Shortly after, he met his future wife, author Edith Thacher, a member of the Writer's Laboratory who was pursuing a teaching career. Born in Kansas City, Missouri, Edith attended a boarding school in Switzerland and received a degree in art history from Radcliffe College prior to her career as a writer of books for young children. While attending the Writer's Laboratory, she wrote her first book, *Hurry Hurry! A Tale of Calamity and Woe,* published by Young Scott Books at the encouragement of Margaret Wise Brown. Clement and Edith were married in 1939 and eventually wrote and illustrated over 75 books together, including numerous picture books on nature and animals drawn from experiences at their Vermont farm. During World War II, Clement painted camouflage in the South Pacific for four years while Edith lived with her parents in San Francisco, California. In 1949, their son Thacher, who would follow the family tradition as a children's author and illustrator, was born. Eventually, the Hurds moved to San Francisco, but often spent summers in Vermont. During the early 1960s, Edith wrote several titles for Harper's "I Can Read" series, including *Come and Have Fun* (1962). Clement experimented with impressions of linoleum cuts, driftwood boards, rice paper, and bits of plants and twigs in his illustrations for Edith's *Christmas Eve* (1962) and for titles in their nature book series, including *The Day the Sun Danced* and *Rain in the Valley (1968)*. One of their last collaborative efforts was a series of books devoted to mother animals. Clement died of pneumonia in 1988 at the age of eighty after suffering from Alzheimer's Disease for four years. Edith died in 1997 at the age of eighty-six.

Major Works

As an alternative to folk and fairy tales, the Hurds wanted to create picture books that stimulated children's imaginations with the experiences of their immediate surroundings. To this end, they collaborated with other artists and authors on books appealing to children's senses, emotions, curiosities, and interests. In two of Clement's most popular illustrated works, *The Runaway Bunny* and *Goodnight Moon*, both written by Margaret Wise Brown, his creative use of color enhances the mood of Brown's narrative. Seeing the bunny cloud blowing its white, icy breath in *The Runaway Bunny*, readers sense little runaway bunny's coldness. Likewise, as the pages of *Goodnight Moon* are turned, the text becomes more soothing and repetitive and the shades of the pictures gradually become darker and darker, lulling the child to sleep. Clement's fervent illustrations invite children inside the story. Unconventionally designed and filled with detail—from the toy house in a corner on the floor to a scene from *The Runaway Bunny* hung on the rabbit children's bedroom wall—*Goodnight Moon* has comforted thousands of children with its secure universe of a comb and a brush and a bowl full of mush and a quiet old lady whispering hush. Clement once remarked that an eighteen-month-old child burst into tears when he could not crawl into the warm, cozy room. Critics have also noted that Edith's simple but descriptive information books, five of them written with Margaret Wise Brown, satisfy children's curiosities about what people do at their jobs or how something works. Books such as *Speedy, the Hook and Ladder Truck* (1942) and *Benny, the Bulldozer* (1947) describe fire trucks, tugboats, planes and trains, or the parts of an engine or the typical day of a fireman or man in a manhole—the "stuff that a six-year-old boy's imaginative play is made of," Edith once explained. Clement's exact pictures attempt to answer children's questions about some of the typical activities they see every day. A reviewer for *The New York Herald Tribune Books* commented that Edith's "machinery" books give children experiences they need for their "own particular purpose in living" and will last for several years.

Together, the Hurds produced a series of "I Can Read" books for elementary readers, including *Last One Home Is a Green Pig* (1959) and *Come and Have Fun*, that present basic concepts in a humorous way using easy-to-read vocabulary. The Hurds also popularized a series of nature and wildlife books that make science accessible and exciting to very young children. Often featuring animals as main characters, these tales explore ecology, conservation, geology, migration, and agriculture in habitats such as the sea, jungle, forest, and farm. *The Day the Sun Danced* evokes themes of birth and renewal as a small rabbit awakens his animal friends to watch the sunrise. The fresh, deep colors and wood-grained textures evoke the warmth of the sun and highlight the natural beauty of the spring landscape. Similarly, *Rain and the Valley* conveys the cycle of life in a rural setting through one farmer's abuse of his farmland and another's restoration of it. The woodcut illustrations are presented in three colors to indicate the contrast between dryness and vitality. In 1968, Clement also collaborated with Edna Mitchell Preston to produce *Monkey in the Jungle*, which *Publishers Weekly* acknowledged as the "cream of the crop" for its natural illustrations. Continuing to focus on animals with the Johnny Lion books and such titles as *What Whale? Where?*

(1966) and *The Blue Heron Tree* (1968), the Hurds also published the award-winning *Catfish,* a book hailed by *Horn Book* for its irresistibility and humor and its "effective, easy-to-read-prose" complemented by "breezy black-and-white drawings splashed with brilliant red." With the publication of *The Mother Beaver,* the Hurds introduced a series of animal books chronicling a mother's care and nurturing of her offspring. The mother animal series features beavers, deer, whales, owls, kangaroos, and chimpanzees, giving facts on feeding and rearing, playing, and interactions with other animals. Each tale is told with sympathy and warmth using accurate information and pictures that embellish the natural habitat of the animals.

Awards

The Hurds received a Spring Book Festival picture book honor for *The Day the Sun Danced* and *Catfish* and a Children's Book Showcase award for *The Mother Beaver.* Clement Hurd received the *Boston Globe-Horn Book* illustration honor for *Monkey in the Jungle.* Edith Hurd was awarded a Spring Book Festival "Younger Honor" for *The Bad Little Duck-Hunter* (1947), and *Sandpipers* (1961) was recognized as a *New York Times* Best Illustrated book.

GENERAL COMMENTARY

Publishers Weekly

SOURCE: "Clement Hurd: Children's Book Illustrator As Artist and Exhibitor," in *Publishers Weekly,* Vol. 189, No. 6, February 7, 1996, pp. 106-08.

The field of children's book illustration, according to Mr. [Clement] Hurd, "is related to painting and graphics, but is specialized in that the artist must keep the ultimate audience more firmly in mind than the 'pure' painter who primarily tries to satisfy himself. This audience, an ever new and wide-eyed group, responds freely to what interests it, and turns away from what does not. Since children are not intellectual snobs or stylists, it is a matter of direct involvement or rejection.

"Having illustrated more than 50 books in 28 years, however," Mr. Hurd continued, "I don't feel any more sure now of creating pictures that speak directly to children than I did the first time I approached a manuscript. When your audience is so fresh and full of wonder, it seems to me that a book for them must share some of this freshness."

Clement Hurd considers himself an artist rather than an illustrator and recalls that the author, Margaret Wise Brown, once said the best thing about his illustrations was that he was not an illustrator but a painter. This remark, he feels, is particularly true about his favorites

among the books he's illustrated: *The Runaway Bunny, Goodnight Moon* and *Christmas Eve, Wingfin and Topple* and *Wildfire, The So-So Cat* and *The Day the Sun Danced.*

When he had his first book published in 1938 by W. R. Scott, Inc., Mr. Hurd recalls, "There was a wonderful sense of cooperation and enthusiasm among all of us working to create fresh and good children's books for a younger age level than had been aimed at previously. My illustrations for Margaret Wise Brown's *Bumblebugs and Elephants,* and then for *Town* and *Country,* were done in flat bright colors, showing simple objects. These were called the youngest books ever made, because they were aimed at the two- and three-year-olds. Leonard Weisgard was working at that time with Miss Brown on *The Noisy Books,* which became classics because of their direct sensory appeal, which invited the child's participation.

"As I progressed in the field I became more conscious that, when creating for children, one has to think of the adult, too. An embryonic book has to pass the test with many adults—the editor, designer, and printer (who must interpret it sympathetically in producing the book), and the adult purchaser—before the child can judge it.

"About eight years ago, I began experimenting with weathered wood and old boards lying on the beach outside my San Francisco Bay studio. The grains and textures in these woods made very interesting effects when printed on rice paper, and soon began creeping into my books. I used them very timidly in *The Diggers.* The technique also seemed right, especially with the paper quite wet, for the underwater setting of *Wingfin and Topple;* it gave a richness to the setting for *Christmas Eve;* it worked for fire and smoke in *Wildfire;* and it helped make *The So-So Cat* suitably scary. Although it is a technique which will not suit all stories, in the right place it offers a richness that would look overworked and fussy if painted by hand.

"Since those early days, the field of children's books has come of age. There is now an overwhelming number of books published annually, ranging from purely commercial products designed with the lowest common denominator in mind, to the purely creative expression of serious artists. The latter group interests me greatly, but I sometimes wonder if all of these interest the children. There is an ambivalence in this type of work, as to whether one is creating primarily to please the child or to satisfy the artist. Both are important and should not be incompatible."

Barbara Bader

SOURCE: "Golden Books," in *American Picturebooks from Noah's Ark to the Beast Within,* Macmillan Publishing Company, Inc., 1976, pp. 285-88.

Best, however, 'rightest,' [of the Little Golden Books] were the jolly little workman ballads on which Edith Thacher Hurd collaborated [with Margaret Wise Brown]—

ballads because, prose or verse, they are celebrations, hero narratives running along on repetition and rhythmic sounds and phrases. Say *The Man in the Manhole* plus *The Little Fireman,* but homelier, livelier; to be formal, less archetypal and more anecdotal. A little house catches on fire, a policeman calls in the alarm, and the *Five Little Firemen* snap to.

"'Sparks!' shouts the First Little Fireman. He puts on his white helmet, twirls his black mustache, and jumps into the little red Chief's car with its shiny brass bell. Cling, clang!"

With those words, I can feel again my children's excitement and recall our fondness for those little firemen: for the Second, "round as a pumpkin," who drives the hook-and-ladder, "the biggest fire engine of all"; the Third, who "has muscles as big as baseballs, he is that strong" ("He runs up the ladders and carries people down the ladders—that Third Little Fireman"); the Fourth, ready to "squirt lots of water"; and the Fifth, only human— "I sneeze in the smoke."

Then "Clang, clang, whoo, whee" . . . , and we're at the house of the Hurricane Jones family where the commotion climaxes in the cook's last-minute escape. "She is too fat to carry and too big to jump into a net and too jolly to stay and burn up in the flames. So they shoot up the life-line for the Hurricane Jones's jolly fat cook to slide down. 'Jewallopers!' says she. 'It was getting warm up there.'"

There would be no excuse for repeating all this good-natured horseplay, whatever my affection for it, were it not so rare in small children's books, where a void exists between burlesque or buffoonery, on the one hand, and drollery on the other. Here is honest, concerned humor—with a special citation for the cook "too fat to carry and too big to jump into a net and too jolly to stay and burn up in the flames."

Seven Little Postmen does as well, because it has a letter with a secret, a surprise, and lippety-lap rhyme that bounces it along from one little postman to the next—"Stamp stamp, clickety click,/The machinery ran with a quick sharp tick./The letter with the secret is stamped at last/And the round black circle tells that it passed/Through the cancelling machine/Whizz whizz fast!" The pictures are Tibor Gergely's again too, and they have the robust humor that the Hungarian-born Gergely shares with H. A. Rey, and a punch and a zip the match of the most rambunctious text.

Quieter and gentler, but not torpid, is *Two Little Gardeners,* an eager, intimate processional from planting to harvest which has some of the loveliest long-looking pictures of any of the Little Golden Books. Comes spring . . . "And the worm turned in the ground. The groundhog cast his shadow, and the two little gardeners"—a boy and a girl—"came out of their house to plant their garden." There are weeds and drought to contend with, and unwelcome animals and bugs; but there are animal friends and allies

too, and together they populate the pictures: the setting is all outdoors. The floppy-eared dog is always there too, taking shelter under the gardeners' umbrella and, the next morning, peering at the "little green sprouts sprouting out of the ground." He has his share of the harvest, we assume, seeing him stretched out under the table where "they ate and they ate and they ate"; and when the remaining food is stored away—the peas, beans and beets canned, the onions "dried and hung in big bunches," the potatoes and pumpkins put into bins—and the little gardeners sing a little song, he gives what looks to be a little howl.

So varied are the Little Golden Books that it is easier to define them by what they are not than by what they are; but in any respect *Two Little Gardeners* is atypical. It packs no wallop, it is not an enlargement or simplification of experience: it is not something anyone can immediately understand, to use a general criterion. It yields itself up to careful reading—unto "round little radish seeds, thin black lettuce seeds, round wrinkled pea seeds" ("And tiny parsley seeds and tomato plants and potato eyes"). It is inflected and gradual—no strong contrasts, no suddenness. And it has pictures to dwell on.

Joseph Stanton

SOURCE: "'Goodnight Nobody': Comfort and the Vast Dark in the Picture-Poems of Margaret Wise Brown and Her Collaborators," in *The Lion and the Unicorn,* Vol. 14, No. 2, December, 1990, pp. 67-76.

Many of the best known books of Margaret Wise Brown and the artists with whom she collaborated are famous for the comforts they are thought to offer. I believe, however, that it is the understatedly dangerous contexts in which those comforts are offered that gives them their poignancy. The kinds of dangers and the comforts so quietly presented in Brown's books are, it seems to me, powerful contraries that resonate at the psychic core of the parent-child bond. The simplicity of Brown's picture-book-length poems and the rightness of the pictures that visualize them have made these unpretentious little books into important artistic events in the lives of innumerable children and their parents.

Two motifs that occur again and again in Brown's work are the runaway-child and the child-alone-in-the-wide-world. Although they obviously overlap, and the second motif is always at least partially present whenever the first motif is in operation, it is important to distinguish them because the plots driven by these two motifs polarize the parent and the child figures in two different, but strangely complementary, ways. The runaway-child plot involves the rescue or return of the child, whereas the child-alone-in-the-wide-world plot leaves the child by him- or herself while finding a satisfactory resolution within that aloneness.

Brown had a passionate yet unsentimental view of children and childhood. One important aspect of the dynamics of the parent-child relationship in Brown's books is the rebellious aggressiveness of the child. It was remarked, by Brown as well as others, that she saw herself as a child. . . .

The runaway-child motif is perhaps most famously captured by Brown in *The Runaway Bunny.* It is, of course, comforting that the little bunny who wanted to run away from his mother was answered successfully at every turn by that loving mother. There is wonderful, unqualified love in this willingness to run after the child who, of course, does not really want to get away. She will run after him simply and absolutely because he is her little bunny. The back and forth of this poetic dialogue has a marvelous cadence of real conversation that children (and their parents) enjoy. If he becomes a fish, she will become a fisherman. If he becomes a rock on the mountain, she will become a mountain climber. If he becomes a crocus in a hidden garden, she will become a gardener. And so on. There is great comfort to this. No matter what he does or how he strays the mother's love is so great that she will find a way to be there to catch him in her arms and hug him.

But at the same time as the comfort is enforced by the mother's satisfactory and satisfying rebuttals, the child's stated plans of escape name the far reaches of the wide world. Each of the episodes sets the child dangerously apart in another way. This constant reenactment of the mother striving to reach the strayed child suggests that the process could go on forever, and suggests, subtly, by the very heroism of the mother's effort, the drama could, at some future time, end differently. The prospect of loss and abandonment is dangled again and again, and it is in the very repetition that the dangerousness of the wide world is made apparent.

Obviously, Margaret Wise Brown's predilections have dictated the nature of this poetic dialogue, but the artist, Clement Hurd, contributes importantly to the quality and effectiveness of the finished work. His pictures for this book are of two kinds. There are the black-on-white line drawings that illustrate some of the basic details of each episode, and then for each episode there is a full-color painting, covering two facing pages, that presents the heart of the action, the mother's dramatized and in-costume readiness to rescue her baby. These large, uncaptioned pictures give Clement Hurd's painting equal partnership with Brown's writing.

From Goodnight Moon, *written by Margaret Wise Brown. Illustrated by Clement Hurd.*

Hurd's pictures reinforce and go beyond the text in several important ways. The bunnies are without facial expression and, indeed, show no signs of having mouths. This expressionlessness is an important support to Brown's unsentimental agenda. One has but to recall the many children's books with grinning animal protagonists to appreciate the importance of this expressionlessness. (In the "Curious George" books, for example, everything smiles, even fish that are about to be eaten). Despite their lack of emotion, this mother and this child appear eminently huggable. Likewise, the gorgeous world of Clement Hurd's picture looks deliciously soft and gloriously colorful. The richness of the colors is exciting as well as comforting. The red walls of the living room scene have, for instance, a Matisse-like intensity that will be transformed by Clement Hurd into "the great green room" of Brown's *Goodnight Moon.* The joyous, bright magic of Hurd's pictures lights up this little book and serves to further overwhelm the dark undercurrent of potential loss; however, as I have already stressed, the repeated runnings away keep the possibility of loss alive.

In a sense, the last picture in *The Runaway Bunny* encapsulates the theme of this essay. The mother and child are sheltered in the warm food-filled comfort of their burrow, while outside the vast, indifferent universe of fields and starry skies stretches into the distance. Here again, we have an anticipation of *Goodnight Moon.* . . .

The best and most famous of Brown's child-alone-in-the-wide-world plots is *Goodnight Moon.* I expect to hear some objections. It might be pointed out that this child is neither alone nor out in the wide world. *Goodnight Moon* is, in fact, renowned for its cozy comforts. The child is protected by "the quiet old lady whispering 'hush'" and sheltered by "the great green room." It is my contention here, however, that this book has been so profoundly moving to so many children and adults precisely because Margaret Wise Brown poetically invokes, with the considerable help of Clement Hurd's pictures, both a comforting interior space and an overwhelming exterior space. I can think of no other book that provides the kind of experience this one does, although it has had numerous imitators.

The book embodies an uncomplicated, yet subtly modulated, process. Preparatory to going to sleep, a child, illustrated as a bunny in the same style that was used in *The Runaway Bunny,* says goodnight to the world of his bedroom, as well as to the world in general. As these goodnights proceed the room gradually darkens, from page to page, while the moon-filled sky gradually brightens. Part of the magic here is the result of the nature of the voice that speaks the goodnights. Unlike most books in the goodnight genre—a genre that has become an industry, in part because of the legendary popularity of Brown's classic—*Goodnight Moon* does not feature a parental figure helping a child to say his or her goodnights. Here the child's point of view is all we have. The child has complete authority here. Everything in this universe revolves around the child as a central "human" presence, and this presence names its universe.

There is a problem here, however. The voice speaking in *Goodnight Moon* does not sound like the voice of a child. It is a knowing voice, a whimsical voice, a voice that sees and understands what the child sees and understands in the universe the book creates. It is, of course, the omniscient voice of Margaret Wise Brown at its poetic best. Brown has found here a powerful vehicle for her voice. The oracular nature of this authorial naming of the universe taps into the power of a basic type of myth that has "comforted" people of all ages. It is, in essence, a creation myth in a kind of end-of-the-world (rather than beginning of the world) pattern. Of course, the end-of-the-world here is merely a saying of goodnight to the world, but the mythic weight of this ritualistic naming of things is implicit in the satisfactions this simple little book provides.

The bright pictures of Clement Hurd are key to the success of this book. I have not attempted to determine to what extent Brown "conceptualized" the contents of the pictures. Some information on that score would undoubtedly be available to a researcher. Brown is well known to have done layouts of her concepts in advance of the give-and-take of discussion with the artist. Because she was an important editor as well as a highly-in-demand author, she was in a better position to genuinely collaborate than are most children's book authors. In addition, many of the artists she worked with, like Clement Hurd, were close personal friends.

There is an enormous amount that could be said about the interface of words and images in this book. I will limit myself to a few observations. In the pictures, as in the poem, the child is the center of this universe. Although the child-bunny is in bed throughout the book, he is the active protagonist around which the action revolves. He changes his position and what he is looking at from one frame to the next. His shifts are not highly dramatic. Sometimes he is partially under the covers; sometimes he is sitting or crouching on top of them; but everything in the scene is clearly oriented around him and what he is looking at. His stance always relates in some way to what is being named. By contrast, "the quiet old lady whispering 'hush'" is a virtual statue. She is sometimes absent, with her knitting equipment left on her rocker, but when she is present she is always in the same position, one hand on her lap and the other raised to her mouth to signal the quiet she demands. It is significant that she is described simply as "an old lady," with no indication of any connection to the child. The child is essentially alone in the world of this book. The old woman is not treated as a parent or even as a person. She is just one of the features of the landscape. The child sits alone in a universe that extends from delightfully trivial details such as "a comb and a brush and a bowl full of mush" to the vast outside that includes stars, air, and even the whimsically puzzling "nobody."

Although the old woman stays put, other creatures of the room move about in ways that delight young consumers of this book. The kittens play themselves into several positions and, most delightful of all, there is a mouse that changes position radically from one frame to the next.

The changing position of the tiny mouse serves as a "find-me" game for young readers, yet even the mouse seems influenced by the ongoing naming of the world. He, too, seems to be saying goodnight to many of the named things. The stance of the mouse plays a kind of musical counterpoint to the stance of the child-bunny.

It is with regard to light and dark that I would like to tie together the strands of my interpretation of **Goodnight Moon.** In this reverse creation myth we meet the child in the midst of his world of things—his pictures, his toys, his socks, his old woman whispering "hush," and so forth. As the room darkens the things are gradually lost in a dark that is only slightly mitigated by the nightlight inside the toy house and a lingering fire in the fireplace. What becomes dominant in the concluding pictures is the moon and the sky that has changed to a bright blue to give us a sense of the brightness of a moonlit night once interior house lights are dimmed. Although the now familiar but dimmed details of the room are overwhelmed visually by this marvelous evocation of the moon-struck night, the child and his point of view are still strongly present in the speaking voice of the poem. He is securely present in the center of his universe, yet he is completely alone in that godlike eminence. The child is regarding, at the last, a vast dark of "noises everywhere" in which the child is alone but unafraid. The child is finally lost in his sleep while the universe gleams on without him.

TITLE COMMENTARY

📖 *HURRY HURRY: A TALE OF CALAMITY AND WOE; OR A LESSON IN LEISURE* **(written by Edith Thacher Hurd and illustrated by Mary Pepperell Dana, 1938; reprinted with illustrations by Clement Hurd, 1960)**

Ellen Lewis Buell

SOURCE: "Hurry, Suzie," in *The New York Times Book Review,* November 13, 1938, p. 38.

Once in a while Suzie's nurse said "Quickly," but mostly it was "Hurry." Hurry to school and hurry home, hurry to meals and hurry to bed, until Suzie, who felt that otherwise she might have liked Nurse, wished, quite justifiably, that she might never have to hurry again. Her wish was fulfilled in three episodes; rather harrowing ones for Nurse, but so entirely in keeping with her character that Suzie was able to view them with the calm satisfaction of one on whom justice smiles at last.

How Nurse failed to heed the lessons painfully experienced in a manhole and an elevator and was finally reformed in a glue factory is too good a story to have its edge dulled by repetition here. It is only necessary to say the tempo of Suzie's life was satisfactorily adjusted by

circumstances which are as ludicrous as they were logical, and that the story is told with a fine sense of narrative in a style as brisk as was Nurse's manner.

Bulletin of the Center for Children's Books

SOURCE: A review of *Hurry Hurry,* in *Bulletin of the Center for Children's Books,* Vol. XIV, No. 4, December, 1960, p. 59.

For the beginning reader or to be read aloud, a mildly amusing book about Miss Mugs, who always got into trouble because she was in too much of a hurry to be careful. Taking care of Suzie while her parents were away, Miss Mugs tried to hurry Suzie along so that she wouldn't be late for school. Tangling with leashes, falling into a manhole, scooped by a steamshovel, and drenched in glue, Miss Mugs finally learned her lesson. Although the slight theme is drawn out, the exaggeration is a form of humor most children enjoy. The question does arise as to how Suzie ever did get to school on time after all the delays; and, if she did, how early the trip began?

📖 **THE WORLD IS ROUND (written by Gertrude Stein and illustrated by Clement Hurd, 1939; reprinted with new illustrations, 1967, and in a round edition as *The World is Not Flat,* 1986)**

Myra Cohn Livingston

SOURCE: A review of *The World Is Not Flat,* in *Los Angeles Times Book Review,* March 9, 1986, p. 1.

It is fascinating to speculate how Gertrude Stein might react to this newest edition of **The World Is Round,** bound (literally and figuratively) to attract Stein devotees and the child-listeners for whom the story was written. First published in 1939 and again with alterations in 1967 by Young Scott Books of New York, the book has traveled across country. Now Arion Press of San Francisco has added a splendid dimension by offering the heroine Rose's adventures in a rose-red *round* format, together with a more conventional square-shaped essay on its publishing history, "The World Is Not Flat." For whimsical effect, there is a red-and-blue balloon—all three packaged together in a rose-pink box.

It is perhaps unprecedented in publishing history that in slightly less than half a century, Stein's book should be issued in three varying formats, all interpreted by the same illustrator, Clement Hurd. To view these three editions together is to marvel how Hurd's illustrations remain vital and fresh, yet how significantly changes in the world have affected the pictorialization and attitude toward children's responses.

Stein insisted in 1939 that the heroine, Rose, "look French," that the pages be pink and that the type be blue—Stein's favorite color. For the second edition, in 1967, Clement

Hurd and the publisher, William Scott, could ignore these strictures. White paper and a new black typeface were introduced; rose was used for the endpapers and as one of the illustrative colors. Hurd, while retaining his original concept for the pictures, recut them in wood and linoleum blocks. Thus, Rose and Willie and a number of animals were transformed from pink into black. In the Arion edition, the use of these same blocks printed in a warm blue seems a stroke of genius on the part of Hurd and Andrew Hoyem of Arion Press. The world is still round, but the children, no longer French-Thirties-Pink or Sixties-Black, have transcended ethnic and national barriers, just as Rose conquered her fears, carved her name around the tree trunk and climbed the mountain.

Equally meaningful in terms of changed attitudes is Rose's response to the "Night of Fear" and "Night." No longer, as in 1939, are there jagged rocks, a menacing waterfall. The fearful blackness of night sky and mountain of the 1967 edition have vanished. Nor does Rose hold up her hands to ward off the blinding light. In this new edition the blue of mountain, the splay of foaming water, and Rose's content as the beacon light envelops her firmly establish that today's children must of necessity respond quite differently in a world where fear resides not in nature but in forces outside its province. . . .

And what of the children for whom the story is intended? Will they laugh, be intrigued or puzzled to read how Rose wondered "would she have been Rose if her name had not been Rose." In 1939, the eminent critic-editor Louise Seaman Bechtel voiced belief that Stein had instilled spirit and warmth into prose that was ordinarily, in other children's books, dull and lackluster. Language in 1986 has changed; it is even more pedestrian in most books today. Perhaps children will view Stein's sentences as impossible, lacking proper punctuation. Surely *The World Is Round* would be banished from the language arts curriculum of most schools.

But what a joy for anyone who is or can remember being a child, thinking without periods or proper sentence structure, making connections between words and ideas that are more apt to lead to nonsense than sense, and weaving into story every event of life. The prose is as syncretistic as the child's mind; indeed almost paleological in its concept, connecting together through rhyming words that insist it be read aloud, as verse:

> *Well anyway just then the hay went away, hay has that*
> *way and the water went away and the car did stay and*
> *neither Rose nor Willie were drowned that day.*

📖   ***THE RACE*** (written and illustrated by Clement Hurd, 1940)

Marjorie F. Potter

SOURCE: A review of *The Race*, in *Library Journal*, Vol. 65, No. 17, October 1, 1940, p. 813.

The reviewer has used this book with the age children for whom it is intended, namely the two and three years olds, but with no appreciable applause. The text is an attempt at a modern fable. The monkey and the duck have a race. They use all the modern means of transportation—bicycle, bus, taxi, boat, fire engine, train, and airplane—with first the monkey and then the duck in the lead. The illustrations by the author are in the bold colors young children like and are simplified in detail. This sounds as if the book had all the proper ingredients for success. But it does not have that necessary touch of true inspiration that makes such stories as *The Three Little Kittens* really beloved. Recommended for collections that can afford it as something to try; or for those centers working extensively with preschool children who feel they need more "here and now" picture-books.

The New York Times Book Review

SOURCE: "For Nursery Age," in *The New York Times Book Review*, November 10, 1940, p. 34.

With all the picture books being produced today there is no over-supply of those appealing to the nursery ages. This one has the qualities that a 3-year-old child loves, simplicity, clarity, variety and action.

The suspense and fun seem just right for very small children and those old enough to read the brief text by themselves will approve this picture book. The bright colored drawings in flat reds, greens, blues and yellows are humorous and dramatic. They are composed of familiar objects with small details that make entertaining discoveries for close young observers. The text has the simplicity of an animal fable, but this is one fable streamlined for speed.

📖   ***THE ANNIE MORAN*** (1942)

May Lamberton Becker

SOURCE: A review of *The Annie Moran*, in *New York Herald Tribune Books*, Vol. 18, No. 33, April 12, 1942, p. 6.

The Annie Moran was a tug who had seen her best days. The dispatcher gave her only easy jobs to do, and the call was usually delayed till there was but one tugboat waiting. "Go into the harbor and dock that little oil tanker at Dock 3" came a call through the megaphone, and the Annie Moran, who had never found out that she was old, went shug-a-shug, put the tanker into her slip and whistled for a bigger job to do. She is not "personified" by a face or any human sign, in these precise, plain, colored pictures of harbor craft in action, but children from five to ten, who naturally personify beloved objects without painting faces on them, will understand at once that this little tug has feelings like anybody, and that they are beginning to wear down.

From The Runaway Bunny, *written by Margaret Wise Brown. Illustrated by Clement Hurd.*

The worst is when she is tied to a big steamer and pulls so hard she pulls out her own stern bitt. Then all she is allowed to do is to tow sand barges—until a freighter takes fire one foggy night, close by the dock. There are no new tugs around, no Diesel tugs; there is only the Annie Moran just going home. So she pulls till the fireboats get there, and no other boats catch fire and the sailors are saved, and everybody cries, "Hurrah for the Annie Moran!"

So far as story goes, this is the most ambitious of the Hurd collaborations for little children: it has a real plot. The pictures keep the same particular charm; the tug itself on the end papers is exact as a diagram, and all the scenes are meant for little children who want to know exactly what you are talking about. In this case, it is a tug who does not talk but has a character of her own.

📖 **THE WRECK OF THE WILD WAVE (written by Edith Thacher Hurd and illustrated by Frederick T. Chapman, 1942)**

The Horn Book Magazine

SOURCE: A review of *The Wreck of the Wild Wave,* in *The Horn Book Magazine,* Vol. XVIII, No. 5, September/October, 1942, p. 341.

Drawn from the log of the *Wild Wave,* a clipper ship sailing from San Francisco, in 1858, these shipwreck adventures have an authentic ring which cannot be questioned. Young Captain Knowles of Cape Cod, with a crew of thirty men and ten passengers, struck a reef in the South Seas and knew many hardships before getting home to Brewster. Seven of the ship's company made for Pitcairn's Island, only to find it uninhabited at that time. Their boat was broken up in landing, but after several months they built another in which they reached the

Marquesas Islands. The tragic situation of a ship pounded by the sea in the old sailing ship days stands out clearly in this true record of an American mariner.

Ellen Lewis Buell

SOURCE: "Pitcairn Island," in *The New York Times Book Review,* November 22, 1942, pp. 30-31.

The dramatic settling of Pitcairn Island is well known to readers of the "Bounty Trilogy," but there is another chapter in its history, less spectacular but dramatic enough to catch the imagination of anyone with a touch of sea-fever in his blood. On that incident, duly recorded from anxious day to anxious day in the log of Captain Josiah Knowles of Brewster, is this story based.

It was in 1858 that the captain took his clipper ship out of San Francisco. He was young, but as a Cape Codder he was seasoned, and only a badly charted map was responsible for the crashing of the Wild Wave on the desert island of Oeno. All hands were saved and much provender, but there was little hope of a ship passing that bare remote isle, so Captain Knowles, his mate and five picked men set out in a longboat for Pitcairn Island, 100 miles away.

The trip was hard, the landing dangerous, but it was sheer tragedy to find the inhabitants had left the island two years before and when their boat was crushed by the tide the men were trapped. How they foraged for food and made their homes in the deserted village is told in a straightforward narrative which seems to catch the forthright accents of the young captain. There is tragedy in the story of the enigmatic gentlemanly sailor Sir Christopher, and courage and grim humor in the captain's determination to build another seaworthy boat. The trip across the burning waters to the Marquesas is a fitting end to a tale which holds the unfailing interest of all stories of men cast, remote from civilization, upon their own wits and fortitude.

The Junior Bookshelf

SOURCE: A review of *The Wreck of the Wild Wave,* in *The Junior Bookshelf,* Vol. 8, No. 2, July, 1944, p. 80.

This story, which has in it the ingredients of a splendid exciting tale, is about a shipwreck and the lives of the survivors on Pitcairn and another island. Like so many American stories for children, it is based on an authentic eye-witness' account of the adventures, but also like many other stories based on fact, and indeed true to those facts, it lacks fire. Interesting it certainly is, but the manner of its telling is pedestrian, and the author would seem to have been at pains to avoid the risk of making her story too exciting.

📖 *THE RUNAWAY BUNNY* **(written by Margaret Wise Brown and illustrated by Clement Hurd, 1942; reprinted with new illustrations, 1972)**

May Lamberton Becker

SOURCE: A review of *The Runaway Bunny,* in *New York Herald Tribune Books,* March 15, 1942, p. 6.

There is a rich background to this up-to-date, affectionate picture-book. The student of folksong recognizes a baby's variant of the old chansons in which a persistent suitor follows the elusive beloved through successive changes of form—reminding one of less affectionate duels of magicians in the Arabian Nights. That duel now becomes a duet between mother and baby. They are rabbits, but a human baby at once identifies himself with the bunny, who said to his mother, "I am running away," to which she replied: "If you run away, I will run after you, for you are my little bunny."

His first change is into a fish, mother becoming a fisherman: those pictures are fairly realistic, for the two-page spread shows one in the brook and the other in boots and line. When he is a bird and his mother the tree, the figures call for just a little more effort of comprehension, so that when one reaches Bunny as a boat, with a vast gray cloud-rabbit pushing his sails from the sky, even a little child has been prepared to get the idea at a glance. In the end the babys says, "Shucks, I might as well stay where I am and be your little bunny"; the mother says, "Have a carrot," and the pictures close on a purely domestic note.

Pictures and text are in complete collaboration. Brilliant in color, the large scenes show the dreams, while realistic black-and-whites show that this is really a mother-play.

Barbara Bader

SOURCE: "The Emotional Element: Harper and the Most of Margaret Wise Brown," in *American Picturebooks from Noah's Ark to the Beast Within,* Macmillan Publishing Company, Inc., 1976, p. 256.

When Clement Hurd first did the illustrations [for *The Runaway Bunny*] in 1942, he was not accustomed to working in separations in shades of gray and the results fell short of his expectations; in 1972, prevailing upon Ursula Nordstrom to let him redo the book (a steady seller regardless), he prepared new drawings for the black-and-white text pages, remade some of the color spreads, and conceived an entirely new one for the last opening—a picture that one former child (a carrot-lover too) pronounced simply, "Heaven."

Old or new, flat and bright like the pictures for *Goodnight Moon,* or more atmospheric, more lyrical, the illustrations are one in that they dare the impossible, even the absurd—a bunny bird flying to a bunny tree, a bunny wind blowing a bunny boat—and because of Hurd's gentle, grave honesty, make it utterly natural. He imagines himself into the child/bunny world wholly, turns the runaway bunny into a sailboat by simply extending his ears, and has credit left, as it were, for a pennant waving on top (where a bunny-*shaped* boat all togged out would have been an affront). There is no cleverness, nothing to marvel at; the magic is in the image, not in the making.

📖 *SPEEDY, THE HOOK AND LADDER TRUCK* **(1942)**

May Lamberton Becker

SOURCE: A review of *Speedy the Hook and Ladder Truck,* in *New York Herald Tribune Books,* Vol. 19, No. 12, November 15, 1942, p. 30.

Here is a book for very little boys who don't want animal stories or fairy tales at all: what they want is lots of pictures of trucks or tractors or anything that moves in the magical way of motors. This is the story of a hook and ladder truck such as little boys love even when too small to go unescorted to the firehouse—unless they live on the same block—and watch their scarlet beloved angle itself across the street and away.

If you think its detailed information is too advanced for a five-year-old, it all depends on the one who gets the book. If he is of the engineering type, all these details thrill him as he listens, even if he cannot take it all in, and the book will last him for several years. Speedy puts out a brush fire, then a smoky, then a blaze in a deserted wooden hotel that taxes all his energies. The pictures are so plain—and so full of bright scarlet—that a little boy follows the action as he listens. There is a place among picture books for one like this, and no personal preference for poetry or folklore should altogether deprive a child in one's charge of some experience with "machinery" books he needs for his own particular purpose in living.

THE MAN IN THE MANHOLE AND THE FIX-IT MEN (written by Edith Thacher Hurd and Margaret Wise Brown under the joint pseudonym Juniper Sage and illustrated by Bill Ballantine, 1946)

Virginia Kirkus' Bookshop Service

SOURCE: A review of *The Man in the Manhole*, in *Virginia Kirkus' Bookshop Service*, Vol. XIV, No. 20, October 15, 1946, p. 521.

One of the most successful and original books of the season—and a MUST for small boys' Christmas lists, particularly small boys in the city, boys (and girls too) who are endlessly curious about what's going on above, below and on the city streets. This book goes about minding everybody's private business,—the hole in the roof, the cracked plaster, the leaky pipes, the telephone wires, the wrecked taxi, the road needing repair—and perhaps most fascinating of all, the loose joint way under the street where the man in the manhole goes. In prose that sings, and drawings with enormous vitality, this book should jump right off the counters. We are told the author is an old hand under a pen name. Anyhow, he (or she?) has a fascinating, lilting text, and has made a book that lends itself to story and play. Bill Ballantine's pictures have the appeal of the comics—but are *good*.

The New York Times Book Review

SOURCE: "Story-Pictures for the Very Young," in *The New York Times Book Review*, November 10, 1946, p. 42.

Every child wants most of all to be an underground fixing man when he grows up—on that day when he watches a workman disappear down a manhole with his wrench and crowbar. Another time he dreams of being a lineman—as he watches that workman swing up a high pole to fix the wires. Through this book he can be these fix-it men and many more as he studies Bill Ballantine's pictures of strong, friendly workers using the huge tools of their different trades. There's Tonio who climbs down into the tunnel to fix a leaking pipe and the telephone man who climbs up to mend wires broken by the storm. There are cement-mixer crews to mend bumps in the road; carpenters, painters and other fix-it men to mend the world as it breaks down. The story that accompanies these men at their work describes how they do their job, step by step. Story and pictures are full of life and action and will stimulate good play activity for the child who plays alone or for groups of children. This book is a must for children three to seven.

GOODNIGHT MOON (written by Margaret Wise Brown and illustrated by Clement Hurd, 1947)

Virginia H. Mathews

SOURCE: A review of *Goodnight Moon*, in *The New York Times Book Review*, September 7, 1947, p. 35.

Rhythmic, drowsy phrases are set to pictures that complement them perfectly in this new go-to-sleep book for very little children. Warm and bright in color, the illustrations show all the cozy, familiar details of a big cheerful nursery, with a bunny tucked into bed ready for sleep. First he takes a look around the room and recognizes its contents while the lamp shines brightly; then, as the room darkens, he says goodnight to all the real and imaginary things he knows are there. The sound of the words, the ideas they convey and the pictures combine to lull and reassure when bedtime and darkness come. The rhythm of the little story is like the sing-song of disconnected thoughts with which children so often put themselves to sleep, and should prove very effective in the case of a too wide-awake youngster.

Anne Thaxter Eaton

SOURCE: "Stories for Happy Hours," in *Christian Science Monitor*, September 30, 1947, p. 14.

In these days of hurry and strain, a book for little children which creates an atmosphere of peace and calm is something for which to be thankful. Such a book is **Goodnight Moon** by Margaret Wise Brown, with pictures by Clement Hurd. In a large, green-walled room a bunny (perhaps of all animals a little child's favorite) is tucked up in bed. Around are toys, and pictures such as a child loves, a little old lady bunny quietly knitting and the moon peeping in through the window.

"Good night" the bunny is saying to all the familiar things, his toys, the three little bears sitting in chairs, the clocks and socks, mittens and kittens, finally "good night stars, good night air, good night noise everywhere." As the drowsy text proceeds, the room, in the lovely double-spread pictures, with all its familiar objects, seems gradually to darken. An ideal bedtime book with its rhythm, its atmosphere of cozy security, its poetry and childlike imagination.

May Lamberton Becker

SOURCE: A review of *Goodnight Moon*, in *New York Herald Tribune Weekly Book Review*, October 26, 1947, p. 10.

Sleepy stories have a special place in nursery equipment, as every mother knows. This one combines a softly repeating, rhyming text with pictures for the most part in full color, together creating an atmosphere of going to sleep so contagious that the eyelids of a reviewer may begin to droop if he is writing on a warm day. In a great green room, it says, there was a telephone and a red balloon—here they are in a full-page picture full of furniture details, and with a wideawake rabbit in a little pink bed. There was also, as you next see, "two little kittens and a pair of mittens, and a little toyhouse and a young mouse and a comb and a brush and a bowl full of mush and a quiet old lady who was whispering hush"—she was also a rabbit. Then, as the colors of the pictures gradually deepen, you begin saying goodnight to everything you have mentioned. "Goodnight kittens and goodnight mittens, goodnight clocks and goodnight socks, goodnight nobody, goodnight stars, goodnight air, goodnight noises everywhere" . . . till the room is lighted only by the stars.

Remembering how for years I have put myself to sleep, when needed, by going over the names of the guests at the Kenwigs's evening party in *Nicholas Nickelby* or the articles of furniture in a room described in *Sketches of Boz,* I can testify that the principle involved in this cozy little book is sound.

Barbara Bader

SOURCE: "The Emotional Element: Harper and the Most of Margaret Wise Brown," in *American Picturebooks from Noah's Ark to the Beast Within,* Macmillan Publishing Company, Inc., 1976, pp. 258-59.

In *Goodnight Moon,* it is the close of day, and a room first brilliant with light darkens at each color opening as, outside, the moon rises and brightens the sky.

> In the great green room
> There was a telephone
> And a red balloon
> And a picture of—

Here, as Dorothy White remarks, "one should turn the page," but her daughter wasn't ready. "'You haven't said about the rabbit on the bed.' She held the page down and went round the room pointing out all the things I hadn't said." Then on to a picture of "The cow jumping over the moon" and "three little bears sitting on chairs" . . .

> And two little kittens
> And a pair of mittens
> And a little toy house
> And a young mouse
>
> And a comb and a brush and a bowl full of
>   mush
> And a quiet old lady who was whispering
>   "hush"

To interrupt the text is to do violence to it, and Mrs. White correctly points out that the intervals between page turnings are apt to be long when [Clement Hurd's] pictures offer much to look at and a child has much to say.

To give primacy to delivering the text, on the other hand, is to do violence to the child. Margaret Wise Brown, one suspects, would say to let the specific rhymes go and rely on the rhythm and reiteration to carry over, as they do.

> Goodnight room
>
> Goodnight moon
> Goodnight cow jumping over the moon
>
> Goodnight light
> And the red balloon
> Goodnight bears
> Goodnight chairs

Goodnight to clocks and socks . . . to comb and brush; good night to nobody, goodnight mush; "And goodnight to the old lady whispering 'hush.'"

> Goodnight stars
> Goodnight air
>
> Goodnight noises everywhere.

The old lady is gone, the cats are curled on her chair; the room is dim, in a deep shadowless shade save for the lights blazing in the toyhouse and the fire blazing on the hearth; the rabbit is asleep. Through the windows the sky is bright, the moon and the stars shine; the mouse sits on the sill.

Quietly, from picture to picture, the mouse has moved about, the only significant action in the course of the book. Hardly noticeable, he is never unnoticed. Turning the pages alone, a youngster will retrace his route; looking on—for the umpteenth time—point him out as soon as the page turns. (Some books children should *own,* and this is one of them.) Like the questions in the Noisy Books that have to be answered, he has to be accounted for; he brings the audience into the story.

Praising the pictures, Dorothy White speaks of the text as "inferior . . . the barest commentary"; and notes that her daughter "has very much more to say about the book than the author has." Exactly. In saying less, the author allows the artist to say more, and the child to find more—to find the old lady knitting (the author doesn't say that), the cats playing with the yarn (or that), the extra blanket, the slippers, the fire. But why are we looking so hard? Because "In the great green room/There was a telephone/And a red balloon. . . ." And would we be listening so intently were it not a 'great green room,' a 'telephone,' and a 'red balloon'—a real telephone, mind you, beside the child bunny's bed.

Of all of Margaret Wise Brown's writings, *Goodnight Moon* is probably the most abstract in form and concrete in substance; the closest to Gertrude Stein and to the utterances of children; the most circumscribed and, as put into pictures, the most difficult to exhaust. What about that mouse, for instance, inhabiting a room in a house?

accepted by the family, untouched by the cats? (But they are rabbits, we remind ourselves, wavering.) For all the dear mittens and socks, the great green room is at the last—a mystery.

Leonard S. Marcus

SOURCE: "A 50th Anniversary Retrospective," in *Goodnight Moon,* HarperCollins Publishers, 1997.

Children, like writers, need rooms of their own, places—whether real or imaginary—of peace and well-being and unconditional love, places where a secure sense of self can begin to grow. That solid sense of being at home in the world is one of the great gifts the adult world has the power to bestow on its children. That is the gift that three generations of children have happily found in the hypnotic, mystery-laden words and joyful pictures of **Goodnight Moon**. . . .

In one of those apparently effortless creative acts that comes of a lifetime of preparation, Brown set down the text of **Goodnight Moon** in nearly finished form on awaking one morning in early 1945. The mercurial author who told friends that she "dreamt" her books seems in this instance to have literally done so. She called the new book *Goodnight Room.*

That morning [editor] Ursula Nordstrom became the first person to have the manuscript read aloud to her—over the telephone, by the author herself. . . .

Hurd worked on the illustrations for most of [1946]. "The bunny is younger and the old lady is lovable if not 'fairy story,'" he assured Brown and Nordstrom in March. "One reason why I can't get the fairy story feeling is because I don't really like [fairy tales] and think of all the old ladies [in them as] witches."

Confining the action of a picture book to a single room—even the "fabulous room" that Nordstrom told Hurd to devise—was a strikingly original plan. (In 1948, Alfred Hitchcock, with a rather different effect in mind, would attempt a similarly bold exploration of psychological space in his experimental thriller *Rope.*) In the first preliminary layout hashed out by the author, editor, and artist, an identical panoramic view of the room was to be shown in each full-page color spread. It was Hurd's more fluid (and cinematic) idea, however, to subtly vary the field of vision and scale from page to page, thereby gently but firmly guiding the reader through the great green room. . . .

Not everyone liked the book. The New York Public Library's Anne Carroll Moore, who had reacted strongly against Bank Street's efforts to grow literature in the laboratory of modern social science, pointedly declined to place **Goodnight Moon** on the library's prestigious annual list of recommended titles.

Over the next few years, sales slackened off predictably as newer titles (including a breathtaking thirty-two picture books by Brown herself) moved to the fore. What happened next, however—an unanticipated surge in sales in 1953, followed up by a nearly uninterrupted increase in annual demand ever since—was to become the stuff of publishing legend. No one knows for sure why it happened. Parents over the years seem to have discovered the book and told their friends about it, again and again. . . .

By the 1990s **Goodnight Moon** had become all but synonymous in pop cultural shorthand with kids' bedtime books and rituals. It had also been discovered as a convenient springboard for the observations of columnists, cartoonists, and parodists with something to say about the chances for a happy childhood, or a good night's rest, in late-twentieth-century America.

Amid all the commotion, Brown and Hurd's remarkable little book went on offering "readers who fear the dark," as *The New York Times* had said, "a world that is warm and safe and inviting." And on reconsideration the New York Public Library now honored **Goodnight Moon** as one of its "Books of the Century," noting in its 1996 centennial exhibition catalogue that "few books," whether intended for children or adults, "have been as cherished."

TOUGHY AND HIS TRAILER TRUCK (1948)

Margaret Ernst

SOURCE: A review of *Toughy and His Trailer Truck,* in *New York Herald Tribune Weekly Book Review,* September 5, 1948, p. 8.

Father, driving the family car, may hate the huge trucks that slow him up, but his children are always interested, always want to know what's inside the house-like creatures, where they are going, who drives them. Edith and Clement Hurd, in short, easy sentences and detailed pictures, wrap all this information into their story of Toughy the truck driver and his truck. Lucky 'Leven. There is plenty of suspense, too, from Toughy's tangle with a cop to his much more trying engagement with storm and ice on a mountain road.

Children who liked the Hurds' **Engine Engine No. 9** and the rest of their automotive-minded tales will love **Toughy and His Trailer Truck** too. It is good reading for beginners, as well as for those a little younger who are still read to.

THE GALLEON FROM MANILA (written by Edith Thacher Hurd and illustrated by Frederick T. Chapman, 1949)

Ralph Adams Brown

SOURCE: "Intrigue and Piracy," in *The New York Times Book Review,* October 9, 1949, p. 26.

Felipe and his father, the Duke de Torres, were determined to forestall the efforts of Manila's new governor to rob the merchants and people of the city. Sixteen-year-old Félipe discovered the details of the governor's plot, was captured, kidnapped and placed aboard a galleon sailing for New Spain.

The tempo of this story is rapid, filled as it is with the suspense of intrigue and piracy. The unsuccessful effort to thwart the governor, the storm at sea, the effort to kill Félipe, the violent battle—all provide excitement and danger to satisfy the longing of a teen-aged boy. The sixteenth-century background is richly detailed and generally accurate. The characterization sometimes lacks depth, but the story is exciting enough to carry the reader past such places.

Louise S. Bechtel

SOURCE: A review of *The Galleon From Manila*, in *New York Herald Tribune Book Review*, Vol. 26, No. 13, November 13, 1949, p. 20.

In Manila, in 1709, a cruel and crafty Spanish governor tried to make a fortune by tricking his real admiral, and sending a fake one in the galleon sailing for Acapulco in New Spain. Felipe, son of one of the decent nobles who opposed him, was victim of the hatred of one of the double-dealing Spaniards; he was held for ransom as a prisoner on the galleon, and endured horrible sufferings on the long voyage. But at last, after a battle with an English privateer, he used his wits to deliver up the villain to his father on a pursuing ship. He was then appointed an officer for the return trip, under the real admiral general, fulfilling his greatest ambition. Meanwhile, his father had gotten the best of the bad governor at Manila.

The romantic oldtime atmosphere, on shore and at sea, the excitement and suspense as Felipe's life is often at stake make this a most readable thriller for teen-age boys, though one rather wonders why the author chose this strange period.

WILLY'S FARM (1949)

Margaret E. Martignoni

SOURCE: A review of *Willy's Farm*, in *Library Journal*, Vol. 75, January 5, 1950, p. 112.

Rich in feeling for American farm life, these little vignettes are excellent for reading aloud to small children; nine-and ten-year-olds might enjoy reading them for themselves. Solid text and picture-book illustrations make it difficult to predict just what the audience will be. Both stories and pictures give a vivid impression of a farm as seen through a little boy's eyes.

Ellen Lewis Buell

SOURCE: "Country Boy," in *The New York Times Book Review*, January 8, 1950, p. 18.

Willy's proud interest in everything that happens on his father's farm, his sense of personal possession in it, give a special feeling of validity to these short stories or sketches of farm life. Willy enjoys everything from making maple sugar (as who doesn't?) to the first blizzard. His enthusiasm over his spring garden, the new calf, the fine crop of hay is contagious. Some of the sketches are pretty slight, but altogether, and combined with Mr. Hurd's many pictures, they add up to a good picture of farming through the seasons, full of the sights, smells and tastes which are the country boy's heritage. Readers of 6 to 9 will also gain from this book an elementary knowledge of the sources of food, which in these uncertain days is important.

Saturday Review

SOURCE: A review of *Willy's Farm*, in *Saturday Review*, Vol. XXXIII, No. 3, January 21, 1950, p. 44.

The theme and characters in this story are going to amuse and satisfy little boys and girls. Willy feels that the farm, which really belongs to his father, is largely his own responsibility. He allows his father and mother, his grandfather, and the hired man to have a share in it. Escorted by Willy, we see the changes of the seasons on the farm, the "sugaring" in spring, the planting, the cultivating, and the harvesting. We see the new-born animals grow into middle-aged animals, encouraged and cared for by Willy and his assistants. The story ends at Christmas time, when grandfather tells the story of the Christmas bells and hangs the old bell at the very top of the Christmas tree. The drawings follow the story on every page. We predict a long life for the story of Willy's farm.

Louise S. Bechtel

SOURCE: A review of *Willy's Farm*, in *New York Herald Tribune Book Review*, March 5, 1950, p. 8.

If a boy from five to eight has not already too many farm stories at hand—and there are too many—this is a very good one. Mrs. Hurd has really watched and listened to a small boy enjoying farm life, sharing the work, thinking the whole place is his own, singing his little songs about it all, finding the new-born lamb and calf, eating too much at the Fourth-of-July picnic, watching what goes on at the creamery, helping to snake logs, making maple syrup.

The pictures vary in a peculiar way in actual drawing ability, and they are a far cry from Mr. Hurd's bold art work in his classic *The Race*. But they offer much of the exact detail small boys will like, and a genuine farm atmosphere that matches the text. The large format and the division of the seasons by colors set the book apart from the run of farm books, as the text well deserves.

📖 *RUN, RUN, RUN* (written and illustrated by Clement Hurd, 1951)

Virginia Kirkus' Bookshop Service

SOURCE: A review of *Run, Run, Run,* in *Virginia Kirkus' Bookshop Service,* Vol. XIX, No. 14, July 15, 1951, p. 345.

A bingity-bangity cat and dog chase which toddlers will love to follow in this exuberantly illustrated book. The little dog thought this was a good day for chasing a cat and so—down the street, and across, in a truck until the cat decided she would chase the dog, and so—up the street, and through coal chutes and windows, run, run, run. Full page black and white illustrations by the author of leaps and bounces all around the town. Simple, satisfying action.

The Horn Book Magazine

SOURCE: A review of *Run, Run, Run,* in *The Horn Book Magazine,* Vol. XXVII, No. 5, September, 1951, p. 320.

Run, run, run—in the early morning a lively cat and dog chase each other up one street and down another, into a cellar and out through a kitchen window, up the street again until all tired out each reaches his own welcoming home. "That was a good run!" Into the pictures for this simple tale Mr. Hurd gets so much action and detail that small children will go through the book quickly the first time to learn how the race comes out; and then turn the pages over and over again to see all the things that are happening as the dog and cat race by. One of Mr. Hurd's best books.

Louise S. Bechtel

SOURCE: "More Cats," in *New York Herald Tribune Book Review,* September 30, 1951, p. 10.

When Clement Hurd did his color picture book, *The Race,* long ago, he made a lasting contribution to the pleasure of very small children. . . . Now in a large black and white picture book, *Run, Run, Run,* he offers another chase. The few words are done in a striking black script. It is quite funny, with a dog chasing a cat and the cat then chasing the dog. But there is nothing memorable about either story or pictures.

📖 *ST. GEORGE'S DAY IN WILLIAMSBURG* (1952)

Elizabeth Hodges

SOURCE: A review of *St. George's Day in Williamsburg,* in *Library Journal,* Vol. 78, No. 6, March 15, 1953, p. 530.

The Hurds have re-created the festival held every St. George's Day in restored Williamsburg, showing in lovely colored pictures and brief text the exciting doings of the day—theatricals, cudgeling, dancing on the green, the greased pig race, etc.—as experienced by a colonial boy. Aided by historians and architects of Colonial Williamsburg, the Hurds have presented an authentic picture of colonial Virginia in holiday mood. Especially recommended for elementary social studies.

Louise S. Bechtel

SOURCE: A review of *St. George's Day in Williamsburg,* in *New York Herald Tribune Book Review,* April 26, 1953, p. 12.

The Hurds give us a picture of Williamsburg alive which will please young visitors to that now so neatly reconstructed place. Here is eighteenth century spirit as no costumed guides can recreate it. Children will recognize famous buildings in the background, but it is the variety of people and unusual doings (catch the greased pig, crack the stone on a strong man's chest, knock the man down with a quarterstaff), which will interest them.

Mr. Hurd's style is admirable. In two soft colors, one a nicely varied basic brown, he manages to suggest the period, never with Hogarthian vigor, perhaps more in the mood of Rowlandson.

📖 *SOMEBODY'S HOUSE* (1953)

Bulletin of the Center for Children's Books

SOURCE: A review of *Somebody's House,* in *Bulletin of the Center for Children's Books,* Vol. VI, No. 7, March, 1953, p. 51.

Two small children watch the building of a house from the time the shovel starts excavating for the cellar until the new family moves in. The workers are far more willing to stop and explain each step to the children than would happen in real life and the children are allowed to climb over the unfinished building in a way that should not be encouraged because of the danger involved. The information is interesting and the illustrations are especially helpful in explaining some of the processes. However, because of the fictionalized style the usefulness of the book is limited.

Virginia Kirkus' Bookshop Service

SOURCE: A review of *Somebody's House,* in *Virginia Kirkus' Bookshop Service,* Vol. XXI, No. 5, March 1, 1953, p. 148.

We have yet to see a child who doesn't get all excited at the whole process of house building—watching the foundations laid, running over floor frames, digging into putty left by friendly workmen. Here's a book to recapture the urge. Jimmy, Jenny and their parents get a new house in the country and have a warming time indeed as all the stages are accomplished. Fine to read aloud or for older brothers and sisters who know something about construction. Action and detail ring the rafters in Clement Hurd's drawings.

Ellen Lewis Buell

SOURCE: "Building Homes," in *The New York Times Book Review,* March 29, 1953, p. 24.

The easiest way to learn about houses is to watch the day-by-day construction of one in company with a patient adult who will answer all the important questions. The Hurds' newest informational picture book, **Somebody's House,** offers children a similar fictional experience. Jimmy and Jenny watch the building of a frame house from the time the architect draws the plans (with advice from the children) to the moment the new neighbors move in. Each step in the construction of the house is explained clearly—the why as well as the how—of such absorbing processes as pouring the foundations, wiring the house, shingling the roof. The pictures are far from decorative, but they are explicit. This book ought to give children a respect for the thought, skill and care which have gone into the making of their own houses.

Louise S. Bechtel

SOURCE: A review of *Somebody's House,* in *New York Herald Tribune Book Review,* May 24, 1953, p. 8.

Jenny thought she would hate anyone who built on Blueberry Hill. Jimmy was not so sure. After a talk with the architect, they couldn't wait to watch it all happen. So, on pages half large type and half flat-color pictures, we learn all about it. Carpenters, masons, electricians, plumbers, painters, all play their parts, and we meet them and see them in action pictures and diagrams. At last comes the new family. It is a happily conceived factual book, for a wide age range of small would-be builders, or for kibitzers like the children in the story, or for a family who are just acquiring a new home. There is nothing else like it on this age level. Mr. Hurd's exact drawings are just right, giving the details small boys long to know, besides the dramatic action as the house nears completion.

NINO AND HIS FISH (1954)

Ruth O. Bostwick

SOURCE: A review of *Nino and His Fish,* in *Library Journal,* Vol. 79, No. 9, May 1, 1954, p. 864.

A delightful picture book about little Nino who lived near Fisherman's Wharf in Monterey. Because the fishing had

been poor and there was no money for cake, Nino's wish for a birthday party seemed hopeless until he decided to catch a big fish and serve that. How he caught the biggest fish of the day and exchanged it for the biggest party makes an appealing story which children under ten will enjoy. Full-page illustrations in deep blue and soft rose. Recommended.

Louise S. Bechtel

SOURCE: A review of *Nino and His Fish,* in *New York Herald Tribune Book Review,* May 16, 1954, p. 14.

Nino has the great idea of catching his own fish for his birthday party, since the sardine fishing has been too poor for him to expect the usual cake. So he goes along salmon fishing, with his father and the fishing fleet from Monterey. And every one he knows comes to the most wonderful fish birthday party to eat the "biggest fish of the day, caught by Nino of the Santa Rosa." Clement Hurd's two-color pictures combine original, bold, poster-like forms with exact details of Fisherman's Wharf, the boats, the guests. There is occasional intrusive local detail in the telling, but the whole leaves a vivid sense of a gay, real slice of life. Neither story style nor art style is unified, so that the whole just misses real distinction.

Virginia Haviland

SOURCE: A review of *Nino and His Fish,* in *The Horn Book Magazine,* Vol. XXX, No. 3, June, 1954, p. 171.

This gay picture book set in Monterey village and harbor will delight small children, both as an unusual birthday story and as an account of a little boy doing a grown-up job. Nino, a fisherman's son, says, just before his birthday, "What if I should go fishing and what if I should catch a fish of my own? A great big fish! Then I could invite all my friends and we would eat fish for my party." Three-color action pictures show that Nino catches the biggest fish of the day and that he has a party far more exciting than he had planned.

LAST ONE HOME IS A GREEN PIG (1959)

Virginia Kirkus' Service

SOURCE: A review of *Last One Home Is a Green Pig,* in *Virginia Kirkus' Service,* June 15, 1959, p. 400.

All the excitement and tempo of a race are incorporated into this tale of a duck and a monkey. The penalty of the race they propose is so dire that they explore every possibility which will prevent them being the last one home, and, consequently, "a green pig". Ripping across a world washed with green and red, the two animals employ their own momentum, plus the momentum of every available vehicle. The young reader is painlessly introduced, not only to the mannerism of monkeys and ducks, but also to a vocabulary which features trucks, boats, planes, horses, buses and bicycles. Clement Hurd, who has previously cooperated with his wife in illustrating *St. George's Day in Williamsburg, The Devil's Tail,* and *The Fox In The Box,* etc. captures the excitement of speed in an original and thoroughly convincing manner in his freely executed paintings.

Booklist

SOURCE: A review of *Last One Home Is a Green Pig,* in *Booklist,* Vol. 56, No. 2, September 15, 1959, pp. 56-57.

Racing each other home a duck and a monkey use their wits—and many different kinds of conveyances—to avoid being the last one home and "a green pig." This "I can read" book is unnecessarily drawn out and overlong for the average first or second grader reading by himself but the action and excitement of the story and pictures should hold the attention of the better independent reader. Satisfactory for libraries needing a variety of material for beginning readers.

📖 **THE GOLDEN HIND (written by Edith Thacher Hurd and illustrated by Leonard Everett Fisher, 1960)**

Virginia Kirkus' Service

SOURCE: A review of *The Golden Hind,* in *Virginia Kirkus' Service,* June 15, 1960, p. 452.

Francis Drake is without a doubt one of the most colorful figures of Elizabethan England. In this story of his voyages, his exploits against the Spanish pirates, his conflicts with mutinous and jealous men, and his explorations of waters on which English ships had never sailed before, the author is strongly partial to her hero. Edith Thacher Hurd, who has written many books for young readers, boldly conveys the man, his accomplishments and his times in simple terms, and it is considerably more stimulating than other informative texts written for beginning readers.

Saturday Review

SOURCE: A review of *The Golden Hind,* in *Saturday Review,* Vol. XLIV, No. 3, January 21, 1961, p. 75.

Sir Francis Drake is the key figure in this story about the Age of Exploration. Although the voyage with which the book is concerned is described in rather routine fashion, the honesty with which the author records Drake's piratical treatment of the Spaniards and hints at the complicated morality of the times makes this an unusual book for school children.

📖 **COME AND HAVE FUN (1962)**

Virginia Haviland

SOURCE: A review of *Come and Have Fun,* in *The Horn Book Magazine,* Vol. XXXVIII, No. 6, December, 1962, pp. 595-96.

As an Early I Can Read book (for first graders) this has a small vocabulary and the familiar old play of cat at mouse's hole and cat-and-mouse on the run. These limitations are largely compensated for by the verve and humor of the pictures and by the fast, rhythmic pace of the telling. "'Come out,' said the cat/ 'Come out and have tea.'/ 'Oh, no,' said the mouse/ in his safe little house./ 'I know what cats like best/ for their tea!'"

Zena Sutherland

SOURCE: A review of *Come and Have Fun,* in *Bulletin of the Center for Children's Books,* Vol. XVI, No. 10, June, 1963, p. 162.

For the beginning independent reader, a brief and simple story with gay and simple illustrations. The text, half of which is in dialogue, will be useful for supplementary reading practice; as a story it is an improvement on the saga of Dick and Jane, but it is only moderately interesting. "The mouse would not play, so the cat went away. The mouse looked out of his little mouse house 'Where is the cat?' said the mouse. 'He will run after me if I come out of my little mouse house.' The cat sat and sat. The mouse sat and sat."

📖 **JOHNNY LION'S BOOK (1965)**

The New York Times Book Review

SOURCE: A review of *Johnny Lion's Book,* in *The New York Times Book Review,* November 7, 1965, p. 56.

The unusual book-within-a-book technique is admirably handled, though it may be a bit sophisticated for the youngest readers without some guidance. More experienced readers (late second or early third grade) will enjoy the gay pictures and understand the central idea that adventures in a book are almost as exciting and interesting as real ones.

Saturday Review

SOURCE: A review of *Johnny Lion's Book,* in *Saturday Review,* Vol. XLVIII, No. 46, November 13, 1965, p. 54.

> One day Mother Lion
> said to Father Lion,
> "Johnny can read."

"Oh, really?" said Father Lion.
"Yes, really," said Mother Lion.
"I am going out to buy him
a new book,"
said Mother Lion.

Children will enjoy this brightly colored book because they will share Johnny Lion's struggles and ultimate triumph. Grownups will be amused because they know all about Johnny who can't read. It is one of life's mysteries why publishers go on producing more and more children's books of all kinds if children do not read them. But, of course, they do read the books. And I'm sure that the best of the Harper I Can Read books are read to tatters by those who, like Johnny Lion, have discovered the joy of words on a printed page.

Priscilla L. Moulton

SOURCE: A review of *Johnny Lion's Book,* in *The Horn Book Magazine,* Vol. XLI, No. 6, December, 1965, p. 625.

Johnny Lion's identification with Oscar P. Lion, the principal character in his first book, constitutes one of the more original and amusing themes in a series for beginning readers. Since Johnny now can read, Mother Lion buys him a book; Johnny reads and rereads it while Father and Mother Lion are out hunting. Oscar P. Lion disobeys his parents, leaves home, goes hunting, escapes with his life, and loses his way. When Johnny's parents return, Johnny tells them about the perilous adventures he had during their absence—Oscar P. Lion's, of course. Lovable lions, drawn with light, curving line and colored with gold and red, are cuddly soft and endearing.

From Come and Have Fun, *written by Edith Thacher Hurd. Illustrated by Clement Hurd.*

THE DAY THE SUN DANCED (1965)

Virginia Kirkus' Service

SOURCE: A review of *The Day the Sun Danced,* in *Virginia Kirkus' Service,* Vol. XXXIV, No. 3, February 1, 1966, p. 104.

The illustrator has made the sun dance through the imaginative use of color impressed in wood grains and the delicate color work does convey a sense of the intensifying heat from the sun. It's a winter into spring commentary. The text describes the animal activity stimulated by the approach of warm weather as well as the rebirth of plant life. Like the numberless other juvenile titles celebrating seasonal changes . . . these declarative sentences are completely rural wildlife oriented. Both author and illustrator have successfully suggested the simultaneity of nature's response to spring. The color suggests the speed and noise. The text is hushed mood piece writing.

Margaret F. O'Connell

SOURCE: A review of *The Day the Sun Danced,* in *The New York Times Book Review,* March 13, 1966, p. 26.

Spring comes when the sun rises "glorious gold-bright" to warm and stir the wood to life. Edith Thacher Hurd celebrates this event with a gentle tale of the rabbit who rouses the fox, deer and hibernating bear to watch the sunburst. It is a simple, eloquent, if sentimental, evocation of the signs of nature's renewal: the new leaves and flowers; the birds and the young animals. Clement Hurd's stunning woodcuts have an appealing spontaneity and naturalness.

RAIN AND THE VALLEY (1968)

Kirkus Service

SOURCE: A review of *Rain and the Valley,* in *Kirkus Service,* Vol. XXXVI, No. 7, April 1, 1968, p. 399.

Mountain rain runoff makes valley; valley grows green and flourishes; man cultivates, pastures cows, neglects need to retain rainwater; valley becomes dustbowl for many years; new farmer arrives, plows and plants properly, replenishes trees, builds dam for pond; valley grows green again. In minimal text and atmospheric woodcuts, it's the cycle of life according to the canon of conservation and the trouble is that it's too compressed and abstract for the young child who's not already familiar with geologic, ecological and agricultural transformation, and too cursory for the older child who is. Each of the areas is best approached separately, as they can be in effective introductions for this age level.

Marjorie Lewis

SOURCE: A review of *Rain and the Valley,* in *School Library Journal,* Vol. 14, No. 9, May, 1968, p. 72.

In **The Day the Sun Danced,** the Hurds treated a poetic subject poetically; however, the same approach and format fails in this attempt at arty early childhood science information on why good farmland can become dry and worthless. The text, arranged in lines as though it were poetry, is arid as a dust bowl. The vocabulary is simple enough for independent reading in early grades, but switching tenses from present to past and back again is confusing. The impressionistic woodcuts are crude and depressing; when color is used, it is often muddy. Suggested related science experiments are printed on the last two pages. This is the kind of book some adults may think makes science exciting but which has no record of fostering excitement in children.

Wayne Hanley

SOURCE: A review of *Rain and the Valley,* in *Appraisal: Children's Science Books,* Vol. 2, No. 3, Fall, 1969, p. 11.

I give this volume a high score for its superb woodcuts, half of which appear in three colors. Although they are of a sophisticated quality that may be beyond childish comprehension, I suspect most children would be intrigued by them. Despite gross oversimplification, which I accept as necessary in presenting the complex subject of man's degradation and restoration of land to children, the text is not misleading.

📖   *MONKEY IN THE JUNGLE* **(written by Edna Mitchell Preston and illustrated by Clement Hurd, 1968)**

Publishers Weekly

SOURCE: A review of *Monkey in the Jungle,* in *Publishers Weekly,* Vol. 194, No. 11, September 9, 1968, p. 64.

It's not a new device, but it seems to be *this* year's device, this pattern of introducing children to a group of animals, birds, what-have-you, with a simple story line. *Monkey in the Jungle* is the cream of the crop—so far—this story which introduces its small readers to many animals in a jungle as they watch a small monkey resist going to bed. Maybe it seems the cream of the crop because it is Clement Hurd who illustrates the monkey and the jungle.

Diane Farrell

SOURCE: A review of *Monkey in the Jungle,* in *The Horn Book Magazine,* Vol. XLV, No. 2, April, 1969, p. 163.

Every small child will feel empathy for the little monkey who makes such outrageous statements as: "I will NOT go to sleep"; "I don't know how"; "I can't"; "I will stay up all night and all day/ and all the next night and all the next day/ and ALL THE TIME. So there!" The elephant threatens to spank him, and the lion threatens to eat him; but the little monkey swings through the jungle—away from his parents, away from the TORTOISE, away from the SNAKE, the LEOPARD, the CROCODILE, away from all the animals that are rushing and roaring and crashing through the jungle to catch him—until he falls with a bump into his mother's arms and drifts to sleep while the jungle night grows dark and still. The rhythmic repetitions of the text change the conversation of the animals into a chant that becomes a prose lullaby. The illustrations are vigorous and humorous prints—with lush tangles of foliage in muted tones of orange, yellow, and green, and with bulky shapes of animals dissolving into the shadowy jungle and becoming more completely hidden as night draws near.

Mary W. Hammond

SOURCE: A review of *Monkey in the Jungle,* in *School Library Journal,* Vol. 15, No. 9, May, 1969, p. 78.

When a baby monkey stubbornly refuses to go to sleep at night, he upsets all the other animals in the jungle and subsequently leads them on a wild, merry chase, which culminates in their eventual peace as the now tired little monkey drops off to sleep. The simple text, highly repetitive and often awkward, sometimes tries for rhythm, sometimes tries for rhyme: ("swinging high/swinging low/ never looking where to go"). Clement Hurd's block prints in black, green, red, and yellow are the highlight of the oversize book: his double-page spreads of the wild jungle, becoming progressively darker as night falls, are convincingly well executed. This might serve as a read-aloud item, especially for contrary three-to-five-year-olds who would rather monkey around than nap.

📖   *THIS IS THE FOREST* **(1969)**

Kirkus Reviews

SOURCE: A review of *This Is the Forest,* in *Kirkus Reviews,* Vol. XXXVI, No. 18, October 1, 1969, p. 1068.

"Each little animal has its place in the forest. The birds and the insects, each has its place in the forest of pine trees." In these literary (i.e. semi-poetic) and ecological terms, the death and rebirth of a pine forest are depicted. Felled by fire, it rises again in soil readied by a slow process of decay and burrowing and scattering, of living and dying, until first one and then many pine seeds take root. While a sense of continuity and interdependence is conveyed, the particulars don't stand out—largely because the "moles and shrews . . . spiders and ants, tumblebugs and doodlebugs, slugs, snails and little gray sow bugs," towhees and thrushes, the brown creeper and the red-headed woodpecker and the others mentioned by name can't be distinguished in the fuzzy illustrations. And the lyricism dissipates attention at the same time the pictures fail to reward it.

CATFISH (1970)

Ethel L. Heins

SOURCE: A review of *Catfish,* in *The Horn Book Magazine,* Vol. XLVI, No. 3, June, 1970, p. 291.

Some years ago, the author and the artist produced a very funny book about a sulky cat who imagined himself speeding along at the wheel of his master's car (*No Funny Business*). But Catfish, a bold and brazen feline, who lived with a man called Mush Mouth in the little town of Nevermind, completely outstrips his predecessor. Catfish first had a tricycle, but tearing around town, he smashed it up; next he demolished a "high-speed/ low-speed/ stop-and-go/ whiz-bang/ bicycle"; and finally he had to be forcibly parted from a splendid red motorcycle by Mr. Fix-It-Fine the Mayor, and Mighty Mince Meat the Police Chief. When two gangsters held up the town bank, Catfish, roaring after them in the bank president's car, apprehended the thugs in a wildly noisy chase. But Catfish, the "cool cat," the fastest cat in town, wanted no medal for bravery. He got, instead, a "bright, new, shiny very, very fast . . . AUTOMOBILE." What small child could resist this tale of a cheeky four-legged speed demon, told in effective, easy-to-read prose and in breezy black-and-white drawings splashed with brilliant red?

Kathlyn K. Lundgren

SOURCE: A review of *Catfish,* in *Library Journal,* Vol. 93, No. 10, June 15, 1970, p. 2302.

This original story has a certain appeal in its action-packed, red-white-and-black cartoon drawings. Also, the vocabulary is simple enough for beginning readers and is in a modern vernacular. However, the story gives the impression that it doesn't matter what one does as long as things turn out right. A speed-crazy, careless cat gives chase in a stolen car to bank robbers; through a lucky coincidence, Catfish captures the robbers, and saves the cash. He becomes a hero and is rewarded with an automobile even though he has been unreliable and a hazard on a tricycle, bicycle and motorcycle, and his irresponsibility is actually given applause.

JOHNNY LION'S BAD DAY (1970)

Zena Sutherland

SOURCE: A review of *Johnny Lion's Bad Day,* in *Bulletin of the Center for Children's Books,* Vol. 24, No. 2, October, 1970, p. 28.

Intended as a book for independent reading, the story seems more appropriate for reading aloud, both because of the subject and because of the occasional difficult polysyllabic word. The illustrations have movement and humor but are repetitive, the story is gay and charming. Little Johnny Lion, in bed because of a cold, keeps urging his mother not to give him medicine, and mother's calm handling of this is exemplary. He has a series of bad dreams (attributed by mother to illness and by Johnny to the medicine) and then—finally—one in which he is triumphant. Happily he bounces into his parents' bedroom to have a cuddle, falls asleep, and has a dreamless night to end the bad day. A light touch, a familiar situation, and a balanced combination of real events and the dozing dreams of illness.

THE MOTHER BEAVER (1971)

Kirkus Reviews

SOURCE: A review of *The Mother Beaver,* in *Kirkus Reviews,* Vol. XXXIX, No. 8, April 15, 1971, p. 439.

A year in the life of a female beaver that begins with her making a nest in the family lodge and giving birth to four kits. The reader follows her as she feeds them, takes them out to eat and swim, protects them from an otter, works with her older offspring and their father to repair the dam, winters with her family in the lodge, and mates with the male in early spring. The cycle ends as the mother beaver waits in the lodge to deliver a new litter. A pleasant enough chronicle that will convey to the receptive a feeling for the rhythms of nature, the book will disappoint children seeking information about beaver dams and their construction, the beaver's role in conservation, the uses of their fur, or other uniquely beaverish aspects of the animal's existence. Adequate colored woodcuts on each page depict the beavers' activities and their homes.

Eleanor Glaser

SOURCE: A review of *The Mother Beaver,* in *Library Journal,* Vol. 96, No. 13, July, 1971, p. 2358.

This very simple beaver story concentrates on the mother beaver and her kits. The mother and father get the lodge ready for the young they are expecting. The father takes their one- and two-year-old young to a den on the shore while the mother remains in the lodge to bear her kits alone. A few days after they are born they are able to swim, and the mother leads them underwater to where the father and other young are. After a very brief visit she returns with the kits to the lodge and cares for them until they are bigger and stronger. The story covers their growth to their membership in the beaver colony. The detailed blue, green and yellow block prints are attractive and appropriate to the well-told story.

WILSON'S WORLD (1971; British edition published as *Wilkie's World*, 1973)

Kirkus Reviews

SOURCE: A review of *Wilson's World*, in *Kirkus Reviews*, Vol. XXXIX, No. 15, August 1, 1971, p. 803.

Wilson likes to paint, and in his painting he reiterates the process of creation, producing world, sun, plants, animals, cave people, other people, cities, highways—until the picture is crowded with people and smoke and Wilson writes "Phooey" on his picture and starts all over. The second time there is not too much of anything and the world is beautiful because "everybody cares" again. Like Wilson's first picture, the book moves from a promising start to a murky conclusion; the ease with which Wilson undoes the damage makes the ending flatly pious. The pictures, though, are clear and fresh and affecting; they make Wilson's renewed world something to care about.

Melinda Schroeder

SOURCE: A review of *Wilson's World*, in *School Library Journal*, Vol. 18, No. 2, October, 1971, p. 103.

After awhile this book becomes both pretentious and monotonous. Like God, Wilson, aged six or seven, decides one day to create the world, but he does it with paints at his easel. He begins with a picture of the earth, adds the sea, sky and sun, and then progresses through time at the speed of light, from dinosaurs to monkeys and chimpanzees, cave dwellers, towns and then crowded cities, American pioneers, and, finally, to a smoky brown likeness of New York City or Los Angeles on a day when the pollution is at a particularly "unsatisfactory level." Wilson, understandably disgusted, writes "PHOOEY, PHOOEY, PHOOEY" under the sordid sight. Then he starts all over with a brand-new piece of paper on which he paints a brand-new world with brand-new people who care about their world and do not pollute, overpopulate, or deplete its natural resources. The book opens like a tablet, with the majority of the dominantly red, blue, yellow and green traditional-style pictures (depicting vistas more proficiently than people) vertical double-page spreads. The writing is only fair, and the cataloguing of the phenomena and inhabitants of Wilson's two worlds is tedious.

Children's Book Review

SOURCE: A review of *Wilkie's World*, in *Children's Book Review*, Vol. III, No. 5, October, 1973, p. 138.

It was predictable that environmental pollution would become a voguish topic with today's writers for the young and *Wilkie's World* is a prime example of the sort of confused and oversimplified thinking which too often characterises this new genre.

Wilkie paints a (garbled) picture of the evolution of the modern world in which city life is seen as the ultimate evil: 'too many cities and too many people . . . so much smoke and so much smog' (a view which ignores the far more pressing problems of over half the world and reduces those of the 'developed nations' to a cliché).

Wilkie's solution is to paint a 'brand new world' in which 'they're not building too many houses or too many cities' (nothing is said about how they disposed of 'too many people'!) This brave new world is shown as a romantic rural paradise with a small country house beside a winding river, the old folk relaxing on the porch, father and son fishing and Wilkie swimming in the unpolluted waters. All this surrounded by a good three hundred acres of unspoiled countryside on which sheep, cattle, horses and poultry are grazing while white rabbits gambol unmolested beside a group of cats and dogs. True, on the horizon we see three scattered blocks of high-rise flats (looking a bit like Christian's Celestial City) but we are not invited to consider what life is like for the thousands of people who live there.

This is not just a book of surpassing silliness—it shows a criminal lack of responsibility in its approach to the real and complex issues which face young children in the future.

THE MOTHER WHALE (1973)

Booklist

SOURCE: A review of *The Mother Whale*, in *Booklist*, Vol. 70, No. 8, December 15, 1973, pp. 445-46.

The birth of her baby and its first two years are described in terms of the mother whale's actions in this quiet narrative that captures the rhythm of the sea and its inhabitants. The blue and green block prints provide a visual tranquility and sense of vastness that match the mood established in the text as readers observe the baby's birth tail first, his rapid growth, and, finally, the mother's mating again with the bull whale. In much the same style as their book, *The Mother Deer*, the Hurds have imparted a sense of the wonder in nature's cycles.

Zena Sutherland

SOURCE: A review of *The Mother Whale*, in *Bulletin of the Center for Children's Books*, Vol. 27, No. 7, March, 1974, p. 111.

A description of the life cycle of the sperm whale begins with the birth of a calf, describes the mother's care and the baby calf's growth to independence, the challenge of an old bull by a young male, and the courting and mating of the whale mother that brings, months later, the birth of another baby whale. Simple, quite smooth in style despite

He climbed a big tree.

Lots of good things to eat

ran under the tree.

But little Oscar P. Lion

was afraid to jump down

and eat them.

From Johnny Lion's Book, *written by Edith Thacher Hurd. Illustrated by Clement Hurd.*

the simplicity, and judicious in the amount of information provided for the intended audience, the book is illustrated in attractive if repetitive block prints: blue, green, and black scenes of the dark whale bodies in the blue-green sea.

Beryl B. Beatley

SOURCE: A review of *The Mother Whale*, in *Appraisal: Children's Science Books*, Vol. 7, No. 3, Fall, 1974, pp. 25-26.

Another handsome companion to the author's **The Mother Beaver** and **The Mother Deer, The Mother Whale** follows the same format and pattern as those earlier volumes. In simple, strong, but not limited prose, the life of a mother sperm whale is told from the birth of her baby, a mere 2,000 lb., to the time when her next baby is born (a sperm whale's gestation period is 16 months, and weening takes over two years). Although the text is minimal, four to six lines on each of the 32 pages, a great deal of information is given so that the child to whom this is read or who reads it himself will understand how and

where the great whales live, who are their enemies and who are their companions, and get a feeling from the prose of the vastness of the oceans and a satisfying amount of information on the sperm whale. The beautiful block prints in blues and greens and black cover every page and add to the atmosphere, although they are more likely to be appreciated by the adult introducing the book.

THE MOTHER CHIMPANZEE (1977)

Publishers Weekly

SOURCE: A review of *The Mother Chimpanzee*, in *Publishers Weekly*, Vol. 213, No. 6, February 6, 1978, pp. 101-02.

The warm sympathy and authentic information in the books about animals produced by the Hurds rate them A for excellence. Critics and little naturalists have appreciated the couple's stories and pictures on mothers and babies of the beaver, the deer, whale, owl and kangaroo. Now the team brings us into the jungle, to experience the daily lives of the primates. The older male and female chimps run to see their mother's new baby girl as the story begins. In the following episodes, the amazingly humanlike family life is described in simple but touching words and atmospheric pictures. The ending portrays the female baby, now an adult, but still bound by love to mother, brothers and sisters.

Denise M. Wilms

SOURCE: A review of *The Mother Chimpanzee*, in *Booklist*, Vol. 74, No. 12, February 15, 1978, p. 1009.

Key scenes in this picture book introduction to chimpanzees are familiar ones seen in older treatments of the animals: the mother cradles her youngest child as siblings look on, grooming interaction soothes, rain makes the two miserable, the young chimp wanders off while her mother pokes out termites, a baboon becomes a temporary playmate. The flow of typical events in the lives of this pair is smooth, and the text is admirably simple. Green linoleum cuts highlighted with brown and black are sometimes muddy but still eye-catching in their angular proportions. A credible addition to a good series.

John R. Pancella

SOURCE: A review of *The Mother Chimpanzee*, in *Appraisal: Children's Science Books*, Vol. 12, No. 2, Spring, 1979, pp. 27-28.

The story is more about the life of a young chimpanzee than a mother. There is information on the rearing and feeding of the young, play activities, and some interactions with other animals such as a baboon and leopard. There is a dedication to Jane Goodall, whose recent field research probably was the basis for much of the content. The drawings will be welcomed by primary readers because they capture chimps in natural poses and closely relate to the text. Every page is illustrated, but the three-color line drawings are uneven in detail and realism. Some are oversimplified and others more comic than natural. There is not much information here: the range is from twenty to about seventy words per page.

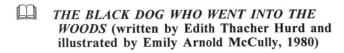 *THE BLACK DOG WHO WENT INTO THE WOODS* (written by Edith Thacher Hurd and illustrated by Emily Arnold McCully, 1980)

Marilyn R. Singer

SOURCE: A review of *The Black Dog Who Went Into the Woods*, in *School Library Journal*, Vol. 26, No. 8, April, 1980, p. 95

The death of the family dog is treated with sensitivity and an original slant in this quiet, easily read little book that also gives some good insights into family dynamics. The

youngest member of the family is the one who intuitively understands and accepts that their old dog has gone off to die. His parents and older siblings, in an effort to protect him, deny it and insist on looking for Black Dog in the woods. After hours of searching and futilely calling (the dog is deaf), Benjamin puts his foot down: "'I don't think we should look for Black Dog anymore,' he said. 'Black Dog doesn't want us to look for her.'" During the next few days, the rest of the family keeps on looking, until one evening they finally agree with Benjamin. That night, the full moon shines in each one's window and brings a special goodbye dream from Black Dog. The next morning, typically, it's Benjamin who dares to jump right in with the truth. "Everyone was quiet at breakfast the next morning. Only Benjamin said 'Black Dog came in the night to say good-bye to me.'"; this helps everyone else open up. Maybe Benjamin's ability to speak the truth comes from his being the youngest, without the burden of having to shield anyone; nonetheless, his perceptivity and inner strength make him a welcome hero. He's reflective of the book itself, spare but sweet. And there's a pleasing wholeness to the world within the story, a spiritual undercurrent that connects all the elements—the family, the animals, the woods, the moon, the spirit.

Kirkus Reviews

SOURCE: A review of *The Black Dog Who Went Into the Woods*, in *Kirkus Reviews*, Vol. XLVIII, No. 9, May 1, 1980, p. 576.

The pet who dies here is called Black Dog; little Benjamin, who senses that "Black Dog has gone into the woods and died," is referred to—and addressed—as Youngest One; and that's indicative of the self-consciousness throughout. Benjamin, as the youngest, might be more closely attuned to Black Dog's feelings than the others—hence his hunch that she's gone off to die. But his sister is given to say solemnly, "Only the youngest one could still talk to her." What happens in the course of many texty pages is the family's acceptance of Benjamin's hunch—sealed by the dreams each of them has about Black Dog, dreams in which she says goodbye to each in an appropriate way. And: "Benjamin did not say anything more about Black Dog after that." An earnest attempt to concretize the ineffable that shows its hand too plainly.

Zena Sutherland

SOURCE: A review of *The Black Dog Who Went Into the Woods*, in *Bulletin of the Center for Children's Books*, Vol. 33, No. 11, July-August, 1980, p. 215.

The youngest of three children, Benjamin, dolefully reports that their old dog has disappeared; he is sure that she has gone off to the woods to die. For days the members of the family search for Black Dog, and finally they admit that Benjamin is probably right. One night each member of the family has a dream about Black Dog, a dream in which each remembers some incident. At breakfast they talk about the way Black Dog had come in the night to say farewell to them and, the book ends, "Benjamin did not say anything more about Black Dog after that." The illustrations [by Emily Arnold McCully], line and wash, softly echo the quiet poignancy of the story; while the fact that each member of the family had a dream about the dog on the same night, after she had been missing for days, is not quite credible, this is a sensitive handling of adjustment to a pet's death, written with direct simplicity and restraint.

UNDER THE LEMON TREE (1980)

Kirkus Reviews

SOURCE: A review of *Under the Lemon Tree,* in *Kirkus Reviews,* Vol. XLVIII, No. 7, April 1, 1980, pp. 435-36.

A beckoning Mediterranean farmyard, an injustice to be righted, a danger to be thwarted, and lots of animal sounds to chime in on—so who cares if the actual plot is old hat? Tethered "under the lemon tree" is a gray donkey whose braying at the stealthy approach of a fox wakes the rooster, the chickens, and the ducks—and thus puts the fox to rout. But the also-roused farmer and his wife, unaware of the fox's presence, indignantly exile the donkey to a distant fig tree. Then the fox returns, snatches up the farmer's pet rooster, and streaks off—only to be intercepted again by the sleepless donkey's EE-AAW-EE-AWW-EE-AAW. This time of course the farmer and his wife are properly grateful, and the donkey is restored to her lemon-tree domain forever. That tree is a vital presence, not a picturesque prop; the animals are scatty, the couple is comical; and even the fox is saved from villainy—she's "looking for something for herself and her five little foxes to eat." However modest, it's the kind of thoughtful, assured performance one expects of the Hurds.

Kristi L. Thomas

SOURCE: A review of *Under the Lemon Tree,* in *School Library Journal,* Vol. 26, No. 9, May, 1980, p. 58.

An unoriginal quasi-fable of the fox-in-the-henhouse variety. A farmer's donkey raises the midnight alarm, rouses the barnyard, and frightens the intruder away. The farmer, seeing nothing amiss but disliking the ruckus, opts for a good night's sleep and moves the donkey far out into the fields. The fox returns, steals the farmer's prize rooster, and is only stopped in his pre-snack tracks by an accidental encounter with the self-same beast, whereupon the donkey is returned to his place of former esteem. The illustrations have a fuzzy comfortableness but are notable chiefly for the stylized silent-movie mugging of the farmer and his wife; the language is serviceable if not exciting. Nothing to crow about, but then, nothing to bray about either.

Karen M. Klockner

SOURCE: A review of *Under the Lemon Tree,* in *The Horn Book Magazine,* Vol. LVI, No. 3, June, 1980, p. 287.

A little gray donkey lives under the lemon tree in a farmer's yard. Each night he awakens the other animals by his noisy bawling to warn them of an approaching hungry fox. So the farmer decides to rid his yard of the nightly racket by moving the donkey to a spot further away from the house. But the donkey is still able to help the farmer save his favorite white rooster from the fox's attack—thus winning back his old spot under the lemon tree. Framed pictures, similar in style to the work of Ardizzone, show each scene in soft tones. Daylight settings are brightened by the lemon tree and sunshine. Most of the nighttime scenes darkened with blues and grays convey an almost dreamlike feeling, although some are less effective because of their unusually dark tones. The old-fashioned quality of the story is complemented by the childlike simplicity of the illustrations.

SONG OF THE SEA OTTER (written by Edith Thacher Hurd and illustrated by Jennifer Dewey, 1983)

Kirkus Reviews

SOURCE: A review of *Song of the Sea Otter,* in *Kirkus Reviews,* Vol. LI, No. 21, November 1, 1983, p. J-196.

A slightly older, slightly fuller book in the gentle, musing tenor of **The Mother Chimpanzee** or **The Mother Whale**—similarly concerned with the young otter's growth to independence, but most especially with his discovery of where he belongs: not in "the great mysterious sea" (which he explores), nor on land (where he takes refuge in a storm), but in the little harbor his mother first sang to him about. "Sleep./ My little sea otter baby./ The waves to rock you,/ The deep water below you,/ These are your two worlds./ My little sea otter child." The young otter does learn to gather shellfish, break them with stones on his chest, and eat the contents; he drifts about on a bed of kelp, grooms himself, sleeps. But there's a teddy-bear look to the drawings, [by Jennifer Dewey], and a mushyness (and patterning) to the text, more suitable to picture books than to true-life accounts.

Miriam Lang Budin

SOURCE: A review of *Song of the Sea Otter,* in *School Library Journal,* Vol. 30, No. 7, March, 1984, p. 160.

Hurd tells a story about the early years of a sea otter's life in a harbor on the Pacific Ocean. She recounts how the otter learns to swim and find his own food, then describes his exploration of the ocean. Supposing that he becomes curious about the world where the sun sets, she also imagines that he dreams of the land, only realizing that it is not a hospitable place for him after he is tossed there by the waves of a storm. If *Song of the Sea Otter* is a less distinguished book than Hurd's previous science books, it is partially because she attributes thoughts to the sea otter instead of sticking to facts. She also attempts to introduce the evolution of the otter, but the oversimplified description is vague and difficult to understand. Dewey's realistic pencil drawings adequately portray the world of the sea otter for the most part, but some of them are indistinct. There is a substantial amount of information in this book, but it is muddied by Hurd's uncharacteristic anthropomorphizing of the otter.

Charlotte W. Draper

SOURCE: A review of *Song of the Sea Otter,* in *The Horn Book Magazine,* Vol. LX, No. 2, April, 1984, pp. 209-10.

The song of the mother sea otter lulls her newborn to sleep while defining his world: "The waves to rock you / the deep water below you." But since the baby learned to swim a few weeks after birth, his curiosity impels him to explore beyond the protected harbor which is his natural habitat. He swims in the ocean, meeting dolphins and whales, and attempts to gain the dry land where his ancestors and those of related aquatic mammals lived millennia ago. "Perhaps, without even knowing what had happened millions of years before, this was why the young otter dreamed of the land." Although a lyrical evocation more than an objective discussion, the text provides specific information about a large number of sea creatures in the ecosystem. With her usual clarity, the author introduces concepts such as the food chain, evolution, migration, and life cycles, never losing sight of the reader's emotional identification with the otter. Soft black-and-white drawings carry the listener along with the sea otter's adventures and are sufficiently detailed to identify the flora and fauna mentioned in the text.

Additional coverage of the Hurds' life and career is contained in the following sources published by Gale Research: *Contemporary Authors New Revision Series,* Vol. 24; *Major Authors and Illustrators for Children and Young Adults; Something About the Author,* Vol. 64; and *Something About the Author Autobiography Series,* Vol. 13.

Anne (Inez) McCaffrey

1926-

American author of fiction.

Major works include *Dragonflight* (1968), *The Ship Who Sang* (1969), *Dragonsong* (1976), *Killashandra* (1985), *The Rowan* (1990), *Black Horses for the King* (1996).

INTRODUCTION

McCaffrey, affectionately dubbed the "Dragon Lady," is best known as the creator of Pern, a former colony of earth inhabited by flying, telepathic dragons and their human riders. She has written more than twelve titles in the series "Dragonriders of Pern," which includes the *Dragonflight, Dragonquest* (1971)*,* and *The White Dragon* (1978) trilogy and the popular "Harper Hall" trilogy for young adults. While adept at building credible science fiction universes—she has published a number of series and single titles about other planets in addition to Pern—McCaffrey tends to emphasize the personal over the technical in her stories. As a result of her emphasis on people and feelings and her use of classic fantasy elements such as dragons and near feudal societies, critics have often labeled her novels as fantasy. McCaffrey argues, however, that her books are based on solid scientific principles; her dragons are biogenetically engineered, not imagined. The emotional focus, fast-paced action, and strong characters—particularly talented, determined women and child protagonists—blended with credible science make her stories appealing to both teen and adult readers across genres. With *The White Dragon*, McCaffrey was the first science fiction writer to achieve best-seller status and she has continued to write best-selling novels ever since. As she related to *Booklist* interviewer Pat Monaghan, "If you tell a good story, anybody will read it. It doesn't have to be fantasy or science fiction. It could be anything."

Biographical Information

McCaffrey was born in Massachusetts on April 1, 1926, a date she finds fateful since in the same month and year, Hugo Gernsback began publishing *Amazing* and *Fantastic* magazines. Raised in Upper Montclair, New Jersey, McCaffrey was one of three children. Unlike many women of her day, she credits her parents for instilling in her the "notion that I would do well in school and college; marry; have children; and DO something with the rest of my life." She graduated cum laude from Radcliffe College in 1947 majoring in Slavonic languages and literatures. Shortly after marrying in 1950 she became housebound due to illness and began reading the science fiction magazines that came with her furnished apartment. Entranced by the magical worlds, she started writing her own stories when new stories didn't come out fast enough.

She sold her first story in 1952. She later wrote *The Ship Who Sang* in response to the grief she experienced by her father's death. She credits this story with teaching her how to use emotion as a writing tool and it remains her favorite story. McCaffrey's first published novel was *Restoree* in 1967. By 1970, she was an established writer and mother of three grown children. After a divorce from her husband, she moved to Ireland where she continues to write in a cottage named "Dragonhold."

Major Works

The premise for the series "Dragonriders of Pern" is the constant struggle the human inhabitants face against deadly spores called Thread. In *Dragonflight*, the first book of the series, McCaffrey introduces her popular dragons and the special bond they have with their human riders that enables them to ward off the spores. The next two novels in the series, *Dragonquest* and *The White Dragon*, complete the trilogy of the adventures of the dragonriders. The other titles in the series expand on different aspects of Pern originating from these first three novels. *Dragonsdawn* (1988), for example, chronicles the original settlement of Pern and the creation of the dragons through biogenetic engineering. Within the series is another trilogy, called the "Harper Hall" series, which parallels the first three books but is aimed specifically toward young adult readers. *Dragonsong, Dragonsinger* (1977), and *Dragondrums* (1979) follow the adventures of a musically talented teenage girl, Menolly, who is forbidden to play her harp and sing because she is a girl. With determination and assistance from her friends, young fire lizards that are cousins to Pern's dragons, Menolly faces the dangers of Thread and the challenges of surviving on her own. The popularity of the Pern books has inspired a cassette of music titled *Dragonsongs,* a board game and computer games. *The Ship Who Sang,* McCaffrey's personal favorite, is about a severely handicapped young woman who is cybernetically linked to a spaceship so that her body becomes the ship. Remaining titles in the series were done as collaborations, a practice McCaffrey has used with other series as well. *Killashandra,* part of the "Crystal Singer" series, chronicles the adventures of Killashandra Ree, whose musical ability allows her to cut crystal indigenous to the planet. The crystal, used in space travel, lengthens the life of its cutters, but unfortunately affects their brains. *The Rowan* is expanded from one of McCaffrey's earliest stories, "Lady in the Tower" (1959). In this introduction to another series of adventures, the Rowan is an orphan with supreme telepathic abilities. Raised by psychologists to be a Prime, a powerful telepath monitoring the commerce of human-settled space, the Rowan's responsibilities restrict her access to other humans. Using her unique ability, she connects mentally with another Prime who seeks her help in warding off an alien invasion and with whom she eventually finds love. In *Black Horses for the King,* McCaffrey's first historical novel for young adults, she retells the Arthurian tale through the eyes of a Roman Celtic youth named Galwyn. McCaffrey, who raises horses in Ireland, combines knowledgeable horse lore with a coming-of-age story to create the legend of a charismatic young Arthur who imports great Libyan horses to Britain to carry his warriors to military triumph against the Saxons.

Awards

McCaffrey won the Hugo Award for the novella "Weyr Search" in 1968 and the Nebula Award for the novella "Dragonrider" in 1969. Both novellas were later combined to produce *Dragonflight.* She was the first woman to receive the Hugo Award and received the E. E. Smith Award for fantasy in 1975. McCaffrey was awarded ALA Notable Book Citations for *Dragonsong* in 1976 and *Dragonsinger* in 1977. She also received the Children's Book Showcase Award and the *Horn Book* Fanfare Citation for *Dragonsong* in 1977. She won the Gandalf and Ditmar Awards for *The White Dragon* in 1979 and the Balrog citation for *Dragondrums* in 1980. McCaffrey received Science Fiction Book Club Awards in 1986 for *Killashandra,* in 1989 for *Dragonsdawn,* in 1990 for *The Renegades of Pern* and *The Rowan,* in 1991 for *All the Weyrs of Pern,* in 1993 for *Damia's Children,* and in 1994 for *The Dolphins of Pern.*

AUTHOR'S COMMENTARY

Pat Monaghan with Anne McCaffrey

SOURCE: In an interview, in *Booklist,* Vol. 90, No. 14, March 15, 1994, pp. 1300-01.

It was a fine soft day, as they say in Ireland—meaning it was drizzling cold rain. Anne McCaffrey picked us up at the Dublin Area Rapid Transit Station in Bray, a half-hour outside the city, in the hills of County Wicklow. "Look for the white car with 'Dragonhold' on the side," she'd said cheerily when we called from the little seaside town.

Dragonhold was the name McCaffrey gave to the little bungalow she bought 20 years ago. She calls her new home and horse farm Dragonhold Underhill. We pictured a medieval castle, but it is a four-bedroom cottage with swimming pool, large cats that bask on the kitchen table in the warmth of hanging lights, and stuffed dragons decorating the traditional turf-fireplace.

BKL: *Just for background, what are your books and the series into which they fall?*

McCAFFREY: We have first [assumes radio-commercial voice] the enormously popular **Dragonriders of Pern,** now 12 volumes; [normal voice] there are also three Pern reference books, in case you get lost among the many names and places. Then there's **Decision at Doona,** that's three books. **Then Dinosaur Planet,** that's five; the **Ship Who Sang** is five. There are three in the **Crystal Singer** series—there won't be anymore, I think. There are now five in the **Damia's Children's** series, which came from the second short story I ever published; Berkley Putnam wanted me to do a romantical series, and my agent suggested I expand on "The Lady in the Tower." I did so.

And then you have a few novels that aren't in series.

I have a few one-offs, and most are going to stay that way. But I may do another one about horses. I would like to do some set in Ireland, some romances, just old-fashioned romances, gothic novels as we called them in the seventies. Slightly out of the ordinary, but still gothic novels.

What books did you finish this year?

Oh jeez, I have to go back and think. The first one was **Chronicles of Pern: First Fall** then **Lyon's Pride,** then **Power-Line,** which is a collaboration with Elizabeth Scarborough—Annie, I call her. Now I don't actually have to lift my fingers to the keyboard until October or November to start next year's books.

How many books a year do you write?

Seems like I'm writing three. Two myself, one collaborative.

*How did you begin the collaborative series [**The Powers That Be**] with Scarborough?*

We were talking after dinner and got to thinking, Why don't we do a book together? I said, "Hey! They haven't done one based on an arctic planet. Let's use our Alaskan experiences and see what we can come up with." So we decided on our main characters and what we were going to do with the story in general. She had certain characters that she wanted to write, and I had certain characters. She does baddies much better than I do, and I do love scenes better. But you can't tell where one of us stopped and the other picked up, because by rereading and working over the pages, we sounded alike.

Is the voice that emerged a combination of your two voices?

Yes, I think so. Because everyone was wrong who said, "Obviously, McCaffrey wrote this part" or "Obviously, Scarborough's experience led to this." One critic said, "This is a seamless collaboration," which we both took very much to heart: finally, someone is reading us as we should be read!

How, in practical terms, did the collaboration work?

Annie came to stay here, and we worked together. Each one would pass the disk when things started running dry. Then the other would build on what had been written and go over it, and that way we went back and forth. I'd print out, and we'd go over it again together. Then Shelly Shapiro, my Del Rey editor, was visiting with her husband and her lovely child. She read the first bits of it and liked it, and we sold it to her. She told us, "You've got more than just one book here." She wanted to go on with it. Sure, sure, why not? So we did a three-book contract. We had a lot of fun doing the second one. I still don't know what our editor thinks about it because we turned it in only the end of July.

Did you do the same thing with it, where you wrote part and she wrote part?

Yeah, back and forth.

So it wasn't a division of duties, with one person doing an outline and the other one filling it in.

No, no. It's much easier to work face-to-face. That way, you're not tied to an outline, and Annie and I don't like to write outlines anyway. The two books I wrote outlines for—I never wrote them. So I trained my editors, since I always produced a good novel, to let me run with the situation I started at the beginning. But my other collaborations, they were all my ideas. I wrote a full novel outline, and the collaborator took over from there and embellished it. Some of the embellishments were excellent.

Did you use any of your characters, your locations, in the collaborative books?

I've done five **Ship Who Sang** books. The one with Mercedes Lackey was the best. She writes in the same vein I do. She did an absolutely beautiful job. I ended up crying. And the one Jody Lynn [Nye] did was a hoot, the best writing she's done so far. We each had different ship partners in these books. We didn't use the original ship, *Helga,* at all—she's mentioned, but she's not used, because *Helga* is my property—no one gets to work on her. Yeah, I don't know if I would do another *Helga* novel. She was sort of my escape valve during the dissolution of my marriage, and now I'm happily divorced.

Going back to your noncollaborative work, why do you prefer people to read the Pern series in the order of writing rather than the chronological order of the stories?

I think it gets you into the Pern society better to read it that way. If you start with **Dragonsdawn** (1988), half of the fun of **Dragonflight** (1968) is cut off at the knees. If you read the books as they were written, you will be eased into the complexities of the Weirs and Holds and Craftholds and all that good stuff, and you'll meet the characters as they first come on stage.

Are you still doing Pern books?

There's another due out in October [**The Chronicles of Pern: First Fall**], which is actually five shorter stories. One is **"Rescue Run,"** which tells everyone why no one is going to find Pern ever again. I am always hearing, "Why can't we have Earth people on Pern? Why can't the dragons go back to Earth?" Because, honey, there's a certain limitation to how long the dragons can hold their breath. And they can only travel so far exponentially each second, and about as far as they can go is the fifth planet in their own solar system.

But the real fact is, you just don't want those people on Pern.

I don't want it messed up. I just don't want Pern polluted.

How many of your books are still in print?

Everything I've written, including **Cooking out of This World** (1973), is still in print. A writer depends on the royalties coming in from all publications, not just the latest best-seller. I still get as much money for **Restoree** (1967) as I did for the first contract I signed for it. I got $1,200 for that book, and it brings more than that every year. My baby!

Weren't you the first woman science-fiction writer to hit the best-seller list?

The first science-fiction writer. Frank Herbert didn't hit until the following year. It was **The White Dragon** (1978). It was Jody Lynn's first hardcover [as publisher] under her new imprint [Del Rey], and I remember she said, "Well, Anne, we've got so many advance sales on this book, we're going to up our advance printing from 15,000 to 20,000." Before that, Doubleday did 3,000, maybe

5,000, of a well-known author in hardcover, and that was it. There were 85,000 copies printed, and all I'm thinking is, "All those extra books! How can I keep my head up?" Then it hit the best-seller list. We sold 81,433 of that printing.

What did you have that other people didn't have before?

I had a track record with the dragons, two previous dragon books. And *Star Trek* and *Star Wars* had increased the readership, but when women couldn't "get" them, they started reading female writers of fantasy and science fiction. Marion Zimmer Bradley and I are big in that circle. Science fiction has been picking up steam ever since we landed on the moon in 1969. It was ready to break out. A lot of things combined for the **The White Dragon** to be that popular that suddenly.

Are these books science fiction or fantasy?

Science fiction, absolutely. The dragons are biogenetically engineered. They were derived from the genetic material of the fire lizards who were indigenous to the planet.

You raise horses. Are dragons really horses?

No. Horses are stupid. Dragons are smart. But cats are fire lizards. So they're derived from cats.

What is the difference between science fiction and fantasy?

Fantasy uses magic. You set up parameters for a world that doesn't work on Newtonian logic. All my worlds work on Newtonian logic. So it's science fiction.

Who constitutes the audience for science fiction?

The audience is very broad now. Lots of "straight" people—people you would never think would read science fiction—buy it and like it. I had a letter from a woman who's doing a research paper for her local group in Perrysville, Ohio. She was given the topic of women science-fiction writers, and she had never read science fiction. She started out with **Dragonflight,** and despite herself, she got hooked. If you tell a good story, anybody will read it. It doesn't have to be fantasy or science fiction. It could be anything.

How did you get started? Who were your role models?

I wrote because it was a good way to get rid of me in the morning. When I was 8 or 9, my mother would say, "Go up and write a story, dear," and I did. I was always going to write. I used to submit stories to the slick magazines, and they all came back. But I also had been brought up on Kipling, and I found Edgar Rice Burroughs. I preferred John Carter of Mars to the Tarzan series, but Tarzan was better than nothing. When I was 14, I read *Islandia* by Austin Tappan Wright, and it blew my mind, absolutely blew my mind. A lot of that philosophy I adopted as my own, and it stood me in very good stead. In college, I did my thesis on Yevgeny Zamyatin's *We.* After

that, I had quite a few jobs. I had majored in Slavic languages and literature, but I didn't get a job in that.

Not exactly a real career-oriented choice.

No! After college, I got a job writing copy for Liberty Music Shops, then for Helena Rubenstein. Then, after I was married, I was stuck at home with bronchitis, and the only thing to read in the apartment we were renting was *Amazing Stories.* I read *The Star Kings* by Edmund Hamilton, and it blew my mind . . . I forgot to cough . . . I couldn't get enough of it. So I started reading the pulps, and I found that I couldn't stop. So next I tried my hand at writing myself. I ran into Lila Shaffer, the editor of *Amazing* and *Fantastic,* and I tried out a few of my ideas on her, but I published my first story with Sam Moskowitz for *Science Fiction Plus.* It was a thousand-worder; you know, they always need something to fill, and he offered a hundred bucks for a thousand-worder. They made a big play of it, my first published story.

When you moved to Ireland, how many books had you published?

I had about four or five.

Were you able to live on your writing over here?

Oh, no, I barely existed! But I wrote **Dragonquest** (1971) here, and I wrote three of the romances for Dell, and we managed to keep body and soul together on the backlists.

Why Ireland?

It was the artist tax exemption. I wouldn't have to pay income tax here in Ireland. They have a much better school system than you have in the States, and I had two very bright, younger kids. My mother loved Ireland, and I packed my kids, electric typewriter, and moved. That was in 1970, and I've never looked back. There were tough years, what we call the pancake years—[imitates child's voice] "Mother, gee, it would be nice to have pancakes when we wanted them!"—but things worked out very favorably for me. I lived in south County Dublin at first—and then down here. I was 16 years in Dragonhold Junior, and I think Dragonhold Senior will last me the rest of my life.

GENERAL COMMENTARY

Fred Hauptfuhrer

SOURCE: "Dragonlady Anne McCaffrey Slays Them with Another Saga and Earns Best-Seller Bucks," in *People Weekly,* Vol. 21, No. 10, March 12, 1984, pp. 82, 87.

Not since St. George set off on his quest has there been such a flap over dragons. Those fire-breathing creatures bravely ward off evil on the mythical planet of Pern.

Moreover, they are linked telepathically with their humanoid riders, a fearless race descended from earthling space colonizers.

Such is the substance of **Moreta: Dragonlady of Pern,** a whimsical sci-fi tale that caught the imagination of readers and has become a firmly rooted best-seller. Yet Anne McCaffrey, 57, an expatriate American who lives in a bungalow called Dragonhold in Ireland, is not surprised by the interest in her creations. "Dragons have had a bad press," she argues. "I make nice dragons."

She has blithely done so through four adult dragon novels (**Dragondrums** and **The White Dragon** were also best-sellers) and three for teenagers. Her devoted fans respond to the odd mix of adventure, science fiction and medievalism that pervades her writing. There is even a feminist touch: Fertile dragon queens control the planet Pern and are ridden by formidable "Weyrwomen." "I've always had strong women around me," explains McCaffrey, "so it's easy to draw from that."

One of those women was her mother, Anne, a tough-minded real estate agent. McCaffrey's father, George, a Harvard Ph.D. in government, worked for a New York business organization. Following in his academic footsteps, Anne graduated cum laude from Radcliffe, where she majored in Slavic languages and literature.

In 1950, after working briefly as a secretary and copywriter, she married H. Wright Johnson, then a reporter for *Women's Wear Daily.* The marriage produced three children: Alec, now 31, a graduate student in economics at MIT, Todd, 27, an engineering student in Dublin, and Georgeanne, 24, who has worked as her mother's assistant. After the marriage ended in divorce in 1970, Anne settled with the children in County Wicklow, south of Dublin.

It is in these peaceful surroundings that she spins out her fantasies on a word processor. "The books come off the top of my head," says McCaffrey, who first began exercising her imagination back in 1950. Housebound with bronchitis at the time, she began reading science-fiction magazines. "What attracted me was the sheer freedom. With sci fi, you have a universe and all its permutations to play with," she explains.

McCaffrey is a celebrity in her field and is invited to conventions all over the world. Her literary passion has brought McCaffrey the nickname "Dragonlady"—a "term of affection," she says proudly. McCaffrey is now working on an animated TV series on dragons and polishing a new book on the subject. Reflecting on her life's work, McCaffrey deadpans: "I was born on April 1. I think I have lived up to the auspices of my natal day."

J. R. Wytenbroek

SOURCE: "The Child as Creator in McCaffrey's *Dragonsong* and *Dragonsinger,*" in *The Lion and the Unicorn,* Vol. 16, No. 2, December, 1992, pp. 210-14.

The disabled child and the gifted one are often perceived to have little in common with each other or with more "ordinary" children. However, McCaffrey has presented the gifted child *as* disabled in the person of Menolly, the musician/composer heroine of both *Dragonsong* and *Dragonsinger,* showing through Menolly that perhaps "gifted" and "disabled" are not so different, after all, and that both have the same emotional needs as "ordinary" people.

Menolly is a gifted musician. She not only sings and plays almost any musical instrument well, but she writes good and highly singable songs, the kind that make up the incidental music that is the primary entertainment on her world of Pern—where musicians, or Harpers as they are called, are highly regarded, for they not only entertain the people but provide all instruction regarding the lore, history, and survival techniques of their planet through the teaching ballads. Because of her abilities, Menolly's path toward recognition in this highly honored craft should be as easy as that of most talented children once their talent is recognized by someone who can help them. However, it is exactly here that Menolly is different.

Menolly is the youngest daughter of Yanus, Seaholder of an isolated coastal hold on the Northern continent of the planet Pern. In this semi-feudal, intensely patriarchal society, the role of women is severely limited. They are not trained in trades or crafts of any kind, although they are expected to help out with the menial work whenever needed. They are educated as children by the Harpers, but unlike the boys who then take up a trade, they are confined to domestic tasks and wait for their fathers to arrange marriages for them. At best, if they are high up the social ladder, they may achieve some kind of domestic power. As most Pernese live in large, complex social clusters called holds or crafthalls, only the headwoman of a crafthall or the first wife of the head holder ever achieves even that power.

As a girl, Menolly is disadvantaged from the beginning. She is a brilliant musician, taught as much as he knows by the very knowledgeable old Harper of the hold, Petiron. But by the beginning of *Dragonsong,* the first of the two novels, Petiron has died, after sending a couple of Menolly's songs to the Masterharper of Pern, Robinton. Alone, without a champion in the hold of her arch-conservative father, Menolly is forbidden to play her own tunes and is beaten severely when she does. Then, when she slices her hand open cleaning fish, her mother sews the hand together badly, deliberately intending to cripple Menolly so that she can never play an instrument again.

At this point Menolly becomes physically disabled, as well as being gifted, but remains as disadvantaged as before. She is now even forbidden to sing in the evenings with the rest of the people of the hold, once the new Harper comes, lest he discover she taught the children during the months between Petiron's death and his arrival, and the hold be disgraced. With no word regarding her songs from Master Robinton (who is searching for her but does not know who she is), and unable to stand the oppression at home, although she believes herself truly and permanently maimed, Menolly flees her hold.

McCaffrey is thoroughly presenting here the problem of the unacceptable gift. If Menolly had been a boy, there would have been no problem with her going to Harper Crafthall, where her talents would have been trained and developed early on. However, because she is a girl, her ability is *denied* by others, not just ignored. As it is, she is fifteen, emotionally scarred, and partially crippled when she finally gets to Harperhall. It is a long time before she can even be persuaded to openly write music again, the injunction on her not to write having been so strongly and brutally enforced.

But for the true creator spirit, creating is as necessary to life as breathing is. Thus Menolly's disability is also her greatest strength. The need to perform and to create music that drives her from her home keeps her alive as she seeks refuge in uninhabited sea caves where she impresses, or bonds deeply and permanently, with nine firelizards, tiny, arm-length cousins of the mighty telepathic dragons who protect Pern from its most devastating enemy: the deadly thread that falls through the sky at intervals, seeking to devour all organic life. The love of the firelizards for Menolly's music as well as for her encourages her to go with her music, so she continues to play her homemade pipes and writes her own songs for the weeks she lives isolated in the sea caves.

When she is eventually found and taken to Harperhall, Menolly's passion for music gives her the strength to fight for her place there as apprentice Harper against the destructive envy of the only other girls at Harperhall, the paying students. That love of music makes her work with the Healer to restore her hand to full use. Her passion and ability for music wins her the love and admiration of many of the people, masters, journeymen, and apprentices alike, at Harperhall. Most of all, her passion for music gives her the strength to overcome her own inner fear and uncertainty so that she can begin to compose the songs Master Robinton needs so desperately to change the attitudes that nearly killed her, and that broke her heart.

Music, for Menolly, stops being a disability and becomes a source of strength and healing as she finds her own sense of worth. It helps heal her broken heart and the other emotional damage done to her through years of neglect and abuse. And it provides for her a loving community where she finds herself and her true place in her society.

Love, of course, is the other important ingredient in Menolly's healing, but initially for her, it too is tied in directly with her music. In fifteen years she has never before experienced real love, except from the old Harper, and it is not until she reaches her new home, her real home at Harperhall, that she finds true human love, although the love of her nine firelizards has prepared Menolly's heart for human love, to some extent. At Harp-

erhall, Menolly is loved for herself *and* for her gift, both being the two parts of the whole that is she. Without her music, Menolly does not yet exist fully as herself. At first she has trouble accepting the love, approval, and recognition she is generally given at Harperhall, but she is slowly won over when she realizes how much the Harpers, from Master Robinton to the lowliest apprentice, love her music:

> "You wrote a new song?" Piemur brightened. "When'll we get to hear it?"
>
> "When will you get to hear it?" Menolly heard her voice cracking on the last few words.
>
> "What's the matter, Menolly?" . . .
>
> "It's just that it's . . . so different. . . . " She stammered, unable to express the upheaval in her mind, the reversal of all she had been expected to do. . . . She tried to stop the words that were threatening to burst from her, but she couldn't, not with Piemur's face contorted with distress for her. And Sebell quietly encouraging her to speak with the sympathy so plain on his face. . . .
>
> "I can see now why it has been so hard for you, Menolly, to appreciate how important your songs are. After what you've been through," and Sebell gently squeezed her left hand, "it would be hard to believe in yourself. Promise me, Menolly, to believe from now on? Your songs are very important to the Harper, to the Hall and to me. Master Domick's music *is* brilliant, but yours appeals to everyone, holder and crafter, landsman and seaman. Your songs deal with subjects . . . that will help change the set attitudes that nearly killed you in your home hold."

For Menolly, whose music has been brutally suppressed, their love and acceptance of her music is the same thing as loving and accepting her. And because she is now in a deeply supportive artistic community, that naive assumption is, in fact, correct, although for some of her new friends that was not the order in which their love of her came. What heals Menolly, however, is the love combined with her new injunction from the Masterharper himself, the most loving and supportive of them all, to write whatever and whenever she feels she should. He frees her, through his need for her as musician and love of her as individual to become the whole, integrated, healed person she finally becomes, a person who can now create freely and joyously so that she will create more and better than she ever did before.

In these novels, then, McCaffrey presents Menolly as a young person whose gift is a disability, not an advantage, until near the end of the second novel. She is also suggesting that the true creator spirit is a difficult thing for any child or adult to cope with. A gift always has two edges. As Master Robinton tells Menolly, "it is never easy, sweet child, to have a real gift; something else is withheld to compensate" *(Dragonsinger)*. But he goes on to say, "if you won't surrender the mark, you'll never be more than half alive" *(Dragonsinger)*. The drive to create must be obeyed for the individual's life to be full and fulfilled. However, there is always suffering to be undergone, or some price to pay, for that joy of creation.

McCaffrey here presents the young adult reader with a female protagonist with a gift that almost kills her who is initially misunderstood and repressed by those around her. McCaffrey makes Menolly likeable and easy to identify with for readers because of her self-doubt, her fear, and her hurt. Menolly copes with these problems as some abused or neglected children do cope, with the help of a loving, supportive community and by doing something that is really important to her. McCaffrey has been careful to make sure that most readers, gifted or not, can identify with Menolly, and can learn and grow with her. But McCaffrey has done something more, as well. She has presented a heroine who is afire with, even driven by, her need to create music, and for whom nothing in her whole oppressive world equals that need, not even her own life. McCaffrey is showing the reader through Menolly the importance of letting people be themselves and do what they must do, and the tragic or potentially tragic consequences if people are stopped from fulfilling their potential. Further, she is showing the devastating effects of harshly limited, socially accepted roles, sexual stereotypes and expectations that may not only deeply harm the person inhibited by them, but that can also deprive and impoverish the society that inhibits that person.

These novels portray for young people the importance of finding and being what they truly are themselves, and the importance of letting others around them do the same. By using a heroine who is a creator of music which will help change her entire society, McCaffrey makes this message powerful and exciting. Through Menolly, the author also assures one of the most fragile groups of our society, the young adults, that they too have a place in their community, that they too can make a difference.

TITLE COMMENTARY

RESTOREE (1967)

Publishers Weekly

SOURCE: A review of *Restoree,* in *Publishers Weekly,* Vol. 192, No. 8, August 21, 1967, p. 76.

In this well-written and carefully plotted story, the author has constructed a fascinating world that is technologically sophisticated, but culturally quaint and archaic, and her heroine, Sara, snatched out of Central Park by a low-hovering space craft, observes it closely and describes it intelligently. She comes out of amnesia months later on a strange planet in a zombie-like state, working as an attendant in a mental clinic. She is startled to find that she is enclosed in a new body, with golden skin and a short nose. She is a "restoree" and for what that means we refer you to this top-notch science fiction tale.

DRAGONFLIGHT (1968)

Publishers Weekly

SOURCE: A review of *Dragonflight,* in *Publishers Weekly,* Vol. 194, No. 2, July 8, 1968, p. 166.

By the author of **Restoree,** a science-fantasy that readers surfeited with gadge-tridden supermodernistic space epics will welcome. A Terran-colonized planet is threatened every 200 years when it draws near to the orbit of a wandering planet that sends out life-destroying Threads. A super race of Dragonmen and Weyrwomen, who fly their dragons at great height and communicate with them telepathically, has been the defense of the planet, but now their ranks are thinned and their status reduced, and the 200-year cycle is drawing to a close. How they do battle against the Threads makes for an ingenious story.

The Junior Bookshelf

SOURCE: "The Bridge," in *The Junior Bookshelf,* Vol. 33, No. 4, August, 1969, p. 259.

The countryside of the planet Pern and its Weyr satellite is Tolkien-land rather than futuristic space-world. The dragonmen and their splendid beasts, gold, bronze, green and blue, who guard Pern from the Red Star which every two hundred years tries to colonise Pern by terrible Threads from the sky; the Holds of Pern and their Overlords, resemble the mediaeval world of Tolkien's Mark and its inhabitants. Like that world, this is well-thought-out and developed, and is full of the excitement of battle and hidden revenge and love. The menace of the Threads at a time when the Weyr has fallen far below strength is ingeniously combatted by the dangerous power to move between space and time. The loves of Lessa, Pern noblewoman who becomes guardian to Ramoth, the gold female dragon, and F'lar, rider of Ramoth's bronze mate, are considerably more earthy than those of Eowyn and Faramir, though reticently described by modern standards. Nevertheless, the unearthly mysterious worlds in which they move have superficially many similarities, and **Dragonflight** will probably appeal most to those who fall under the spell of *Lord of the Rings.* The fact that the two first parts of the book won separate Science Fiction awards fortunately does not result in a lack of unity in the whole.

THE SHIP WHO SANG (1969)

Publishers Weekly

SOURCE: A review of *The Ship Who Sang,* in *Publishers Weekly,* Vol. 196, No. 11, September 15, 1969, p. 61.

This science fiction prize-winning author's new one is a sure-fire love story for man or machine. The ship of the title is Helva; in her society of the future, malformed babies with perfect minds are separated from their bodies and conditioned to become as one with the ship built for them. The ship is, therefore, basically human, with emotions and the option, having earned enough, to buy herself free from the Confederation and freelance for herself. Helva's fortunes multiply as her love life languishes. Her first "brawn" or human (she is the computerized "brain") is Jennan, with whose musical talents she harmonizes until she is known throughout the galaxy as the Singing Ship.

Richard W. Ryan

SOURCE: A review of *The Ship Who Sang,* in *Library Journal,* Vol. 94, No. 17, October, 1969, p. 3468.

The concept of a spaceship as a living being is cleverly developed in this book by a recent winner of science fiction's Hugo and Nebula awards. The present work may not be up to the standards of her **Dragonflight,** but it is a winning treatment. Helva is a birth-defective baby with a superior brain. Like similar babies, she undergoes special training, treatment, and conditioning, is encased in a protective metal shell, and eventually in a space ship. Through sensory connections she controls, and in fact becomes, the ship, and in company with a succession of pilot-partners—humans in normal bodies—handles a variety of missions for the Central Worlds government. In a special way this is a love story, for Helva (or the XH-824) finally finds her ideal ship partner. For science fiction collections.

Norman Culpan

SOURCE: A review of *The Ship Who Sang,* in *School Librarian,* Vol. 19, No. 1, March, 1971, p. 243.

The plot summary of this adult SF fantasy story sounds corny, but the book is written with much ingenuity, and offers enjoyable light reading for many boys and some girls of sixth-form age and younger. Helva, born deformed but of high intelligence, is educated and conditioned to be built into the structure of a space ship. She has a personality and a character of her own, but remains permanently encapsulated, seeing, hearing, speaking and controlling her space-ship body through highly sophisticated mechanisms wired into her brain. It is customary for such ships, reserved for special missions, to carry one crew, in what may be a short or a permanent relationship. During the course of a number of interesting missions, Helva works with a variety of crew mates until, in the last few pages, she secures the man who loves her and with whom she is in love. Try it: it is much better than in brief space I can make it sound.

 DRAGONQUEST: BEING THE FURTHER ADVENTURES OF THE DRAGONRIDERS OF PERN (1971)

Publishers Weekly

SOURCE: A review of *Dragonquest,* in *Publishers Weekly,* Vol. 199, No. 15, April 12, 1971, p. 85.

The planet of Pern is a pleasant place except during the "Turns" that occur every few generations when a wandering stranger planet in erratic orbit appears in the sky and drops "Threads" that devour every living thing. The only defense is provided by flying dragons that incinerate the Threads, but after long years of peace, the Pern people have become lax and the dragon population is almost extinct. This ecological problem is followed by civil war as well as the threatening Threads. The author writes well and is very inventive. Her story, however, is likely to appeal only to those sword-and-sorcery devotees who have the patience to keep track of a big cast of characters.

Times Literary Supplement

SOURCE: "Future Folklore," in *Times Literary Supplement,* No. 3740, November 9, 1973, p. 1377.

It is not always easy to distinguish SF from science fantasy, and the task is made harder by the epithet "science" when applied to "fantasy". The notion of an occult technology is self contradictory. There is now an amorphous body of escapist literature which booksellers tend to display on their SF shelves, partly because it is often by authors who first made their mark in classical SF but mostly because there doesn't seem to be anywhere else to put it. The books considered here represent what one might call the two wings of the beast grotesquely named "imaginative fiction". To review them as SF and then to say they fail because they are not SF seems as churlish as dismissing *Lear* for being an inaccurate historical drama; nevertheless, they grew from the same roots as mainstream SF even though they owe more to *The Anglo-Saxon Chronicle.*

Anne McCaffrey's book is a sequel to **Dragonflight,** which won the Hugo Award, itself a confirmation of full SF status. (Nobody seems to have denied that to Jack Vance's *The Dragon Masters,* either, so perhaps it qualifies.) Yet there is a minimum of SF in the book, barring the traditional nature of the setting. The distant descendants of earth colonists are living on the planet Pern, which is menaced by a red rogue planet whenever an indigenous life-form, Thread, tries to cross over to the more hospitable Pern. Over the centuries the Pernese have bred and trained their own life-form to combat the falls of Thread. Their "dragons" chew a phosphine-bearing rock and can fly about, charring the Thread in mid-air with their breath. Thus the simple SF basis of the saga. But from that point on the whole landscape of the book is pre-medieval. The Pernese have names like old Norsemen and live hierarchical, ritualized lives in "weyrs" and strongholds. They have knives in their belts and feudal titles and make herbal infusions for dressing Threadburns. Setting the story in the future does not make it SF, though. Revealingly, the Pernese have regressed to an Earthly historical era which Miss McCaffrey finds romantically absorbing, and her book is an account of tribal adventurings. They are vividly seen, yet somehow they are wishfully thought rather than imagined, and unless one is gripped by the world of Pern it all seems very safe and cosy.

📖 *DRAGONSONG* (1976)

Joan Barbour

SOURCE: A review of *Dragonsong,* in *School Library Journal,* Vol. 22, No. 8, April, 1976, p. 91.

An invasion of life-consuming, threadlike spores from the Red Star necessitates a new way of life for the people of Pern. Protected by giant dragons who breathe fire and destroy the spores, the citizens live in cave-like dwellings called Holds. Young Menolly, whose greatest love is music, rebels against the harsh life in a fishing Hold after her father forbids her even to sing. Leaving the safety of the Hold, Menolly is befriended by a group of fire lizards and eventually realizes her dream about becoming a musician. The author explores the ideas of alienation, rebellion, love of beauty, the role of women and the role of the individual in society with some sensitivity in a generally well-structured plot with sound characterizations.

Barbara Elleman

SOURCE: A review of *Dragonsong,* in *Booklist,* Vol. 72, No. 17, May 1, 1976, pp. 1266-67.

The people of Pern have developed huge flying dragons to counteract the periodic fall of threadlike spores that threaten their planet. These creatures and their riders sweep the sky, breathing fire, to protect the people below, who live in cavelike Holds. Menolly longs to see a dragon, but even more, she wants to be a Harper—to sing, play, and write the tunes that come so naturally to her. To escape her father's edict of banishment from the singing because she is a girl, Menolly runs away and seeks refuge in a cave. There she becomes friends with nine fire lizards, small relatives of the huge dragons, and teaches them to sing. One day, caught outside during Threadfall, she is rescued and taken to the home of the dragonriders, where her gift for music is appreciated and honored. McCaffrey uses great imaginative powers in constructing her intricate and intriguing story, and she includes a helpful character chart; however, confusing details of life on Pern should have been either more fully described or eliminated for readers unversed in science fiction. But for any reader, Menolly comes through as a resourceful young girl searching for a way to give vent to her talents.

Zena Sutherland

SOURCE: A review of *Dragonsong,* in *Bulletin of the Center for Children's Books,* Vol. 29, No. 11, July-August, 1976, p. 177.

On an imaginary planet periodically assailed by a fall of corrosive Thread, the inhabitants are protected by tamed dragons whose flames destroy the Thread as it falls. In an isolated district of the planet, fifteen-year-old Menolly lives, her talent as a harper suppressed and derided by her stern father as unseemly for a girl. Running away, Menolly acquires, by imprinting, a band of fire lizards; when she arrives at the planet's ruling community, her skills at composing and at teaching her lizard brood to sing bring her the career she has longed for. Despite a plethora of characters and a rather heavy-handed preface, this is a science fantasy that is cohesive and briskly paced, with sturdy characterization and a fully-conceived society with its mores and customs.

Francis J. Molson

SOURCE: "Juvenile Science Fiction, 1975-1976," in *Children's Literature: Annual of The Modern Language Association Group on Children's Literature and The Children's Literature Association,* Vol. 6, 1977, pp. 202-11.

Anne McCaffrey's **Dragonsong** is . . . superior science fiction. Surprisingly, the novel's plot is slight and unexciting. Menolly, a very musically talented girl, gains her dream of becoming a harper despite parental disapproval and an injury to her hand. More impressive is the novel's portrait of the girl's growth in self-confidence, and most impressive is its setting. McCaffrey has created an original and credible world, Pern, complete with a geography and ecology, and settled by people whose social organizations reflect the physical environment.

Pern is a planet that has been colonized by humans who soon find themselves under attack by Thread, a hostile, carnivorous spore life drifting down from the sky. To defend themselves, the colonists selectively breed a life form indigenous to Pern into creatures that can destroy Thread. These the people call dragons because they spit fire and can teleport through space and time. A select few of the colonists who manifest ESP are recruited to "partner" the dragons, a process called impressing. Because of the necessity to have dragons and their human riders prepared at all times and in all places for defense, the people of Pern develop very specialized social and economic organizations, the Holds. Descriptions of the life and routine of two of the Holds make up a large part of **Dragonsong.** Although a brief preface records the past history of Pern and provides necessary background—a history derived, presumably, from McCaffrey's other adult novels about Pern—enough of the physical texture and culture of Pern exists in **Dragonsong** so that the reader can believe in it. So convincing and attractive is Pern that it seems safe to predict that it will be remembered when many other secondary worlds have disappeared into oblivion.

📖 *DRAGONSINGER* (1977)

Barbara Elleman

SOURCE: A review of *Dragonsinger,* in *Booklist,* Vol. 73, No. 15, April 1, 1977, p. 1170.

Menolly's dream of studying music at Harper Hall, which she so intensely longed for in *Dragonsong,* is finally realized here when Robinton, the Masterharper of Pern, brings her to Fort Hold after hearing her songs. But life at Harper Hall as the only girl apprentice is not easy, especially for one who has accomplished the unheard of—impressing nine fire lizards. Gradually Menolly adjusts, sorting out friends from those who wish her ill, discovering the complexities of life in the Hold, and above all relishing the opportunity to play, sing, and compose. The theme is developed through many related incidents—some tense, some amusing, others dependent on simple day-to-day occurrences at the Hall rather than the exciting, dramatic episodes found in the first book. McCaffrey deliberately paces this story slowly, constructing the many nuances of life at Fort Hold and, most importantly, revealing a girl's struggle to accept and use her very special talent. Although set in another world, where dragons fly and people have fire lizards as pets, Menolly's innermost concerns are wholly contemporary as she seeks to invade what has been a male-dominated craft. Deeply entrenched in the world of Pern from authoring several adult books on the subject, McCaffrey makes references to incidents and people outside the immediate story which may confuse some readers.

Zena Sutherland

SOURCE: A review of *Dragonsinger,* in *Bulletin of the Center for Children's Books,* Vol. 30, No. 9, May, 1977, pp. 146-47.

A sequel to *Dragonsong,* a science fantasy in which young Menolly, who yearns to be a harpist, is roughly treated by her sexist father and runs away to another community of the planet. Her identity as the composer of music that has excited the Master Harper is unmasked, and in this novel Menolly comes to Harper Hall as an apprentice. Her talent and her brood of nine fire lizards stir admiration in some and envy in others, as she struggles through her first term and becomes a journeyman. McCaffrey has constructed a believable fantasy world; the characterization is excellent, the writing style fluent and vigorous, and the plot soundly constructed and briskly paced.

Mary M. Burns

SOURCE: A review of *Dragonsinger,* in *The Horn Book Magazine,* Vol. 53, No. 3, June, 1977, p. 320.

In the sequel to *Dragonsong,* Menolly, having been identified as the unknown apprentice of the deceased harper Petiron, is brought to the Harper Hall to continue her studies. Instead of the punishments she endured at her former home, where her musical talent came into direct conflict with traditional beliefs and attitudes toward women, she finds affection and encouragement from many of her new associates. Despite this recognition, however, she is at first confused by the complexity of the new situation—the rules, the demands of her new masters, the conduct of her nine fire lizards, and the seeming hostility of the other girl students. As a result, she is apologetic and self-effacing, questioning her ability and doubting that she deserves the opportunity given her. In time, however, she realizes with the help of those wiser than she that her talent is worthy to ensure her a permanent place among the Harpers as the maker of new songs to weld the disparate elements of planet Pern into a cohesive unit. Details of the apprentices' lives—rigorous curriculum and teaching methods, food, clothing, and societal relationships—give verisimilitude to a superbly crafted fantasy in the heroic tradition. Yet these details, essential to the evocation of the setting, are so thoroughly integrated into the story that they complement and extend the action rather than serve merely as a framework. Poetic introductions to each chapter appropriately suggest ancient ballads and sagas, thus supporting the motif of song as the cement of a people and the idea that crafters of song are historians and effectors of change. As Master Dominick tells Menolly, "[t]he whole point of the Harper Hall is to extend knowledge. . . . [n]ot to confine it." Unlike many sequels, this maintains the dramatic tensions of its predecessor; however, for fullest appreciation of the author's skill, the two books should be read in correct sequence.

Whitney Rogge

SOURCE: A review of *Dragonsinger,* in *School Library Journal,* Vol. 24, No. 1, September, 1977, p. 132.

A well-thought-out sequel to *Dragonsong* about the planet Pern and the apprentice harper Menolly. McCaffrey's fantasy celebrates the power of music. At Harper Hall, the music conservatory on Pern, Menolly is initially unaware of the extent of her own powers, since, due to her sex, her musical skill had been suppressed in her homeland. Moreover, she encounters hostility because all of Pern's other harpers—who are more powerful than kings in a world where music literally controls minds—are men. Gradually, she gains confidence with the help of new friends, teachers, and nine of the planet's rare fire lizards who themselves are excellent singers with mysterious powers. Though the plot moves slowly and descriptions are sometimes long-winded and repetitive, the transformation of Menolly from a terrified outcast to a woman secure within herself is skillfully handled, making her a sympathetic character with whom many readers will identify.

James Norsworthy

SOURCE: A review of *Dragonsinger,* in *Catholic Library World,* Vol. 49, No. 4, November, 1977, pp. 189.

McCaffrey relates Menolly's life in the Harper Hall after she was brought there by the Masterharper of Pern as his special apprentice. She discovers that many of her fears about a female breaking what she understood to be "absolute" traditions have no place, but at the same time she encounters the problems caused by both ignorance, pride and jealousy. Although McCaffrey has only described a seven day period in Menolly's life, it is so beautifully written and so vivid in feeling that one simply hates to see the last pages come forth. This book is an example of true excellence in writing and it is certainly more than a satisfactory continuation of *Dragonsong.*

📖 THE WHITE DRAGON (1978)

Kirkus Reviews

SOURCE: A review of *The White Dragon,* in *Kirkus Reviews,* Vol. 46, No. 7, April 1, 1978, p. 397.

McCaffrey's popular Dragonrider books—now making the leap to hardcover—are built on one of those "soft" scientific premises dear to a certain portion of the sci-fi audience: on the planet of Pern, the main business of life is surviving the recurrent attacks of a strange menace called Thread. Over a period of eons the inhabitants—now unable to trace their own off-planet origins—have learned to counter Threadfall with the fire-breathing, telepathic, time-traveling abilities of the native dragons. The White Dragon is an oddly small but battle-worthy specimen called Ruth, ridden by the gallant stripling Jaxom. Together they head off a disastrous war with the hostile "Oldtimers," help establish a beachhead on the vast unexplored Southern Continent, and incidentally cast unexpected light on the mystery of the colony's past. Sappy.

Publishers Weekly

SOURCE: A review of *The White Dragon,* in *Publishers Weekly,* Vol. 213, No. 17, April 24, 1978, p. 81.

A prologue summarizing the first two volumes of the saga of the Dragonriders of Pern helps some, but not enough, to make clear who's who and what's what here. Readers who haven't absorbed the lore of the Weyrs, Holds and Crafts and their tensions and rivalries will often be at a loss. Young Jaxom and his white dragon Ruth (a male), previously encountered, mature, fight the deadly Threads from the Red Planet, help open the largely unexplored continent and discover in an ancient spaceship a map, key to major changes for Pern. Once all the necessary background is assimilated, it's a rousing adventure and colorful portrayal of a unique and carefully-worked-out culture.

Booklist

SOURCE: A review of *The White Dragon,* in *Booklist,* Vol. 75, No. 1, September 1, 1978, p. 39.

The third volume in McCaffrey's popular science fantasy series, *The Dragonriders of Pern,* follows the adventures of young Lord Jaxom of Ruatha Hold and his unique white dragon Ruth, who is smaller than other dragons and unusual in mental capability. Disobeying orders, the pair train to fight the destructive silver Thread that falls from the sky and practice traveling back in time—two skills they need when they are thrust into danger. Although those who have read the first two volumes, *Dragonflight* and *Dragonquest,* will be the most comfortable here, the novel is accessible to others since a prologue gives some background. Readers of McCaffrey's juvenile books set on Pern, *Dragonsong* and *Dragonsinger,* will be delighted to once more meet Menolly, who shares some of Jaxom's experiences, and other familiar characters. McCaffrey again succeeds in evoking her lovingly created planet of Pern, its extraordinary dragons, freewheeling fire lizards, and human society and individuals.

📖 DRAGONDRUMS (1979)

Kirkus Reviews

SOURCE: A review of *Dragondrums,* in *Kirkus Reviews,* Vol. 47, No. 8, April 15, 1979, p. 456.

McCaffrey first introduced her Thread-threatened planet of Pern in adult paperbacks, and this third juvenile with the same setting refers to events that occurred in last year's episode, the first adult hardcover installment in the Dragonrider complex. (Complicated? You bet. And hardly worth it.) Here wondergirl Menolly's young friend Piemur suffers a voice change at 14, and so, in the manner of this paternalistic community, he is transferred from his singing Hall to work ostensibly as a drummer's apprentice, actually as a political spy for the beloved Masterharper. Jealous fellow apprentices hassle Piemur as Menolly's Cot-mates did her in a previous adventure; but soon Piemur is far away, stealing and Impressing his own Fire Lizard from a disagreeable and dying local Lord, then hiding in a sack which is smuggled off to the mysterious Southern Continent—where he survives three dread Threadfalls before Menolly and her new lover come to the rescue. Readers might still wonder why young people and adults alike attribute such importance to the little Fire Lizards. McCaffrey too makes very much of very little.

Ann A. Flowers

SOURCE: A review of *Dragondrums,* in *The Horn Book Magazine,* Vol. 55, No. 3, June, 1979, pp. 310-11.

The sixth novel about Pern is the third for young readers, following *Dragonsong* and *Dragonsinger.* By now the history, the inhabitants, and the flora and fauna are well established and make a unique, recognizable world. Young Piemur, an apprentice singer, is distressed when his voice breaks and he loses his central position in the chorus. A saucy, quick-witted, and observant boy, he finds his talents recognized by Master Robinton, the Harper, and by Menolly, heroine of the two earlier books. He becomes apprenticed to the Drummaster as a front for his work as a messenger and scout for the Masterharper, who is deeply involved in politics. But Piemur has troubles with the other apprentices to the Drummaster, for they are jealous of his talents and make his new life very difficult. He is eager to possess a fire lizard, one of the charming, affectionate small relatives of the magnificent dragons who protect the land. When he steals a queen fire lizard egg during a spy mission, he escapes from the vindictive nobleman who owned it, is transported to an almost uninhabited continent, and there manages to get the egg hatched and find a suitable home for himself. Some references to events in the preceding books may not be quite clear, but the breathtaking adventures of the resourceful Piemur make rewarding a return visit to the fantasy world of Pern.

Barbara Elleman

SOURCE: A review of *Dragondrums,* in *Booklist,* Vol. 75, No. 19, June 1, 1979, pp. 1492-93.

Piemur, the rascally, nimble-minded singer par excellence of Pern, suffers a change of voice and is reapprenticed to the Drum Master—actually a subterfuge for the undercover work that Masterharper Robinton and his journeymen Menolly and Sebell have planned for him. Sent to Nabol Hold to investigate the maneuverings of traitorous Lord Meron, Piemur appropriates a coveted queen fire lizard egg, is trapped inside the Hold when word gets out about the missing egg, and unwittingly escapes via a load of grain lifted dragonback to the Southern Weyr. There he impresses his fire lizard at hatching, survives Threadfall and solitude, and is eventually reunited with his friends, discovering a place and a role for himself. Though the story stands alone, those familiar with characters and setting from the author's *Dragonsong* and *Dragonsinger* will enjoy it more. In the first two-thirds of the book, the plot is tightly filled with Piemur's adventures, whereas later the pace shifts to a slower, though still compelling, one concerned with survival. Structurally this breaks the plot, but suspense and continuity are nevertheless maintained through McCaffrey's ability to weave deft characterizations and a good story.

Zena Sutherland

SOURCE: A review of *Dragondrums,* in *Bulletin of the Center for Children's Books,* Vol. 32, No. 11, July-August, 1979, p. 195.

The third book in a science fantasy series (written for young people) is as deftly structured and as smoothly written as its predecessors; again McCaffrey has produced strong characters, new and old, a wholly conceived fantasy world, and a nice balance between problems that are present in any civilized society and a sense of humor that lightens both exposition and dialogue. The protagonist

here is not the masterharper journeyman Menolly, but her protege Piemur, whose life changes when his voice changes; a soloist, Piemur despairs of ever being able to sing again, but he's quick to learn both of his new assignments and enjoys them. He becomes an apprentice message-drummer, and that role is used to mask his more important job, acting as personal scout for the distinguished Masterharper. Piemur has a series of exciting adventures, not the least of which are riding a dragon (used for transport in Piemur's world) and acquiring his very own fire lizard.

📖 *CRYSTAL SINGER* (1981)

Roland Green

SOURCE: A review of *Crystal Singer,* in *Booklist,* Vol. 78, No. 21, July, 1982, p. 1394.

A young woman faced with the prospect of losing her musical career travels to a mining planet, where the mining of crystal requires musical talent but causes irreversible physiological changes in the miners. The novel, originally published as four novellas, chronicles Killashandra Ree's emergence as one of the most successful crystal miners on Ballybran. The seams between the original novellas occasionally show, and some of the heroine's triumphs seem almost too easy. Yet McCaffrey is still supremely gifted at characterization, world building, and creating a mood; it is to be hoped that readers will forgive the book for not being about the dragons of Pern. Highly recommended.

Susan L. Nickerson

SOURCE: A review of *Crystal Singer,* in *Library Journal,* Vol. 107, No. 14, August, 1982, p. 1487.

McCaffrey combines her love of music with an exotic locale to produce the involving and enjoyable story of Killashandra Ree, rejected as a vocal soloist, who joins the Crystal Singers, a guild of miners unearthing the musical crystals of the planet Ballybran. But will her body adapt to the Ballybran symbiont that can either enhance or cripple human abilities? Intelligent, independent Killashandra reminds one of Helga from *The Ship Who Sang.*

Gerald Jonas

SOURCE: "Imaginary People," in *The New York Times Book Review,* August 29, 1982, pp. 10-11.

Anne McCaffrey is best known for her series of novels about the dragonriders of Pern. Her new novel is about the crystal singers of Ballybran. As before, the locale is exotic and meticulously detailed. Her heroine, called Killashandra Ree, is young, beautiful, intelligent, sexy and courageous. And behind the confident spring of Miss

McCaffrey's athletic language, as always, lies a preoccupation with obsession. Obsession on a Melvillean scale is Miss McCaffrey's subject, and her method as well. The planet Ballybran is the sole source of "living crystal," which is indispensable to all the devices that tie the Federated Sentient Planets into a civilized unit, from "tachyon drive systems" to "instantaneous interstellar communication" networks. To mine the crystal you must be able to "sing" (with perfect pitch) the precise note to which each specimen resonates. Crystal singers may get fabulously rich and live long lives, but they also lose their memories, their personalities and their freedom: "Once you sing crystal, you don't stop."

The bulk of the book is devoted to a description of Killashandra's training as a crystal singer and her first successful foray into the crystal ranges. There are some mild plot complications and amusing or romantic encounters with minor characters, but we always return to the scientific, economic, political and psychological ramifications of the crystal singers' trade. It is as if Melville's descriptions of the whaling trade were expanded and Moby Dick and Ahab reduced to mere walk-on parts. While some of Killashandra's colleagues are killed or maimed, their suffering provokes little sympathy, since it is so readily accepted as the inevitable price of the precious crystal. Moreover, despite the temptations, Miss McCaffrey avoids any hint of symbolism; the whole pitch of her narrative invites us to take Killashandra's obsession at face value. So what we are left with is a detailed instruction manual for a trade that doesn't exist. But be forewarned: Crystal singing may not be real, but Killashandra's obsession comes alive, and readers who get past the first 50 pages will find themselves sharing it.

Claudia Morner

SOURCE: A review of *Crystal Singer,* in *School Library Journal,* Vol. 29, No. 3, November, 1982, p. 106.

Proud, talented Killashandra Ree learns she has failed her final audition despite ten years of all-consuming preparation for a career as a vocal concert soloist. By coincidence that day she meets a vacationing crystal singer, joins him for the remainder of his holiday and becomes acquainted with the side effects and risks of crystal singing. When Carrik goes into a coma from which he never awakens, she escorts his body home to Ballybran. She stays on to take a series of entrance exams, which might lead to a career as a crystal singer, or, if she fails, will limit her forever to the planet Ballybran. She is successful because of motivation, self-confidence, ability and luck. The story ends as she accomplishes a difficult job, cutting and placing black crystal on four remote planets so they may have instant interstellar communication. Although it lacks the epic scale of McCaffrey's popular Dragon series, this is a well-constructed story with a strong-willed and courageous young heroine who finds her niche in the workplace. Because of the universal struggle adolescents have with career choices, **Crystal Singer** belongs in any library serving YA science fiction/fantasy readers.

Rebecca Sue Taylor

SOURCE: A review of *Crystal Singer,* in *Voice of Youth Advocates,* Vol. 5, No. 6, February, 1983, p. 45.

McCaffrey's legions of fans may at first be disappointed that this newest work contains not a single dragon. However, they will soon find themselves swept into an intriguing and uniquely told adventure. Young Killashandra Ree finds that her ten years of intense musical training have been wasted when she is told that her voice lacks the quality to make her a solo artist. By chance she meets Carrick, a Crystal Singer of the Heptite Guild from the planet Ballybran. She is soon intrigued by his personality and way of life. There are many mysteries that surround Ballybran and its dangerous occupation. Even as Killashandra discovers each increasingly frightening fact her desire to find and "sing" the rare black crystal grows. Killashandra's personality and motivations are the carefully crafted core to the story that moves steadily toward a satisfying conclusion. Though missing the magical spark that raises some of her earlier works, **The Ship Who Sang, The White Dragon,** to the level of classics, this is the competent, readable, better than most, science fiction one expects from a master "world builder."

MORETA: DRAGONLADY OF PERN (1983)

Publishers Weekly

SOURCE: A review of *Moreta: Dragonlady of Pern,* in *Publishers Weekly,* Vol. 224, No. 13, September 23, 1983, p. 64.

For McCaffrey fans, five and a half years is a long time between journeys to the memorable Dragonworld of Pern, but the engaging tale of Moreta is worth the wait. In the early centuries of the planet's colonization, the Dragonrider heroine Moreta leads the riders and their personally imprinted dragons in a defensive foray to protect Pern from the fall of the Red Star's fatal Threads. External threats are not the only peril. A lethal plague spreads its carnage and threatens the extinction of all earth-spawned life. Action is provided in ample measure along the way, and the bonus in this adventure is a satisfying, sympathetic portrayal of the ability to survive hostile circumstance. Tragedies and even the petty infirmities of characters may punctuate the plot, but the effect is to reaffirm the versatility of the human spirit. For those on an initial visit to Pern, a concise prologue provides useful background detail, while neophytes and veterans alike will appreciate the "Dragondex," a compendium of historical information on Pernese society.

Roy Hoffman

SOURCE: A review of *Moreta: Dragonlady of Pern,* in *The New York Times Book Review,* January 8, 1984, p. 18.

All is well on the planet Pern save the periodic falling of Thread, a deadly spore that destroys all organic matter in its path. To combat Thread, citizens of Pern climb onto the backs of variously colored fire-breathing dragons and soar into the sky. Baby dragons, upon hatching, "Impress" their riders for life, "Impression," according to the book's "Dragondex," being "the joining of minds of a dragon and his or her rider-to-be." The queen dragon, Orlith, Impresses Moreta, the passionate heroine. Orlith carries Moreta aloft and also serves as her therapist, telepathically communicating comfort and wisdom, even crooning "supportively" when Moreta reaches "catharsis" with Alessan, the passionate hero. Unfortunately, a potentially exciting fantasy is buried in many places by Anne McCaffrey's tortured prose. When she focuses on dragons, she is entertaining. The best scenes of the book picture the beasts turning and banking in their demolition of Thread. With humans, though (and the Pernese seem human in every way), Miss McCaffrey seems an alien. The novel is shackled with long, tedious, ersatz-medieval dialogue about dragon-wing mending, family bloodlines and the nature of a viral epidemic sweeping the planet. *Moreta* may appeal to dragon cultists or aficionados of sword and sorcery fantasies that attempt to blend medievalism and science fiction, but the novel won't win many converts to this field.

Debora Bugbee

SOURCE: A review of *Dragonlady of Pern,* in *School Library Journal,* Vol. 30, No. 6, February, 1984, p. 87.

The long awaited addition to McCaffrey's "Pern" series, this is the seventh novel set among the dragonriding inhabitants of the planet Pern. Taking place before the other titles and filling in a previously mentioned chapter in the history of the planet, *Moreta: Dragonlady of Pern* tells the story of the great plague (a form of influenza) which decimates the populace. As their friends die, the healers, harpers and wyerfolk of Pern strive to find and deliver a cure to the isolated victims. McCaffrey has created a science fiction novel of high drama touched with tragedy. The well-constructed characters will be familiar to her fans, yet they are clearly new individuals, and the details of life on Pern are created with her usual thorough attention. However, McCaffrey seems to have some trouble sustaining tension during the build-up to Moreta's final tragic ride. Nonetheless, the final result is a well-written novel sure to please her fans.

Rebecca Sue Taylor

SOURCE: A review of *Moreta: Dragonlady of Pern,* in *Voice of Youth Advocates,* Vol. 7, No. 1, April, 1984, p. 38.

McCaffrey fans rejoice. This popular author has returned to the planet Pern and her magnificent Dragons. Moreta, Weyrwoman of Fort Weyr, is a strong and capable leader.

However, when a deadly plague sweeps through the halls, holds, and weyrs of Pern, there is danger that there will soon be too few dragonriders to fight threadfall. For Moreta, there is also the dilemma of her growing love for Alessan, the Lord Holder of Ruatha.

This work is McCaffrey at her best with well drawn characters both human and dragon. The culture and ecology of Pern is thoughtfully complex. The story moves swiftly toward a heroic, if tragic, conclusion. For fans of the series, Moreta is actually an ancestor of the characters in *Dragonflight, Dragonquest,* and *The White Dragon.* This story takes place in a century before the earlier books. Readers unfamiliar with the unique characters and culture of Pern may find this book frustrating at first but the usual "Dragondex" will help novice readers a great deal. An important addition to a critically acclaimed series.

THE COELURA (1983; reprinted in 1987)

Publishers Weekly

SOURCE: A review of *The Coelura,* in *Publishers Weekly,* Vol. 232, No. 22, November 27, 1987, p. 71.

After an adolescence spent in hunting and other pleasures, 20-year-old Caissa resists her aristocratic father's suggestion that it is time to produce an heir—particularly, since he recommends a dull nobleman as a mate. It is inevitable, then, that she happens to rescue and fall in love with a handsome downed pilot who turns out to be of the right sort of wealthy family. In the bargain she discovers the secret of her planet Demeathorne—the coelura, an endangered lifeform resembling a singing rainbow that produces exquisite, living, empathetic silk. This hothouse dream of love, with its teenage vision of bravura gestures justifying self-indulgence and the flaunting of rules, will please only the most romantic of readers. The extensive illustrations are all too appropriate: they might have been drawn by the inexperienced, self-dramatizing heroine.

Randy M. Brough

SOURCE: A review of *The Coelura,* in *Voice of Youth Advocates,* Vol. 11, No. 1, April, 1988, p. 40.

Baythan, Minister Plenipotentiary of the Federated Sentient Planets to Demeathorn, has arranged for his body-heir, the Lady Caissa, to marry a politically suitable but socially inept nobleman. Young, beautiful, intelligent, wealthy, and impetuous, Caissa loathes the man her father has chosen for her to wed. Upset after an abortive meeting with her intended, Caissa commandeers a space craft and wanders into the forbidden zone of Demeathorn. On a bleak island in the prohibited territory, Caissa discovers a man stranded by the crash of his space vessel. On the same island, Caissa also discovers the mysterious

Coelura: iridescent, magnificent rainbow creatures thought to be nearly extinct on Demeathorn. Caissa eventually returns to civilization with her new friend Murell, initiating a chain of events which will determine not only her own fate, but that of her father, the Coelura, and the planet itself.

The Coelura is a disappointing novel, or more accurately, novellette. McCaffrey shows she can write, but the plot is, to be generous, slight, and her characters lack depth. The book is profusely illustrated, but the drawings add little to the story. The author's name will attract readers, some of whom will undoubtedly find themselves yearning for Pern. A glorified comic book, though not even as interesting as some comic books.

STITCH IN SNOW (1984)

Sally Estes

SOURCE: A review of *Stitch in Snow,* in *Booklist,* Vol. 81, No. 14, March 15, 1985, p. 1030.

Away from her home in Ireland doing a U.S. lecture tour for her publisher, American children's author Dana Jane ("Jenny") Lovell is snowbound for three days in Denver, where she meets mystery man Dan Lowell. The attraction is mutual, and a pleasant companionship slides into an idyllic weekend love affair far removed from either's ordinary life. Later, after they have gone their separate ways, Jenny learns that she is Dan's only alibi for the night his former wife was killed. Positive that he is innocent, she rushes back to Denver, realizing that her feelings for him far surpass those of a brief romantic interlude. The legion of McCaffrey science fiction fans may be surprised and perhaps disappointed by this radical departure from the author's usual fare, but romance readers will relish the book as an endearing, witty love story.

KILLASHANDRA (1985)

Sally Estes

SOURCE: A review of *Killashandra,* in *Booklist,* Vol. 82, No. 4, October 15, 1985, p. 290.

In the further adventures of Killashandra Ree, heroine of *Crystal Singer,* Killashandra accepts a mission to the planet Optheria to install a replacement crystal in a sensory organ and also to investigate the Optherian government's prohibition of interstellar travel. Kidnapped and then stranded on a remote, uninhabited island, she escapes by swimming from island to island, ultimately making her way to a rebel stronghold. She and her abductor, a rebel leader who doesn't recognize her in her changed state (suntanned, bleached hair, almost gaunt), feel a mutual

sexual attraction that develops into a genuine love relationship. Killashandra soon finds herself on the side of the rebels, helps them expose the governing elders, and opens the planet to off-world travel. The stalwart heroine comes across as something of a "Wonder Woman," except that she does *not* bounce bullets off bracelets and she *does* have a voracious appetite for food, alcohol, and sex. All in all, this suspenseful and romantic story exhibits McCaffrey's usual verve in building convincing societies, developing vital characters, and sustaining mood.

Betsy Shorb

SOURCE: A review of *Killashandra,* in *School Library Journal,* Vol. 32, No. 6, February, 1986, p. 103.

Crystal singer Killashandra Ree is desperate to get off the crystal-mining planet of Ballybran, so she takes what at first sounds like a routine assignment replacing a shattered crystal in the main Sensory Organ on planet Optheria. While she is there she is also to find out why Optherians never leave the planet. She is kidnapped and marooned on an isolated island, but escapes, only to encounter her handsome kidnapper Lars Dahl, with whom she eventually falls in love. From Lars she discovers that the Optherian Sensory Organ is not only a musical instrument, but that it also uses subliminal suggestion to keep Optherians from wanting to leave their planet or oppose the planet's rulers. Together they plan sabotage. In this sequel to *Crystal Singer* McCaffrey returns to the more romantic vein of her dragon novels. Killashandra is bratty, feisty and independent. Lars is big and lovable, sometimes shrewd, sometimes simple. They make an unlikely and not always convincing pair. Otherwise, the book is a satisfying adventure for those who like their science fiction spiced with humor.

THE YEAR OF THE LUCY (1986)

Publishers Weekly

SOURCE: A review of *The Year of the Lucy,* in *Publishers Weekly,* Vol. 228, No. 23, December 6, 1985, p. 70.

The ingredients for titillation are here: an exotic, foreign-born sculptor, bastard daughter of a famous Hungarian artist; a husband who travels; a concert pianist who happens by when his car breaks down. But this promising buildup crumbles into the petty business of getting the children off to school, preparing for a church bazaar, putting up with in-laws so overbearing as to be laughable. Though sculptor Mirelle manages some hanky-panky with pianist James, the reader fails to bate the breath. This is less a novel than a series of social notes for a suburban newspaper, each dinner described in excruciating detail, and every neighbor's closet revealing an unconvincing skeleton. Even Mirelle's vaunted artistic ability, the focus of the novel, becomes hard to credit. This is a book filled with earnest conversation that rings false, with hints of conflicts that never take place.

Joyce Smothers

SOURCE: A review of *The Year of the Lucy,* in *Library Journal,* Vol. 111, No. 1, January, 1986, p. 103.

An award-winning science fiction novelist succeeds here with contemporary realism. This psychologically authentic portrait of a housewife-manqué has none of Judy Blume's snappy dialogue or Norma Klein's trendiness, but its superb characterization involves the reader deeply. The setting is Wilmington, Delaware in 1961; the protagonist, a talented sculptor in her thirties who feels overwhelmed by the demands of her cold, preoccupied husband and neurotic mother-in-law. For sustenance she takes a lover, and, reaching out to the past, she sculpts a portrait of Lucy, a deceased friend who supported her in earlier crises. Most McCaffrey fans will be disappointed that this isn't sf, but it will appeal to the growing audience for this type of book. Recommended for libraries that can afford its stiff price.

Publishers Weekly

SOURCE: A review of *The Year of the Lucy,* in *Publishers Weekly,* Vol. 230, No. 3, July 18, 1986, p. 80.

Mirelle Martin finds herself increasingly discouraged by marital turmoil, depleted self-esteem, and a propensity to neglect her artistic talent. Mirelle loves her husband, Steve, but his intense, volatile personality exhausts her, as do his jealous, sometimes violent, tirades. Mirelle stoically endures these outbursts, although the caustic criticism she customarily receives from Steve's overbearing mother wears her down. The elder Mrs. Martin scorns Mirelle largely because she is the illegitimate daughter of a famous singer and the Hungarian painter Lajos Neagu. To placate her mother-in-law, Mirelle conceals her provocative heritage by refusing to seek widespread public attention for her sculptures. Such subservience always outraged her friend Lucy, who, before she died, exhorted Mirelle to be more assertive. Fortunately, the void Lucy left is suddenly filled by concert pianist James Howell, a lonely man who coaxes Mirelle to self-awareness, then falls in love with her. McCaffrey, best known for her science fiction fantasy, depicts Mirelle's predicament with sensitivity and credibility, and she perceptively delineates this troubled artist's creative temperament.

📖 *NERILKA'S STORY: A PERN ADVENTURE*
    (1986)

Publishers Weekly

SOURCE: A review of *Nerilka's Story: A Pern Adventure,* in *Publishers Weekly,* Vol. 229, No. 5, January 31, 1986, p. 366.

The latest of McCaffrey's romantic Pern novels expands on the tale of a minor character in ***Moreta: Dragonlady of Pern.*** Young Nerilka is considered unattractive and overly serious in her own hold, where her peremptory father installs his mistress immediately after his wife's death. Angry and frustrated, Nerilka uses her medical training and her access to the supplies her father is hoarding to help combat the plague sweeping Pern, which has already claimed her mother and sisters. Inevitably, her work with the Healers leads her to Ruatha Hold, whose rugged widower chief, Lord Alessan, sees her worth and marries her. In form, this is basically a Victorian gothic in which a governess tames and marries the gruff master of the house. As such, McCaffrey's legions of fans should enjoy it, but it is a weak entry in the Pern saga.

Peter L. Robertson

SOURCE: A review of *Nerilka's Story: A Pern Adventure,* in *Booklist,* Vol. 82, No. 13, March 1, 1986, p. 914.

This short novel continues the thematic thrust of the Dragonriders of Pern series. As Nerilka grows unhappy at Fort Hold, a plague sweeps over Pern, and her father, Lord Holder Tolocamp, takes a second wife, who is not to Nerilka's liking. The narrative takes the young girl away from her own Hold to Ruatha Hold where she nurses the sick in the terrible aftermath of the plague and where she marries Alessan, Lord Holder of Ruatha. A companion piece to ***Moreta: Dragonlady of Pern, Nerilka's Story*** is told by one of the minor characters in that novel and offers another perspective on many of the same events, including Moreta's death. Although often short on action, the tale is written with McCaffrey's customary simplicity and elegance.

Betsy Shorb

SOURCE: A review of *Nerilka's Story: A Pern Adventure,* in *School Library Journal,* Vol. 32, No. 9, May, 1986, p. 114.

This slight addition to McCaffrey's dragon novels is about a minor character mentioned in ***Moretta, Dragonlady of Pern.*** Nerilka, the plain and ignored oldest daughter of Lord Tolocamp, is appalled when her father abandons her mother and sisters to the plague spreading from Ruatha Hold, then refuses aid to anyone else on the rest of Pern. Nerilka first sends medicines secretly, then sets off (in disguise) for Ruatha, a place she had long wished to visit but had always been prevented from going. There she finds acceptance both for her healing skills and for herself, and she falls in love with the seemingly unattainable Alessan, Lord of Ruatha. This illustrated novella, about the size of a paperback, is not the best of McCaffrey, but it does have an interesting heroine and will satisfy McCaffrey's legions of fans who want to know why Alessan married so shortly after the death of his beloved Moretta.

DRAGONSDAWN (1988)

Sally Estes

SOURCE: A review of *Dragonsdawn,* in *Booklist,* Vol. 85, No. 1, September 1, 1988, p. 4.

Pernophiles, rejoice! At last McCaffrey unfolds her early vision of the colonizing of the beautiful, Earthlike, uninhabited planet Pern. As the novel opens, three ships on a one-way trip with more than 6,000 colonists (most of them having passed the entire journey in deep sleep) are approaching their destination. What follows is the story of the landing and the settling. There is some political infighting and some scheming by bad guys, but, in general, a concerted effort is made to set up a peaceful agrarian society. McCaffrey focuses on a handful of people, mainly the leaders and two young people who are the first to bond with the small, dragonlike lizards native to Pern. All is going well when, after eight years, the colonists experience their first Threadfall—deadly spores that fall from the sky in silver threads devouring everything in their path. When people notice the dragonets helping fight the Thread by breathing fire on it, they decide to genetically create large, intelligent dragons capable of working with their human riders to defend the land from Thread. Rich in detail and characterization, but not as complex in construction as McCaffrey's Dragonriders of Pern series (after all, here the author is working with material familiar to her readers), this will delight Pern fans while satisfying their curiosity about how it all began.

Publishers Weekly

SOURCE: A review of *Dragonsdawn,* in *Publishers Weekly,* Vol. 234, No. 12, September 16, 1988, p. 69.

Readers who for two decades have been following the fortunes of the dragonriders and other inhabitants of the planet Pern will welcome the latest volume, chronicling the early years. It stands very much on its own, however; knowing about the later history of the planet only adds enjoyment. After 15 years of cold sleep, 6000 colonists land on Pern, seeking a simpler existence, escaping the aftermath of interstellar war and an overly technical society. The colony prospers until the consuming Thread—a force that destroys all life it comes in contact with—makes its first appearance. A brilliant bio-engineer attempts to develop a biological weapon to save them, a much larger version of a native life form many of the colonists have adopted as pets: dragonets with the ability to teleport and breathe flame after eating phosphoric rock. The book ends with the first successful result of that experiment. Many richly developed characters people the novel, among them two youngsters, Sorka Hanrahan and Sean Connell, who grow up to become two of the first dragonriders. One hopes McCaffrey, who most recently has been writing in the mainstream (*The Lady*), is beginning a new Pern cycle in which she will tell, in answer to many other questions, whatever happened to the intelligent dolphins that came with the humans to Pern.

Gerald Jonas

SOURCE: A review of *Dragonsdawn,* in *The New York Times Book Review,* January 8, 1989, p. 31

Anne McCaffrey's **Dragonsdawn** is the sixth book in the "Dragonriders of Pern" series, which has brought Ms. McCaffrey a large and appreciative audience. To readers familiar with the series, it is sufficient to note that **Dragonsdawn** comes first chronologically; it tells of the colonizing of the uninhabited planet Pern by a few thousand carefully selected humans, of the colonists' first encounter with the life-threatening spores known as Thread and of the creation (by genetic engineering) of the winged, telepathic, fire-breathing "dragons" who become the colonists' first line of defense against the periodic falls of Thread.

Ms. McCaffrey's evocations of the first Threadfall and the maiden flight of the first Dragonriders will not disappoint her fans. Few are better at mixing elements of high fantasy and hard science in a narrative that disarms skepticism by its open embrace of the joys of wish fulfillment. Only when she strays too far from Thread and dragons into realms of character delineation do her deficiencies as a writer become manifest: the awkward similes ("Had he not pierced the protective gases of a hundred worlds in just the same way, slipping like a penknife under the flap of an envelope, like a man into the body of his beloved?"), the formulaic descriptions ("Her jaw was set in a resolute line, and her lips curved in a curious smile, which her tired eyes did not echo"), the jejune speculations ("Differences! Why did there always have to be distinctions, arrogantly displayed as superiorities, or derided as inferiorities?"). This is prose in too much of a hurry to get to the good parts to pay enough attention to details. Advice to nonfans: skip everything but the good parts.

Eugene La Faille

SOURCE: A review of *Dragonsdawn,* in *Voice of Youth Advocates,* Vol. 12, No. 1, April, 1989, p. 44.

This prequel to the **Dragonriders of Pern** series begins as several thousand colonists reach their new and final (due to a lack of fuel) home—Pern, an Earth-like planet where they can begin again without repeating the mistakes of Earth and the other colonies. However, the colonists are soon confronted by human greed and terror from the skies. Some of the colonists begin searching for rare minerals and hoarding fuel supplies, even going so far as to kill, kidnap, and steal to accomplish their goals. At the same time, deadly spores known as Thread unexpectedly begin to fall, destroying all organic life in their path. The only hope is to fight the Thread with fire and to genetically alter the small, tamable dragon lizards into large fire-breathing dragons to aid in the battle. But will there be time to breed the necessary dragons before all must perish?

This will undoubtedly satisfy most of the fans of the Pern series as it does answer some questions about the settlement of Pern by humans and the early relationship between humans and dragons. Unfortunately, the quality of writing does not live up to that in the earlier novels. The depth of characterization is minimal even for major characters, with the villains being stock portrayals. The plot is limited for such a lengthy novel and the ending is much too abrupt. However, this is bound to be a requested title and is represented by excellent cover art.

THE RENEGADES OF PERN (1989)

Sally Estes

SOURCE: A review of *The Renegades of Pern,* in *Booklist,* Vol. 86, No. 2, September 15, 1989, p. 114.

McCaffrey's latest, which nicely ties together the adult Dragonriders of Pern series and the juvenile Harper Hall series, involves many familiar figures: for example, young Lord Jaxon and his pure white dragon, Ruth, from *The White Dragon,* who play subsidiary roles, and Piemur, also of *The White Dragon* and *Dragondrums,* who is a major figure here, providing a touch of romance and adventure. But McCaffrey adds a wealth of lesser-known or new characters to the richness of the Pern panoply: there's Lady Thella, the vicious leader of a highly organized pack of renegades; Aramina, whose reputed ability to "hear" dragons brings her to Thella's attention; and Jayge, who is bent on revenge for Thella's brutal attack on his family of traders. The relatively unknown southern continent, the setting for much of the tale, is mapped; and the original landing site, described in full in *Dragonsdawn,* is investigated. By leaving a puzzling mystery unexplored and just opening the door on what can be learned about the original settlers, McCaffrey hints at a sequel.

Kirkus Reviews

SOURCE: A review of *The Renegades of Pern,* in *Kirkus Reviews,* Vol. LXVII, No. 17, September 15, 1989, p. 1368.

Another in McCaffrey's popular series about the dragonriders of planet Pern, whose function is to destroy the mysterious, corrosive Thread as it falls from space. Now, as a new Threadfall threatens Pern, Lessa and F'lar will soon teleport into the past in search of the Weyrs of yore, allies desperately needed to fight Thread.

Meanwhile, away from the alluring actions of dragons, riders, and Thread, the renegade Lady Thella has formed a powerful raider band and preys on the wealth of the honest Lord Holders, whose tithes support the Weyrs. Insanely ambitious Thella fears nothing but the dragons, who can observe her operations from above. So she de-

cides to kidnap Aramina, a young girl who talks telepathically with dragons. But, in the attempt, Thella arouses the wrath of young carter Jayge, who vows to track down and destroy her. Another subplot, eventually to link up, involves the colonization of the vast southern continent, where explorers uncover ruins and artifacts of the original colonists of Pern.

Disappointingly little about dragons this time. Otherwise, a pleasant, undemanding, fairly typical McCaffrey diversion—with plenty of plot, overmuch psychologizing, and more chat than action.

Publishers Weekly

SOURCE: A review of *The Renegades of Pern,* in *Publishers Weekly,* Vol. 236, No. 14, October 16, 1989, p. 84.

While recent tales of Pern have dealt with early eras on that turbulent planet, this one begins during the time of *Dragonquest* and continues beyond the closing of *The White Dragon,* focusing on some of the commoners, and how they cope with the return of the life-consuming Thread. A number of lives intertwine, such as that of the trader boy Jayge Lilcamp, whose family is almost destroyed when his father refuses to believe the first Thread warning. Jayge runs afoul of Thella, sister of the Telgar Hold lord but a malcontent and leader of renegades, when she tries to kidnap the refugee girl Aramina, who can hear all dragons. Meanwhile, in the South, the young harper Piemur finds his destiny, and Toric, the first Holder there, schemes for supremacy. McCaffrey paints her colorful world on a still larger canvas, maintaining the complex plots and strong characterization that permeate her work. Timed to coincide with the publication of this book is an illustrated nonfiction companion book, *The Dragonlover's Guide to Pern* by Jody Lynn Nye with McCaffrey. The large-format volume gathers together much known and some new information about Pern and its history.

Christy Tyson and Joel Singer

SOURCE: A review of *The Renegades of Pern,* in *Voice of Youth Advocates,* Vol. 13, No. 1, April, 1990, p. 39.

Pern fans will be thrilled to get this latest in the chronicles of McCaffrey's fascinating planet and its inhabitants. They will enjoy catching up on old friends and meeting new ones. And they'll be pleased to find the details of events hinted at in earlier novels. But they won't find *Renegades of Pern* particularly satisfying as a novel or as a transition piece. Too many characters are introduced but not brought to life, and too many plots sketched out but not developed. There are outlines of wonderful stories here—enough to remind readers of McCaffrey's power as a storyteller—but only true fans will be content with these, with the expectation that future novels will make use of these pieces in more coherent stories. Teen reviewer and Pern fan Joel Singer writes, "Why is it that as authors get older they tend not to write stories focusing on the wonderful characters and plots they created in their younger days and instead go for long, majestic, sweeping masterpieces? Asimov, Heinlein, and now McCaffrey have all done it. *Renegades of Pern* is a parallel novel, set during the time of her original trilogy and telling about new events that we didn't know were happening, as well as old events through new eyes. The only problem is that the viewpoint continually switches—first Piemur, then Sharra, then Toric, and several more new characters—Jayge and Thella, to name two. It makes the novel take on an entirely different tone, that of a historical chronicle rather than a novel of adventure. Lots of exciting things happen, and McCaffrey gives great descriptions of events from different points of view, but the novel as a whole does not really hang together. Don't get me wrong; I loved the book. They excavated more ruins, learned more about the free traders, introduced a new interesting couple, and Piemur finally got laid. It's just compared to the original, it lacks something vital. Maybe it's originality, and I'm being too picky. Anyway, I strongly look forward to the next one in the series and I'll read it anyway. The dragonriders are headed to the stars!"

Buy for fans, and use *Dragonflight, Dragonquest* or *Dragonsong, Dragonsinger, Dragondrums* to bring new readers to this wonderful, complex world.

📖 *SASSINAK* (with Elizabeth Moon, 1990)

Publishers Weekly

SOURCE: A review of *Sassinak,* in *Publishers Weekly,* Vol. 237, No. 6, February 9, 1990, p. 56.

The first in the Planet Pirates series, this science fiction yarn offers a vivid universe inhabited by cardboard citizens. Sassinak, the heroine and the only developed character, steps straight from a formula: When she is 12, pirates raid her native colony, enslaving her and murdering her family. Abe, a fellow captive, befriends her and, when they are emancipated by Fleet (the military), becomes her guardian until he is slain in a barroom brawl. Intelligent and daring, Sass joins Fleet, seeking vengeance on her enemies. She becomes the classic fictional commander: a loner whose entire life is subsumed by the military. Fortunately, Sass's exploits are so expertly recounted that their intrigue and adventure compensate for the hackneyed plot line. Cleverly drawn aliens, supporting characters here, allow the authors to explore various aspects of prejudice. Sass's appraisal of men, however, verges at times on sexist. Hugo winner McCaffrey's works include *Dragonsdawn.*

Roland Green

SOURCE: A review of *Sassinak,* in *Booklist,* Vol. 86, No. 13, March 1, 1990, p. 1268.

This well-done spinoff from McCaffrey's Dinosaur Planet series—and the first volume in the Planet Pirates series—tells the story of Commander Sassinak from her kidnapping by pirate slavers as a young girl to her tenacious fight against pirates in command of a fleet cruiser. The authors together make the concept of space piracy at least plausible, while Moon's nearly unsurpassed skill at realistic military sf raises the book to an even higher level.

Jody McCoy

SOURCE: A review of *Sassinak,* in *Voice of Youth Advocates,* Vol. 13, No. 3, August, 1990, p. 168.

With a central character as potentially captivating as Sassinak, an intriguing futuristic universe, and a name like McCaffrey sharing authorship, how can a book go wrong? Twelve year old Sassinak is captured by space pirates who destroy her colony, kill her family, and enslave her. Her rescue and subsequent acceptance into the Fleet provide the means to achieve revenge. Though there are some wonderful supportive characters in Sassinak's life 'twixt 12 and 40, they fall to the side as the authors rush toward the second volume of the "Planet Pirates" series. Perhaps then Moon and McCaffrey will decide if the characters are more important than the mechanics of the Fleet ships. A great cover and a rousing blurb on the back will get this book to readers who may not be critical of a 333 page introduction to a series.

📖 *THE ROWAN* (1990)

Publishers Weekly

SOURCE: A review of *The Rowan,* in *Publishers Weekly,* Vol. 237, No. 26, June 29, 1990, p. 89

McCaffrey leaves behind the Dragonriders of Pern to write this charming tale of a powerful psi on whom depends the commerce of human-settled space. Through the Nine-Star League, people and goods are instantaneously transported by the telepaths and telekinetics of Federal Telepath & Transport. Orphaned as a baby and discovered to be a potential Prime, most powerful of the psis, the Rowan is raised by psychologists, trained by them and put in charge of the FT&T Tower on Callisto where she lives a lonely life, psychologically impeded, as are other Primes, from moving around the human universe. Then she touches minds with an unknown Prime from recently colonized Deneb VIII who seeks help opposing an invasion of extraterrestrials. The Rowan can't help him because of her phobia, but the new Prime, who doesn't share her disability, teaches her how to transport herself. The two team up to fight the aliens and grow to love each other. In this sensitive portrayal (expanded from the author's first published story, **"Lady in the Tower,"** which appeared in 1959, *Magazine of Fantasy and Science Fiction),* McCaffrey draws a warm and vivid picture of a struggling frontier society.

Paul Stuewe

SOURCE: "Of Some Import," in *Quill & Quire,* Vol. 56, No. 9, September, 1990, p. 64.

Anne McCaffrey's publishers are pulling out all the publicity stops on her latest novel, which tells a staple science-fiction story with mass-market-oriented simplicity. The protagonist is a telepath whose precious powers severely strain the social fabric of her society, a world in which such recently discovered powers of mind are gingerly used for material purposes. McCaffrey has worked out the psychological and economic consequences of these developments with a great deal of care, but regrettably her foregrounds aren't nearly as interesting as her backgrounds. The book's romantic relationships are conducted at a sub-adolescent level, and a couple of surprise attacks from alien invaders seem to have been thrown in to compensate for the generally low level of narrative tension. All things considered, *The Rowan* probably won't do particularly well with mainstream fiction readers, while hardcore science-fiction and fantasy fans may find it rather tame by genre standards.

John Lawson

SOURCE: A review of *The Rowan,* in *School Library Journal,* Vol. 37, No. 2, February, 1991, p. 104.

Rowan, a telepathic, telekinetic three-year-old, is the sole survivor of a mining disaster on a frontier planet. As she matures, her powers grow until she becomes one of a handful of "Primes" with the Federal Telepath & Teleport network, the organization responsible for telecommunications and shipping of cargo throughout the galaxy. Rowan finds herself alienated from humanity and her coworkers due to her unique talents and tremendous responsibilities until she senses Jeff Raven, a fellow talent, on the fringes of explored space. A bonding develops between the two when they are thrown together to help defeat aliens bent on destroying the human race. *The Rowan* was expanded from the short story **"Lady in the Tower"** in *Get Off the Unicorn.* While not as strong a love story as *The Ship Who Sang,* McCaffrey weaves believable characters with a well-written story to produce this entertaining science fiction romance.

📖 *THE DEATH OF SLEEP* (with Jody Lynn Nye, 1990)

Roland Green

SOURCE: A review of *The Death of Sleep,* in *Booklist,* Vol. 86, No. 21, July, 1990, p. 2077.

This novel continues the Planet Pirates shared-world trilogy, begun in the McCaffrey/Elizabeth Moon collaboration, *Sassinak.* It tells the story of healer Lunzie Mespil, who takes to space on the trail of pirates because they have robbed her of her career and family by causing her to spend many years in cryogenic stasis. Lunzie and her world are well drawn and the tale is generally well told. Readers of the first series entry will be fully interested.

John Lawson

SOURCE: A review of *The Death of Sleep,* in *School Library Journal,* Vol. 36, No. 12, December, 1990, p. 135.

Like Dan Davis in Heinlein's *Door into Summer,* Lunzie Mespil is a victim of cryogenic sleep and future shock. On three separate occasions following a deep-space disaster, she is placed in suspended animation totaling almost 90 years while awaiting rescue. Like Ripley in the film *Aliens,* she has lost not just her friends and loved ones, but everything familiar to her. Her story is a study of struggle against adversity as she tries to put her life back together. Because her medical knowledge is obsolete, Lunzie returns to school and becomes the medical officer on an exploratory vessel for the Federation of Sentient Planets. While routinely surveying the prehistoric life of the planet Ireta, she is caught in the middle of a violent racial mutiny. While not as strong a book as *The Ship Who Sang* or most of the "Pern" novels, McCaffrey has created a feisty, likable character in Lunzie Mespil. This well-written yarn can stand alone, but it works best if read with *Dinosaur Planet* (1978), *Dinosaur Planet Survivors* (1984), and *Sassinak* (1990).

Bette DeBruyne Ammon

SOURCE: A review of *The Death of Sleep,* in *Voice of Youth Advocates,* Vol. 13, No. 5, December, 1990, p. 300.

Dr. Lunzie Mespil's specialty is the treatment of psychological space-incurred trauma and that's why she has been hired on the space mining vessel Nellie Mine. Having left behind her 14 year old daughter, Lunzie plans to make some money, develop a reputation, and return for Fiona. She reckons without a meeting with an asteroid belt and is forced to put herself into "cold sleep" in order to survive. When she is awakened, 62 years have passed and Lunzie's world (a variety of colonies throughout the galaxy) has changed drastically. Thus begins her search for a much older Fiona; retraining in her profession; involvement with spies, killers, pirates, etc.

McCaffrey has teamed up with Nye to write what appears to be the first of a futuristic space travel and colonization series. The story is moderately exciting and the cyrogenic aspects are intriguing. Lunzie's family and peers (including lovers) continue to age while she snoozes away the years undergoing no physical change. Although Lunzie is a strong and capable character, some of her actions lack clarification (as in her unreasonable aversion to the Heavy-worlders), and the reader is left pondering why she doesn't more diligently pursue a reunion with her aged daughter. Strangely, the few 20th century carryovers include Rudyard Kipling, coffee, and Carmen Miranda. McCaffrey's name will draw readers but this one misses the boat (and the space ship).

PEGASUS IN FLIGHT (1990)

Sally Estes

SOURCE: A review of *Pegasus in Flight,* in *Booklist,* Vol. 87, No. 5, November 1, 1990, p. 483.

Something of a prequel to **The Rowan,** in which humanity has made it into interstellar space, McCaffrey's latest takes place at a time when Earth is in the process of building its first space platform. Earth is overpopulated and extrasensory perception—or Talent—comes in varying strengths and forms, ranging from telepathy to telekinetics to clairvoyance. Two young people with extraordinary Talent are at the core of events: peppery, streetsmart, 12-year-old Tirla, living on her own in one of the swarming residential areas in a multiethnic 30-story community; and teenage Peter Reidinger, a quadraplegic whose telekinetic abilities enable him not only to move his own body in a seemingly natural fashion, but also to shift huge objects. Longer on character development, world building, and the exploration of psychic abilities than on action, this tale nevertheless has exciting moments; for example, Peter is called in to telekinetically land a space shuttle in a monsoon, and he and Tirla, kidnapped by criminals, help crack a ring that has been abducting minors for slave labor, unlawful intercourse, and organ removal. An atmospheric novel that will fascinate McCaffrey's legion of fans as well as readers interested in the paranormal.

Kirkus Reviews

SOURCE: A review of *Pegasus in Flight,* in *Kirkus Reviews,* Vol. LVIII, No. 21, November 1, 1990, p. 1503.

Long-awaited sequel to **To Ride Pegasus,** the near-future trials and tribulations of a developing group of paranormal-powered Talents.

Gifted telepath Rhyssa Owen, director of the Jerhattan Center for Parapsychic Talents, faces a variety of difficult problems. Prickly, headstrong Ludmilla Barchenka, construction boss of a vitally important space station, needs the help of all the telekinetic Talents she can grab—but refuses to provide satisfactory working conditions and accommodation for the sensitive Talents. Young telekinetic whiz Peter, paralyzed and traumatized after an accident, must be coaxed to develop his ability to transform electricity into kinetic power enough to move spaceships. Streetwise survivor-type Tirla uses her extraordinary knack for languages to manipulate or avoid the swarming kidnappers and child-molesters of the slums; eventually, she will lead Rhyssa to the brains behind an organized gang

of slavers and perverts. Finally, Rhyssa hires outstanding p.r. expert Dave Lehardt and finds herself falling in love with him-despite the fact that Dave lacks all signs of Talent.

Breezy, often absorbing, well constructed—and a refreshing change of scene from McCaffrey's ubiquitous Dragonyarns.

John Lawson

SOURCE: A review of *Pegasus in Flight,* in *School Library Journal,* Vol. 37, No. 4, April, 1991, p. 154.

This book is set shortly after **To Ride Pegasus** and centuries before **The Rowan.** Rhyssa Owen, telepathic granddaughter of Daffyd op Owen, is now director of the Center for Parapsychic Talents, a nonprofit organization that works for the betterment of humanity by predicting disasters, controlling crime, locating missing persons or things, and manipulating material, from heavy equipment to the microscopic. The Center becomes involved with a ruthless head of construction who uses and abuses these talents in the dangerous task of building the first space platform. Tirla, 12, and adolescent Peter become involved in the growing crisis. McCaffrey continues her fascinating parapsychic chronicle in this fast-paced, easy read, and readers are sure to care about her multidimensional, believable characters.

ALL THE WEYRS OF PERN (1991)

Sally Estes

SOURCE: A review of *All the Weyrs of Pern,* in *Booklist,* Vol. 88, No. 3, October 1, 1991, p. 202.

McCaffrey brings her human settlers on the planet Pern full swing in her latest entry, as the past and future meet. In **Dragonsdawn,** she took readers back to the settling of the planet, showing us how it all came about—the first devastating Thread attack, the genetic engineering of the dragons, and the need to abandon the landing site. Here, Lord Jaxom of Ruatha and his white dragon, Ruth, are leaders in the rediscovery of the Landing and the revitalizing of Avivas (the Artificial Intelligence Voice-Address System), which is still extant after 5,525 years of maintaining itself on minimum power. Avivas sets out to educate the Pernians in the sciences that have been long lost in order that they might end the Thread threat for all time. This is an exciting, full-bodied, richly detailed new chapter in the Pern chronicle as the knowledge of the first settlers is united with the wisdom of the descendants. It also mirrors human nature, setting the hide-bound traditionalists against those willing to learn new ways by building on the relearned capabilities. Once again McCaffrey's narrative flows smoothly, maintaining the world and characters she has so lovingly created and setting new challenges for them to meet. A must for Pern fans.

Library Journal

SOURCE: A review of *All the Weyrs of Pern,* in *Library Journal,* Vol. 116, No. 19, November 15, 1991, p. 111.

The dream of generations of Dragonriders draws within reach as, with the aid of an intelligent computer, the possibility of destroying the devastating phenomenon known as "Thread" becomes a reality. Having exposed Pern's civilization to technology in **Renegades of Pern,** McCaffrey proceeds with her customary skill and humor to explore all the ramifications of culture shock. Despite some weaknesses in plot and an odd notion of time travel, the latest novel in a popular series will not lack for readers. Especially for libraries owning the previous Pern titles.

S. J. Rice

SOURCE: A review of *All the Weyrs of Pern,* in *Voice of Youth Advocates,* Vol. 15, No. 1, April, 1992, p. 45.

According to McCaffrey, this is our last visit to the Weyrs of Pern, so it's only fitting and appropriate that it should be one of the best. The current residents of Pern have discovered the master computer center—Artificial Intelligence Voice Address System, or Aivas—installed by the first settlers at Landing. The more forward-seeing of them (such as F'lar, Lessa, Robinton, Jaxom, and Piemur) are quick to see the benefits that Aivas offers, including long-lost knowledge held by the first settlers. But the traditionalists hate and fear Aivas, seeing the knowledge as evil and referring to the computer as the Abomination.

But when Aivas offers the chance to protect Pern from Thread forever by destroying the Red Star, the conflict becomes more than just an abstract disagreement over knowledge. Those opposing Aivas will stop at nothing, including kidnapping and murder, to preserve what they perceive as the ordained way of life. And even if our side (of course) manages to defeat the reactionaries, the destruction of the Red Star involves a trip to her surface—a trip that once nearly killed F'nor. But Jaxom and Ruth—"serving their world as only dragon and rider could, united in mind and heart to their purpose" —destroy the ancient scourge. If, in the end, the death of two friends, one old, one new, provides a bittersweet victory, Aivas' final words are a consolation: "And a time for every purpose under heaven."

Though this novel could be read with reasonable enjoyment by readers unfamiliar with the previous books, some understanding and all resonance would be lost, so it should be recommended as the culmination of a great reading experience. This work is closer in characterization, plot, and "feel" to the earlier works in the series, and so should be a rewarding experience for all those whose dreams inhabit *All the Weyrs of Pern.*

John Lawson

SOURCE: A review of *All the Weyrs of Pern,* in *School Library Journal,* Vol. 38, No. 6, June, 1992, p. 148.

AIVAS, the Artificial Intelligence Voice Address System that was a part of the original colonists' settlement, is unearthed on the Southern continent after having been buried for generations. This latest volume in the Pern saga deals with the reactions of the various lords, dragonriders, and craftsmen as they realize the impact the artificial intelligence will have on their culture and traditions. With its help, F'lar, Robinton, Lessa, Menolly, and all of the other characters YAs have come to care about devise a risky plan to eliminate a serious threat to their environment. While *All the Weyrs of Pern* is not as tight and exciting as the earlier dragonrider books, it is a well-written novel that's sure to appeal to McCaffrey's many fans.

CRISIS ON DOONA (with Jody Lynn Nye, 1992)

Publishers Weekly

SOURCE: A review of *Crisis on Doona,* in *Publishers Weekly,* Vol. 239, No. 8, February 10, 1992, pp. 77-78.

When humans colonized Doona they thought it to be uninhabited. When they discovered another race—the catlike Hrrubans—the two races decided to forego their traditional isolationism and try to share the planet. That treaty is up for review 25 years later, and a conspiracy is afoot to discredit Todd Reeve and Hrriss, best of friends, who have come to symbolize the human/Hrruban cohabitation and, by extension, the treaty. McCaffrey and Nye (coauthors of **The Death of Sleep**) return to the setting of McCaffrey's 1969 **Decision at Doona** for a novel that falls far short of their previous works. The good guys (Todd, Hrriss and their families and friends) are *so* noble and upright and true and the bad guys (Admiral Landreau—who has a longstanding grudge against the Reeve family and the Hrrubans—and his flunkies) are *so* irredeemable that any interest in the conflict is lost. Interactions between catlike aliens and humans have become a stock element in the SF genre, and McCaffrey and Nye have nothing new to add.

Catherine M. Dwyer

SOURCE: A review of *Crisis on Doona,* in *Voice of Youth Advocates,* Vol. 15, No. 2, June, 1992, p. 112.

In the not-so-distant future, Earth has become so crowded and polluted that its people are forced to search for other planets to colonize. They search for uninhabited planets but sometimes, as in the case of Doona, they make mistakes. The Reeve family and other colonists had already settled when they encountered the Hrrubans, a race of two-legged cat-like people who are also colonizing the planet. Despite concerns by both races, the colonists co-exist under a Treaty that is up for renewal. Todd Reeve is the first human to learn the language of the Hrrubans and his best friend Hrriss is Hrruban. Hrriss and Todd are returning to Doona in their spaceship when they violate Treaty-protected space to answer a Mayday call. The call turns out to be a fake. When they finally land on Doona, Todd and Hrriss find themselves in difficulty not only over the Treaty violation but also due to stolen artifacts that are found in their ship. A major political scandal is slowly uncovered, involving the governments of both Earth and Doona. Todd and Hrriss are forced to enlist a number of people to aid them, including Kelly Solinari, one of the Reeves' neighbors, and Nrrna, a female Hrruban. As they try to clear Todd and Hrriss, romance blooms for both couples.

McCaffrey and Nye start their story with a bang. The false Mayday is intriguing, and the roundup of the giant, dangerous snakes when Todd and Hrriss return to Doona is thrilling. The addition of Jilamey Landreau as a tender-foot who becomes a danger to himself and those around him only increases the level of excitement. Unfortunately the excitement is not sustained and the story quickly deteriorates into a slow-moving political tangle. The relationship between Kelly and Todd seems forced, and the friendship between Hrriss and Todd is too perfect. Jilamey Landreau, who provides some lighthearted scenes and is related to one of the major bad guys in the story, disappears entirely after the Hunt. McCaffrey and Nye should have passed on the political intrigue and concentrated on the interaction of the Hrrubans and the Humans.

DAMIA (1992)

Sally Estes

SOURCE: A review of *Damia,* in *Booklist,* Vol. 88, No. 15, April 1, 1992, p. 1412.

Another tale set in McCaffrey's well-crafted universe in which interstellar trade depends on the use of telepathy and telekinetics. Some of the initial events in this second entry in the Rowan trilogy overlap with those that conclude *The Rowan;* however, they are seen from a different perspective—that of Afra, whose strong mental Talent leads to his becoming second in command to the Rowan. Here, the Rowan remains a secondary character; center stage is held not only by Afra, but also by the Rowan's tempestuous and strong-willed daughter, Damia, who inherits much of her mother's stormy nature and grows up to surpass her parents in telepathic powers. A stronger, more controlled novel than *The Rowan,* this one both refines and extends characterizations, especially in inter-relationships and the use of mental powers. The story is also a romance; for Afra, who is close to the Rowan and her husband, becomes mentor and friend to the infant and toddler Damia and, finally, her lover and husband. There are two separate contacts with aliens—one extremely powerful and hostile, almost defeating the combined powers

of the Talented; the other friendly, seeking allies against the deadly invaders defeated by the Rowan and her husband in the earlier novel. A sure lead-in to the trilogy's concluding volume, and decidedly a winning choice for the author's legion of fans.

Library Journal

SOURCE: A review of *Damia,* in *Library Journal,* Vol. 117, No. 7, April 15, 1992, p. 125.

Damia, child of the legendary Rowan and inheritor of her mother's formidable telepathic powers, faces a test of courage and self-control as the planet Deneb is threatened by an insidious alien attacker. This sequel to *The Rowan* extends the story of a remarkable group of people into a second generation. Although the plot verges on the melo-dramatic and the central characters suffer from an over-abundance of self-awareness, McCaffrey's legion of fans will undoubtedly want this. Otherwise, a marginal sf romantic adventure.

John Lawson

SOURCE: A review of *Damia,* in *School Library Journal,* Vol. 38, No. 12, December, 1992, p. 148.

This is the second volume in McCaffrey's latest trilogy. In *The Rowan,* she introduced FT&T, Federal Telepath and Teleport, an organization that, through the use of psi talents, is responsible for interstellar communication. This well-written book centers around Damia (the daughter of Rowan and Jeff Raven) and Afra Lyon, Rowan's second-in-command. The story follows the girl from birth into adulthood, as she becomes a beautiful, young woman who is enormously talented in FT&T. Afra starts out as Damia's babysitter and becomes her friend, teacher, and ultimately her husband. This title climaxes with Damia battling a powerful alien invader. McCaffrey has created another memorable, independent female protagonist and fully fleshed-out, secondary characters who behave in a believable manner. *Damia* is a tighter, stronger story than *The Rowan,* and stands on its own. A superb sci-fi romance.

Eleanor Klopp

SOURCE: A review of *Damia,* in *Voice of Youth Advocates,* December, 1992, p. 293.

This is the second book in a trilogy dealing with the activities of the Federated Telepath and Teleportation System, commonly known as FT&T, whose super psy-chic Primes (I-1s) control and handle speedy shipment of objects and life forms amongst the federated planets with the help of powerful generators. When this money-making ability is first discovered, psychic talent becomes valuable and Talents, as the gifted are known, evaluated on a scale from one down, are correspondingly admired, trained, and rewarded. The FT&T is outside of government and its self-policing Talents maintain high ethical standards. It is said of them that "Cooperation was a primary requirement for all Talented people: civil discord was something intolerable in one with Talent." However, the story does not bear this out, and when it comes right down to it, the Primes for all the hoopla are actually glorified freight handlers, and pretty temperamental ones at that. The book cannot stand on its own. In spite of a 60-odd page recap, the reader who has not read the first book, *The Rowan,* will puzzle over too many things to make reading it enjoyable.

FREEDOM'S LANDING (1995)

Sally Estes

SOURCE: A review of *Freedom's Landing,* in *Booklist,* Vol. 91, No. 16, April 15, 1995, p. 1484.

With this book, McCaffrey opens an exciting and totally convincing new universe far removed from the worlds of the dragonriders, the Rowan, the crystal singer, and the ship-brawn partnerships with which her readers are happily familiar. The Catteni, an alien race of slavers, are settling a habitable but dangerous planet with recalcitrant slaves from a variety of races, including the human; all must learn to cooperate with one another to survive. Among the conscripted colonists is an exiled Catteni noble, Zainal, who is resented by some other colonists because he is a member of the overlord race, and Kristin Bjornsen, a spirited young human who finds herself not only working closely with Zainal but drawn to him romantically. What with the "mechos" that already farm the planet's land, the advanced society that must have created them, the Catteni themselves, and the formidable race that apparently controls the Catteni as just some of the challenges facing the colonists, there can only be more action in the sequels McCaffrey presumably plans.

Library Journal

SOURCE: A review of *Freedom's Landing,* in *Library Journal,* Vol. 120, No. 7, April 15, 1995, p. 119.

When the Catteni conquerers of Earth discover a potentially habitable new planet, a group of human slaves, accompanied by an exiled Catteni lord, become involuntary colonists forced to live or die by their own resources. McCaffrey's latest novel inaugurates a new series set in a universe where humans are pawns in a war between galactic powers. With her customary talent for imaginative storytelling, the author skillfully portrays the environmental and personal challenges faced by the new colonists. Most libraries should consider this a priority purchase.

Publishers Weekly

SOURCE: A review of *Freedom's Landing,* in *Publishers Weekly,* Vol. 241, No. 17, April 24, 1995, p. 64.

With a tale of human and other slaves abandoned by harsh masters on an ostensibly deserted planet, McCaffrey begins another highly readable series about successful survival in difficult circumstances. Kristin Bjornsen, an escaped human slave on the planet Barevi, saves one of the Catteni masters, Zainal, from being killed in a blood feud. When she tries to return him to the capital city, she is caught in a roundup of troublemakers designated for colonization duty. Among those dropped with few supplies on the unexplored new planet, later named Freedom, is Zainal, who turns out to be an aristocrat of his species. After Zainal is again saved from death, this time at the hands of vengeful former slaves, he casts his lot with the castaways, who have turned to former Marine sergeant Chuck Mitford for leadership. In sturdy Robinson Crusoe fashion, the survivors overcome the odds against them, rescue other castaways and find signs of a mysterious civilization that is using Freedom as a giant mechanized farm. They also deal with the few bad apples in their midst. Meanwhile love blossoms between Zainal and Kristin, to the displeasure of some of the other humans. McCaffrey has created another set of winning protagonists and a carefully detailed, exotic background on which to develop a new series.

Brian Martin

SOURCE: A review of *Freedom's Landing,* in *School Library Journal,* Vol. 41, No. 8, August, 1995, p. 171.

McCaffrey begins a new chronicle of human resilience and survival. Earth has been invaded by the Catteni, a race of soldiers who have come to quell opposition and to relocate troublesome cases (both human and alien) to inhospitable worlds. Kristen Bjornsen, a human, and a ragtag group must learn to communicate and begin to build a new life. Further, they must discover what is behind a completely different civilization that is using their planet (nicknamed Botany) as a farm for animal and vegetable produce. Underlying this cooperation is the resentment that some of the colonists feel for Zanial, a member of the race of slavers, and the romantic feelings that Zanial and Kristen begin to feel for one another. With two possible antagonistic alien cultures and their own internal problems, there can only be more interesting scenarios for the settlers of Botany. The characters are especially well developed: teens will be able to identify with their spirit, creativeness, and tenacity to survive despite all odds.

BLACK HORSES FOR THE KING (1996)

Kirkus Reviews

SOURCE: A review of *Black Horses for the King,* in *Kirkus Reviews,* Vol. 64, No. 7, April 1, 1996, p. 534.

McCaffrey turns away from the distant planet Pern to the world of King Arthur in her first enchanting historical novel for YAs. Galwyn Varianus is a quick-witted lad who is forced, after his father's death, to work as a page on his mean-spirited uncle's boat. Fortunately Galwyn meets the young Lord Artos (later, King Arthur), who has set out to breed Libyan horses for his army to ride against the invading Saxons. This larger conflict forms the background for Galwyn's simple, engrossing tale. After spending a few days in the future king's company, Galwyn is swayed by his noble leadership and mercy, so runs away to join Artos's forces. Here, Galwyn learns all about raising horses and grows into a fine citizen of Camelot.

The author deftly recreates the tools and culture of the Arthurian era, but readers may find the prolonged development of the prototypical horseshoe plodding. McCaffrey's fans will no doubt enjoy the camaraderie of Artos's merry band, and her trademark good guy/bad guy characterizations flatten but slightly this enjoyable adventure.

Publishers Weekly

SOURCE: A review of *Black Horses for the King,* in *Publishers Weekly,* Vol. 243, No. 17, April 22, 1996, p. 73.

McCaffrey steps out of her niche as a Hugo and Nebula award-winning fantasy writer to tackle her first historical novel for young adults, retelling the Arthurian legend—minus the Round Table, Guinevere and Merlin—through the eyes of Galwyn Varianus. A Roman Celtic youth, Galwyn helps the future king of Britain, known here as Lord Artos, acquire the legendary Black Horses of his legions. The author's tender reverence for equine history (she raises horses in Ireland) makes for vivid descriptions of frightened steeds in the hold of a ship across the English Channel; it also allows an undue amount of horsey jargon. A teenage boy interested exclusively in horseshoes rings not quite true, yet the well-drawn story moves along at a compelling trot, climaxing in a battle in which horses help Lord Artos reclaim Britain for future mad cows and Englishmen.

Deborah Stevenson

SOURCE: A review of *Black Horses for the King,* in *Bulletin of the Center for Children's Books,* Vol. 49, No. 9, May, 1996, pp. 306-07.

Galwyn resents his tyrannical uncle and employer and relishes his assignment to assist Lord Artos (better known to us as King Arthur) in obtaining war horses and bringing them to Britain. Once in Britain, he casts his lot with Artos, who retains him to translate the local dialects and to look after the horses. Galwyn finds that his talent with horses earns him friends and enemies; he also joins with old Canyd, esteemed horseman, in developing an effective and necessary horseshoe, learning to shape and shoe, and convincing leaders and allies of the shoes' benefit. Developed from a previously published short story, this is an unusual slant both on Arthurian legend/history and on military strategy. McCaffrey keeps to the historical Arthur

and depicts only this early pre-marriage period but ladles the charisma on—this is clearly a leader who is going places, whether on horseback or not. The military importance of the horses and the significance of the small strategic advantage inherent in the use of horseshoes is well-depicted without becoming dryly factual; these horses whinny and prance and thunder across the field of battle as well as playing a crucial part in defense and conquest. Galwyn himself is a familiar kind of narrator, the young person whose gifts and inherent merit raise him above others and bring him close to the great; his hero-worship and his modesty stale a bit but his enthusiasm will be shared by the readers. Arthur fans, historical fictionites, and military buffs can all find satisfying material here, and they'll all think more seriously on the old adage that begins "For want of a nail, the shoe was lost. . . . "

Cheri Estes

SOURCE: A review of *Black Horses for the King,* in *School Library Journal,* Vol. 42, No. 6, June, 1996, p. 153.

Lord Artos has a vision of using great, black Libyan stallions to carry him and his Companions into battle. To procure them, he and his men sail to Burtigala (Bordeaux), then cross over land to Septimania (the French Mediterranean coast). Galwyn, the ship owner's mistreated nephew, is gifted at languages and handling horses, not at sailing; when the ship reaches port, he runs away to join Artos on his trek. Once the mares and stallions reach Britain safely, the lord returns to Camelot and leaves the lad to learn the new craft of farriery. Artos prepares his army to fight the Saxons, and it is Galwyn's job to demonstrate the iron horseshoes and find a way to make them hold up in battle. Tension is introduced by the impending Saxon invasion and by a dismissed employee who seeks to sabotage the mission. The Latin and Celtic names and the large cast take some time to sort out, but become easier to manage as readers get into the story. Galwyn is the only character who is developed, and he matures nicely into a valued member of Artos's team. The book ends after the first Battle of the Glein, leaving readers wanting a sequel. McCaffrey's unromanticized portrait of the times is full of muck and grit, and horse lovers and fans of historical fiction will find much to enjoy in the details. An excellent companion to Rosemary Sutcliff's Arthurian fantasy trilogy.

Ann A. Flowers

SOURCE: A review of *Black Horses for the King,* in *The Horn Book Magazine,* Vol. 72, No. 4, July/August, 1996, p. 467.

The famed author of fantasy has broadened her literary domain by writing a historical novel of Arthur and his times that is both the story of a young man's coming of age and—more unusually—of the introduction of iron shoes for horses. Galwyn is the son of a wealthy trader whose death has left him as the despised and mistreated apprentice to his uncle, the captain of a small cargo vessel. By chance Arthur and his companions, on their way to buy Libyan horses, travel on his ship, and Galwyn escapes from his uncle and attaches himself to the kindly and encouraging Arthur. Galwyn returns to Britain with Arthur's horses and is sent to learn horseshoeing, a novel and deeply distrusted idea at the time, and to be trained in the care of horses. As Galwyn matures, increasing in strength and knowledge, he overcomes his lack of confidence and becomes Arthur's shoeing smith. The wonderful horse lore, the great and charismatic figure of Arthur, and the sympathetic hero all come together to make an engrossing and realistic Arthurian novel. An afternote by the author points out the historical background and the rise and importance of horseshoeing.

The Junior Bookshelf

SOURCE: A review of *Black Horses for the King,* in *The Junior Bookshelf,* Vol. 60, No. 4, August, 1996, p. 158.

This is a book to be read in one go. The young Gladwyn, practically a slave to his cruel and greedy uncle, by chance becomes involved in the scheme of the Lord Artos (Arthur) to build a cavalry force of great horses to help him drive out the Saxon invaders. This takes him to France and later to Chester and other important centres such as Camelot to serve Artos directly. He is schooled in the health of horses by a horse-wise herbalist, and learns to make and fit the horseshoes which will make Artos' horses less prone to injury and disease. He serves Artos as courier and wins golden opinions from those close to him.

Anne McCaffrey claims she had sworn to eschew Arthurian tales but one can't help feeling delighted she changed her mind. The result is a handsomely arranged story with an attractive main character and a wealth of historical background and practical information. No Hollywoodisms here and no Tennysonian romance either, but the goods.

Linda Newbery

SOURCE: A review of *Black Horses for the King,* in *School Librarian,* Vol. 44, No. 3, August, 1996, p. 120.

This is a novel set in Arthurian times which answers a question Anne McCaffrey set herself after reading Rosemary Sutcliff: where did King Arthur get his war-horses? She makes no attempt to emulate the romance and lyricism of Sutcliff's Arthurian tales, or indeed to introduce the well-known characters of Merlin, Lancelot or Guinevere; her tale is based firmly in the practicalities of fifth-century survival and of buying, transporting and caring for horses. The main character, Galwyn, initially ship's boy for his cruel uncle, absconds with Lord Artos (Arthur) and learns the farrier's trade—the new craft of fitting horses with 'sandals' to equip them for the strain of carrying heavy knights and weaponry. The setting is stronger than the plot, which hinges on the build-up to the fight against the Saxons and, with some contrivance, the malevolent intentions of Galwyn's slighted rival, Iswy. If Galwyn were more fallible—he is invariably conscientious, kind and brave, and his loyalty to Lord Artos is never tested—he would be more rounded as a character. However, this is a well-written and thoroughly researched novel which will appeal to confident readers of 10 and above who like an adventure story with a real sense of the past.

Linnett Hunter

SOURCE: A review of *Black Horses for the King,* in *Magpies,* Vol. 11, No. 4, September, 1996, p. 38.

Those readers familiar with McCaffrey's **Dragonquest** series will know only too well her great skill at breathing life into the shadowy figure of myth and fable. Never will I forget the scene as the young dragons emerged from their eggs . . . but that's another story. In this one, it's the young King Arthur who emerges, a courageous flesh-and-blood leader of great vision who inspires all about him. He is seen through the eyes of Galwyn Varianus, a young Roman-Celt who joins Artos (as Arthur is known) on his journey across the Mediterranean seeking the great Libyan horses who will carry the Companions to battle against the Saxons.

The story gallops along. Galwyn is an eager follower of Artos, but the real heroes of the tale are the horses. For anyone wanting a story of equine exploits, wonderfully told, this is a must. The introduction of horse *sandals* is imagined in every convincing detail as Galwyn trains to become the first farrier. . . .

Additional coverage of McCaffrey's life and career is contained in the following sources published by Gale Research: *Authors and Artists for Young Adults,* Vol. 6; *Contemporary Authors New Revision Series,* Vol. 55; *Major Authors and Illustrators for Children and Young Adults; Something About the Author Autobiography Series,* Vol. 11; and *Something About the Author,* Vol. 70.

Barry Moser

1940-

American illustrator and author of fiction, nonfiction, picture books, and retellings.

Major works include *Alice's Adventures in Wonderland* (1982; written by Lewis Carroll), *In the Beginning: Creation Stories from Around the World* (retelling by Virginia Hamilton, 1988), *Little Tricker the Squirrel Meets Big Double the Bear* (written by Ken Kesey, 1990), *Appalachia: The Voices of Sleeping Birds* (written by Cynthia Rylant, 1991), *Through the Mickle Woods* (written by Valiska Gregory, 1992).

INTRODUCTION

Acclaimed for his dramatic watercolors and meticulous wood engravings, Barry Moser has emerged as one of the foremost book illustrators in America, with over 120 books for primary and middle graders, young adults, and adults to his credit. Moser's art complements editions of literary classics by Dante, Virgil, and Herman Melville, but he is perhaps best known for his illustrations accompanying Lewis Carroll's *Alice's Adventures in Wonderland* and *Through the Looking Glass, and What Alice Found There* (1982) and Joel Chandler Harris's Brer Rabbit stories. He has studied under the direction of artists Leonard Baskin, George Cress, and Jack Coughlin, and with Harold McGrath founded Pennyroyal Press—specializing in finely designed and illustrated limited editions—in Northampton, Massachusetts. An associate of the National Academy of Design, Moser has shown his work internationally in both solo and group exhibits. His impeccable style and technique distinguish him from other artists; he often uses wood engravings—a method of relief printmaking invented in the eighteenth century—that he carves himself, and transparent watercolors, opting, however, for a dark palette not typical of the medium.

Moser admits that he is rarely inspired by fantasy or "flights of imagination," instead preferring simple, realistic compositions that focus on character, setting, or objects. He uses light and dark shadings to create dramatic images that leave an indelible impression on the reader. Striving to infuse texts with "the warp and weft of place and voice," Moser views illustration as more than merely enhancing a story—it is equal to and interconnected with text, typography, and overall design. Known for his exquisite calligraphy and careful attention to detail, Moser wants most of all to produce works that are aesthetically attractive. "Handsome books are the result of harmony—the arranging and combining of elements in pleasant and interesting ways that ultimately form a whole," he commented in *Children's Book Critic*. "The books I make . . . are all done for the same purpose—to make a beautiful *book*."

Biographical Information

Moser was born in Chattanooga, Tennessee, in 1940. Though he came from a loving and close-knit family, his childhood passion for drawing was not nurtured in what he described as a "southern male-oriented" home. However, apprenticing in his uncle's woodworking shop provided some creative outlet for his talent, and the experience taught him self-discipline, perseverance, and to strive for perfection. After receiving his secondary education at the Baylor School, a military academy, Moser enrolled at Auburn University in Alabama where he majored in mechanical engineering but immersed himself in his drawing and design classes. He later left Auburn for financial reasons, returning to his home state to study painting at the University of Chattanooga. In 1962, he graduated from college and married artist Kay Richmond. A year later, his first of three children was born. Moser taught typing, mechanical drawing, and occasional art classes at McCallie military academy for five years. With his young family in tow, he moved to Massachusetts in 1968 and landed a teaching position at the Williston Academy. His own art education also flourished; he learned the skills of making etchings and wood engravings, working with type, life drawing, book design, and calligraphy under the direction of Baskin, Coughlin, and McGrath. In 1969, he crafted his first book by hand—setting the type, running the printing press, and folding and gathering sheets of paper for an edition of American painter James Abbott McNeill Whistler's essay *The Red Rag*. Over the next decade he produced some of his best-known art, illustrating such classics as *Frankenstein* (1983) and *The Adventures of Huckleberry Finn* (1985), and collections by poet Robert Frost. In addition, Moser founded Pennyroyal Press with McGrath and Jeff Dwyer, and in the 1980s focused his attention primarily on books for children, illustrating two *Alice* texts and the Brer Rabbit stories, for which he won several awards. His impressive body of work also includes self-illustrated writings for children in the folk tale tradition, such as a recasting of Hans Christian Andersen's *The Tinderbox* (1990) and *Polly Vaughn* (1992), inspired by a traditional English ballad. Moser's works are found in many museums and collections, including the Library of Congress, Harvard University, the London College of Printing, Cambridge University, and the British Museum.

Major Works

Moser's artwork for Lewis Carroll's *Alice's Adventures in Wonderland*—published as a hand-printed limited edition in 1982 by Pennyroyal Press—represents a drastic departure from the pictures done by previous illustrators of the children's classic, most notably John Tenniel. Depriving the reader of the traditional role of "voyeur," in which he or she observes Alice engaged with the other characters in realistically depicted scenes, Moser presents Wonderland—a skewed and sometimes sinister dream world—through her eyes; Alice herself appears in only four of the seventy-five wood engravings, imbuing the characters inside the rabbit hole with an even greater presence. The inhabitants of Moser's Wonderland teeter on the brink of insanity—the Mad Hatter stares intently into space as he hold his teacup upside down, the Queen of Hearts is a cross-eyed, crazed elderly woman, and the Cheshire Cat looks hideous. Moser's use of blacks and shadows to depict these unique characters captures what he refers to as the "calculated pandemonium" of Carroll's text. *In the Beginning: Creation Stories from Around the World*, retold by Virginia Hamilton and illustrated by Moser, contains twenty-five versions of the creation story, including myths from Australia, Greece, China, and Tahiti. Each myth opens with a dark, powerful full-page watercolor by Moser that provides an excellent complement to Hamilton's simple writing style and solemn tone. A book less for children than for young adults interested in comparative religion and cultures, *In the Beginning* brought both Hamilton and Moser critical acclaim and was named a Newbery Honor Book in 1989. In *Little Tricker the Squirrel Meets Big Double the Bear*, Moser collaborated with *One Flew Over the Cuckoo's Nest* author Ken Kesey to create a picture book that is both entertaining and masterful in terms of text and pictures. This fable is about a shrewd squirrel who outsmarts an imposing bear intent on eating every critter in the forest. Moser's evocative watercolors, depicted in rich, deep tones on the book's right-hand pages, convey both a sense of peril and wit.

In contrast to some of the lively folktales Moser had previously illustrated, *Appalachia: The Voices of Sleeping Birds* is a quieter book about the work and domestic lives of people from a region of the country that both the author—West Virginian Cynthia Rylant—and illustrator regard as close to home. The lyrical text conveys a sense of rootedness and generational connection as it details the daily routine and rituals of this coal-mining community and the natural landscape circumscribed by the Appalachian Mountains. Moser, who designed the book as well, leaves a wide border of white space around each picture, creating such a realistic effect that his images, according to *Booklist*, have the "timelessness and humanity of Depression-era photographs." A picture book for older children, *Through the Mickle Woods*, written by Valiska Gregory, is in essence a quest story: a young boy and a grieving king follow instructions left by the dead queen to search the woods for a bear, who, in turn, tells them three stories containing universal truths. In this work, Moser achieves what is of supreme importance to him—a "perfect union" between pictures and text. His opening watercolors are dark and wintry, reflecting the king's sorrow, while the later ones possess a luminescent quality that highlights the story's final message of love and hope.

Awards

Moser received an American Institute of Graphic Arts Award of Merit, 1982-86. He also received several honors for *Alice's Adventures in Wonderland*, including an American Book Award for pictorial design, 1983, Bookbuilder's West Award of Merit, 1983-86, and *Communication Arts* Award of Merit, 1984-86. *Jump!: The Adventures of Brer Rabbit* was recognized as an American Library Association Notable Book in 1986 and a Child Study Association of America Best Book of the Year in 1987. Also in 1987, *Jump Again!: More Adventures of Brer Rabbit* was designated a *New York Times* Best Illustrated Book of the Year and an American Library Association Notable Book. *In the Beginning: Creation Stories from Around the World* was recognized as an American Library Association Notable Book in 1988 and a Newbery Medal Honor Book in 1989. *Appalachia: The Voices of Sleeping Birds* won the *Boston Globe-Horn Book Award* for nonfiction in 1991 and *Little Tricker the Squirrel Meets Big Double the Bear* received an illustration award from the International Board on Books for Young Children in 1992.

AUTHOR'S COMMENTARY

Barry Moser

SOURCE: "Illustrator at Work: Barry Moser," in *Publishers Weekly,* Vol. 226, No. 1, July 6, 1984, pp. 50-51.

In a recent talk before an audience at New York City's Endicott bookstore, Moser, proprietor of the Pennyroyal Press, in an unusually frank look at himself and his techniques, unfurled what might be termed his "philosophy of art for the book."

While reading in my studio one day I came across a letter by George Bernard Shaw to the then prominent engraver, John Farley. The letter was brief but contained four elements that I think are important to any artist who works with the book as his medium. It read as follows: "Dear Sir, As I am old and out of date I have not the privilege of knowing you or your work. But Mr. William Maxwell of Clark's of Edinburgh tells me you can design, draw and engrave pictures as part of a printed book, which you can understand is something more than making a picture and sticking it in a book as an illustration. The idea is that you and I and Maxwell should cooperate in turning out a good-looking volume consisting of a story contained in the enclosed proof sheets (please hold them as very private and confidential) and, say, a dozen pictures. Are you sufficiently young and unknown to read the story and make one trial drawing for me for, say, five guineas, that is, if the job interests you. Sincerely yours, G. Bernard Shaw."

[Moser then selected key quotes from the letter to illustrate his points.]

"If the job interests you." This involves choice of the text. What texts do you do—for the horizon is full of possibilities. A text I choose must seed my mind and have a market. I know it is not popular for an artist to talk about money, but as far as I'm concerned there is no reason to choose a text that has a limited market when you can choose a text that has a broad one.

"Are you sufficiently young and unknown . . . to make one trial drawing for me for, say, five guineas?" I don't want to belabor this point, except to quote from the last sentence of Chapter 32 on Cetacea of Melville's *Moby-Dick:* "Oh time, strength, cash and patience." These are inextricable from the life of the arts. Works take time, the artist needs stamina and patience to stay with it, and funds with which to exist during the project. The sentence is one of the few things I have ever engraved in wood.

"The idea is that you and I and Maxwell should cooperate. . . ." This is a matter of collegiality. The illustrated book, which is different from the typographic book, does not belong to any one person, neither to the author any more than it belongs to the illustrator, any more than, on a different level, to the craftsman who had manufactured its paper, to the designers and punch-cutters who had drawn and cut the punches for its type, to the compositors who had composed the type, to the impositors who had imposed it, any more than it belongs to the pressman who has midwifed the book to a physical reality, nor to the binder, who ultimately cradles it between its boards to give it a substance that allows it to go out to be held in the hand to be read. The art of the book is an act of solidarity and collegiality. It is more closely akin to the-

ater or architecture than to painting or sculpture. Designer and illustrator are craft-fellows to typographers and printers, to papermakers and bookbinders, to editors and publishers. The whole book is spawned in a community of peers.

"Mr. Maxwell . . . tells me you can design, draw and engrave pictures as part of a printed book, which you can understand is something more than making a picture and sticking it in a book as an illustration." This is perhaps the most complex and therefore the most important of the four points. The book is an organic whole, a single voice, a single form. When I see images from a book tacked up on a wall they look out of place. They need to be tied together because that's what they have been designed for.

I don't know where ideas come from. One moment you have none, the next moment you do. Deadline pressure seems to make them flow more readily. Happily, with the *Alice* books I had all kinds of ideas. The creation of illustrations is often a merging of the theoretical and the practical. This was the case of one *Alice* illustration idea I had for the falling-down-the-well dream scene. I discussed this with people in the theater department of Smith College, who were helping me design an authentic period costume, about making an apparatus inside the costume consisting of a pongee cord to which I could hook up one of my daughters. The theory was to attach her to a hanging ring in a gymnasium with me lying flat on my back, taking pictures underneath her, and have her bounce up and down on the cord trying to create a falling effect. But, in practice, it never would have worked, since the gestures of a human form falling in space are different from those of a secured weight on which gravity is acting.

Although I wanted to explore it, I was diverted by information I came by that was to change the nature of my approach. From a concordance to *Alice* then being written by a scholar at the University of Colorado, I was astonished to learn of the number of times the words "death" and "dying" and "lone" and "lonely" came up in the text. It came to me then that reality was the key, not the dream scenes. So I abandoned the falling idea and of ever seeing Alice except when she's awake. The only time we see Alice within the dream is when she sees herself in the looking glass, which is an announcement of the next book, *Alice Through the Looking Glass.* I used the mirror image to play the two books against each other—images from one book being identical in position and outline with images in the other. If you lay the two *Alice* books side by side and flip the pages simultaneously from the back of one book and the front of the other, you find that some illustrations are exact mirror images—duplications. In *Alice in Wonderland,* 10 pages from the back, there is a double spread of the jury that is at the bottom of the page, with two large hats going up into the margin. Close the pages and those two hats close on top of each other and are, in fact, mirror images. Ten pages from the front of *Alice Through the Looking Glass* are two chess sets that do exactly the same thing. In fact, if you pile the books one on top of the other and drive a nail through them both, it would pass through exactly similar points, particularly eyes, in both books. The hatter and the hare in *Alice* and the hatter and the hare in *Looking Glass* are based on the same two images, and if one traced them both they would be identical and the tracings could be interchanged.

Mary Wollstonecraft Shelley's *Frankenstein,* which I recently completed, was a difficult book to do. It was the first one I did using color in the image. I "see" in black and white and I create my images in black and white. But *Frankenstein* changed all that. The book contains 10 color plates and its typography is rigidly black and white. There are no paragraph breaks. Instead, I used tiny crosses for paragraph marks, so there are little black spots all the way through, but the pages are always a rectangle and always mechanically the same, each page 31 lines long. Even at the end of a volume (the book is written in three volumes), I designed the layout of the last page so as to end in a triangular point of type that is 31 lines from the top line.

Color is nonexistent in the book except as it relates to the monster. Ugliness in *Frankenstein* is the book's psychological basis, and I used color to bring it out in a structural sense. I decided the monster had to be very ugly, and in meeting the problem head on I decided to go to color to give him special intensity.

In the middle of the work, the monster comes back and in a monologue tells Frankenstein what he has been doing over the past two or three years. During that monologue, I have shown the monster eight times in what I call conversational portraits—his head turns slightly, gestures change, the light changes. In them, the monster's color becomes more and more complex—the first image is one color under black, then two colors under black, then three colors. Then I play yellow over red over a second red, then the second red over the first red over the yellow, playing it in reverse order. And I continue building color for the subsequent portraits. The frontispiece—a tree being blown apart by lightning—is the motif of the book and is a pale blue overprinted with black. In the book's last image—the last thing the monster says is "farewell"— his face is literally going out of the picture, thrown way up into a corner; his back is also printed with blue.

Once an idea is in place, the search for the image begins. Images can emerge from a lot of research. Some I do in my library, which contains visual material rather than books purely for reading—history, objects, costumes, anatomy, curiosities and the like. This kind of material comes in handy when I'm called in to handle just one aspect of a job, like cutting the woodblocks for *Moby-Dick.* That wasn't my book and I didn't create the illustration concept, but was hired because my hands could cut the blocks. The publisher felt that no one should interfere with, or interpret, Melville's novelistic art. The illustrator should do nothing more than build "stage sets" for it, that is, simply illustrate for the reader authentically detailed elements of whaling at that time. So my woodcuts are of harpoons, tackle, long boats, whales and the like. At the time I thought the approach was a good one. But I have my own ideas about the illustrating of *Moby-Dick* and am longing for a chance to do the book again, but from a dramatic point of view, interfering, as it were, with Melville's work.

In researching, I go as far down into a project as I possibly can. In doing *Huckleberry Finn,* for instance, in order to depict a trip down the Mississippi River I sat on a boat in the middle of the river with a camera to capture the essence of the scene. (I use a camera as a tool to record in a permanent way what my eyes see.)

I may not use a single piece of research I come up with, but it's there. It's part of the well I have to dip into. And no matter what I find, whether I use it or not, it all makes the final work richer.

In creating the image of the monster in *Frankenstein,* I did not rely on conventional research. For instance, I didn't turn to a memory of Boris Karloff, who played the monster in the original film version. To avoid stereotyping and to give the image true ugliness, my 18-year-old daughter and I took a human skull, built up areas with plasticene, covered it with chicken skin and then sewed it with coarse black thread to create the suture lines. I must have taken over 300 pictures of it, and it was from those pictures that the image was created.

I bought a 500mm lens for my camera, which I am using specifically to capture faces of outpatients at the State Mental Hospital in Northampton, Mass., for the day I do my own *Moby-Dick.* I want to use such faces as the crew of the *Pequod.* I can't capture them by sketching, because I'm not that fast or that good. But standing unobtrusively at a distance with a 500mm lens, I can do it.

When I get into a project I live an intense life. When I did *Alice,* I'd get up at 4 o'clock in the morning and work for 17 hours a day, seven days a week, for eight or nine months and damn near killed myself. As Bernard Shaw said, "Whiskey makes it possible."

Barry Moser

SOURCE: "Artist at Work: Illustrating the Classics," in *The Horn Book Magazine,* Vol. LXIII, No. 6, November/ December, 1987, pp. 703-09.

Frequently I am asked, "What's it like to illustrate a story someone else has illustrated so well before, like *Alice in Wonderland*?" Robert Frost said that education is a matter of taking a kid from where he is to "where he ain't." The statement is also true of illustration. The task of the illustrator is not merely to supply pictures for a text but to take the text from where it is to where it "ain't." Where it "ain't" may closely parallel the author's intentions; on the other hand, the story may be taken to a point never imagined by the author.

When the latter situation occurs, it is always a surprise

for me because I see the role of illustrator as that of a servant, a servant to the literature. I never intentionally contradict nor do I take unreasonable license with a text. But regardless of how illustrations do or do not parallel the author's intentions, if I have done my job well, I will have at least provoked the text with images, which, in the hands of the reader, will seem holistic and inseparable from the typography and the story.

Typography is an invisible art. If the reader is aware of it, it hasn't been done well and therefore isn't art. Illustration, on the other hand, is hardly invisible; but if it interferes with the reading of the text, it is contradictory to the function of the book and should be deleted. The pictures must seem to have grown there, as if they were inevitable, an organic part of the whole. Though illustrations may occur unexpectedly and dramatically, as elements in the literature do, they should occur with reason and never disrupt what John Gardner calls the "vivid and continuous fictional dream."

When I begin a project, much of my time is spent in the procrustean bed—designing typography; writing specifications for typesetting; organizing and proportioning margins; figuring out the cadence, scale, and placement of illustrations; and designing tables of contents, chapter openings, and title pages (which always come last). Only when these things are accomplished to my satisfaction, until they seem invisible and inevitable, do I begin inventing images.

Some people apparently believe that inventing images for a text closely associated with particular illustrations is the most daring, intimidating, even sacrilegious project an illustrator can undertake. For instance, when I began to illustrate Lewis Carroll's *Alice in Wonderland,* Leonard Baskin told me that he thought it was foolish to compete with John Tenniel. I did not then, nor do I now, see it as foolish. I do not see art as a matter of competition. I see other artists as colleagues, not adversaries. It would be foolish for me or any other artist to think that new illustrations would not be compared with their historic antecedents. It would be equally foolish to think that contemporary illustrations will replace historical illustrations. What inevitably happens is comparison.

I have also illustrated *Divine Comedy, Moby-Dick, Frankenstein,* and *The Wonderful Wizard of Oz* (all University of California). When I made illustrations for Dante, I put my work in the arena with Botticelli, Blake, Dore, Lebrun, Baskin, and Rauschenberg. When I made new images for *Moby-Dick,* I knew my work would be compared to Rockwell Kent's. How could I not risk comparison with the great Celluloid illustrators when I illustrated *Frankenstein* and *The Wonderful Wizard of Oz*? Boris Karloff's monster and Judy Garland's Dorothy are fixed in the public's mind. Though neither book was accurately treated by its film interpretation, those two images pose the most difficult problems of overcoming archetypical preconceptions, Alice and Ahab notwithstanding. Film is a powerful illustration medium. After all, that is what film-making is—telling illustrated stories in a continuous,

spatiotemporal, photographic medium. By contrast, book illustration is staccato, pictorial, and static. Illustrations for a book, like stills from a film, carry the action or personality of the story in a continuous line throughout the entire suite of static pictures, giving movement and establishing an overall pattern. Illustrations punctuate the text with atmosphere, timbre, and cadence—isolating characters, establishing settings, and depicting events.

As intimidation is virtual, one must be assertive, daring, self-assured, iconoclastic, and somewhat sacrilegious when illustrating anew the great texts. Botticelli, Blake, and Lebrun are certainly intimidating. Artists like Doré, Flaxman, Stradanus, and Tenniel are less awe-striking. I am always surprised that John Tenniel's name inevitably surfaces as the sine qua non of book artists. When I study the Tenniel pictures, I see only quaintness, not greatness. I am neither overwhelmed nor even impressed by the gestures, the draftsmanship, the characterizations, the embellishments of his drawings.

I found *Alice* accessible, first of all, because I had never read the book to myself or to my children. I was only casually aware of the Tenniel illustrations. Second, I found illustrating *Alice* accessible because I discovered that the little girl for whom Lewis Carroll wrote the story, Alice Liddell, was a dark-haired child-beauty with whom he was most definitely in love and that he used her likeness in his own illustrations for the story. His photographs of Alice Liddell as a beggar maid are masterpieces of subtle Victorian eroticism. In the most famous she leans against an ivy-covered wall, her tattered dress exposing a naked shoulder and leg, her feet bare, one hand on her hip, the other in a drooping gesture of begging. In his holograph version of *Alice,* which he originally called *Alice's Adventures Under Ground,* Carroll pasted in a photograph of Alice Liddell as a *cul de lampe* at the tail of the final verso. In the other illustrations Carroll drew a dark-haired heroine. No doubt he had his Alice in mind. Yet, when he instructed Tenniel-and he instructed Tenniel frequently in matters of illustration-as to the physiognomy of Alice, he sent him a photograph of Mary Hilton Badcock to use as a model. The photograph of little Miss Badcock shows a rather pretty-though haughty, blond child, sitting in a straight-backed chair, arms folded impudently, a ribbon in her hair, and wearing strapped patent-leather shoes. Why Carroll changed his mind so drastically about the image of Alice is subject for dispute and speculation.

So a key to illustrating *Alice* anew was found in Carroll's original illustrations and with his original inspiration, Alice Liddell at age ten. The result was that my Alice is dark. She is not based directly on Alice Liddell, however, but on my own daughter, Madeline, who at the age of ten, was a spitting image of the real Alice. Furthermore, since the story is a dream sequence and since it is rude to accompany people on dream journeys, I simply moved my illustrator's point of view to within Alice's head and peered out. I depicted what I imagined she was seeing, representing the story as I had seen it in my first reading, through her eyes, from her point of view. Hence, we never see

Alice seeing, except once when she espies herself in a looking glass.

For these rather simple and obvious conceits, my *Alice in Wonderland* has been praised for being original and different. It is. It is different not for the sake of being different; it is different from the core out—intrinsically, organically, and philosophically different. In contrast to John Tenniel's drawings stand the drawings of A. B. Frost for the tales of Uncle Remus. For me they were far more intimidating. Though many consider Frost a lightweight, his images for Joel Chandler Harris's tellings of the black American folk tales gave me serious pause before I could get a grip on *my* Brer Rabbit. I have reflected on that often and have concluded that it was because I associated Frost's drawings with my first readings and therefore made them sacrosanct. This is the primary reason people accept only the Tenniel pictures as the authentic *Alice* illustrations. Otherwise, why did the designers of "Alice in the Palace," say, hark back to Tenniel. Or Arthur Rackham? Is it because Tenniel's are definitive? Is it because people, afraid of falling short by comparison, distrust their own creativity and doubt the worth of their own ideas? I believe the latter is the case.

Thinking back, I find it odd that I don't hold Walt Disney's Brer Rabbit sacrosanct, because my first exposure to the Uncle Remus tales was as a child, in knickers, when I saw *Song of the South* at the old State Theater in Chattanooga. That must have been 1946 or 1947. Later, in college, when I read the Brer Rabbit stories, I remember being proud that I could read the thick and sometimes difficult dialect. Having been reared and educated in the South, I, of course, had an ear for the dialect. Later, as a parent, I quite naturally chose to read these stories to my daughters. Later still, as a teacher, I read them aloud to my teenage students: the "Wonderful Tar-Baby Story" and the tale that explains why Brer Possum has no hair on his tail. Many years later, when my career in books began, one of my fondest dreams was to someday illustrate an edition of Uncle Remus tales.

The opportunity came when five of the stories were adapted by Van Dyke Parks and Malcolm Jones. The book was called *Jump!* I balked at first because it was an adaptation, and, as I said before, I was very used to Mr. Harris's rendering of the dialect. I balked, too, because I knew that I had to invent characters who were free from the influence of A. B. Frost and would have to stand in comparison to his—my comparisons if no one else's.

When I read the Parks/Jones adaptations, my first reservations disappeared. These adaptations were, I felt, masterful. Van Dyke Parks was raised in Mississippi, Malcolm Jones in South Carolina. They had not only a good ear for the dialect but the enviable ability to retain all the flavor and grit of the original text without condescension or bowdlerization and without being self-consciously white.

My second reservation was not so easily dissipated. Mr. Frost's gestures, draftsmanship, characterizations, and embellishments are wonderful, impeccable, and uncanny.

From Jump Again! More Adventures of Brer Rabbit, *written by Joel Chandler Harris, adapted by Van Dyke Parks. Illustrated by Barry Moser.*

He must have raised rabbits, lived near a rabbit farm or a zoo, or had children who were local animal husbands, because his observation of the animal form is so competent and keen. He understands better than most animal anatomy, and, more important, he understands animal gestures. Although the talent of the German illustrator Wilhelm von Kaulbach comes close to Frost's, his ability to commingle animal gesture and anthropomorphic gesture is short of miraculous. His vignettes fixed Brer Rabbit and Brer Fox in my mind.

To establish my independence from Frost at the outset, I felt that my pictures for *Jump!* had to come from a different point of view. I looked for an idea that would move along the atmosphere, character, and setting coherently and yet be intrinsically different. I never found one. Unlike *Alice,* over which I had complete control, *Jump!* and its sequel, *Jump Again!,* were commissions which had a specific audience—children. With *Alice* I had only to entertain myself, but here I had to entertain children, and it was to that end that I commenced my watercolors for *Jump!,* using the same conventions as the others who have illustrated Harris: James H. Moser, Church, Frost, Kemble, Conde, and Beard.

My first efforts were tenuous: searching for the right format, the right medium, the right mood. The formula for overcoming intimidation is to disregard it and get to work. By dint of hard work, I finally began to emancipate my vision. The pictorial conceit, the characterizations, the mood, and the timbre grew free from my antecedents. I set the stories in southern locales that I know well—Tennessee, Georgia, Alabama, Mississippi. I chose a dusty palette, punctuated with moments of brilliant hue. I placed the stories anachronistically in various parts of the twentieth century using photographs by Walker Evans, Doris Ulmann, Ben Shahn, Jacob Riis, Lewis Hine, Marion Post Wolcott, Russell Lee, and Dorothea Lange as primary resources.

Inevitably, my images took on their own life, quite apart from the resources. While they have much in common, they are quite distinct from the Frost illustrations. Fortunately for me, neither Frost nor the others dealt with the image of Miss Meadows. Frederick S. Church inappropriately figured Miss Meadows's "gals" to be white women —although Miss Meadows's species is never told. The omission happily left room for at least one original contribution to the literature: since many adult readers see that Miss Meadows's place is obviously a "cat house," what else could Miss Meadows be but a cat? In the book she's a cat who's been around the block lots of times.

Illustration is, as George Bernard Shaw said, something more than making pictures and sticking them into a book.

TITLE COMMENTARY

📖 *ALICE'S ADVENTURES IN WONDERLAND*
(1982; written by Lewis Carroll)

John Ashbery

SOURCE: "A Brilliant New 'Alice'," in *Newsweek,* Vol. XCIX, No. 9, March 1, 1982, pp. 74-75.

Alice started the whole thing when she glanced at the book her sister was reading and wondered: "And what is the use of a book without pictures or conversations?" Since then, generations of artists, from Arthur Rackham to Ralph Steadman, have applied themselves to providing the pictures for Lewis Carroll's *Alice's Adventures in Wonderland.* None, however, has succeeded in dethroning Carroll's original illustrator, Sir John Tenniel, whose views of Wonderland have become as closely identified with that splendidly irrational kingdom as Carroll's text.

Now, a new contender, wood engraver Barry Moser, has entered the lists with a formidable undertaking: a magnificently produced, hand-printed limited edition (350 copies) of *Alice,* published by Moser's own Pennyroyal Press. (Pennyroyal, he explains, is "a plant grown by all self-respecting witches.") The 75 wood engravings that illustrate it were shown recently at the Mary Ryan Gallery in New York City, in an exhibition timed to coincide with the 150th anniversary of Carroll's birth on Jan. 27, 1832.

That show is over, but anyone willing to part with $1,000 can own Moser's *Alice,* which comes bound in beautiful violet leather to match the ink that Carroll often used for his letters to children. (The University of California Press is publishing a more moderately priced trade edition later this year.)

Savvy Children: Moser, a 42-year-old Tennessean and sometime Baptist preacher now happily transplanted to Massachusetts where he teaches at the Williston-Northampton School, is perhaps the foremost wood engraver in America. He has already illustrated two out of three volumes of Dante's *Divine Comedy* and an edition of Virgil's Aeneid for the University of California Press and recently has done a widely acclaimed limited edition of *Moby-Dick,* published by Arion Press in San Francisco. His *Alice* pictures are as violent an antidote to Tenniel's quaint realism as anything that Alice imbibed from a medicine bottle, and everything about this new edition seems to be whispering "Drink me—if you think you can stand the consequences." There have been some far-out visual interpretations of Alice before, but none so convincingly elaborated into a world view where innocence and malignancy are inextricably intertwined. This isn't an "adult" Wonderland—it's for savvy children, too—but it has an enigmatic profundity that sets it apart.

It was Moser's decision to present Wonderland as seen through Alice's eyes, thus depriving the reader of his role as a "voyeur"— "There can be no voyeurs to dreams," he says. So we see Alice herself only four times, the last a close-up, in strong, raking light and shadow, with the other characters engraved in the paper as faintly as a watermark, a technique that reproduces the very texture of a dream. Moser discovered that Maddy, the youngest of his three daughters, bears a startling resemblance to photographs of the young Alice Liddell, for whom Carroll wrote the book. So he used Maddy as his model for Alice and found that her tousled hair fit Carroll's allusions to Alice's unkempt locks better than the prim coiffure of Tenniel's version.

The rest of the population of Wonderland has undergone stranger transmogrifications. The Mad Hatter holds a teacup firmly upside down; his bemused stare reminds us that hatters in nineteenth-century England were thought to go mad from exposure to chemicals used in their trade. Moser's hatter is a caricature of the poet Allen Mandelbaum, who translated the Aeneid and the Dante that Moser illustrated. The puppy that chases Alice is a frightening behemoth, and the Cheshire Cat is a far cry from the moonfaced one we know—Moser modeled it after "the hairless Sphinx, a ridiculously rare feline, which like a mule cannot reproduce itself." The creature is shockingly ugly, but that's because Moser considers the Cheshire Cat "a moment of sanity, and sanity is sometimes ugly, in a world where beauty is presented as insane."

Garden: Elsewhere Moser artfully attenuates the shocks. The White Rabbit exudes the hauteur of a French maitre d', yet remains a rabbit for all that. Tenniel's huffy Queen of Hearts has been updated to a cross-eyed, crazed elderly woman with a few shreds of dignity remaining. Some of the images hover on the edge of delirium, like that of the March Hare's house—a thatched brick cottage from which a pair of chimneys shaped like rabbit ears protrudes. Often Moser is most effective when he is most straightforward. The door to the garden which Alice finally unlocks is realistically drawn, but it seems about to burst open with the pressure of the madness behind it.

Moser's wood-engraving technique is never less than dazzling. Unlike most of his colleagues, including Tenniel, he engraves the wood blocks himself, rather than having a technician do it from a drawing. That technical skill may explain why his blacks are so richly Cimmerian and his shadows—the result of an infinity of closely packed, hair-thin black lines—are as insubstantial as the real thing. In a few places one could feel that technique has triumphed over content, as in the final portrait of Alice, which is a bit too suggestive of conventional fashion illustration.

Bravura: Nevertheless, the book captures what Moser calls the "calculated pandemonium" of the text with as much bravura as another recent Carroll offshoot, composer David Del Tredici's "Final Alice," a current best seller among classical records. In depicting his heroine's misadventures from a modern-day viewpoint, Moser has amplified Alice's own words: "Dear, dear! How queer everything is to-day! And yesterday things went on just as usual."

Edward Guiliano

SOURCE: A review of *Alice's Adventures in Wonderland,* in *Fine Print,* Vol. VIII, No. 3, July, 1982, pp. 103-06.

"And what is the use of a book," thought Alice, "without pictures or conversations?" Barry Moser shares with Alice the same iconic regard for print. On the heels of his acclaimed illustrated editions of **Moby-Dick, The Divine Comedy,** and **The Aeneid,** he has brought along an extraordinary **Alice.** It is a splendid marriage of textual editing, literary scholarship and criticism, artistry, and craftsmanship. Publishers like to speak of the publication of a major book as a publishing "event," and although many works are described as such, few of course are: The Pennyroyal **Alice** is. . .

Moser's illustrations to the Pennyroyal **Alice** are . . . the book's most stunning element. Although John Tenniel's illustrations to *Alice in Wonderland* complement and enrich Carroll's text so much and are so wedded to it in the reader's mind that subsequent illustrators must think thrice before attempting a new interpretation, there have been floods of illustrated editions of **Alice.** It seems that **Alice** has become the challenge by which book illustrators are known and judged. Following Tenniel, only a few artists, in my opinion, have been worthy of the task: Arthur Rackham, Peter Newell, Charles Robinson, Willy Pogany, Mervyn Peake, and Ralph Steadman. Barry Moser can now be added to that list.

Moser's **Alice** is distinguished on several counts, starting of course with Moser's supreme gifts as an illustrator and wood engraver. (Unlike Tenniel, Moser does his own engraving.) I need not argue that Moser is one of the preeminent book illustrators now at work in the world, and despite his prodigious achievements, he is, at age forty-two, in the early throes of a brilliant career. Notably, the Pennyroyal **Alice** with its seventy-five wood engravings is perhaps the most lavishly illustrated edition of **Alice** ever, and its iconography is unique.

For one thing, Moser has elected a point of view for his illustrations that has not been seen before. His engravings—beyond the decorative ones—reveal the Wonderland world as seen through Alice's eyes. We see Alice herself only at the beginning, catching a couple of glimpses of her in looking-glasses, and in her sister's dream. *Alice* is not a first-person narrative; it has a third-person narrator who is not above making asides and passing an occasional judgment on the action. But Alice is the reader's surrogate in Wonderland, and that is why Moser's bold decision to reveal Wonderland through our heroine's eyes is successful; it is also reflective of contemporary reinterpretations of *Alice.* Moser's illustrations draw us into Wonderland; we see Wonderland creatures and landscapes that have sinister, bizarre, and threatening overtones because that is how they burst upon Alice's consciousness. Moser has captured an element that many readers find in **Alice,** that many readers perceive through Alice's consciousness, and an element that is not evident or at least not compellingly so in most previously illustrated editions: the "calculated pandemonium" that is Wonderland. The Moser/Alice vision of Wonderland is a complex vision that will speak sharply and eloquently to readers of **Alice.**

Although Moser's iconography is a mad hatter's hat out of which any semiotic conjurer could pull an endless commentary, this is not the place to begin. (Curiously, only recently have Tenniel's illustrations begun to be analyzed profitably.) With seventy-five illustrations, though, it is natural that some of the Pennyroyal's illustrations "work" better than others and that some are more appealing than others. Determining the merits of the experience of illustrations, however, is subjective, so I will only say that among my favorite drawings in the Pennyroyal **Alice** are the two renderings of the rabbit hole, the Mock Turtle, and the Dormouse—some of the rather more traditional drawings. The Mock Turtle is a great lark that plays off the reader's familiarity with Tenniel's version. For his drawing Tenniel depicts the Mock Turtle with the body of a turtle and the head of a cow, and Moser counters with the body of a cow and the head of a turtle. His Dormouse is a great success, and I defy anyone not to be engaged by it. One set of illustrations that bothers me is the decorative floral designs that accompany the prefatory poems. I am especially unsettled by the grapes and vine preceding "To All Child-Readers"; this illustration is jarringly out of step with both the mood and vision of those that follow. Moser justifies it in his afterword as a symbol for Christ taken from St. John's Gospel, the fifteenth chapter—hardly the first association that comes to mind when opening up **Alice.** His final illustration, however, is a triumph. It is an oversized fold-out of Alice waking from her dream, printed in black over a montage of Wonderland characters and creatures that appear apparation-like in white against a buff background.

Joseph Parisi

SOURCE: A review of *Alice's Adventures in Wonderland*, in *Booklist*, Vol. 79, No. 12, February 15, 1983, p. 760.

Though Tenniel has become synonymous with *Alice*, several other illustrators have depicted her adventures, including Steadman, Dalí, and Carroll himself. In approaching this classic, the incisive designer, printer, and wood engraver Barry Moser takes yet another, and refreshingly different, tack: seeing Alice's dream from *her* point of view. In his pithy and thought-provoking preface, the distinguished scholar James Kincaid points out that Carroll's masterpiece is many things to many readers—adults, children, psychoanalysts, mathematicians, logicians, linguists, philosophers, literary critics—but, from whatever perspective, the book remains a dear and disturbing excursion. It is that edgy perplexity that Moser perfectly captures. Graced with his brilliant woodcuts and glossed with precise and witty red-ink marginalia, this presentation is an altogether beautiful example of the bookman's art. . . .

Leonard S. Marcus

SOURCE: "Alice's Adventures: The Pennyroyal Press Edition," in *Children's Literature: Annual of The Modern Language Association Division on Children's Literature and The Children's Literature Association,* Vol. 12, 1984, pp. 175-84.

For more than one hundred years, a parade of artists like hopeful suitors in the fairy tale about the glass mountain have tried their hand at illustrating one or both of Lewis Carroll's *Alice* books. For all that time the woodcut engravings by Sir John Tenniel, prepared for the earliest published editions under Carroll's watchful eye, have somehow remained so nearly synonymous with Wonderland-and-Looking-Glass reality as to seem the inseparable twin of Carroll's elusive art.

Yet if none of Tenniel's successors—excluding for the moment the artist to whose work we will soon turn—can be said to have supplanted him altogether as the *Alice* illustrator of record, memorable images, garden-glimpses as it were of alternative Wonderland visions, have come down to us in the versions of Harry Furniss, Arthur Rackham, Charles Robinson, Willy Pogany, Salvador Dali, and Ralph Steadman, among others. . . .

The Pennyroyal *Alice's Adventures in Wonderland,* in both its trade and limited editions, is a tall, elegantly designed and produced book, illustrated with finely rendered, black-and-white woodcut engravings by Barry Moser. Moser, who is also its designer, is proprietor of the Pennyroyal Press and director of the Hampshire Typothetae of Northhampton, Massachusetts. . . .

Certain visual details of the Pennyroyal *Alice* recall details of the author's life and of *Alice's* earliest published editions. The shade of blue in which chapter headings are printed, for example, is Oxford blue. The spine of the trade volume and the complete binding and slipcasing of the deluxe limited are red cloth, a festive allusion to the bright red covers of the first printings overseen by Carroll—and to his attendant notion that of all colors, red is the one children find most pleasurable. . . .

Once supposed to have been an attentive reader of *Émile,* Carroll may also be imagined to have had Rousseau's memorable assault on the drabber ranges of juvenile literature in mind—"I detest books. . . . Reading is the scourge of Childhood. . . . What do books teach? . . . Words, words, words!"—when he supplied Alice with her own more temperate, though no less sharply expressed, opinion about literature as a whole: "And what is the use of a book . . . without pictures or conversations?"

Carroll, in any case, wasted no time in assuring readers that *his* book was well supplied with pictures and dialogue worth the trouble of lingering over. Moreover, having overseen his collaborator's progress with a fastidiousness that Tenniel would eventually find maddening, Carroll, as much Wonderland's impresario as its author, had made certain that in image and text *Alice* would be all of a piece. Wonderland chaos is chaos of a highly ordered variety.

For readers encountering Lewis Carroll's fantasy for the first time through the Pennyroyal edition, comparison between Moser's art and Tenniel's may be of little concern. But, the Tenniels being as widely dispersed throughout the world as they are—in advertising, on theater posters, on rubber stamps and drinking mugs as well as in editions of Carroll's actual writings—relatively few readers are likely to experience the Pennyroyal without some prior knowledge of the earlier Wonderland graphics. Children of course are somewhat more likely to do so than adults, and the Pennyroyal, at least in its trade version, is not so much of an *edition de luxe* that older children cannot relax with it and be entrusted with it (though it is plainly not a book to be handled with sticky fingers except at one's peril). From a critical standpoint, the main question to ask about the book remains how well it succeeds on its own terms, but comparison to Tenniel is inevitable and so must also be considered. Moser himself seems to have been mindful of this reality as he went about his task.

Many features of the Pennyroyal *Alice* work exceedingly well on terms distinctly (and perhaps intentionally) different from those laid down by Tenniel. On the level of pure graphics, the predominance of black-over-white in Moser's woodcuts is an ingeniously apt Looking-Glass inversion (if not merely a pleasing chance reversal) of the white-over-black impression of the earlier artist's images.

And whereas Tenniel's characteristic line is incisive, steely clear, a stylistic mirror-equivalent for Carroll's lucid, marksmanlike prose, Moser's line is rougher, ruder, more tactile, less predictable, engaging us at gut level in Wonderland's labyrinth of unsettled meanings and fugitive emotions. Illustrations in the Pennyroyal *Alice* emerge from rigorously ordered bundles of these nervelike textural incisions, with certain bundles set against others in contrapuntal rhythmic patterns, or forcefully juxtaposed with solid areas of black or white. In the most effective images—the portraits of the Caterpillar, the Duchess, and the Queen, among others—this skillful linework results in a shimmering moiré effect similar to that achieved by the nineteenth-century French illustrator Gustave Doré in his visionary engravings for (among other works) Coleridge's *Rime of the Ancient Mariner*. The moiré illusion, thus exploited, charges Wonderland with an aura of the uncanny and implies for the characters portrayed a swarming, turbulent inner life or under-life. Readers become enmeshed in a dimly lit chimera-world, a nightmarish vision that strongly hints at the probability that Wonderland, if discoverable at all, must lie somewhere along the trunk-line to the Inferno.

Moser's most ambitious departure from Wonderland-according-to-Tenniel, however, consists of his abandonment of a traditional approach to illustration that is so often the one chosen that we tend to think of it as the only possibility the illustrator has; namely, the convention of illustration as theatrical tableau, under the terms of which scenes from the author's imagined world are presented for an ideal observer perched as it were (and as Carroll often found himself during day trips to the London theater) in one of the house's preferred stalls.

The Tenniels not only conform to this theatrical convention but accentuate it, leaving vague or altogether omitting background scenery so that the page itself can become the primary scene. Carroll's artful use of dramatic dialog, of descriptive writing so finely compressed as to approximate stage directions for the reader's imagination, and of slapstick routines directly inspired by the contemporary English Harlequinade—all contribute to Wonderland's subtly theatrical edge and flavor. The Tenniels' staged quality likewise quickens our sense of Wonderland as an illusion-world of a particularly ambiguous kind: equally a cunning mirror on reality and a manic negation of reality. In the Tenniels, all the world's a stage within a stage within a stage . . . onward to infinity. It is thus (and in the unsparing precision of the artist's caricature, the bite of his satire as of his line) that Tenniel's woodcuts merge so fully with Carroll's elliptical tale.

Moser, like certain experimental theater directors of the sixties and seventies who felt the urgent need to abolish what they perceived to be an artificial barrier separating the actors from their audience, has taken a more confrontational approach to representing Carroll's fantasy. He has attempted to have us come face to face, as Alice herself does, with the towering Caterpillar, the absurdly menacing Hatter, the imperious, murderous Queen; to illustrate Wonderland in the first person. The artist explains:

To illustrate *Alice* entails a certain indelicacy, for *Alice* is a story of loneliness. Its illustrators, beginning with Carroll himself and including Tenniel, Rackham, Steadman, Pogany, Furniss, and Dali have intruded on the privacy of Alice's adventure, standing apart and observing Alice in her dream. They have been voyeurs, and yet there can be no voyeurs in dreams. In the Pennyroyal *Alice,* the images of Alice's dream are always seen from Alice's point of view, for after all the dream *is* Alice's dream . . .

These observations, which seem novel enough both as a critique of earlier attempts at illustrating Carroll's work and as a program for a new edition, overlook one essential feature of the Wonderland narrative: that Carroll interposes himself as an all-seeing presence, an observer looming Cheshire Cat-like at the very edge of Alice's dream. For example: "'Curiouser and curiouser!' cried Alice (she was so much surprised, that for the moment she quite forgot how to speak good English)." "'You ought to be ashamed of yourself,' said Alice, 'a great girl like you,' (she might well say this), 'to go on crying in this way!'" "'Who cares for *you?*' said Alice (she had grown to her full size by this time). 'You're nothing but a pack of cards!'"

The intrusiveness to which Moser objects is thus actually an element of the author's tale. One may of course call this "voyeurism," too. ("Call it what you like," as the Cheshire Cat, sorting out growls and purrs, chillingly advises Alice.) But one would still be left to ponder what purpose such deftly planted dramatic asides—stage whispers more pointed at times than the Duchess's chin—serve in establishing the peculiarly convincing tone and atmosphere and world of the most memorable dream episode in modern literature. Carroll's asides are unsettling, and they disrupt our capacity for believing in the Wonderland dream and more especially for identifying ourselves with Alice.

Adventure fantasies, generally, arouse an overwhelming wish for identification with the hero, for the essence of all such tales of escape is the impulse *to see what happens next* as only the hero is in a position to do; to venture farther into the unknown than one has yet gone in one's own experience. This of course is the motive which impels Alice down the rabbit hole, and, once in Wonderland, sustains her from one puzzling encounter to another, despite periodic doubts suffered at the hands of a well-developed Victorian conscience and of the less time-bound human fear of being overwhelmed by chaos.

Yet Carroll would disturb this wish of ours to escape *like* Alice and *as* Alice, reminding us sharply, as he does at many turns, of the foolishness of certain of her thoughts, actions, and remarks; praising her tongue-in-check for her struggles to remain good in a world where goodness has no apparent referent or value; or merely witnessing her predicament with an amused detachment and unflinching objectivity such as one might well expect of the accomplished and disciplined logician and portrait photographer that Carroll also was, but hardly of an author intent on transporting us deeper and deeper into a conventional type of escapist fantasy. We recoil from Alice emotionally at such moments, though only to be drawn back to her moments later by her next casual leap into Wonderland's rarefied state of pure possibility.

Carroll's purpose in thus dividing our loyalty toward her would seem nonetheless to be dramatic in nature, an attempt to involve us more directly in her ambiguous plight. In dreaming, the self at times adopts the double role of actor and observer, the better to sort through its dilemmas from a clarifying distance; Alice's adventure is essentially a dream of this kind. In Wonderland she becomes radically divided over the matter of her self-identity: "I can't explain *myself* . . . ," she says in one of many expositions of her situation, "because I'm not myself, you see . . . " As readers we find that out of our own confusion of feeling toward her comes a strangely immediate insight into Alice's central predicament. It is as though Carroll, turning Coleridge's formulation on its head decided that it is not so much art as the self which is a fiction requiring of us a "willing suspension of disbelief." Paradoxically, it is in not being quite certain how to feel toward Alice that we as readers experience Wonderland firsthand.

Moser's premise that there can be "no voyeurs in dreams" turns out, then, to be misleading in nearly all its consequences; for not only does Carroll observe Alice's dream; Alice herself does. Illustrating Wonderland from her point of view (in the literal sense of what she saw) does not necessarily yield a more faithful impression of her dream than do the Tenniels; in fact the Tenniels may themselves be said to represent Alice's vantage point—that is, that side of it which consists of detached, intensely concentrated self-observation. Moser's work does not so much correct the earlier illustrations as complement them as no previous *Alice* edition has done. The Pennyroyal also leads us to imagine some future Wonderland that will somehow accommodate both aspects of Alice's double dream.

Even within the limits proposed by Moser, however, more inventiveness might have been shown in illustrating Alice's psychic dislocation, the inner division she experiences between body and mind, as for example when she grows so tall that her feet no longer seem a part of her and she is led to consider sending Christmas presents down to them. Except for one fugitive glance of her catching sight of herself in a mirror, no such instance of Alice looking at Alice has been recorded.

Instead, and as if to emphasize the pervasive mood of loneliness that Moser has found at the story's emotional core, his heroine perceives Wonderland as a series of isolated details—the White Rabbit's watch and gloves, the key to the garden, the bottle standing before a mirror—and as a gallery of monolithic, masklike heads of ferocious intensity edged with whimsy. Few dramatic scenes or actions are portrayed. Characters, rarely seen much below the neck, do not often meet within an illustration's or a double spread's frame.

Alice's reeling contortionist changes of physical size are cleverly implied in the shifting scale of certain images.

The Caterpillar appears, end-to-end, both as the immense and billowingly lugubrious overlord first encountered by shrunken Alice, and as the three-inch creature more familiar to her, and ourselves. The giant puppy that tiny Alice meets after escaping from the Mad Hatter's inhospitable table is depicted close-up—all eyes, nose, and fangs to the bewildered little girl. This last image, intended to make us relive Alice's fright, is however too abstract—*too* close-up—to be very menacing. More visual information is needed for us to accept the dog's menace as real. In certain instances, then, seeing Wonderland from Alice's viewpoint actually becomes a hindrance to imaginative sympathy. Nearly all of Moser's more fully rendered portraits are by contrast bracingly immediate in their claims on our attention. We find ourselves staring at them, warts and all; and one by one they return our gaze.

From the Pennyroyal illustrations, a deep sense of loneliness emerges as from all the failed Wonderland attempts at even the slightest forms of social contact. But in Carroll's text, more so than in Moser's engravings, the feeling is modified, lightened somehow, by the mad persistence with which all press onward with their wildly wrongheaded experiments at society. One misses in the Pennyroyal an illustration of the assembled Tea-Party and the Queen's Croquet-Match. (Moser's cursory depiction of the trial is among the least effective images.) Although lonely, Alice is scarcely overwhelmed by her loneliness. "I almost wish I hadn't gone down that rabbit-hole," she shrewdly remarks early on, "and yet—and yet—it's rather curious, you know, this sort of life!"

Comic characters, Mary McCarthy has observed, are the "incorrigible" ones, those characters who do not learn. Wonderland society is made up entirely of incorrigibles—comic to us and isolated from each other precisely because their experience teaches them nothing.

In the *Alice* books, society is comic theater, as much a fiction to be credited by a "willing suspension of disbelief" as is the self, that mysterious phenomenon which conventional middle-class Victorians so confidently aspired to under the grave rubric of "individual character." For Carroll, character does not exist, only characters. Alice, dreaming, discovers all sorts of characters within herself: a Mad Hatter and a savage Queen as well as an Alice. All are her and not her. To accept such difficult self-knowledge requires a tolerance of more chaos than Alice apparently can bear. She prefers to wake up, to "grow up," to insist that her dreams are her dreams alone.

THROUGH THE LOOKING-GLASS, AND WHAT ALICE FOUND THERE (1983; written by Lewis Carroll)

New York Times Book Review

SOURCE: "Woodcuts from Wonderland," in *New York Times Book Review,* November 13, 1983, p. 13.

Lewis Carroll's *Through the Looking-Glass, And What*

Alice Found There, designed and illustrated by Barry Moser, who first published it as a limited edition from his Pennyroyal Press, is a wonderful spectacle. It is a companion to Mr. Moser's Pennyroyal edition of *Alice's Adventures in Wonderland* that won an American Book Award as best illustrated book of 1982 and is also issued in a trade edition by California.

In *Through the Looking-Glass,* as in its predecessor, Mr. Moser's woodcuts look through Alice's eyes; we see only what she saw. (One exception is the Jabberwock which Alice only heard about; here the beast is the frontispiece.) This is truly a looking-glass world; where Alice saw things backward or as mirror images, so do we. A few characters resemble some in *Alice's Adventures* (Mr. Moser used some people he knows as models for both books) and a few resemble historical figures; the White Knight is Lewis Carroll himself, and if you look closely at Humpty Dumpty, you will see former President Richard Nixon. The book includes a beautiful guide to the chess game underlying the story of *Through the Looking-Glass* and, as an appendix, the **"Wasp in a Wig"** episode which was cut by Carroll from his original and only rediscovered in manuscript in the 1970's.

California has also published a trade edition of Mr. Moser's limited edition of **"The Hunting of the Snark."** In five mysterious woodcuts one can search for the boojum, thus joining the famous hunt in the poem. All these exquisitely printed California editions of Mr. Moser's Pennyroyal originals have eloquent introductions by James R. Kincaid of the University of Colorado. They should delight anyone who loves Carroll, and he could hardly be introduced more elegantly to anyone who does not know him.

Joseph Parisi

SOURCE: A review of *Through the Looking-Glass, and What Alice Found There,* in *Booklist,* Vol. 80, No. 9, January 1, 1984, p. 666.

Follo.....ng the brilliant *Alice's Adventures in Wonderland* illustrator Barry Moser has produced, if such is possible, an even more sumptuous sequel. Although Alice's further adventures, on the other side of the mirror, take place but six months later, the story is now of a much darker hue, perfectly captured in Moser's 92 exquisite and imaginative wood engravings, many of them based on actual personages, including the Reverend Dodgson himself. As editorial collaborator [James] Kincaid observes, this is a most ambivalent book, both for Alice and her creator; as the child rushes gladly yet reluctantly toward adulthood, she loses the charms of youth, while the author mourns the passing of childhood friendships, as evanescent as they are inevitable. The ambiguity, melancholy, and complexity of the book are reflected with great subtlety and mirror much of the earlier volume; and as there, the editor's marginal rubrics are as witty as they are concisely informative. A faithful reproduction of the original Pennyroyal edition, the volume is a beautiful

instance of the bookman's art; and at this price, an unbelievable bargain.

Zena Sutherland

SOURCE: A review of *Through the Looking-Glass, and What Alice Found There,* in *Bulletin of the Center for Children's Books,* Vol. 37, No. 8, April, 1984, p. 144.

Moser, whose design and wood engravings for *Alice's Adventures in Wonderland* won the American Book Award for 1983 in the Design/Pictorial category, does it again. Dramatic black and white pictures, large scale to fit the oversize pages, are highly textured, often using parallel lines, and often grim in their domination of a page. The layout is spacious: the wide margins have often interesting notes, although the small type (red or blue) is not easy to read. Although this can, like any edition of Carroll, be read by children, it seems more appropriate for the scholar (young or old) who may be interested in the marginal notes, the preface, and the concluding notes that accompany the text.

THE ADVENTURES OF HUCKLEBERRY FINN (1985; written by Mark Twain)

Donald A. Barclay

SOURCE: "Interpreted Well Enough: Two Illustrators' Visions of *Adventures of Huckleberry Finn,*" in *The Horn Book Magazine,* Vol. LXVIII, No. 3, May/June, 1992, pp. 311-19.

If Mark Twain's *Adventures of Huckleberry Finn* is not the most frequently illustrated novel in history, it is close to it. *Adventures of Huckleberry Finn* entered the world during a golden age of illustration, a time when sales of novels depended on the quality and quantity of their illustrations. Since that time, Twain's novel has been reborn in some eight hundred editions, many of which are illustrated. While in some of these editions the artwork consists of no more than a token drawing or two, there are many that contain enough serious, thoughtfully executed illustrations to allow the artist to make a statement about his reading of *Adventures of Huckleberry Finn.* Among the most notable of these artistic statements are those of Edward Windsor Kemble, the first illustrator of the novel, and Barry Moser, illustrator of a centennial edition. While the work of Kemble and Moser is strikingly different, comparison of their work on *Huckleberry Finn* leads to insights into how the various elements of illustration affect the look of the final product, as well as how illustration is used to suggest certain readings of a novel. . . .

Though the number of illustrations in Moser's version seems small in comparison to [E. W.] Kemble's, it is typical of post-Kemble editions of *Huckleberry Finn* illustrated by important artists. . . .

Some scenes from the novel have been depicted so often

as to have become clichés, which perhaps explains why artists like Moser have given up trying to pump freshness into these moments and have moved away from producing straight narrative illustration. Many of Moser's illustrations are nonnarrative portraits which resemble period photographs. Some of these portraits have round frames, like daguerreotypes, and the depicted characters' eyes are often blanked out as if the subjects had blinked during a long camera exposure. Moser's nonportrait illustrations edge toward the narrative, but instead of literally depicting the action of the novel, these illustrations are snapshots of objects and settings. Moser shows a frightening steamboat shooting sparks into the night sky but doesn't actually depict it running down Huck and Jim's raft; he shows Peter Wilks's grave back-lit by lightning but doesn't show the eager, angry crowd gathered for the exhumation. The effect is quite different from the mostly narrative standard set down by Kemble and taken up by the majority of illustrators who followed him. Highly atmospheric, Moser's illustrations give the reader the feeling of flipping through an antique photograph album rather than of being led through the story in a narrative sense.

Despite the atmospheric appeal of Moser's illustrations, there is something to be said for the use of narrative illustrations in a literary form as dependent on plot as the nineteenth-century novel. Some moments from *Huckleberry Finn* almost demand to be narratively illustrated. The scene of Huck and Pap at the Widow's is such a moment: there is tremendous drama as Huck confronts the wicked father who has been hunkering in the darkened room, waiting for the unsuspecting boy, and few illustrators of the novel have failed to recognize the scene's potential for depicting a primal conflict between father and son. The moment is also attractive because it is Huck's first direct contact with evil and so allows the artist to set the terms by which the dark side of the novel will be approached. Artists who wish to give full play to the novel's humor can tone down Pap's appearance. Kemble, whose emphasis is basically comic, draws Pap to look more "no' count" than evil, and in the moment of discovery Huck is shown with his hands on his hips, striking a defiant pose to his scruffy father. Rockwell also downplays Pap's malevolence, hiding the brutal father's features behind a comically wild beard. Following a darker path, Worth Brehm, the second American artist to illustrate the novel, shows Pap from Huck's point of view—a glowering head that "cussed me for putting on frills and trying to be better than him." Thomas Hart Benton's Pap is a mean, sharp-faced hillbilly, radiating ignorance and hate. Darkest of all is Moser's depiction of Pap as a disfigured, scar-faced monster. It is hard to imagine the next illustrator of the novel depicting Pap more negatively than Moser, even though illustrators have tended to make Pap increasingly hideous over the years.

The vileness of Moser's Pap raises the issue of whether illustrations for *Adventures of Huckleberry Finn* should have a comic or a serious emphasis. Kemble's illustrations are overwhelmingly comic. He was a cartoonist, after all, and was hired largely because Twain had been amused by a Kemble cartoon on the possible uses of electricity.

Ironically, one of Kemble's suggested uses was to electrify one's doormat in order to fend off subscription book salesmen. While few of Kemble's illustrations for the novel are serious, and none are truly dark, most of Moser's illustrations are both. Not only is Moser's Pap a monster, but almost every character is drawn to look mean or ugly. Scars, missing teeth, and warts abound. Even Mary Jane Wilks—who is good, young, and pretty in the novel—is made to look ugly. And her younger sisters fare much worse. Moser also gives a smug, selfish face to the Widow Douglas, the loving Christian foil to Miss Watson's stern, self-serving Puritanism. If Moser's vision of the bulk of the novel's characters is not spelled out in his portraits, the illustrations entitled "Huck's Surrogate," depicting a pig with its throat cut, and "Miss Sophia's Testament," depicting pigs in church, make his vision quite clear.

The great exception Moser makes is in his illustrations of Jim, who appears nearly Olympian in his beauty and dignity, especially in comparison to Moser's cast of hideous white characters. Just as Moser's dark vision of the novel is part of the hundred-year progression toward more serious readings of the novel, so too is his ennobling of Jim part of a long progression away from Kemble's Jim Crow art. Though only a few of Kemble's illustrations of Jim are blatant, rolling-eyed-darky exaggerations, there is much subtle racism in Kemble's portrayal of Jim, as shown in the illustrations depicting Jim taking submissive positions to whites. Despite Kemble's racism, however, a few of his drawings manage to make Jim look noble, such as the illustration of Jim asleep at the steering oar and the illustration showing Jim heroically insisting on a doctor for the wounded Tom Sawyer, a boy whose game-playing has caused Jim raftloads of trouble.

Besides presenting a super-heroic view of Jim, Moser's illustrations also differ from Kemble's in their explicitness. Moser shows Pap in gruesome death, naked and shot in the back, and he shows the King naked as he dances "The King's Cameloopard." Among the post-Kemble illustrators of *Adventures of Huckleberry Finn,* Moser is not alone in depicting nudity—Benson drew bare-breasted witches, and many illustrators have shown, discreetly, a naked, dancing King—but Moser's depiction of nudity is distinctly explicit. This freedom to be explicit was not granted to Kemble, an artist confined by the moral standards of his day. . . .

The shock some readers feel upon seeing Moser's illustrations underscores something that Twain himself understood when he censored Kemble's depiction of the camp meeting. In censoring Kemble, Twain recognized that text can get away with more than illustrations. This is a tribute to the immediacy of illustration as well as an acknowledgment of the power of illustration to shape a reader's interpretation of a novel even before the reader has cast an eye on the first word of the text. As with any power, illustration is a power to be used, and Twain certainly used illustration both to sell copies of *Adventures of Huckleberry Finn* and to present an immediately accessible image of his novel as a bit of good, clean fun spiced with a few moments of danger and sentiment. It takes a more-than-casual reading to discover the disturbing side of *Huckleberry Finn* that lurks below the surface visual image, and one suspects Twain knew that it was the casual reader who was most likely to be influenced by illustration—as well as most likely to censor *Huckleberry Finn* with a battle axe if the illustrations sent the wrong message. That Twain knew he could get into more trouble over a picture than a phrase is clear from the pains which he and his publisher, Charles L. Webster, took to stamp out all traces of the infamous obscene plate that held up production of the first American edition of *Adventures of Huckleberry Finn.*

The later producers of illustrated editions of *Huckleberry Finn* are doing nothing new in using illustrations for purposes economic and political. There is really nothing surprising in the fact that illustration is still used to sell Twain's novel as something it may not entirely be: a children's book; a plea for total racial equality; a knee-slapping comedy; or a journey to the depths of the psyche. What is surprising is that new illustrated editions of *Adventures of Huckleberry Finn* continue to appear to this day, some seventy years after the golden age of illustrated fiction. Why, in an era when readers neither expect nor demand illustration with their fiction, is Twain's book still being illustrated by first-rate artists such as Barry Moser? It may be because *Huckleberry Finn* still carries the cachet of a children's book, and children's books are frequently illustrated. It may be because readers of this very nostalgic novel feel comfortable being immersed in the nostalgic experience of reading an illustrated novel. Or it may be a reflection of the general conservatism of the book arts: since the first edition was illustrated, then later editions should be illustrated as well. Perhaps it is the result of all three of these circumstances. Whatever the causes, it seems likely the tradition of illustrating *Adventures of Huckleberry Finn* will continue. While it is hard to imagine the year 2084 giving birth to an illustrated edition of *Catch-22* or *The Handmaid's Tale* or any other novel that was not originally part of the illustrated-novel tradition, an illustrated bicentennial edition of *Huckleberry Finn* seems a sure bet. It is almost certain that an illustrator not yet born will put a hand to the task of artistically interpreting the novel once again; will set out to shape the characters, setting, and spirit of the novel for a generation still capable of appreciating, through words and pictures, the humor and humanity of Mark Twain's, and maybe this nation's, greatest novel.

IN THE BEGINNING: CREATION STORIES FROM AROUND THE WORLD (retelling by Virginia Hamilton, 1988)

Kirkus Reviews

SOURCE: A review of *In the Beginning: Creation Stories from Around the World,* in *Kirkus Reviews,* Vol. LVI, No. 18, September 15, 1988, pp. 1403-04.

A leading author and illustrator collaborate in a fine compilation of creation myths—a basic component of any folklore collection.

Each of the 25 stories is told in spare, dignified language appropriate to its source and is followed by a brief discussion of its origin and type. While many cultures are included, there is more emphasis on presenting a variety of mythological figures and interpretations than on equal representation. Five stories come from the Americas, from Eskimo to Mayan; four from the Pacific, including Australia; five from Africa. There are a few stories from Europe and Asia, five from the ancient Mediterranean world (including three of the Greek myths), and the concluding piece is from Genesis, shining as the brightest in this bright firmament. Moser's dark, powerful portraits of the Creators are dramatically framed in stark white.

A rich mix of fascinating stories, making an excellent introduction to myths and their cross-cultural connections. Memorable bookmaking.

Betsy Hearne

SOURCE: A review of *In the Beginning,* in *Bulletin of the Center for Children's Books,* Vol. 42, No. 2, October, 1988, p. 37.

The adaptation of 25 diverse creation myths is an ambitious undertaking, and this book succeeds in that it brings the stories together for comparative reading and suggests powerful metaphors, both in printed and graphical statements. [Virginia] Hamilton has ranged across African, Asian, South and North American, Mediterannean, Australian, and European cultures for source material and rendered the retellings with her customary intelligence, though not with the rhythmic familiarity that characterized *The People Could Fly. . . .*

Moser's paintings are powerful, in some cases relying on suggestion, as in the mystical blue oval for **"Bursting from the Hen's Egg: Phan Ku the Creator"** and in others fostering the comedy of strict detail, as in the profile of Warm Dog, duped by the Russian Altaic devil Ulgen. There are few juvenile collections against which to measure this—Penelope Farmer's *Beginnings: Creation Myths of the World* is out of print; the book is badly needed and handsomely done.

Janice M. Del Negro

SOURCE: A review of *In the Beginning: Creation Stories from Around the World,* in *School Library Journal,* Vol. 35, No. 4, December, 1988, p. 127.

Twenty-five creation myths from such diverse cultures as China, Tahiti, Micronesia, and Australia. Illustrated with 42 dramatic, full-color paintings [by Barry Moser], this is a handsome representative collection. [Virginia] Hamilton's introduction briefly defines creation myths and places them within the formal cultural structure that gives them authority. Her commitment to stay true to the simplicity of style of many creation myths results in some brilliant retellings, complete with the clarity of vision and fluidity of language synonymous with her work. While most of these retold myths are highly successful, others lack the precision of the "perfect word" associated with Hamilton. (One example is the jarring use of the modern word "aide," as in aides to a god in a Zambian creation myth.) Although the placement of the explanatory notes at the end of each myth is less effective than if they were placed at the beginning, the book is handsomely designed. Each myth opens with a striking full-page painting, each of which is truly evocative and powerful in design and content. Text and illustrations together result in a strong, effective piece of work.

Trevor Dickinson

SOURCE: A review of *In the Beginning: Creation Stories from Around the World,* in *Books for Keeps,* Vol. 74, May, 1992, p. 29.

Virginia Hamilton's **In the Beginning** is a truly remarkable collection of 25 Creation Myths (including two Old Testament stories) supported by 41 unique illustrations from Barry Moser. Together, in a beautifully produced book, with text of carefully shaped simplicity, both stories and pictures make demands. Coming from a wide range of cultures, the tales remind us of humanity's obsession with its origins. They show, sometimes comically, sometimes with quiet pain, the different attempts by diverse cultures to explain their worlds; and they show, more importantly, the similarities in our efforts to explain.

Marcus Crouch

SOURCE: A review of *In the Beginning: Creation Stories from Around the World,* in *School Librarian,* Vol. 40, No. 3, August, 1992, pp. 113-14.

Virginia Hamilton has assembled twenty-five versions of the story of the creation and retold them in a characteristically bald, unemphatic style. Equal numbers are from the African and Asian continents, three are from Greece, and there are three remarkable stories from oceanic islands of the southern hemisphere.

Hamilton excels in conveying vast concepts in the simplest of sentences. Here is the opening of an Australian creation: 'In the beginning, all was darkness forever. Night covered the earth in a great tangle.' While retaining the same terse style, she adapts it to the mood and matter of each culture, from the one comic story, from Togo, about the God who unwisely spread out his heaven not five feet above the earth and was constantly being bumped by men passing below, to grim stories of conflict between parents and children or between brothers, from Iceland or India, and gravely eloquent accounts from the Pentateuch.

The book has full-page colour plates by Barry Moser which match the sombre text and tackle valiantly such concepts as Chaos or the Cosmic Egg. Both text and pictures are unlikely to appeal to young children; the whole book in fact is most likely to speak to young adults interested in comparative religion and culture. It is very suitable as a basis for classroom discussion or for use in assembly. That way it may well justify the relatively large outlay. The book is produced with due regard to the importance of the content and the author, and in absolute terms represents very good value.

📖   ***EAST OF THE SUN AND WEST OF THE MOON: A PLAY* (written by Nancy Willard, 1989)**

Kirkus Reviews

SOURCE: A review of *East of the Sun and West of the Moon,* in *Kirkus Reviews,* Vol. LVII, No. 7, April 1, 1989, p. 556.

In beautiful format, a dramatic version of a Norwegian folktale.

While the imaginative set directions here may be too complex for amateur productions. [Nancy] Willard has created a truly magical "folk-play" that begs for production. Though references to VCRs and multi-speed bicycles may jar traditionalists, and having one of the trolls' freed captives say, "Free at last. Thank heaven we're free at last" *is* a bit much, the fairy tale mood is, overall, consistently maintained. Willard's imaginative embellishments include giving the four winds (one male, three female) more clearly delineated personalities than they have in the folktale, becoming perfect subjects for [illustrator Barry] Moser's powerful illustrations. Vibrant and earthy, his paintings are especially suitable to this robust tale.

With unique style and wit, Willard and Moser have produced a fine translation of an old favorite into a new genre.

Karla Kuskin

SOURCE: A review of *East of the Sun and West of the Moon,* in *New York Times Book Review,* July 9, 1989, p. 34.

Princes disguised as animals, gifts of unending riches—such shared themes mark myths and have kept us faithfully in their thrall down the years. ***East of the Sun & West of the Moon*** is a classic Norwegian variation on *Beauty and the Beast,* with echoes of those quest tales in which a young innocent sets out to find a lost love in some impossibly distant land.

By turning the narrative into a play, the poet and novelist

Nancy Willard has chosen a form designed to bring the past into the present. The action is introduced by the four winds, who take the role of the chorus and, as in the original tale, eventually lead the heroine to her true love. There is some entertaining dialogue and exuberant rhythmic verse. But wonderful fairy tales unfold with the concision of dreams. Reworking this one into a three-act drama has required letting out the story's formerly invisible seams. In addition to the original characters, puppets, talking objects and animals painted on scrims get into the act. Bits of stage business are drawn from sources as diverse as Walt Disney's *Fantasia* and a Marx Brothers routine. Along the way, stretches of current phrasing jar with more formal fairy-tale language.

This uneasy alliance of once upon a time and right now is also apparent in Barry Moser's watercolors, which are handsomely laid out and generously framed with white on big pages. They include a few glowing, moody landscapes and a series of portraits of the primary players. The bear as the prince whose beauty is a linchpin of the plot is bear-bearded, overweight and looks like an aging tenor. This makes him a startlingly incongruous lover for Mr. Moser's fresh-faced, totally contemporary woodcutter's daughter. The happy couple must be 40 years and, at least, several worlds apart. The shining star of this rogue's gallery is the bear as himself: big, beautiful and soulful, just the kind of bear a girl would fall for. If he didn't turn into a tenor.

JUMP ON OVER! THE ADVENTURES OF BRER RABBIT AND HIS FAMILY (1989; written by Joel Chandler Harris)

Betsy Hearne

SOURCE: A review of *Jump on Over!: The Adventures of Brer Rabbit and His Family,* in *Bulletin of the Center for Children's Books,* Vol. 43, No. 2, October, 1989, p. 33.

How can you lose? Brer Rabbit has perennial appeal and Barry Moser just gets better and better. Here are five more stories: **"How Brer Rabbit Frightened His Neighbors," "Brer Rabbit and Brer Bear," "Why Brer Wolf Didn't Eat the Little Rabs," "Another Story about the Little Rabs,"** and **"Brer Fox Gets Out-Foxed."** Just for the record, Brer Rabbit frightens his neighbors by wearing the tin coffee pot, cups, and plates he has bought for his family. He fools Brer Fox by enticing Brer Bear into a goober-patch trap for a dollar a minute. He tricks Brer Wolf into chasing Brer Fox by persuading the former that the latter's blood tastes like molasses. He comes home to find that even his children have, with the helpful advice of a friendly bird, outfoxed Brer Fox. And he persuades Brer Fox that a team of horses has sunk into quicks and by judiciously planting a few tails. No child can resist such a trickster, and no adult can resist Moser's sly portraits, with their varied perspectives, uncanny draftsmanship, and sparely detailed southern settings.

Ethel L. Twichell

SOURCE: A review of *Jump on Over! The Adventures of Brer Rabbit and His Family,* in *The Horn Book Magazine,* Vol. LXVI, No. 2, March/April, 1990, p. 213.

The third volume of Brer Rabbit stories includes five lesser known escapades of the incorrigible scamp. Although the plots seem somewhat blander variations of other stories, the same colorful dialect and ebullient humor of the earlier books also enlivens and enriches these. Once more an ingenious Brer Rabbit is up to his tricks of eluding ambush by his old enemies, tempting slow-witted Brer Bear into the same trap which has snared him and deftly acquiring Brer Fox's horses, wagon, and cornmeal. Whether it is Brer Rabbit prancing "terbuckity-buckity" into town to buy a coffeepot or poor old Brer Bear being *"blippity-blipped"* with Brer Fox's cane, the sounds and cadence of the speech are those of the born raconteur. [Moser's] illustrations are, as usual, witty and utterly beguiling. Brer Rabbit in his pinstriped suit, derby hat, and natty tie is a slick rabbit gentleman, not merely a dressed-up animal, and Brer Fox outfitted with lofty hat and bibbed overalls is a perplexed farmer who just happens to have a bushy tail. The strong characterization of the animals seems to leap out of the pictures, adding rich drama and playful humor to the endless struggle of Brer Rabbit's wits against the greater strength and size of Brer Fox, Brer Bear, and Brer Wolf.

THE BALLAD OF BIDDY EARLY (written by Nancy Willard, 1989)

Denise Wilms

SOURCE: A review of *The Ballad of Biddy Early,* in *Booklist,* Vol. 86, No. 8, December 15, 1989, p. 838.

As she did in *A Visit to William Blake's Inn,* [Nancy] Willard turns to a fascinating historical figure for inspiration to summon up original poetry and storytelling. Biddy Early, a nineteenth-century Irish woman, became known for her healing powers and her ability to tell the future. Willard's poems celebrate Biddy Early's mysterious power and elaborate on the bare bones of legend to fashion a character who is both powerful and compassionate. The picture can be fascinating, the images rich: "I've sixty sleek sparrows to carry my wishes, / my clock is a thistle, my servant a bee. / So pay me with goslings and roaring red roosters / and ponies and pigs, and I'll set them all free." The verses illuminate Biddy from various angles. Some tell stories of the woman ("How Biddy Hid Mick the Moonlighter's Sleep in Her Sleeve"); in others, she herself speaks; and in some lines her beloved animals sing her praises. Moser's watercolors emphasize the mysterious aspects of the poems, with haunting portraits of the characters whose paths cross Biddy's door. This doesn't have the glamorous graphics and dazzling appeal the Provensens provided in *William Blake's Inn,* but it could work nicely as a centerpiece for poetry and literature units.

Leda Schubert

SOURCE: A review of *Ballad of Biddy Early*, in *School Library Journal*, Vol. 36, No. 3, March, 1990, p. 233.

These 15 poems praise Biddy Early, the wise woman of Ireland's County Clare who lived from 1798 to 1874. Beginning with the ballad of the title, Willard invites listeners in with limericks, songs, and poems. The poems tell of magic and mystery, witchcraft, the supernatural, and murder; how nature and animals revered Biddy Early; how she read the future and cured illness. There are limericks from her cat, a song from her speckled hen, and a final remembrance from her friends. Meter, rhyme, structure, and rhythm vary throughout. Each of Moser's luminous watercolors focuses on a single element; his irregular rectangles rest on white pages and play with light and dark. They are exquisitely composed of haunting images, showing thick-walled cottages, gleaming Irish pipes, eerie cats. Like *A Visit to William Blake's Inn* this is not for everyone, but the rich word play and imagery of the poetry and the power of the art should thrill readers who seek enchantment.

THE TINDERBOX (1990; adapted by Moser from the story by Hans Christian Andersen)

Kirkus Reviews

SOURCE: A review of *The Tinderbox*, in *Kirkus Reviews*, Vol. LVIII, No. 16, August 15, 1990, pp. 1165-66.

In a cogent afterword, Moser explains why he has set his familiar story just after the Civil War: he wished, like Aaron Copland, to "use an American idiom . . . in the not so distant past." A valid approach, and certainly preferable to the condescending oversimplifications so often visited on Andersen in the name of accessibility. This is Moser's first attempt at retelling; the resulting story, tuned to a Tennessee lilt, has a laconic flavor and wry humor that surely would have appealed to Andersen, different as they are from his own. The witch has become a "curmudgeon" who falls from a cliff rather than being gratuitously murdered; the violence that precedes the soldier's elevation to mayor at the end has also been considerably muted, with no loss to the story. In his usual style, Moser's beautiful paintings are not so much illustrations that carry the story forward as searching portraits and vignettes that give it added depth. A creative presentation that will appeal to storytellers and other adults as well as to young readers.

Patricia Dooley

SOURCE: A review of *The Tinderbox*, in *School Library Journal*, Vol. 36, No. 10, October, 1990, p. 113.

Purists will be horrified. This is not just a retelling, but a complete reimagining of the tale. Moser keeps the struc-ture: a war-weary soldier acquires a tinderbox, ventures into a glittering underworld, and braves three huge dogs. The box' magic gives him access to wealth and to love: for the latter he nearly hangs, but the tinderbox saves him and all ends happily. Everything but the action, however, is Moser's: time, place, characters, idiom. The hero is an ex-Confederate. Instead of a witch, the old curmudgeon who sends him after the box is an east Tennessee mountain man. The dialect is Appalachian country; the heroine is the green-eyed daughter of an absentee politician and his domineering wife (removed by the dogs so the young couple can triumph). Moser's superb watercolors are chiefly portraits of the principals: the old codger; the country girl; the open-faced hero, Yoder Ott—and the three dogs, whose eyes are not *quite* as big as wagon wheels or windmills. Their vivid individuality convincingly links the real, the historic, and the fantastic, giving a new, distinctly American life to the tale. Moser's reincarnation of this story is as magical as any fairy-tale transformation. Andersen would be envious.

Carolyn Phelan

SOURCE: A review of *The Tinderbox*, in *Booklist*, Vol. 87, No. 4, October 15, 1990, p. 438.

Moser retells Andersen's classic fairy tale as it might have happened in the Tennessee mountains just after the Civil War. A young soldier on his way home meets an old codger (rather than the traditional witch). The mountain man lowers the soldier down a rock cliff to a cave where he finds three magical dogs atop their treasure chests and, of course, the tinderbox. Preserving the main elements of the story, Moser uses dialogue along with the illustrations to create the Southern setting. Designed by the illustrator, the book features wide margins and thick, cream-colored paper. Its text appears on odd-numbered pages, each of which faces a full-color painting, often an arresting portrait of a single character. From the dark, mysterious painting on the dust jacket to the thoughtful afterword, this adaptation shows both imagination and integrity, and Moser tells his tale with such conviction that it seems more like a comfortably settled immigrant than a foreigner on American soil.

Ethel L. Heins

SOURCE: A review of *The Tinderbox*, in *The Horn Book Magazine*, Vol. LXVII, No. 1, January/February, 1991, p. 65.

In 1835 Hans Christian Andersen published four fairy tales in the first of his little books for children. "The Tinder Box" and two other stories were not original literary creations but free retellings of favorites recalled from his childhood, and he wrote them down in a crisp, conversational manner. "These I have told in my own way: where I thought it fitting, I have changed them and let imagination freshen the colors in the picture that had begun to fade." Andersen's "The Tinder Box" bears a noticeable resemblance to "Aladdin and the Wonderful Lamp"—as a child, Andersen knew *The Arabian Nights*—and it closely parallels the Grimms' "The Blue Light." Rather than adapting the story, Barry Moser, like Andersen, has actually recast it in his own way. Indeed, it is inaccurate to credit Andersen as the author, for although Moser closely follows the pattern and the plot, he gives the narrative a fresh setting, along with its distinctive idiom and characters. Retaining the substance and the spirit of the tale, he endows it with ironic wit and an integrity of its own. Moser places the story in Appalachia, with the hero an impoverished soldier returning from the Civil War; the heroine is the comely, overprotected daughter of the henpecked mayor and his vigilant, tyrannical wife; according to Moser, "the ogre-curmudgeon is an East Tennessee mountain man, the likes of which I saw many a time as I grew up there." An extraordinary artist with an instinctive dramatic sense, Barry Moser has placed opposite each page of text a strikingly imaginative painting that adds to the tension of the action or suggests the essential nature of the characters, both animal and human.

📖   *SKY DOGS* (written by Jane Yolen, 1990)

Publishers Weekly

SOURCE: A review of *Sky Dogs,* in *Publishers Weekly,* Vol. 237, No. 39, September 28, 1990, p. 101.

In this lyrical tale drawn from Blackfoot legend, an old man recounts the origin of his name, He-who-loves-horses. He describes the coming of horses, "Sky Dogs," from across the plains, and the wonder and awe he and his people felt when they first saw these "big . . . elk, with tails of straw." He-who-loves-horses, then a lonely boy, learns to care for and ride the beautiful animals, and his knowledge and abilities help him earn a place on the council of warriors—and a sense of self-worth. His story is made all the more poignant by the elderly narrator's revelation that "now I sit in the tipi, and food is brought to me, and I do not ride the wind." Moser's sun-and-earth-toned watercolors, of the plains and of the main character as both boy and man, are lovely and haunting.

Kirkus Reviews

SOURCE: A review of *Sky Dogs,* in *Kirkus Reviews,* Vol. LVIII, No. 19, October 1, 1990, p. 1399.

Drawing on Native American tales, [Jane] Yolen creates her own story (as she meticulously explains in a note) about how horses might first have come to the Blackfeet: An old man tells why he is called "He-who-loves-horses." When he was a boy, three large beasts (so awe-inspiring that people called them "Sky Dogs") arrived bearing dying members of a hostile tribe, and stayed to become an important part of his tribe's life and lore. Yolen's dignified, lyrical style turns the episode into an event that resonates with significance; Moser's stunning

watercolor illustrations—in sunset gold and the rich hues of shadowed sandstone—shine with the glory of remembered youth. An excellent complement to Goble's fine books about Native Americans.

Leone McDermott

SOURCE: A review of *Sky Dogs,* in *Booklist,* Vol. 87, No. 4, October 15, 1990, p. 453.

Drawing on a number of Blackfoot Indian stories, [Jane] Yolen has fashioned a spare, realistic tale of how the Blackfeet first acquired horses. A young boy of the Piegan band relates the time when three Kutani Indians arrived on doglike animals as big as elk. Many Piegan feared the strange creatures, but Long Arrow pronounced them "sky dogs," a gift sent from heaven by Old Man the creator. This simple, undramatic account, which focuses largely on people's immediate reactions, has a feel of authenticity. Young readers, however, might have benefited from more details on how the horses changed the Indians' way of life. Moser's sweeping watercolors drawn on handmade paper glow in sunset tones and range from detailed portraits to silhouettelike panoramas.

Patricia Dooley

SOURCE: A review of *Sky Dogs,* in *School Library Journal,* Vol. 36, No. 11, November, 1990, pp. 100-01.

Many legends reflect the radical difference the advent of the horse made in the life of the Plains Indians. In fluid storytelling style, [Jane] Yolen melds the mythic and the realistic modes in the emotions and reactions of her narrator, a motherless Piegan boy, on the day the first "sky dogs" come to his band. Fear and disbelief are tempered by wonder and gratitude. The horse brings the hero a substitute mother and status in the tribe, as it would bring success to all the Plains people. Goble's retelling in *The Gift of the Sacred Dog* emphasizes the legendary over the realistic, and his slick, flat, brightly colored illustrations are the antithesis of Moser's. Moser's palette is all ochre, yellow, and umber, red earth and golden sky. Against the low horizon and dry prairie, humans and horses loom, at once significant and insignificant. Two portrait roundels are as revealing and moving as Catlin's or Bodmer's 19th-century "noble savages." Writer and artist together have produced a fine evocation of a place and a people.

📖   *LITTLE TRICKER THE SQUIRREL MEETS BIG DOUBLE THE BEAR* (written by Ken Kesey, 1990)

Betsy Hearne

SOURCE: A review of *Little Tricker the Squirrel Meets Big Double the Bear,* in *Bulletin of the Center for Children's Books,* Vol. 44, No. 2, October, 1990, p. 34.

"Don't tell me you're the *only* youngsters never heard tell of the time the bear came to Topple's Bottom? He was a huge high-country bear and not only huge but *horrible* huge. And hairy, and hateful, and *hungry!* Why he almost ate up the *entire Bottom* before Tricker finally cut him down to size, just you listen and see if he didn't. . . ." And listen kids will, to this language that plays like Carl Sandburg's and doesn't fool around when it comes to plot. Folktale elements emerge without seeming either self-conscious or precious. After Big Double eats a couple of little ground animals, just to whet his appetite, he finds himself eye to eye with Tricker the tree squirrel, who admits to being impressed: "you may have been a little short-changed in the thinking department but when it comes to running, jumping, and climbing you got double portions." In addition to music and wit in the words, which will sustain repeated read-aloud sessions, there's wild satire and more action than usual (without loss of control) in the masterful watercolors with which Barry Moser portrays this archetypal cast. Lots of writers and painters who have concentrated their artistry on adults can't switch to children without loud tonal flaws, but [Ken] Kesey and Moser have proved the exception. Like the hazelnuts ripening in the tree below Tricker's "cottonwood high rise," this picture book is *"just about perfect!"*

Kirkus Reviews

SOURCE: A review of *Little Tricker the Squirrel Meets Big Double the Bear,* in *Kirkus Reviews,* Vol. LVIII, No. 20, October 15, 1990, p. 1457.

This rollicking tall tale, based on a story told to [Ken] Kesey by his grandmother, was published twice, "in different form," in books for adults; this is its first appearance in a format that will also appeal to children. Both story and telling are splendid. Big Double is "HONGRY! . . . grumpy grouchy bedtime bigtime hongry . . . when I hit the hay tonight I got six months before breakfast so I need a supper the size of my sleep." In classic style, he catches and gulps down three other animals, the chase amusingly escalating each time; but the squirrel who has been watching turns the tables with a satisfyingly funny, appropriate trick. Moser contributes a dozen of his grand watercolor portraits and superbly crafted scenes, nicely touched with humor: a rabbit, grimacing and cleaning his ear with a parsnip; the bear, seen from a vertiginous perspective, hurtling downhill after the luckless rabbit. Kesey's frequent italics aren't essential, but they're expertly placed and remind the reader that this is the sort of lively, comical tale that demands reading aloud—a perfect picture book to share with older children.

Connie C. Rockman

SOURCE: A review of *Little Tricker the Squirrel Meets Big Double the Bear,* in *School Library Journal,* Vol. 36, No. 12, December, 1990, p. 104.

Big Double the Bear comes down from the high ridges one fine fall morning, terrorizing the creatures of Topple's Bottom until Tricker the Squirrel defeats him through courage and cunning. The characters are reminiscent of those in the Brer Rabbit stories, and the plot is similar to "Sody Salleratus" from Richard Chase's *Grandfather Tales.* But this story is [Ken] Kesey's own, told in a vigorous, colorful style that invites reading aloud, demonstrating how much new life can be breathed into old stories with rich and vital language. His style brings each character into sharp focus, and that style is perfectly matched by Moser's sly, witty, and wonderfully evocative full-page watercolors, among his best yet, employing varying perspectives and a highly effective use of light and shadow. An exceptionally well-designed book with a fine juxtaposition of text, pictures, and generous margins, this one is sure to be a favorite.

Booklist

SOURCE: A review of *Little Tricker the Squirrel Meets Big Double the Bear,* in *Booklist,* Vol. 87, No. 9, January 1, 1991, p. 924.

Since [Ken] Kesey's adult novels, *One Flew over the Cuckoo's Nest* and *Sometimes a Great Notion,* are really fables at heart—mythic salutes to rugged individualism—it should come as no surprise that the writer's first venture into children's literature also draws heavily on the fable tradition. Kesey's hero, a squirrel known as Little Tricker, is every bit the individualist that Randall Patrick McMurphy was, but rather than the ultimately suicidal defiance with which McMurphy challenged Big Nurse, Tricker opts for cunning as his weapon against an even bigger foe, Big Double the Bear, who comes down from the High Country with the intention of eating every critter in Topple's Bottom. He's off to a good start until he meets up with Tricker and gets his comeuppance, Tom Sawyer-style, restoring tranquility to the Bottom and proving once again that brains can beat brawn. It all works superbly, due in equal measure to Kesey's graceful handling of the folk idiom ("The night shifts and the day shifts were shifting very slow. . . . The birds hadn't quite woke up and the bats hadn't quite gone to sleep") and to Moser's evocative watercolors, which appear in rich, deep colors on the book's right-hand pages and capture both the story's humor and its sense of peril. Kesey and Moser are a winning combination; let's hope we see more of them.

APPALACHIA: THE VOICES OF SLEEPING BIRDS (written by Cynthia Rylant, 1991)

Barry Moser

SOURCE: "Appalachia: The Front Porch," in *The Horn Book Magazine,* Vol. LXVIII, No. 1, January/February, 1992, pp. 28-30.

I am honored by this award, and I thank you. But I remind myself and my benefactors that, as John Donne preached in 1624, "No man is an island, entire of itself; every man is a piece of the continent, a part of the main." I accept this award with gratitude, humility, and the recognition that I am simply "a part of the main." A part of the main which I share with Cynthia Rylant, without whose quietly brilliant text my design and images would never have come about; and with our editor, Bonnie Verburg, without whose vision the project would never have been; and with our ingenious production manager, Warren Wallerstein.

The Greek poet Heraclitus said that "in the tension of opposites all things have their being." This is obvious to all of us who draw or engrave or write or paint. Nowhere, however, is this notion more vivid to me than in my memories of childhood.

Memories of summer evenings, for instance, when the family gathered on my aunt Velma's screened-in front porch. Her old metal glider, upholstered in green-and-white-striped canvas, squeaked with age—as did her green, scallop-shaped lawn chairs that we had brought in from badminton to get away from the bugs; they now buzzed at the screen trying to get at the floor lamps that glowed through amber-colored paper shades. African violets flourished in white wrought-iron stands near the front door. A hemp rug tickled little feet. I remember my belly tight with Sunday dinner: fried chicken and milk gravy; turnip greens and buttermilk biscuits; a watermelon as likely as not—a round one, like a cannonball, dark Hooker's green, which my uncle Bob "plugged" earlier in the afternoon to make sure it was ripe. Or better still, a tart blackberry cobbler or homemade ice cream made with fresh Georgia Belle peaches.

Food in my family—that is to say, our meals—provided sustenance, ritual, fellowship, communion, and a setting wherein stories were told, usually about somebody in the family: about a cousin over in Decherd; or about a woman up in the hollow who nursed a baby that was too old to be nursed; or about the people across the road who got drunk the night before and set about fussing and screaming and throwing things at each other.

And when my folks talked about things they didn't want me or my brother, Tommy, to understand, they dropped into pig Latin.

This is what we did before Velma and Bob bought their television set in 1953. No one read books—not that I remember, anyhow. My mother read *Reader's Digest* and an occasional novel like *Forever Amber;* Aunt Velma read Mary Baker Eddy's *Science and Health;* and my daddy came home from work late in the afternoon and sat on the couch and read the *Chattanooga Times* and the *Chattanooga News-Free Press.* I, as a child, had no books to speak of, was not read to insofar as I remember, and did not begin to read *seriously* until, as an adult, I learned how to engrave wood, how to set type, and how to print books.

But, those summer evenings of stories and pig Latin did

From The Farm Summer 1942, *written by Donald Hall. Illustrated by Barry Moser.*

foster an interest in language and storytelling (albeit storytelling with pictures)—interests which are now the primary focuses of my life, outside my own family.

The day-to-day language of my childhood, however rurally poetic, was neither elegant nor literate. Rather, it was common and bigoted. Aunts and uncles, mother and father said things like "that woman never did have no common sense, did she?" and "that dog shore likes to chase 'coons, don't he?" We in my family did not speak, nor did we have any interest in speaking, any foreign languages (except pig Latin), being, as we were, xenophobic—skeptical of and hateful toward all things foreign, which included Unitarians, Congregationalists, Jews, Catholics, and Yankees (including anyone who lived north of the Kentucky state line or west of the Mississippi River). And of course it included *all* people of color.

The playful language of Velma's pig Latin, my uncle Floyd's funny stories about family and neighbors, and even the sweetness of my mother's loving voice comforting me from the despair of a nightmare are today diminished in my memory by the seemingly ubiquitous language of their hate and bigotry.

I see my childhood now as having been marred by verbal stains. At that time I had no consciousness of the stains, nor any notion that the stains would become, later in life, scars. I was a polite and obedient child, and never questioned or challenged my family when they made racist remarks. But I do remember not understanding their bigotry and not accepting their hate. I accepted their words, certainly, because they were just that—*words*. But I never understood why I shouldn't sit in the back of the bus when black folks were sitting there (would they hurt me?), or why I couldn't drink from water fountains marked "colored" (would I catch something?), or why I couldn't kiss my mother's black friend, Vernita (would her black rub off?).

As I grew older, and began first questioning and then rejecting my family's values, I became aware of other prejudices: like, for instance, those against artists and intellectuals and those against anybody who embraced a different concept of the Almighty God from the concept they *knew* to be true.

So, like a latter-day Huck Finn, I lit out for New England with my own little family and became an expatriate southerner.

Now, at fifty—and due in large measure to the commissions, encouragement, and support Harcourt Brace Jovanovich has given me—I have begun to weave both memories and scars into my work. I have become like the dog Cynthia Rylant writes about, Prince or King, who wanders home after being lost for a couple of weeks and who searches out that corner of the yard he knew he had to find again before he could get a good sleep.

But it is not enough to have only memories and scars. As Rilke said, "One must be able to forget [the memories and scars] when they are many, and one must have the great patience to wait until they come again. For it is not yet the memories [and scars] themselves. Not until they have turned to blood within us, to glance and gesture, nameless and no longer to be distinguished from ourselves—not till then can it happen that in a most rare hour the first word of a verse arises in their midst and goes forth from them."

Hazel Rochman

SOURCE: A review of *Appalachia: The Voices of Sleeping Birds,* in *Booklist,* Vol. 87, No. 11, February 1, 1991, p. 1128.

Together, writer [Cynthia] Rylant, from West Virginia, and artist-designer Moser, from Tennessee, have made a loving book, spare in line and word, remembering their home and how their people see themselves. In contrast to the exuberant tall tales Moser has illustrated recently, the view of Appalachia is understated—with a rooted, sometimes melancholy sense of community. Like the murmur of conversation on the front porch or around the kitchen table, the focus is on the rituals of chores and church and food and daily work and the company of good dogs that can be trusted "running the mountains." Yet beneath the surface of common things, there's also a deep unspoken feeling of mystery and connection: "Most of them are

thinkers, because these mountains inspire that, but they could never find the words to tell you of these thoughts they have." Moser's realistic watercolor portraits—each one alone on a page with a wide border of white space—have the timelessness and humanity of Depression-era photographs, like the portrait of the coal-miner in his pit-dirt, with his large hands and exhausted face. Just as moving are the landscapes with human figures seen from behind, like the small girl carrying water from the creek to a house in the hills. An exquisite still life of a kettle on an iron stove is extended by the prose, both domestic and lyrical, on the facing page. Rylant's idiom captures (with no dialect or false nostalgia) the colloquial voice, hesitant ("Most would probably rather not meet anyone new") and also rock hard ("Many of them are coalminers because the mountains in Appalachia are full of coal which people want and if you are brave enough to travel two miles down into solid dark earth to get it, somebody will pay you money for your trouble"). Like Carson's *Stories I Ain't Told Nobody Yet,* this is a book to share across generations.

Barbara Chatton

SOURCE: A review of *Appalachia: The Voices of Sleeping Birds,* in *School Library Journal,* Vol. 37, No. 4, April, 1991, p. 137.

This gentle collaboration is clearly not a picture book for young children. It is instead a richly simple work for older readers in which [Cynthia] Rylant's elegant prose is echoed in Moser's realistic paintings. Rylant reveals Appalachia by starting with its dogs, then describing their owners, what they do, how they live, and their thoughts and feelings through the seasons of the year. At the end, readers meet the dogs again, "running the mountains like all good dogs in Appalachia." As with all of her books, Rylant selects words carefully to evoke images. Moser has used family pictures and those of well-known photographers of Appalachia such as Walker Evans and Dorthea Lange as the basis for some of his watercolor paintings. Each is set squarely against the white background of the left-hand page, and each has the shadings and intensity of a photograph. The pictures echo the feelings of Rylant's text, with hounds, children, and older adults who stare out at readers with thoughtful intensity. Students who want to learn more about the Appalachian region can use this book as a starting point, and it might be combined with Rylant's other books as it picks up on many of the themes and topics she has previously raised. It should also encourage original writing or art as it reveals how illustrations and words can interact, how prose can illuminate a painting, and how simple paintings can bring power to prose.

Elizabeth S. Watson

SOURCE: A review of *Appalachia: The Voices of Sleeping Birds,* in *The Horn Book Magazine,* Vol. LXVII, No. 5, September/October, 1991, p. 613.

Taking her subtitle from a passage by James Agee, the author conveys with a marvelous economy of words the essence of the very special part of America where she was raised. A poetic text projects emotion as well as information as it flows along, describing the good dogs named Prince and King; the hard-working people with names like Mamie and Oley and Boyd; the kitchens where leftovers are kept warm; the days and the seasons. In describing the dogs and people, the author tells volumes about the place, while Moser's watercolors capture the scene perfectly. The paintings, framed by wide white borders, are placed opposite a similarly sized block of text, producing an attractive, focused book design. The book is a treasure—simply a beautiful combination of text and art.

📖 ST. JEROME AND THE LION (retelling by Margaret Hodges, 1991)

Roger Sutton

SOURCE: A review of *St. Jerome and the Lion,* in *Bulletin of the Center for Children's Books,* Vol. 45, No. 1, September, 1991, p. 12.

A somewhat fragmentary saint's tale is given cohesion and interest by Barry Moser's scrupulous watercolors and [Margaret] Hodges' simple and dignified adaptation. When a wounded lion calls at Jerome's monastery, the monk heals him and gives him a home and work, guarding the donkey at pasture. But the lion falls asleep, and the donkey is taken by merchants on their way to Egypt. The lion, ostracized by the monks who believe he has eaten the donkey, eventually gets the donkey back and he—and the merchants—are forgiven. "'God has taught us a lesson,' said Jerome. "Here is our trusty friend, proved innocent by a miracle.'" The compassion is clear, so is the story; a subplot about the jealousy of Jerome's dog for the lion is more obliquely resolved (but tenderly illustrated with a gold-toned silhouette). All of the pictures glow with different lights: the monastery walls washed in night light; the hard hot sun on the laboring lion, performing the missing donkey's tasks; the candlelight that guides Jerome in his nightly translation of the Bible. The last picture is puzzling, setting Jerome and the lion against a background of the crucifixes on Calvary. Children will, however, appreciate the solemnity of the portrait, and the noble friendship between saint and beast. The design is open and handsome; a source note is included; the book is dedicated to librarians, "because Jerome is their patron saint."

Shirley Wilton

SOURCE: A review of *St. Jerome and the Lion,* in *School Library Journal,* Vol. 37, No. 9, September, 1991, p. 246.

As in the pre-Christian legend Androcles, the Christian Saint Jerome, first Latin translator of the Bible, is credit-

ed with the good deed of removing a thorn from a lion's paw. Paintings throughout Christian times picture St. Jerome with the grateful lion at his feet. [Margaret] Hodges, using Renaissance interpretations of the legend that show the saint with a dog and donkey, as well as the lion, has shaped a story that includes all three animals. The rescued lion, set to the task of guarding the donkey, fails to keep him safe from thieves. The monks who surround the blessed saint speak out against the lion, but kindly Jerome defends him. The lion gives up his favored place in St. Jerome's study to the dog and takes on the domestic role of donkey, becoming a beast of burden. One day the thieves return with their caravan, led by the donkey. The lion is redeemed, the donkey is returned, and the wisdom of Jerome restores peace and justice to the community of men and animals. A moral tale, handsomely illustrated with Moser's dramatically highlighted, dark-shadowed watercolors, this gentle story is well suited to church libraries and to situations in which the values of trust and kindness and "innocent until proven guilty" are to be discussed.

Carolyn Phelan

SOURCE: A review of *St. Jerome and the Lion,* in *Booklist,* Vol. 88, No. 3, October 1, 1991, p. 333.

St. Jerome was a fifth-century monk who built a monastery in Bethlehem, translated the Bible into Latin, and in the legend recounted here, gained a lion's devotion by removing a thorn from its paw. When the monastery donkey disappears one day, the monks accuse the lion of having eaten the animal it was sent to guard. Jerome makes the king of beasts take the donkey's place as a beast of burden. When the donkey returns, Jerome realizes the faithfulness of the lion, who takes up his old place by his master's side. While the writing is good, the tale lacks the essential drama of *Saint George and the Dragon* [Margaret] Hodges' best-known retelling. Set into a handsomely designed and beautifully made volume, Moser's sensitive, full-color illustrations bring the main characters and the setting to life in a series of evocative scenes and portraits. A natural for libraries in parochial schools and churches, and with its themes of courage, kindness, and justice, a welcome addition to other libraries as well.

Mary M. Burns

SOURCE: A review of *St. Jerome and the Lion,* in *The Horn Book Magazine,* Vol. LXVII, No. 6, November/December, 1991, pp. 753-55.

A blue casing incised in gold; parchment-like endpapers; and judiciously placed calligraphic decorations give additional luster to a beautifully designed, magnificently illustrated, memorable retelling of an appealing legend: the story of St. Jerome, translator of the Bible into Latin, and of the lion who became his constant companion. The voice of a true storyteller informs the story as the daily life of the monastery which Jerome founded is described—a routine that demanded contributions from each occupant, whether human or animal. Thus it is that the lion whose paw Jerome cures is also given a particular responsibility: the guarding of the communal donkey. But when it is stolen by a passing caravan, the lion, accused of eating his charge, is forced to take the donkey's place as a humble beast of burden. Then, miraculously, he is redeemed from his ignominious state when the real culprits return, and he rescues the missing donkey. Jerome duly notes the injustice which has occurred, forgives the erring merchants, and offers them hospitality in a manner befitting his innate nobility. The spirit of dignity underlying the story is echoed in Barry Moser's splendid, glowing illustrations. Executed in watercolor, they evoke a variety of textures and impressions—from the hot sands of the desert to the modulating blues of a moon-illumined nightscape. The modeling of his figures, shaped by light and shadow, is superb.

KASHTANKA (written by Anton Chekhov; translated by Richard Pevear, 1991)

Patricia Dooley

SOURCE: A review of *Kashtanka,* in *School Library Journal,* Vol. 37, No. 11, November, 1991, p. 116.

Kashtanka is a small, rusty-red "half dachshund and half mutt." On a freezing Moscow day she gets separated from her master (an alcoholic cabinetmaker), and is adopted by a stranger who turns out to be a circus clown. Kashtanka meets the pig, goose, and cat performers the new master has trained, and learns tricks herself. Life seems good, but at her circus debut the cabinetmaker's son recognizes Kashtanka and she runs to his call. Following them home, her interlude with the circus master and his retinue " . . . now seemed to her like a long, confused dream." Young readers who expect strict logic in stories may also be confused; the cabinetmaker treats Kashtanka harshly and barely feeds her, while the circus trainer is kind and the dog enjoys learning tricks. But the charm of the tale (in a masterly translation) lies in its dog's-eye view of the world. From that perspective, her dogged, illogical loyalty to her original family makes perfect sense. The sophisticated appeal of Chekhov's prose is matched by Moser's watercolors. As usual, simplicity, elegance, and drama characterize these pictures. Closeup portraits of the animals are particularly striking. Although standard picturebook audiences might find this title too subtle, for slightly older readers (and literature-loving parents) it's a dog story with a difference.

Kirkus Reviews

SOURCE: A review of *Kashtanka,* in *Kirkus Reviews,* Vol. LIX, No. 22, November 15, 1991, p. 1468.

After the little dog Kashtanka is separated from her master, who spends the day wandering from customer to tav-ern to relative, she is taken in by a man who feeds her better than her master ever did and begins to train her: he's a clown whose act already includes a boar, a cat, and a goose. When the goose suddenly dies, Kashtanka is pressed into service—and is recognized and reclaimed by her original master and his son, who happen to be in the audience. The rather long, quiet story has been "translated for young readers" (does this mean adopted? We couldn't find the original, but the style seems less rich and colorful than in Chekhov's other stories); it is illustrated with Moser's usual gallery of skillfully wrought paintings, including several incisive portraits (the half-madeup clown could be Olivier), appealing glimpses of the dog, and some memorable compositions. Not essential, but good bookmaking.

THE ALL JAHDU STORYBOOK (written by Virginia Hamilton, 1991)

Kirkus Reviews

SOURCE: A review of *The All Jahdu Storybook,* in *Kirkus Reviews,* Vol. LIX, No. 21, November 1, 1991, p. 1402.

In 1969, [Virginia] Hamilton published *The Time-Ago Tales of Jahdu,* four tales about a trickster boy-hero who expressed his sense of freedom by "running along" and whose favorite exclamation was "Woogily!" Like those in *Time-Ago Lost* (1973), they were set in a framing story about "Mama Luka" in "a fine, good place called Harlem," telling her stories to young Lee Edward. Now Hamilton drops the framing story, adds a central section ("Jahdu Adventure") with four new pieces (including one involving the giant Trouble as a robot and one in which Jahdu encounters several folkloric characters), and tightens and reshapes the whole. By eliminating the explicit celebration of pride in the black experience, she highlights the rich blend of creation myths, philosophies, and folklore that inspired these tales; they seem more universal here than they did in the earlier setting. But they are still not easy; like the later books in the *Justice* series, they can be hard to follow, their events imposed by symbols that seem arbitrarily intertwined. Still, the language is vigorous and masterfully honed, while the character of lively, powerful, self-defining Jahdu has appeal even though some of his adventures are less than compelling. Moser contributes the attractive design and 20 beautifully painted glimpses of the scenes and characters in Jahdu's world.

Helen E. Williams

SOURCE: A review of *The All Jahdu Storybook,* in *School Library Journal,* Vol. 38, No. 1, January, 1992, p. 109.

A collection of 11 previously told tales and 4 completely new ones. In the original stories, *The Time-Ago Tales of Jahdu, Time-Ago Lost,* and *Jahdu,* Mama Luka entertains her young charge, Lee Edward, by plucking stories about

Jadhu out of the air and tasting them before passing them on. In these reconstructed versions, Mama Luka has been removed and Jahdu emerges as the central character, an "all-out trickster, magical and devilish, good and bad, imp and elf." These mythical tales are set in a fantastical place and time to convey mystery, adventure, humor, and enjoyment. Moser's striking watercolors show texture and consistency of drama without ever portraying the diminutive fellow graphically. Readers and listeners will find delight and wonder in these tales. A storyteller's treasure.

📖 *NOAH'S CATS AND THE DEVIL'S FIRE* (written by Arielle North Olson, 1992)

Hazel Rochman

SOURCE: A review of *Noah's Cats and the Devil's Fire,* in *Booklist,* Vol. 88, No. 11, February 1, 1992, p. 1034.

In a traditional Romanian variant of the biblical story, the devil sneaks onto the ark disguised as a mouse, makes mischief, and nearly sinks the ark with everyone on it. Just in time, the cats pounce on the devil mouse, and one of them swallows the fiend, fiery eyes and all, and spits him out into the ocean. The telling is cheerful, in colloquial folktale style ("Well, the devil mouse was furious . . ."). Noah's in control—nothing bothers him. In menacing contrast, Moser's full-page watercolors are full of danger and struggle—not only the lurid view of the monster, his snout, claws, and slithery skin lit with hellish red, but also the pictures of the ark, like a world under swirling, dark green water, with people and animals barely discernible in the storm and driving rain. Noah's cats save the ark, and the floods go down. But Moser's magnificent cover painting—a still black cat watching with fiery eyes—makes us wonder if the demon left something of himself behind. Design, story, and art enrich each other in a haunting picture book.

Kathy Piehl

SOURCE: A review of *Noah's Cats and the Devil's Fire,* in *School Library Journal,* Vol. 38, No. 5, May, 1992, p. 107.

As the animals board the ark, the devil confronts Noah and demands a place. He is turned away, but turns himself into a mouse and slips on board. He tries to aggravate Noah in various ways, but the partiarch interprets every act positively. Furious, the devil-mouse starts gnawing a hole to sink the ark. However, his plan fails when he entices the other two mice to join in his scheme, and Noah notices the three of a kind instead of the requisite two. One of the cats swallows the devil-mouse and then spits him into the ocean where he becomes a viper fish. The Romanian tale on which [Arielle North] Olson bases her text has parallels in other Eastern European stories that pit the good cat against the evil mouse. However, the story will be unfamiliar to most children. Moser's dark and brooding watercolors create a suitable air of malev-

olence. With glowing red eyes, the devil is appropriately menacing and ugly. However, most of the other pictures are also so dark that details are obliterated, which will greatly reduce the book's effectiveness with all but the smallest group. Moser's cover illustration of a staring cat is unforgettable in its powerful gaze at readers.

Ann A. Flowers

SOURCE: A review of *Noah's Cats and the Devil's Fire,* in *The Horn Book Magazine,* Vol. LXVIII, No. 3, May/ June, 1992, pp. 347-48.

Spectacularly beautiful and vivid illustrations [by Moser] add drama to a delightfully retold folk tale from Rumania. The devil is determined to join Noah and his animals on the ark, but Noah defies him with the help of his cats. The devil steals on board anyway, disguised as a mouse and hiding under the lion's mane, but he is singularly unsuccessful at his goal of causing trouble—until he hits upon the clever notion of chewing a hole in the hull. But Noah notices him, and when one of the cats catches him and spits the piping hot devil-mouse into the sea, the cat is changed forever; now all cats have eyes that gleam in the dark and fur that makes sparks. The artist has created incredibly memorable images—from the blackest cat that ever was, with glittering greeny-yellow eyes, to a bright red devil-mouse with red eyes and spikes down his back.

📖 *POLLY VAUGHN: A TRADITIONAL BRITISH BALLAD* (1992)

Hazel Rochman

SOURCE: A review of *Polly Vaughn: A Traditional British Ballad,* in *Booklist,* Vol. 88, No. 13, March 1, 1992, p. 1270.

Moser retells an old English ballad in the voice and setting of his Appalachian roots. It's a story of innocent lovers, sweethearts since childhood, destroyed by a muddle of accident, family grudge, and community violence. As Moser says in an afterword, it's the stuff of tabloids; it's also from the world of country music. A few days before their wedding, Jimmy shoots Polly when he mistakes her for a deer in the woods. Her vengeful father calls it murder, and Jimmy's arrested, tried, and found guilty by a judge and jury of good, strong hunters. There's a moment of light when Polly's ghost appears in a veil of snow—first, to Jimmy in his cell and, then, to those who taught him that hunting was a badge of manhood. But they hang him in the snow. Moser's language is vivid and immediate, though the ballad loses some of its melancholy power by being recast in prose, and the type is cramped. The full-page illustrations, almost all portraits, are full of character and emotion, from the gentle lovers to their fierce, hardy parents. Tabloid or not, Moser paints no stereotypes: you look and look at those jurors, the small-town "characters," and see their narrowness, their hypocrisy, and their need.

Kirkus Reviews

SOURCE: A review of *Polly Vaughn,* in *Kirkus Reviews,* Vol. LX, No. 7, April 1, 1992, p. 469.

As he did with Andersen's *The Tinderbox* (1990), Moser transplants a traditional British ballad with interesting parallels to *Romeo and Juliet* to Appalachia, a likely enough setting for the tragedy of a young man who, mistaking his beloved for a deer, shoots her and then is hanged for murder. The transformation from song to story is less satisfactory: though Moser's narrative reads smoothly, it runs to rather prosaic explanations, whereas a ballad's power is derived from leaving all but the essentials to the imagination. The book is handsomely designed, including one of Moser's compelling portraits or set pieces on each double spread (but not the original ballad, about which readers are sure to be curious). It's not necessarily an anti-hunting story, but it does raise the issue; certainly it's a love story with appeal for older children and possibly teenagers. A mostly successful attempt to clothe a classic tale in new attire.

Publishers Weekly

SOURCE: A review of *Polly Vaughn,* in *Publishers Weekly,* Vol. 239, No. 17, April 6, 1992, p. 65.

Refashioning a "traditional British ballad" into a tragic Southern love story, Moser—who illustrated Cynthia Rylant's *Appalachia*—again displays compassion for the prideful people of the rural South. Childhood sweethearts Polly Vaughn and Jimmy Randall are determined to marry despite their fathers' longstanding feud. But a hunting accident leaves Polly dead in her lover's arms and Jimmy sentenced to hang for her murder. Steeped in the transcendent power of true love, the legend holds that a veil of snow swelled up in the courtroom and "taking on a form like a pale and translucent young woman" futilely admonished the jury: "You judge my Jimmer wrongly." Moser's distinctive watercolor portraits, featuring expressive, imperfect faces, crystallize emotions with the stillness of photographs. The supernatural elements here seem somewhat at odds with the text's gritty realism—perhaps because the ballad format allows realism and fantasy to coexist more easily than in Moser's straightforward prose. Nonetheless, he fleshes out his version with compelling detail, infusing the tale with what he terms "the warp and weft of place and voice."

Helen Gregory

SOURCE: A review of *Polly Vaughn,* in *School Library Journal,* Vol. 38, No. 7, July, 1992, p. 86.

Montagues and Capulets, Hatfields and McCoys, Randalls and Vaughns: echoing literary history, Jimmy Randall proposes to childhood sweetheart Polly Vaughn, despite a long-standing family feud. A week before their wedding day, mistaking his bride for a deer, Jimmy accidentally kills her and is brought to trial for murder. Polly's ghost is the only one to defend Jimmy and the lovers are reunited only in death. Moser fleshes out an Appalachian ballad with full characters and a vivid setting. After a few cloying kidbits and countryisms, such as "kinleygarten," "chile," "Jimmer," he lets the story, as good stories will, tell itself. Dark watercolor character studies are typical of Moser's impeccable style. Artistic in every way, the illustrations, layout, print, even the paper are an experience in fine bookmaking. The redheaded lovers are not pretty, just real, almost breathing. The traditional ballad came from England and Ireland where it was known as "Molly Bawn." Moser quotes two lines from one version in his afterword. Complete words and music would have been a plus, but all those who enjoy a romantic ghost story will never forget Polly Vaughn.

BEAUTY AND THE BEAST (retelling by Nancy Willard, 1992)

Linda Boyles

SOURCE: A review of *Beauty and the Beast,* in *School Library Journal,* Vol. 38, No. 10, October, 1992, p. 123.

From a first glimpse of the jacket, readers will know that this is not just another retelling of an old story, but something entirely different. And so it is, for [Nancy] Willard and Moser have reworked the foundations of the tale to create a book that startles and surprises (and absolutely satisfies) readers. While the plot is remarkably true to the original, the setting will catch readers off guard—New York at the turn of the century. The rough-hewn, prosaic American backdrop may seem at odds with the magic of the tale, but Willard's poetic prose, filled with vivid images and intricate period detail, and Moser's strong, evocative black-and-white wood engravings root the tale firmly and naturally in this place; the characters fit it perfectly. Beauty is a sturdy, pragmatic young woman—kind, courageous, and rational. She is human enough to resent her sisters' greed, while her intelligence allows her to see the Beast's sorrow and gentleness despite his ugliness. And this is a truly horrible beast—one that walks upright with a grossly distorted, but all-too-human face (rather like George C. Scott as Mr. Hyde). This is a masterful collaboration, with text and illustration anticipating and echoing each other. The language is direct, yet rich in images; the pictures are solidly rendered, with delicately sensuous undertones. They have an intriguing depth and dimension, like old photographs that capture real moments in time. This is an astonishing and beautifully made book, with an original vision and unique voice. Don't miss it.

Kirkus Reviews

SOURCE: A review of *Beauty and the Beast,* in *Kirkus Reviews,* Vol. LX, No. 20, October 15, 1992, p. 1318.

In a briefer recasting of Leprince Beaumont's beloved

tale than McKinley's fine novelization (1978), [Nancy] Willard grounds the story in the opulent materialism of the late 19th century, with Beauty's father as a wealthy New York merchant; their country retreat is in the Hudson Valley, where the Beast's magical Victorian mansion fits right in with a region renowned for supernatural happenings. Willard's telling is brisk but lyrical, of course, the lovely romantic touches delicately balanced with wry humor. There are but two sisters here, as self-serving as Cinderella's; in an abruptly vengeful conclusion, they become a pair of andirons. Otherwise, the tone is gentle, with much of the interest in the enchanting details of the Beast's magical home and garden. Moser provides 14 wood engravings, handsome but rather austere for attracting much of the book's natural audience. There are telling (but distancing) portraits of Beauty and her sisters; a poignant take on the beast—deformed face, haunted eyes; the brooding mansion; and, representing the denouement, a chaste pair of hands, not quite clasped. A felicitous retelling, in an elegant format that leaves plenty of "scope for the imagination."

Betsy Hearne

SOURCE: A review of *Beauty and the Beast*, in *Bulletin of the Center for Children's Books*, Vol. 46, No. 3, November, 1992, p. 94.

The time is early in the twentieth-century, the place is New York, and the plot is a fairy tale fictionalized in the way "Beauty and the Beast" has inspired authors and artists to assay for more than a hundred years. True to this tradition, Willard names and develops the characters, elaborates the setting, and joins hands with an impressive artist who lends her descriptions graphic weight—heavy weight, in this case. Romantics may be slightly jarred by the contrast between the author's lush prose ("Maples washed the air with a warm honeyed light and lit up the road like torches") and Moser's stark black-and-white wood engravings, which project an aura of American Gothic gloom. At the same time, it's a relief to get away from the rosy cartoons that have deluged the market since the release of Disney's film, and the bookmaking here will attract readers who think they're too old for fairy tales but are in fact exactly the right audience for this one. Those who have enjoyed Willard and Moser's sophisticated collaboration in *East of the Sun and West of the Moon* or *The Ballad of Biddy Early* will gravitate to this one as well.

Nancy Vasilakis

SOURCE: A review of *Beauty and the Beast*, in *The Horn Book Magazine*, Vol. LXVIII, No. 6, November/December, 1992, p. 734.

Nancy Willard's version of this classic tale appears in a lavishly produced volume bearing a haunting, gilt-lettered jacket and illustrated inside with dramatic black-and-white wood engravings set off by scarlet initial chapter letters.

Author and artist have apparently collaborated closely on this project, drawing inspiration from several print and film sources. Willard has set her story in nineteenth-century New York City and outlying areas. Research excursions to Hudson River Valley mansions resulted in Moser's Victorian architectural exteriors and period portraits of haughty, elegantly dressed gentry. The author's whimsical prose style is at its most controlled; her descriptions of the Beast's enchanted palace represent Willard at her imaginative best. Her industrious, inquisitive heroine is the very model of courtesy and kindness—"when you met her, she remembered your name, and when you spoke to her, she listened"—though not so virtuous that she's not above answering in kind when her sister makes a cutting remark. Beauty's father and two sisters are equally well drawn; indeed, the dynamics at work among these family members almost overshadow Beauty's interaction with the Beast, a disappointingly tame fellow for the most part. This is a storybook rather than a picture book, a splendid gift of sure-fire appeal to middle-grade lovers of fairy tales.

THROUGH THE MICKLE WOODS (written by Valiska Gregory, 1992)

Helen Gregory

SOURCE: A review of *Through the Mickle Woods*, in *School Library Journal*, Vol. 38, No. 12, December, 1992, p. 112.

A page urges his mourning king to honor the queen's last wish and go with him into the winter night of the mickle woods to find the bear. Once in the cave, the impatient monarch is ready to turn back, but the wise bear has stories to tell and the boy wants to listen. After three healing parables, the grieving man can look forward to the new day. Moser's large, dramatic, ink, watercolor, and gouache illustrations realize the telling. For each of the bear's stories, he frames a smaller picture against snow-dappled trees. The art is among the best of a master painter. Unfortunately, although [Valiska] Gregory's similes are apt, there are far too many, and they lack the power of metaphor or plain straight telling. She averages over two per page, weighing down the story, distracting readers, and breaking the pace. She is better than this; less ornate, her bear's fables sing, teach, and comfort. Overall, however, the tale is as rich as its artwork. Beyond its power as story, it could help those dealing with grief.

Deborah Abbot

SOURCE: A review of *Through the Mickle Woods*, in *Booklist*, Vol. 89, No. 7, December 1, 1992, p. 675.

In this elegantly written and illustrated picture book for older children, a king is grief-stricken by the loss of his queen. A boy gives the king a box containing the late queen's ring and a letter instructing the king to go to the mickle woods to find the bear. Together the two make their way through the snowy mickle woods to the cave of the bear. After the bear accepts the ring, the king is impatient to return home, but the overpowering presence of the bear forces him to listen as the bear spins three yarns, each conveying a universal truth. The king's sorrow begins to ease, and by the end the boy and the king are bound together by their memories of the dead queen. Many of Moser's paintings display a dark, wintry feeling closely matched to the opening tone of the text. Others, with a luminescent quality, shed a light that proclaims the messages of hope and love. For each of the bear's tales there is a framed image, set against the snowy, gray, forested background of the mickle woods. The vehicle of a story within a story works well here, as the author's pen traces a pattern that heals and the artist's brush fills in paintings that liberate.

Elizabeth S. Watson

SOURCE: A review of *Through the Mickle Woods,* in *The Horn Book Magazine,* Vol. LXIX, No. 2, March/April, 1993, pp. 202-03.

Reminiscent of "Good King Wenceslas," this tale brings another king and his young friend into an equally snowy

From When Willard Met Babe Ruth, *written by Donald Hall. Illustrated by Barry Moser.*

woods in search of solace. Unwilling yet compelled by his dying queen's last words, "Do one thing more for me, my king, my love. Into the dark and mickle woods go forth to find the bear," the saddened king sets forth with the youngster, Michael, whom the queen had befriended. The bear is found to be a master storyteller whose pointed references allude to the beauty and importance of life and ultimately begin to ease the king's grief. The language and phrasing are as pleasing to the ear as the story is to the heart. Moser's solid dark castle, barely visible in the snow spotted landscape, sets the scene and mood beautifully; the approach to the bear's den is equally dramatic. The combination of text and facing full-page illustrations succeeds in producing an effective presentation of the poignant tale.

📖 **THE MAGIC HARE** (written by Lynne Reid Banks, 1993)

Publishers Weekly

SOURCE: A review of *The Magic Hare,* in *Publishers Weekly,* Vol. 240, No. 27, July 5, 1993, p. 69.

An irrepressible hare dances his way through 10 stories, which take him from an English meadow to Transylvania to the moon. Along the way, he uses humor, wiles and magic to improve the situations of those he meets—teaching good manners to a bad-tempered queen; helping a timid orphan overcome her fear (and her appetite for hare); defanging a vampire. With her widely varied settings and diverse characters, [Lynne Reid] Banks (the *Indian in the Cupboard* novels) delivers abundant amounts of fantasy; her stories also function as parables, aptly demonstrating the rewards of such qualities as curiosity, spontaneity and self-acceptance. Her most compelling tales are those in which the hare, as trickster, faces an intractable situation or foe; when he is simply deploying his magic powers the narrative moves with considerably less tension. Moser supplies a single full-page watercolor—in most cases a portrait of a central figure—to accompany each tale. His illustrations vary in mood and expression from tender to terrifying, and provide strong, often strikingly dramatic touchstones for the text.

Kirkus Reviews

SOURCE: A review of *The Magic Hare,* in *Kirkus Reviews,* Vol. LXI, No. 14, July 15, 1993, p. 930.

Ten fanciful tales about a hare with magical powers who rescues maidens from vampires, dragons, or their own fears; christens a tiny flower that had been overlooked (the harebell, of course); makes an end of one horrible giant and reforms another; cures assorted royalty of their hiccups, greed, and bad temper; and meets his match in a black witch who works white magic to turn Hare into a human for one brief, uncomfortable moment. Wonderful readalouds (though a few end rather abruptly, and some

British expressions may need explaining), with humor, suspense, and some implied messages about environmental responsibility and valuing one's own talents. Moser *(Jump! The Tales of Brer Rabbit)* may be the best illustrator of rabbits since Beatrix Potter; this one has startling green eyes and a bit of a grin. The ten full-page portraits here pose colorful characters against dark backgrounds; the villainous ones are most satisfactorily revolting. A refreshing alternative to standard fairy tales.

Janice Del Negro

SOURCE: A review of *The Magic Hare,* in *Booklist,* Vol. 90, No. 2, September 15, 1993, p. 149.

[Lynne Reid] Banks has taken the traditional folklore figure of the hare and fashioned her own version of the trickster character. Her creation has many traditional characteristics—the rabbit is smart, mischievous, helpful, and devious—and it also has magical powers that are often used to save the day. During the course of the 10 original tales included here, the hare gives a spoiled queen a lesson in manners, cures a prince of hiccups, and names a lonesome flower. Moser's paintings are sometimes dark, sometimes gruesome, and always effective: the faces of his giants are truly scary, and his vampire is satisfactorily gory. The stories are occasionally uneven (some have promising openings but fall flat). On the whole, however, they will make unusual and intriguing read-alouds for groups of older children.

FLY! A BRIEF HISTORY OF FLIGHT (1993)

Kirkus Reviews

SOURCE: A review of *Fly! A Brief History of Flight,* in *Kirkus Reviews,* Vol. LXI, No. 16, August 15, 1993, p. 1076.

As a kid, Moser says, he loved to draw pictures of airplanes, and he still does. Choosing key moments in aviation history, he accompanies three-quarter-spread watercolors with a brief text (expanded in lengthy "Historical Notes") and an idiosyncratic timeline, running along the bottom of each page, ranging from the invention of ice cream to the Russian Revolution. ("1936, *Life* magazine first published. 1939, film *The Wizard of Oz* appears. 1940, penicillin developed," etc.) Who's to say his priorities are wrong? The illustrations are evocative and handsomely structured—but, for the subject, static. Good browsing.

Dorcus Hand

SOURCE: A review of *Fly! A Brief History of Flight,* in *School Library Journal,* Vol. 39, No. 10, October, 1993, p. 145.

Moser's love of aviation shines through in this survey of 16 episodes from the history of modern flight. He opens with the invention of the hot-air balloon and concludes with the space shuttle. The first section is done in a picture-book format and offers a rich watercolor painting and a brief description of each incident with a timeline of concurrent historical events and inventions along the bottom of each spread. The latter half of the book is devoted to "Historical Notes" that describe the occurrences in greater detail and smaller print with minimal illustration for more able readers. An extensive bibliography is appended. Fans of Moser's fine artwork, as well as those with an interest in the ever-popular subject, will want to include this outstanding title.

Stephanie Zvirin

SOURCE: A review of *Fly! A Brief History of Flight,* in *Booklist,* Vol. 90, No. 4, October 15, 1993, p. 438.

This nicely designed book melds Moser's lifelong interest in planes with his love of art. In a series of 16 attractive double-page spreads, which begins with a depiction of the Montgolfiers' balloon and its crew of animal aeronauts, Moser uses words and watercolors to capture milestones in aviation history. The impressive paintings are evocative rather than intricately detailed, but they show the beauty and variety of the aircraft—from George Cayley's three-winged glider to *Sputnik 1* and the space shuttle *Atlantis.* A timeline, concluding with 1992, puts the achievements described into historical context. Moser's text, though brief, contains enough to pique curiosity, and his pictures are certain to attract browsers. His notes, written for an older reader than his main text, are a lively elaboration of the history presented in each spread. Kids as old as junior-high age will find this section of interest, and the bibliography, containing a number of adult books, provides follow-up material for a variety of readers.

James R. Hansen

SOURCE: A review of *Fly! A Brief History of Flight,* in *Science Books & Films,* Vol. 30, No. 3, April, 1994, p. 83.

This nice little picture book provides children with a "short, chronological, episodic history of men and women and their flying machines." Wisely, the author begins not by reaching back thousands of years to the Chinese kite and the aboriginal boomerang, but by moving right to the "First Ascent," the original manned flight of the Montgolfier hot-air balloon in 1783. The wondrous story then proceeds, in the first half of the book, through a series of beautifully illustrated vignettes showing the achievements of Sir George Cayley, Otto Lilienthal, and the Wright brothers, up to the Space Shuttle and the *Gossamer Condor.* An especially nice touch is the running time line at the bottom of each page, which tells the young reader what else was going on in the world at the time of the event depicted, in fields like science, politics, sports, and the arts. The second half of the book, entitled "Historical Notes," presents a visually mundane version of the same story. The text of this half is more detailed and adult, but the overall presentation less satisfying. The approach taken in the first half of the book should have been extended to the second. A few more pretty pictures would also make the. . . price a bit more palatable.

THE DREAMER (written by Cynthia Rylant, 1993)

Ilene Cooper

SOURCE: A review of *The Dreamer,* in *Booklist,* Vol. 90, No. 5, November 1, 1993, p. 519.

[Cynthia] Rylant and Moser combine their talents, and the sum is more than their considerable parts. Rylant casts her own creation story, starting with a young artist who lives alone and spends his days as artists do, daydreaming. But then, as artists also do, he decides to make what he sees in his mind. First, he cuts out a star. So delighted is he with the results that he keeps making stars until he is surrounded by the heavens. Then his imagination shows him the earth and the sea and the animals. He feels such love for his creation, such an explosion of joy, that he wants to tell someone, someone who is an artist as well. So he draws another artist, and soon the world fills up with artists. "The first young artist, still a dreamer, has always called them his children. And they, in turn, have always called him God." Rylant's text, exceptionally moving in places, can also border on the sweet, but when that happens, Moser is always there with his incredible art to lift the words to a higher level. Along with handsome, expected vistas, there are also unexpected scenes: the artist (only his hands are seen) cutting out stars, or the family-of-man portrait, with every person unique. This book is a reminder that the oldest stories can always be refashioned in new ways to touch the heart.

Kirkus Reviews

SOURCE: A review of *The Dreamer,* in *Kirkus Reviews,* Vol. LXI, No. 22, November 15, 1993, p. 1466.

An all-star rendition of the creation makes an appropriate entry for the Blue Sky imprint's inaugural list. [Cynthia] Rylant brings the Creator down to earth in a conversational, unassuming narrative, depicting him as a shy young artist who dreams, tests new ideas, and makes other "artist[s] in his own image" in order to have someone to share the pleasure in his works. He "has always called them his children. And they, in turn, have always called him God," the author concludes, finally equating the artist with the deity. Moser's elegantly simple compositions reflect the straightforward tone and sense of a primeval beauty within the everyday world; he shows the stars being clipped out with scissors held in sturdy hands, while the artist also appears as a misty figure beneath the dramatic

silhouette of an aging pine, imagining the animal kingdom yet to come. An attractively developed concept, nondoctrinal yet reverent, that would be interesting to compare to Eric Carle's *Draw Me a Star.*

Karen James

SOURCE: A review of *The Dreamer,* in *School Library Journal,* Vol. 40, No. 2, February, 1994, p. 91.

"There once was a young artist who lived all alone, quietly, and who spent his days as most young artists do: daydreaming." What follows is a sentimental and personal vision of the Biblical Creation story. Rylant chooses her words carefully, and the text has a certain ineffable quality, but not the transcendent power of James Weldon Johnson's emotional poem, *The Creation,* or the heroic simplicity of Leonard Everett Fisher's *David and Goliath.* However, **The Dreamer** is a handsome, well-designed book. From the title page, sprinkled with stars, to the parchment-colored endpapers, it has a clear, open, almost pristine look that suits the text. Moser's signature watercolors include some evocative images. All that readers see is the creator's hands—cutting out stars, extending the globe of the world against the heavens, drawing with a pen. Readers are looking over the artist's shoulder, or by extension, are doing the creating themselves. The story is heartfelt, but it lacks the complexity of thought found in Rylant's novels, or even in her easy-to-read "Henry and Mudge" series. For libraries looking for another interpretation of the Creation story, this is a visually attractive choice, but not a first purchase.

TUCKER PFEFFERCORN: AN OLD STORY RETOLD (1994)

Hazel Rochman

SOURCE: A review of *Tucker Pfeffercorn: An Old Story Retold,* in *Booklist,* Vol. 90, No. 13, March 1, 1994, p. 1265.

Moser sets the Rumpelstiltskin fairy tale in a contemporary southern gothic setting. From the beginning you notice everyone's name: names have power in this story. The company boss, Hezekiah Sweatt, the meanest and richest man in the mountains, hears a "crazy tale" that a 19-year-old widow, Bessie Grace Kinzalow, can spin cotton into gold. She denies it, but Sweatt locks her up in a shed and threatens to kill her baby if she doesn't provide the gold by morning. Strong-willed though she is, she can't fight the powerful boss and his thugs. Then a peculiar little man appears in the night and spins the gold for her. One day he returns and demands her baby as his price—unless she can guess his name. As in **The Tinderbox** (1990), Moser intensifies the mystery of the traditional story by bringing it close to home. The colloquial voice—both comic and scary—roots the tale in a strongly realized place, and Moser's full-page watercolors portray ordinary people in the community: from the miners swapping tall tales at the company store to fearless young Bessie Grace in her overalls, dreamy and strong, holding her late husband's jacket around her. The glaring boss in suit and tie is right out of a gangster movie. The strange, little bald man in a denim jacket, might—perhaps—be living down the road. There's just the right touch of menace in the cover portrait: smiling Bessie Grace cudding her baby, the little man a dark silhouette in the golden background.

Joanne Schott

SOURCE: A review of *Tucker Pfeffercorn*, in *Quill & Quire*, Vol. 60, No. 4, April, 1994, p. 42.

At Sweatt's Company Store, one of the story-swappers gains credibility for his tales by giving his characters real local names. His final story, of a woman who can spin cotton into gold, arouses the interest of Mr. Sweatt, the meanest and richest man for miles around, who demands that the woman be brought to him. Almost before the reader realizes, the story of Rumpelstiltskin is unfolding, with Barry Moser using a technique similar to the story-swapper's. The setting is a specific one of southern cotton fields and mines, and the heroine is a young miner's widow. The usual mode of folklore, where distance and anonymity provide safety, is no longer in operation. Threats here are real: " . . . if'n that there cotton ain't gold by mornin' . . . I'd just hate to think what might happen to yore sweet little ol' baby." The final events play out in much the familiar way, though Bessie Grace gets to keep most of the gold because the peculiar little man has disposed of her captor.

Moser's use of colourful dialect and his realistic detail in text and illustrations bring new dimensions and interpretation to the story, demonstrating vividly that the archetypes from old folktales can be found in more familiar places. All the fear and the dark side of human nature that lurk in the old tale spring to the surface. In this retelling, though, the Rumpelstiltskin story is no longer appropriate for a young child.

Roger Sutton

SOURCE: A review of *Tucker Pfeffercorn*, in *Bulletin of the Center for Children's Books*, Vol. 47, No. 10, June, 1994, p. 311-12.

With that ominous little man on the cover, this probably isn't a *Bulletin* for someone's bedtime reading. The same goes for Barry Moser's spooky revisioning of Rumpelstiltskin, here known as Tucker Pfeffercorn, the name sought by the desperate Bessie Grace, who, sans palace helpers, all on her own, discovers the name of the hateful imp in order to save her young daughter, Claretta.

And it wasn't her stupid boasting father who got her into

the mess, either. Bessie, a comely young widow, is the victim of a story spun by company store porch-sitter Jefferson Tadlock, who decides to spice up his yarn about a woman who can spin cotton into gold by giving her the name of that "little ol' widow woman up on the hill," Bessie Grace. Unfortunately, local land baron Hezakiah Sweatt is listening in and locks Bessie into his shed along with a half bale of cotton: "If'n ya want yore baby back, ya best get to work, cause if'n that there cotton ain't gold by mornin' . . . why, I'd just hate to think what might happen to yore sweet little ol' baby." Southern humorist Florence King would call Sweatt a "bad good ole boy," and Moser's portrait, complete with mean squint, mean mouth, and big ol' belly, sets us firmly down in mountain-gothic country. You wouldn't want to mess with this sucker.

Nor with his evil, tiny twin. Bessie Grace's cotton-spinning savior first appears hanging from the rafters of the shed—all we see of him are his pointy little feet while Bessie Grace looks from below. He doesn't ask for any payment the first night—"'I don't want nothin,' he said in a sweet voice. 'Not now, no-how'"—but when on the third night Bessie Grace desperately promises him anything, he says "Ya got a deal," only returning for payment after Sweatt has mysteriously disappeared and Bessie Grace escapes—with the gold—and gives what-for to Sweatt's thugs. Safely home with her baby, Bessie Grace is reading her Bible when the little man reappears: "Ya said anything, an' the anything I want is her!"

"Rumpelstiltskin" is a pretty scary story to begin with; what's gained by its transplantation into local legend? "Inside many of us/ is a small old man/ who wants to get out," writes Anne Sexton in her version of the tale, and both Sexton and Moser know the power of story brought (down) home. The Appalachia he evokes is not real, exactly; it's a literary backwoods rooted in the popular American imagination. Bessie Grace is an angel from a country song, complete with grit and resourcefulness; Hezakiah Sweatt and the little man himself are Carson McCullers grotesques. By putting a European folktale into an American context, old roots in new soil, Moser surprises our expectations—*that's* not supposed to happen *here*—so we see the story and the setting each in a new light, whether it's the hard-baking glare on the faces of Sweatt's henchmen or the white-hot glow of the emerging gold as Tucker Pfeffercorn spins it from the wheel. An excess of portraits often makes a picture book static, but Moser has here succeeded in making each (and the illustrations are almost exclusively portraits) work as narrative art, from the cover watercolor of Bessie Grace and Claretta in a tender embrace while the shadow of Tucker lurks behind, to the upside down, eye-popping rage of Tucker when Bessie Grace names his name. In a mischievous turn that makes manifest the intense fusing of text and art throughout the book, Moser mirrors Tucker's furious found out stamping on the ceiling with a corresponding upside-down reversal of his words: "The devil told ya! The devil told ya!"

Just as folktales proceed from archetypes—the trickster,

the fool, the princess—stories come from characters. And while it would have been easy for Moser to employ "characters"—hillbilly jim-cracker-dandies—he gives us instead real strength and terror, sometimes in combination. Tucker Pfeffercorn is wicked for sure, but in the picture mentioned above of the gold-spinning, there's an aura of sacred flame that gives his demonic features nobility, and reminds us that his magic is indeed marvelous. And Bessie Grace is nobody's fool. After she takes care of Tucker, she takes care of herself: "She gave a good bit of the gold to her church, but most of it she kept. A few months later, she and Claretta moved to Cincinnati, where they lived happily ever after." Let's wish them the best, but people probably tell stories there, too, when they find them hanging from the rafters or standing beside the crib. And as Jefferson Tadlock learned, stories can cause trouble. Sleep tight.

📖 ARIADNE, AWAKE! (written by Doris Orgel, 1994)

Hazel Rochman

SOURCE: A review of *Ariadne, Awake!*, in *Booklist*, Vol. 90, No. 17, May 1, 1994, p. 1599.

Ariadne is the young princess who helps Theseus defeat the Minotaur; it's her thread that guides him back through the twists and treachery of the labyrinth. The myth has always focused on Theseus as hero; in fact (except for those familiar with Strauss' opera *Ariadne aux Naxos*), most of us can't remember who Ariadne is. Now [Doris] Orgel puts Ariadne center stage and lets her tell the story from the beginning. Always a rebel, she hates her cruel father, King Minos of Crete, who keeps the Minotaur imprisoned in the labyrinth and feeds him on human flesh. Then Theseus arrives, one of the 14 Athenians who are the required annual tribute to the monster. Dazzled by Theseus' beauty, power, and attention, Ariadne loves him and helps him; she leaves home and sails away with him—and then wakes up to find that he has abandoned her on an island. Ariadne tells her story with simple drama, and the book design is spacious and beautiful.

Moser's watercolors, however, are sunlit and idyllic, with little sense of the darkness and terror that are also part of the story. His full-front view of the Minotaur is a mistake, maybe because it jars our own images; it's not nearly as compelling as his woodcuts for *Frankenstein* (1984), which kept the monster mysterious and distanced. What is heartrending is the view of Ariadne on the shore, searching the horizon for a sail, waiting for Theseus to return. This version of the story shakes you up. Theseus is undoubtedly a hero who sacrifices himself for others; does he deliberately mislead Ariadne? The treachery is a shock, but just as astonishing is the way that Ariadne recovers from her pain and finds love and joy with the god Dionysus. Orgel shows that the young woman's perilous journey is also a personal one of leaving home and transforming herself.

Betsy Hearne

SOURCE: A review of *Ariadne, Awake!*, in *Bulletin of the Center for Children's Books,* Vol. 47, No. 10, June, 1994, p. 330.

[Doris] Orgel's version of the Theseus myth is related by Ariadne and begins—after a brief prologue describing Pasiphae's passion for a sacred bull, and the Minotaur that's born as a result—with Ariadne's early memory of trying to find and comfort her bestial half-brother in the Labyrinth. She's almost killed in the process and is punished by her tyrannical father, so when Theseus appears and wakes her own passion, she determines to save his life in defiance of her King Minos. Her appeal to Daedalus for help, the golden thread he gives her, Theseus' killing the Minotaur, and their escape from the guards all lead to Theseus' abandoning Ariadne on the Isle of Naxos, where she's saved by a satyr and wedded to Dionysus. Like Nancy Willard's *Beauty and the Beast,* also illustrated by Barry Moser, this is a tale that's been fictionalized far beyond its usual length but not quite to the full development of a novel. Gracefully written and cannily illustrated with vivid portraits (though Minos looks more like a Viking raider than a king of Crete) or scenes playing on unexpected perspectives, the book will especially appeal to readers who think they've outgrown picture-book editions of myth but aren't ready for dense historical fiction such as H. M. Hoover's *The Dawn Palace: The Story of Medea*.

Patricia Dooley

SOURCE: A review of *Ariadne, Awake!*, in *School Library Journal,* Vol. 40, No. 6, June, 1994, p. 152.

A prologue sets the stage for readers: King Minos angered the god Poseidon and as punishment saw his wife enamoured of a bull. She died at the birth of the product of that union: the Minotaur, now immured and fed an annual sacrifice of Athenian youth. This fictionalized, first-person narrative begins with 10-year-old Ariadne as she tries to approach her monstrous half-brother, only to learn a brutal lesson about his—and her father's—nature. The core story begins five years later, as Ariadne watches the Greek prince Theseus arrive to be sacrificed—and instantly falls in love with him. In quick order she helps him escape, is abandoned on Naxos, and is rescued from despair by a satyr who introduces her to Dionysus (who in turn introduces her to wine). The god marries her on the spot, just after spelling out the lesson of the tale: "Even love that ends in pain and grief is precious as a stop along the way toward greater love." Who could quarrel with this consoling moral, even if Ariadne's rebound is rather precipitous? The prolific Moser gets better and better, though his bull-headed Minotaur is more pathetic than terrifying. Minos looks like a Viking, but Theseus and Dionysus clearly represent opposing male types. Ariadne, with her button-nose and straggling red locks, doesn't look much like a Cretan or a princess, but perhaps the idea is that the young teenage target audience will identify with the face above the flowing robes. The emotional heroine, and the romantic and sexual themes, may make the myth material more than palatable to middle-school readers.

Mary M. Burns

SOURCE: A review *Ariadne, Awake!*, in *The Horn Book Magazine,* Vol. LXX, No. 5, September/October, 1994, pp. 589-90.

In conventional retellings of the ancient story of the Minotaur, the Greek hero Theseus is at the center, celebrated for his cleverness in securing the assistance of the Cretan princess Ariadne to escape from the labyrinth in which the creature is confined. In this work of fiction based on the Greek legend, Doris Orgel has chosen to turn the spotlight on Ariadne, exploring her motivation for aiding and abetting the enemy, her reaction to being abandoned on Naxos, and her final triumph as the wife of the god Dionysus. The result is a romantic—but not saccharine—tale which traces the development of a headstrong preadolescent into a determined young woman. The expansion of the legend adds dimension to Ariadne's character and immediacy to the story. The style is contemporary in feeling, reinforcing the concept that ancient tales have universal applications. Barry Moser's luminous watercolors capture the essence of Ariadne's longing in a series of dramatic tableaux, emphasizing her personality rather than the terror of the conflict with the Minotaur.

THE FARM SUMMER 1942 (written by Donald Hall, 1994)

Kirkus Reviews

SOURCE: A review of *The Farm Summer 1942,* in *Kirkus Reviews,* Vol. LXII, No. 10, May 15, 1994, p. 698.

The noted poet and author of *Ox-Cart Man* describes a nine-year-old's summer on his grandparents' New Hampshire farm while his dad's in the South Pacific and his mother works "on a secret project . . . for the war effort." Peter flies across the country but ends his journey in a buggy; [Donald] Hall rounds out an evocatively detailed description of traditional farm life with Peter's reunion with Dad back home in San Francisco. But the chief glory of this beautifully crafted book is Moser's watercolor art, in which the details-from the sun glancing off Peter's freshly ironed shirt to the contrast between the military bearing of a newel post and the more relaxed stance of the uniformed father as he welcomes his son—are statements of pure design as well as singularly pleasing depictions of the warm relationships, wholesome setting, and exquisitely observed farm animals. Nostalgia at its best.

Lee Bock

SOURCE: A review of *The Farm Summer 1942,* in *School Library Journal,* Vol. 40, No. 6, June, 1994, p. 101.

[Donald] Hall delivers precisely what his title promises—a straightforward family reminiscence that is comfortable and richly detailed. Peter, nine, is sent to spend the summer on his grandparents' New Hampshire farm while his father is on a destroyer in the South Pacific and his mother is working on a secret government project. Whatever insecurities the boy might have are soon dismissed as he finds comfort in the routines of the farm and the loving presence of his grandparents. He lends a hand as they salt the sheep, milk the cows, and hay, and listens intently to news on the radio. The summer passes peacefully without crisis—no turning point, no high drama—other than that which is implied by the wartime backdrop. The voice of the story is warm, and, as in real-life family storytelling, occasionally a bit long-winded, while at the same time leaving listeners wanting to know more. Moser's full-page watercolor illustrations are surprisingly bright and photo-real, expertly complementing the story. He focuses at times on a simple straw hat that Peter wears just as his father did as a boy, linking him visually to the past. The painter's skill in rendering animals, in capturing people's thoughtful expressions, and his careful inclusion of period details will encourage readers to linger. In the summer of 1942, a window to the past opens and Peter steps through it. Readers can do the same.

Deborah Stevenson

SOURCE: A review of *The Farm Summer 1942,* in *Bulletin of the Center for Children's Books,* Vol. 47, No. 11, July/August, 1994, p. 358.

It's 1942; Peter's father is off at the war and now his mother is called to New York, so nine-year-old Peter must spend the summer on his grandparents' New Hampshire farm. There Peter encounters rural life ("Lady Ghost pulled them in the buggy along the road past old farmhouses to a long white house with green shutters where his grandmother waited with gingersnaps and rhubarb pie") and hears about the war distantly over the radio. When the summer ends, Peter regrets leaving the farm but enjoys returning to his San Francisco home, especially when his father, home on leave, welcomes Peter back. This is an evocative account of daily farm life, gently tidied through backward-looking eyes but still full of interesting detail. There's little plot, however; the quiet mention of how much Peter misses his father makes that absence part of the background rather than the thrust of the story, and the narrative sometimes keeps its smoothness by leaving terms ("streamliner," for instance) unexplained. Barry Moser paints an all-American kid on an all-American farm, although the art has a stillness that conveys historical distance; the pictures sometimes extend the story and once contradict it where the illustration shows Peter and a local girl playing outside and the text keeps them firmly inside. Kids might enjoy sharing this with grandparents or grand-parent figures, who can explain the period features and expand with stories of their own.

PILGRIM'S PROGRESS (retelling by Gary Schmidt, 1994)

Carolyn Phelan

SOURCE: A review of *Pilgrim's Progress,* in *Booklist,* Vol. 91, No. 5, November 1, 1994, p. 501.

[Gary] Schmidt provides a clear, simple retelling of Bunyan's allegory. In this classic story, Christian leaves his home in the city of Destruction and sets out to find the Celestial City. Nearly drowned in the bog called the Slough of Despond and almost executed in a city named Vanity Fair, he is helped by such characters as Evangelist, Goodwill, and Hopeful, and hindered by Apollyon, Despair, and Deceiver, as he makes his way to his heavenly destination. This beautifully designed book has large, heavy pages, each divided into two columns by a single, scarlet line. Moser's watercolor paintings, mainly portraits of the characters dressed in clothing from many eras and places, thoughtfully interpret the text. A beautiful edition, recommended for any library with an audience for the classics.

Tom Ferrell

SOURCE: A review of *Pilgrim's Progress,* in *New York Times Book Review,* November 13, 1994, p. 30.

The story of John Bunyan's *Pilgrim's Progress* is easily told, because there is not much of it. An anonymous (unless it is Bunyan) narrator falls asleep. He dreams he sees a man standing "in a certain place," holding a book and carrying an immense burden on his back. This is Christian, who immediately cries out, "What shall I do?" Christian briefly explains to his wife and children that fire from heaven is about to destroy their town, gets a bearing from a bystander named Evangelist, and takes off at once, pleas of wife and children notwithstanding, for what we soon learn is the Celestial City.

Not for a moment do we doubt that Christian will arrive at his goal, but in his path lie all manner of allegorically named pests and enemies who divert him, thrash him, imprison him, try to kill him, with little apparent logic of narrative or theology (why should he encounter Mr. Worldly-Wiseman before he loses his burden at the Cross, and Formality and Hypocrisy later, and Giant Despair later yet?). Never permanently defeated, Christian struggles on, with occasional help both human and divine, overcoming or escaping what is, quite literally, just one damned thing after another. At length this Indiana Jones of Protestant Christianity enters the Celestial City. The narrator wakes up. . . .

If any earthly power can restore *Pilgrim's Progress* to the children's library, this handsome version ought to do it,

with its large, elegant pages, sharp typography, acres of white space and above all Barry Moser's watercolor illustrations. His facility in rendering lights, shadows and textures in this unforgiving medium is a wonder to see, and so is his figure drawing. Since *Pilgrim's Progress* is short on physical description, Mr. Moser has freely assigned period and character: while Christian is a short-bearded young man of the 1990's in jeans and a baseball cap, Mr. Worldly-Wiseman is a plump, self-absorbed Cavalier who can hardly open both eyes to sneer, and Simple is a long-faced moron with an ax murderer's haircut and an over-size mail-order suit of, say, the 1880s.

Kate Hegarty Bouman

SOURCE: A review of *Pilgrim's Progress,* in *School Library Journal,* Vol. 40, No. 12, December, 1994, p. 130.

[Gary] Schmidt's retelling is much more accessible than the original version, which was written in the late 1600s. Although the number and extent of Christian's encounters with various temptations and trials on his journey to the Celestial City are reduced in this retelling, the flavor of his adventures is maintained. Schmidt has kept Bunyan's straightforward names such as Ignorance, Obstinate, Hopeful, Despair, Faithful, etc. for the players. The text is beautifully illustrated with Moser's colorful, realistic watercolors. His mix of both historical periods and ethnic groups is a fascinating way to extend the text spatially and temporally. For example, Christian is wearing a baseball cap but he also wears armor. Help is a portly gentleman in green overalls and a pinstriped shirt, while Evangelist is a distinguished African American in a white suit. An interesting, accessible version of an old classic that many YAs have heard about, but not all have read.

WHEN BIRDS COULD TALK AND BATS COULD SING: THE ADVENTURES OF BRUH SPARROW, SIS WREN, AND THEIR FRIENDS (written by Virginia Hamilton, 1996)

Publishers Weekly

SOURCE: A review of *When Birds Could Talk & Bats Could Sing,* in *Publishers Weekly,* Vol. 243, No. 8, February 19, 1996, p. 214.

With impressive aplomb, [Virginia] Hamilton follows the ambitious *Her Stories* with eight animal tales, reworked from 19th-century originals recorded by a slave owner's daughter. The stories are told in the *cante fable* tradition, with plenty of rhyming and singing, and an apparently artless ease ("Well, Miss Mockingbird reeled the song off as pretty as you please"). They must be read aloud. And they will be—the foibles, squabblings and occasional good deeds of Miss Bat, Bruh Buzzard and Sis Wren are our own. The self-deceived Miss Bat's two stories epitomize the book. She shakes loose all her beautiful feathers, then casts away all her songs, so that she will not be like any bird . . . and soon she most certainly is not. The reader will laugh, ruefully, at her pride, recognizing the moral ("For pride has a way of taking a fall every time") long before it appears as the satisfying conclusion. A wonderful complement to the front-porch voice of the stories, Moser's bright watercolors vibrate with dozens of birds confronting the reader in their best hats and bonnets, their faces alive with contentment, irritation or panic. These vaguely Disneyesque characters strut through formal full-page compositions and flutter, flounce and perch among the lines of type. It's unusually warm and down-to-earth work for Moser, some of his best, and helps to make this book, if not the most serious of Hamilton's collections, one of her most enjoyable and accessible.

Janice Del Negro

SOURCE: A review of *When Birds Could Talk & Bats Could Sing,* in *Booklist,* Vol. 92, No. 16, April 15, 1996, p. 1440.

[Virginia] Hamilton's eight lively retellings of tales from the American South feature feuding birds, foolish bats, and hummingbirds with attitudes. In one story, Blue Jay and Swallow bring fire to humankind; in another, Hummingbird loses her voice in a battle with the wind. Each tale is written in the style of a *cante fable* (a story that includes a song or verse and ends with a moral). The moral, printed in italics, enhances and reflects the oral nature of the stories, which Hamilton roots in the work of Martha Young, a nineteenth-century Alabama folklorist who collected black folktales and songs and wrote original stories in the African American tradition. Dialect has been eliminated, with the stories retold in an easygoing style that gracefully lends itself to reading and telling aloud. The layout is exceptionally appealing and effective—from the full- and double-page-spread watercolors and generous use of white space to the enlarged typeface and extra leading. Moser's finely detailed watercolors have an inherent humor that makes the characters especially vivid, and the jacket illustration is a wonderful, slyly funny collection of bird personalities. The text, the layout, and the illustrations work together seamlessly in this beautifully designed, well-crafted collection.

Jennifer Fleming

SOURCE: A review of *When Birds Could Talk & Bats Could Sing,* in *School Library Journal,* Vol. 42, No. 5, May, 1996, pp. 104-05.

[Virginia] Hamilton's hilarious and accessible retellings of eight bird and bat stories based on African American folk-tales are a joy to read. They are kin to the Bruh/Brer Rabbit stories, and were originally assembled by a Southern journalist, Martha Young, in the 1880s. Hamilton takes care to document and explain her sources. Some of these selections were collected from folklore and others Young herself created; together they form a cohesive, delightful

whole. Moser has glowingly illustrated all manner of creatures in his illustrious career, but the flighty feathered ones he creates here are among his best. He skillfully and with great glee defines a cast of hat-wearing wrens, jays, buzzards, and even a self-obsessed, singing bat with a serious attitude problem. There is also one painting that looks suspiciously like Moser himself—in comically gruesome disguise, of course. The dynamic duo that created *In the Beginning* has succeeded again with this lively collection.

Betsy Hearne

SOURCE: A review of *When Birds Could Talk & Bats Could Sing,* in *Bulletin for the Center of Children's Books,* Vol. 49, No. 10, June, 1996, p. 336-37.

Drawn from post-Civil War African-American stories collected by Martha Young, a wealthy white woman raised on southern plantations, these stories acquire new life with Virginia Hamilton's lyrical idiom and Barry Moser's fun-poking pictures. The cast is largely avian. Sis Wren and Bruh Sparrow lose an argument about the ownership of an impossibly large pumpkin ("Pick on your own size. For it's no use squabbling over what's too big for you to handle"), Miss Bat loses her beautiful feathers and songs because of inordinate pride, Bluejay and Swallow steal from old Firekeeper (who looks a lot like old Barry Moser), Bruh Buzzard loses his top to an aggrieved victim, Hummingbird loses her voice to Old Wind, Cardinal acquires red feathers but almost loses his gray wife when he cleans up Bruh Deer after a hunter's gunshot, and Brown Wren tries to fly too high ("You were born down there. . . . Get used to it"). . . .

Along with his signature portraits (take a gander at loop-eyed Bruh Buzzard), Moser has injected the collection with spirited action and sprightly colors, as well as a varied page design that will wake up sleepy readers. These pictures are as loud as birdsong on a country morning. The compositions are bold, the humor sly, and the drafting uncannily accurate even as it's indulgently anthropomorphized. Although independent readers will be able to handle this oversized picture book on their own, don't miss the fun of reading it aloud.

📖 ***WHEN WILLARD MET BABE RUTH* (written by Donald Hall, 1996)**

Kirkus Reviews

SOURCE: A review of *When Willard Met Babe Ruth,* in *Kirkus Reviews,* Vol. LXIV, No. 5, March 1, 1996, pp. 374-75.

The national pastime gets a bit of much-needed luster from the poet's touch. Young Willard Babson makes the acquaintance of Babe Ruth one day when he and his father pull the young, just-married pitcher's auto out of a

New Hampshire ditch. From there, [Donald] Hall builds a beautiful story about the twining of two lives over 20 years; one a farm boy, rapt in the pleasures of baseball and mesmerized by Ruth's style; the other, "the best who ever played the game of baseball." Hanging over every event is the penumbral melancholy of those years, from the end of the First World War through the middle of the Great Depression—when baseball helped anchor a storm-tossed population. That feeling is enhanced by Moser's nostalgic watercolors, each an achingly sentimental tableau. Hall salts the tale with fine historical tidbits—from the mention of "Fibber McGee and Molly" to Al Smith's run for office—as he moves the story to its emotional climax when Willard's daughter, a baseball fan named Ruth, meets her hero. A heartfelt piece of Americana from two old pros.

Bill Ott

SOURCE: A review of *When Willard Met Babe Ruth,* in *Booklist,* Vol. 92, No. 14, March 15, 1996, p. 1262.

You hear a lot of twaddle about how baseball unites generations, but as with most clichés, there is a resonant truth in there somewhere, if only the speaker or writer or illustrator has the talent to reinvent it.

[Donald] Hall and Moser have the talent to do just that. There is nothing remarkable about this story: a 12-year-old New Hampshire farm boy and his father, both avid baseball fans, are herding their geese across a country road one day when a slick roadster swerves to avoid the animals and winds up in the ditch. Yes, the driver of the roadster just happens to be Babe Ruth, star pitcher of the Boston Red Sox and young Willard's favorite player. The Babe gives Willard a baseball glove, and the family myth is begun. Years of Babe worship follow, extending even beyond the unfathomable trade of Ruth to the hated Yankees and encompassing a new generation, in the form of Willard's daughter, Ruthie (that's right, named after the Babe). What lifts all this beyond twaddle is Hall's ear and Moser's eye for detail. We feel and see the way the world was then—before television, before cyberspace—when the rhythm of the seasons had tangible meaning and when baseball talk was a good way to get through the harsh New England winter. Moser's nostalgic but never cloying full-page watercolors, characteristically sharp despite the abundance of earth tones, give Hall's carefully chosen words additional life. But despite the nostalgia, both words and pictures draw their energy from the sense of universality they bring to the experience of hero worship. We all need the power of myth to endure the dreariness of quotidian life, and for many of us, it is sports stars, from Achilles to Babe Ruth to Michael Jordan, who supply what we most crave.

Tom S. Hurlburt

SOURCE: A review of *When Willard Met Babe Ruth,* in *School Library Journal,* Vol. 42, No. 5, May, 1996, p. 113.

Hall pens a gentle tale of a time when both life and baseball were less complicated than they are today. In 1917, while 12-year-old Willard and his father are tending the sheep and geese near their New Hampshire farm, a roaring automobile slides into a ditch while trying to stop. The boy and his father use their ox team to pull out the roadster of the Boston Red Sox star pitcher Babe Ruth. Willard receives Ruth's glove as a gesture of appreciation and is forever a fan of the pitcher soon-to-turn slugger. The story follows the lives of Ruth on the ballfield and Willard as he matures into a man and raises a family. He meets the legendary star one last time in 1935 (he had a second meeting with him at Fenway Park in 1918), when he takes his daughter to Braves Field to watch the Bambino in one of his last games. Moser's graceful watercolor paintings are featured throughout the book and are similar in style to his works in Richard Wilbur's *A Game of Catch* and Willie Morris's *A Prayer for the Opening of the Little League Season.* Shelve this title with the chapter books where it's most likely to get in the hands of its intended audience.

Ellen Fader

SOURCE: A review of *When Willard Met Babe Ruth,* in *The Horn Book Magazine,* Vol. LXXII, No. 5, September/October, 1996, p. 589.

Twelve-year-old Willard is obsessed with baseball (his father has given him a love of the game). One afternoon in 1917, he and his father help pull Babe Ruth's car out of a ditch, and the best left-handed pitcher in the sport rewards Willard with one of his mitts. Many years later, Willard's daughter Ruth reveals a love of the sport as well, and on her tenth birthday her father arranges a trip to Braves Field in Boston to see Babe Ruth play. Willard's reunion with the man he worshipped for so many years is an eye-opener since he is a tired-looking "forty years old and fat," but Babe Ruth remembers the family. Poet [Donald] Hall peppers his story with carefully chosen details—the hardship of the Great Depression, the 1928 election in which Ruth poses with a "Vote for Al Smith" sign pinned to his coat, the fun of listening to radio shows on the Arrow cabinet radio—that give the story a vibrant sense of time and place. These details add up to an understated but poignant story of pure and simple hero worship that passes through three generations of a family. Moser's watercolors play down the sentimentality that could have overwhelmed the book; instead, his pictures are filled with insightful portraits of Babe Ruth and of Willard's red-haired family, and with enough farm and rural scenes to clearly establish the book's setting. The full-page, full-color paintings every few pages break up the book's five chapters into easy-to-read-aloud innings.

Additional coverage of Moser's life and career is contained in the following sources published by Gale Research: *Major Authors and Illustrators for Young Adults; Something About the Author Autobiography Series,* Vol. 15; and *Something About the Author,* Vol. 79.

Jacqueline Woodson

1964-

African-American author of fiction and picture books; editor.

Major works include *The Dear One* (1991), *Maizon at Blue Hill* (1992), *I Hadn't Meant to Tell You This* (1994), *From the Notebooks of Melanin Sun* (1995), *The House You Pass on the Way* (1997).

INTRODUCTION

Regarded as one of the most talented and intelligent writers for young people to have emerged in the 1990s, Woodson is praised for expanding the scope of literature for middle graders and young adults by addressing mature topics and confronting stereotypes in explicitly feminist novels and stories. Credited for offering valuable perspectives on provocative social issues in poetic, eloquent prose, she is recognized for her understanding of and sensitivity to the young as well as for her insight, honesty, nondidactic approach, and strong characterizations. Woodson generally explores themes centering around identity; her protagonists, usually bright, sensitive young women, survive difficult personal and social situations through inner strength and the support of their family, friends, and community. The characters encounter such issues as coping with the death of a parent, accepting themselves or their parent as gay, and dealing with the possibility of losing a close friend; in addition, her fiction covers such topics as teen pregnancy, adoption, divorce, mental illness, anorexia, and sexual abuse. Woodson is often acknowledged for her candid treatment of racism: she explores the effects of bigotry among both blacks and whites and underscores her works with a subtle message about the destructiveness of racial and sexual prejudice. Although she provides no easy answers, she is acknowledged for her hopeful attitude toward her teenage characters.

Woodson is occasionally criticized for allowing her social conscience to intrude on the narrative flow of her books; however, most reviewers commend her works as moving, articulate affirmations of both self-esteem and diversity. "As always," noted Hazel Rochman, "Woodson confronts bigotry with truth and sadness." Diane R. Paylor commented, "When it comes to choosing the subject matter for her books, Jacqueline Woodson is fearless." Paylor further concluded that her "understanding of young readers has established her as one of the foremost African American women writers of young adult books." Michael Cart praised Woodson's novels for their "thematic richness, strong female characters, and convincing demonstrations of friendship's power to breech the walls society erects between people of different race and economic conditions."

Biographical Information

Born in Columbus, Ohio, Woodson grew up in Greenville, South Carolina and Brooklyn, New York. She admitted that she never felt at home in either place, a feeling intensified by being raised as a Jehovah's Witness. At the age of six, Woodson was sexually molested by her mother's boyfriend; the abuse continued until she was thirteen. She started writing stories and poems when she was in the fifth grade and was chosen as the editor of a school magazine. Another turning point came following the resignation of Richard Nixon in 1974; when Gerald Ford became president instead of George McGovern, a candidate whom Woodson felt embodied Martin Luther King, Jr.'s dream for racial equality, she felt abandoned and angry. She explained, "The word *democracy* no longer existed for me. I began to challenge teachers, and when they couldn't give me the answers I wanted, I became sullen, a loner. I would spend hours sitting underneath the porch, writing poetry and anti-American songs. . . . The world became a place that didn't welcome me and the people I loved, and in response I stepped outside of the world. From this vantage point, I watched and took notes." When she was in seventh grade, Woodson's English teacher told her that she wrote well and that she should make sure that the career she chose was one she liked. This encouragement prompted her decision to become a writer. Woodson admitted that "another influence was picking up books and not seeing people who looked like myself or who came from the same neighborhood as I did. I knew that I wanted to write about communities that were familiar to me and people that were familiar to me. I wanted to write about communities of color. I wanted to write about girls. I wanted to write about friendship and all of these things that I felt like were missing in a lot of the books that I read as a child."

As a result of the abuse she experienced, Woodson spent her adolescence disassociating herself from, as she wrote, "intimacy, uncomfortable situations, physical pain," and becoming sexually promiscuous. She became depressed and even suicidal as she entered her twenties; however, at the age of twenty-four, Woodson decided to begin the process of healing: "By my will, my strength, and the grace of God," she explained, "I survived." As a young woman, Woodson also came out as a lesbian. After graduating from college with a degree in English and a concentration in British Literature and Middle English, she worked as a drama therapist at a residence for runaway and homeless children in New York City. Woodson then moved into academia, becoming a fellow at the MacDowell Colony and at the Fine Arts Work Center in Provincetown, Massachusetts, as well as a faculty member in the M.F.A. writing program at Goddard College. She continued writing, receiving *The Kenyon Review* Award for Literary Excellence in Fiction for a work directed to adults before turning to literature for children and young people.

"I write about black girls," Woodson remarked, "because this world would like to keep us invisible. I write about all girls because I know what happens to self-esteem when we turn twelve, and I hope to show readers the number of ways in which we are strong. . . . I don't believe gay writers must always have gay characters. I think we must tell all of our stories. . . . I believe first and foremost that we must write the truth, and this can only be a good thing." She concluded, "My plan is to keep writing books that transcend the lines. . . . I want to leave a sign of having been here. The rest of my life is committed to changing the way the world thinks, one reader at a time."

Major Works

Woodson's first book, *Last Summer with Maizon* (1990), is the first of a trilogy for middle graders that chronicles the lives of Margaret Tory and Maizon Singh, eleven-year-old African-American girls who live in Brooklyn and are best friends. The girls find their friendship shaken when Margaret's father dies suddenly and Maizon accepts a scholarship to Blue Hill, an elite boarding school for girls in Connecticut. While outgoing Maizon is away, the introspective Margaret begins to find herself as a writer. At school, Maizon learns that she is marginalized as one of only a few black students. After a few months, she

decides to give up her scholarship and return home, where she and Margaret will attend a school for gifted children in their neighborhood. Most reviewers found *Last Summer with Maizon* a successful first novel. Observing Woodson's insight, Karen Braillsford remarked, "Woodson writes with a sure understanding of the thoughts of young people" and offers a "mature exploration of grown-up issues. . . ." A critic in *Junior Bookshelf* commented that Woodson "has a gift not only for insight but also for dialogue. Sometimes it glitters, sometimes glows but it always has bite and gives a dramatic edge to what might have been not much more than a sorry tale." The second book about Maizon and Margaret, *Maizon at Blue Hill*, describes what happened to Maizon while she was at boarding school in the first volume of the trilogy, focusing on her experience with racism. For the first time in her life, Maizon is in a minority, and she is uncomfortable with both the inquisitive white students, who see her as different, and the cliquish black students, who stick together exclusively while dismissing a biracial girl as an "oreo." After evaluating her situation, Maizon realizes that she needs to return to Brooklyn, where she can just be herself. Hazel Rochman commented that *Maizon at Blue Hill* "frankly confronts issues of color, class, prejudice, and identity without offering Band-aids of self-esteem." A reviewer in *Publishers Weekly* claimed that this "simply told, finely crafted sequel . . . neatly avoids predictability while offering a perspective on racism and elitism rarely found in fiction for this age group." Alice F. Stern noted, "We are in the hands of a skilled writer here." In the third volume of the series, *Between Madison and Palmetto* (1993), the bond between Margaret and Maizon—now eighth graders—is tested when the latter develops a relationship with a white girl who has moved into the neighborhood. In addition, Maizon is dealing with the reappearance of her father after a twelve-year absence. Margaret, who is still dealing with the death of her own father, becomes anorexic. At the end of the novel, Maizon has accepted her father, Margaret has accepted her body, and both girls have retained their close friendship. Writing in *Booklist*, Hazel Rochman commented, "What's most interesting is the story of friendship between Maizon and Margaret and their funny banter, their tension, their enduring bond." A *Kirkus Review* critic noted, "In simple, delicately tuned language, each interaction is evoked in dialogue that explores the choices these thoughtful characters confront, while their close-knit community . . . comes nicely to life." In addition, Alice F. Stern noted, "This series is an impressive addition to young adult literature."

Although the "Maizon and Margaret" trilogy is generally considered inoffensive, several of Woodson's books are regarded as controversial. *The Dear One* is a young adult novel that features twelve-year-old Afeni (Swahili for "dear one"), an African-American girl who lives with her mother in a middle-class Philadelphia suburb. When her mother brings home Rebecca, the pregnant fifteen-year-old daughter of one of her mother's college friends from Harlem, Feni becomes jealous. The girls gradually begin to trust and care for each other with the support of Feni's mother and a lesbian couple, one of whom attended college with the mothers of both Feni and Rebecca. At the end of the novel, Rebecca gives birth to a daughter whom she names Afeni before giving her up for adoption. Critics acknowledged the sustaining circle of black sisterhood that is at the center of the book; a reviewer in *Publishers Weekly* called the novel a "paradigm for understanding between social groups. . . . Woodson's deep understanding of and concern for the role of black women in society is evident. . . ." However, after publishing *The Dear One,* which also includes alcoholism, divorce, and mental illness, Woodson was no longer invited to appear in front of young people. Woodson's next novel for young adults, *I Hadn't Meant to Tell You This*, is often considered her best and most popular book as well as one of her most controversial. The story outlines how two motherless teenage girls, one black and one white, help each other to find personal strength. Set in a suburb of Athens, Ohio, the novel is narrated by Marie, who is black and middle-class. When Marie meets Lena, a poor white girl, the two are connected by their grief over the loss of their mothers. Jeered by both their black and white schoolmates, the girls become close friends. As their friendship progresses, Marie confides to Lena that her father stopped touching her when she became an adolescent; Lena tells Marie that she is being sexually abused by her father, who has also made advances to her younger sister. At the end of the novel, Lena, facing her anger, takes her sister and runs away from home. Marie, whose friendship with Lena has helped her to deal with her mother's desertion of their family and her father's coldness, resolves to tell her friend's story. A reviewer in *Publishers Weekly* commented that Woodson "confronts sticky questions about race head-on with the result that her observations and her characterizations are all the more trustworthy. Her approach to the incest theme is less immediate but equally convincing . . . . Woodson's novel is wrenchingly honest and. . . full of hope and inspiration." Carolyn Polese called *I Hadn't Meant to Tell You This* an "exceptional book. . . . Far from being a diatribe on child abuse, this novel explores the complex and often contradictory responses of individuals—and society—to the plight of abused children." Furthermore, Michael Cart concluded, "Woodson's talent, intelligence, and compassionate understanding of her characters find their finest expression in . . . *I Hadn't Meant to Tell You This.*"

From the Notebooks of Melanin Sun is the first of Woodson's books to feature a male protagonist. In this novel for young adults, thirteen-year-old Melanin, who has been named for his beautiful dark skin, is shocked to discover that his beloved single mother is in love with a white woman, a fellow student from her law school class. Mel agonizes about what will happen to him when his friends find out, wonders if homosexuality runs in his family, and is concerned that the close relationship with his mother will be destroyed. Mel works out his confusion through notebook entries in his journal that tell the story along with his first-person narrative. At the end of the novel, Mel realizes that his love for his mother transcends anything else; after a discussion with his mother's girlfriend, he accepts her and their relationship. A critic in *Kirkus Reviews* predicted, "Melanin Sun's inner journey will leave

readers moved and reassured." Moreover, Roger Sutton noted, "This is one of the most unpreachy . . . accounts we've had of gay parents; it's also a rare YA novel in its belief that parents deserve lives of their own." Woodson's next novel, *The House You Pass on the Way,* also raises questions about homosexuality and race. The story focuses on fourteen-year-old Evangeline, the middle child in her county's only mixed-race family. Friendless and isolated, Evangeline, who has defiantly changed her name to Staggerlee after the folk ballad hero, has fond remembrances of kissing a girl in grade school. When Staggerlee meets her cousin Trout, another self-named fourteen-year-old, the girls become confidantes, and Staggerlee finds the courage to admit her dawning sexual preference. At the novel's close, Trout writes to Staggerlee to let her know that she is in love with a boy, and Staggerlee realizes that she and her cousin have begun to follow their own paths. Susan P. Bloom called *The House You Pass on the Way* a novel "that feels far more expansive than its brief length. . . . [The] reader feels grateful that Woodson has whispered her lyrical story to us. . . ." A critic in *Kirkus Reviews* commented, "A provocative topic, treated with wisdom and sensitivity, with a strong secondary thread exploring some of the inner and outer effects of racism."

Awards

Maizon at Blue Hill was named a Best Book for Young Adults by the American Library Association in 1992 and *I Hadn't Meant to Tell You This* was given the same designation in 1994. The latter was named a Coretta Scott King Award honor book in 1995, a designation also given to *From the Notebooks of Melanin Sun* in 1996. *From the Notebooks* also received a Lambda Book Award in the children's and young adult books category, as did Woodson's adult novel *Autobiography of a Family Photo* in the category of lesbian fiction.

AUTHOR'S COMMENTARY

Jacqueline Woodson

SOURCE: "A Sign of Having Been Here," in *The Horn Book Magazine,* Vol. LXXI, No. 6, November/December, 1995, p. 711.

My first realization of the way the world worked came when I was nine or ten. Nixon was president, and Watergate was just beginning to surface. As I watched reports of the scandal, and as Nixon's involvement slowly unfolded, I remember thinking, Good, now Nixon is going to get kicked out of office and we'll get who we really want—McGovern. McGovern was my first "American dream." Everyone in my neighborhood had been pushing for him. Over and over again, I heard how McGovern *cared* for black people.

When Nixon finally stepped down, I was not only surprised that Ford took his place, I was devastated. For the first time, I had believed that America was going to begin to exist as a nation, that we could live as Martin Luther King, Jr., had dreamed—in solidarity, coexisting, helping each other. I was a child, and in my child's mind I really believed this.

My life changed that year. I became sad and disconnected from other children. I cried often for what seemed to be no reason and felt I was outside of the world. I believed I had been cheated out of something. The word *democracy* no longer existed for me. I began to challenge teachers, and when they couldn't give me the answers I wanted, I became sullen, a loner. I would spend hours sitting underneath the porch, writing poetry and anti-American songs. Vietnam encircled my neighborhood, and I watched men come home half-alive, addicted to heroin, destroyed. We were all, as Carson McCullers so elegantly put it, "unjoined" people, living in a world that newscasters came into only when a murder or a three-alarm fire swept through our neighborhoods. The bitterness of Vietnam, the scandal of Watergate, poverty, inadequate housing and education—the list goes on—became our everyday experience. I took this in and didn't react. The world became a place that didn't welcome me and the people I loved, and in response I stepped outside of the world. From this vantage point, I watched and took note.

This is how I began to write.

And, too, this is how I began to read: searching the pages of the books available to me for people like my people; reading the books where I found tiny pieces of myself over and over again. I didn't grow tired of reading these books, because I couldn't afford to. What else was there? So few books published in the 1970s reflected the existence of marginal people—and already, at nine, ten, eleven, I understood myself to be marginal. Every white face on my television, in my textbooks, in my newspaper reiterated the fact that I was not a part of the majority. I wasn't. And never would be. And when this was all figured out, I realized I didn't want to be. But then, who was I? And who were the many others like myself? Why weren't we visible? How could we become so? These days, when I hear the backlash against multiculturalism, I want to scream. How dare people want us to be invisible again, to give up the tiny bit of visibility we've fought so hard for, been arrested for, died for?

It's hard for me to talk about myself in the context of gayness without talking about the part of me that is black, because all of this continues to be threatened by people who believe that no part of me should be in the world. As a writer who is black and gay but neither a black writer nor a gay writer, I do not feel as though I have a responsibility to only these two communities but a responsibility to write beyond the systems of oppression in *all* communities. As people who exist on the margins, we do have a different view of the world, and it is our responsibility to refocus. In the course of refocusing, we may help a child who is coming out or struggling with abuse or with family or with health to acquire a clearer vision of the world and thereby grow up stronger.

I write about black girls because this world would like to keep us invisible. I write about *all* girls because I know what happens to self-esteem when we turn twelve, and *I hope to show readers* the number *of ways in which we are strong.* This strength isn't about getting into a great school or having the most popular boyfriend or getting on the cheerleading squad. It can be as complex and as simple as crossing a class and color line to befriend someone, or running away or coming home, or discovering Audre Lorde and sharing it with a friend, or, as in the short story **"Slipping Away"** from *Am I Blue?,* as simple and as complex as acknowledging difference and letting it happen. I don't believe gay writers must always have gay characters. I think we must tell *all* of our stories. Many of my own aren't about gayness, yet are written with an awareness that has arisen from acknowledging who I am. I believe first and foremost that we must write the truth, and this can only be a good thing.

There has been some backlash against my truths. When I wrote **Last Summer with Maizon**—which I would later term my "good" book because it was about family and friends—I was invited to read and speak in many places. Then I wrote **The Dear One,** in which I dealt with teenage pregnancy, lesbianism, and alcoholic recovery, and while reviews were still good, I was no longer invited to appear in front of young people. In fact, the first person my publisher sent the book to for a cover illustration refused to do it because she found the book "offensive." Even after **Maizon at Blue Hill,** another relatively "nice" book, school visits were few and far between. Yet I often wonder, If every book had been like **Last Summer with Maizon,** and I was a young woman with a wedding band on my hand, would I get to visit schools more often?

As a black writer in the predominantly white world of children's books, I have to acknowledge racism as well as homophobia. I must acknowledge that there are white reviewers who will only see the bigotry of my black characters and completely ignore the overt racism of my white ones. In the same respect, there are those who zero in on the dysfunction of the gay characters and completely ignore it in the straight ones. In dealing with many levels and many identities, I realize that we will sometimes see what we want to see and disregard the rest.

I don't believe I can write a book about a fourteen-year-old girl who is a lesbian because I've never known any and don't believe they exist. I can, however, write about a fourteen-year-old girl who is struggling with her identity as she watches her friends interact with boys and realizes that isn't what she wants, a fourteen-year-old girl who sees a lesbian couple on the street and fears this may be who she is. I believe identity is fluid, that young people are exploring their identities. As adults, we need to show them their options while giving them space to make their own decisions. Too often I've seen young girls who are labeled *lesbians* fiercely act out against the label, whereas if they were allowed to just *be* they might become happier, better adjusted adults. In my writing I deal with the many layers of identity. There isn't just one kind of gay or white person or person of color or mother or father in the world; there are all kinds, and we have to be open-minded enough to allow for the existence of each.

I believe young people want honesty. If you tell a story as you remember it at their age, they'll read it. If you talk down to them or try to show them how much you've learned, they'll turn away. When I sit down to write, I return to the places of my tenth, twelfth, or fourteenth year of living. I don't explain anything, because at that time I had no explanation. Life just was. I am compelled always to write about living and how living molds us. I feel compelled to write against stereotypes, hoping people will see that some issues know no color, class, sexuality. No—I don't feel as though I have a commitment to one community—I don't want to be shackled this way. I write from the very depths of who I am, and in this place there are all of my identities. I have to write about issues I feel most passionate about; I love black people first and foremost, and my books will always deal with blackness in some way, shape, or form. My writing began from this place of simple adoration for the amazingness of black people and moved forward as I grew up and out to encompass my other loves as well.

I think the mistake many make in dealing with "other" is that they pigeonhole difference. All of the black books come out during Black History Month; all of the books about women during Women's History Month; all of the gay books come out in June. If there is one black child in a classroom, teachers will search high and low for a book about blacks for that child—or only then begin to think about blackness. But what about the white children? What about putting a book that deals with blackness into the hands of a white child? What about giving an admittedly straight reader a book with gay characters, or a child who lives with both parents a book about a single-parent household? Every month should celebrate diversity. Young people are eager to see beyond their own existence, and we must respect this. They must be allowed to transcend color, class, or sexuality; to grow bigger, more whole.

In *The Dear One,* a novel about a working-class, poor, pregnant teenager who gets sent to live with an upper-middle-class mother and daughter, women find ways of helping each other across class and generational lines. In the end, a baby is born—another girl—with the hope that she will take these women's strengths into the next generation. In *I Hadn't Meant to Tell You This,* Marie and Lena, two motherless twelve-year-old girls—one black, one white; one rich, the other poor—find a common ground across lines of color and class and ignore the world beyond this ground. What they learn from each other will be passed on somehow; maybe readers will challenge their own and their parents' racism and classism. Maybe they'll find new ways of speaking, of telling their stories. Maybe marginal people will realize they don't have to be silent, that everyone has a story to tell and a reason to be here.

My plan is to keep writing books that transcend the lines.

I know I will get angry letters from teachers and young people who don't approve of the stories I tell, and I will read these letters with the understanding that these same people don't believe that blacks, gays, and working-class poor people should exist equally with people who don't fit into these categories. I've lived long enough to understand the depth of hatred in this world. It has destroyed a lot of self-esteem, killed people, ravaged neighborhoods and families. This hatred is highly visible, cratered into our society like potholes.

But I want to leave a sign of having been here. The rest of my life is committed to changing the way the world thinks, one reader at a time.

GENERAL COMMENTARY

Rudine Sims Bishop

SOURCE: "Books from Parallel Cultures: New African-American Voices," in *The Horn Book Magazine,* Vol. LXVIII, No. 5, September, 1992, pp. 616-20.

Males are not prominent in Jacqueline Woodson's work, which features strong, independent black women and girls. In her first novel, ***Last Summer with Maizon,*** Margaret's and Maizon's friendship withstands the death of Margaret's father and Maizon's enrollment in a boarding school in Connecticut. With Maizon away and her personality no longer dominating, Margaret's own talent as a writer blossoms. In the meantime, Margaret waits in vain for news from her friend, who is unhappy in the cold and inhospitable environment of the private school and reluctant to let her loved ones know. After three months, Maizon leaves school and is lovingly welcomed home by her grandmother, Margaret, and her other friends. Both girls will attend a school for gifted children in their own community. In spite of its sometimes blurred focus, the novel is appealing in its vivid portrayal of the characters and the small community they create.

My first impression on reading Woodson's ***The Dear One*** was that here was a "black woman's novel." Her characters—college-educated professional women, a privileged pre-adolescent girl, and an underprivileged child-woman—are all convincingly familiar. But the story centers on Afeni, whose name means "the dear one" in Swahili. On the morning of her twelfth birthday, Afeni learns that the pregnant daughter of one of her mother's college friends will come to live in her home and be looked after by her mother and another of her college friends. They live in an upscale suburb, while Rebecca has grown up in a low-income family in Harlem, a situation ripe for conflict. Initially, Afeni tries to shut Rebecca out, but, encircled by the love and support of the older women, the girls work through their differences. When the baby is born, Rebecca names her Afeni. Although some readers may be put off by some of the social issues dealt with in this book—lesbianism, alcoholism, teenage pregnancy—adolescents will find it engaging in its frank and straightforward approach.

Both [Rita] Williams-Garcia and Woodson demonstrate considerable talent as novelists. Their work will appeal to readers, in middle grades and beyond, who may recognize in the main characters and their problems something of themselves. At the same time, these two writers continue to expand the scope of African-American children's literature by incorporating some uncommon themes, such as intraracial social class conflicts and the education or miseducation of gifted black youngsters. In these books, even the inevitable encounters with racism are complex and thought-provoking. We can all look forward to their future work.

Diane R. Paylor

SOURCE: "Bold Type: Jacqueline Woodson's 'Girl Stories'," in *Ms.,* Vol. V, No. 3, November/December, 1994, p. 77.

When it comes to choosing the subject matter for her books, Jacqueline Woodson is fearless. Her five novels for and about young adults have addressed alcoholism, lesbianism, racism, class tensions, and other real stuff. "People say you can't put all that material into a book for young people because it'll distress them or they won't be able to absorb it all," she says. "But I believe children's minds compartmentalize—they will put stuff away until they're ready to deal with it."

Woodson's understanding of young readers has established her as one of the foremost African American women writers of young adult books. Now the Brooklyn-based Woodson has written her first adult book, *Autobiography of a Family Photo,* a gripping series of vignettes about life in a dysfunctional African American family during the Vietnam war. She was interested in the Vietnam era because there are so many raw, unexplored feelings about how it affected African Americans. "You'd see the neighborhood changing and everyone coming back and being addicted to heroin or having lost their minds or their arms or legs," she says. "But nobody was talking about it. That's the way stuff is in black neighborhoods. The community weaves back into itself after the damage has been done." The novel follows an unnamed narrator through her childhood as she searches for identity, love, and sanity amid a family and community in disarray.

"Girl stories" have always been Woodson's mission, beginning with a trilogy exploring the complexities and strength of the friendship between preteens Maizon and Margaret. In *The Dear One,* a pregnant fifteen-year-old girl from Harlem moves in with an upper-middle-class black family where the mother is a recovering alcoholic whose best friend is a lesbian. *I Hadn't Meant to Tell You This* depicts the unlikely friendship between a poor white girl from a racist family and an upper-middle-class black girl.

Woodson says she learned at a very young age that the world is not a girl-friendly place. "Girls are desperate for identity and love," she says. "Society says if you go out and do A, B, and C, this is how you can get it. This is who you can become. And the girls do A, B, and C and they realize that they were lied to. I want to show young people that there are other ways."

Having spent her adolescence being shuttled between South Carolina and New York City, Woodson never quite felt a part of either place—a feeling intensified by being raised as a Jehovah's Witness. Although no longer a Witness, Woodson has retained the religion's "be in the world but not of the world" ideology. "I've been in the children's publishing world long enough to know I'm on the outside of it," she admits. "I'm never going to write best-sellers." She says people often judge her work by who she is. "I have these qualifiers: Jacqueline Woodson, African American, lesbian writer. No one ever says 'Hemingway, a misogynist, anti-Semitic, white, male writer.' How come I can't just be a writer?"

"I'm always happy when someone comes up to me and says, 'I read your book and I really loved it; it changed my life.' It's like, wow, I really touched this person. Which is what I want to do as a writer."

TITLE COMMENTARY

📖 *LAST SUMMER WITH MAIZON* (1990)

Karen Brailsford

SOURCE: A review of *Last Summer with Maizon,* in *The New York Times Book Review,* July 29, 1990, p. 33.

"Almost twins. We're best friends, jumpin' side by side," chant the eleven-year-old Margaret Tory and Maizon Singh as they skip rope in their Brooklyn neighborhood. "Turn around, touch the ground, up and give me five." They clap palms together. "Almost twins—could be cousins—coolest girls alive!" *Last Summer with Maizon,* a first novel by Jacqueline Woodson, chronicles the strain that threatens the two girls' friendship as they cope with the death of Margaret's father and confront their impending separation, brought about by Maizon's acceptance at a boarding school. A drama therapist in a New York City residence for runaway and homeless children, Ms. Woodson writes with a sure understanding of the thoughts of young people, offering a poetic, eloquent narrative that is not simply a story of nearly adolescent children, but a mature exploration of grown-up issues: death, racism, independence, the nurturing of the gifted black child and, most important, self-discovery.

Ms. Woodson draws both characters' personalities with deft strokes as she details Margaret's evolution into a poet and the girls' realization that behind Maizon's brio hides a child who doesn't know everything after all. Though they claim to be "almost twins," they are quite dissimilar in style and temperment. Maizon leaps off the page garbed in a most outrageous outfit: a red and black dress copied from a magazine by her grandmother, large gold hoop earrings that weigh down her earlobes, errant eye liner and red globs of blush on her cheeks. Often thoughtless—even her grandmother admits she may be smart but doesn't always display common sense—Maizon is nevertheless envied by Margaret. "Sometimes it didn't seem fair. Maizon had everything," she grumbles to herself.

But throughout the novel, Ms. Woodson hints that Maizon is certainly jealous of Margaret as well, For instance, Maizon, who sports a short Afro, combs Margaret's mane "longingly." She also wishes she belonged to a family like Margaret's, with parents and a brother like Li'l Jay, the inspiration for the most poignant sentence in *Last Summer with Maizon.* Margaret goes into her little brother's room on the rainy night of her father's death and finds Maizon watching the sleeping toddler: "His thumb crept slowly to his mouth and soft sucking sounds mingled with storm." (Maizon's own mother died in childbirth, and her father deserted her shortly afterward.)

Quiet and introspective, Margaret first appears with her legs dangling over the edge of the fire escape as she writes an entry in her diary. It becomes clear that though Maizon is always loud and vocal, it is Margaret whose voice will eventually be heard. "I feel like I'm on one of those balance beams we have in gym class—balancing between today and tomorrow," she writes.

Some vibrant characters round out the cast. There is Ms. Dell, a hefty woman with an unusual shade of blue eyes. She has strange powers that enable her to foresee Margaret's upcoming trials. "Gonna learn about strength this summer," she quietly predicts. Hattie, Ms. Dell's 19-year-old daughter, writes poems that she says live inside her head, not on paper. Maizon's guardian and grandmother, a Cheyenne Indian, clicks knitting needles while spinning tales of the reservation.

As the plot unfolds, we realize that Maizon's departure is a blessing. "I feel like sometimes Maizon kept me from doing things," Margaret says. "Now I don't have any excuse not to do things." She then goes on to write an award-winning poem documenting the summer anguish. "My pen doesn't write anymore," it begins. "It stumbles and trembles in my hand." Let's hope Jacqueline Woodson's pen writes steadily on.

Roger Sutton

SOURCE: A review of *Last Summer with Maizon,* in *Bulletin of the Center for Children's Books,* Vol. 44, No. 2, October, 1990, pp. 49-50.

"Gonna learn about strength this summer, Margaret," says

downstairs neighbor Ms. Dell, whose powers of prophecy are well-regarded by Margaret and her best friend, Maizon. It is a hard summer for Margaret: her father dies of a heart attack, and Maizon has applied for admission to boarding school, leaving Margaret with the prospect of facing sixth grade by herself. While this first novel prefers conversation over action, the best-friendship of two young black girls in Brooklyn is honestly portrayed, including the little swipes of meanness that jostle with the shared care and loyalty to make a bond. Margaret's grief over her father's death is hard and convincing, but she seems unrealistically comforted by some cathartic poetry-writing. Maizon's trials at boarding school are offstage, hinted at by her lack of letters to Margaret and only revealed for certain when she decides to come back to the city. Although underdeveloped, this story will appeal to readers who want "a book about friends"; they will learn enough about this pair to wish them well.

Susan Schuller

SOURCE: A review of *Last Summer with Maizon,* in *School Library Journal,* Vol. 36, No. 11, November, 1990, p. 121.

When her best friend wins a scholarship to a boarding school for gifted students, Margaret is devastated. Then, in Maizon's absence, she discovers her own abilities, including success in the smartest class at school and winning a poetry contest. Still, when Maizon leaves the boarding school after only three months, Margaret, Maizon's grandmother, and the other adults in their Brooklyn neighborhood are glad to have her back. Woodson quickly establishes the strong ties between the two girls and paints a vivid picture of the supporting characters and their surroundings. However, once Maizon goes away to school, the focus of the story blurs. Because Maizon neither writes nor calls, other characters speculate that she is finding the work too difficult because she's not the brightest student anymore. Surprisingly, the eleven-year-old's decision to leave is made without any adult input. Later, readers receive only a brief explanation when Maizon comments that many of the girls hated her because she was smart and black. Margaret's growth is conveyed through only two brief episodes at school, yet this is a major development in the story. While readers will certainly be drawn into the book by the warmth and tenderness generated by the characters, as well as the descriptive images of cinnamon-scented kitchens and distant trains in the twilight, the narrative gaps may leave them wondering just what happened and why, and whose story this is meant to be.

A. R. Williams

SOURCE: A review of *Last Summer with Maizon,* in *The Junior Bookshelf,* Vol. 55, No. 4, August, 1991, pp. 183-84.

Brooklyn is the setting for Mrs. Woodson's at times

melancholy tale of pre-teenage friendship between two girls of different blood. The last summer of the title is the one they shared before Maizon was to be separated from Margaret by taking up a scholarship at a boarding school. Maizon, though, is a different proposition from her erstwhile friend: energetic, vivacious, with her afro hair and bright clothes, her trendy dancing, her marked intelligence, 'always out in front', yet with a tendency to not always tell the truth about herself. Something might be owed to the rumoured Cherokee strain in her? She appears a mite superficial to the point where she seems to understand less clearly the coming loss to Margaret who has also at this point lost her father and is in the way of losing her mother to the demands of breadwinning and the care of a younger child. Li'l Jay spends much time in the care of a ground-floor mother and daughter, Ms Dell and Hattie, the one wise through living and the other wary through the gift of second sight. The pair are Margaret's domestic mentors although neither spoils her or panders to her grief. Through her teacher, Ms Peazle, more sympathetic and perceptive than she sounds, Margaret is made to sublimate her sadness over Maizon and the summer gone, and no word for so long, in prose and verse compositions laid upon her as a school exercise, the author's pleasing device to give the reader insight in an oblique way. It helps her bear with Hattie's and Ms Dell's appraisal of the absent girl: 'She didn't have any common sense, Margaret.' It comes as no surprise that Maizon fails to adjust to life at Blue Hill; she had no best friend there. So, she returns, changed but still ripe for another venture in friendship. Woodson has a gift not only for insight but also for dialogue. Sometimes it glitters, sometimes glows but it always has bite and gives a dramatic edge to what might have been not much more than a sorry tale.

📖 *THE DEAR ONE* (1991)

Publishers Weekly

SOURCE: A review of *The Dear One,* in *Publishers Weekly,* Vol. 238, No. 28, June 28, 1991, p. 103.

Feni's visitor Rebecca, 15, comes from Harlem, is pregnant and is sleeping in Feni's room. It's almost too much for the 12-year-old to bear: she sees little enough of her corporate-executive mother without having to entertain her friend's daughter. Feni is determined to dislike Rebecca—until she realizes that the older girl's toughness is just a facade that hides a strong, nurturing young woman. When Rebecca's baby is born and she prepares to leave, Feni is faced with the unexpected prospect of losing her new friend. Peopled with strong African American female characters, this paradigm for understanding between social groups is written in a warm, rich style that creates an immediate intimacy with the players and issues. Woodson's deep understanding of and concern for the role of black women in society is evident as she eloquently introduces the reader to teenage pregnancy, alternate life-styles and adoption in her moving, powerful story.

Kirkus Reviews

SOURCE: A review of *The Dear One,* in *Kirkus Reviews,* Vol. LIX, No. 15, August 1, 1991, p. 1018.

Second-novelist Woodson gives thoughtful consideration to the impact of a pregnant teenager on the 12-year-old daughter of a friend who takes her in.

Afeni (Swahili for "Dear One") is still coping with her grandmother's death and her parents' divorce when her mother invites Rebecca, 15, daughter of a childhood friend who now lives in Harlem, to share their suburban home until her baby is born. Rebecca finds it as hard to deal with a group of caring women (which includes recovering alcoholics and a lesbian couple) as Afeni does to share her room with a stranger whose concerns are her boyfriend and the baby she's about to give up. Still, in their time together the two form a bond that enables each to grow in understanding and love.

Minimal plot, but the characterizations are rich, warm, and memorable; Woodson draws a frank, realistic picture of a community of African-American women who thrive while bravely confronting a myriad of problems and life situations. Though the writing is occasionally a little slapdash, this is a strong, original, and life-affirming book.

Roger Sutton

SOURCE: A review of *The Dear One,* in *Bulletin of the Center for Children's Books,* Vol. 45, No. 1, September, 1991, p. 26.

Twelve-year-old Feni's middle-class life in a black suburb of Philadelphia is rocked when Rebecca, fifteen, pregnant, and from Harlem, comes to stay. The girls' mothers are friends from college; a third friend, who lives nearby with her female lover, is also helping Rebecca through her pregnancy. Mama and Marion feel an obligation to Rebecca's mother, a sad alcoholic, but Feni feels scared and pushed-around: "Don't tell me it's *our* decision because it's not! I don't care how tight you and Clair were at Spelman, our house isn't some home for pregnant girls! This is my life, too, now and I'm going to decide who I do and don't want in it!" The best scenes in this book are the angry ones, such as Feni's confrontations with Rebecca, or when Feni reminds her mother of past alcoholic abuses, but the story too often slides into sermons on recovery, black and gay pride, self-esteem, and open adoption. The conflict between the two girls seems pushed out of the way rather than credibly resolved. But when it's fierce, it's real.

Ellen Fader

SOURCE: A review of *The Dear One,* in *The Horn Book Magazine,* Vol. LXVII, No. 6, November, 1991, p. 746.

Because she is still trying to adjust to her beloved grandmother's death and to the divorce of her parents, Afeni finds the announcement made on the morning of her twelfth birthday particularly disturbing: Rebecca, an unmarried, pregnant daughter of a college friend of her mother's, is coming to live with them until her baby is born. The differences between the two girls, one from a suburban Pennsylvania middle-class African-American home and the other a street-smart product of Harlem, cause tension in the house and a silence between them that seems unbreakable. But a group of strong, close-knit women, each of whom has had her own out-of-the-ordinary situation to deal with—including alcoholism and coping with being a lesbian in a suburban community—rallies around the fifteen-year-old Rebecca, providing her with emotional support, clothes, medical attention, and childbirth classes. Over time, the girls grow to understand and respect each other, and Rebecca decides to name the about-to-be-adopted baby Afeni, which means "the dear one" in Swahili. While the story has all the trappings of a familiar problem novel, it rises above the limits of that genre by offering portraits of richly developed characters, a setting unusual in a book for young adults, and a satisfying emotional conclusion. This strikingly original book holds special appeal; readers will immediately recognize the frankness and honesty with which Woodson tells her story.

MAIZON AT BLUE HILL (1992)

Hazel Rochman

SOURCE: A review of *Maizon at Blue Hill*, in *Booklist*, Vol. 88, No. 21, July, 1992, p. 1931.

Seventh-grader Maizon Singh, black and smart, reluctantly leaves her Brooklyn neighborhood, her best friend, and her beloved grandmother to take up a scholarship in a private Connecticut girls' boarding school. The classes are small, the place is beautiful, most people are quite nice to her, and her grades are A+. But she can't fit in. For the first time in her life, she's a "minority," and she hates it. She's furious with those whites who fear her as something different; she's not entirely at ease with the small group of rich black girls, who tell her not to mix at all ("We have to stick together"), and she closes herself off from her funny, free-spirited white roommate. Contrary to all our formula expectations, Maizon doesn't finally find her place there and settle down. She can't take the loneliness, and she leaves to go back home. Like Williams-Garcia's *Fast Talk on a Slow Track,* Woodson's story frankly confronts issues of color, class, prejudice, and identity without offering Band-aids of self-esteem. As in the first book about Maizon, *Last Summer with Maizon,* we're not just told she's smart: she thinks and reads, and one of the best scenes here is her class discussion of Morrison's *The Bluest Eye,* about a dark-skinned, brown-eyed girl who cannot see her own beauty. Good readers could go on from Maizon to Cary's *Black Ice,* with its candid recollections of being one of the first black recruits in an eastern prep school.

Publishers Weekly

SOURCE: A review of *Maizon at Blue Hill,* in *Publishers Weekly,* Vol. 239, No. 41, September 14, 1992, p. 126.

Maizon, 12, wins a scholarship to Blue Hill, an exclusive, girls-only academy in Connecticut. She reluctantly leaves her Brooklyn home for unfamiliar surroundings, apprehensive about being one of only five African American students at the school. She soon meets three older African American enrollees, who boast of their affluent backgrounds and isolate her from the other girls—including Pauli, the offspring of a mixed marriage, whom they detest for "assimilating." Maizon resents such manipulation, and the trio consequently shuns her. Erecting a shield against further hurt, the girl becomes achingly lonely. Maizon senses she's an oddity at the essentially all-white Blue Hill and in her frank and engaging narrative admits to resisting the place, where racial insults are often seen in innocuous remarks—yet in fact only the three African American girls indulge in obviously bigoted comments. This simply told, finely crafted sequel to *Last Summer with Maizon* neatly avoids predictability while offering a perspective on racism and elitism rarely found in fiction for this age group.

Alice F. Stern

SOURCE: A review of *Maizon at Blue Hill,* in *Voice of Youth Advocates,* Vol. 15, No. 4, October, 1992, p. 235.

Readers of Woodson's wonderful *Last Summer with Maizon* will remember Margaret's loneliness facing the school year without her best friend Maizon. Maizon had been accepted on scholarship at a prestigious boarding school in Connecticut. At the end of *Last Summer with Maizon,* Maizon has returned to Brooklyn after deciding to leave Blue Hill. What happened to Maizon at Blue Hill and why did she decide to leave? *Maizon at Blue Hill* answers those questions. One of a handful of black students, Maizon has no trouble adjusting to the academics at school, but is wondering how she fits in socially. Most of the other black girls, who have been at the school for several years, keep to their own group. They encourage Maizon to join them, but she is not sure she wants to restrict herself. Most of the white girls, however, are uncomfortable around her at best; some are downright racist. By Thanksgiving, Maizon has decided to return to Brooklyn and try to find some other way to be herself—smart, black, and from Brooklyn.

Maizon is a strong, interesting individual. Woodson's gift at characterization extends to her secondary characters as well, all of whom ring true. She raises some important questions about identity and self-esteem, but these issues are generated from the characters, and not the other way around. We are in the hands of a skilled writer here. Unlike *Last Summer with Maizon, Maizon at Blue Hill* is written in the first person. It doesn't have quite the same magical quality as the first book, but is engaging nevertheless. Woodson is a real find.

Kirkus Reviews

SOURCE: A review of *Maizon at Blue Hill*, in *Kirkus Reviews*, October 15, 1992, p. 1318.

In the second of a trilogy, Maizon describes her experiences as a scholarship student, one of five blacks at an exclusive girls' school in Connecticut: events offstage in *Last Summer with Maizon*, which focused on friend Margaret in sixth grade in public school back in Brooklyn. Woodson neatly stacks her deck so that Maizon typifies a bright, conscientious girl deciding to bow out of a situation so alien that she finds it untenable; still, the author provides enough range among other characters to make the story believable, while Maizon herself is poignantly real. Though Maizon had described herself as an outcast at Blue Hill, the "true" story here is more complex: three of the other black girls (all older) have given up on whites and stick exclusively together, deriding the fourth—raised by her white father—as an "oreo." Confronted by their ultimatum and stung by the insensitivity of some of the whites, Maizon decides to be friends with no one; and though she eventually responds to her nice roommate and has real liking for some fine teachers, loneliness is the overriding factor in her decision to "find a place where smart black girls from Brooklyn could feel like they belonged." Deeply felt and intelligently written. . . .

📖 *BETWEEN MADISON AND PALMETTO* (1993)

Hazel Rochman

SOURCE: A review of *Between Madison and Palmetto*, in *Booklist*, Vol. 90, No. 2, September 15, 1993, p. 152.

Woodson's *Maizon at Blue Hill* was a candid, intense story about a smart African American seventh-grader who won a scholarship to an elite prep school and suddenly found herself a "minority." But the sequel, in which Maizon is back home in her Brooklyn neighborhood, never quite comes together as a novel. Part of the problem stems from Woodson's strength. She doesn't push for certainty; she raises crucial issues and conflicts—about growing up female, about family, about racism and separatism—but resists the temptation to resolve them with a neat and tidy formula. A lot happens: Maizon's father, who deserted her as a baby, suddenly arrives and wants her to accept him; her best friend, Margaret, develops bulimia; a white girl, new to the changing neighborhood, wants to be friends. But nothing is really developed. Abrupt shifts in point of view are hard to follow. What's most interesting is the story of friendship between Maizon and Margaret: their funny banter, their tension, and their enduring bond.

Publishers Weekly

SOURCE: A review of *Between Madison and Palmetto*, in *Publishers Weekly*, Vol. 240, No. 45, November 8, 1993, p. 78.

Completing the trilogy begun with *Last Summer with Maizon* and *Maizon at Blue Hill,* Woodson revisits her heroines Margaret and Maizon as their close friendship is newly tested. Undergoing the transformations of adolescence, they also find their Brooklyn neighborhood changing, with new buildings erected and white people, such as Carolyn Berg, moving in. Lately, Maizon has been spending more time with Carolyn, and Margaret feels excluded. Developing physically, Margaret also feels overweight, a misperception that leads to symptoms of bulimia and a near-starvation diet. Maizon, meanwhile, struggles with the sudden appearance of her father, who has contacted her for the first time since he left her with her grandmother following her mother's death in childbirth. As in the previous novels, Woodson stresses the importance of friends and family, but the impact here is somewhat diluted by the movie-of-the-week problems that challenge the two girls. Her candid assessments of relations between blacks and whites are as searching as ever, however, and her characters just as commanding.

Roger Sutton

SOURCE: A review of *Between Madison and Palmetto*, in *Bulletin of the Center for Children's Books,* Vol. 47, No. 4, December, 1993, p. 136.

Having left boarding school, Maizon has come back to her old neighborhood, which is changing—gentrifying—rapidly. Maizon's best friend Margaret is changing too: frightened at the changes puberty is making to her body, Margaret has taken to excessive dieting and making herself throw up. Maizon herself faces a big change when her father, gone since Maizon's birth and the simultaneous death of her mother, comes back, eager to try again with his daughter. While there's a lot of incident and preaching about self-esteem, the book doesn't have much plot momentum. Margaret's mother has a wise talk with Margaret, and while Maizon constructs her own relationship with her father without excessive interference from her (saintly) grandmother, it's just too easy. What works best here is the slice-of-life portrait of Margaret and Maizon's friendship: close, sometimes uneasy or prickly, but ultimately affirming.

Alice F. Stern

SOURCE: A review of *Between Madison and Palmetto*, in *Voice of Youth Advocates*, Vol. 17, No. 2, June, 1994, p. 95.

A visit to the world of friends Margaret and Maizon and their families and neighborhood was a treat in the first two volumes of this trilogy (*Last Summer with Maizon* and *Maizon at Blue Hill*). This third volume stands up to the first two. The theme this time is change. Margaret and Maizon are pleased with their new school, but there is a new girl hovering on the edge of their twosome, threatening to upset the balance and tradition of their friendship. The girls are reaching puberty, and are becoming concerned with the changes in their bodies, and the type and pace of these changes. Their neighborhood is being fixed up, but this raises the possibility of rent increases and people being forced to move. Finally, perhaps most significantly, Maizon's long-absent father suddenly appears.

Woodson is covering familiar YA territory here—adolescent body image, parental and family tensions, appearance of a third party in a two-party friendship. This is a lot of ground to cover in just over 100 pages, but she manages admirably. Woodson explores with humor and heart and is not forcing any heavy-handed messages. Rather, she has created a community of vibrant, interesting, likable, *real* people whose lives and feelings speak for themselves. This series is an impressive addition to young adult literature.

I HADN'T MEANT TO TELL YOU THIS (1994)

Hazel Rochman

SOURCE: "Friend on the Edge," in *Booklist,* Vol. 90, No. 12, February 15, 1994, p. 1072.

In a quiet, beautiful friendship story, two young teenagers resist the bigotry in their school and the sorrow in their families and help each other find the strength to go on.

Marie tells the story; she's black and smart, part of the well-dressed crowd in her middle-class black suburb near Athens, Ohio. Lena is a poor white girl, new at school, one of those living in the "crevices at the edge of town." Both have lost their mothers—Lena's mother died of breast cancer; Marie's left two years ago to find herself—and grief is one of the things that connects the girls. The other kids sneer at Lena as white trash and call Marie an Uncle Tom for befriending the scruffy girl. Lena is dirty and unkempt, but not only because of poverty and loss. She tells Marie a secret and swears her to secrecy: "My daddy does things to me." The sexual abuse is quietly told, spelled out in terms of the rage and helplessness that Lena says she feels, her need to get out of the house as fast as she can and take her little sister with her.

Woodson's last book, **Between Madison and Palmetto,** also about friendship, was poorly developed, with too much happening all over the place. In contrast, this brief novel is controlled, each chapter like a film cut, with its own tight structure and falling beat, whether the scene is the crowded school cafeteria or Marie's kitchen. The casual dialogue is sharp with pain, soft with affection; as much is said in the spaces between the words as in what is spoken. "Ain't got no quarter to call for help," Lena says just before she takes off with her sister and runs away.

Through Marie's eyes, we see people in muddle and conflict. The characters are complicated. Marie's mother walked away from her, but it was she who taught Marie to look at people without stereotyping. We feel the mother's absence and, also, her desperate need to get away. Marie's college-professor father is a bigot who sees the world in "black and white," but he's a loving parent to her, and his grief at his wife's leaving is heartfelt. The girls' friendship isn't idealized. They quarrel and hurt each other, even as they get close. At first Marie succumbs to the pressures around her and turns on Lena. In anger she calls Lena a liar, accuses her of wanting attention, of liking what her father does to her. But their friendship helps both girls find joy and courage. They know from bitter experience that catastrophe can hit you anytime. Neither trusts the world, but you can see "how they're planning to blast through it."

The racism and class prejudice on all sides is graphically confronted. "Must be trash," Marie's father says when he first hears she has a white friend. A veteran of the 1960s civil rights movement, he wants separation from the white world that he hates for hating him. Marie challenges him: how come he doesn't want her to say *nigger,* but it's okay to say *white trash?*

Woodson's fine novel **Maizon at Blue Hill** dramatized the pain of the outsider who suddenly finds herself a "minority" in a fancy prep school. This time the minority is white, and the black teenager is shocked into awareness of the segregation and the privilege she's taken for granted. With all these issues, the novel could easily have drowned in politics and social problems. In fact, there is a didactic chapter that seems patched on, where the friends read aloud together from Audre Lorde's *The Cancer Journals* about her battle with breast cancer, and they find messages that help them in a harsh world. In **Maizon at Blue Hill,** Woodson did the same thing with Toni Morrison's *The Bluest Eye,* showing kids talking about books and ideas as part of growing up. But even the messages are uncertain, opening out to possibilities rather than offering slick answers.

There's a bittersweet moment when Lena's little sister, Dion, meets Marie for the first time and glares at her: "You ain't told me she was black," Dion accuses her sister. Right. That's how it is when you make a friend. The candor is welcome here and the hope.

Roger Sutton

SOURCE: A review of *I Hadn't Meant to Tell You This,* in *Bulletin of the Center for Children's Books,* Vol. 47, No. 7, March, 1994, p. 239.

Two girls: one black, one white; one comfortably middle-class, the other poor; both motherless. Even as they acknowledge how unlikely it is, Marie and Lena do become friends, although their bond is threatened when Lena tells Marie, who doesn't want to hear it, that she is being sexually abused by her father. Explicitly feminist in both theme and poetics, the book turns a lot of stereotypes around, with Lena, the white girl, being the underprivileged outsider in a mostly black town. Marie is popular, voted best-dressed, and her father is a university professor, but both father and daughter are still dislocated since Marie's mother walked out, now in touch only via postcards sent with beautiful drawings and oblique poems from foreign places. Marie wonders why her father never touches her. Lena wants her (widowed) father never to touch her again: "just if he didn't look at me. If he made believe I wasn't even in the world, that would be better." The bleakness of Lena's life is unrelieved; when Marie loyally suggests that she'd like to kill Lena's father, Lena replies, "Then what?," and the novel ends with Lena running away with her little sister Dion when their father starts to molest her as well. While the structure is a little neat, this is probably the best book Woodson has yet written. The girls' friendship is awkward, sometimes angry as Woodson acknowledges that no one can be meaner than your best friend. All the emotions played out here are rough-edged and ambivalent, as are the frank discussions about race. The story, told through a series of recollected vignettes from Marie's point of view, has an elegiac quality that gets to the heart of both girls' dilemmas in a way that a more prescriptive problem novel could not, and the spare writing generally allows events to speak for themselves. It's a book that has the courage to let things hang in the air.

Publishers Weekly

SOURCE: A review of *I Hadn't Meant to Tell You This,* in *Publishers Weekly,* Vol. 241, No. 16, April 18, 1994, p. 64.

This sensitive yet gritty novel about incest may be Woodson's strongest work to date. Marie, the eighth-grade narrator, lives in an all-black suburb of Athens, Ohio, with her father; her mother, who has inherited money from her own parents, sends arty messages from the far-flung locales she has toured since leaving the family two years ago. Ignoring the sneers of her friends—and her father's warnings—Marie befriends "whitetrash" Lena, the new girl at school. Woodson confronts sticky questions about race head-on, with the result that her observations and her characterizations are all the more trustworthy. Her approach to the incest theme is less immediate but equally convincing—Marie receives Lena's restrained confidences about being molested, at first disbelieving Lena, then torn between her desire to help her friend and her promise not to tell anyone. Lena has tried all the textbook solutions—including reporting her father to the authorities—and has learned that outside interference only brings more trouble. Marie, struggling to cope with her mother's desertion, must accept Lena's disappearance, too, when Lena and her younger sister first decide to run away and then do flee. Told in adroitly sequenced flashbacks, Woodson's novel is wrenchingly honest and, despite its sad themes, full of hope and inspiration.

Carolyn Polese

SOURCE: A review of *I Hadn't Meant to Tell You This,* in *School Library Journal,* Vol. 40, No. 5, May, 1994, p. 136.

This exceptional book is told from the viewpoint of Marie, a popular eighth grader in a predominantly black, middle-class school. When a poor white girl shows up mid-term, Marie finds herself drawn to Lena; both have recently lost their mothers. Despite social and familial pressures, an awkward friendship develops. Then Lena blurts out that her father is molesting her. Marie avoids her, unable to face the awfulness of what she's been told. When Lena confronts her, Marie in turn doubts that she is telling the truth, blames her friend, and then feels impotent rage. Lena shouts back, "'Don't be hating me. It ain't about *me!*'" Far from being a diatribe on child abuse, this novel explores the complex and often contradictory responses of individuals—and society—to the plight of abused children. With searing honesty, Woodson shows Lena's father for the damaged and pitiful person that he is. She raises questions for which society has no answers. By skillfully weaving together themes of abandonment, emotional maturation, and friendship across social and economic barriers, the author goes far deeper than the typical "problem novel." Lena's tragedy—her only recourse is to take her sister and run—is balanced by Marie's ability to come to terms with the loss of her mother and by her decision to tell her friend's story so that "maybe someday other girls like you and me can fly through this stupid world without being afraid." Lena's hope lies in the fact that she does break through, express her anger, and get out. While there are no easy answers for either girl, there is honesty, growth, and love in their relationship that gives young readers hope for the future.

Lauren Adams

SOURCE: A review of *I Hadn't Meant to Tell You This,* in *The Horn Book Magazine,* Vol. 70, No. 5, September/ October, 1994, pp. 601-02.

As she enters the eighth grade, twelve-year-old Marie is still reeling from her mother's sudden departure two years earlier. Her father has tried to explain that "'sometimes people have to go away . . . to live'" and to reassure her that the two of them will be all right. But Marie knows that they are "a little wrong. A different kind of family now." Marie is part of the popular group at school, led by her best friend, Sherry. Both girls come from the well-off black community that makes up the majority of their Ohio suburb and is sharply divided from the poor white transient population of the town. But on the third day of school, dirty, raggedy-looking white girl Lena Bright appears and is drawn immediately to Marie, and gradually Marie's fascination with Lena develops into a strong bond between them. Lena also has lost her mother, to cancer, and Marie finds she can tell her things that she could not discuss with Sherry—things Lena implicitly understands. Yet Lena has a sadness that runs even deeper than Marie's, and she confides to Marie that her father has been sexually abusing her. Marie angrily denies this possibility at first; she is further confused because she misses the hugs from her own father, who has stopped touching her altogether since she reached adolescence. When Marie allows herself to see the truth of Lena's horrifying secret, she urges her friend to tell someone and seek help. The story is told in retrospect in Marie's distinctly mature, thoughtful voice; she regrets the loss of childhood innocence taken by the harsh realities of the world. She tells us she "had never questioned anybody's happiness before [her] mother left," but by the end of the novel she is full of questions, and "feeling a hundred years older than everyone." Though Marie keeps her friend's secret, as promised, until Lena has gotten away, she tells the story now in hopes that "other girls . . . can fly through this stupid world without being afraid"—perhaps soaring off the swings as Lena does in Marie's dream, singing Jimi Hendrix's lyrics "S'cuse me while I kiss the sky." Woodson's characters are deftly drawn, whole individuals; her spare prose, crystal images, and the staccato rhythm of the short chapters combine to create a haunting and beautifully poetic novel.

FROM THE NOTEBOOKS OF MELANIN SUN (1995)

Hazel Rochman

SOURCE: A review of *From the Notebooks of Melanin Sun,* in *Booklist,* Vol. 91, No. 16, April 15, 1995, p. 1494.

"If she was a dyke, then what did that make me?" Melanin, 13, is appalled when his mother tells him she loves a woman, Kristin, a fellow student in her law school class. What's more, Kristin is white, and Mel has no room for whites in his world; he keeps away from their hatred and racism. His loving, single-parent mother has always made him proud that he's so dark. How can she love a white woman? What will his friends and all the people in their Flatbush neighborhood say? Will the girl he likes dump him? As always, Woodson confronts bigotry with truth and sadness. This new novel doesn't have the taut structure of *I Hadn't Meant to Tell You This;* there are too many of Mel's sensitive notebook entries. What's beautifully dramatized here are Mel's hesitant social encounters: the scenes on the street, at the kitchen table, on the beach. Woodson writes dialogue that captures the lilt and drift and sudden spurts of conversation. There's intensity in the pauses between words and in the most casual line. The story builds to an exquisite climax when Mel finally talks to Kristin and finds that she cares, as he does, about the fragile species on our planet.

Kirkus Reviews

SOURCE: A review of *From the Notebooks of Melanin Sun,* in *Kirkus Reviews,* Vol. LXIII, No. 10, May 15, 1995, pp. 717-18.

The close and loving relationship between a teenager and his single mother takes a heavy hit in this intense story. . . .

Melanin Sun, 13, is unpleasantly surprised when Encanta

Cedar's latest dinner guest turns out to be a woman—and a white woman to boot; that's nothing compared to his dismay when Encanta, after much sighing and hesitation, reveals that they are lovers. Mel's first reactions are predictable; except to say hurtful things, he clams up, retreating behind headphones and notebooks, rehearsing the common misconceptions about gays (freely using the words "fag" and "dyke"), and agonizing over what will happen when his friends find out. Fortunately, Melanin Sun has inherited his mother's courage and intelligence, so after thinking hard about how central she is to what he truly values and trusts, he passes from rage to resentment to bewilderment, and, finally, acceptance. In Woodson's graceful, sometimes tender prose, most of the characters shine with very human complexity, each a melange of dreams and concerns, moods, hopes and doubts. Melanin Sun's inner journey will leave readers moved and reassured.

Publishers Weekly

SOURCE: A review of *From the Notebooks of Melanin Sun,* in *Publishers Weekly,* Vol. 242, No. 20, May 15, 1995, p. 74.

Woodson's perceptively wrought novel imaginatively tackles such weighty issues as racism and sexuality. At age 13, Melanin Sun, an African American boy growing up in Brooklyn with his single mother, sometimes longs for the days when life was as "simple as chocolate cakes and Lego sets." Instead, his feelings grow more complicated after his mother explains that she is gay and in love with Kristin, the white woman whom she has recently invited home. "You're a dyke! A dyke!" he screams at her, enraged. His shock and sense of alienation are quickly exacerbated when the neighbors begin to gossip and he becomes the object of cruel taunts. Through Melanin's voice, Woodson frankly expresses the resentment and confusion of an adolescent desperately struggling to reestablish normalcy. She shatters stereotypes even as she evokes the tenderness of a mother/son relationship. Offering no easy answers, Woodson teaches the reader that love can lead to acceptance of all manner of differences.

Roger Sutton

SOURCE: A review of *From the Notebooks of Melanin Sun,* in *Bulletin of the Center for Children's Books,* Vol. 48, No. 11, July/August, 1995, p. 401.

Named by EC, his mother, for the beauty and strength of his black skin, thirteen-year-old Melanin Sun is beginning to feel that his mother has a secret, and he's not at all easy about her new friend, Kristin: "She was white. White white. Like Breck Shampoo-girl white but with glasses." When EC tells him the truth ("I'm in love, Mel . . . I'm in love with Kristin") he feels angry and betrayed, embarrassed that his friends will find out, scared that—despite his sexy feelings for friend Angie—he could be gay too. Most of all, he's frightened that the close bond he's had with his mother will now be lost forever.

Problem never overwhelms story in Melanin's touching and vulnerable account of finding a new understanding of himself and his mother's implacable need for adult bonds ("I need friends my age and a lover"). While friend Sean responds with derision and anger, Melanin's other friend Ralph lightens things up with a report of his mother's reaction: "She said she saw EC day before yesterday and she looked happier than anything. Mama said she should go out and find herself a woman if that's what it's all about." Both EC and Kristin are a bit idealized in their patience with Mel's sullen rebellion, but his gradual rapprochement with the women is realistically paced and his resolution with his friends and girlfriend about the subject is left open. This is one of the most unpreachy—and in the person of EC, unapologetic—accounts we've had of gay parents; it's also a rare YA novel in its belief that parents deserve lives of their own.

Claudia Morrow

SOURCE: A review of *From the Notebooks of Melanin Sun,* in *School Library Journal,* Vol. 41, No. 8, August, 1995, p. 158.

Fourteen-year-old Melanin Sun has a lot to say—not out loud, but in notebooks he keeps. Named for his dark skin, he knows about being on the outside of things. "Difference matters," he writes early on. What follows is not the usual identity crisis, however. His mother, a law student who sometimes acts more like a best friend, tells him she's in love with a woman—a white one, at that. His reaction is negative, strong, and hurtful. Nonetheless, at the end, Melanin seems to have sorted out his feelings—slowly, believably—and recognized in his mother and her lover a vulnerability he feels himself for other reasons. He comes around because of who he is, not because it's the "right" thing to do. Woodson has made Melanin an affecting and memorable, even admirable, character. Once thought "slow" in school because of his reticence, he is in fact a well-read, gifted young man with a talent for writing. The author effectively alternates excerpts from his notebooks—the thoughts intended for his own eyes only—with first-person descriptions of the action. Unfortunately, neither the cover nor the title will draw kids in; the book will need introduction and perhaps booktalking.

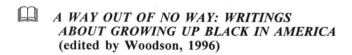

A WAY OUT OF NO WAY: WRITINGS ABOUT GROWING UP BLACK IN AMERICA (edited by Woodson, 1996)

Hazel Rochman

SOURCE: A review of *A Way out of No Way: Writings about Growing Up Black in America,* in *Booklist,* Vol. 93, No. 12, February 15, 1997, p. 1017.

Some anthologies are personal. They represent not just the best or the chronological, but *my* best, what the compiler has read and loved and can't wait to share. Woodson

communicates that excitement in her introduction to this fine collection: what it was like for her as a young adult to find writers such as James Baldwin, Toni Cade Bambara, and Langston Hughes, writers who showed her home and offered a way out of no way. In addition to the earlier writers, Woodson also includes some great contemporary pieces by Jamaica Kincaid, Ntozake Shange, and others. A few excerpts aren't easy to read as self-contained stories, but they will make readers search for more by these writers. The longest entry is Paul Beatty's "Big Bowls of Cereal," a witty, irreverent, painful, occasionally scatological poem that combines street talk and sophisticated allusion. In brief notes at the back, Woodson talks about each author and what the piece has meant in her life. Her comment on Bambara's "Gorilla, My Love" is eloquent: "At the core of the story is a strong-willed girl with a broken heart: It speaks to the strengths and weaknesses in all of us."

Gebregeorgis Yohannes

SOURCE: A review of *A Way Out of No Way: Writings about Growing Up Black in America,* in *School Library Journal,* Vol. 43, No. 7, July, 1997, p. 99.

This compilation of 18 excerpts, stories, and poems includes selections from such distinguished African-American writers as James Baldwin, Toni Morrison, Langston Hughes, and Gwendolyn Brooks. Most of the fiction and verse are taken from previously published works, such as Hughes's "Passing" from *The Ways of the White Folks* (Random, 1990); Anna Deavere Smith's "Look in the Mirror" from *Fires in the Mirror* (Anchor, 1993); the title story from Toni Cade Bambara's *Gorilla My Love* (Random, 1992); and an excerpt from Ernest J. Gaines's *A Lesson Before Dying* (Knopf, 1993). More than just a coming-of-age compendium, this work covers all aspects of African-American life. The themes include social relations, community, love, lust, murder, treachery, loyalty, sadness, and joy. There is also humor. For instance, Paul Beatty's poem "Big Bowls of Cereal" is a funny and moving diversion into myriad possibilities and situations for youth trembling on the brink of adulthood. The entries in this collection, selected and introduced by Woodson, show a wide range of writing styles and content. This title will afford young adults the opportunity to sample the work of noted African-American authors and see the "bigger world."

THE HOUSE YOU PASS ON THE WAY (1997)

Kirkus Reviews

SOURCE: A review of *The House You Pass on the Way,* in *Kirkus Reviews,* Vol. LXV, No. 13, July 1, 1997, p. 1038.

A newfound confidante and a breath of common sense clears away a teenager's guilt and dismay over her dawning sexual preference in this thoughtful, deceptively low-key story from Woodson.

The middle child in the county's only mixed-race family, Evangeline defiantly changed her name years ago to Staggerlee, after the anti-hero in a ballad, but the finger-pointing has driven her within herself, leaving her friendless and lonely—lonelier still for the memory of the pleasure she took in kissing a girl in grade school. Along comes Trout, another self-named teenager, from a branch of the family that had cut off her parents after their marriage. The attraction is quick, strong, and mutual; Trout's visit may be a short one, but it's long enough for each to open up, find the courage to say the word *gay*—and to remember that they're only 14, too young to close off options. Woodson takes readers another step down the road when Trout later writes to admit that she's gone head over heels for a guy, and Staggerlee, though feeling betrayed, realizes that she and Trout are both growing and going their own ways. A provocative topic, treated with wisdom and sensitivity, with a strong secondary thread exploring some of the inner and outer effects of biracialism.

Publishers Weekly

SOURCE: A review of *The House You Pass on the Way*, in *Publishers Weekly,* Vol. 244, No. 37, September 8, 1997, p. 77.

"Sitting big and silent with all her family's land spread out beyond it," Staggerlee Canan's house, once belonging to her famous grandparents, stands as a refuge from the townspeople's gossip about her parents' "mixed" marriage. Here the pensive 14-year-old can quietly contemplate all the ways she is different from her classmates and her older sister, "smart, popular" Dotti. Staggerlee has never had a close friend besides Hazel back in sixth grade, the first and only girl she ever kissed. But when her cousin Tyler (called "Trout") comes to spend the summer, the two girls are drawn together by their common heritage and longings. As soft-spoken and poetic as the heroine herself, Woodson's prose gracefully expresses Staggerlee's slow emergence from isolation as she and Trout grapple with their shared secret (Trout traces in the dirt by the river: *"Staggerlee and Trout were here today. Maybe they will and maybe they won't be gay."*). Minor characters—Staggerlee's gregarious father, her independent, conspicuously white mother ("it's only three, four white women in all of Sweet Gum") and her four diverse siblings—add depth and complexity to the heroine's small world. Using a nondidactic approach, the author gently probes questions regarding racism and homosexuality in this poignant tale about growing pains and the ongoing process of self-discovery.

Susan P. Bloom

SOURCE: A review of *The House You Pass on the Way*, in *The Horn Book Magazine,* Vol. LXXIII, No. 5, September/October, 1997, pp. 583-84.

In a novel that feels far more expansive than its brief length, Woodson takes us inside the confused mind of her fourteen-year-old protagonist. Staggerlee's internal sense of difference extends beyond the externals of being the daughter of a racially mixed marriage and the grandchild of a celebrated martyred couple who were victims of a bombing during the civil rights movement. Still, Staggerlee is unable to articulate her own sense of apartness. With the hushed intensity that marks this reflective book, Staggerlee can only identify her feelings as "something deeper—something lonely inside of her. Something quiet." Setting her novel in the winter, a time of stilled emotion, Woodson allows Staggerlee to relive the past summer as an awakening to thoughts and feelings that have lain dormant, waiting to be voiced. When her cousin Trout came to visit for the summer, Staggerlee's strong and growing feelings for her cousin confirmed her own suspicions that she, like Trout, might be gay. Now, only months later, Staggerlee holds a letter from Trout that reveals her cousin's changing emotions and inability to speak about other than how she feels at the moment, a moment that holds not only a boyfriend, but also remembrance of a sweet summer with Staggerlee. Resisting the less subtle exploration of girl meets girl and falls in love and lives happily ever after . . . Woodson crafts a more complex examination of gayness in the emerging adolescent. As Staggerlee wonders if someday there will be "someone she could whisper her life to," the reader feels grateful that Woodson has whispered her lyrical story to us, a story still awaiting, like all young lives, its conclusion.

Deborah Stevenson

SOURCE: A review of *The House You Pass on the Way*, in *Bulletin of the Center for Children's Books,* Vol. 51, No. 2, October, 1997, pp. 71-72.

Staggerlee's family is pretty much on its own, since her African-American father's relatives all cut the family off when he married Staggerlee's mother (a white woman), and the community is similarly suspicious of the family. Stag is therefore quite excited when her cousin Trout visits, thinking that perhaps this will help her get a better idea of her place in the world. She and Trout find common ground in their family concern and in their questions about their sexuality, since both girls are drawn to female friends and contemplate the possibility that they might be gay. The book is sympathetic and lyrically written, and Staggerlee's search for self will resonate with many young readers. The exploration of sexual identity is unforced and open-minded, with both the possibility of longterm orientation and youthful questioning acknowledged. Most of the action here is internal, and the narrative feels like a series of vignettes, so it's a particularly good fit for short-story fans.

Lynne B. Hawkins

SOURCE: A review of *The House You Pass on the Way*, in *Voice of Youth Advocates,* Vol. 20, No. 4, October, 1997, p. 250.

Staggerlee's name is her own, changed from her given name, Evangeline, to a proud name from a song her grandfather sang on stage. Her grandparents were well-known performers and civil rights activists killed in a bombing during the summer of 1969. Her father, who moved back to his childhood home in Sweet Gum, has been ostracized by his sisters for marrying a white woman. Staggerlee and her siblings have felt the sting of taunts that they are not entirely African American. She loves her family and is proud of her grandparents, but she, at fourteen, is confused about exactly who she is. The death of one of Daddy's sisters prompts the other, Ida Mae, to write them saying that her adopted daughter, fifteen-year-old Trout, wants to meet them all and to stay with them this summer. It is for Staggerlee an abrupt request after twenty years, for it is an opportunity to meet and learn about the family she has never seen. Trout becomes the outspoken and honest friend Staggerlee has been needing. As her feelings for Trout grow, Staggerlee realizes why Trout, who admits that the visit was not her idea, was sent to Sweet Gum.

Woodson writes beautifully about feelings and issues, and this slim novel is packed with them. Racism is discussed clearly, family barriers are built and torn down, and sexuality and young women's coming-of-age are explored. The house you pass on the way, the summer one must pass through on the way to becoming one's self, is a painful, growing place more often explored for young men than young women. Woodson stops well short of being sexually explicit. And while the reading level is appropriate for middle schoolers, the ideas explored—racism, family barriers, homosexuality—might draw older YAs who are ready to think about complex issues.

Additional coverage of Woodson's life and career is contained in the following sources published by Gale Research: *Contemporary Authors*, Vol. 159 and *Something About the Author*, Vol. 94.

CUMULATIVE INDEXES

How to Use This Index

The main reference

Baum, L(yman) Frank 1856–
1919 .... **15**

list all author entries in this and previous volumes of *Children's Literature Review:*

The cross-references

See also CA 103; 108; DLB 22; JRDA
MAICYA; MTCW; SATA 18; TCLC 7

list all author entries in the following Gale biographical and literary sources:

AAYA = *Authors & Artists for Young Adults*
AITN = *Authors in the News*
BLC = *Black Literature Criticism*
BW = *Black Writers*
CA = *Contemporary Authors*
CAAS = *Contemporary Authors Autobiography Series*
CABS = *Contemporary Authors Bibliographical Series*
CANR = *Contemporary Authors New Revision Series*
CAP = *Contemporary Authors Permanent Series*
CDALB = *Concise Dictionary of American Literary Biography*
CDBLB = *Concise Dictionary of British Literary Biography*
CLC = *Contemporary Literary Criticism*
CMLC = *Classical and Medieval Literature Criticism*
DAB = *DISCovering Authors: British*
DAC = *DISCovering Authors: Canadian*
DAM = *DISCovering Authors: Modules*
      DRAM: Dramatists Module; *MST*: Most-Studied Authors Module;
      MULT: Multicultural Authors Module; *NOV*: Novelists Module;
      POET: Poets Module; *POP*: Popular Fiction and Genre Authors Module
DC = *Drama Criticism*
DLB = *Dictionary of Literary Biography*
DLBD = *Dictionary of Literary Biography Documentary Series*
DLBY = *Dictionary of Literary Biography Yearbook*
HLC = *Hispanic Literature Criticism*
HW = *Hispanic Writers*
JRDA = *Junior DISCovering Authors*
LC = *Literature Criticism from 1400 to 1800*
MAICYA = *Major Authors and Illustrators for Children and Young Adults*
MTCW = *Major 20th-Century Writers*
NCLC = *Nineteenth-Century Literature Criticism*
NNAL = *Native North American Literature*
PC = *Poetry Criticism*
SAAS = *Something about the Author Autobiography Series*
SATA = *Something about the Author*
SSC = *Short Story Criticism*
TCLC = *Twentieth-Century Literary Criticism*
WLC = *World Literature Criticism, 1500 to the Present*
YABC = *Yesterday's Authors of Books for Children*

CUMULATIVE INDEX TO AUTHORS

Author Index

CUMULATIVE INDEX TO NATIONALITIES

Nationality Index

CUMULATIVE INDEX TO TITLES

Title Index

Title Index

Title Index

Title Index

Title Index

Title Index

Title Index

Title Index

Title Index

Title Index